BODYGUARD OF LIES

Volume II

BODYGUARD OF LIES

Volume II

Anthony Cave Brown

1817

HARPER & ROW, PUBLISHERS

NEW YORK, EVANSTON

SAN FRANCISCO

LONDON

Contents

Illustrations

BODYGUARD OF LIES

Fortitude South

THE PILOT of General George S. Patton's C-47 transport let down on instruments and broke cloud over the gentle landscape of Buckinghamshire, sighted Ivinghoe Beacon and the violet approach lights at Traveller's Rest, and then landed at the American air force base at Cheddington. It was January 26, 1944, a dull and misty morning, and there were no bands to welcome the general; neither was there a guard of honor. Patton was met somewhat coldly at the farthest edge of the airfield by General J. C. H. Lee, the chief quartermaster of the U.S. army in England, and by Commander Harry C. Butcher, U.S.N., the Supreme Commander's naval *aide-de-camp* and diarist (who had actually come to collect Eisenhower's dog Telek). When his kit had been stowed in the boot of a Packard that bore no stars, Patton was driven into London where he was received by Eisenhower at Hayes Lodge. There the Supreme Commander gave Patton certain explicit instructions that marked the start of the key stratagem of the war in Europe.

Patton was not sure what was in store for him when he arrived in England. His flamboyance, brutality and indiscretion had all damaged his reputation and career. Yet no one could contest his ability as an army commander. He had displayed that ability during Torch when the Allies captured 1000 miles of African coast in seventy-six hours. As a result of his brilliance as a tactician and disciplinarian in Sicily, he and his armored forces had received the lion's share of the honors in a thirty-nine-day campaign which cost the Axis 167,000 casualties (including 37,000 Germans), at a price of 16,769 Allied troops. But it was the very violence with which Patton had conducted this battle that had got him into trouble; in a fit of nervous anger and impatience he had twice slapped the faces of shell-shocked American soldiers as they lay in hospital. Eisenhower wrote him a "blistering epistle" of reprimand for his "despicable" conduct. The President castigated him for his "reprehensible conduct." An angry howl of protest swept the United States, his court-martial was demanded, and Eisenhower was not able to obtain an operational command for Patton during the Italian campaign, as he had planned.

But in the strange way that bad publicity is sometimes good publicity—or can be turned to good use—the furor worked in favor of A-Force, the Allied deception organization in the Mediterranean. Aware of the German belief that Patton was certain to be in the place of main action, and looking for such an Allied field commander to give substance to the early Zeppelin schemes, Brigadier Clarke asked for and obtained the services of the flamboyant general. Suddenly, Patton appeared in Corsica to support rumors that the 7th Army was about to land in northern Italy; then he was seen at Malta, "inspecting amphibious forces"; a little later he was found to be at Cairo, "having discussions with the British about an invasion of Greece"; and at Christmas he was back at 7th Army headquarters at Palermo in Sicily, "preparing for operations in the Adriatic." Then he disappeared, and while the Abwehr and the SD scoured the Mediterranean for news of his whereabouts, he slipped quietly into England.

Despite the disgrace he was in, Patton expected to get more than he got: command of the U.S. 3rd Army under Montgomery, whom he detested, and Bradley, about whom he was patronizing. As Eisenhower told him that evening at Hayes Lodge, according to the Neptune plan, the 3rd Army, after the breakout from Normandy, would rush for and take the Breton port of Brest, which was essential as a supply base. But, Eisenhower went on, 3rd Army was still in the United States, and while it was on the high seas, Patton must lend his services to another force. Before, and even after, his own army had assembled in Britain, Patton must appear to be the commander of FUSAG, the Quicksilver force that was at the very core of Fortitude.

According to the Quicksilver scenario, FUSAG would consist of the 1st Canadian Army, which would make the assault on the Pas de Calais with one Canadian and three American infantry divisions, and one Canadian armored division. The four armored and four infantry divisions of the American 3rd Army would constitute a follow-up force, and behind them were fifty more divisions, so the story went, in the United States awaiting shipment to the Pas de Calais when FUSAG had established its beachhead. Most of these forces, with the exception of the fifty divisions in the United States, did—or would—

exist; but they belonged either to Montgomery's or Bradley's commands and would invade France through Normandy. Yet this was the force that the Germans must be led to believe was poised and ready to strike the Pas de Calais. And even if FUSAG existed in name only, its commanding general had to be unquestionably real. That was where Patton came on stage. He had a reputation for daring and brilliant unorthodoxy among the Germans, just as the Americans and the British admired Rommel's tactical cunning. The Germans were sure that he would be in the spearhead of the invasion. The LCS and CSM knew that and so, once more, Patton was to be used for the purposes of deception.

As the leading figure in Quicksilver, Patton would be expected to heed one imperative: absolute discretion. From now on, Eisenhower told him, everything he did and said would have to be most carefully orchestrated to the score of Fortitude and Quicksilver. A single major blunder might—almost certainly would—destroy the stratagem, and the Germans might—almost certainly would—divine what the Allied strategy really was. But silence and discretion were not among Patton's strong points, as Eisenhower knew well. With those weaknesses in mind, he gave Patton a word of warning:

> You persistently disregarded my advice [about making statements to the press and appearances without permission], but it is not just advice any longer. Well, from now on it is an order. Think before you leap, George, or you will have no one to blame but yourself for the consequences of your rashness.

Patton, a "master of flattery," was deferential and said "he certainly would be more careful as to the place where he has a tantrum. . . ." Then he went off to his own quarters at 22 Mount Street, Mayfair, where, so it was said afterwards, he broke his undertaking to the Supreme Commander almost immediately. He took a dislike to his quarters—they were rich, ornate, and "queer"—and exploded to his aide: "Whoever picked this Goddamn place has a genius for cloak and dagger. It seems to be the ideal hideout for a fellow like me they're trying to keep under wraps." He said to a friend: "Sandy, let's get the hell out of this Goddamn crib. I'd rather be shot in the streets than spend an evening sitting around this sink of iniquity." And with that declaration—according to a biographer—he went to see Robert E. Sherwood's play *There Shall Be No Night* with Alfred Lunt and Lynn Fontanne at the Haymarket Theatre. After the show, he first visited the stars' dressing rooms to pay his compliments, then went on with the Lunts to the Savoy Hotel for a party. His presence at the Savoy was noted by the press—it was a headquarters for the American newspapers—and also came to the attention of the security authorities at Supreme Headquarters.

Patton's transgression was so flagrant that it may well have been intentional—or so it was later suggested. For Patton was not to be "kept under wraps" at all; to give substance to Quicksilver, his presence in England as an army group commander was to be brought to the attention of the German intelligence system in a variety of ways. Little or nothing was done to conceal his activities. He was constantly calling on Eisenhower and Bradley in Grosvenor Square; he was received by Brooke and made a Knight Commander of the Most Honourable Order of the Bath; he lunched with Tedder, the deputy Supreme Commander; he went to Euston to board a special train which took him to Scotland to meet the advance guard of the 3rd Army; he paraded magnificently before a bevy of British generals and admirals at Greenock as the *Queen Mary* steamed in—thousands of American soldiers aboard the liner saw and cheered him; he inspected a German prisoner of war compound; he hobnobbed with the British gentry and nobility; he was driven in the grand manner to visit Montgomery; he occupied the pew of the Master of Peover Hall at the local church near his headquarters at Knutsford in Cheshire. In short, the only thing the CSM did not do was to announce Patton's presence in Britain in the press. A brief announcement to that effect finally appeared in the Los Angeles *Times,* but meanwhile, two XX-Committee double agents, Tricycle and Treasure, had already informed their German controllers of Patton's whereabouts, and on March 20, 1944, FHW stated in a bulletin: "It has now been clarified . . . that General Patton, who was formerly employed in North Africa and is highly regarded for his proficiency, is now in England." That same day, Eisenhower's headquarters announced vaguely that Patton had relinquished command of the 7th Army for another army command.

Patton disliked his assignment in Britain before the invasion. As one of his biographers would write: "Patton appreciated the importance of (Fortitude) but did not enjoy his role in it. He was especially chagrined that his clearly secondary—as a matter of fact, fictitious—part in (Neptune) removed him from the planning of the campaign. . . ." Moreover, Patton came to suspect that his indiscretions —of which there were several—were deliberately blown up out of all proportion to call the Germans' attention to himself and his command.

Such certainly appeared to be the case in an episode that came to be called the "Knutsford Affair."

In April 1944, Patton disobeyed Eisenhower's orders not to make speeches or public appearances without permission and accepted an invitation to be the principal guest at the inauguration of the "Welcome Club," which had been established by the villagers of Knutsford, close to Patton's headquarters, for American servicemen. He was assured that he would be there unofficially and that there would be no ceremony. But when he arrived he discovered, to his dismay, that there were a crowd, a brass band, an honor guard of British women auxiliaries to welcome him—and a number of press photographers. Patton requested that no photographs of him be taken, and the photographers agreed. Told that there were no reporters present, he then proceeded to make a few bellicose remarks, among them the declaration that ". . . since it is the evident destiny of the British and Americans to rule the world, the better we know each other the better job we will do." It was that remark—an insult to Russia—which was quickly splashed across the headlines of the world press.

How the press obtained the story, and how it got out of Britain, which was under total censorship at the time, would never be clear. It could only have been accomplished through a blunder in the censor's department, which had been told to be especially alert for all news concerning Patton and to delay the transmission of all telegrams until Smith's approval had been obtained, or through some official connivance, although not necessarily the Supreme Commander's. As it happened there had been an official representative of the British government present at Knutsford; his name was Mould. It was almost certainly he who released the text of Patton's speech. But on whose authority? And for what reason?

Whatever the reason, the reaction was immediate, and Patton suddenly found himself in the center of another raging controversy. Windows began to rattle at the Kremlin, the White House and at the St. George's Hotel in Algiers where de Gaulle was quartered, but not in Britain where the statement was suppressed. The ensuing storm caught Marshall at a most embarrassing moment; he was seeking to win congressional approval to appoint a number of officers to the permanent rank of general, including Patton. As a result of his bombast, so Marshall said in a signal to Eisenhower, not only had Patton's fitness for command been brought into serious question, but he had imperiled the entire permanent promotions list.

The controversy could not be quelled, particularly in the United

States; but Marshall, although he was greatly perturbed, left it to Eisenhower to decide whether or not Patton should be replaced. Eisenhower, his nerves already stretched to concert pitch over other menaces to the success of Neptune, expressed his displeasure in a personal letter to Patton: "I am thoroughly weary of your failure to control your tongue and have begun to doubt your all-round judgment, so essential in high military position." But in a signal to Marshall he admitted that Patton was indispensable to Neptune. He may have been aware that the Knutsford leak was intentional; he certainly gave orders to use Patton's name for deception purposes later on. In any case, he decided to retain Patton in command.

Patton was contrite, but he suspected that there was some other explanation for the incident. In his reply to Eisenhower's letter, he wrote: "You probably are damn fed up with me . . . but certainly my last alleged escapade smells strongly of having been a frame-up in view of the fact that . . . the thing was under the auspices of the (British) Ministry of Information (whose representative) was present." And then, expecting to be cashiered, he wrote in his diary with welling bitterness: "I feel like death, but I am not out yet. If they will let me fight, I will; but if not, I will resign so as to be able to talk, and then I will tell the truth, and possibly do my country some good." He had already ordered his batman to begin packing when the furor ended as suddenly as it had begun. Eisenhower called Patton to say that he was to keep his command. But in another entry in his diary, Patton wrote: ". . . this last incident was so trivial in its nature, but so terrible in its effect, that it is not the result of an accident. . . ."

Was the "Knutsford Affair" part of the Fortitude deception scheme? If it was, then the Allied high command had gambled not only with Patton's reputation but also with his career. They were certainly not above that kind of manipulation, but there was never any proof at the time. Only after Fortitude was buried did evidence emerge that the LCS and the Allied Supreme Command, for reasons of deception, had indeed played with Patton's reputation. But the devices used to advertise Patton would prove to be artless compared to the stratagems that were employed to create his fictitious command—the Quicksilver army group, FUSAG.

Quicksilver began where such a force would have to begin, in America, and the opening note was sounded by a double agent whom J. Edgar Hoover had christened "Albert van Loop." Described as "51, a swarthy, somewhat corpulent, shy man looking at the world

with squinted eyes through thick-lensed glasses," van Loop was Dutch
by nationality. But he had served in German intelligence in the First
World War as a specialist in the U.S. army, and when the Americans
entered the Second World War, Canaris reemployed him. After extensive training, van Loop was sent to Madrid, his mission to infiltrate the
United States. He was to approach the U.S. legation and state that he
had been press-ganged into the Abwehr but now wanted to offer his
services to the OSS or the FBI. He was to reveal one cipher (while
concealing a second) and hope that the American authorities would
accept him as a defector, send him to the United States and give him a
job. Then when their suspicions were relaxed, van Loop could begin
his real business—reporting the movement of American divisions to
Britain and the Mediterranean.

But instead of double-crossing the Americans at Madrid, van Loop,
to all appearances, double-crossed the Abwehr. He announced that he
really did want to go to America and work for the FBI or the OSS. To
prove his sincerity he produced *both* his ciphers and *all* his transmission schedules, wavelengths, call signs and security checks. His real
cipher was an ingenious double transposition system based on the
Dutch prayer book, while his operating instructions were very cleverly
concealed in secret ink amid the clefs and staves of the score of the
Dutch national anthem.

With these revelations, Madrid decided that, whatever else he was,
van Loop was a German spy, and as such would have some value to
the FBI. He was sent to the United States via Lisbon and Buenos
Aires, and when he reached New York the third week of June 1943,
he was taken into custody by the FBI, and kept under guard—it was
said—at an FBI safehouse in the Queens district of New York. His
ciphers and operating instructions were taken over by an expert
wireless operator on the staff of Dr. George Sterling's Radio Intelligence Service, a section of the Federal Communications Commission.

Quicksilver got under way when, acting under the general supervision of Joint Security Control, which provided supervision of the
FBI, the new van Loop opened communication with Hamburg in late
September 1943. Over the following weeks the RIS operator impersonating van Loop transmitted a careful blend of truth and fiction
until it was apparent that Hamburg trusted him. Then in a secret ink
report he explained that he had done exactly as he had been told to do
—give himself up to the Americans—and that, after a period of interrogation and surveillance, he had been released and had gone to work

as the "night manager" of the Henry Hudson Hotel, on West 57th Street in New York. This, he explained, was especially suited to his assignment since the U.S. army used the hotel extensively for lodging American officers going to England. He was able, he wrote, to see the lists of troopships proceeding from New York, and these, together with the lists of officers, revealed the designations of the divisions en route to Britain.

Some of the information sent in van Loop's name was accurate, for it was considered inevitable that, sooner or later, the Germans would be able to identify the real divisions for themselves, usually through the press or prisoners of war. But at the same time, information was sent about departing units that did not exist, at least on the Allied order of battle maps, in the hope that the Germans would believe that they were part of the Quicksilver assault force assembling in Britain. Did Hamburg trust van Loop's despatches? Apparently it did, if the yardstick of that trust was the amount of money he was paid. He had extracted some $55,000 from the Abwehr by February 1944.

That was not the end of the van Loop case, however. The FBI sent Hamburg a total of 115 messages in van Loop's name, but when his file was captured and examined after the war, it was discovered that the Abwehr had received 231 wireless messages from him—some of them in a cipher other than the one based on the Dutch prayer book which the FBI was using. According to Ladislas Farago, the intelligence historian who investigated the incident, van Loop had managed to outwit the FBI, whose surveillance of him was not as expert as it might have been. With a new supply of money smuggled to him by his wife, who arrived in the United States with $10,000 sewn into her girdle, he reverted to his original loyalty, made contact with another German agent in America, and through him established communications with his German controllers. Van Loop was not a double but a triple agent.

Even so, the Germans appear not to have doubted the information about Quicksilver transmitted by the fictitious van Loop, perhaps because the real van Loop was ignorant of the FBI transmissions and did not bother to inform his controllers of the possibility that he was being impersonated. The bureaucratic confusion that followed the SD's assumption of the command of the Abwehr may also have made it difficult to sort out evidence indicating which German agents in America or Britain might be under control. Whatever the case, the Allied deception agencies in dealing with double agents were treading a narrow and dangerous line throughout the Quicksilver stratagem.

When the fictitious Quicksilver forces began to arrive in Britain, the stratagem was taken over by the British deception agencies, and a series of calculated leakages began to appear in the press: "2/lt. N, of O, Falls Church, Va., on active service in England with the 9th Airborne Division, a sophomore of Johns Hopkins, has announced his engagement to Miss P of Norwich, England." Or on the radio: "This is the American Forces Network. Here is *Sweethearts' Playtime*. Private M of the 315th Reconnaissance Troop, 11th Infantry Division, on duty somewhere overseas, is twenty today; and here is *Six Lessons from Madame Lazonga*, as requested by his fiancée, Miss R, of Great Neck, New York . . ." This type of announcement was sufficient to alert FHW—whose men read and listened to everything—to the possibility that these formations really existed, but *that trick was as old as the hills*. Thus, in addition to these seemingly harmless leaks, the CSM began to generate wireless sounds that simulated the presence of an army or divisional headquarters, a regiment or an armored battalion, in the fairly confident hope that the excellent German wireless intelligence service would be listening in. Moreover, the Quicksilver army group had to be seen as well as heard. There had to be troop concentrations, tank parks, petrol dumps, hospitals, pipelines, sewage farms—all the weft and warp of life created by the existence of a million men. And so these military installations began to appear on the British landscape—fabricated, much as Hollywood might create a film set, out of lumber, rubber, wire and cardboard.

Even this, however, was not considered to be enough to fool Roenne and the other intelligence experts at FHW. This point was acknowledged by Masterman who would later write:

> Speculations, guesses, or leakages, would have little or no effect on the German military mind, for the German staff officer would make his own appreciations and his own guesses from the facts put before him. What he would require would be facts . . . (including) the location and identification of formations, units, headquarters, assembly areas and the like.

This kind of intelligence could come only from double agents under XX-Committee control, agents who were, it was hoped, trusted by the Germans.

The XX-Committee had a number of such agents they could use; early in January 1944 there was a total of twenty under British control, nine of whom had wireless, with many other similar channels open to the LCS overseas through MI-6's penetration of the Abwehr and the SD. But the committee was the first to realize that an agent was trusted by the Germans only in direct relationship to the excellence and truth of the intelligence he had transmitted in the past. Which of these agents did the Germans really trust? And could the XX-Committee trust any of them? After all, they were spies, one or two of whom had changed sides two and three times. No matter how elaborately Quicksilver was being staged, a single false note, intentional or unintentional, could destroy the illusion. Furthermore, as Masterman would note, "An agent who, in spite of all precautions on our part, turned out not to be believed by the enemy, might wreck the whole enterprise, or, even worse, his messages might be 'read in reverse' and the true target of attack be exposed instead of concealed by him."

In consequence, it was decided that the "orchestra" employed to spread the "facts" of Quicksilver would be small instead of large. The "first violins"—to use the jargon of espionage—would consist of Garbo, whom the Germans considered their best agent in England; "Brutus," a Pole who worked for MI-6 in France after the fall, and had agreed, so the Germans thought, to work for the Abwehr as an agent in Britain; "Treasure," a Frenchwoman of Russian origins; and Tricycle, the winning but weasely Yugoslav businessman who was regarded both by the Germans and the British as the very best type of European idealist. Other agents—the "second violins"—would be used in the operation, but these four would carry the main themes of Quicksilver and its allied deceptions, particularly Skye. But as the sly men of the XX-Committee put these strange musicians to work, they would again come perilously close to disaster—for themselves, for Fortitude and Quicksilver, and for Neptune.

Garbo was a Spaniard. That was all that would be known about him personally. But Masterman later wrote: "Connoisseurs of double cross have always regarded the GARBO case as the most highly developed example of their art. . . ." He was, it was said, equally hostile to Nazism and communism, had been compelled to hide for two years in one house during the Spanish Civil War, and seemed to have had ambitions to become a professional spy for the British in either Germany or Italy. He offered his services to MI-6 at Madrid in January 1941, but his offer was rejected, and so Garbo presented himself to the Germans. He went to see Wilhelm Leissner, an old Abwehr hand who, as "Gustav Lenz," was chief of the Abwehr in Iberia; and Lenz, after what Masterman called "characteristically lengthy and involved negotiations," decided to send Garbo to England in July 1941 "with a questionnaire, secret ink, money, cover addresses, and the German blessing. . . ."

Garbo did not go to London at all; when he arrived in Lisbon he decided to stay there. And it was from Lisbon that he began to fabricate intelligence reports about the British Isles, using a few well-known guides and reference books. But such were his talents that his reports had the ring of authenticity, and in some cases came very close to the truth. The Germans grew to trust him, perhaps because he always reported what they wanted to hear. They also believed that he employed three sub-agents in various parts of Great Britain to assist him in his work. But by February 1942, MI-6 had learned of Garbo. Ultra revealed that the Germans were making preparations to intercept a big convoy which was supposed to have left Liverpool for Malta. As Masterman wrote: "Only later did we establish the fact that GARBO was the sole inventor and begetter of this convoy, and thus responsible for a great expenditure of useless labour on the part of the enemy. It became clear to us at this stage that GARBO was more fitted to be a worthy collaborator than an unconscious competitor." He was brought to England as an XX-Committee special agent.

There was no need to create a spy network for Garbo; he had already done that himself. He was also a tireless worker. Posing as the employee of a large fruit and vegetable importer who did much business with Iberia from Covent Garden market, he spent seven days a week, averaging six to eight hours a day, drafting secret letters. In all, he would compose 400 secret letters and 2000 wireless messages between Torch and Neptune; and the Germans financed him to the tune of £20,000 ($96,000)—handsome reward indeed. During 1943 he was used to pass over the greater part of Plan Starkey; and if that plan was a short-term failure, it was a long-term success, for in the course of the operation Garbo gave the Germans what was the embryo of the Quicksilver order of battle.

By the spring of 1944, Garbo had fabricated an even more extensive network in Britain; he was informing Lenz that he employed fourteen agents and eleven well-placed contacts, including one in the Ministry of Information, where most Allied secret matters were discussed at one time or another. He also had an agent in Canada, busily inflating the order of battle of the 1st Canadian Army, and another in Ceylon, spying on Mountbatten, the Allied Supreme Commander in Southeast Asia, who knew most things about Neptune. He used two wireless operators and had reporting posts all over southwestern, western and eastern Britain—handily for Quicksilver. Master-man would observe: "The one-man band of Lisbon (had) developed into an orchestra. . . ." Thus it was that agents who did not exist began to report an army group that did not exist.

Did the Germans trust Garbo? Obviously they did, for they sent him the cipher (for his own use) which they used themselves in wireless communications between Madrid and Hamburg and Madrid and Tangier. The possession of that cipher released "The Bomb" at Bletchley for other duties and played an important part in the liquidation of the enemy intelligence services in time for D-Day—at least in the Mediterranean. When the Germans changed the cipher key, as they did from time to time, they entrusted Garbo with the new one, too—and the Bletchley cryptanalysts continued their work with little inconvenience.

A character no less singular than Garbo, and no less important to Quicksilver, was codenamed "Brutus" by the XX-Committee. He was, in reality, Captain Roman Garby-Czerniawski, an officer of the Polish General Staff who, in 1940, was in his mid-thirties. A man of extraordinary abilities, he was both a pilot and an Olympic skier, and his professional mind had been sharpened by a period in the cryptanalytical service of the Polish General Staff, the service that broke the main Soviet military cipher during the Russo-Polish War of 1920 and later helped Britain obtain Enigma. With the destruction of the Polish armies by the Wehrmacht in 1939, Garby-Czerniawski made his way to Paris; and he was in the service of Polish intelligence there when the French surrendered in 1940. He then went underground, and as "Paul" founded Interallié, an MI-6 *réseau*. But in 1941 he was betrayed by his cipher clerk, Mathilde Carré, and arrested by the Abwehr while in bed at his home at St. Germain-en-Laye. His captor, Hugo Bleicher, one of the best of the German counterintelligence agents in France, had succeeded in turning Mme Carré's loyalties when she became jealous of Paul's relationship with another young woman in the *réseau*. He was taken to Fresnes Prison to await execution; but then the Abwehr conceived another use for his services, and his life was spared.

For many months Colonel Joachim Rohleder, the chief of the Abwehr department responsible for the penetration of the British secret agencies, had combed the jails for British agents who might be turned and sent to England as German agents. His attention fastened upon Garby-Czerniawski for the same reasons that he had been employed by the British in the first place; he was a first-rate intelligence officer, cool, brave, patriotic and dependable, despite his indiscretion over Carré. Rohleder presented Garby-Czerniawski with a proposition—if he would go to England as a German spy, the one hundred members of Interallié who were now under arrest would not be executed but rather treated as prisoners of war. Garby-Czerniawski considered the proposal and countered with one of his own. He demanded that, in return for his services, the Germans must promise that Poland would be granted full national sovereignty after the war. Rohleder could not give him such a guarantee, and their negotiations collapsed. Then Germany invaded Russia, and Garby-Czerniawski, calling Rohleder back to his cell, declared that he now realized that Russia, not Germany, was Poland's natural enemy, and that if the jailed members of Interallié were treated as prisoners of war, he would go to England and, as he put it, "work for peace."

A formal contract was struck between the Abwehr and Garby-Czerniawski, who was now rechristened "Armand," and the details of his "escape" were arranged. These were put in the hands of Hugo Bleicher, who would write:

> I received a strange commission at the beginning of July 1942. I was to fetch Armand out of Fresnes prison allegedly to go to an interrogation in Paris, but I was to allow him to make an escape on the way. . . . The whole business was mysterious in the extreme. It appeared to me that Armand had a special mission from a very high quarter in German Military Intelligence Headquarters. . . . My duties had hitherto been to catch spies. Now I was to help the chief of a big spy organisation to escape. It was a grotesque situation. It had been impressed on me that this flight of Armand might become known to the French Resistance. I must also ensure that the S.D. should get no wind of it. In order that the news should reach the Resistance in the most natural manner, I took with me to Fresnes one of my agents who I knew to be working for the other side. Of course, I did not let him into the secret.

Armand's "escape" was cleverly planned. Bleicher and Raoul Kiffer, the French double agent, were to pick up Armand from Fresnes in an Abwehr car, and when the car approached a sharp bend in the road at Pont Orléans, they would see a stalled German army truck. As the car slowed down, Armand was to leap out and make off. Bleicher and Kiffer would give chase and even fire some shots, but Armand was to disregard all challenges and make for an Abwehr safehouse on the Boulevard Massena. There, if he had not already succeeded in removing them by other means, his handcuffs would be taken off, and he would be given fresh clothes, false papers representing him to be a courier of the Rumanian Embassy at Paris, some money and some travel papers. He would then go to Lyon where he would rendezvous at the Hôtel Beaux Arts with Bleicher, who would arrange his passage into Spain.

Garby-Czerniawski "escaped" on Bastille Day 1942 exactly as planned, although the Abwehr car failed to avoid a collision with the stalled truck, which added an unexpected note of authenticity. The French resistance learned of his escape, informed London and two weeks later Armand had made his way across the Pyrenees over a British escape line. He met first with a British escape line officer at Madrid codenamed "Monday," but later he met and was briefed by General Erich Kuhlenthal, the second in command of the Abwehrkriegsorganisation in Iberia. At these meetings Armand was given a list of intelligence targets to tackle when he reached England. He was instructed how to build a wireless transmitter from parts generally available in British shops; he was given a supply of *G-Tinten*— shoulder pads impregnated with the slightly yellow secret ink made from pyramidon; and he was introduced to the *Mikropunkt* system of microphotography. He was also given an Abwehr cipher based upon *The Story of St. Michele* by Axel Munthe. Then Armand drove with Monday to Lisbon, where he was to catch a BOAC DC-3 to England. He had, of course, told Monday everything.

Armand arrived in England in January 1943 and he was taken, as was usual, to the Royal Patriotic School at Battersea for interrogation, clearance and observation. His case was then passed to the XX-Committee to see if he might be of service as a double agent. The committee hesitated to use him at first, for the Germans knew that he had once worked for MI-6 and might do so again. In that event, they might not trust Armand and read what he was sending them "in reverse." Nevertheless, it was decided to employ him, but not on operational matters, and he was given his third code name in eighteen months— Brutus. Soon, however, it became clear from the nature of the questions they sent him that the Germans did trust Brutus; and it was decided to "build him up" as a liaison officer between the Polish and the Royal Air Force—a position in which Brutus might be expected to learn much about Neptune. It was a fortunate decision, for when a disaster occurred to thin the ranks of the XX-Committee special agents, a new and greater burden would fall upon Brutus. The man whom the XX-Committee had not been inclined to trust would become the main agent for the transmission of Quicksilver.

Treasure was more appropriately codenamed than Brutus, for she added small, dainty touches of authenticity to Quicksilver. Her real name was Lily Sergeyev, she was twenty-six, a Frenchwoman of Russian origins, and she had first come to the attention of the British secret service in 1937 through her uncle, General George de Miller, the leader of the Czarist Russian exiles in Paris. In appearance Treasure would be described as having a "rough-hewn Slavic face . . . marred by a square chin but mellowed by her gently sloping brow and sensitive eyes. She wore her rich auburn hair down to shoulders that were firm and broad, giving her a somewhat masculine appearance. But Lily was all woman—tender, skittish, vital, highly-strung, and set in her ways." Judged by her German and British controllers alike as intelligent but temperamental and difficult to handle, she cared nothing for her personal safety because she believed that she was dying of leukemia. (In fact, she would still be alive in 1971.)

At the outbreak of war Miss Sergeyev was in Lebanon on the leg of a Paris-Saigon cycle ride. An anti-Communist because of her Czarist background, she decided to return to Paris and offer her services to MI-6. But before she could make contact with Dunderdale, Paris fell to the Wehrmacht, and Miss Sergeyev conceived another plan. She presented herself for employment in the Abwehr, and after much expensive wining and dining, the Abwehr agreed to take her on. But Miss Sergeyev intended to defect and was using the Abwehr only to provide her with papers and money to get to Iberia. And this, in June 1943, she managed to do.

The Abwehr refused to equip her with a transceiver and ciphers. No Abwehr female agent had been so equipped for service in the field by 1943, for Canaris disliked and distrusted women agents; he felt they were too susceptible to emotional involvement and lacked the objectivity of men. Thus Miss Sergeyev would communicate with her controllers by secret writing. But when she reached Madrid, she surrendered to the British Embassy and, unknown to the Germans, told an official of her mission for the Abwehr. She was given papers allowing her entry into England by air from Lisbon and, on her arrival, she was detained for interrogation by the security authorities at the Royal Patriotic School. Her loyalties finally established, Miss Sergeyev was offered "secret work"—XX-Committee work, although she was never told that such an organization existed or what her work would be. The Committee was somewhat uneasy about her, but they needed a female agent for the special tasks they had in mind. And so Miss Sergeyev became Treasure.

Treasure soon opened contact with her controller through a letter box in Lisbon, using a secret ink preparation. She reported that she had enlisted in the British women's army service which, in fact, she did do later on. Her credentials established, she notified her controller that she had met a staff officer of the American 14th Army at Bristol. Bristol was, in truth, the headquarters for the American assault army for Neptune, the 1st; the 14th Army did not exist other than for the purposes of deception. Treasure then reported that 14th Army headquarters had moved to Little Waltham in Essex, directly facing the North Sea and the Pas de Calais, the area in which the fictitious FUSAG was supposed to be assembling. It was a movement that pleased Treasure, she said, because now the 14th Army was close to London she would be able to see her friend more often. Treasure also reported on real American and British units which were being used to give substance to Quicksilver, but, of course, she lied about their locations, misrepresented their missions and disguised their affiliation with the army groups that would actually take part in Neptune. All this information filled in some of the details of the broader picture of FUSAG being presented to the Germans by the other members of the Quicksilver chorus; and if Treasure reported the precise location of a military unit, there was certain to be a characteristic pattern of wireless traffic coming from that area to verify her story when the German wireless intelligence service listened in.

When Ultra surveillance of the Abwehr's traffic between Madrid and Berlin showed that Treasure was in good standing with the Germans, she announced the bitter news that she had "broken off her friendship with her friend at 14th Army"; "he would be going to France soon and there would be no hope of her following." But, she announced happily a little later, she had found somebody else in the U.S. Judge Advocate General's branch at Cheltenham who was in a position to provide her with most valuable information. It appeared that it was the custom of the U.S. Army to make out monthly crime reports, division by division, which were used, among other things, as a barometer of morale and divisional efficiency. Would such reports be useful? Indeed they would, Treasure's controller replied. So the CSM arranged for the preparation of such reports that excluded the divisions about which the Germans knew nothing or which the Allies wished to conceal, and included those in FUSAG which they wished to reveal. Quicksilver was becoming a reality. But, unknown to the LCS and the CSM, there was serious trouble ahead. It involved the case of Tricycle.

Tricycle, the young Yugoslav whose real name was Dusko Popov, came to the XX-Committee by a more direct route than many of its double agents. While studying at Freiburg University before the war, he had become friendly with a fellow student named Johann Jebsen. Popov later entered the shipping business; and Jebsen, who would become a figure of importance in the Abwehr, and was, apparently, connected to it even when he was at Freiburg, made vague suggestions to his friend that he might wish to increase his income and status in Germany by spying for Germany against the British. The suggestion was repeated to Popov in 1940 when he called at the German Consulate in Belgrade to arrange some documentation in connection with the sale of two ships to Germany. But Popov's loyalties lay elsewhere. He contacted the MI-6 representative at Belgrade, and it was agreed that he should continue to appear interested in the Abwehr's approaches. Then, the Abwehr asked Popov to go to England to collect some secret *courrier* from a member of the Yugoslav Embassy in London who was in the employ of the Abwehr. He reported his mission to MI-6, which then arranged his papers, and he arrived in London on December 20, 1940. There, Masterman wrote: "He was interrogated and created a most favorable impression . . . we had in him a new agent of high quality who could plausibly meet persons in any social stratum, who was well established with the Germans at the instance of an Abwehr official [Jebsen], and who had an excellent business cover for frequent journeys to Lisbon or to other neutral countries." Menzies, too, would find Popov useful in the conduct of MI-6 business. His Abwehr connections would serve as a valuable link between MI-6 and the anti-Hitler conspirators, including Canaris, in the German secret intelligence service.

Popov was also well connected at the Yugoslav court; and when MI-6 arranged the evacuation to London of King Peter, Popov, now known as Tricycle, was able to represent to the Germans that, through the King, he had entrance into circles close to the Prime Minister. This claim, which Tricycle was able to substantiate with choice bits of information about life at Storey's Gate, including intelligence about Churchill's health, enhanced his prestige with the Abwehr enormously. His business cover required him to travel to Lisbon frequently, which the British allowed him to do, and Tricycle was soon trained and equipped to transmit intelligence from Britain to his controller at Lisbon, a certain Karsthoff, by all available means, including wireless, secret writing and microphotography. This intelligence was, of course, supplied by the XX-Committee, and enough of it was useful and true that Tricycle steadily rose in the estimation of the Abwehr.

It was in June 1941 that Tricycle was instructed by the Abwehr to go to America to report, among other matters, the defenses of Pearl Harbor. The British permitted him to go, passing his case on to their colleagues in the FBI. But Tricycle did not prosper in the United States; J. Edgar Hoover wanted no spies in America, and Tricycle returned to Lisbon in October 1942, explaining that his poor performance in America was due to the Abwehr's failure to send him adequate funds. That error was corrected when he was given a large imprest with which to return to Britain and expand his network. From that point on, Tricycle became the Abwehr's second most trusted agent, and he expanded his network in Britain as he had been asked to do. He already had "Balloon," a British army officer who had resigned because of debts, and "Gelatine," an Austrian woman expatriot in London who had worked for MI-5 and had been recruited by Tricycle as an Abwehr spy without knowing that he was working for the British. Then he added "Meteor" to his string, who was a member of King Peter's inner circle and a "Yugoslav of good family, high character, and patriotic principles. . . ."

In July 1943, Tricycle was back in Lisbon, this time to see his old friend Jebsen. Jebsen had risen in the Abwehr and had been sent by Canaris to Lisbon, possibly on Schwarze Kapelle business. During their reunion he said enough to Tricycle to indicate that he was disenchanted with Hitlerism, and Tricycle reported to the XX-Committee on his return to London that Jebsen was ready and willing to sell out to Great Britain. It was through "Artist" (as Jebsen came to be called by the XX-Committee) that Tricycle enlisted another agent in his network—"Freak." Freak was also a Yugoslav officer, and in December 1943, after he had been trained by the Abwehr as a wireless operator, he arrived in England and promptly joined Tricycle. Yet another Yugoslav from the Belgrade establishment, "The Worm," joined the network at about the same time and, during his interrogation, confirmed Tricycle's impression that both Artist—and Canaris— were wavering in their allegiance to the Third Reich. Thus, by the turn of 1943–44, the "Yugoslav Ring" of Abwehr agents around King Peter was wholly controlled by the XX-Committee through Tricycle. And this was more than fortunate for Allied security during the Neptune period, for King Peter resided at the Savoy Hotel and was frequently to be seen at the American Bar with Allied generals and war correspondents.

Artist's usefulness to the XX-Committee was still in question, however. But when Tricycle again visited Lisbon in November 1943,

Artist gave him much important information regarding V-weapons and the Schwarze Kapelle, which strengthened his belief that he might be enlisted as a resident agent in Lisbon. Two MI-5 men were sent from London to check both Tricycle and Artist, and when they returned with a favorable report, it was finally decided to enlist Artist. But an aura of doubt remained, for Artist might pose a very serious threat to the security of the "Yugoslav Ring." If his treachery was detected by the Abwehr and he was forced to talk, he might bring down both Tricycle and Garbo, for Artist believed that Garbo was a German spy in Britain, and he would naturally warn the British. Then, if the Abwehr learned that Garbo had not been arrested, it would logically conclude that he, too, was under British control. The XX-Committee was apprehensive about Artist, and for good reason; but there his case rested—for the time being.

In February 1944, Tricycle returned to Lisbon on his most important mission of the war: Quicksilver. He carried with him detailed information about the Allied order of battle in Britain for the invasion which, he informed his controller, Karsthoff, had been gathered by Balloon, Gelatine, Meteor, Freak, The Worm and their sub-agents. In fact, the information was the framework of the Quicksilver order of battle which had been fabricated by the XX-Committee. It was a bold move, for the success or failure of the Quicksilver deception now depended entirely upon whether or not the Abwehr trusted Tricycle. If it did, all the calculated leaks and the reports from other double agents under XX-Committee control would serve to enhance the deception; if it did not, Quicksilver would be revealed as a hoax before it had scarcely begun. For reasons that would not be clear, Karsthoff reacted angrily to Tricycle's intelligence, describing it as "warmed-over gossip." But Tricycle protested against the accusation and demanded that it be sent to Berlin for assessment. This Karsthoff did; and fortunately for Quicksilver, the reaction of FHW was quite different. FHW saw what the LCS and the CSM intended it to see—the embryo of FUSAG assembling in southeastern and eastern England. As Roenne would write in a bulletin to Hitler and OKW on March 9, 1944: "A V-mann dispatch . . . has brought particularly valuable information. . . . The authenticity of the report was checked and proved. It contains information about three armies, three army corps and twenty-three (divisions) among which the location of only one need be regarded as questionable. The report confirms our operational picture."

Roenne's acceptance of Tricycle's despatch was yet another major victory for the LCS and CSM strategists—one comparable to Fortitude

North. If FHW continued to believe in the existence of FUSAG, it would have far-reaching consequences not only upon the success of Neptune but also upon the outcome of the war. Thus, from its very inception, Quicksilver seemed to be a success; and between February and May 1944, the LCS, the CSM and the XX-Committee, working on that assumption, leaked additional information about FUSAG through the "Yugoslav Ring," Garbo and his network, Treasure, and by a variety of other special means. But all that time, unknown to the Allied deception agencies, the entire Fortitude fabrication was dangerously close to failure.

The first near-disaster concerned the case of Jeff, the Abwehr agent who, with his partner Mutt, had come ashore in 1941 on the Moray Firth. Though Jeff had turned sour and was jailed at Dartmoor for "recalcitrancy," he had managed to get in touch by means of secret writing with one Erich Carl, warning him not only that Mutt was working for the British, but also that he was working for the XX-Committee, the existence of which was unknown to the Germans. Carl, a member of the German War Graves Commission who was being detained in Britain, was repatriated when he grew seriously ill, and returned to Germany with information that might have destroyed Fortitude. But the German secret intelligence services remained unaware that their agents in Britain were under control, perhaps because their reports were more convincing than any information to the contrary, or perhaps because of the bureaucratic chaos that followed the Abwehr's absorption by the SD. Again, Fortitude had escaped by a whisker.

A German agent in Lisbon who was not under XX-Committee control posed another threat to the deception. His name was Paul Fidrmuc, his German code name was "Ostro," and he was the Iberian representative of an American pharmaceutical firm. Like Garbo before he was recruited by the committee, Ostro had invented a string of agents in Britain and was supplying the Germans with intelligence reports that were products of his own imagination. When his activities were uncovered, the British took little notice at first; but then his reports began to come uncomfortably close to the truth. "It was not impossible," Masterman would write, "that OSTRO might by a fluke give the exact area of the attack on the Continent, and thus destroy the deception plan." It was decided that Ostro must be eliminated, but MI-5, MI-6 and SOE could not quite catch him. He continued to operate, but as imaginative as he was, he never uncovered the secrets of Neptune. He reported that the Allies would come ashore at the Pas de Calais.

Plainly, the success of Fortitude depended upon a good deal of luck, and suddenly, as D-Day neared, it seemed that luck had run out for the Allied deception agencies. The SD, as part of the *ratissages* that followed the Solf tea parties and the defection of the Vermehrens and their associates from Turkey, had grown suspicious of Artist, the weakest link in the Fortitude-Quicksilver chain. For one thing, Artist was a frequent guest of Frau Vermehren, Erich Vermehren's mother, who had her home in Lisbon; and for another he was suspected of financial irregularities. Neither at the time nor later was it clear whether the SD was aware of Artist's connection with Tricycle. In any event, its agents arrested Artist early in May at his villa among the gardens of Lapa. He was drugged, packed into a tin trunk, and taken through Spain and France into Germany as diplomatic baggage. His interrogations began at the Prinzalbrechtstrasse; and even if it seemed that the SD was chiefly concerned, at least at the start, about his association with Frau Vermehren and his financial dealings in Lisbon, under interrogation he might reveal everything he knew.

The XX-Committee soon learned of Artist's fate through Ultra, and while it appeared that his arrest had more to do with money than with treachery, this was, as Masterman wrote, "small consolation." Under the circumstances, the XX-Committee was compelled to assume that Artist would tell all. As Masterman put it: "On the most optimistic estimate . . . we had lost one of the most important cases, or sets of cases, just as D Day approached; on the most pessimistic, the whole deception through double-cross agents was in danger." Prudence dictated that Tricycle and the "Yugoslav Ring" be retired from the Quicksilver chorus, although, curiously, Garbo and his network would remain operative in the later stages of the deception, perhaps because Artist knew only that he was a German agent in Britain, not that he was under XX-Committee control.

It was now that Brutus was elevated to new importance in the deception, for the LCS and the CSM could not simply abandon Quicksilver at this late date. To have done so would have necessitated a complete revision of Allied plans, both actual and deceptive, for the Normandy invasion, and that was an operation so vast that SHAEF was unwilling to undertake it. SHAEF, however, did turn its attention to Ultra to establish, if possible, whether the truth of Neptune lay bare before the Fuehrer's eyes. If Artist had revealed that Tricycle was a double agent, the Germans could assume that all of the information he had passed to them was false, FUSAG would be exposed as a fiction, and an invasion of the Pas de Calais as an improbability. To the horror of the Allied planners, Ultra revealed that Hitler was ordering considerable reinforcements in the Normandy area, although it also showed that he was *not* reducing his garrisons at the Pas de Calais. Whether Ultra revealed the actual text of the order that led to the sudden reinforcement of Normandy would not be established. But General Blumentritt, Rundstedt's Chief of Staff, sent this signal to all commands at 8 P.M. on May 8, 1944:

> The Führer attaches extreme importance to Normandy and the defense of Normandy. In the coming enemy offensive, very strong landings by air and heavy bombing raids, as well as the main attacks from the sea, are to be expected. . . . High Command Army Group B will report its plans for submission to (OKW).

If this signal was intercepted—and it may well have been—it might have seemed that Neptune's security had collapsed. Not until the eve of D-Day would the Allied high command be certain that Artist had not blown Quicksilver. It was, therefore, a period of extreme anxiety at Supreme Headquarters and the LCS, for no one could know that Artist would behave as he did. He was murdered soon after D-Day without revealing anything of his own or of Tricycle's connections with the British. But, ironically, even if he had, Quicksilver might still have been assured of success, not only through the skillful efforts of the Allied deception agencies but also through an intrigue at FHW that was among the most extraordinary acts of treason in the history of the Third Reich.

The man chiefly responsible for determining the order of battle of the western powers before D-Day was Colonel Alexis Baron von Roenne, a tall, slim, sarcastic and pious Junker who seemed to be a *Flügelmann* of the officers of the old German Empire. As chief of FHW, he performed his work with the fastidiousness for fact and detail, for precision and intelligent objectivity that was the hallmark of a staff officer of his age and class. He was a master of the diplomatic phraseology used by the General Staff when it studied the power of an intended victim; there was never a word too many. General Ulrich Liss, a chief of FHW during the campaign against France in 1940, would remember of him: "He was an excellent man in all respects—a man who set very high standards for himself and his men. He had also a perception of political and military matters that was akin to genius. He had a clear and realistic mind, and he was able to make decisions with the speed of lightning." It came, therefore, as a great sense of shock when, four years later, it was discovered that Baron von Roenne had cooked the books at FHW.

Roenne was of a caste which made such conduct quite incomprehensible. He came from the aristocracy east of the Elbe River that was the very spine of German military science and power. His family was one of the oldest in the Reich. They had always been King's men; they had always worn the royal cloak. Their baronetcy was bestowed upon them by Frederick the Great for the parts they had played in the battles he waged from Zorndorf to Leuthen, from Rossbach to Mollwitz. They were patricians of old Prussia, and Roenne's conduct had been molded by a social code that was so rigid that—for example—it was forbidden to talk to a jockey in public. The rules of etiquette were severe; even more severe was the code of loyalty and discipline. If an officer violated that code, far better to shoot himself than to go on living in a world that treated him as an outcast.

Roenne, in a sense the brain of the German army in the West, came to FHW in 1939, after an impeccable career. He had served with distinction in the First World War with one of the Kaiser's finest, the 9th Potsdam Infantry Regiment; Hindenburg was his colonel-in-chief. But because his family lost their estates in the Bolshevik revolution in Courland just after the war, he was compelled to resign his commission in order to restore the family's fortunes. He became a banker, but when Hitler began to rearm and a career as an army officer was attractive once more, Roenne returned to his regiment. He did well and was selected for the War Academy, a school only for those officers who were likely to reach the highest rank. After graduation—the courses were so demanding that it was said that a man who had attended the War Academy never smiled again—he was admitted to the General Staff. By the outbreak of the second great war he was chief of Group France, the branch of FHW responsible for studying the military power and intentions of the French Republic.

It was as head of Group France that Roenne's excellence as an intelligence evaluator first came to the attention of Hitler. The Fuehrer was then planning his offensive against Poland, but because the Wehrmacht was so small in 1939, it would be impossible to invade Poland and still maintain a strong defense in the West. It was imperative to know what the French and the British reaction to an attack against Poland would be. Hitler asked for a special study, the task was given to Roenne, and he wrote a report stating that in his opinion the western powers would only assemble their armies; they would not attack Germany while Germany was invading Poland. The report confirmed

Hitler's own impression. He vanquished the Poles and the western powers did nothing. Roenne was proven correct and thereafter he enjoyed the favor of the Fuehrer. That favor was confirmed when, again in response to a request from Hitler for a special evaluation, Roenne predicted that if the German panzers struck across the Meuse between Givet and Sedan, the French army would collapse. Hitler attacked that sector, and again Roenne was proven correct. The fact that the French army was defeated so quickly was—as Liss would state—due in no small part to the shrewdness of Roenne's appreciations. The Fuehrer awarded him the *Deutsches Kreuz.*

When Hitler began to prepare for the invasion of Russia, Roenne, bent upon retrieving the family estates in Latvia, volunteered for service in the northern sector of the eastern frontier. He went to battle and behaved with gallantry, but was wounded badly before his regiment got to Tukkum. After spending many months in hospital, he returned to FHW; and then, in early 1943, largely as a result of Hitler's insistence, he was appointed its chief. It was a position of great influence and power, for Roenne enjoyed the complete confidence of the Fuehrer, and only he had all the facts at his fingertips. Every scrap of intelligence about the western powers poured into FHW's headquarters at Zossen, and it was Roenne who put all the pieces together in his weekly and monthly reports for OKW and the Fuehrer. Seldom, if ever, did anyone question his authority or challenge his opinions.

Roenne's loyalty to Hitler and to the Third Reich would seem, under these circumstances, to have been above suspicion. But, in fact, he was a confirmed conspirator of the Schwarze Kapelle. Just when he set out on this dangerous path would never quite be determined. It probably began with the trap of the *Fahneneid,* the humiliation of General von Fritsch and the dismissal of General Beck. He was appalled by the SS pogroms in Poland, and he detested, as did so many others of his class, the gutter behavior of the Nazis and what the general staff considered to be their lack of military professionalism. Roenne had worked very closely with the Abwehr and had formed a high, respectful regard for Canaris, and a close friendship with Oster. Roenne and Oster were often to be seen riding together, practicing the *haute école* in the Tiergarten, the Potsdam Cavalry School and the Brandenburg woods. Gradually Roenne fell under Oster's spell, and then under the influence of Stauffenberg, whom he had known well since their days together at the War Academy. Roenne had no post in the Schwarze Kapelle, and neither did he have any tasks, except to keep the leadership closely informed with relevant political and military intelligence. He remained at FHW, in a position that enabled him to render the Fuehrer the greatest service—or disservice. For it was his job to estimate the strength of the forces ranged against Germany by the western powers, and to discern the truth of Allied intentions in Europe during 1944.

From the start of his attack on the Allied order of battle for D-Day, Roenne was bedeviled in a number of key areas of intelligence acquisition—and without good acquisition there could be no good evaluation. Ever since the British had retreated to the home islands after the debacle of Dunkirk, it had been virtually impossible for FHW to establish with certainty the strength of British forces. Now, with the build-up of forces in preparation for the invasion, it was even more difficult to obtain accurate estimates of Allied strength. Furthermore, Roenne was well aware that the Allies were systematically and on a large scale attempting to mislead OKW about their military strength and intentions. As early as Starkey he wrote in a report to the Fuehrer: "The multiplicity of the at times utterly fantastic reports about allegedly imminent operations . . . reveals an intention to deceive and mislead." Yet, Roenne and FHW had been deceived and misled by operations such as Mincemeat and by the Cicero case. But could the Allied deception agencies mislead them about the secrets of Neptune?

It seemed at first that they might not, for Roenne reported in his first major assessment of 1944 that he had conclusive evidence that the Allies would make their decisive stroke that year not in the Balkans but in France. He followed up this bulletin with another on February 8, 1944, in which he advised that:

> In 1944 an operation is planned outside the Eastern Mediterranean that will seek to force a decision (in the world war), and, therefore, will be carried out (from England) with all available forces. This operation is probably being prepared under the codename of *Overlock* and the distribution of enemy forces and troop movements clearly point to England as a point of departure.

How, with most of the sources upon which he depended for his intelligence in disarray or under Allied control, had Roenne been able to make this excellent and—for the Allies—dangerous assessment? It was a question that would not be answered until thirty years later when documents concerning the extent to which the Germans had penetrated Allied secrets were finally declassified. These documents revealed that the omnipresent German wireless intelligence service had obtained, through a variety of eavesdropping techniques, the information upon which Roenne had based his estimate. When, late in December 1943 and early in January 1944, Allied troops and assault shipping began to move from the Mediterranean to England in preparation for Neptune, German Y service analysts noted the rising crescendo of wireless traffic in the British Isles and a decrease in the Mediterranean theater, despite Allied attempts to use false wireless traffic to conceal the movement. Clearly, all of the British Isles were becoming an armed camp.

The German Y service also detected the arrival in Britain of the élite American 82nd Airborne Division from Italy—an event that confirmed Roenne's belief that England would be the springboard for the invasion. The Y service had been listening in on the 82nd's traffic for over a year and knew intimately the pattern of its wireless nets, the characteristics of its transmissions and even the names and home addresses of its operators. When the 82nd dropped out of sight in Italy, the Germans began to look for it in England; the radio nets which the division had left behind to make it seem that it was still positioned in the Mediterranean displayed few of the characteristics the Germans had studied for so long. Such was the excellence of SHAEF's wireless security plan that the 82nd's presence in Britain was not detected upon arrival; but then, early in February, the Germans picked up a radio net in Britain that they could not identify and overheard a signal *en clair* concerning paternity proceedings instituted in the United States against an American soldier. They also collected the reply which stated that the wanted soldier was in England with the 82nd Airborne and that the lawyers could interview him at the divisional command post at Banbury. The cat was out of the bag. Nevertheless, OKW at first refused to believe the report that the 82nd was in England. One high officer of German wireless intelligence would recall that Jodl's office replied facetiously that, unless the division had been transported by submarine, then it must still be in the Mediterranean; no transports had been observed by Abwehr agents on either side of the Pillars of Hercules. The Y service responded by bringing to Cherbourg the wireless analysts in Italy who were so familiar with the 82nd's wireless traffic. They placed the net under special observation, noted exactly the same characteristics as they had noted in Italy, and were able to provide indisputable evidence that the division was indeed in England.

The German Y service would prove to be an even more dangerous threat to the secrets of Neptune in the months ahead; but while its surveillance of the British Isles indicated that the Allies were planning a cross-Channel attack, that evidence alone was not sufficient to permit Roenne to conclude that there would be no invasion of the Balkans. As a result Hitler would not be able to withdraw his divisions from the Balkans to reinforce the Channel and Russian fronts. Equally, Roenne did not have the evidence to disabuse the Fuehrer of the prospect of an invasion of Norway if he withdrew his divisions from there, or of a strike across the Adriatic and an invasion of Germany through the Ljubljana Gap if he withdrew his forces from Italy. Nor was he able to predict, in the winter of 1943–44, *where* the Allies would land in France, so that OKW was compelled to divide its forces in northwestern Europe among no less than five sectors: The Netherlands, the Pas de Calais, the Normandy-Brittany area, and the Biscayan and Mediterranean coasts of France. The stratagems of Bodyguard and Fortitude, it appeared, were having the desired effect upon Roenne.

But even the most skillful deception campaigns would have fallen far short of success had Roenne been able to deduce with accuracy the strength and location of the Allied armies in Britain. With that kind of intelligence, it would have required little more than common sense to eliminate all but the Normandy-Brittany sector as the point of the major Allied attack. Concealing the Allied order of battle from the Germans was therefore at the very core of the cover and deception plans surrounding Neptune; and Roenne's reaction to Quicksilver in particular would be of crucial importance. The carefully calculated leaks to the press and radio, the reports from the XX-Committee's double agents, were often for the benefit of Roenne. It was Roenne and FHW that must be misled if Quicksilver was to succeed. For Roenne had the Fuehrer's ear. As Colonel Anton Staubwasser, who served under Roenne as chief of Group England until he became Rommel's chief of intelligence before the invasion, would state: ". . . it is known to me that the opinions held by Hitler and *OKW* [about the invasion] were based principally on the information supplied by FHW and did not deviate from that department's ideas in essentials."

How, then, did Roenne and FHW assess the Allied order of battle? Did Roenne believe that the Quicksilver force really existed? Did he believe that FUSAG was assembling in southeastern Britain and that Patton would lead this mighty army group against the Pas de Calais? The answer would prove to be far more complicated than the Allied deception agencies could have guessed. For just as Quicksilver got under way, the stiff, proud and hitherto impeccably honest Roenne was engaged in a deception of his own—an intrigue that would have a profound effect upon the outcome of Neptune.

It began at the end of 1943 when a newcomer joined the staff of FHW—Lieutenant Colonel Roger Michel, who succeeded Staubwasser as chief of Group England. A boisterous and heavy-drinking man—FHW, for all the primness of its chief, as Gehlen would say, "had a reputation for sloth" and for "throwing drinking parties on the most tenuous of pretexts"—Michel was born at Zaalen, not far from the Swiss frontier at Lake Constance. He was the son of a south German schoolmaster and his English wife; and as Staubwasser would later state, Michel, as a young man, spent time in England as a member of the German national rugby team. According to Staubwasser, he was "tall, sporty and athletic . . . and in spite of his baldness he had a youthful manner. He had a jolly, easy, happy disposition, and was said to be a good comrade." Staubwasser would further testify to Michel's fondness for "alcohol and women," but he would also remark that "In his work he was said to be reliable and he had a quick understanding of essentials. He was above average intelligence."

Michel's area of responsibility at FHW was England, and in January 1944 he approached Roenne with a complaint that was fully justified. As part of the continuing battle between the Abwehr and the SD for command of the Reich's intelligence system, and in order to prove to Hitler that its sources, intellect and objectivity were superior to the army's, the SD had consistently *halved* Michel's estimates of the Allied order of battle. Roenne was well aware of the truth of what Michel told him; but, as he explained, he saw no way of preventing SD interference. The system required that all FHW reports be filtered through the SD in order to "ensure their accuracy" and to be certain that they corresponded with the information and evaluations of the SD.

By March the situation had become serious, for Hitler, believing that the halved estimates of Allied strength came from Roenne, whom he had had every reason to trust, was removing divisions from the West. Roenne, in fact, believed he should reinforce the Atlantic Wall; but what could be done? Since the downfall of Canaris and the dissolution of the Abwehr, the SD had become more powerful than ever. It was Michel who proposed a solution. He suggested that from now on FHW should *double* its estimate of the number of Allied divisions in Britain. Then, when the SD halved it, which was done now almost as a routine, an estimate that was pretty near the truth would find its way to the Fuehrer's desk. Michel's suggestion was contrary to all the principles of FHW, and of Roenne himself. But the idea took hold in his mind.

When Roenne became desperate about the apparent lack of reality at Hitler's headquarters concerning the dangers from England, he approached Colonel Lothar Metz, his operations officer, about the proposal. Would Metz assist? Metz refused instantly and advised Roenne to have nothing to do with the scheme either. What would happen, he asked, if the SD accepted rather than halved the estimate? If that did happen, Metz warned, no one at OKW would be able to establish the truth of the situation in England—unless Roenne admitted what he had done. And that admission would certainly cost him his career, and probably his head.

But then Metz was transferred from FHW, and when he had gone Roenne did as Michel had proposed. He began to submit reports to Hitler that exaggerated Allied strength in Britain. This was serious enough; worse was to follow. The system required that evidence be available to substantiate the existence of divisions mentioned in FHW's estimates. But where was this evidence to be obtained? Michel had another suggestion; FHW should accept as true all of the leakages and reports about the strength of Allied forces in England. This intelligence was, of course, being deliberately fed to the Germans as part of Quicksilver, and Roenne knew very well that it might be a deception. But confident that the SD would halve his estimate, he went ahead with a major survey of Allied military strength in the British Isles. His survey was sent to the SD in May 1944; and it was then that the unexpected happened. Just as Metz had warned, the SD—possibly because the man who was doing the halving had been transferred—*accepted* and promulgated Roenne's inflated estimate. His survey reported that there were eighty-five to ninety Allied divisions assembling in Britain, together with seven airborne divisions, instead of the thirty-five (including three airborne divisions) which was the reality. This was the estimate that found its way onto all the charts throughout the Wehrmacht.

Thus, the Allied deception agencies had an unwitting ally in Roenne. For this survey of Allied strength in England prior to D-Day conformed in all respects to the Quicksilver order of battle. From May on the fictitious FUSAG became a reality to the Fuehrer and OKW, and no amount of maneuvering on Roenne's part could alter that reality. He discovered that it was much easier to put Allied divisions on an order of battle chart than it was to get them off; and indeed, as evidence continued to pour into FHW supporting the existence of eighty-five to ninety Allied divisions in Britain, Roenne himself began to believe that he might have been right in the first place. By the time the SD learned that it had been tricked, it would be too late to make any corrections; the last battle had been joined.

Roenne would pay for his intrigue with his life. But the progenitor of the scheme, Michel, escaped retribution, a fact which would lead to the suspicion in postwar Germany that he had been an agent for either the British or the American secret services. This suspicion increased when Michel was freed long before the rest of the General Staff was released from internment, appeared at Heidelburg wearing an American uniform, and announced that he was employed in the U.S. Counter-Intelligence Corps. But Michel did not remain in West Germany long. He soon fled into the Russian zone, thereby compounding a wartime mystery with a peacetime defection.

Whether or not Michel was an Allied agent is of incidental importance, just as it is useless to speculate whether Roenne's act of treachery was motivated by a desire to protect Germany or to pull the Fuehrer and the Third Reich down. Whatever the case, between them Roenne and Michel helped complete the tangled web that the Allied deception agencies spun around Neptune—a web that trapped the Fuehrer himself and would impede him in all his plans to meet the invasion.

7

Nuremberg

WHILE ROENNE'S INTRIGUE was a major factor in OKW's acceptance of Quicksilver, it was not the only one. OKW had a strong belief in the loyalty, reliability and competence of its main agents in England during the build-up for Neptune. Rarely was the intelligence gathered from these men questioned. Why did OKW not suspect that at least some of them, and perhaps even all, might be under British control?

There were several reasons: the chaos of the German intelligence services; the astuteness of Allied deception; the fact that the controlled agents generally transmitted information that conformed to OKW's own beliefs, and to military logic; and the fact that much of what agents such as Garbo and Brutus sent could be, and was, verified by aerial reconnaissance and wireless intelligence. But another reason for OKW's confidence was that its principal agents in Britain had supplied the Reich, over a considerable period, with intelligence that had proven to be correct. In short, the British high command, and later Supreme Headquarters, were often telling the Germans the truth, their motive being to establish and maintain the credibility of the agents under Allied control—"a necessary preliminary," Masterman would write, "for the passing over of the lie." The stratagem worked, for the performance of these agents had been so consistently valuable to the Germans that they came to accept as fact their information about the existence of Quicksilver and the deceptive strategy implied in Fortitude.

That being the case, what was the nature of the true intelligence the Allies—and particularly the British—were willing to reveal in order to ensure the success of Fortitude? Since the value of intelligence in war is measured in death and destruction, were the Allies willing to leak information detrimental to their own cause? Were they willing to risk or even sacrifice their own men to set up a deception scheme? Were some men and operations considered expendable in order that larger, decisive operations might succeed? After the war, Masterman deliberated these questions and replied: "We never gave the enemy information that would have cost Allied lives." But Masterman's military master for Neptune, General Sir Francis de Guingand, Montgomery's Chief of Staff and the 21st Army Group officer who ensured that deception conformed to strategy and tactics, disagreed. The British high command, he said, did indeed make such sacrifices. "On at least one occasion," de Guingand recalled, "the deception people were authorized to reveal the target of a major air attack on a German city to the Germans beforehand in order to reinforce the credibility of an (XX-Committee) agent who was to be used to mislead the German high command during Neptune." He said he seemed to remember that the city was Stuttgart, and the month in which the stratagem took place was March 1944. But he could not be sure that it was not Nuremberg in that same month. He was certain, however, that the incident took place just before the Allied heavy bomber forces were switched from Pointblank to tactical support of Neptune, which occurred on April 14, 1944.

Was de Guingand correct in his assertion? If so, the reasons for such an action might be traced beyond the demands of deception to Allied strategy governing the prosecution of the air war against Germany. Pointblank, the Allied Combined Bomber Offensive that preceded the invasion, had as a major objective the systematic destruction of the German industrial heartland. It was also the policy of the American and British air forces conjointly to compel the Luftwaffe to battle—or to force it to diffuse its strength by guarding theaters remote from France and Germany—so that it might be eliminated as a source of danger on D-Day. As the Pointblank directive said, the destruction of the Luftwaffe was second to none in priority. To obtain that objective, the USAAF in Washington instructed Wallace Carroll, chief of the European department of OWI, the American political warfare agency, ". . . to bait the *Luftwaffe*. Do *everything* you can to make the Germans come up and fight." The RAF, said Carroll, agreed with and cooperated in the policy; the purpose of this "cruel expedient," he continued, was to "save lives in the long run." " 'If the aim of the air force is achieved,' I told a meeting [of the New York office of OWI], 'the sacrifice which may now be made will mean the saving of thousands, even tens of thousands, of lives on the beaches when the Allied armies land on the Continent!' " The Anglo-American high command did not dispute the tragic logic of this policy. Eisenhower would tell Butcher: "One of the duties of a General is to determine the best investment of human lives. If he thinks expenditure of 10,000 lives in the current battle will save 20,000 lives later, it is up to him to do it."

Carroll, in accordance with his instructions, and with the knowledge and cooperation of the British, launched "Huguenot," a political warfare operation to lure the Luftwaffe into the air. It was prosecuted with great success but, as Carroll would recall, "no other propaganda campaign ever caused us so much heart-burning," because through it the Allied air forces encountered "more rather than less opposition in their raids." Propaganda was only part of that campaign, however, for Carroll wrote that U.S. heavy bomber forces were sent out "over routes which had been deliberately selected to bring out the maximum opposition from the Germans." There is no doubt that air commanders were aware of this strategy, for Eisenhower's diarist, Butcher, wrote on April 22, 1944: "General Spaatz [the commander of the U.S. Strategic Air Force in Europe] is not too crazy about it but admits that the strategic planes are supposed to draw the fire of the *Luftwaffe* over Germany." Spaatz himself would announce that he was prepared to take "more than ordinary risks to complete the task [of destroying the Luftwaffe as a prelude to Neptune], including the risk of exceptional losses."

While this strategy was a ruthless one—for American casualties were bound to increase—it was no more ruthless than the general means being used to fight a total war. However, the flight tactics of the Americans made them well able to take care of themselves. American bombers were heavily armed and armored, they flew in close formation to mass their firepower against attackers—the B17 was accurately called the Flying Fortress—and they were escorted by hundreds of long-range fighters that were the equal of most if not all the Luftwaffe's fighters. Their power was such that—as General Walter Grabmann, the commander of the German 3rd Fighter Division, would state—the Americans by the spring of 1944 no longer "had to bother about special maneuvers to mislead the defence." Moreover, just before D-Day, as Grabmann continued, "Their fighter preponderance was such that, in fine weather particularly, they could send out whole formations in advance to shatter the Germans before they were in position." The Americans, therefore, would have everything to gain by forewarning the Germans of the target for the day; such forewarning would virtually guarantee large numbers of Germans to shoot down.

Even so, American casualties in the three months before D-Day were extremely heavy. The 8th Air Force lost nearly 10,000 men, 800 heavy bombers and over 500 long-range fighters. And when the losses of the other U.S. air forces involved in the enormous bombardment of Europe before D-Day were included—at times it seemed that almost the entire continent between the Channel and Potsdam was covered with the smoke, fumes, ash, sound and aircraft of war—these casualties were almost doubled.

The RAF supported, indeed it was the instigator of, Pointblank in all its objectives. But British flight tactics were different from the American. British bombers sacrificed heavy defensive armament in return for much heavier bomb loads than the Americans were able to carry; they relied upon the cover of darkness, cloud and deception to avoid heavy losses, and they usually operated without fighter protection and in streams rather than formations, which meant that, on clear nights at least, they were extremely vulnerable to attack by radar-equipped night fighters. Thus the British would have a great deal more to lose by deliberately forewarning the enemy of the target of an attack to bait the Luftwaffe or to establish the credibility of a double agent. Yet de Guingand stated that they did just that.

If de Guingand was correct—and no one in the Allied high command was less likely to be in error, or less capable of exaggeration—the raid in question must have occurred during March 1944. That month Bomber Command did indeed attack Stuttgart, the great industrial city of 400,000 people on the Neckar River in Württemberg. The city was raided on March 1/2 and March 15/16, but neither raid showed signs of German foreknowledge. In the attack on Berlin on March 24/25, German night fighters shot down 72 of the 811 bombers that took part in the raid; but the heavy casualties were probably caused by factors other than foreknowledge. Of all the raids of the period, the only one that showed signs of German foreknowledge was the attack on Nuremberg by ninety squadrons of Bomber Command on March 30/31.

The circumstances of the Nuremberg raid were most unusual, and it was suggested, both at the time and later, that it might have been betrayed. The Royal Institute of International Affairs' *Chronology of the Second World War* used the word "ambush" in its report of the attack —with all that word's connotations of lying in wait and foreknowledge. Flight Lieutenant Alfred Price, a serving officer of the RAF and the author of *Instruments of Darkness,* a study of electronic deception in the Second World War, was not prevented by the Ministry of Defence from recording: "Since the war there have been suggestions that the Germans had some foreknowledge that the night's target was to be Nuremberg and had arranged their defences accordingly." Then even the official British air campaign historians, Sir Charles Webster, the president of the Royal Academy, and Dr. Noble Frankland, a director of studies at the Royal Institute of International Affairs, found something strange about the strategy employed in the attack. "This was," they wrote in *The Strategic Air Offensive Against Germany 1939–1945,* "indeed a curious operation. . . . The plan of action . . . abandoned most of the tactical precepts which for a long time had governed Bomber Command operations. . . . The normal ruses seemed to give way to a straightforward declaration of intention and the German fighter force was presented with a unique opportunity. . . ."

What was the intention of the raid on Nuremberg? By mid-March, the Allies' daylight raids over the continent had dealt the enemy such a severe blow that they had, through actual operations and Huguenot, achieved a large measure of daytime aerial superiority over France and the Low Countries. Moreover, American long-range fighters had established an important degree of sovereignty over the daylight skies of Germany. And the combined attacks of Bomber Command and the U.S. Strategic Air Forces in Europe had compelled the enemy to concentrate upon the defense of Germany rather than the Channel countries, thus reducing the Germans' ability to defend Normandy on D-Day. But in darkness air superiority had not yet been won, and it was expected that most of the Germans' air operations against Neptune would be conducted by night air crews. Therefore, it was vital to bring on an immense night battle where the best of the German night fighters might be destroyed. That, certainly, was a principal intention of the raid.

The choice of target—Nuremberg—reinforced that intention. For while Nuremberg was an important military target (equipment for tanks, aircraft, aero-engines and armored cars was produced there), it also had a special political and psychological significance. It was at Nuremberg in 1934 that Hitler had proclaimed that "The German form of life is definitely determined for the next thousand years"; and every year since then, the Nazi hierarchy, amid a vast Teutonic ceremonial, had dedicated itself anew. A successful raid against this Nazi shrine would demonstrate the impotence and the looming destruction of the Third Reich, and the Luftwaffe could be expected to defend the city with determination. But to bait the Luftwaffe, were the British willing to expose RAF air crews to even greater dangers than those normally associated with such a raid? And to ensure that the Luftwaffe took the bait, and to establish the credibility of a double agent, were they willing to forewarn the Germans of the raid? These were the central mysteries of the Nuremberg attack.

The mystery began from the moment Air Chief Marshal Arthur Harris, the C-in-C of Bomber Command, took the chair at his routine morning conference on March 30, 1944, at his headquarters in a hillside near the Buckinghamshire town of High Wycombe. The first order of business was the weather. Mr. Magnus Spence, the Command meteorological officer, presented his forecast; and while he was hesitant about making a positive prediction, he did say enough to suggest that the weather over Germany that night might not favor Bomber Command. It might favor the defense. The half-moon might be very brilliant, high winds might break up the bomber stream, and he could not guarantee that there would be cloud to hide the bombers from the night fighters. In short, weather conditions might be the direct opposite of those in which the Command preferred to operate—pitch-black, windless, cloudy nights.

Despite this forecast, Harris proceeded to announce the target for that night: Nuremberg. His announcement caused some surprise, for Nuremberg was not one of the targets on his current directive. Moreover, it was deep inside Germany. Even if weather conditions favored the raid, the bomber stream would be over enemy territory for so long that a major air battle was almost inevitable. There was cause for even greater surprise when Harris announced the route the Command was to take to reach the target. His plan was to gather almost the entire might of the Command over The Naze, a headland in eastern England, proceed to and cross the Belgian coast near Bruges, and fly directly to Charleroi in Belgium. At Charleroi, the bomber stream was to proceed in a straight line some 265 miles to Fulda, across the German frontier near Frankfurt; and at Fulda, it was to change course again and fly directly to Nuremberg.

It was this route—and particularly the "long leg" from Charleroi to Fulda—that provoked in Air Marshal Sir Robert Saundby, deputy C-in-C of Bomber Command, what would be called his "mounting apprehension" about the raid. Harris himself had recently ordered that, because of the heavy casualties suffered in the Leipzig and Berlin raids earlier that month, bomber streams should henceforward be split up to approach their targets from different directions in order to confuse and split night fighter defenses. Now he proposed to send a single stream to Nuremberg. Moreover, it would follow a route that would take it close to the thick concentration of German night fighter bases around the Ruhr, and directly over the fighters' assembly beacons at Aachen (codenamed "Ida") and Frankfurt ("Otto"). These tactics, as well as the depth of the target, seemed to confirm that luring the Luftwaffe to battle was a primary objective of the raid. But Saundby was concerned about the extraordinary dangers of the route, and when the conference ended, he voiced his concern to Harris. Harris replied merely that if the weather did turn definitely against Bomber Command, the operation could always be canceled at the last moment.

Before proceeding with the detailed planning for the attack, Saundby telephoned Air Vice Marshal D. C. T. Bennett—the air officer commanding (AOC) the Pathfinder force, which consisted of picked crews who would lead the bomber stream to Nuremberg and then mark the target with flares for accurate bombardment—to tell him about the route. Bennett protested immediately that the long leg was inviting disaster and told Saundby he would prepare a route himself, one that would avoid, so far as possible, the night fighter beacons and bases, and which would contain the usual "dog legs" to confuse the German night fighter controllers about the destination of the bombers. Saundby agreed to present Bennett's route to Harris. But when he held his usual telephone conference with the AOC's of the bomber groups, he found that they agreed with Harris's "straight in, straight out" route. It meant, they contended, that the bombers would be in and out of Germany much more quickly than if they took the route that Bennett was proposing. It was decided that the "straight in, straight out" route should stand. Informed that his opinion had been overruled, Bennett was overheard to remark: "The blood is on their heads."

By noon, Saundby and his staff had completed the detailed planning for the raid, including diversionary operations. To turn the Germans' attention away from the bomber stream, and to pin down the 1st German Fighter Division in northern Germany, fifty Halifaxes were to fly across the North Sea, simulating the approach of a much larger force in flight to Hamburg or Berlin. Their flight would be scheduled so that they approached the German coast at the same time that the main force approached the Belgian coast nearly 300 miles away to the southeast. Then, as the main force crossed the coast, Mosquitos would fly three missions, again simulating much larger forces threatening Aachen, Cologne and Kassel.

These were usual diversionary tactics, designed to confuse the Germans for as long as possible about the actual destination of the main force, and thus split their defenses. But the plan also called for some seventy to eighty long-range Mosquito night fighters to accompany the main force to engage the German night fighters as they were taking off or landing at their bases, or as they tried to penetrate the bomber stream. These were not usual tactics, and they again confirmed that the primary purpose of the raid was to lure the Luftwaffe to battle. The British intended to tempt the Germans into the air with a stream of lumbering bombers flying a long and dangerous route, and then shoot them down with night fighters. It was a risky strategy, but the bomber stream would have the protection of the Mosquitos and, it was hoped, the weather. All those concerned with planning the raid were convinced that it would be canceled if late weather forecasts proved unfavorable.

But reports from Spence's meteorological flights that afternoon confirmed his earlier predictions. There would be no high cloud over Germany, and weather conditions were such that the bomber stream would leave contrails—those tell-tale trails of frozen vapor that would pinpoint the location of every bomber. Furthermore, over Nuremberg itself there would be thick cloud at bombing altitude, which meant that the Pathfinders would not be able to mark the city accurately, and therefore the bombers might not be able to bomb accurately. Plainly, the weather would favor the defense, and it now seemed certain that Harris would cancel the raid.

It was not canceled. At the main briefings, which took place between 5 and 6 P.M. that afternoon and were attended by all the men who would fly that night, there were general expressions of surprise—and even of dismay—when the target and the route were revealed. Perhaps because they anticipated such a reaction, or perhaps because they had been misinformed by Bomber Command, briefing officers misled the bomber crews about the dangers of the route. To explain why the bomber stream was being routed through Flak Valley, a hellspot near Cologne where anti-aircraft defenses were very deep and effective, the crews at Coningsby bomber base were told, according to Martin Middlebrook, an historian of the Nuremberg raid, that "the Germans were known to have moved their fighters to the coast in readiness for the shortening raids of the less deep spring nights and would not be expecting a deep penetration." The crews at Lissett bomber base were told that "the defences covering southern Germany were weak and the gap near Cologne [Flak Valley] would be 'virtually unprotected.'"

Many bomber crews were also misled about the weather. Middlebrook would write that:

> . . . at station level, every effort was made to keep from crews the un-
> pleasant fact that they were to fly a constant course for 265 miles
> through a well-defended part of Germany in bright moonlight but with
> little chance of cloud cover. On at least eleven stations, the crews were
> given the specific forecasts that there would be cloud cover at opera-
> tional flight on this outward flight.

Flight Sergeant Tom Fogaty of 115 Squadron would remark that "we were assured that there would be ten-tenths cloud cover for most of the way." The crews of 102 Squadron were told that "it should be a milk-run . . . (because) cloud and fog would completely black-out the Continent and that they could therefore expect practically no night-fighter opposition for some time (until) after they had crossed the enemy coast."

There can have been only one reason for misinforming the bomber crews; if they had been told the truth there might have been—given the heavy casualties they had suffered in recent operations—serious refus-als to fly. As it was, there were further protests about the route, but they were useless. Harris, it seemed, was determined to mount the raid however vulnerable the bomber stream would be because of the route and the weather. Apparently, an attempt to destroy the Luftwaffe night fighter force warranted such risks. But did it warrant the addi-tional risk of deliberately forewarning the Germans of the attack? Whatever the answer to that question, the bomber crews would soon discover that the Germans were ready and waiting for them.

At about 4:30 P.M., General Wolfgang Martini, the chief of the German signals intelligence service, having examined all data from the technical surveillance of the RAF's electronics traffic, sent a signal to General Hans-Juergen Stumpff, the C-in-C of the Reich Air Defense Command. Martini expressed the opinion that the RAF was preparing for a major attack that night. But he did not say what he thought the strength of the attack would be. Neither could he say where he felt the attack would be delivered. There was little that was unusual about this appreciation. Martini knew Bomber Command's procedure, RAF wireless and radar equipment was always tested before the aircraft were loaded with fuel to prevent sparks from detonating petrol fumes. Martini's technical intelligence experts had detected heavy test transmissions that morning; therefore it could be assumed that the

RAF was preparing for an attack that night. However, there was something unusual about the signal Martini sent between 5 and 6 P.M. He said he thought that between seven hundred and eight hundred bombers would attack Germany that night. How he could have been so close to the truth is not clear. It was possible, but not probable, that he deduced the number of bombers that would take part in the raid from his observations of the strength, location and pattern of British test transmissions. But he could not have deduced with any certainty that Germany would be the target that night; Bomber Command was striking everywhere from Murmansk to Milan. Had Martini made an inspired guess, or had he had some forewarning of the attack?

Whatever the source of Martini's assessment, Stumpff's headquarters at Berlin-Wannsee, the great underground command post on the outskirts of Berlin, began to prepare the crews, and arm, fuel and service the aircraft of no less than six air divisions, and to bring some of the most distant squadrons to airfields closer to Otto and Ida. Again, that was not unusual. But Stumpff's later disposition of his forces would be unusual indeed.

Shortly before 10 P.M. that night, the quiet of the English countryside was shattered as thousands of Koffmann starters exploded in clouds of acrid blue smoke; propellers began to revolve, and 898 British and 10 American aircraft connected with the raid began to move. At 10 P.M. exactly the first greens were fired from the towers and the first bombers began to roar down the runways, lifting up over the silvered countryside. Fifty-five of the aircraft soon aborted the operation through technical failure and returned to base, leaving 843 flying toward Germany. Once airborne, the main force clawed for the operating altitude and formed into the great bomber stream, Bomber Command's tactic for overwhelming each line of German defenses by a sheer profusion of targets; the bombers would pass over any given point on the ground at an average rate of forty a minute. As the bombers left the British coast on a southeasterly heading, the bombaimers flicked switches to arm the bombs, the gunners test-fired their machine guns, the navigators worked under the glow of amber lamps plotting the track of the planes across the pink-printed charts of northern Europe. By the time it was out over the Channel, the force occupied a volume of sky some 65 miles long, 10 miles wide and 1 mile deep—a great thundering phalanx moving forward at nearly 4 miles a minute. But there was trouble ahead. Almost immediately high winds began to disorder the stream, and the bomber crews were astounded to find that the sky was as clear as a summer's night. They were, they discovered, naked in the moonlight.

As the main force neared the Belgian coast, the fifty Halifaxes in the diversionary force approached the German coast at Heligoland Bay, feigning a raid against either Hamburg or Berlin. If Stumpff was uncertain about which of the two forces was the main one, he would be compelled to keep the two fighter divisions in northwestern and northern Europe in place and the bombers destined for Nuremberg might slip through Flak Valley into central Germany. But Stumpff knew which was the main force; his technical intelligence men informed him that the northern force was not using the H2S precision bombing radar, which was always the case with a major attack. Therefore, it was the diversionary force, and Stumpff ordered all fighter squadrons of the 1st and 2nd Fighter Divisions to rendezvous with the 3rd Division over Ida and Otto. The weather made it impossible, Stumpff reasoned, for the main force to be going anywhere other than central Germany. The Luftwaffe was concentrating almost all the fighter defenses of Germany and western Europe along the exact route that the bomber stream would fly. Was it a coincidence, or did Stumpff have some foreknowledge of the route and destination of the attack?

It was the Luftwaffe's customary strategy to intercept a bomber stream long before it reached its target, but that night the German fighters were among the stream exceptionally early. Flight Sergeant Ronald Gardner of 103 Squadron would recall:

The fighters were waiting for us shortly after we crossed the coast, as if they already knew our target and route. And they were in force. Never have I seen so many gathered at one point during my tour of operations . . . (the sky) was full of Me-109s and 110s. . . . Normally, flying in the leading wave, we were seldom attacked by fighters until well into France or Germany. . . . Usually the fighters took at least half an hour to get amongst us.

It was now that other factors intruded to ensure the looming catastrophe. The spoof raids by Mosquitos on Cologne, Kassel and Aachen were as accurately interpreted by Stumpff as had been the Halifax feint at Hamburg and Berlin. He left the spoofs to the flak as his night fighters concentrated on the bomber stream. German ground controllers used voice radio communications to help the night fighters home in on their targets, and the RAF employed giant transmitters to jam their frequencies with sounds of ringing bells, shouts, massed bands, long speeches by Hitler and Goering, interminable passages from Goethe. More often than not, the ground controllers' orders were successfully blocked; but that night, the jamming was not fully effective. The Germans normally changed their frequencies at random to confuse the jammers, but on this occasion, as the Bomber Command signals officer would report: "The enemy displayed . . . unusual subtlety (in avoiding the RAF's jamming transmissions) in that he appeared to be making his frequency changes in step with our Group Broadcast times. . . ." How the Germans were able to do this would remain a mystery, for it was not yet technically possible to scan and locate an open frequency automatically. Was it, again, a coincidence, or did they have some foreknowledge of the main force's signals plan?

The German night fighters also used radar to direct them to their targets, and that night, for the first time, they used a new type—the SN-2. The Mosquitos that were accompanying the bomber stream to pick off the night fighters as they rose to the attack were not able to home in on this new system. The Germans eluded them both in the air and on the ground. Few of the Mosquito attacks against the fighter bases were successful; all of the fighters had taken off by the time the Mosquitos arrived, and the bomber stream was virtually defenseless except for its own guns.

The weather completed the tragedy. The bomber stream was flying in brilliant moonlight at an altitude that produced luminous contrails. Flight Sergeant Robert Truman of 625 Squadron would recount: "You could see them clearly; the sky was full of contrails. I remember thinking that if they were so clear to us then they must be equally clear to the night fighters and that, if they were anywhere about, they could not fail to get onto us."

The night fighters were all about by the time the stream reached the first of the two beacons, Ida. Stumpff had concentrated between 200 and 250 aircraft in the area; and he had calculated the estimated time of arrival of the main force and the flight time of the fighters, which was of very limited duration, with remarkable precision. They were up in strength and "fresh"; each had a full fuel load and could stay in the stream, falling upon the bombers like falcons on disordered geese. The night sky was filled with deadly beauty as the fighters dropped their flares, which were hardly necessary in the bright moonlight, and opened fire with cannon tracer. Flying Officer George Foley, a radar operator in one of the Pathfinders, would remember: "I knew things were going very badly when I heard the captain call out over the intercom, 'Better put your parachutes on, chaps, as I have just seen the 42nd go down.'"

At RAF Kingsdown, the British wireless intelligence post in the tip of the Kentish peninsula, the operators all knew that a disaster was in the making. The German night fighters' voice radio bands were filled with the Nazi greeting *Sieg Heil!*, followed by the transmitting aircraft's call sign—the procedure for announcing a kill. By the time the main force had reached the end of the long leg at Fulda, the landscape below was marked by a necklace of fifty-nine crashed and burning bombers. Flying Officer L. Young of 103 Squadron later recalled: ". . . one could navigate on the blazing wrecks below." Flight Sergeant Ronald Holder of 460 Squadron, who had flown eighty-six missions over Germany before this one—an almost unheard-of number—recorded:

> It was a story of the perfect air ambush. . . . The ground controllers had to guess where we were making for, and they guessed correctly. . . . There were enemy fighters everywhere. We were sitting ducks, with no cloud cover to shield us. . . . Before this hellish action we had bombed many big German cities . . . but this was our first real experience of encountering the full fury of the enemy's fighter force . . . and it was terrifying.

At approximately 12:45 A.M. the first Lancaster turned southeast at Fulda toward Nuremberg, which was now only 75 miles away—twenty minutes' flying time. But this course change, which was intended to fox the Germans into thinking that either Berlin or Leipzig might be the target, had seemingly been anticipated. Stumpff had scrambled fresh squadrons into this final leg before the bomb run. Moreover, Nuremberg had been warned that it might be the target shortly before midnight—some seventy-five minutes before the attack was due to start, while the bomber stream was far away and could still have gone in any direction. Shortly afterwards—perhaps forty minutes before 1:10 A.M., Zero Hour for the attack—the sirens sounded the preliminary *Öffentliche Luftwarnung*. The main alarm—the *Fliegeralarm*—was sounded at 12:38, even before the bombers reached the end of the long leg, thirty minutes before Zero Hour. Again, it seemed that the Germans had foreknowledge that Nuremberg would be the target, for normally, given RAF tactics, the Germans were able to provide their cities with only a few minutes' warning, if any at all.

There were 643 bombers left in the stream; casualties and aborts had removed one out of every five aircraft that had taken off from England. But still—if all went well—the force approaching Nuremberg was big enough to wipe the city off the map. Furthermore, the

Pathfinder force and the force responsible for marking the target were virtually intact. But all did not go well. Light white clouds began to appear below, making the bombers, as one pilot put it, appear to the night fighters above like flies on a white tablecloth. By the time the marker force reached Nuremberg, the cloud cover was nearly 2 miles thick and totally obscured the city. The marker flares—red and green cascades called "Christmas trees" and huge mushrooming ground flares—disappeared into the thick cloud and could not be seen by the bomb-aimers aboard the main force. But other flares, inaccurately dropped, could be seen, and it was on these that the main force bombed. Some damage was caused to the industrial areas of the city, but in general damage to the rest of Nuremberg was slight.

Then came the flight back to England. The night fighters had shot their bolt, but they did muster enough force to catch and shoot down more bombers on the way home. How many would not be clear, for although ten heavy bombers were lost on the return flight, some were aircraft that had been disabled in attacks before they reached the target, or while they were over it. But these casualties did not mark the end of the agony that night. More aircraft were lost over the English countryside, or in the Channel, crashing either through the miscalculation of exhausted pilots or because they had been shot to pieces and simply fell apart in the turbulence. Such was the distress of the force that, as James Campbell, a British journalist, would write:

> The air over half of England that foggy dawn hummed with Mayday calls as wireless operators tapped out desperate emergency signals in the knowledge that they could not remain airborne much longer. And from control towers of fog-shrouded bases equally frantic signals flashed back to the bombers, diverting them to fog-free airfields where grim-faced controllers fought the clock to sort out landing priorities and get the flak-battered aircraft down as swiftly as possible. . . .

When the aircraft did get down, many of the crews were extremely angry, bitter and suspicious. The Pathfinder leader, Wing Commander Daniels, found Bennett, his AOC, waiting for him as he got out of his aircraft. Daniels exclaimed: "Bloody hell! Why did we have to go that way?" At the debriefings, the crews' attitudes were similar. Flight Lieutenant Stephen Burrows would recall the debriefing at Dunholme Lodge base: "It certainly appeared to me that Jerry was waiting for us, and there were rumors that the raid had been leaked. In fact, it was said quite openly during (debriefing)—with lots of derogatory remarks being made." Flight Sergeant Ronald Gardner, a Pathfinder with 103 Squadron, would recall: "Everyone I talked to after the raid was sure that it had been leaked." Pilot Officer Merril of 463 Squadron summed up the general opinion when he wrote in his debriefing report: "Fighter activity from leaving position B [Charleroi] to the target was such that enemy may have been aware of the route taken by the main force."

Now came the reckoning. The raid was a disaster for Bomber Command, yet the dimension of that disaster would remain obscure. All that was said about losses on the main BBC newscast on March 31 was that ninety-six bombers had failed to return. When two of the missing aircraft turned up, the total was reduced to ninety-four; but an official analysis would show that ninety-five bombers had been lost, a further ten were total losses upon crashing in England, one was later scrapped because of the severity of its battle damage, and seventy more sustained damage that put them out of action for between six hours and six months. Furthermore, a Halifax taking SOE agents to Belgium that night had been shot down, as well as a Mosquito taking part in airfield attack operations supporting the Nuremberg raid. That brought the known total to 108 aircraft for the entire night's operations. In all, 745 crewmen were killed or wounded and a further 159, some of whom were wounded, were taken prisoner. But that may not have been the end of the casualty list. Intelligence documents which were not intended for general circulation are said to have revealed that 53 bombers had, in fact, crashed in England, bringing the total to 160 aircraft; while yet another source, one that was only semi-official, would increase the number of crashes to 66 and the total to 178. Whatever the actual total, the RAF had suffered its heaviest casualties of the war, and the crew loss was higher than that for the entire Battle of Britain. German losses, on the other hand, totaled five aircraft, with five more damaged seriously and three less seriously. German dead, civil as well as military, totaled 129.

With the hindsight of history, it seemed incredible to the RAF and its historians that the Nuremberg raid was mounted at all. The destruction of the German night fighter force was an important military priority, and the choice of Nuremberg as a target, as well as the route and tactics employed in the raid, plainly indicated that Bomber Command was being used as live bait, just as Spaatz was using his command. But why undertake such a mission on a night when the weather promised to favor the defense? Saundby would speculate:

. . . I always had the impression that (Churchill) exerted pressure on Harris to make the raid before Bomber Command was switched to the

(*Neptune*) operations and attacks on pre-invasion targets in France. Nuremberg was the place where Hitler held his big rallies, and Churchill was persistent in that it must be bombed (now). . . .

Harris would deny, however, that Churchill demanded the city be attacked that night, adding that on one occasion the Prime Minister had told him that he did not expect Bomber Command to fight both the enemy *and* the weather. Harris would further state that it was doubtful that he would have gone ahead with the operation if he had known more accurately what the weather would be that night. He would also defend the route and tactics used in the raid:

> In sending the force in one stream to Nuremberg we thought we would fool the German night-controller, who we considered would not believe it. We had used in the past so many tactics and diversions—making out that such-and-such a city was to be the target and then heading for the real one—that we hoped that the straight run to Nuremberg would fox the Germans into thinking that we would, as in the past, suddenly turn off before the city was reached and deliver our attack elsewhere. . . .

It is certain, of course, that neither Churchill and Harris nor anyone else concerned with planning the raid intended that Bomber Command should suffer such heavy losses in the pursuit of aerial supremacy for D-Day. In fact, shortly after the Nuremberg raid, the British withdrew their support from Huguenot. Clearly, the operation had backfired. The Luftwaffe had been lured to battle, but it was the RAF that suffered the devastating casualties. The city of Nuremberg was scarcely touched. Everything, it seemed, had gone wrong: the weather, a grave miscalculation of the German reaction to the novel tactics of the raid, the ineffectiveness of the diversionary raids, the failure of the Mosquito night fighters to protect the bomber stream—all contributed to the tragedy. But what of the contention that the Germans were given forewarning of the raid? If so, would that not, above all, have sealed Bomber Command's fate?

There were several indications that the Germans knew of Bomber Command's plans in advance—the early appreciation of the size of the raid, the fact that the German night fighters were concentrated at exactly the right place and the right altitude for an ambush, the alerts passed to Nuremberg before the bomber stream turned into the final leg of its run. Moreover, British airmen who had been shot down and were being held prisoner at the time of the raid would state after the war that during the afternoon of the 30th—about five hours before the bomber stream took off—they were told by Luftwaffe intelligence interrogators at the main interrogation center at Oberursel, near Frankfurt, that the target for the raid that night was Nuremberg. At least one prisoner claimed that he saw that someone in the Luftwaffe had marked the route to be taken, with the target, on a wall map in the room where he was questioned. Prisoners taken after the raid would state that they were told by their interrogators at Oberursel that the route and target were known to the Luftwaffe at four o'clock in the afternoon on March 30.

While it was common for interrogators on both sides to claim more knowledge than in fact they had, in order to demoralize prisoners and persuade them that there was no point in keeping silent, these statements, if the prisoners concerned reported correctly, at least warranted further investigation. But neither Bomber Command nor the British intelligence authorities pursued the allegation—an odd fact in itself. A document which surfaced in the RAF archives after the war would add to the mystery. It was the Raid Plot, upon which was noted the exact crash position of each missing aircraft. It had been compiled not only from RAF intelligence and records but also from the findings of RAF intelligence teams in Germany after the war and from captured German records. The person who had investigated the raid and compiled the map had written in large capital letters on top of the document: "THEY KNEW WE WERE COMING," and "CARELESS TALK COSTS LIVES." Middlebrook would draw attention to this document in his book on the Nuremberg raid which was published in 1974; but when the Public Records Office in London was asked to supply the Raid Plot in 1975, the document with the superscription was not provided.

Few of the British principals in the disaster ever said very much about the raid. Air Vice Marshal Bennett, the Pathfinder AOC, was said to have told James Campbell, who was investigating the affair, that "It was caused, . . . and was not merely accidental." Campbell would find it "strange" that Harris made no mention at all of the raid in his memoirs after the war. He would also find it strange that Churchill dismissed it with one short paragraph in a work of six volumes. Their reticence, however, might be attributed to the fact that the raid was, by its very nature, sacrificial, just as were other British and American raids of the period that were intended to entrap the Luftwaffe. The difference, in this case, was simply the magnitude of the sacrifice. Yet the contention that the Germans were given foreknowledge of the raid as an additional incentive to come up and fight—

and, at the same time, to establish the credibility of a double agent—cannot be discounted, particularly in light of de Guingand's remark.

If this was, in fact, what happened, it seems quite clear that Harris was not privy to the stratagem. It was Churchill who, again, appeared to occupy the center of the web. Harris may well have been under pressure from the Prime Minister to launch the raid, but every high commander was under similar pressure to mount extremely risky operations to obtain the preconditions of intelligence, security and safety for the invasion. Harris accepted the risks of a deep-penetrating mission even under adverse weather conditions, and he sought to counter those risks with diversionary operations and fighter protection for the bomber stream. He could not have predicted the outcome, nor could he be held responsible. But once it had been decided to undertake such an operation—and Churchill as Minister of Defence was one of two or three men who were informed of Bomber Command's targets in advance—it may also have been decided to add one of the sinister touches to which Churchill was addicted.

The dangers of forewarning the Germans of the raid were obvious, but so were the dangers of the novel tactics employed in the raid. Just as Harris hoped that the Germans would be fooled by such a "straightforward declaration of intention," so it was possible that Churchill thought that they would disbelieve, and fail to act upon, a forewarning. Furthermore, a double agent could not tell the Germans very much more beforehand than they would learn for themselves from radar and wireless intelligence once the main force was airborne. All other factors being equal, the probability was that Bomber Command would suffer no greater losses through foreknowledge than if there had been none.

The advantages of such a stratagem, however, were numerous. The Germans were keenly interested in obtaining foreknowledge of the RAF's and the USAAF's targets during this period. Any agent who could provide such information, even if it resulted in a major defeat for the Luftwaffe—which was the intention of the Nuremberg raid—would soar in the estimation of the German intelligence services. Who, in the future, would dare disbelieve reports from an agent who had warned of any of the Allies' major targets at this time? His information had merely to be true; it need not have been so detailed and specific that the Luftwaffe would be able to thwart the attack or inflict severe casualties. In fact, an agent who supplied that kind of information might be immediately suspect, for how would it be possible that he could reveal the details of one raid and of no other?

If a double agent was used to warn the Germans of the Nuremberg attack, Garbo or Brutus would have been logical choices. The Germans believed that Brutus actually served on an air staff, and that both men had sub-agents connected with Allied air headquarters. Both Garbo and Brutus were, significantly, playing central roles in establishing the deceptions of Fortitude and Quicksilver in German minds; they would also play a crucial part in a later, even more daring deception to prevent the Germans, it was hoped, from launching the massive panzer counteroffensive that the Allies expected shortly after D-Day. Because the success of military operations that involved millions might depend upon the credibility of one or two double agents, Churchill may well have considered it essential to tell the Germans the truth about Nuremberg, if only in broad outline, to prime them for the lies of Fortitude.

If the Germans had foreknowledge of the raid, and acted upon it, here was grim evidence indeed of the truth of Masterman's remark that "the larger the prize the higher must also be the preliminary stake." Miscalculation, misfortune, coincidence, perhaps even foreknowledge, had combined to provide Goering with a major victory. In an Order of the Day he proclaimed triumphantly: "The enemy has been dealt the heaviest nocturnal defeat so far in his criminal attack on our beloved homeland." The German night fighter pilots were the heroes of the hour, while among the pilots and crews of Bomber Command there was a profound bitterness against those who had planned and ordered the attack. There were too many empty seats at breakfast the morning after the raid, too many "chop girls"—the girl friends of missing airmen who were, through superstition, shunned by the survivors. There they stood, at Flying Control, at the ends of runways, in the messes, at the bars, lonely, disconsolate, silent reminders of the lives that had been lost in an operation that was intended to save lives on D-Day.

Aerial Stratagems

THE LYSANDER AIRCRAFT landed at Manston just after midnight and taxied over to the SOE/MI-6 hardstanding in the southeast corner of the field. The bulky form of Commander Dunderdale came out of the darkness to open the aircraft door and help two passengers down the steps. They were "M. Pierre Moreau," a nervous, bespectacled French railway official who had been exfiltrated earlier that evening from his home near Lyon, and his wife, who was wrapped in an old fur coat. When the trio was in the brightly lit crew room, Mme Moreau took the coat off, and Dunderdale noted that she was heavily pregnant. By daybreak, M. and Mme Moreau were at Brown's Hotel on Piccadilly; and there, after they had slept, bathed and eaten, Moreau received a caller. He was Professor Solly Zuckerman, a brilliant anatomist whose range of studies extended from apes to the effects of bomb blast on the human frame. Now he was concerned with another study in which Moreau would play an important part—the destruction of the French railroads.

Before Moreau arrived, a major disagreement had been raging for weeks between the Supreme Command and its airmen on the one hand, and Churchill, the War Cabinet and the Anglo-American heavy bomber barons on the other. The dispute centered upon the huge Allied heavy bomber force and how it was to be employed in direct support of Neptune. Eisenhower demanded that it must be used not only in bombing enemy cities but also in massed attacks to destroy the rail centers of western Europe—rail centers through which the panzers and German reserves must move to reach Normandy. At the request of Air Chief Marshal Sir Trafford Leigh-Mallory, the C-in-C of the Allied Expeditionary Air Force (AEAF), Professor Zuckerman had produced a plan for a ninety-day attack against eighty rail targets in western Europe. The plan went to Tedder, the deputy Supreme Commander, it was codenamed "Transportation," and it received Eisenhower's strong support. He insisted that, since the first five or six weeks of Neptune were likely to be the most critical, it was essential to take every possible step to ensure that the assault forces obtained and held the largest possible foothold in Europe, an objective that would be difficult to achieve if the Germans were able to rush major reinforcements by rail to Normandy.

The military advantages of destroying the major rail centers of western Europe were self-evident, but the political implications of the Transportation plan raised a host of objections. The War Cabinet, upon hearing that the plan might kill 20,000 and injure 60,000 Frenchmen and Belgians, took what its Minutes described as a "grave and on the whole adverse view of the proposal." Churchill supported this view and at a Defence Committee meeting on April 26, 1944, stated that if the western powers proceeded with the plan, then "we should build up a volume of dull hatred in France which would affect our relations with that country for many years to come." He wired Roosevelt to ask him to order Eisenhower to find some other means of delaying the panzers. But Roosevelt was unwilling to interfere. After consultation with the Joint Chiefs of Staff, he replied to Churchill: "I am not prepared to impose from this distance any restriction on military action by responsible Commanders that in their opinion might militate against the success of Overlord or cause additional loss of life to our Allied forces of invasion." His cable was decisive; western Europe was to be turned into a railway desert in the interests of Neptune.

M. Moreau was a man of considerable importance to that aerial campaign. As a lifelong and senior official of the French railway system, the Société Nationale des Chemins de Fer (SNCF), he knew as much as any man about the military capacity of the system, and of German plans for its use in the event of invasion. Moreau had been approached by MI-6's *réseau* in Paris, Jade Amicol, which had important connections within the executive of SNCF, and had agreed to go to England and place his knowledge and experience at the service of Neptune. He brought with him the set of three volumes which constituted the latest operating manual for the French railways, together with extensive material about German plans for their operations in the event of an invasion. And with the end of the political dispute over Transportation, he joined the Railway Research Service (RRS), which had been established to survey northwest Europe's rail yards, sidings, stations, sheds, tracks, repair shops, roundhouses, turntables, signals systems, switches, locomotive and rolling stock resources, and bridges. Moreau's particular job would be to assist the RRS in selecting targets whose destruction would have the maximum effect upon the ability of the Germans to move their reserves up to Normandy.

Moreau placed his wife in the care of an obstetrician, and then went to work. He was a nervous, sensitive man who seemed to his colleagues to be the archetype of the French civil servant—fussy in sums and in life—and it was not long before a crisis developed. Mme Moreau bore a son and Moreau, who was a Jew, insisted that since he was in England on British government business, the British government must pay all the expenses of the birth—including the circumcision. MI-6 agreed to pay the obstetrician's fees but the paymaster balked at paying for the circumcision. This, he said, should be charged against the AEAF and the RRS. But as neither had funds for such purposes, both refused to pay. Moreau reacted by stating that he would resume his work only when he was reimbursed for the expense. The world might be involved in a cataclysmic war, but the French attitude toward money had not changed, and neither had the spirit of English bureaucracy. Aware of French punctiliousness about small sums, Dunderdale decided to raise the matter at the next meeting of the Air Council. He did so, mentioning the question of the circumcision fee under the heading of "any other business," and the chairman, Marshal of the Royal Air Force Sir Charles Portal, "put his hand in his pocket and produced a half-crown. The other members of the council did likewise, and there was shortly enough to meet the bill."

Moreau resumed work, but in a state of increasing agitation. For as Transportation got under way, he began to realize that he was contributing to a national disaster in French life by helping destroy the railroads. Apparently unaware of the enormity of Allied airpower, he listened aghast to the radio stations at Paris, Vichy and Brussels which reported the casualties and damage caused by his and the RRS's work. He reacted very strongly when he heard that the French cardinals had issued an appeal to British and American episcopates to halt the campaign. And he finally stopped work altogether when, on May 23, 1944, he heard the Nazi-controlled Radio Paris describe the devastation:

> The French railway system is in complete chaos. The Allies have successfully pulverized into rubble whole marshalling yards. They have destroyed countless locomotives and have made scores of railway stations unusable. The rest of the destructive work which could not be

done by the Allied pilots has been accomplished by experienced squads of saboteurs. . . . The temper of the population, especially that of Paris, is rising because no food is available, nobody can travel, and there are severe restrictions in the use of electricity. . . .

It was also reported that, by the third week of May, 6062 civilians had been killed in the campaign.

Moreau refused to do any further work for the RRS, waited in England until France had been liberated and then went home. Long after the war, Dunderdale received a letter from the SNCF stating that Moreau had retired and had applied for his pension after forty years of service. Unfortunately, the letter pointed out, there was a period of broken service in the spring of 1944 which Moreau could not explain satisfactorily. He asked that the SNCF approach the Foreign Office for the information; he could say nothing. But neither could Dunderdale. For MI-6 did not officially exist, and therefore had never employed anybody. Moreover, Dunderdale was not sure what effect his words might have upon Moreau's pension if the SNCF discovered that he had played a role in the wartime destruction of the French railways.

Transportation was only one aspect of the gigantic aerial campaign waged by the Allied air forces prior to D-Day; and just as the Battle of the Atlantic was fought to destroy the Kriegsmarine, so the prize in the air was the destruction of the Luftwaffe and, coincidentally, the obliteration of the industrial centers that supplied the German war machine. With the virtual elimination of the U-boat threat and victory in North Africa in 1943, the aerial campaign came to dominate Allied priorities, for the Luftwaffe posed a dual hazard to Neptune. Allied planners feared that even a handful of German planes might create havoc in the crowded sea lanes and beachheads of the Neptune assault area, just as they had done at Bari. And the Luftwaffe, which had at its disposal a complete paratroop army of at least five divisions, might react to Neptune by making a mass drop on the ports of southern England, on London, or on the beachhead zones. Indeed, it was discovered after the war that such a plan had been drawn up by Goering, and it might have been attempted if the Germans had been able to obtain foreknowledge of the time and place of the invasion, if the Luftwaffe had available the transport aircraft necessary to carry the paratroopers to the target—and if the Allies had not been able to achieve aerial supremacy and wipe out a paratroop armada before it reached the French bases from which it would have to operate.

Victory in the air, however, was not simply a matter of which side had the greatest number of aircraft. There were the additional imperatives of keeping Allied casualties to a minimum and, as important, of concealing from the Germans the truths about Neptune that might be deduced from the patterns and intensity of the pre-invasion aerial campaign. The German air intelligence service was large, experienced and extremely capable, and it existed for the sole purpose of confounding Allied aerial attacks. Through its surveillance of Allied tactics, formations and targets, its cryptanalytical and wireless intelligence activities, and its techniques for blinding or jamming radar systems and radio navigation devices, it had the means to predict, and perhaps even prevent, Neptune. Thus deception, and in particular the fictions of Fortitude, became the dominant influence on the pre-invasion aerial campaign. Aerial warfare itself was new, and it called forth a catalogue of stratagems as ingenious, and as ruthless, as any practiced against the enemy on land or at sea.

There were, first of all, systematic attempts to deceive the German wireless intelligence service. It was known that the Germans monitored Allied air force wireless traffic and assumed from certain characteristic patterns that a major strike was in the offing. Therefore, false wireless traffic was broadcast to keep them continuously, and needlessly, alert; and in the special context of Neptune, dummy traffic similar to the real traffic that would occur on the eve of D-Day was broadcast to coincide with large-scale pre-invasion exercises so that, it was hoped, the enemy would conclude that Neptune itself was just another exercise. Deceptive traffic was also broadcast in the clear or in an easily breakable code so that the Germans would think they had intercepted some important piece of information through a security leak. This was a familiar ruse, however, and was employed very sparingly lest the Germans see the truth behind a lie too easily obtained.

Aware that if the enemy could not see what was going on in England, he could certainly hear it, the strategists of the aerial campaign began broadcasting false wireless traffic that revealed, or so it appeared, that the main concentration of Allied air power was located on the flat fields of East Anglia—the Quicksilver area—while the real squadrons in southwestern England were kept silent or transmitted their signals by landline. American and British aircraft also flew deception missions coincidentally with real air strikes, broadcasting false wireless traffic to suggest that their point of departure and return was East Anglia. But above all, the principal stratagem in the wireless deception campaign was simply to produce so much false traffic that the German wireless intelligence facilities were completely swamped. And to add to their burden, the Allied air forces systematically attacked all the wireless stations in both the Neptune and Fortitude areas, culminating in a massed raid of one hundred Lancasters upon the headquarters of the German signals intelligence service in northwestern Europe, located at Ferme d'Urville near Cherbourg. The raid was so effective that, as a subsequent photographic interpretation report stated: "The station is completely useless, the site itself is rendered unsuitable for rebuilding the installations without much effort being expended in levelling and filling in the craters." This and other raids against German wireless stations served another purpose; they compelled the enemy to resort to hastily-built installations to restore communications, which rendered secret traffic much more liable to the depredations of Ultra. The *maquis,* meanwhile, were busy cutting telecommunications cables, again forcing the Germans to resort to wireless transmission.

The selection of targets was perhaps the most ruthless of the Allied aerial stratagems. While laying waste to western European rail centers, the Allied air forces were also dealing with the road and rail bridges. But to suggest that the invasion would occur in the Pas de Calais, only the bridges over the Seine were attacked before D-Day; those of the Loire and the other rivers were not attacked until afterwards. Thus, between April 21 and June 5, 1944, all the bridges over the Seine between Rouen and Paris were successfully sent crashing into the water. Rommel himself witnessed one such attack when 8 Thunderbolts of the U.S. 9th Air Force wrecked the 725-foot steel girder railway bridge over the Seine at Vernon with 8 tons of bombs. In all, thirty-six bridges suffered a similar fate. Coastal batteries, radar sites, airfields, tank parks, petrol and oil dumps, headquarters (but not those which were serving the purposes of Ultra), and, particularly, V-weapons sites were also devastated from the air. And since most of these targets were located in the Fortitude area, their destruction served the purposes of deception admirably. A Top Secret memorandum entitled "Cover and Deception in Air Force Operations, European Theater of Operations," would sum up the basic strategy of the campaign. Since it was "absolutely vital that neither the target date nor target area be indicated by the bombardment intensity or pattern," the memorandum stated, "the coastal defences in the Pas de Calais (the cover or fictional assault area) were attacked equally, and sometimes twice as heavily, as those in Normandy." For every pound of bombs dropped inside the assault area, two pounds were dropped outside it; and because German aerial defenses were much stronger in the

Pas de Calais than elsewhere, this stratagem would result in a significant increase in casualties among the Allied air crews.

Air operations to supply the resistance movements of Belgium and northern France, as well as reconnaissance flights over enemy-occupied territory, followed a similar pattern. Throughout the pre-invasion period, supply missions flown into the Fortitude area out-numbered those into Normandy by a ratio of two or three to one, while false reconnaissance missions were flown with the same thor-oughness over the Fortitude area as over the area where Neptune would actually land. The reconnaissance pilots themselves were, of course, not informed which was the cover area and which the real target, although the "Cover and Deception" memorandum indicated that they may have been led to believe that the Pas de Calais was the assault area—in case they were shot down and interrogated. It can be assumed that these operations, too, resulted in an increase in casual-ties, a portion of which must be charged to the Fortitude account.

How much were the Allies willing to spend in the campaign to defeat the Luftwaffe and guard the secrets of Neptune? Allied losses were particularly heavy in the raids against the rail centers of Aachen, Hasselt, Juvisy, Lille and Trappes, giving rise once again to the specu-lation that the Germans might have been fed foreknowledge of the at-tacks to induce the Luftwaffe to come up and fight. Moreover, Win-gate would recall that the RAF was prepared to hand over to the Germans the latest model Spitfire fighter reconnaissance aircraft in a game of deception that was a variant of both the Meinertzhagen strat-agem and Mincemeat. A German fighter pilot who was taken prisoner, a man known to be both fanatically *führertreu* and a skilled pilot, was taken to the RAF base at Leuchars in Scotland "for interrogation." The RAF intelligence officer in charge of the prisoner excused himself midway through the interrogation to, as he put it, "see a man about a dog." A few moments later, RAF ground crews brought up the Spitfire in full view of the German. They fueled the aircraft, turned the propeller, and then with great cries of "There's the NAAFI wagon," went off for tea. The sky-blue aircraft was so beautiful in line that it was said that no real pilot could resist flying it; and that was what the German was supposed to do, for the air deception staff had planted a set of false maps in its cockpit. The cockpit hatch was left open, there was not a soul in sight. It would have been a simple matter for the German to leave the office where he was being interrogated (the RAF intelligence officer had not locked the door), climb in the cockpit and take off. But, according to Wingate, he did nothing but sit by the window looking at the Spitfire, waiting patiently for the intelligence officer to return.

It was known that the Luftwaffe had been badly beaten in the great air battles of the winter and spring of 1944. But how badly? In spite of claims to the contrary, Ultra failed at this crucial time to provide the Supreme Command with an accurate estimate of the Luftwaffe order of battle. In fact, estimates of Luftwaffe strength and capability "varied so widely," as the American official history, *Cross-Channel Attack,* would note, "that they might have been drawn from a hat." There were several reasons for this gap in SHAEF's knowledge, among them the rivalry between the American and British air intelligence services and the rigid security imposed upon the Luftwaffe intelligence that Ultra was able to provide. But the Germans were becoming more wily; the game of intelligence and counterintelligence had gone on for so long that the Luftwaffe had learned to guard its secrets. As a result, there was a fundamental difference of opinion between the Pentagon and the Air Ministry about German strength in the air, and both, in the event, would prove to be exaggerations. Thus, as D-Day approached, the Supreme Command was infected with a profound unease that influenced all its plans. In spite of the massive pre-invasion aerial campaign, the Luftwaffe remained a grave threat to Neptune. Aerial operations, including those mounted to give truth to the fictions of Fortitude, were intensified. In all, between April 1 and June 5, 1944, the Allied air forces launched just over 20,000 missions against targets in northern France and Belgium, dropping 200,000 tons of bombs. Even before the campaign had ended, the effect was considerable. But the cost was grievous. Over 12,000 Allied airmen and 2000 aircraft were lost during those last few weeks of aerial *Blitzkrieg.* French and Belgian civilian deaths totaled some 12,000 people; and most of the Allied and civilian casualties occurred north of the Seine rather than to the south of it—in the Fortitude area. The Allies would lose almost as many men in the aerial preparations that cut a path for the invading armies as those armies would lose in the invasion of France. Was it all necessary? The Supreme Commander thought so, for he would report to the Combined Chiefs of Staff: "No single factor contributing to the success of our efforts in Normandy could be overlooked or disregarded. Military events, I believe, justified the decision taken. . . ."

A vital component of the pre-invasion aerial campaign was the attacks against German radar sites along the Channel coast, attacks which again served the interests of both Neptune and Fortitude. If the Allies were to achieve tactical surprise on D-Day, the enemy radar system that guarded the invasion area had to be seriously or completely deranged. But to conceal the particular interest of the Allies in Normandy, sites in other areas were even more heavily bombed, again increasing the human and material cost of the campaign. In all, twenty-six of forty-two radar sites were put out of action between the Channel Islands and Ostend. But in a new and sophisticated twist to the techniques of aerial warfare—and deception—several of these sites were purposely left operational. For throughout this period the Allies were testing and perfecting a unique variety of ruses that would be put to use on D-Day. All involved so-called radio or electronic countermeasures (RCM's or ECM's), which were designed specifically to trick the German radar equipment that was allowed to survive.

During April and May 1944, the final tests of a series of ECM deceptions were being made at Tantallon Castle on a headland overlooking the Firth of Forth. There, in a hut under the red ruins of the castle, electronic scientists from TRE and the American-British Laboratory 15 (ABL-15) at Harvard, led by Dr. Robert Cockburn and including Dr. Joan Curran, had assembled the latest in the German arsenal of radar equipment, "pinched" as long ago as February 1942 in the raid on Bruneval and updated by bits and pieces captured in Africa, Sicily and Italy. The group was first concerned with the ECM known as "Window."

Window was the British code name for the dipole; its American code name was "Chaff," and it consisted of strips of foil which could be unloaded in large quantities from an approaching bomber stream to create an effect upon radar screens not unlike that of a blizzard upon the human eye; it became impossible to distinguish objects. But in the simplicity of the dipole lay its vulnerability. Quite early in the war, both Britain and Germany had discovered the effectiveness of the dipole; but because both sides had radar networks upon which they depended heavily for protection, and because they were unaware that they shared the same secret, each was reluctant to use it for fear of revealing the secret and inviting retaliation. The decision not to use dipoles had involved the highest Allied and Axis commands. Goering had ordered the technical reports describing their effectiveness destroyed by fire; Churchill was prepared to accept very heavy RAF casualties to protect British radar. But the British finally tipped their hand in the great raid on Hamburg on July 26, 1943, and had been using Window ever since to confound the German radar screens.

It was not done without reason, for the British had perfected a new weapon of electronic warfare that the Germans did not have. Dr. Curran, an outstanding radar scientist, had discovered that when dipoles were dropped from a few aircraft under calculated and controlled circumstances, they produced echoes on radar screens that resembled an entire air fleet. She had carried her experiments forward and also discovered that an electronic device, which she called "Moonshine," could be built and installed in ships or aircraft. Moonshine received the pulses of the enemy radar, and amplified and returned them to produce symptoms on radar screens somewhat similar to those produced by a large number of ships or planes on the move. In short, Moonshine could make it appear to the enemy, without his knowledge that he was being tricked, that large formations of ships or aircraft were approaching him when, in fact, only a few Moonshine-equipped craft were.

The potential of Moonshine for making feints against the Germans' coastal defenses, in order to lure their formations away from the point actually to be attacked, had been recognized immediately by Professor Edward Neville da Costa Andrade, the brilliant but quaint scientific member of the LCS. He recommended that the device be action-tested, and on April 6, 1942, nine Defiant fighters equipped with Moonshine had circled over Portland to suggest that a large group of American bombers was approaching Cherbourg. Ultra vigilance showed that thirty German fighters—the entire daytime air defense for the port—rose to meet the nonexistent threat. On April 17, 1942, Moonshine was used to lure the Luftwaffe away from an actual attack; as Moonshine Defiants circled over the Thames to duplicate the pulses created by bomber streams assembling for a raid, Ultra showed that the Luftwaffe controller launched 144 fighters to meet the deception thrust. To meet the actual attack—a raid by Fortresses of the U.S. 8th Air Force against Rouen—the controller put up seventy fighters. Its effectiveness as an airborne deception proven, Moonshine was put on ice and electronics scientists worked on further refinements for use on D-Day.

To test the results of the combined use of Window and Moonshine, Drs. Cockburn, Curran and their assistants at Tantallon required the services of a fleet of Stirlings and Lancasters, the Canadian destroyer *Haida* and a number of other sea and air craft. Stirlings flew over the test area at an exact altitude and an exact speed, dropping bundles of Window at predetermined intervals. Lancasters equipped with search radar flew above them in equally complicated patterns, while *Haida* and a small fleet of minesweepers sailed into the Firth trailing Filberts, naval balloons with radar reflectors built inside. *Haida* and the minesweepers were ordered to "Moonshine" the search radar of the Lancasters, and when they did so, the combination of Window, Moonshine and the Filbert reflectors created impressions on the scientists' scopes that resembled a vast mass of shipping which covered some 200 square miles and was approaching the shore at exactly the speed a real invasion fleet would move. The tests were a success, and "Taxable" and "Glimmer"—electronic deception operations to make it appear that two great fleets were approaching the French coast between Le Havre and Calais as the real invasion fleet steamed into the Bay of the Seine—were approved for use in Fortitude between midnight and daybreak on D-Day.

Now Dr. Cockburn, again using *Haida* and the minesweepers, tried another ruse. When the test fleet had reached a point 10 miles off the headland, it stopped and moored its Filbert floats. Then the Lancasters and Stirlings flew over the area, and all scopes and Moonshines were switched on. But this time great noise amplifiers on the boats began to make sounds like the squeals and rattles of anchors being dropped, and of landing craft being lowered. Then a number of high-speed motor launches swooped in to lay a smoke screen. Visually, aurally, electronically, and from all angles, it looked as if there was a large invasion fleet lying just offshore, engaged in all the activities that preceded a seaborne assault. It was a more elaborate version of the trick used to divert the German response to Montgomery's attack at El Alamein, and it would be used again to divert their response to the Normandy assault.

Well satisfied, Cockburn turned to his next and last electronic deception. Aircraft again flew over the area, and at an appointed time, place and altitude hundreds of dummy paratroopers were dropped through a Window screen. When they hit the ground, they exploded with the sounds of a ground battle: machine-gun fire, pistol reports, the snap of rifles. A few real SAS troopers were dropped along with the dummies, and when they landed, they switched on amplifiers and records of gunfire, soldiers' oaths, cries for help, thuds. They also unleashed a chemical preparation which, in the form of light smoke, created the smell of battle. Those tests, too, were successful, and would form the basis of "Titanic," a stratagem to attract the enemy's attention to the landing of dummy paratroop brigades and divisions, while the real airborne invaders were dropped into other areas.

The tests over, Cockburn and his team returned to London to begin work on equipping the various naval craft that would be used in these deceptions, while air crews continued to perfect the extraordinarily precise flying techniques that would be necessary—techniques that would require the installation in each aircraft of a wholly new system of automatic pilotage. The ECM deceptions had worked well in Scotland and would be employed operationally on D-Day. A new military science had been created for this moment—electronic spoofing. If it succeeded in confusing and confounding German technical defenses, electronics would be confirmed as a new dimension of war, a weapon as revolutionary as the rifle, the machine gun and the tank.

Security

THE SPRING OF 1944 was a peculiar time in the history of England. As D-Day neared and millions of strangers crowded the countryside with even stranger vehicles, a great fog descended upon the island—a fog of security, the handmaiden of deception. Never before had such extraordinary precautions been taken to protect the secrets of a military operation; never before had Britons been so suspicious, so cautious. Busybodies and informers flourished, every village bobby kept his eyes and ears open for German spies, and ordinary human indiscretions assumed the proportions of crime. The campaign which the British government had begun at the outbreak of war—"Careless talk costs lives"—was intensified to an extraordinary degree. A social historian of the times would write: "Urging others not to spread rumours became a national occupation. Newspapers harangued their readers, clergy their congregations, headmasters their pupils. Special anti-rumour rallies were even held in some places." Security became an obsession, enveloping every aspect of every life; not even the King or the Prime Minister could do or say as he pleased.

When Eisenhower arrived in London as Supreme Commander, he had used his new pro-consular powers to urge the British government to take the most extensive and unusual security precautions in its history. He wrote to the British Chiefs of Staff: "It will go hard on our consciences if we were to feel, in later years, that by neglecting any security precaution we had compromised the success of these vital operations." With that letter, Britain became, temporarily, a police state isolated from the rest of the world. Overseas cabling privileges were withdrawn from all but the most trusted newspapermen. The press growled but—with one grave exception—honored the restrictions. Churchill himself advocated the censorship of the press, for Captain

B. H. Liddell Hart, the British military writer who worked for Eisenhower making assessments of the personalities and abilities of enemy high commanders, showed him that it was possible to have made reasonably accurate deductions about Allied intentions between June 1943 and February 1944 simply by reading the main British and American newspapers. At the same time, every telephone call made by a soldier or an official, every letter in every sensitive part of Britain, every telegram, could be, and frequently was, monitored. Foreign and troops' mail was delayed, travel in and out of England was forbidden to all except essential personnel, and a ban was imposed on all visits in and out of a broad swath of the British Isles from the northern tip of Scotland to Land's End.

Restrictions on the military were even more severe, and Eisenhower warned every man under his command soon after his arrival:

> The rules of security are known to us all—a guarded tongue and safe-guarded documents. It rests with each of us to ensure that there is no relaxation of these rules until success is achieved. All commanders will ensure that the highest standard of individual security discipline is maintained throughout their commands, and that the most stringent disciplinary action is taken in all cases of the violations of security.

A special procedure was instituted for the protection of all documents that revealed the time and place of the invasion. This was the "Bigot procedure," which took its curious name from the stamp "To Gib" that had appeared on the papers of all officers traveling to Gibraltar for the Torch invasions. To confuse the curious, the letters had been reversed, and for Neptune the Bigot designation was retained as the highest general security classification of the times. In the main, only Bigots could see Bigot documents; and to become a Bigot was as difficult as joining a good club. The most thorough security checks were made on candidates on both sides of the Atlantic, and even after clearance a Bigot's behavior and performance in England were liable to the most intimate scrutiny. But inevitably there were security breaches, even among Bigots, some of them serious and even terrifying in their gravity.

One of the first was a mysterious affair that began late in March 1944 when General Clayton Bissell, the chief of U.S. army intelligence at the Pentagon, received information from the FBI that a package of very secret papers had broken open by accident at a U.S. army mail sorting office at Chicago. Four unauthorized persons had seen the contents of the package in the headquarters of the U.S. army post office, and another ten had seen the documents when they reached the Chicago post office; no attempt was made, it appeared, to reseal the package. The sender was "Sergeant Thomas P. Kane," a man of German extraction who was a secretary to General Robert W. Crawford, chief of the ordnance supply section at Supreme Headquarters in London. Kane had sent the package, somewhat oddly, to "The Ordnance Division, G-4," but the address he wrote was that of his sister in Chicago, who lived in a predominantly German quarter of the city.

The situation was quickly brought to the attention of General Thomas J. Betts, the assistant chief of intelligence at Supreme Headquarters. It was a serious situation indeed, for as Betts later said:

> There lurked in the background the nagging doubt as to how long this had been going on, and whether or not it was still continuing. The documents were very important, for they revealed the target date and place of the invasion and schedules for the build-up and breakout. The mercy was that we had six weeks to investigate the affair and see whether we must recommend that changes be made in the Neptune plans.

An FBI check of Kane and his family showed that, so far as anyone knew, all were perfectly loyal American citizens with no history of any connection with pro-Nazi organizations. Kane was summoned before a departmental tribunal and admitted that the handwriting on the parcel was his. But he could not explain why he had put such secret documents into an envelope and posted them to his sister except, as Butcher (Eisenhower's diarist) noted, that his sister had been seriously ill, he was overtired, and he was thinking of her. "The clumsy handling would indicate that no professional spy was involved," Butcher continued, "but nevertheless important facts, including strength, places, equipment and target date have been disclosed to unauthorized persons."

The FBI was instructed to keep all persons who had seen the documents under surveillance. A court-martial was recommended for Kane, but no action was taken, although he too was kept under observation, his telephone was tapped, and he was not allowed to leave his quarters until after D-Day. That was not the end of the episode, however, for there were security men in both London and Washington who were convinced that the leakage was in some way connected with the Chicago *Tribune,* which was regarded with extreme displeasure by the two governments for having published information that the Allies had broken the Japanese naval code. Suspicion would again arise about the paper when it was discovered that, shortly before D-Day, one of the editors of the *Tribune* had tried to leave Britain in a U.S. transport despite a total ban on all travel from Britain by any unauthorized person. But no connection between the Kane case and the *Tribune* was ever established, and the editor in question was apparently guilty of nothing more than irresponsibility.

No sooner had the Kane case ended than another security breach occurred, this time involving a friend of Eisenhower's himself. He was Major General Henry Jervis Friese Miller who, at fifty-four, was one of the U.S. army's most able officers. He had been graduated from West Point with Eisenhower in 1915, and had then advanced through the ranks of the U.S. cavalry to become the general commanding the Air Service Command. He was now, for the invasion, the quartermaster of the U.S. 9th Air Force, and he was a Bigot.

On the evening of April 18, 1944, Miller attended a dinner party for American Red Cross nurses given by General Edwin L. Sibert, chief of intelligence in the U.S. European Theater of Operations and later G2 to Bradley's 12th Army Group. The party was held in a public dining room of Claridge's and during the conversation Miller complained of his difficulties in obtaining supplies from the United States. Then he declared to the nurses, without even gracing the secret with a whisper, that the invasion would take place before June 15, 1944. Sibert, who overheard the remark, was furious. It was a gross breach of security, and the next morning he reported the matter to Bradley. Bradley also knew and liked Miller, but as he later said: "I had no choice. I telephoned Ike . . ."

Eisenhower was quite merciless; after a quick investigation he ordered Miller to return to the United States on the next boat and reduced him to his substantive rank, that of lieutenant colonel. "There were officers," wrote Bradley, "who afterward contended that Ike had acted with unnecessary harshness but I was not among them. For had I been in Eisenhower's shoes, I would have been no less severe. . . . At the same time this punishment reassured the British that we would not tolerate any loose talk."

Miller sought the claims of friendship and wrote in a letter to Eisenhower: "I simply want to ask you to have me shipped home in my present grade [i.e., major general], there to await such action as the fates have in store for me." He also strongly protested his innocence, but to no avail. Eisenhower replied to him confidentially: "I know of nothing that causes me more real distress than to be faced with the necessity of sitting as a judge in cases involving military offenses by officers of character and good record, particularly when they are old and warm friends." But, he continued, ". . . it was because of your long record of efficient service that I felt justified in recommending only administrative rather than more drastic procedure in your case."

Almost immediately after the Miller case, there occurred another embarrassing security breach for which the British were responsible. In April 1944, a deputy to Brigadier Lionel Harris, chief of the telecommunications department of SHAEF, reported that he had lost the SHAEF communications plan for Neptune as he was going home by train via Waterloo Station. And he said he had no idea how or where he had lost it. This seemed odd, for the plan was as bulky as *Gone With the Wind;* and Harris formed the impression that the man had been drinking. But the loss of the plan was the most serious imaginable, for it contained in every detail all the wireless nets and ciphers to be used during the assault. From that information, which was priceless in itself, an experienced wireless intelligence expert could also have deduced the layout, strength and disposition of the assault forces, and something of the time and place of the invasion.

In all, the document—had it got into German hands—would have made Neptune impossible to undertake unless the American and British governments were prepared to accept defeat on the Far Shore. But just as Harris was about to go and explain the catastrophe to Smith, the lost property office of Scotland Yard called to report that it had a briefcase belonging to an officer at Norfolk House. Inside, the police officer said, were some documents marked "Bigot" and "Top Secret" which appeared to be connected with wireless, and (so the story went) some socks and a bottle of beer. The police officer asked if the documents were important, and if so, could Norfolk House send someone round for them, as he had nobody in his office to send? Harris himself hurried across St. James's Park to retrieve the briefcase. It had been found by the driver of a taxi that had dropped a passenger at Waterloo.

The documents contained in another briefcase were never found. In March and April, the Luftwaffe mounted a series of very sharp raids on the official quarter of London; and in one of these, a string of bombs landed between Norfolk House and St. James's Palace, riddling Norfolk House and its intelligence section with shrapnel. More grievously, a bomb that dropped in the street near the palace blew to pieces the officer in charge of the Fortitude and Quicksilver wireless deceptions, Lieutenant Colonel Finlay Austin. Austin was carrying his briefcase when he was killed, and in it were the master documents of the Fortitude wireless plan. They were never recovered. It was assumed—but not without extensive forensic and police inquiry—that they had simply disintegrated in the flash of the aluminum-based high explosive in the bomb. However, the Fortitude wireless game was discontinued for a short time while a new commanding officer was briefed and trained.

Only a very few weeks before the invasion, the third serious security breach occurred in the American high command. This time the offender was a naval officer, "Captain Edward M. Miles," who was an aide to Admiral Harold R. "Betty" Stark, the C-in-C of U.S. naval forces in Europe and one of the top Neptune planners. The plaintiff was Air Chief Marshal Sir Trafford Leigh-Mallory, the C-in-C of the Tactical Air Force for Neptune, who wrote to Eisenhower that Miles had revealed in public "details of impending operations to include areas, lift, strength and dates." The indiscretion had taken place at a party given by Colonel Sir William Dupree, the Portsmouth brewer, and Leigh-Mallory complained that Miles was "apparently intoxicated."

Eisenhower, on May 21, 1944, wrote to Stark to say that he was "disturbed, not to say alarmed" by the report of Miles's indiscretion, and went on: "If this report is even partially true . . . , then I must say that the greatest harm could result from this indiscretion. I know that you will take prompt and effective action. . . ." Two days later Stark replied that he was sending Miles home. "I see no alternative. He will be a distinct loss and I have no replacement at present, but that can't be helped."

Meanwhile Eisenhower had written to Marshall to say that the Miles indiscretion had given him the "shakes," and that he "would willingly shoot the offender myself." But in Washington, Miles was given the chance to redeem his career, although privately he made it known that he had been the victim of an intrigue. After a period of doldrums, he was rehabilitated, given command of a transport division at Okinawa during the assault in 1944, and awarded the Bronze Star with Combat Distinction. He also distinguished himself during the invasion of the Philippines.

The Miller and Miles cases were serious blows to Eisenhower, for they seemed to reflect upon the discretion and responsibility of the U.S. staff in London. An occasional unguarded tongue or unguarded document was perhaps inevitable in a command the size of SHAEF, but not even coincidence could satisfactorily explain a security leak that was traced to quite a different quarter. In May 1944, a British officer was traveling to work by train and, as usual, passing the time by doing the crossword puzzle in his morning newspaper, the *Daily Telegraph*. The number of the puzzle was 5775, and 17 Across asked for a four-letter word that was "One of the U.S." The answer was "Utah," and the officer, who was a senior member of the Supreme Commander's staff, was surprised to see it, for he knew most of the principal code names for Neptune, and Utah was the name of one of the two main American beachheads in Normandy. Later he was even more surprised when he was doing puzzle number 5792 and found that the answer to the clue: "Red Indian on the Missouri" was "Omaha"—the code name for the other main American beachhead. Later still, tackling puzzle number 5797, he found that the answer to the clue "But some big wig like this has stolen some of it at times" was "Overlord"—the code name for the entire Allied strategy in northwest Europe in 1944. There was even more to come, however. Puzzle number 5799 asked for an eight-letter word for "This bush is a centre of nursery revolutions." The answer was "Mulberry"—the code name for the amphibious harbors that were being built for the invasion in the greatest secrecy. And finally, a fifth code name appeared as a solution. The clue was "Britannia and he hold to the same thing." The answer was "Neptune"—most priceless of all the code names of the period, that of the invasion itself.

By this time the security authorities had already begun to look into this strange affair, but despite the most thorough investigation into the backgrounds of the compilers, nothing sinister was found. One of them was Leonard Sidney Dawe, a schoolmaster living a perfectly respectable life in the small London dormitory town of Leatherhead. The other was his friend Neville Jones, another schoolmaster. Dawe had been the *Telegraph*'s senior crossword puzzle compiler for more than twenty years. He explained that quite often his puzzles were compiled six months ahead of publication; and if this was so, he had created the puzzles before the authorities had created many of the code words. His explanation was accepted and the case was closed. But even twenty-five years later, at a symposium to mark the 25th anniversary of D-Day, George M. Elsey, the president of the American Red Cross and a U.S. naval historian, suggested that there was more to this episode than was ever proven. "Was it really coincidence?" he asked. "Were those rustic British schoolteachers who compiled the puzzles really so naïve and innocent?" The answers to those questions will never be known.

Basic to the security of Neptune was Eisenhower's order that no one in uniform with any knowledge of the invasion be sent on operations where there was the danger of capture. But despite that order, SHAEF security learned, on the morning of May 7, 1944, that Air Commodore Ronald Ivelaw-Chapman had been lost on an RAF bombing raid against an ammunition dump at Le Mans. Since Ivelaw-Chapman held the rank equivalent to a brigadier general in the American air force, SHAEF security asked the Air Ministry to make inquiries about his knowledge of Neptune. The first part of the Air Ministry's report was reassuring; Ivelaw-Chapman was the commander of the bomber base at Elsham Wolds in Lincolnshire, and would therefore have no knowledge of the invasion plans. But the second part of the report caused a storm, for he had been on the Planning Staff at the Air Ministry shortly before going to Elsham Wolds, he had had contact with Morgan at COSSAC, and he was a specialist in paratroop movements. Ivelaw-Chapman might have some knowledge of the paratroop operational plans for Neptune. Moreover, said the Air Ministry, his presence on the raid had *not* been authorized.

Later, Ivelaw-Chapman would protest that his flight over enemy territory that night had been authorized, although he admitted that he was flying as "additional aircrew." Whatever the case, his loss was of major concern at SHAEF. Was he alive or dead? Inquiries among the crews of the fifty Lancasters on the raid disclosed that Ivelaw-Chapman's aircraft—the only one that was shot down—had been intercepted fifteen minutes from Le Mans on the homeward run. A number of the crewmen had been seen bailing out over open country, and it was probable that Ivelaw-Chapman had survived—as indeed he had. He had landed safely and was in the hands of a fragment of "Donkeyman," an F section *réseau* which operated across the Eure and the Orne. There were hidden dangers there, however, for Donkeyman was led by Roger Bardet, a Frenchman turned German agent, apparently without the knowledge of SOE.

A wireless message from Donkeyman brought the first news that Ivelaw-Chapman was alive, and SHAEF decided that every effort must be made to get him out of France. It was for this purpose exactly that the British had formed MI-9, an escape organization with lines that ran all over Europe. SHAEF contacted Lieutenant Colonel Airey Neave, and asked him to exfiltrate the missing air commodore. Neave, a peacetime lawyer who ran a section of MI-9 from the War Office, and who had himself escaped from Colditz Castle near Leipzig in January 1942 and made his way to Switzerland, contacted "Burgundy," the code name of a French agent who had established what came to be called the Burgundy Line which carried escaping Allied soldiers, airmen and agents from Paris to Douarnenez, the small port between Brest and Quimper in Brittany. Could Burgundy locate Ivelaw-Chapman and fly him out? Burgundy agreed to try and, finally, at the very end of May, he succeeded. Ivelaw-Chapman, in civilian clothes, was in hiding with *résistants* about 60 miles from Le Mans, and a Lysander was scheduled to pick him up on the night of June 8/9, 1944. But as Ivelaw-Chapman himself would state, ten hours before the Lysander was due, Gestapo agents raided the house where he was hiding and arrested him. Fortunately, he had managed to elude capture until after the invasion had begun. But curiously, Ivelaw-Chapman would recall that the Gestapo did not interrogate him about Neptune at all; they were interested only in who had given him his French identity papers. Neither did his Luftwaffe interrogation officer at Oberursel near Frankfurt ask him about anything other than the order of battle of Bomber Command. Apparently the Germans were more concerned with routine police and intelligence matters than with Neptune operational plans.

Another worry for SHAEF security authorities concerned the Supreme Commander himself. In 1942, when Eisenhower first arrived in London as C-in-C of ETOUSA, he met and formed a relationship with his driver, Kay Summersby, an Irishwoman in her early thirties who had been a model and film extra before joining the British Auxiliary Territorial Service (ATS) as a private. Mrs. Summersby was divorced from her first husband and had met and was engaged to an American colonel when Eisenhower appeared on the scene. The colonel was later killed in action in Tunisia, where Mrs. Summersby was sent when Eisenhower established his headquarters in Algiers. She became his confidential secretary, chauffeuse, hostess and companion, remaining a member of his "official family" throughout the North African campaigns.

When Eisenhower came to London as Supreme Commander for Neptune and Overlord, Mrs. Summersby followed and, although she was a British citizen, he arranged that she be given a commission in the American Women's Army Corps. She spent much time at Eisenhower's quarters at Telegraph Lodge, was seen frequently at his side on important social occasions and in due course Eisenhower wrote to Marshall asking his advice about whether he might divorce his wife Mamie and marry Mrs. Summersby. Marshall rejected the proposition angrily, warning Eisenhower that if he persisted it would cost him his career.

Despite official disapproval and embarrassment, Eisenhower did persist in the relationship, and because Churchill especially feared the consequences if it became known to the Germans—particularly Goebbels—that Eisenhower had taken a mistress, the affair was one of the most carefully guarded secrets of the pre-invasion period. It was known to the security authorities, however, and they were concerned on a number of counts. The first was the question of Mrs. Summersby's origins; she had been born Kathleen McCarthy-Morrogh on the island of Inish Beg, off the coast of County Cork; and as an Eiranean she was technically disqualified from any contact with Bigots or with invasion secrets. Yet, as was well known, the senior staff at SHAEF discussed most secret matters quite openly in front of her; and for a time, when Butcher was posted to other duties, she kept the Supreme Commander's secret diary. Her proximity to Allied secrets was even more alarming because she was known to visit, from time to time, the American bar at the Savoy Hotel, a haunt for American foreign correspondents, and she was in the habit of dining occasionally with Frank McGee, the eminent American journalist and, later, television personality. McGee became infatuated with Mrs. Summersby and disapproved of her relationship with Eisenhower. Smith, who knew of the triangle, begged the Supreme Commander to be cautious, and he was.

The situation would have been little short of melodrama had it not been for the stakes involved. One high-ranking American intelligence officer would later remark that there was absolutely no question of Mrs. Summersby's loyalty and discretion. McGee, too, was absolutely dependable. The security authorities saw to that. But SHAEF was haunted, he recalled, by what might happen if Goebbels heard of the affair—or if Eisenhower and Summersby fell out. They did not fall out. Mrs. Summersby remained at Eisenhower's side until July 1945 when he was called back to the United States to embark upon the career that eventually took him to the White House.

Of all the dangers to the security of Neptune in the anxious months before the invasion, one of the most serious came from Churchill himself. Addicted to the telephone, he was forever calling Roosevelt from his private telephone booth, which was covered in blue damask and stood like a sedan chair outside the conference room in the War Bunker at Storey's Gate. While he was always guarded in what he said, and always used code names when discussing plans and operations with the President, much could have been deduced from Churchill's terminology. But he was sure that the connection was secure from eavesdropping. Was the line not "scrambled" by the Bell A-3 device? What Churchill did not know—until Ultra told him—was that the SD was indeed tapping the connection, and had been able to do so since September 1941.

The conversations between the President and the Prime Minister were routed through the American Telephone and Telegraph Company's switchboard at 47 Walker Street, New York, where, in a special locked and guarded room, they were mangled by the A-3 system and rendered incomprehensible, it was thought, to anyone tapping the radiotelephone link. Moreover, the operators handling the calls constantly moved the link from one radio frequency to another, more or less at random. The Germans soon learned that the A-3 existed, however, and found a means not only to unscramble parts of the conversations but also to keep track of the frequency changes. Using the technical and manpower resources of the giant Phillips electrical engineering works at Eindhoven in Holland, they established a large radiotelephone interception and unscrambling station on the Dutch coast near The Hague. From there they listened in to the conversations between the Prime Minister and the President, and for a time the operation was remarkably successful. In one call between Churchill and Roosevelt, the Germans learned for the first time that Italy was secretly negotiating surrender to the western powers. This same call also revealed that Cockade was a trick, thus adding to all the other strikes against that ill-fated stratagem.

The installation was still operational and effective as late as January 1944 when, as Schellenberg would write, another conversation between Churchill and Roosevelt "disclosed a crescendo of military activity in Britain," which corroborated "the many reports of impending invasion." Other conversations revealed that the western powers' main attack in 1944 would come not through the Balkans, as had been thought possible, but through France. Fortunately for Neptune, the unscrambling operation, and the other intelligence operations with which it was associated, did not permit the Germans to deduce that there would be no operations at all in the Balkans. Nor did they learn where and when in France the Allies would strike. They might well have, but American experiments had demonstrated that the Allies must regard the A-3 as insecure for half the time it was in use, and Ultra intercepts of German diplomatic traffic revealed, upon analysis by British security authorities at Storey's Gate, terminology and facts that could have been extracted only from Churchill's talks with Roosevelt. A new scrambling system was installed and in operation by February 1944; and to make certain that the Germans did not penetrate that system as well, the RAF bombed and destroyed the recovery station near The Hague late that same month. A dangerous tap on Allied communications was successfully closed.

Neptune was not merely a military operation; neither was Overlord just a strategic design. Both were the forces of destiny. Every country in the world had a stake in their outcome, and the governments-in-exile of the Allied nations, as well as the ambassadors and agents of the neutrals, were gathered at London in the months that preceded the invasion clamoring for information. London became, literally, Istanbul-on-Thames, and the ensuing bedlam posed a very serious security problem for Supreme Headquarters. What nation, if any, could be trusted to keep the secrets of Neptune?

In the first place there was the question of how much—or how little —should be told to the representatives of France and Russia. In both cases the answers were complex and dangerous. The Russians were part of the triumvirate that formed the main core of the Grand Alliance. They had undertaken to synchronize the Red Army's main summer offensive with Neptune in order to pin down as many German divisions as possible on the eastern front. Moreover, they were a party to the deceptions of Bodyguard. Yet, as the russophobes in high places in London pointed out, who could say that the Russians themselves would not betray the secrets of D-Day to the Germans? They remembered the ominous conduct of Ivan Maisky, the Russian ambassador in London, over the invasion of North Africa. As the Torch convoys were being prepared in British and American ports, Maisky, who had been told of the operation in the strictest confidence, revealed the operational plan in a conversation with two reporters. Why had he done this? He was not a man who could fail to appreciate the importance of secrecy in military operations. The russophobes—and they dominated the British military hierarchy—thought that Maisky had revealed the plan because Stalin believed that Torch could bring the Red Army no immediate relief in the desperate campaigns of late 1942 and had sought to force the western powers into an early invasion of northern France by making Torch impossible to execute.

If the British were suspicious of Maisky, they had a positive paranoia over his successor, Feodor Tarasovich Gousev, a wooden ex-butcher whom Cadogan had dubbed "Frogface." He had been a high functionary of OGPU, the Soviet secret police, and chief of the Second European Department of the People's Commissariat for Foreign Affairs. As such, the British feared, he had been unhealthily connected with the *Gesellschaft zur Forderung gewerblicher Unternehmungen,* literally the Society for the Furthering of Industrial Enterprises, the cover organization behind which the Russian and German general staffs had worked to create German arms factories and training grounds in Russia, and whose offices the German General Staff had used to train Russian officers. It was this organization which had also enabled the Germans to perfect the techniques of *Blitzkrieg* warfare. Who could tell whether cooperation still existed between the German and Russian militarists? Who could tell whether Stalin might, if it suited him, reveal the Neptune plans just as he had done with Torch? He might well see an advantage in the failure of the invasion, for it would create a power vacuum throughout western Europe—a vacuum that only the Russians could fill. With these suspicions in the background, the decision was taken; the Russians would be told no more than the target date of the invasion. They would not be told where on the Channel coast the invaders would land. Furthermore, they would be told nothing of the Allied order of battle, and nothing of Fortitude South other than that the Quicksilver army group actually existed.

The French question was equally delicate. The confusion of loyalties among the French both inside and outside France, the conflicts between individual interests and patriotic duty, the power of the conqueror to obtain secrets from the French, the deep national sickness engendered by the calamity of defeat in 1940, the known intention of some members of the French high command to prevent the Allies from making their homeland a battlefield—all combined to compel the Supreme Command to make an incontrovertible decision. It was impossible to know which Frenchmen could really be trusted; therefore none should be trusted. As a result, all American and British officers who were connected with the French forces in Britain and elsewhere were ordered not to consult the French regarding Neptune operations of any kind. It was a decision that would create great bitterness between the French, the British and the Americans in the postwar world.

The variety of exiled kings, queens and princes that were assembled in London at this time posed another serious security problem, not because their own discretion was in question, but because they were usually surrounded by a large entourage of relatives, advisers and attendants, some of whom might well have conflicting loyalties. Like the French, the representatives of all other governments-in-exile at SHAEF were to be kept completely in the dark about Neptune.

The diplomatic representatives of the neutral nations in London presented an even more difficult security problem than exiled royalty. For they, too, moved in the highest circles and their reports to their governments could easily fall into enemy hands—and sometimes did. Further, there were men on embassy staffs and in the foreign offices of neutral governments whose particular business it was to feed information to the Germans. There was only one way to plug these potentially dangerous leaks. Eisenhower, armed with the almost absolute authority of a plenipotentiary, "requested" the complete suspension of all communications from every diplomatic representative in London excepting those of Russia, the United States, and the Dominions. It was a sign of Eisenhower's authority and Churchill's fears about D-Day that the request was granted. All embassies were notified of the suspension and were informed by the Foreign Office that in the unprecedented circumstances created by the military operations impending in the present year—a statement calculated, no doubt, to add to the uncertainty and tension of the pre-invasion period—transmission or receipt of coded telegrams was forbidden. The only exception would be most urgent matters and these were to be presented to the Foreign Office for transmission in British cipher over British systems by British personnel. The British would also be responsible for deciphering and delivering the message, and for handling any reply.

The Foreign Office note also dealt with diplomatic mail. Diplomatic bags—by tradition sacrosanct and inviolable—would be opened, their contents censored, and any material that might bring aid and comfort to an enemy removed. Incoming mail, telephone calls and telegrams would also be liable to delay and even to interception. Moreover, no member of any diplomatic or consular staff or his family would be permitted to leave the country under any circumstances. Each embassy was reminded of the law about entry into the quarantined coastal zones, and some embassies were advised that their officials were not free to travel without the permission of the Foreign Office. Finally, a total ban was placed on the use of all embassy wireless equipment; and to make sure that the ban was obeyed, the Radio Security Service extended its special watch for sounds of clandestine wireless traffic to include the embassies. The Corps Diplomatique at the Court of St. James's was now, for all practical purposes, cut off from the rest of the world. The quarantine was an unprecedented violation of the traditions of international diplomacy, yet no more severe than the restrictions placed on all military personnel and the entire civilian population of the island.

The wisdom of the decision to hobble foreign diplomats for the period of the invasion was soon made evident by a major security alarm that involved a member of that corps. On April 21, 1944, "Lord Haw-Haw," the renegade Anglo-American William Joyce, who was employed as a commentator by Berlin radio, said in a broadcast:

> We know exactly what you intend to do with those concrete units. *You* think you are going to sink them on our coasts in the assault. Well, we are going to help you boys. We'll save you the trouble. When you come to get underway, we're going to sink them for you.

No broadcast during the build-up for Neptune caused greater consternation and fear, for Joyce was clearly referring to the Mulberry harbors, one of the most carefully guarded Allied secrets.

There were two Mulberries, each of which cost some £20 millions ($96 million) to build, consumed some 2 million tons of concrete and steel, and had occupied a work force of 20,000 men for eight months. To move them at the time of the invasion would require the services of every available tug in Britain and on the eastern seaboard of the United States; a fleet of 74 merchantmen was needed to build and service them; to run them required a work force of 11,000 men; and each, floating up and down with the tide, had a capacity to handle 12,000 tons of equipment every day—the capacity of Dover or Port Elizabeth at that time. But their gigantic size and cost apart, their existence was being kept an especial secret since they were the lynchpin of the Neptune strategy.

The Germans were convinced that the Allies would land near a major port at the outset of an invasion, and then attempt to seize that port to supply the invasion forces. The Allies, on the contrary, intended to land in a part of Normandy that was without major port facilities, using the Mulberries, which were to be anchored off the invasion beaches, to supply their forces. Such a strategy had a number of advantages. The Allies would not have to undertake a frontal assault on one of the heavily fortified French Channel ports—an extremely hazardous venture, as the disaster at Dieppe had proved—the area of Normandy to be attacked was relatively lightly garrisoned, and the location of the assault would in itself contribute to Neptune's surprise. The danger of the plan was that if the Germans learned of the existence of the Mulberries, they might conclude the truth of Allied strategy. Joyce's broadcast seemed to indicate that the Germans had indeed discovered the secret of the Mulberries; and Admiral Edward Ellsberg, who was involved in the Mulberry project, would recall that the effect of the broadcast was extremely demoralizing. The men who were at work at Selsey Bill, the point off the Sussex coast where parts of the Mulberries were being assembled, became very apprehensive. Even Eisenhower himself was concerned, and acting to avoid panic, he telegraphed Washington for fifty Coast Guard picket boats to be used to rescue the crews if the Mulberries were destroyed. "Goebbels had done a first-class job on us," Ellsberg would write.

Had the Germans really learned about the Mulberries? The Supreme Command looked to Ultra for the answer. Baron Oshima had made another tour of the Atlantic Wall and had been very fully briefed by Rundstedt on what the Germans expected the Allies to do. During the briefing, Rundstedt had referred to the existence of the very large structures off Selsey Bill, but stated that he had information that they were anti-aircraft gun towers. It was this information that Oshima telegraphed to Tokyo; and when it was intercepted and decrypted, the sense of relief at SHAEF was intense. Moreover, despite Joyce's remark, there had been no changes in German dispositions along the Channel coast traceable to knowledge of the Mulberries.

The scare died, but not before questions were asked about how the Germans had learned the structures were at Selsey Bill in the first place. It was thought possible that the man at least indirectly responsible had been Count Oxenstjerna, the Swedish naval attaché in London and the same man whose reports to his government were being shown to Karl-Heinz Kraemer, the Abwehr agent in Stockholm. The Allied secret agencies had been aware of the link between Oxenstjerna and Kraemer for some time, and while his reports were carefully monitored, he was allowed to remain at his post. But finally, early in April, he had been asked to leave the country; the Admiralty "did not quite like Oxenstierna's avid interest in the Royal Navy and the aggressive manner in which he went after sensitive information." He returned to Stockholm, unaware of why he had been expelled, and there perhaps made some mention of the structures at Selsey Bill. In that event, the information would have found its way to the Abwehr, which had thoroughly penetrated the military administration of Sweden. Whatever the Abwehr's source, the information was incorrect; and it was noticed with satisfaction that, with Oxenstjerna's recall, Kraemer's naval reports suddenly dried up.

Allied measures to protect the secrets of D-Day were not confined to England; they extended to every country of Europe and every corner of the globe where Axis agents might be at work to penetrate the screen of security that protected Neptune. Nowhere were these agents harder at work than in the neutral nations; but by the spring of 1944, the British and the Americans had trained a powerful battery of diplomatic and economic weapons on Stockholm and Madrid, in particular. Slow to respond at first, Sweden and Spain would soon find themselves bested in the battle of the chancelleries. Yielding to the formal pressure of diplomatic "grand remonstrances" and the more compelling threat of economic reprisals, they gradually began to withdraw the favors granted to the Axis governments. The ban on all diplomatic communication to and from their representatives in Britain further served to blind the Axis; but one major watchtower remained uncomfortably close to Neptune—the German and Japanese diplomatic, military and intelligence missions in Dublin.

It seemed harsh and ludicrous to level the big guns of Allied diplomatic and economic warfare on the poor, rural republic of Eire. Moreover, America had strong sentimental ties with the Irish; and Ireland, in spite of her neutrality, had permitted 165,000 of her men to leave the country and serve in the British armed forces. Several of Britain's best generals—Montgomery included—were Irish or Orangemen; and the Irish had behaved with gallantry and distinction in the Allied cause. They had won no fewer than seven Victoria Crosses and many scores of other high awards. Yet both England and America were determined to neutralize German efforts based in Dublin to discover the secrets of Neptune.

When the United States entered the Second World War, the western powers had hoped that, seven hundred years of Anglo-Irish bickering notwithstanding, the Irish Free State would abandon her position of strict neutrality and join the Grand Alliance. It was a lost cause; the Irish President, Eamon de Valera, rejected the suggestion. Irish-American relations remained correct but cool; Roosevelt, however, was particularly embittered and disillusioned by the refusal of de Valera to permit American aircraft and warships to be stationed on the west coast of Eire. Had this been possible, Anglo-American losses in the Battle of the Atlantic might have been much less severe, and the battle itself won much sooner.

Then an incident occurred that aggravated the tensions between the two countries. In April 1943 an aircraft carrying General Walter Bedell Smith crash-landed near Athenry, about 15 miles inland from

Galway Bay. It had developed engine trouble and, finding an emergency airstrip near Oranmore blocked with obstacles, put down on the grounds of an agricultural school. Nobody was hurt, but Smith, his staff and his crew were quickly surrounded by courteous yet firm officers of the Irish army and held at a nearby hotel while the situation was sorted out with Irish army headquarters and the Foreign Ministry. For a time it seemed that Smith might be interned, just as the Irish had interned other combatants of the warring powers who had arrived in neutral Eire. In the event, strong diplomatic representation by the American minister at Dublin, David Gray, brought results, and Smith was taken to Belfast, British territory, to continue his journey to Washington from there.

In the early months of 1944, relations between the Allies and the Irish were jolted even more sharply when both the OSS and MI-6 reported that "a great deal of information pertaining to Allied activities in England and Ulster comes from the German embassy in Dublin. This Legation, which is heavily staffed, has succeeded in infiltrating agents into England. . . . The Germans attribute great importance (to information) obtained from Irish sources." The Irish question, which had been permitted to smolder, now blazed; and when it was learned that the Irish government had arrested two SD agents with wireless transceivers in Galway just after they had landed by parachute, Roosevelt decided the time had come to act. On February 21, 1944, after consultations with the British government, Gray presented a peremptory note to de Valera. Commenting, threateningly, that Irish neutrality "continues to operate in favor of the Axis powers and against the United Nations on whom your security and the maintenance of your national economy depend," the note demanded that the Irish close the German and Japanese missions in Dublin, seize their wireless equipment, imprison all Axis agents, and sever all relations with Berlin and Tokyo.

The chief cause of American concern was the suspicion that Axis agents were spying on the U.S. 15th Corps, which was stationed in Ulster and would soon join Patton's 3rd Army in Britain. That kind of information would have been very useful to the Germans, and very damaging to the Allies. Perhaps for that reason, Gray, finally exasperated by the Irish attitude, telegraphed the State Department to recommend that, unless de Valera quickly complied with the terms of the note, U.S. forces in Ulster should cross the frontier, arrest the Axis diplomats and close down their missions by force. It was an extraordinary recommendation to make, and one that might have involved the United States in guerrilla warfare with the IRA and, perhaps, the Irish army. News of this telegram evidently reached the Irish military authorities for, almost immediately afterwards, the army was put on a state of alert, all leave was canceled, all bridges between Eire and Ulster were mined, and all frontier posts and strategic positions manned. Whether or not Gray's recommendation was considered seriously, Irish-American relations had never been worse.

De Valera replied to Gray's note, in somewhat leisurely fashion, on March 7. Remarking on the rumors sweeping Dublin of an imminent American invasion, he reminded Roosevelt, first of all, that Eire had been assured in 1942 that the United States had no intention of violating her neutrality. He then expressed surprise at the terms of the note and assured the American government of "the uniformly friendly character of Irish neutrality in relation to the United States." But he concluded:

> The Irish government are, therefore, safeguarding, and will continue to safeguard, the interests of the United States but they must in all circumstances protect the neutrality of the Irish state and the democratic way of life of the Irish people. Their attitude will continue to be determined not by fear of any measures which would be employed against them but by goodwill and the fundamental friendship existing between the two peoples.

In short, de Valera called Roosevelt's bluff, confident that any military move against Eire would cause bad blood in the large Irish-American electorate in the United States. Indeed, when news of the American ultimatum was published, it had raised a storm of protest, and de Valera knew that Roosevelt could not back up his demands with force. The wily Irish President had won the round, although Irish Special Branch men did raid the German and Japanese missions in Dublin and seize their wireless equipment.

The United States, which had undoubtedly undertaken the negotiations because of the centuries-old enmity between Britain and Ireland, was forced to stand down. But the stakes were high, and Britain and Churchill took up where America and Roosevelt left off. On March 14, 1944, Churchill announced a policy in the Commons "designed to isolate Great Britain from southern Ireland" and also "to isolate southern Ireland from the outside world during the critical period of the war that is now approaching." He added that he much regretted, in view of the large numbers of Irishmen fighting in the British armed forces, that it was necessary to take these measures. Nevertheless, from now until further notice all Eire's ships and aircraft would be prevented from leaving her coasts for foreign ports, the telephone and air services would be cut between England and Eire, and the menace of economic sanctions would be maintained. The German and Japanese diplomats would therefore be unable to leave the country or to communicate with the outside world. These measures were immediately put into effect, and with that, Germany's western window on Neptune was shut.

Allied planners readily acknowledged that an operation the size of Neptune could not possibly be undertaken without extensive dress rehearsals. Accordingly, as the winter's storms gave way to the spring's zephyrs in the Channel, Allied forces began a series of triphibious exercises to acquaint themselves with the difficulties and dangers of combined attacks on a hostile shore. But as these exercises grew in magnitude, worries concerning the security of Neptune's secrets grew apace. Might not the enemy be able to deduce from the volume of wireless traffic and the troop movements involved in these exercises just when the invasion would take place? And since most of the activity was centered in southern and southwestern England, might he not also deduce that the assault would be launched from those areas and that the most probable target would be Normandy? Because both were very serious risks, it became necessary for the LCS and the CSM to launch a stratagem to disguise the truth of the exercises. Brutus, Tricycle and Garbo were all instructed to inform their German controllers that the full dress rehearsal for Neptune, an operation codenamed "Fabius" after the Roman general of the Second Punic War who foiled Hannibal by dilatory tactics and avoidance of direct engagements, was not the last but the first of many exercises that would be needed before Neptune could be launched around July 20, 1944. To support that *ruse de guerre,* Churchill, at Eisenhower's request, made deceptive references to "many false alarms, many feints and many dress rehearsals" in a fifty-minute review of the state of the war on March 26, 1944. His remarks were also designed to disguise the truth of the exercises from the members of the French resistance, who, if they mistook the nature of these very large and provocative operations, might rise up prematurely and be decimated. But the crisis, when it occurred, came from an unexpected quarter.

Although Allied air and naval superiority had all but immobilized the Kriegsmarine, there was one branch of the German navy that was far from inert: E-boat squadrons, the very fast torpedo boats which marauded Channel waters. E-boat squadrons were fully alert to the prospect of fat pickings along the English coast, and the nature of their forays suggested that they might be getting some good intelligence from somewhere—possibly wireless intelligence. In any case, nine E-boats sailed from Cherbourg on the night of April 27, 1944, not to maraud but with a specific objective: a convoy off Portland Bill, the easternmost extremity of Lyme Bay. Instead they intercepted Exercise "Tiger," an American dress rehearsal for the Utah assault, en route from Plymouth to Slapton Sands. What happened that night may have been purely coincidental, but even so, the curtain of deception and secrecy surrounding Neptune was seriously rent.

Slapton Sands in south Devon, a long, wide and sandy beach beneath low hills, had been chosen for Tiger because the topography resembled that of Utah beach in Normandy; and it was just after midnight on April 28 when eight 5000-ton LST's edged into Lyme Bay in Indian file. The sea was smooth, the night clear but dark, the ships blacked out and almost invisible against a quarter moon that was low and setting. As the ships approached a point 11 miles offshore, the Tiger force—the U.S. 4th Infantry Division and the 1st Amphibian Engineer Brigade—prepared for "H-Hour," that time when the troops would clamber into the assault boats for the long run in to the beach, when the Sherman amphibious tanks would rumble into the sea through the bow doors and the engineers begin to blast passages for them through the maze of obstacles, wire and mines strung along the beach.

Aboard the command ship, Commander Ben Skahill and the deputy commanding general of the assault force, General Theodore Roosevelt, were uneasy. They were in dangerous waters, they had only one escort, the British corvette *Azalea,* and both the troops and the LST's were—it was thought then—irreplaceable. Furthermore, the troops and LST's were about to rehearse for the first time the tactics they would use on D-Day. As Lieutenant Colonel Ralph Ingersoll, deputy chief of the Special Plans Branch, the deception organization at Bradley's headquarters, would explain:

> The exercise concerned was the first which involved a full rehearsal of the actual assault formation that would be employed [in Neptune]. It was complete with such secret weapons as rocket boats and (amphibious) tanks. In Africa and Sicily, and at Salerno, the engineers and infantry had had to go ashore first to make it practical and relatively safe

to bring in the armor. But in Normandy we were about to try reversing the process, sending in the armor first, self-floated.

Hence the need for a full-scale rehearsal—and the strictest secrecy.

As H-Hour approached, all crews were at General Quarters, and between decks the infantry, the engineers and the tank crews were at their assault stations, waiting for the hooter to announce the start of the exercise. Then it happened. Tracer fire was suddenly directed toward LST 507 from the port quarter, and a moment later a torpedo hit the ship. The main engines stopped, the ship began to burn as fire leaped from one fuel tank to another; then it exploded. In that moment, 94 of the 165 sailors and 151 of the 282 soldiers aboard were killed or thrown into the water and drowned. The men aboard LST 531 saw LST 507 blow up, and then their ship, too, was struck by a torpedo. It caught fire from end to end, exploded, rolled over and sank. Only 28 of the 142 sailors and 44 of the 354 soldiers aboard were saved.

Astern, aboard LST 289, Lieutenant Harry J. Mettler watched the fires directly down the path of the moonlight, but he could see no targets—only flames. Were they being attacked by E-boats or a submarine? Nobody knew and before it was possible to call the convoy commander on the radiotelephone, a torpedo was sighted coming directly toward the ship. Mettler shouted to the crew of the 40-mm cannon in the stern to try to destroy the torpedo with gunfire. Then he ordered full right rudder as the gun opened up and, for a moment, he thought he had eluded the 20-knot projectile. But the torpedo was a new type that homed onto the noise of the screws; like a shark chasing a mackerel it closed in and hit the ship in the stern. The explosion blasted the cannon and its crew over the boat davits, the stern deck plating rolled up, the screws began to race, the engines stopped, fire broke out. Mettler, displaying marvelous presence of mind, lowered five of the assault boats and they took the ship in tow. But four men were dead, eight were missing, and twenty-two were wounded or burned.

The Tiger assault force quickly called for protection, the exercise was canceled and the surviving LST's scuttled safely back to Plymouth. A major disaster had occurred. In less than ten or fifteen minutes 630 men had been killed or drowned; another 8 would die in hospital from wounds, and many more were burned or wounded. Two LST's had been sunk and a third had been crippled (leaving Neptune without a single reserve LST), a brigade of amphibious tanks had been lost, and incalculable damage had been done to the morale of the men.

When the news reached Supreme Headquarters, Eisenhower forbade any public announcement to guard the secrecy of the exercise and prevent even graver damage to the morale of the Neptune assault forces. Then it was learned that one of the German E-boats, after attacking the LST's, had turned and scanned the water with a searchlight, while others had cruised through the survivors before the entire squadron sped away under the cover of smoke and darkness. The loss of men and LST's was serious enough; but the report of searchlight activity caused profound fears at Supreme Headquarters. What had the Germans been looking for? Had they picked up any prisoners? And if so, who were they? There were Bigots aboard the LST's, and it was feared that the Germans had captured one of them and would make him talk. Never before had the security of Neptune been in such grave jeopardy.

General Betts, deputy chief of intelligence at SHAEF, and Colonel Gordon Sheen, chief of the SHAEF security branch, went among the oil-soaked survivors at dawn with a list of the Bigots who had taken part in the exercise. One by one they were all accounted for, but there were still a large number of missing men who had *some* knowledge of Neptune's secrets. What had become of them? For they, too, knew enough to be able to compromise at least part of the Allied strategy—the tactics to be employed, for example.

Betts ordered that every man who was missing must be found, every corpse must be recovered and his identity checked. Divers and frogmen swam down to the wrecks, entered the compartments, wriggled between the sunken tanks, and brought up the identity discs of the corpses they found. It would have been impossible to account for every man; the tide would have taken some corpses. But most were found, and at an Admiralty inquiry into the disaster, it was thought impossible that the Germans had captured any prisoners—a claim that was disputed by the men of the Tiger force who were still angry at the lack of escort protection for the exercise.

Had the Germans taken any prisoners? Even if they had not, what had they been able to deduce about Allied strategy and tactics from the location of the Tiger exercise and the composition of the assault force? No one knew. At Montgomery's headquarters, according to Ingersoll: "There was a whole day . . . when it was seriously contemplated trying to alter the operation [Neptune] because of the knowledge which the enemy must now be presumed to have—the detailed knowledge of almost everything we planned."

Other sources of intelligence, including Ultra, were checked in an attempt to discover if the Germans were making the sort of changes in their dispositions that might be expected if they had new information about Neptune; and to the consternation of Supreme Headquarters, apparently they were. For it was only a week after the Tiger calamity that Hitler issued his command instruction to watch Normandy. In obedience to that command, the Germans began almost to double the anti-tank and anti-aircraft defenses of Normandy, the Cherbourg peninsula and Brittany, and two new divisions especially trained to combat paratroopers were ordered to precisely the area where American airborne divisions would land on D-Day. Why had Hitler suddenly focused his attention on Normandy? Was he merely taking all possible precautions, or was Neptune's destination no longer a secret?

As the invasion neared, SHAEF anxiously examined the possible reasons for the new German movements. Artist's fate remained a major concern, or perhaps the Germans had captured American soldiers in the assault rehearsal at Slapton Sands. It was also possible that not all the German agents in England had been apprehended, or, the most frightening prospect, that some German cryptanalytical feat comparable to Ultra was laying bare the reality of Allied plans. Not until after the war was over would the Allies learn what had been behind that sudden flurry of German movement only weeks before D-Day. The reason was traced, once more, to the German wireless intelligence service, the one arm of the Reich's intelligence-gathering system that the Allies had not been able to cripple.

The German wireless intelligence and cryptanalytical service—the Funkabwehr—had been responsible for a remarkable series of triumphs throughout the war. It would claim total penetration of French codes and ciphers, including machine ciphers; and it had consistently broken into every Russian cryptosystem from the highest commands down to battalions. As for the United States, a high officer of the Funkabwehr would later claim that German wireless intelligence had had no difficulty in penetrating American radio communications because of extremely poor security. The same was not true of the British; they had learned their lesson in North Africa. The Funkabwehr official would state that British radio communications were the most effective and secure of all those with which German wireless intelligence had to contend, adding that the higher-echelon cryptosystems of the British were never compromised during the Sec-

ond World War. But while the Germans had not been able to penetrate the systems, they were quite successful in analyzing the characteristic patterns of British wireless traffic—particularly the traffic of the
RAF signals service. The Funkabwehr official would state that the
RAF was not aware that it was responsible for revealing many
carefully guarded plans of the British army and thus for many losses
and casualties; and he would add that the only possible explanation
was interservice jealousy, which led the RAF to overestimate the quality and security of its wireless communications and to refuse to let
them be subject to the supervision of the army.

During the build-up for the invasion in England, the lid of security
was clamped down even tighter on both British and American wireless
units, and a crisis enveloped the entire German wireless intelligence
system. Once again, it was forced to rely on an analysis of the distinctive patterns of Anglo-American wireless transmissions, and upon an
occasional leak, like the one that had revealed the presence in England
of the American 82nd Airborne Division. With this kind of surveillance, the Germans were able to piece together only a very vague
picture of the structure, location and strength of the Anglo-American
armies confronting them, a picture that was further obscured by the
false wireless traffic that filled the ether. But then, in late April, they
made a simple discovery that threw a blinding light upon some of the
Allies' secrets. After an intensive study of the wireless traffic of both
British and American divisions, Funkabwehr analysts realized that
when they heard the distinctive traffic indicating that an air liaison
official had been assigned to a division to provide a link between
ground and air forces, it could be assumed, first, that it was an assault
division and, second, that it was preparing for offensive operations. In
a relatively short period of time, the Funkabwehr heard all the
divisions in southern and southwestern England broadcasting air liaison traffic, and they deduced, with considerable accuracy, that the invasion was imminent and that the axis of the attack would be in the direction of Portsmouth/Plymouth and Le Havre/Cherbourg.

That was what happened late in April and early in May. The
problem then, as the Funkabwehr officer would state, was to convince
Hitler that the intelligence was accurate. Hitler tended to distrust
wireless intelligence as a source of information on military planning;
but on this occasion, to the surprise of the Funkabwehr, he believed it.
Realizing that Normandy was indeed vulnerable to attack, he ordered
the reinforcements that had been noted with such concern at SHAEF.
He did nothing, however, to weaken the garrisons defending the rest of

the Channel coast: he was, as SHAEF hoped in its most optimistic appraisal of the reasons for the reinforcements, merely taking all possible precautions.

Unknown to SHAEF, however, the Germans had obtained a significant hint of Neptune's destination through their ingenious penetration of the wireless communications of Allied assault forces. And they had acted upon it. Also unknown to SHAEF, they had discovered an even more dangerous clue through their penetration of wireless communications of a different sort. Generals and even prime ministers might be hushed up, whole governments might be intimidated into silence, but the security of the wireless traffic between SOE and its agents in France was extremely difficult to monitor and maintain. The Germans had been quick to spot this chink in Allied armor, and while SHAEF worried about loose talk and missing Bigots, a security leak that might endanger the success of Neptune had already occurred.

The Wireless Game

THE LYSANDER PILOT picked up his landmark in the moonlight—the castle of Angers with its moats and seventeen round towers—and looked out for the silvered water at the point where the Loire joins the Sarthe. He circled the area, saw the A light flashing from the meadows below, came down to 300 feet, taking care to see that the speed of his high-winged monoplane did not drop off too much, and then put his spatted wheels down onto the meadow grass. He stopped, taxied back toward the A light and dropped the aircraft's ladder, keeping his motor turning. Three women agents of SOE—Noor Inayat Khan, Cecily Lefort and Diana Rowden—stepped out into the night to be received by Henri Dericourt. Then, having taken the secret mail aboard, the pilot pulled out his boost control override and climbed rapidly away. It was a routine mission; but it was also a mission that would have mysterious and even sinister implications. For all three women were doomed to be captured and executed by the SD; and it was later alleged that they had lost their lives through an intricate weapon of war called the wireless game.

The wireless game was quite as old as wireless itself. In its simplest form, it consisted merely of preempting one of the enemy's channels of communication, a channel that he trusted as a reliable source of intelligence, and using it to transmit false and misleading information. XX-Committee operations were a prime example of this form of the game. With the capture of an enemy agent and his wireless set, ciphers, schedules and other paraphernalia, the transmission of deceptive information could begin—with or without the cooperation of the agent—and could continue as long as the Germans did not suspect that the agent or his set were under British control.

The wireless game was not, however, a British monopoly. The Germans, who called it *Englandspiele* or *Funkspiele* (wireless game), played it, too. SOE agents and wireless posts on the continent frequently fell into German hands, and with the captured sets and ciphers the Germans maintained communication with London, usually in the hope that they would receive instructions that would reveal something of Allied military intentions, as well as information about agents and *réseaux* that had not yet been detected, and about the time and place of the arrival of new agents and drops of stores and money.

The success or failure of these games as they were played by both sides almost always hung upon whether the players learned the system of security checks on the set they were manipulating. The British, extremely wary of wireless deception, sent their agents into the field with a "bluff" check and a "true" check, both of which usually consisted, with many variations, of an arrangement to misspell words at certain places. The assumption was that if an agent was captured and forced to reveal his "bluff" check, the absence of his "true" check in any transmission would still alert his controller that he was operating under duress. The Germans soon learned of this system, however, and once they had captured an agent, they did not stop at torture to learn his checks. But even if they did so, it was sometimes possible to tell that a set was under enemy control by the operator's "fist"—his style of transmission. Each agent had certain characteristics of transmission that were familiar to his controller, and any significant variation in the way a message was sent could warn a controller that an agent was being manipulated or impersonated.

Thus a wireless game was extremely difficult to establish and sustain even in its simplest form. But the game was capable of an additional refinement that was even more risky, yet presented an excellent opportunity to counter deception with deception. If, as often happened, the British learned that one of their wireless posts was under enemy control, they could, if they wished, continue transmission, and in so doing send instructions and information that would deceive and mislead the Germans. But the key to the success of this double game was normality; the British could in no way reveal that they knew the post was in enemy hands. They had to continue to respond to inquiries and requests from the controlled post just as they would normally, including sending in arms, ammunition, stores and money that would inevitably be captured by the Germans.

There was, however, a much more sinister aspect to sustaining this form of wireless deception. Part of the normal operation of a wireless post was to arrange for the reception of incoming agents; and if the

British stopped sending agents into certain posts, the Germans would naturally suspect that they had discovered the post had been captured, and the game would collapse. On the other hand, if the British continued to send in agents to posts they knew to be in enemy hands, the agents would most probably be caught and executed. A wireless game may have been worth the loss of money and military supplies, but was it worth the sacrifice of Allied agents and sympathizers?

Such men and women could also be involved in yet another refinement to the game—the cipher trick. The object of this *ruse de guerre* was to send operators into the field with ciphers that the British knew the Germans would be able to decrypt. By establishing this kind of wireless leak, deceptive instructions and information could be passed to the agent and thence to the enemy. But again, to sustain their credibility, traffic with the agent involved must appear to be normal—and normality presupposed sending in not only arms, ammunition, explosives and money, but also other agents. And the agent using the cipher would sooner or later be detected, arrested—and almost certainly killed.

After the war, the British were accused by both the French and the Dutch of deliberately ignoring the security checks and other warnings that would indicate a wireless post was under control and then sending in agents—some seventy of them—to receptions they knew would be German, all for the purpose of maintaining a channel of communication down which, at some stage, it might be possible to pass deceptive information. The British were also accused of using women agents to play cipher tricks. Aware that the Germans might be suspicious if they were able to read too easily an exchange of ciphered signals between London and a male agent, the British—so the allegation went—used women agents for this purpose on the grounds that the Germans believed that no Englishman would be so ungallant as to involve a woman in such a maneuver.

These were ugly charges which were, of course, denied. But had the British, in their determined pursuit of surprise on D-Day, once again made a "nice assessment of profit and loss"—the lives of a few agents against the lives of hundreds if not thousands of Allied soldiers on the Norman shore? It was undeniably true that, after the collapse of the Prosper empire, SOE did not immediately shut down a number of wireless posts that had been connected with Prosper and had then fallen into German hands. As a result, large consignments of money, arms and war stores would be dropped to the Germans, not the French; and a number of F section agents would be met by German, not French, reception committees. Were the British unaware that these posts had been captured, or were they playing wireless games as a part of Fortitude's attempts to mislead the Germans about the time and place of the invasion? If the former were true, they could be accused only of making a monumentally tragic blunder; if the latter, they were guilty of trading human life for tactical advantage on D-Day. But if this was, in fact, a sacrifice the British were willing to make, what did they hope to gain by it?

The allegation that the British sacrificed their own agents in wireless games and cipher tricks centered mainly on the tragic case of a young woman called "Madeleine." Her real name was Noor Inayat Khan; Noor was her first name, Inayat her surname, and Khan denoted her high birth, for she was an Indian princess. Her father was Inayat Khan, the leader of the Sufi sect of Mohammedan mystics, and the family was a direct descendant of Tipu Sultan, the eighteenth-century Sultan of Mysore and the last Muslim ruler of southern India, a warrior and intriguer who, in the service of Napoleon, gave Arthur Wellesley much trouble. Inayat Khan and his wife, the Begum, had come to Europe to found Sufi "Lodges of Blessing," his mysticism intrigued Rasputin, and they were invited to the Kremlin. There, on New Year's Day 1914, Princess Noor was born, but riots soon forced the family to flee the Russian capital. After many adventures, they settled in Paris where the "Light of Womanhood"—which was what Noor's name meant—went to school, finished at the École Normale de Musique, and, shortly before the outbreak of the Second World War, was earning her living as a writer of children's stories for Paris radio.

Just before the fall of France, Noor came to England with her brother, Vilayat. She enlisted in the Women's Auxiliary Air Force as 424598 Aircraftwoman 2nd Class Norah Baker, and was trained as a wireless operator. Then, while awaiting a posting, she saw orders inviting personnel who could speak French and work wireless to volunteer for "special duties." This she did, and found herself in a dingy room at the War Office being interviewed by SOE for what was called "secret work." She was accepted for training and was enrolled as a "nurse" in the First Aid Nursing Yeomanry—the customary form of cover for female agents sent by SOE to the field. This, Gubbins thought, might induce the Germans to behave more tolerably toward them if they were caught. She was also given a temporary commission as a flying officer in the WAAF—again, to improve her chances if she was caught.

It was now that one of the first mysteries that surrounded Princess Noor began to emerge: why was she accepted by SOE at all? For she was, one of her training officers reported: "A splendid, vague, dreamy creature, far too conspicuous—twice seen, never forgotten." Her appearance, her accent, her bearing, all were such as to attract attention, which an SOE agent was not supposed to do. Shy, of slight build, with dark eyes set in a thin olive face surrounded by long dark hair, Noor was a gentle, graceful and charming young woman. But although in character she was said to be as "strong and flexible as a rapier-blade," her head tutor in clandestinity, Colonel F. V. Spooner, reported adversely on her because he considered her "too emotional and impulsive to be suitable for employment as a secret agent." Spooner later said that he had "really stuck his neck out and gone to considerable lengths in his endeavours to prevent (Noor) from being sent to France as an agent. Not only was she too sensitive and easily hurt, but her inexperience . . . rendered her too vulnerable from a security point of view." Further, a tutor at Beaulieu in the New Forest—where she underwent part of her tuition in clandestinity—said she had "*no* sense of security," and wrote on her training reports: "She has an unstable and temperamental personality and it is very doubtful whether she is really suited to work in the field."

In spite of these and other unfavorable comments, Noor was deemed acceptable for service; Starkey was approaching and F section was very short of wireless operators. Buckmaster wrote the single word "nonsense" on her adverse reports (he said later he was convinced of Noor's ability to withstand the dangers of the field), and she was assigned the post of wireless operator to Émile-Henri Garry, the chief of "Cinema," a *réseau* on Prosper territory near Le Mans. She and two other women agents landed in France on the night of June 16/17, 1943, and it was alleged that, with the help of Dericourt, her arrival was witnessed by the SD, whose agents were hiding behind the hedges of wild roses on the edge of the field. But, if so, the Germans did nothing except watch, for the three women made their way to Angers Station, where they split up and Noor boarded a train for Paris.

Although she succeeded in getting through the German *Feldgendarmerie* controls at the station, Noor was, it was obvious, quite lost when she arrived, late on June 17, at the home of her organizer, Garry, at 40 rue Erlanger in Auteuil, a wealthy district of Paris. She confessed that she had not eaten anything since leaving England because she did not know how to use her French ration book or restaurant food coupons. Moreover, Garry had received no instructions from London that she was coming—a dangerous omission, for lesser men than Garry would have treated her as a Gestapo penetration agent. But touchingly, Noor presented Garry and his fiancée with a bunch of carnations. Both were appalled that she had been sent on such a mission.

Nevertheless, Noor was accepted by the Prosper network and taken to its operational headquarters, the École Nationale d'Agriculture, near Versailles, the next day. She was given temporary lodgings in the home of one of Prosper's lieutenants, Professor Alfred Balachowsky, but her habits immediately betrayed her British background; her hostess noted that she put the milk in the cup before the tea, when the reverse was the custom in France—a small matter but one that would attract the sharp eyes of the SD. Then she dyed her hair blonde, which instantly called attention to her coloring; and it was soon necessary for Balachowsky to scold her for leaving her cipher on the hall tallboy.

Within a week, Noor had settled into lodgings on the edge of the Bois de Boulogne; and there again, her hostess, who was a Prosper sub-agent, had to scold her for leaving her cipher open at the day's grid. She then established a wireless post in an apartment at the rue de la Faisanderie, not far—certainly not far enough—from SD headquarters on the Avenue Foch. But for all her carelessness, she was not afraid; or rather, she was in control of her fear. She was said to have obtained the assistance of her next-door neighbor, a German, in putting up her aerial; she explained that it was a clothes line.

Noor arrived in Paris at a dangerous time. The Prosper network had begun to collapse, and she was forced to find new lodgings. But she did keep her wireless post in the rue de la Faisanderie; and through Garry, she learned of the arrests of Prosper and his lieutenants, and reported the *ratissage* to London. London responded by telling her to lie low. This she did for a week or so; but then her inexperience and carelessness showed themselves again. Wearing a navy blue scarf wrapped around her head like a turban, which emphasized her Indian features, she went on a sentimental journey to her home of the 1930's, visiting school friends on the way. Bodington of F section, who flew to Paris to investigate the extent of the Prosper disaster, saw her briefly during this period—August 1943—and heard enough from Garry to recommend to London that she be brought home. She should have gone out on the night of August 15, 1943, when Dericourt was to handle two Lysanders to evacuate Bodington, Scientist, and some survivors of the Prosper collapse. But although everyone else went, Noor remained behind; she refused to obey her order to leave until a replacement operator had arrived.

Almost incredibly, Noor survived in Paris for another two months, although the SD knew of her existence, for in the secret *courrier* that Dericourt was regularly showing to H. J. Kieffer (the chief of the SD's counterespionage service in Paris) were letters from Noor to friends and relatives in England. But her whereabouts were unknown until Renée Garry, the sister of the Cinema organizer, sold her address to the SD for 100,000 francs (£500 or $2400). Noor was arrested in her Paris apartment on or about October 13, and within minutes found herself at Gestapo headquarters. It was another grave loss for F section, for she was the last F section wireless operator in the Paris area.

Princess Noor was calm when taken and calm when interrogated. Her SD inquisitor, Kieffer, came to admire her and spared her much. He soon lost patience with her, however, for she made not one but two escape bids while at SD headquarters on the Avenue Foch. Both times she got only as far as the street before she was recaptured; but she was becoming a nuisance, and so she soon found herself at Badenweiler concentration camp where she spent many months, most of them in chains and solitary confinement.

Noor was made of sterner stuff than her SOE instructors had realized, but she had, once again, been careless. For when she was arrested, her wireless, her ciphers and all of her back traffic with London were also seized—everything, in fact, that Josef Goetz, the SD's wireless expert, needed to play a convincing *Funkspiele* with London. Noor had recorded all her back traffic in a child's exercise book, which the SD found on her bedside table. And with this invaluable background information, Goetz, impersonating Noor, reopened the Cinema circuit and began transmissions to London. London responded, but cautiously, for her messages did not ring quite true. Goetz needed Noor's help to ensure the success of his game, but she consistently refused to give it and the game was played without her.

At Christmas, the British were still suspicious; the style of "Noor's" transmissions suggested that she was being impersonated. But Goetz pressed the game forward; he signaled London that Cinema was ready to receive an arms drop. London replied that it would send in twelve containers at a given time and place, but in the event, only one container was dropped, which led Goetz to believe that "London had twigged." Buckmaster was, indeed, nervous; he went to see France Antelme, SOE's senior French adviser, and showed him all of "Noor's" transmissions. Antelme said that on balance he thought that she was free, and by the end of the year Buckmaster was inclined to agree, even though Noor's London controller was certain that she was being impersonated. Nevertheless, F section sent in 500,000 francs to the false Cinema. Goetz was definitely encouraged. He asked for more arms and London responded with large drops. But were the British really unaware that Noor's set was under German control and that Cinema receptions were, in fact, German receptions? Or were they countering Goetz's deception with a deception of their own?

Whatever the case, Goetz's *Funkspiele* now took a tragic turn—for the agents involved. Still apparently unaware that Noor was being impersonated, the British began to send in agents—seven in all—to the false Cinema. On the night of February 7/8, 1944, the first four—all of them so inexperienced and ill-trained that their mission seemed to be sacrificial—were dropped together near Poitiers. They were R. E. J. Alexandre, a twenty-two-year-old French aircraft fitter; an American called Byerley who was his wireless operator; a Canadian, Deniset, who was to have been Noor's replacement; and Jacques Ledoux, an Anglo-Frenchman who was to have established a new circuit, "Orator," at Le Mans. All were immediately captured.

Then came Goetz's finest hour. It was the capture of Antelme himself, who was also dropped to a Cinema reception; and the circumstances of his capture were as curious as everything that had gone before. Byerley, the American wireless operator in the first drop, had been instructed by F section before his departure to send certain special messages if he landed and got away safely. This was an unusual procedure, and one used only in cases where a reception committee—in this case Cinema—was suspected by SOE of being of doubtful loyalty. In fact, Byerley's set soon came on the air—it was again being worked by Goetz—but the special messages were not transmitted. That, in itself, should have been enough proof that Cinema was under German control, and Antelme's departure should have been canceled; or at least he should have been parachuted into a circuit that was known to be safe. But, on the contrary, SOE sent him in; and the Germans knew he was coming.

Antelme, a wealthy French aristocrat of forty-three who had important connections in the French banking and industrial hierarchy, was one of F section's most valuable and valued organizers. He had already completed three dangerous missions (for which he had been made a Member of the Order of the British Empire) when, in July 1943, he was appointed an adviser to F section. His knowledge of conditions in the field, and the agents and *réseaux* there, made his opinions always important and sometimes decisive. But in February he asked to be returned to the field, and he was allowed to do so. Antelme was aware of F section's suspicions that Cinema might be under German control, but despite the clear warning implicit in the absence of the special messages from Byerley's transmission, F section sent the false Cinema a request for a reception for Antelme and his party on the night of February 28/29, 1944. Cinema replied that the reception committee would await Antelme at a ground south of the village of Poigny, five miles from Rambouillet.

Goetz was jubilant, and passed the details of Antelme's arrival to Kieffer. He, in turn, aware of Antelme's importance in the SOE hierarchy, and with one eye on his own career, invited his SS chiefs to be present at the drop. On the appointed night the entire area of Rambouillet was sealed off by SS and SD parties and a local curfew was imposed. Promptly at 10:45 P.M., the German reception committee heard a plane overhead. It circled and by quarter-moonlight a stick of three dropped first: Antelme; his wireless operator, Lieutenant Lionel Lee; and his courier, Madeleine Damerment. Then the plane came round again and dropped eight large containers of war stores and several packages of other equipment. Antelme was the first to land; he struggled out of his shrouds, found himself looking into the muzzle of a Walther pistol, and was handcuffed. In an "imperial fury" Antelme cried, "I have been betrayed!" Then he and the two others were collected and taken to the Avenue Foch, where they were placed in solitary confinement, emerging only for interrogation and torture. None spoke and all were, in consequence, handled with great brutality.

With Antelme's capture, Goetz was quick to see the potential for another valuable *Funkspiele*. After nearly a month of silence, he opened communications with London on Lee's set; and, it appeared, he succeeded in hoodwinking SOE for a time, despite the fact that Lee's special security checks were not present in the transmissions, and Goetz pretended that Antelme had been injured in the drop and could not communicate with London directly. (In reality, he was sent to Gross Rosen concentration camp and shot.)

Under the circumstances—the special imperatives of the invasion—it might be expected that SOE would have been especially vigilant for signs of *Funkspiele* over Antelme's mission; and there were indeed such signs. But not for several critical weeks did SOE detect them. Why? And again, if Noor's set and the Cinema circuit were suspect *before* Antelme was dropped, why was he sent in at all? Did SOE—at the instruction of either the LCS or the CSM—continue its transmissions for some deceptive purpose? If so, what was accomplished by it?

The games being played on Noor's and Lee's sets gradually faded out as both sides tried to trick the other. But Goetz continued to play the deadliest *Funkspiele* of all with a wireless set captured from "Butler," another F section agent who had preceded Noor into the field and who was arrested just before she was. Butler was François Garel, a veteran F section organizer who had been parachuted blind into the Sarthe on March 23, 1943, with a wireless operator, Marcel Rousset, and a courier, Marcel Fox. They were dropped badly and lost all their baggage, including Rousset's wireless set. But fresh equipment—wireless, crystals, ciphers—was dropped to Rousset and, by May 1943, Butler and his crew had formed a *réseau* and were at work selecting rail and telephone targets to be blown when the Allies invaded. Garel survived the Prosper mousetraps for a time, but the Germans were aware of his existence, and through tenacious if routine detective work, they caught him, along with Rousset, Fox and a second courier, as they lunched at a safehouse in Paris.

At first Rousset denied his identity, but when Gilbert Norman confirmed that he was Butler's wireless operator he agreed to help Goetz in a *Funkspiele*—but for a reason. He told Goetz that his wireless security check consisted of no more than an agreement with London to transmit in English for Garel and in French for Fox; in fact the reverse was true. Goetz believed him and sent a message in English in which Garel asked for funds. London did not react to the warning. Butler's London controller merely asked why he had changed his *modus operandi,* and with that piece of sleepy stupidity the *Funkspiele* began.

Rousset was taken to Ravitsch concentration camp but, in order to answer some awkward questions from London, he was brought back to Paris to help Goetz prepare the answers. He was kept at the SD offices on the Place des États-Unis but, while sweeping a corridor, he bowled his guard over, broke through a window into a garden, hopped over a wall into a convent, and used the convent's telephone to call a girl friend. She brought him clothes and documents; then he tried to find a means to warn London again that his set was under German control. But he failed, and as a result, Goetz continued to play a *Funkspiele* that would not end until noon on D-Day. In response to instructions transmitted by the false Butler, large quantities of money and stores—and a succession of agents—were sent to German reception committees; and with Butler, Goetz would obtain his major prize: one of the three secrets of D-Day—*when* the Allies would invade.

The German victory concerned the BBC *messages personnels,* the "alert" and "action" messages which were assigned to every *réseau* in preparation for D-Day. The opening lines of Paul Verlaine's poem "Chanson d'Automne," were just such a message, and they were originally assigned to Butler. The first line was the alert: *"Les sanglots longs des violins d'automne"*—and it signaled Butler's sabotage squads to stand by. The second line was the "action" message—*"bercent mon coeur d'une langueur monotone"*—and it meant that they were to begin operations at midnight on the night that they received it. From November 1943 on, however, SOE withdrew the original *messages personnels,* and under circumstances of great care and secrecy they were replaced by new alert and action messages. It was a security precaution, in case the Germans had discovered the meaning of the messages assigned to the *réseaux* that had been captured in the Prosper *ratissage*—as indeed they had in the case of the Butler circuit. It was also part of the *messages personnels* stratagem in which Dericourt participated, for the British were aware that the Germans knew of the *messages personnels* system, although they did not know what individual messages meant or to whom they were directed. In fact, some messages had been revealed to the SD by Dericourt in Prosper's *courrier,* and it was the intention to broadcast these compromised alert and action signals, as well as other dummy messages directed to nonexistent *réseaux,* during the D-Day period to confuse and mislead the Germans about where and when the Allies would invade. But one of the *messages personnels* that should have been withdrawn was reassigned to an actual circuit—"Ventriloquist," an SOE *réseau* in the Loire-et-Cher. It was the Verlaine couplet.

Why a message originally assigned to a *réseau* that had fallen into German hands was to be broadcast on D-Day as an operational instruction will remain a mystery. The Germans would suggest that it was the work of an agent of their own inside SOE headquarters, a suggestion that was investigated and not proven. It was possible that SOE was unaware that Butler was under German control, in spite of the many indications to the contrary; it was also possible that SOE was playing a wireless game with Butler. But in either case, reassigning the Verlaine couplet was probably no more than an administrative blunder. Whatever the reason, the Germans now had a means to discover when the invasion would take place.

In the event, the Germans were not sure to whom the message would be directed, nor precisely what it meant. They thought it was a general call to arms to all railway resistance squads in France to begin operations against the Wehrmacht in support of the invasion when, in fact, it was designed solely for the Ventriloquist circuit. The Germans were also uncertain about the timing involved in the broadcast of the *messages personnels,* for this intelligence bulletin, which was sent out to all commanding generals in France, Belgium, Holland, Denmark and Norway, was slightly in error:

> The first part of this signal, up to and including the word *"l'Automne,"* will be broadcast by the English radio on the 1st and 15th of given months, while the second part is scheduled to be broadcast to mean that the landings would ensue during the next 48 hours, the time counted from midnight on the day of the initial transmission of the signal.

This interpretation was not quite accurate, but it was close enough to the truth so that all the Germans had to do was wait for the second line of the Verlaine couplet to be broadcast over the BBC and they would know that D-Day was to occur within forty-eight hours. It was the gravest breach of the entire security program that attended the invasion. If the Germans had obtained nothing else through *Funkspiele,* that alone would have justified all the effort that went into the game. But what justified the efforts of the British, efforts that included thousands of pounds' worth of arms, ammunition and stores that were dropped to the Germans—and, so it seemed to many Frenchmen, the deliberate sacrifice of scores of agents?

After the war, the allegations that SOE had betrayed some of its agents—and particularly the party of three women agents of which Princess Noor was a member—for the purposes of wireless and military deception received very wide circulation in Europe. But the evidence cited would never have been sufficient, or even admissible, in a court of law. In the euphoria of victory in France, and with the enormity of the problems of putting the country back on its feet, the matter got little further than heady and passionate gossip at the Brasserie Lipp, the politicians' and journalists' restaurant in St. Germain-des-Prés. In Holland, however, similar allegations were taken much more seriously, and a Royal Commission was established to investigate them. Some evidence was produced that SOE, to sustain wireless games which were intended to make it seem that the Allies would invade Holland, had indeed sent in agents in response to wireless communications from *réseaux* that SOE knew—or suspected—were in enemy hands. After much evasion, the British Foreign Office permitted Dutch investigators to interview high officers of both MI-6 and

SOE who had been involved in secret operations from London into Holland. The investigation foundered without a definite conclusion; but the Foreign Office, which became responsible for settling SOE's affairs after the war (SOE was closed down by the then Prime Minister, Clement Attlee, on the grounds that peacetime Britain wanted no "socialist international"), did issue a statement. In substance, it declared that the allegations that Dutch agents had been betrayed for reasons of tactical and strategical deception were both "repugnant" and "untrue."

What therefore was the truth? In the first place, the British never denied that they countered German *Funkspiele* with wireless games of their own. Nor, to sustain those games, did they deny sending in large drops of money and stores to posts they knew were under German control. The reason was both simple and ingenious; and by way of explanation, Foot, in his official account of SOE's activities, cited R. A. Bourne-Patterson, the Scots accountant who was Buckmaster's deputy. Bourne-Patterson, in SOE's secret (and unpublished) after-action report, stated, according to Foot, that drops were made to German-controlled posts "in order to give time for new circuits to establish themselves." This, obviously, was sound and successful strategy, for the Germans concentrated on the compromised circuits while SOE set up new circuits in preparation for the invasion. Moreover, British wireless games were played chiefly with circuits in the Fortitude area between the Seine and the Scheldt, and it was in that area, which included the Pas de Calais, that the attentions of the Germans were successfully fastened, when they might have been concentrating more profitably and dangerously on the region between the Seine and the Loire, which included Normandy.

But was SOE, on its own initiative or under instructions from some other secret agency, prepared to pay for the success of its wireless games with the lives of agents as coinage? Were agents, particularly women agents, used to plant deceptive cipher traffic on the Germans at the expense of their own lives? Were men and women considered no more important than money and stores to sustain wireless games? Foot denied it. With Noor and Antelme in mind, he wrote: "It was certainly never any part of F section's intention to send them straight to their death; nor indeed were their deaths intended by anybody else on the allied side." He added: "They were unfortunates who happened to be caught on an exposed flank while it was exposed." That might suffice as a statement of position, but not as an explanation. For while

SOE might have stopped short of using Noor and others to set up wireless games, it was not above taking advantage of the capture of their sets and ciphers once it had occurred. And that is, perhaps, what Henri Dericourt meant to imply when he was challenged by Miss Jean Overton Fuller, the British author who attempted to find some rational reason for Noor's fate. "The ways of headquarters were impenetrable," Dericourt said enigmatically. Pressed further by Miss Overton Fuller to say whether or not Noor was a deliberate sacrifice, he added, "My theory—I won't tell it to you—is not as crude as that."

It would have been crude indeed for SOE or any other secret agency to rely upon such unpredictable means to initiate a deception. Their stratagems were far more skillfully prepared and executed than that. And if they were willing to use a *Funkspiele* to their own advantage once it had been set up, that would explain why they continued transmissions to wireless posts that had almost surely been captured by the Germans in the wake of Prosper, and why they frequently ignored the security check systems. Colonel George Starr, the controller of a large *réseau* in Gascony, would state that at great peril to himself he had warned London on two occasions that wireless posts were in enemy hands; but he had been told to mind his own business—London knew what it was doing.

But did London know what it was doing in every case? Apparently not, unless it was conceded that the British were willing to sacrifice the lives of agents the stature of Antelme, and give away one of the secrets of D-Day to sustain wireless games.

How, then, to explain these sinister aspects of the mystery? Was it, as has been suggested, departmental muddle, overwork at headquarters, the inefficiency of wireless and security staffs, the amateurishness of SOE itself? SOE was, in fact, that sort of organization. It had been set up in haste for the purposes of war; it had no established bureaucracy; it recruited hurriedly and widely in a social range that extended from pimps to princesses. Errors and casualties were, under the circumstances, bound to occur. And that, in addition to the extreme cleverness with which the Germans played *Funkspiele,* may well have been at least one reason for the high price that SOE paid for the success of its wireless games. But there could have been another that was also related to the peculiar circumstances of the organization and the times. It is possible that SOE did indeed suspect that these posts were under German control, but was not absolutely sure. As long as only money and military supplies were dropped to suspect posts, it did not really matter. That was considered a small enough price to pay to plant deceptive information that might influence the outcome of an Allied military operation. But when it came to sending in agents, SOE, working under the extraordinary pressures of Neptune and Fortitude, was forced to gamble. Other, riskier gambles had paid off; tragically, some of the gambles taken in conjunction with the wireless games did not.

The reasons for the deaths of Noor, Antelme and others will never be known. Secret services rarely make reports that might later come back to haunt them. Who can talk to the dead; who among the living dares talk publicly? Perhaps the final judgment in this sad but heroic affair must be left to the pragmatist. These men and women had volunteered for operations in the lonely, gray outer marches of the war —a world where the only standards were survival, defeat or victory. Were they not liable to betrayal, torture and execution at any time, often for mundane reasons: dislike, jealousy, the desire to purchase the loyalties of a mistress, or even to settle an old score? It was in the very nature of their work that their lives must be considered forfeit the moment they left the shores of England. Were the secret agencies not justified in using them for any purpose, if their lives—and their deaths —served the objectives of Fortitude? What did these agents exist for, but to confound and confuse the enemy? These were, the pragmatist might argue, desperate, pitiless days that demanded desperate, pitiless action. As Baumer, the American representative on the LCS, would state after the war: "I know that the British were in a stop-at-nothing mood before the invasion. The only thing that mattered was the success of Fortitude, and it was impossible for Fortitude to have been a success without sacrifices."

Princess Noor did not survive the war. She spent months in various concentration camps, in chains part of the time. Then at Dachau, on the morning of September 14, 1944, Noor and three other women agents of SOE were taken from their cells "into a sandy yard," Foot recorded, "and told to kneel down by a wall. They saw the old bloodstains in the sand, and knew their fate. They knelt two by two, each pair holding hands; an SS man came up behind them and shot each of them dead, neatly, through the back of the neck." Their corpses were burned.

But Noor was not forgotten by England. On April 5, 1949, at Gubbins's nomination, she was posthumously awarded the George Cross for "acts of the greatest heroism or of the most conspicuous courage in circumstances of extreme danger." Gubbins also arranged to place a plaque in the wall of a church at the back of Harrods in Knightsbridge. Every year someone has left a little bunch of spring flowers at the foot of the plaque.

11

The French Labyrinth

In April 1944, Field Marshal Rommel and his intelligence officer, Colonel Anton Staubwasser, visited the Gothic ramparts of Mont St. Michel on the Emerald Coast of Brittany. They were not interested in the renowned antiquities of the fortress-abbey; they had spent a week in Brittany surveying the formidable defenses of the area. Brittany was in Rommel's command; indeed, it was one of his most important sectors. In it were four great ports—Brest, Lorient, St. Nazaire and St. Malo; the existence of these ports alone, said Staubwasser, was sufficient reason for the Allies to invade. There was another reason. In the Breton moors, in the hilly woodlands intersected by gorges, ravines and tumbled rocks, in the prairies of sunken fields and pollarded oaks, there lurked one of the most ardent *maquis* in France. Their secret organizations had been especially difficult for the Germans to penetrate, for the Bretons were an insular, suspicious, mystical and clannish people and their Celtic lore, their Celtic tongue, their legends of Merlin and Viviane, Tristan and Iseult, the Grail, the town of Is, their Patrons, the Pardons—all served to permit them to move and communicate in ways that were almost completely mysterious to the stolid and procedural Gestapo.

Ethnically and linguistically the Bretons—there were about 3 million of them—were closer to the West Countrymen of England and the Welsh than they were even to the French. They hated their German conquerors, and Staubwasser's intelligence bulletins were filled with reports of gunrunning and *parachutage;* of mysterious meetings in the shades of the menhirs—strange megalithic remains that rose like phalluses all over Brittany; of five and twenty ponies trotting through the dark, laden with explosives and ammunition; of agents, phantom-like, running on the infiltration and exfiltration routes to and from the

Breton coves; of Lysanders coming in with mail, men and wirelesses. The BBC broadcast messages in the Breton tongue that could have no meaning except to a Breton—and Staubwasser was well aware that the resistance was at work in the peninsula to provide bases from which the Allies could gradually move against the Breton ports. Or the Allies might invade the peninsula, take the ports, and then move northeast to cut off the German troops in the Cherbourg peninsula. Whatever their strategy, Brittany was certain to play an important part in the inevitable invasion.

Across the English Channel, a SHAEF syndicate was even then completing plans for the special operations that would take place in Brittany in conjunction with Neptune. The syndicate held its meetings in Room 64 at St. Paul's School, the great red-brick Gothic building that stood beside the road to Heathrow. Montgomery had attended St. Paul's (as had Milton, Pepys, Marlborough, Judge Jeffreys, and Major John André), and it was now his headquarters. The chairman of the syndicate was Brigadier R. F. K. Belchem, Montgomery's chief operations officer and the former commander of the 1st Royal Tank Regiment. The Americans were represented by Colonel Charles M. Bonesteel III, a Virginian who had been a Rhodes Scholar and would go on to command an American army. SOE was represented by Buckmaster; and Colonel Joseph Haskell (who would become a president of the National Distillers and Chemical Corporation of New York) was there for OSS. Colonel Ian Collins, a former Commando, represented the Special Air Service (SAS), the élite *banditti* who did much work for MI-6, and had been formed in Egypt to operate in the role of uniformed guerrillas behind enemy lines. There were others— RAF and USAAF men, representatives of Combined Operations, some civilians from the political warfare agencies, a couple of naval officers. But there were no Frenchmen; while it was France that was to be invaded, and France that was to be the battlefield, no Frenchman was to be privy to Neptune operational planning.

The dominant matter before the syndicate was to devise ways and means to delay the enemy reserves—and particularly the panzer, panzer grenadier, attack and paratroop divisions—that Rundstedt and Rommel would use to launch a full-blooded counterattack in Normandy. After the assault itself, no other matter was of such importance. To blunt this counterthrust, the Neptune planners were depending heavily on the deceptions of Fortitude and Quicksilver to pin down the powerful German forces in the Pas de Calais, where, it was hoped, they would be held to oppose an invasion that would never materialize. But nothing was to be left to chance, and the Neptune planners had also devised an extraordinary program of bombing, deception, guerrilla, harassment and diversion to prevent German forces in every corner of France from assembling to counter the invasion. To keep SHAEF informed of the movements of the German armored divisions, MI-6 and OSS were now, in April, embarking on "Sussex." Over a hundred intelligence teams (the British teams were called "Brissex" while the Americans were "Ossex") were being dropped to form an arc from Avranches through Orléans to Amiens to watch crossroads and rail junctions through which the panzers must move to reach Normandy. And to slow down and disconcert that movement, SOE had already put into action a number of plans. "Vert" called for concentrated sabotage against the railroads; "Tortue," similar action against bridges and highways; "Bleu," the destruction of the Wehrmacht's electrical supply systems; and "Violet," the disruption of the Germans' telecommunications systems.

There were other plans for the sabotage of locomotives and rolling stock and of railway turntables. All bridges were being sabotaged or destroyed by air attack, as were all petrol and lubricants dumps that could be found. Scores of thousands of road mines and tire-bursters that were made of cyclonite plastic explosive and resembled cattle droppings—the invention of Julian Huxley, the zoologist—were being flown or parachuted in to resistance groups to lay in the paths of the panzer columns. F section organizers were giving courses to *résistants* on how to neutralize telecommunications lines without the Germans being able to find the breaks—a thumbtack was usually enough to short a signals cable. Others were being told that a cube or two of sugar in a petrol tank was enough to keep one Panther tank with all its crew and maintenance staff immobilized for several days. Still more *résistants* were being told which German signposts must be taken down or pointed in the wrong direction. Railwaymen were being shown how to jam points and turntables with a single steel bolt, gangers how to derail flats or jam the gates of level crossings, signalsmen how to keep signals arms at the halt when they should be at the proceed, switchboard operators how to immobilize a teleprinter circuit with a feather in an armature. As Gubbins said, it was intended that the Germans should see "the sun, moon and stars at H-Hour." In all, there were 1188 rail, 30 road and 32 telecommunications targets selected for destruction the moment London issued the *messages per-*

sonnels for H-Hour; and several hundred more were still being reconnoitered by May 1, 1944.

Sabotage, however, was only one of the roles that the SHAEF planning syndicate proposed for the French resistance at H-Hour. There was another—guerrilla. But that would pose problems of great sensitivity and complexity, as well as political dangers for the future. Should the Supreme Commander order a national insurrection by the French against the Germans at H-Hour? The arguments for such action were numerous and persuasive. For one thing, if all France broke out into general guerrilla activity, this itself would serve not only to confuse the Germans about Allied intentions but also to delay the movement of the enemy reserves. Moreover, the Germans would be compelled to detach large numbers of *Feldgrau* for police actions and to protect the Wehrmacht's lines of communications, installations and headquarters. But, the syndicate recognized, such an insurrection would lead inevitably to a bloodbath and the destruction of the *maquis*. The Germans, despite their preoccupations in Normandy, would still be too strong; and the *maquis,* despite the heavy *parachutage* before D-Day, too weak. The *maquis* leadership would be exposed and decapitated, leaving the vast body of the resistance flopping around uselessly until eventually it collapsed and died.

The syndicate therefore made plans for what came to be called "bloc operations"—the calling out of the resistance zone by zone as the military need for such operations arose. There would be no national insurrection. Bloc operations would be ordered in such a manner that the Germans would not be able to deduce from the outbreaks of guerrilla where and when the Allies planned each successive military move. There would be only local insurrections; and, the syndicate decided after many meetings, the first main battlefield for the *maquis* would be the Breton departments of the Côtes du Nord and Morbihan. Here, on the night of D-Day, the *maquis,* armed and commanded by special Allied units that were to be established in the area, would cut Brittany off from the rest of France and generally harass German forces if and when they began to move toward Normandy. The second stage of their operations would begin when the Americans broke out of their bridgehead in Normandy. Neptune called for Patton's 3rd Army to burst out of the Cherbourg peninsula into Brittany to take and hold the Breton ports. But in the event that Patton's tanks moved too swiftly for the infantry to keep up, the Breton *maquis* would serve as infantry. They were to hold the towns and villages through which the tanks would pass, secure the various viaducts across the gorges on the road to Brest, guard Patton's flanks and rear, and superintend his prisoners.

The *message personnel* that would signal the beginning of general guerrilla in Brittany was: *"Le chapeau de Napoléon, est-il toujours à Perros-Guirec?"* It was a message of some significance to the Bretons since "Napoleon's hat" was the local name of a famous rose-red granite rock at the holiday resort of Perros-Guirec. But would the Bretons, or, indeed, the *résistants* throughout France, obey the *messages personnels?* The Americans at SHAEF were particularly concerned about the way the French resistance had been manipulated, and the Avis system used, for the purposes of the Starkey deception. General Robert A. McClure, who was chief of psychological and political warfare at SHAEF, wrote to General Dallas Brooks, the military chief of PWE:

> These *Avis,* as originally conceived, were an excellent device for communicating operational requirements to the French. It is a pity that during the summer [of 1943] one or more *Avis* tended towards deception rather than information, and this inevitably lowered their future credibility. This makes it all the more important, therefore, that the *Avis* device should be repositioned in the French mind.

It was a clear rebuff to the deception agencies, and at McClure's request, the BBC broadcast this message to reestablish the credibility of the Avis:

> You have always been promised that, when the time comes, you would be given clear and unmistakeable instructions as to the part which you are to play during any large-scale military operations affecting your country.
>
> In the past you have heard *Avis* which, in the name of the Allied High Command, gave you certain warnings and instructions.
>
> These *Avis* have not always been closely followed by the operations to which their warning in fact referred. This has led to some confusion and even misgiving as to the validity and authority of these *Avis.* It is important at this stage of the war that the greatest clarity should exist among you as to the scope and purpose of these warnings.
>
> The purpose of all *Avis* is to coordinate, while safeguarding your interests, your activities with the military plans of the Supreme Allied Commander in whose name they will be issued.
>
> For military reasons, it will not always be possible to give the reasons underlying the instructions contained in *Avis;* they must, however, be interpreted literally. They will mean exactly what they say and will be dictated by important military considerations.

On no account should an attempt be made to read between the lines, whatever interpretation may be placed upon them by enemy rumours and propaganda.

The broadcast stressed the importance of obedience to the Supreme Allied Commander, and therein lay another uncertain factor in SHAEF's plans for the invasion. For the *résistants* were of many stripes—Protestant, Catholic, Communist, Gaulliste, Pétainiste, loyalist, secessionist. Would they listen to London or to some other voice? It was a conundrum that might influence the outcome of D-Day —a conundrum rooted in the peculiar personality and influence of General Charles de Gaulle.

When MI-6 brought de Gaulle out of France in 1940 at Churchill's orders, the ungainly, lonely, arrogant and passionate Frenchman was to be the "Steward of France." Neither the British nor the American governments regarded him as more than the leader of the French resistance. He was an outlaw in his own country, and he would shortly be declared a traitor and deserter and sentenced to death for grand treason. But de Gaulle saw himself as the personification of the renaissance of French national, military and spiritual glory; and from the moment he arrived in London until the moment four years later when he returned to France, he never ceased to intrigue to ensure that he and his disciples were accepted as the legitimate leaders of France. His attitude and actions brought him into conflicts of ever-intensifying gravity with both Churchill and Roosevelt. Finally, Roosevelt would recommend that British troops arrest de Gaulle and hold him in exile. And Churchill would declare that "We call him Joan of Arc, and we're looking for some bishops to burn him."

Although it was MI-6 that put him in business, it was not long after his arrival in London that de Gaulle and MI-6 began to war. In an early move, he founded his own secret service, the Bureau Centrale de Renseignements et d'Action (BCRA), largely with MI-6 help and finance; but instantly de Gaulle saw it as an instrument by which he would ruin his opponents and obtain the leadership of France. He appointed André Dewavrin, a passionate, extremely literate and articulate synarchist, as the spymaster of the new France. Slim, sly, quick and bloodless in appearance, Dewavrin seemed to be the archetype of the intellectual at war—a young man prepared to stop at nothing. His enemies regarded him as charming and dangerous; and his organization would be accused of political murder in London, of using "Gestapo-like methods" in processing French exiles to ensure their allegiance to Gaullism, of intellectual thuggery, and of discriminating in the arming and supply of the French resistance to ensure that, at the moment of liberation, de Gaulle would emerge as the head of the nation.

The British secret agencies, which had centuries of experience in dealing with such men, regarded de Gaulle and Dewavrin as revolutionary exiles who would naturally maintain secret communications with their homeland. And since their homeland was dominated by a pro-Nazi puppet government, it had to be assumed that their communications would fall into the possession of the Germans. In consequence, BCRA was kept under observation, and even penetrated. De Gaulle came to believe that the British secret services suborned Frenchmen to spy upon him personally, which was probably true. It was certainly true that, from the very outset, the distrust between de Gaulle and the British was intense.

That distrust increased markedly over a question of French discretion when, in September 1940, Churchill embarked upon "Menace," the large expedition mounted at the height of the Battle of Britain to enable de Gaulle to plant his standard at Dakar, from which, it was hoped, he would raise the French African colonies to support the British. Menace was a prodigious enterprise: battleships, cruisers, destroyers, an aircraft carrier, sloops and assault landing craft. The planning was Anglo-French, and surprise was not only considered desirable for the success of the operation, it was essential. But a French diplomat betrayed the expedition to his government at Vichy, which, in turn, informed the Germans; and a month before the forces of Menace sailed, Frenchmen all over London were heard drinking toasts *"à Dakar."* The result was inevitable; everyone knew Menace was coming and the damage suffered by the task force was severe. The expedition was both a humiliation and a disaster for the Royal Navy and for de Gaulle personally. Relations between the Free French and England were severely strained, and never again would the British inform the French of any military undertaking until it was unavoidable, or until the French were in such a position that they could not possibly pass the information on.

The mutual suspicions of the British and the Gaullistes did not diminish during the middle years of the war. In fact, they intensified; and nowhere were they more pronounced—or more dangerous—than in F section operations in France. De Gaulle was convinced that SOE was no more than an instrument of British imperialism and attempted to gain control of its operations. He was rebuffed, for as Gubbins, who

regarded de Gaulle as a troublemaker among the brave, wrote to a colleague on January 22, 1942: "It is clear that we cannot build
up a proper secret army in France under the aegis or flag of de
Gaulle . . ." Gubbins believed that Britain must support anyone who
would kill Germans; and if the Gaullistes proved less effective than,
for example, the Communists, then it was the Communists who must
get the guns. Menzies, too, tended to back others than de Gaulle and
believed, as he wrote in January 1942, that "de Gaulle had not a great
following but only a symbolic value." Nevertheless, de Gaulle succeeded in winning widespread loyalty among the French *résistants,*
but as Gubbins warned in August of 1942: ". . . de Gaulle is busy
furthering his political ends . . . (his) agents do not appear to be
making any attempt to fulfil their primary role of executing an active
sabotage and subversion policy." Brooke and others in London expressed similar opinions; in their view, the Gaullistes were developing a resistance movement in France for the primary purpose not of
fighting the Germans but of taking over France when the Allies liberated the country.

For their part, the Gaullistes (and particularly Dewavrin of BCRA)
continually criticized SOE, alleging "bad faith and sharp practices."
The collapse of Interallié (Menzies's main *réseau* in Paris after the
fall) and of the Prosper network did little to cool the savage words and
opinions that made life at the top of the Allied secret hierarchy
tiresome and difficult. There were staff officers in both MI-6 and F
section who opined that Gaulliste intrigue was involved in both disasters; while the Gaullistes accused MI-6 and F section of staffing its
réseaux in France with Britons, Frenchmen and cosmopolitans who
were there to reestablish Aquitaine when the last trumpet sounded.

Then, at a time when everyone was clearing his desk for Neptune,
there occurred another of those minor contretemps which confirmed
the Allies in their suspicion that the French were not to be trusted. It
was called "the great coding row" and it had its origins in the fate of
Jean Moulin. Moulin, who was appointed by de Gaulle as his delegate-
general in France, headed the Conseil National de la Résistance
(CNR), a centralized organization of Gaulliste resistance leaders. It
did not last long. There was a meeting of the CNR in an apartment, a
shouting match ensued, the Germans were listening nearby, somebody
sold Moulin; and when the CNR next met at Caluire, a suburb of
Lyon, the SD arrested a round dozen of its commanders, Moulin
included. Moulin was murdered when he refused to talk and the
French resistance was left leaderless. The collapse of the CNR was

followed almost immediately by the collapse of Prosper, and the SOE hierarchy, realizing that unless something was done immediately the French resistance would be useless on D-Day, demanded that the Gaullistes actively decentralize their organization in France. This, of course, was not what the London Gaullistes and the BCRA wanted at all; it was only by the centralization of authority over the resistance that their power could be ensured. Nevertheless, they appeared to obey SOE's demand. They handed in a telegram at SOE headquarters for transmission to the field. It was in cipher but it was accompanied by a plain-language text which showed that all BCRA had done was to split France into two zones, instead of the one that had existed under Moulin. Two resistance high commands might be better than one, but it was only a slender guarantee of security. Therefore, SOE returned the telegram to BCRA, declaring that it would not be sent until it specified distinct cellularization.

BCRA countered with a new telegram, in the same cipher, but accompanied by a new plain-language text which showed that the Gaullistes had done as they had been commanded—ordered fundamental cellularization. However, an SOE staff officer noted that there were the same number of cipher groups in the first as in the second telegram. Suspecting a trick, SOE called in its cipher expert, Leonard Marks, a Pickwickian man who was said to do *The Times* crossword puzzle in fifteen minutes, and Marks exposed the two telegrams for what they were—the same. In turn, BCRA accused Marks of having used a purloined copy of the main French cipher to unbutton the telegrams. But indifferent to the accusation, Marks said that if BCRA would care to write a telegram on any subject in the same cipher, he would break the cipher in their presence. BCRA did so; and so did Marks.

The telegram was finally sent when BCRA did what it had agreed to do. But that was not the end of the affair. The Gaullistes, and particularly Dewavrin, were incensed by the ease with which their cipher had been broken. If the British could break their ciphers, they argued, so could the Germans; and as Dewavrin would comment, "If this were true, then it was surely criminal of the British to allow us to go on using them." Tempers cooled, but inescapably, "the great coding row" infected Allied thinking about the security precautions that must be taken with the French over Neptune. When the British, at Eisenhower's request, ordered a total ban on the transmission of all telegrams unless they were sent in British, American or Russian ciphers, no exception was made for the traffic between de Gaulle's headquarters at Algiers and its SHAEF representatives in London. Moreover, to reinforce security procedures, the Gaullistes were only allowed to send those agents to France who had been cleared by British authorities. No one else—not even the couriers of de Gaulle's mail —would be permitted to leave the country until after D-Day. But once again, the Gaullistes attempted to sidestep the Supreme Command— and this time they succeeded in a contretemps that was called *"l'affaire Socrate."*

Allied policy toward the French resistance was governed by the decision that there should be no national insurrection in France on D-Day. The maximum the Allies expected and would order was local sabotage and guerrilla. But the situation within France was so flammable that no one could be sure that the whole nation would not explode on D-Day. Therefore, and very properly, General Pierre Koenig, the Gaulliste representative at Supreme Headquarters, asked permission to send an agent to France to give the necessary instructions and advice to the leaders of the resistance movements. But SHAEF rejected the suggestion on a number of grounds: that the resistance had been and would continue to be informed by agents who were already there and were in touch with London by wireless and *courrier;* that to run an agent at this time (late April) might endanger Neptune if the agent was caught and compelled to talk; that the Germans were engaged in a major *ratissage;* and finally that the candidate who had been selected for the task of instructing the resistance, Lazare Racheline, alias "Socrate," was extremely well known to the SD—his face appeared in every wanted book in France. Therefore, SOE/OSS directed—ordered —that Socrate must not leave England, and he was refused all the necessary security documents that would (it was thought) permit him to leave the country. But BCRA ignored the order and, despite the fact that England was completely sealed off to all unauthorized travelers, prepared to run Socrate.

Socrate was an expert in exfiltration; it was he who had helped establish the *Vic* escape route from Paris across the Pyrenees to the Iberian capitals and Gibraltar. A man of steady nerves and complete discretion, he knew how to hide and how to go on the run in a state that was totally controlled by a ruthless counterintelligence service. He also knew how to elude the British security authorities, for, incredibly, he traveled to France on *Var,* the Admiralty-controlled Paris-London escape line which ran through Brittany. There would be no record that he had any of the papers necessary for such a journey; he traveled in much the same way as a man who takes a train without paying for his ticket. Somehow Socrate succeeded in insinuating himself into a party of agents who were being run from London to France. Under official escort, he was taken with the others to a hotel at Torquay, Devon; and there he was cleared for his journey by torpedo boat to Brittany by, among others, the deputy director of the Admiralty's Irregular Operations Division. He was closely checked to ensure that he neither rattled nor shined, boarded the MTB and set sail across the Channel, under Spitfire and MTB escort, in time to arrive off the Breton coast two hours after sunset. When the *Var* reception committee's papers were verified, Socrate and the other agents went ashore in a rowboat, wearing gas capes to protect them from tell-tale spray. Then they were taken up the steep path to the Maison d'Alphonse, a safehouse belonging to a fisherman called Giquel. Socrate had eluded every check, and confounded even the most practiced security authorities.

In Paris, Socrate met with leaders of the resistance and obtained their written acknowledgment of orders to launch only those operations in conjunction with the invasion that were authorized by London. News of the agreement was conveyed by wireless through SOE to BCRA in London; but SOE had not known that Socrate was out of the country. In fact, he had been forbidden to leave. As Socrate was making his way back to England over *Vic* and the Pyrenees, an almighty thunderstorm burst over the heads of the security authorities. How had Socrate got out of England? How much had he known about Neptune? How much had he seen of the invasion preparations? How trustworthy was he? How trustworthy were the resistance leaders he had met in Paris? Everyone feared that Socrate might get caught up in the *ratissage* and tell all he knew. There was some relief when SHAEF learned that he was "discretion incarnate"—as Foot would describe him afterwards—and he made his way back to London safely. Nevertheless, he was received with none of the usual courtesies granted a man returning from the field. Socrate would never reveal how he had got out of the country (it was presumed that BCRA had arranged it in some fashion) and the matter was not pursued, for D-Day arrived just as the interrogation began.

This latest Gaulliste trick strengthened SHAEF's conviction that the Free French could not be trusted, and confirmed the wisdom of the decision to tell them nothing of Neptune. The fear that the embargo would affect the Supreme Command's ability to control resistance operations was outweighed by the suspicion that the Gaullistes might take some last-minute action that would be equally detrimental to Neptune. It was, however, the reliability of the resistance itself that caused the greatest concern. SHAEF recognized that the majority of the French people were pro-Allied and detested their conquerors. It was also recognized that several hundred thousand men and women might emerge on D-Day to form what de Gaulle called "the army of the shadows." But the vast body of the resistance movement was neither experienced, disciplined, united nor armed. And the hard core of guerrillas was not thought to be strong. In February 1944, MI-6 reported that it doubted whether there was a single band of 2000 men who were prepared to act together in all France—out of a nation of 40 millions at that time. By May 1944, the most optimistic SOE/OSS report estimated that there were not more than 125,000 Frenchmen with Allied guns. The figure of 85,000 was considered to be the realistic one; and of these, not more than 10,000 were believed to have ammunition for more than a day's fighting. The only *résistants* who were experienced in guerrilla were the *réseaux* under the control of F section and the Communists; and while the Gaullistes were the most numerous, they were, with a few important exceptions, the most unreliable, the most penetrated, the most inexperienced in guerrilla, the least ideologically dedicated, and the worst equipped.

The Supreme Command—and particularly its American component—viewed Neptune as the most decisive action of the Second World War; nothing could be left to chance—although, as in all military operations, chance might be a deciding factor. But why increase the already great risks by entrusting any information or military operation to the French resistance which was so badly fractured by Gaulliste-Communist rivalry and in such jeopardy from the SD? In March 1944 the Communists had begun an all-out attack on the Gaullistes, branding their leaders as self-serving crypto-Fascists, while the Germans were using every ruse, including the circulation of leaflets and orders purporting to come from SHAEF or de Gaulle, in an attempt to make the resistance expose itself prematurely. To bring the FFI into hatred and contempt, the SD arranged the assassination of popular personalities, derailed civilian trains, disorganized the lives of whole towns—and then blamed these actions upon F section, upon de Gaulle, upon SHAEF, and upon the Communists. The Gaullistes committed similar actions—and blamed them on the Communists; and the Communists blamed such actions upon everybody. Proclamations for Gaulliste insurrections were issued by the Communists in order to make them show their hands to the Germans; and the Gaullistes did likewise to the Communists.

As seen from London—particularly by the Americans—France was a devil's brew of politics. But it was not one, the British argued, that could be ignored. If France was to reoccupy her place among the nations of the world, her people had to be given the opportunity to liberate themselves and to assist the Allies. In fact, their assistance would be invaluable to Neptune. But, factions in London argued, was it worth arming the French? They recalled Wellington's warning: "I always had a horror of revolutionising any country for a political object. I always said, if they rise up themselves, well and good, but do not stir them up; it is a fearful responsibility." It was a fearful responsibility indeed, for even if the *résistants* complied with Allied orders during the invasion, might they not use the arms and ammunition against each other after the liberation? There were the most alarming stories that the Gaullistes and the Communists had lists of 40,000–50,000 people who were to be impeached or executed. Would it not be better to instruct the French nation to lie low and use conventional means, combined with Anglo-American guerrilla forces of proven reliability, to destroy the Wehrmacht?

Churchill was adamant; the French must be allowed to play a part in their own liberation. Despite the antagonisms between the Gaullistes and the Communists, F section had succeeded in expanding its London-oriented networks. Whereas after the collapse of the Prosper and Scientist circuits there were barely thirty *réseaux* of any consequence left in all France, now, in the spring of 1944, there were sixty. Thus it was finally decided by the syndicates sitting in those high-ceilinged rooms in the order and calm of Hammersmith that the resistance would be used in conjunction with Neptune, but if it was to be effective it must be heavily reinforced with drops of arms, ammunition and supplies. Equally important, the F section and OSS organizers already in the field must be reinforced by men of judgment, tolerance, authority, bearing—and experience in the craft of guerrilla. They must be exemplary men around whom the *maquis* would rally, arm, train and then fight according to Eisenhower's orders. The men to fulfill these difficult tasks would be the "Jedburghs."

The concept of the Jedburghs—and other teams with similar missions but different names, such as "Cooneys," "*Missions Interalliés,*" and the American Operational Groups—emerged from the need to impose discipline and control upon the French *maquisards*. The Jedburghs took their name from their quarters during training: Jedburgh, a royal burgh on the Jed River in the Scots border country of Roxburghshire, a place famous for its abbey and infamous for "Jeddart Justice," in which a man was hung first and tried afterwards. Each

Jedburgh was to consist of one Briton, one American and one Frenchman, lest they be accused of being agents of British imperialism. And each man was to be handpicked both for his high intelligence, his skills as a partisan, his personal courage, his ability to command respect, and his fairness—for a Jed, as they were known for short, was expected to be captain, judge, confessor, and quarter- and paymaster—to say nothing of demolitions expert, gunsmith, linguist, marksman, poacher and doctor. The Jedburgh teams were to be dropped into France by parachute from the evening of D-Day onwards, as far as possible they were to wear uniforms—although some did not and therefore risked being shot as spies—and their main task was to locate *maquis* bands, arm and equip them, and then make them conform and operate to the dictates of the requirements of the orthodox land battle. In a sense, each Jed would have to be a man much in the mold of Lawrence, able to operate behind enemy lines quietly, efficiently and impressively.

Plainly, not too many men existed with the high qualifications necessary for the tasks they had to undertake. Only the British had formed a reservoir of such men: the Special Air Service brigade, which was composed of two regiments of Britons, two battalions of Frenchmen, and one "international squadron" which was much like the Foreign Legion in its composition and the history of the men in it. The OSS provided about one hundred of its best young officers, among them Major William E. Colby, a twenty-four-year-old Minnesotan and a graduate of Princeton. Later, as a member of the CIA, Colby would become station chief in South Vietnam, head of the CIA's Far Eastern operations division, and, in 1974, director of the CIA.

All the special forces teams underwent long, intensive training in the multiple crafts of guerrilla: physical fitness, silent killing, silent movement, unarmed combat, knife and rope work, the use of both Allied and enemy small arms, fieldcraft, elementary Morse, raiding tactics, railway demolitions. About eighty Jed teams would be deployed during Neptune, and a total of about three hundred inter-Allied, MI-6, OSS, SAS, SOE, BCRA, PWE, Cooney, Brissex and Ossex teams would cast a variety of balls among the German skittles. Some twenty Missions Interalliés, each consisting of between two and twenty-five men, would go in to train and stiffen the resistance, along with four purely American Operational Groups, each of thirty-four men, assigned the same mission. In addition, no less than 2200 officers and troops of the SAS, each man superbly trained in guerrilla and clandestinity, would be dropped behind the front, sometimes equipped with armored jeeps to maraud like cavalry. In all, therefore, there would be something like 5000 agents and soldiers organizing and leading the French resistance by and after D-Day—a formidable number indeed to train, equip and maintain.

In the special context of Allied strategy, the Jedburghs' chief mission would be in Brittany, where they would attempt to tie down as many as possible of the German troops stationed there. Then they would arm and train the *maquisards* into organized battalions ready to take to the field when Patton's 3rd Army broke out of the beachhead and moved to capture the Breton peninsula. But as D-Day approached, and as the Jedburghs and other special forces teams were grouped under strict security control at Milton Hall, Castor, about 60 miles north of London, it seemed that an old concept about how they might be used to support Fortitude was being resurrected, a concept that dated from "Plan Torrent."

Torrent was Fortitude in all but name; it was first promulgated secretly by COSSAC on September 20, 1943, and even though the British had been severely criticized for using agents and the French resistance in deception schemes, it again advocated the use of F section agents and special forces teams such as the Jedburghs for the purpose of deception. In its specifications for the special means to be employed in support of Torrent, the plan included this paragraph:

> *Patriot Forces.* The general sabotage in and around the Pas de Calais-Belgium area will be increased and specially briefed organisers will be sent to this area to spread rumours [that the invasion was imminent in that area] and to initiate certain limited action by resistance groups about three weeks before the target date of *Overlord* [then the code name for the invasion].

The paragraph did add the stricture that "This action must in no way prejudice the potential value of resistance groups to Operation Overlord"; but nevertheless it was a clear declaration of the Allied intention to use—and, if necessary, to sacrifice—agents and resistance groups to support a deception.

The plan met with immediate opposition from Gubbins. In the heavily garrisoned Pas de Calais, it was all but impossible for an individual intelligence agent to operate, let alone special forces teams. The plan was discarded. But toward the end of May, some of the Jeds—particularly those to be dropped into Brittany—began to detect an attitude among their briefing officers that not only reflected the extraordinary dangers of their mission but also smacked of sacrifice.

Captain B. M. W. Knox of the OSS, the American leader of Jed team "Giles," noted that attitude as he prepared for his drop into the Breton province of Finistère. He had been fully trained in the crafts of guerrilla warfare, including the techniques of silent killing, under a policeman who had learned his trade from the Tongs of Shanghai, and safe-cracking, under one of England's leading country-house burglars. Knox, an outstanding classics scholar at Cambridge who would become Professor of Greek at Yale and then Director of Hellenic Studies at Harvard, recalled:

> While we were wonderfully trained in the most advanced techniques of clandestine work, we were not privy to what the high command planned. We never quite knew what our function was, beyond the mission prescribed for us in our operational orders. If we were part of some larger strategical scheme, we did not know it. Neither was it desirable that we should have known; we might have been captured and forced into talking. But it was quite clear to us that our unit commanders did not expect us to come back. But this was very carefully camouflaged: had we known perhaps some of us would have had second thoughts about going in at all. There were, at the same time, indications that we were sacrifices of some sort. You know how careful the military is in making you sign for anything of value—binoculars, prismatic compasses, special watches, rum, wireless sets, special pistols, sovereigns, fishing gear, that sort of thing? When I went to the stores to draw my special equipment, the officer concerned said he was not too bothered about a signature as it would not mean much. That was a sign that we were regarded as lost—together with our equipment —the moment we got on the plane. But none of us had the slightest doubt that what we were doing was absolutely right and, of course, that carried us through; nobody, not one man, bugged out. They were baying to get into the field.

Strictly speaking, it was not SHAEF's intention that the special forces teams, or the French resistance itself, be used in Fortitude as live bait to attract German units away from the front during the first difficult days and weeks of Neptune. Nevertheless, the word "diversion"—a synonym for deception in the military lexicon—appeared with frequency in the Jeds' orders. The orders for one Jed team going into eastern Brittany stated: "You will go to the Morbihan, organise the resistance movement already there, and prepare that movement for the greatest possible diversion of German troops away from the lodgement area." Such instructions were, of course, a departure from the declared purpose of the Jeds, which was to help the French liberate themselves. But the effect of their missions, as well as the missions of the other special forces teams, and the activities of the resistance in areas remote from the Normandy beachhead, would inevitably serve the purposes of Fortitude. No one complained, at least among the Jeds. This was total war, the issues were too great to consider the niceties of words and intentions, and the Jeds were the first to agree that if the French were to be liberated, the enemy must be tricked.

It appeared, however, that in order to ensure the success of Neptune, the Gaullistes must also be tricked. Despite the elaborate nature of the special operations that would be undertaken in the field, Eisenhower considered the danger of disobedience among the French resistance so serious that he decided to ask his superior authority, the Combined Chiefs of Staff at Washington, for permission to take Koenig into his confidence. On May 8, 1944, he wirelessed Washington:

> In order that arrangements can be made for the coordinated action by French resistance groups, it has become imperative that General Koenig, head of the French mission here, be given certain general information in connection with forthcoming operations. It is therefore my intention to give him personally but to *no* other member of the French mission, under pledge of secrecy, the name of the country in which the main attack will take place and the month for which it is scheduled. . . . Recent restrictions on communications other than by British (cipher) are considered adequate safeguard against leakage to Algiers.

Eisenhower's telegram brought the sharpest reaction; he was to tell the French nothing of Neptune, nothing whatsoever. But Eisenhower pressed the point and sent another message in which he warned that "The limitations under which we are operating in dealing with the French are becoming very embarrassing and are producing a situation which is potentially dangerous."

Indeed, the situation was already dangerous. The specter of a national insurrection on D-Day could not be quelled, despite every Allied precaution. Moreover, there were clear signs that Eisenhower's authority over the resistance movements was being undermined, and that the Communists at least were issuing orders for an insurrection on D-Day. Some Gaulliste leaders were warning Frenchmen working for SOE/OSS that if they continued to do so they would be regarded and treated as traitors after the liberation. And the rivalry between the Gaullistes and the Communists was still so intense that it might easily lead to major civil disturbances, if not outright civil war, in the rear of the Allied armies.

Eisenhower won a small concession. After consulting with the Brit-

ish, Roosevelt replied personally to the Supreme Commander's plea
for a more reasonable treatment of Koenig. Eisenhower could inform
him of the month in which the landings would take place. But that still
left the tricky question of when Koenig should be informed of the
broadcast schedule for the *messages personnels,* those cryptic alert
and action messages endorsed, at least in theory, by both Koenig and
de Gaulle, which were designed to set in motion the selected acts of
sabotage and guerrilla that would be essential to Neptune in confusing
the Germans and delaying their response to the invasion. Three
hundred twenty-five messages had been prepared and circulated to
resistance groups throughout France, and under the original concept
of bloc operations, it was intended that only a fraction of the alert
messages would be broadcast, commencing June 1, with a corresponding number of action messages broadcast a few hours before
H-Hour. However, as early as April SHAEF had realized that
confining resistance activities to Normandy and immediately adjacent
areas would not serve to delay the movement of German reserves to
the beachhead from other parts of France. Moreover, the Germans
might deduce from guerrilla operations concentrated in Normandy
and adjacent areas that Neptune was *the* invasion and Fortitude
merely a feint. It was therefore decided that the plan for bloc operations must be expanded. All of the *messages personnels* relating to
the invasion phase of Neptune must be broadcast prior to H-Hour.
The dangers of such a plan were obvious. Under the tensions of the
moment, the resistance might boil over in a general insurrection.
SHAEF could only hope that the *résistants,* under the direction of
orders from London and the leadership of the special forces teams,
would do precisely what their messages instructed them to do, and if
the rest of France kept calm, there would not—could not—be an uprising.

Gubbins, Bruce and Mockler-Ferryman, the chief of the London
Group of SOE, were informed of the change of plans; but Mockler-
Ferryman would not accept verbal orders. He insisted upon having
them in writing, for there was a SHAEF-Gaulliste accord that the
Supreme Command would do nothing to provoke a general uprising in
France in support of Neptune, and Mockler-Ferryman was wary of
the possibility that increasing the number of *messages personnels*
broadcast prior to D-Day would be tantamount, in the eyes of the
French, to calling for an insurrection. He received his orders in a letter
issued by the operations staff of SHAEF. In the event, Mockler-
Ferryman's apprehension was well founded, for both SOE and the

Supreme Command would later be accused of triggering a French revolution in support of Neptune and Fortitude, and of sacrificing the lives of thousands of ill-armed, ill-trained Frenchmen to save the lives of American and British fighting men.

Koenig must be told of this change of plan—but when? There could be no doubt that he would know that all of the *messages personnels* were being broadcast. A Gaulliste officer had been made responsible for writing the messages, he knew roughly what each meant and the areas of France to which they applied, and undoubtedly he had given Koenig this information. If Koenig thought that SHAEF was ordering a general insurrection, betraying its agreement to the contrary, he would almost certainly try to stop or countermand the instructions being sent out to the field.

Two courses of action were, therefore, open to SHAEF. The first was to tell Koenig well in advance. But this was contrary to Eisenhower's orders from the Combined Chiefs and from the President and Prime Minister; and with this kind of advance information, Koenig would be able to deduce where and when the invasion would take place, and would inform de Gaulle in Algiers. The SHAEF security staff suspected that de Gaulle's Algiers headquarters was infiltrated by the German intelligence services—as indeed it was. The first course of action was ruled out as too dangerous, and it was decided to inform Koenig only a matter of an hour before the action messages were to be broadcast. Gubbins and Bruce would undertake the task personally, and it was hoped that Koenig's soldierly good sense would prevail, that he would see that the Supreme Command had no choice in the affair, that he would issue orders to the resistance to obey SHAEF's commands, and only those commands, and appeal to the rest of France to keep calm. This last hope was a fragile one, for not all Frenchmen had civilian wireless sets on which they could listen to the BBC and receive Koenig's orders. SHAEF recognized the grave moral and political consequences that might arise if, as a result of this second course of action, the French nation rose up en masse. But once again, the security of Neptune was more important than any other consideration.

The question of when de Gaulle was to be informed of the invasion was even thornier. The Supreme Command felt that he must be invited to Britain prior to D-Day, if only to broadcast an appeal for calm in France during the invasion period. But when should he come? If he came too soon he might learn too much and inform Algiers—and so the Germans. If, on the other hand, he came too late, he would certainly consider it an offense to his personal dignity and the honor of France. Churchill and Roosevelt conferred and the decision was taken; de Gaulle was to be kept at Algiers until a day or two before the invasion. Then he would be invited to London by Churchill personally, who would send a government minister and his private York to fetch him. But on his arrival, Eisenhower would tell him only enough about Neptune to permit him to conclude that it was not *the* invasion, but only its start. Moreover, his communications with Algiers would be strictly controlled by the British after his briefing so that neither he nor his staff might slip any information out of the country. The self-proclaimed leader of the French nation was to be treated not as a statesman, but as an ambitious and untrustworthy general.

De Gaulle would never forget, or forgive, this final insult. But at the end of the war, when the Allies captured the SD archives, it was discovered that the only entirely accurate report that the SD had received about Neptune was from a colonel on de Gaulle's staff in Algiers. How had he obtained this intelligence, which was dated June 4, 1944? Was it a shrewd guess, or had de Gaulle, who was the only Frenchman who knew the Neptune plan in any detail before D-Day, managed to find a way of circumventing the controls on his communications from London? The answer will never be known; but mercifully for the Allies, the report, which was, in fact, circulated by the German command to its army on the invasion front, had then been filed away and forgotten among the dross of 250 other, less accurate intelligence reports that the Germans received about Neptune just prior to the invasion.

12

Canaris's Last Throw

FIELD MARSHAL ROMMEL's headquarters were at the Château de La
Roche Guyon, the sprawling home of the ducs de la Rochefoucauld in
the steep hills beside the Seine more or less midway between Paris and
Rouen. Nearby was the village of La Roche Guyon, little more than a
group of cottages, shops and an inn clustered around the fifteenth-cen-
tury church of St. Samsom; but the area was extremely heavily
guarded. Sentries were everywhere, pillboxes were set in the chalk
outcroppings, there were numerous anti-aircraft guns, and Rommel's
bodyguard commander had sited an observation post in an old tower
on the highest hill above the château. But on the evening of April 15,
1944, Rommel was not concerned with his personal safety; he was
concerned with politics. He sat in his office on the ground floor of the
château, his back to the rose gardens and the French windows, his
feet under a massive Renaissance desk. On one wall there was an old
Gobelin tapestry. On another, the hooded, ironic face of François duc
de la Rochefoucauld, the seventeenth-century writer of maxims, and
an ancestor of the present Duke. Facing Rommel was his new Chief of
Staff, General Hans Speidel. It was a most important encounter in the
history of the Schwarze Kapelle. For Speidel was a dedicated and veteran member of the conspiracy; and Rommel, who spoke with despair
of the military and political policies of the Third Reich, now authorized Speidel to arrange a meeting with the other German conspirators
in the West.

The meeting took place a month to the day after Rommel's conversation with Speidel in a lodge deep in the Forêt de Marly, where the
Sun King had hunted. The site was surrounded by Rommel's bodyguard of grenadiers of the 21st (Africa) Panzer Division stationed
near Caen, men who were the remnants of the Afrika Korps and had

sworn to defend their beloved marshal even unto death. Overtly the meeting was called to discuss measures for the defense of the Channel coast. But covertly, as Speidel would write, it was a "comprehensive conference on the necessary measures for ending the war in the West and overthrowing the Nazi régime." Present, in addition to Rommel and Speidel, were General von Stuelpnagel; General von Falkenhausen; General Heinrich Baron von Luettwitz, the commander of the 2nd Panzer Division; and General Gerhardt Count von Schwerin, the commander of the 116th Panzer Division—the army's two most powerful panzer divisions in the West. Schwerin was the general staff intelligence officer who came to London on the eve of war to see Menzies, Godfrey and Cadogan. The meeting at Forêt de Marly was a solemn one, for the 5th and 8th armies of the Allies had just broken through the Gustav Line in Italy and the German 10th Army was in the process of being surrounded and, it was feared, annihilated. The news from the Russian front was equally bad, and to the generals it was a signal of the beginning of the end for the army and the Reich.

The Marly meeting was concerned primarily with the steps the Schwarze Kapelle was prepared to take to achieve an armistice with the Allies, steps which included: (a) the evacuation by German forces of all territory in the West; (b) the arrest of Hitler by the army, to be followed by a trial by the civilian judiciary; (c) similar trials for all political criminals; (d) a continuation of the fighting in the East on a shorter line; (e) a revolution to overthrow the Nazi government before the invasion began, by mid-June 1944 at the latest; and (f) the promulgation of a temporary government under the leadership of Beck. Rommel was said by Speidel to have accepted the role of leader of the rebellion as he was the only one who had the "undisputed esteem" of the people and the armed forces; and he undertook, with the Allies, to keep order after the revolution. It was also agreed that, so far as possible, the 2nd and 116th panzer divisions should be held in Rommel's command and kept out of military operations in the West so that they would be available to the conspirators to put down any resistance from the SS. There was only one strong area of disagreement between Rommel and most of the other conspirators; it was on the question of assassinating Hitler. Rommel believed that to kill Hitler would be a mistake. It might create a martyr out of him and make the possibility of civil war a probability. Furthermore, it was the duty of the people who had elected him to try, convict and punish him.

This disagreement had not yet been resolved when a third meeting took place at Speidel's home in Freudenstadt on May 28, 1944. Rommel was not present at the meeting for security reasons; he was too well known, and if he was seen going to Speidel's home with men who were suspected conspirators, he too might become suspect. The purpose of this meeting was to integrate the activities of the western conspirators with those of Stauffenberg in Berlin and Tresckow in the East—for Tresckow was, despite the failure of Flash, still very active. And since the Flash conspiracy, the Schwarze Kapelle had become a fundamental if covert part of the German military-political scene. Stauffenberg's organization had representatives in every important command center in the German army, as well as adherents at all the major intelligence, signals, operations and supply centers, in the military governments of the occupied territories, and in all German *Wehrkreise* or "military districts" into which the Reich had been divided for the purposes of administration, mobilization and industry. The main axis of the conspiracy, however, was Paris-Berlin-Smolensk, and would remain so; and the original Valkyrie plan to seize all key points in Germany had been retained and polished.

The conspirators' contacts with the western powers were now, so the Schwarze Kapelle believed, well established. Gisevius, stationed in Switzerland as a vice consul, was in constant and apparently trusted communication with Dulles; and Otto John was able to travel, apparently at will, between Berlin, Madrid and Lisbon to keep in touch with the OSS and MI-6. A third channel had opened up through a senior staff officer with the German Foreign Trade Commission in Paris who was in contact with Colonel William Hohenthal, the American military attaché at Madrid, baiting his opening gambits with a diagram of the German command structure and order of battle in the West. A fourth and most significant channel was also in the process of being created: General Ulrich Liss, the former chief of FHW, now an infantry division commander in the East who was in Berlin recovering from mortar shell wounds, was under the instruction of Colonel Hansen, the chief of Amt Mil, to be ready to fly to Stockholm and from there make contact with his old friend General Kenneth W. D. Strong, who was about to become Eisenhower's chief of intelligence in London. Hansen himself had a fifth channel through a British agent in southern France; while a sixth contact existed between a German officer, Theodore Steltzer, and a British agent with the Norwegian resistance movement. And above all there was Canaris—a man with several channels to London.

The main task of the Freudenstadt conversations was quickly accomplished. The plotters worked out a system of communications among the major centers of the conspiracy—communications which only the conspirators would use and which were designed to prevent the SS and SD hierarchy from communicating with each other. At the plot's command center at the great offices of the Home Army on the Bendlerstrasse, the C-in-C, General Fromm, continued his tacit support for the plot; while Olbricht, his Chief of Staff, was about to be appointed his deputy, and Stauffenberg was about to be appointed Olbricht's successor—an appointment that would give him direct and personal access to the Fuehrer. The Valkyrie plans were amended and placed in Olbricht's safe. All proclamations and orders to the public and the army were reviewed, approved, or sent back to small planning syndicates for further study and development. Trusted panzer and cavalry units were selected by the Schwarze Kapelle to seize the key power centers—Berlin, Paris, Munich, Hamburg, Dresden, Frankfurt, and the like. And the police and detective services of Count Helldorf, the police president of Berlin, were employed to watch and report the movements of the Nazi hierarchy. In short, the Schwarze Kapelle was prepared to move swiftly and ruthlessly. There must be no regard for matters of conscience such as the *Fahneneid*. Even high treason was now justified.

The conspirators were working under circumstances of the greatest danger, for Himmler and the Gestapo were aware that there was a massive plot against the Fuehrer. During a conversation with Canaris in late May or early June, Himmler declared that he knew all about the Schwarze Kapelle, and he knew how to deal effectively with such malcontents as Beck and Goerdeler. Canaris relayed this grim warning to the conspirators, but they took little heed. Artur Nebe, the chief of detectives and one of the hierarchs of the Gestapo, was still a member of the Schwarze Kapelle; and he kept the conspiracy informed of what the Gestapo knew and intended. Moreover, Nebe recognized that Himmler, who often intimated that he might become head of state in any post-Hitler government, was curiously ambivalent about the Schwarze Kapelle. Much that was enigmatic was concealed behind those thick, powerful pince-nez; in a world of rapidly changing loyalties it was not impossible that Himmler, the Schwarze Kapelle's second deadliest enemy after Hitler, might become the conspirators' best friend—which, if it was known in London and Washington, could not have done the conspiracy much political good.

In fact, Himmler knew less than he claimed about the composition of the plot, but a good deal more than the plotters themselves would have wished. In March, the Gestapo had arrested Captain Ludwig

Gehre, the Abwehr officer who was probably responsible for organizing the passage to MI-6 of the Lisbon Report. By watching Gehre's home, the Gestapo had also obtained a lead to John; and shortly, Kaltenbrunner would issue warrants for the arrest of both Gisevius and Goerdeler. However, these arrests did not mean that the central citadel of the conspiracy—the Home Army and its links with the commands—had been penetrated; and in late spring 1944, the Schwarze Kapelle appeared to stand well and firm.

Rommel would surely become the conspiracy's greatest asset. His stature was such that his determination to seek a political settlement of the war would command obedience at home and respect abroad. But the Schwarze Kapelle could not know to what end the Allies intended to put their respect for the field marshal. The British were even then laying plans for "Gaff," an operation to confuse the German army in the West during the opening stages of Neptune by murdering or kidnapping Rommel. It was one of the more ironic situations of the Second World War; at the precise moment that Rommel was making plans to surrender, provided honorable terms could be obtained and, if possible, before D-Day, the Allies were planning to assassinate him. This was not the only irony in the situation. The conspirators had determined to launch their revolution *before* D-Day because they considered that to do so after the Allies had landed would lessen their bargaining power; and from the best information at their disposal, they had scheduled the *coup d'état* for mid-June, expecting the invasion after that date. The Schwarze Kapelle's plans had been infected by Fortitude, just as it was infecting the military planning of the entire German high command. The grand deception operation that had been conceived to save life on D-Day was now contributing to the certainty that D-Day would, in fact, take place.

In pursuing its plans for revolution, the Schwarze Kapelle believed that the western powers, and particularly the British, were weakening in their insistence that they would neither offer nor accept any terms other than those of Unconditional Surrender. Were London and Washington, confronted as they now were with Neptune's inevitable cost in lives and treasure, prepared to modify the stringent terms of that declaration? The situation on the eve of the invasion was a curious one.

Throughout the winter and spring of 1944, there had been a prolonged debate about the wisdom of the doctrine of Unconditional Surrender between the soldiers and the politicians. In general, the former advocated a redefinition of Allied terms on the grounds that Unconditional Surrender was stiffening German resolve and so making the tasks of the fighting men more difficult. However, many of the latter insisted that any abatement of the terms would be taken as a sign of Allied weakness and would be exploited by the German propagandists to make their men fight even harder. But as the invasion neared, it became clear that this political belief was largely confined to the White House, and, fearing a holocaust in France on D-Day, powerful factors in both London and Washington sought a modification of Roosevelt's policy. The British Joint Intelligence Committee had asked its American counterparts what were called "pertinent questions" about the wisdom of Unconditional Surrender. The questions stirred new inquiries into the doctrine among the Pentagon's highest committees and divisions; and after much discussion the Joint Chiefs of Staff submitted a memorandum to the President on March 25, 1944, which read in part: "The Joint Chiefs of Staff are of the opinion that a restatement of the formula of unconditional surrender should be made . . . at an early date so that it may establish a favorable condition precedent to *Overlord.*"

The Joint Chiefs, the highest U.S. military authority under the President in his capacity as C-in-C, then submitted to Roosevelt a draft of what he should say to the German army and people. In essence, the JCS proposal reiterated demands for the Unconditional Surrender of the Nazis and the Wehrmacht, but at the same time it gave the German people and ordinary soldiery some hope. The key parts of the memorandum read: ". . . it is not our purpose to extinguish the German people or Germany as a nation. . . . It will be a main task of Allied military occupation to create the conditions for the rebirth of a peaceful German society. . . . Only unconditional surrender can provide the necessary basis for a fresh start." What the JCS sought to achieve was a differentiation in the doctrine between the German people and their "gangster overlords," and to reassure the German people that the Allies had no intention of destroying the German nation, but only the Nazis and the Wehrmacht. The State Department also thought that the doctrine could usefully be modified in its application toward Hungary, Rumania, Bulgaria and Finland to induce them to surrender. And General Frank N. Roberts, chief of the Strategy and Policy Group of the Pentagon's Operations and Plans Division, the man chiefly responsible for executing the Americans' contributions to Bodyguard and Fortitude, saw the proposed proclamation of a modified formula for Unconditional Surrender as a "psychological blockbuster" that should be "keyed to (Neptune)" in order to "reduce German resistance to the cross-Channel attack."

Even Eisenhower had bitten the bullet. At the surrender of the German army in Tunisia in 1943, he had declared that he would never receive a German general, except for the purposes of intelligence, nor would he give enemy commanders the honors of war. But now, perhaps under the influence of Smith, he modified his view and accepted the advocacy of his propaganda chief, McClure, that the policy of Unconditional Surrender be "restated" shortly before D-Day so that the *Feldgrau* would see that it was "good business" to surrender rather than fight.

For a few days both the JCS and SHAEF awaited the President's reply in a mood of hopefulness. Might it not be possible, after all, to *walk* ashore instead of fighting ashore? Surely Roosevelt would not turn down such a powerfully backed suggestion? But on April 1, 1944, the President, in a reply that rang with vengeance, moral cleansing and cynicism about the intentions and capabilities of the Schwarze Kapelle, did reject the proposal. He declared:

> The trouble is that the reasoning of the (JCS) memorandum supposes a reconstitution of a German state which would give active cooperation apparently at once to peace in Europe. A somewhat long and personal experience in and out of Germany leads me to believe that German Philosophy cannot be changed by decree, law or military order. The change in German Philosophy must be evolutionary and may take two generations. To assume otherwise is to assume, of necessity, a period of quiet followed by a third world war.
>
> I think that the simplest way of approaching this whole matter is to stick to what I have already said, (a) that the United Nations are determined to administer a total defeat to Germany as a whole (b) that the Allies have no intention of destroying the German people. Please note that I am not willing at this time to say that we do not intend to destroy the German nation. As long as the word "Reich" exists in Germany as expressing a nationhood, it will forever be associated with the present form of nationhood. If we admit that, we must seek to eliminate the very word "Reich" and what it stands for today.

The President's declaration surprised even Marshall, who remarked to Dill that "they were up against an obstinate Dutchman who had brought the phrase out and didn't like to go back on it." Roosevelt's reaffirmation of the harsh doctrine of Unconditional Surrender made the invasion an inevitability. But Eisenhower, fully aware of the hazards of both the invasion and a prolonged battle on the European mainland, made one last attempt to get for the Germans what his diarist called a "white alley": a route down which the enemy could surrender with honor. On April 14, 1944, he received Edward R. Stettinius, of U.S. Steel, who was shortly to become Secretary of State, and Eisenhower asked him to cable Cordell Hull about the Supreme Command's views. This Stettinius did, stating:

> In conversation this morning with General Eisenhower and General Smith they raised with me and expressed the considered opinion that the term "unconditional surrender" should be clarified by announcing the principles on which the treatment of a defeated Germany would be based. This seemed to them highly desirable in view of the accumulated evidence that German propaganda is interpreting the words "unconditional surrender" to strengthen the morale of the German army and people. In order to offset this the generals thought it very necessary to create, if possible, through our own propaganda (a) a mood of acceptance of unconditional surrender in the German army such as would make possible a collapse of resistance similar to that which took place in Tunisia; and (b) to create a mood in the German General Staff as a result of which necessary political steps might be undertaken by a German "Badoglio" [i.e., the Italian field marshal who led the Italian nation out of the war by revolution against Mussolini] for unconditional surrender.

Stettinius's telegram went on to reveal that "General Smith rather than General Eisenhower" recommended that, after this governmental announcement, the Supreme Commander should call upon the German commander in the West to surrender. This call, Smith had evidently suggested, should be "recited in soldierly terms," and should be made *after* the bridgehead had been established. Finally, Stettinius's cable declared:

> General Smith expressed the opinion that from all available evidence, in default of such declarations, it would be impossible to exploit the crisis in the German army which will undoubtedly arise immediately after a successful Allied landing.

SHAEF was obviously well informed, through MI-6's special contacts with the enemy, of the state of mind of the German generals. On May 23, 1944, an important report was circulated to all SHAEF's commands which said in part:

> In the German Army, as in German political life, authority is exercised at the top and almost always obeyed at the bottom. For that reason, political trends among the generals in the German Army are

of great significance. Should the *Wehrmacht* suffer severe setbacks [through Neptune] the generals may play a decisive role in determining the future. There has been some evidence of friction between Hitler and his higher commanders as a result of German retreats . . . when the generals recognize defeat as inevitable, they may be unwilling to fight on until Germany is reduced to chaos. The generals are likely to believe themselves in a position to get better terms from the conquerors than the nazis. . . . If the first weeks of invasion indicate that the (Allies) cannot be stopped, high-ranking officers of the German Army, recognizing the war-weariness of the German people, may act quickly against Hitler. Politically and psychologically that would be the moment for them to stage a coup. To a majority of German general officers the future of Germany is more important than the future of Hitler. . . . Trends among the German generals during the first weeks of successful invasion will (therefore) merit the closest analysis. . . .

The report amounted virtually to a prophecy, and as such must have been of immense importance and encouragement to Eisenhower. A revolt against Hitler led by his own generals, even if it was unsuccessful, would dramatically disconcert German opposition to the invading Allied armies. If it was successful, like the revolt that deposed the Kaiser, Berlin would lie shimmering, and not far away. It was, perhaps, too much to hope, at this late stage, that such a revolt might precede the invasion and that Neptune itself would prove unnecessary. Although the Rankin contingency plans for unopposed landings on the European mainland remained in readiness at SHAEF, Eisenhower seemed irrevocably committed to launch the invasion—and Rommel irrevocably committed to oppose it. Otherwise, Eisenhower and Rommel were not far apart; both now advocated communication across the drawn lines of battle. But would Churchill or Roosevelt permit such a contact? How many lives, how many cities, how much treasure might be saved if Allied and German generals could negotiate a surrender that would be mutually acceptable? It was a moment of extraordinary opportunity.

The Prime Minister made the first move. On May 24, 1944, he rose before Parliament and spoke of the enemy less ferociously than usual, stating merely that, while Unconditional Surrender gave the enemy no rights, it relieved the Allies of none of their duties. "Justice," he declared vaguely, "will have to be done and retribution will fall upon the wicked and the cruel." McClure's Political Warfare Branch at Supreme Headquarters then prepared a statement for Eisenhower. It was touched up by Robert Sherwood, the playwright, who was an executive of the OWI, and finally polished by William Phillips, the Supreme Commander's American political adviser. The speech was to be a "fireside chat" by Eisenhower to the German soldier, broadcast *after* the Allies had secured a beachhead in Normandy. Its object was, by redefining, explaining, and making more palatable the implications to German honor of Unconditional Surrender, to weaken the determination and powers of resistance of the *Feldgrau* in France. The speech was sent to Washington, but no word of approval or disapproval came back from the White House. There was only silence. Roosevelt did, however, yield to pressure for modifications of Unconditional Surrender so far as it affected Rumania, Hungary, Bulgaria and Finland—but not Germany. Further than that the President would not and did not go. But there was no explosion, as might have been expected—for the Supreme Commander, who was but an instrument of Anglo-American political policy, had no right or power to influence or change that policy. He had greatly exceeded his powers in even permitting such an address to be written without the express, written authority of London and Washington. The explosion came from Churchill on May 31, 1944.

The Prime Minister, already concerned about the extent of the powers that Eisenhower had assumed, particularly those related to security, wrote an angry letter accusing him of "begging before we have won the battle." "This is a matter which really must be dealt with by Governments, and cannot be made the subject of fireside talks," Churchill wrote. "I never read anything less suitable for the troops (on the eve of battle)."

The contretemps with Churchill on the eve of Neptune was one of Eisenhower's earliest lessons in statesmanship. He had trodden where wise men fear to tread—into the area of coalition politics. He did not try again. Unconditional Surrender remained in force, unmodified, for Germany. Nevertheless, the political climate and the inclination—to say nothing of many opportunities—for secret contacts between the Supreme Command and the Schwarze Kapelle continued to exist on both sides of the English Channel. And as if to confirm that these contacts might yet be exploited, a familiar figure was at work behind the scenes. Admiral Canaris reappeared once again at a critical moment in the history of the Third Reich.

In preparing the plans for Neptune and allied operations, the SHAEF syndicates enjoyed a unique advantage. They had before them detailed intelligence about German strength, dispositions, fortifications, supply and telecommunications routes, morale and much else that was, with a few important exceptions, almost complete. No military commander in history would be better informed than Eisenhower on the eve of D-Day, and for that information, at least in part, he could thank Canaris.

Canaris's role in, once again, betraying top-level German secrets to the Allies during the pre-Neptune period would remain obscure. But there can be little question about his involvement, for it would be affirmed by men who were in a position to know of it, among them General James O. Curtis. From late February to early May 1944, Curtis, then a colonel, was the senior American intelligence evaluator in the Operational Intelligence Centre of the Supreme Command. Colonel E. J. Foord was the chief of the section, and the other members of OIC included Major John Austin, an Oxford don in peacetime and a future professor of metaphysics, and Colonel Eric Birley, another don who used to spend his leaves establishing the order of battle of Caesar's 10th Legion in Britain. Together these men were responsible for much the same tasks as those of FHW, sifting the nuggets of truth from the dross of hundreds of thousands of bits of intelligence that arrived each month that spring. And when the nuggets had been weighed and analyzed to establish their substance and value, they were incorporated into the intelligence bulletins known as Neptune *Monitors*. But from the beginning of his involvement in operational intelligence, Curtis, who prided himself on the excellence of his relations with the British, felt that he was not wholly trusted by them. His job demanded skepticism and thoroughness, and he was not disposed to accept the authenticity of material placed before him until he knew more about its origins. Curtis said later that he was well aware that the British had most secret sources of intelligence, but he felt that he could not advise the U.S. army commanders with absolute confidence unless he knew as much about the sources of the material reaching his desk as did his British counterparts.

For that reason, Curtis decided to ask Foord where so much intelligence of the highest grade was coming from. According to Curtis, he heard nothing from Foord about his demand for a day or two; and then Foord, after a meeting at Norfolk House, took him into an anteroom. There, he revealed what Curtis had already guessed: that much of the high-grade intelligence was obtained through Ultra intercepts of OKW's and Hitler's own wireless traffic. But to the revelation concerning Ultra, Foord added the astonishing information that some of the material reaching Curtis was coming from Canaris. Curtis would later elaborate in a witnessed statement:

> I first heard the name Canaris in February 1944. My duties required me to check the authenticity of certain information reaching my desk. We had a system of grading information at SHAEF which ranged from A1 to F6, so that the highest grade and most authentic information was graded A1 while the lowest grade and the least authentic information was graded F6.
>
> It is not usual to get large amounts of A1 but I noticed that a surprising amount of A1 information was coming through. It was necessary for me to know the source, and so I inquired at a meeting of the Order of Battle intelligence section. A British officer, E. J. Foord, took me quietly on one side [Curtis here inserted, "Just two in the room"] and said that the source was Canaris personally. Foord said: "The only reason that I am telling you this is that we want you to regard this information as being priceless and copper-bottomed." The source, said Foord, was known to only a few men—men like Roosevelt, Churchill, Ike, Montgomery, etc.
>
> His most important service was to give us substantially the complete order of battle plans for the German Army, together with the plans they had worked out for coping with the invasion.

Curtis would remember, even after twenty-three years, how surprised he was at hearing this information. "I was, at first, afraid to go to sleep in case I talked in my sleep," he said. He would add that Canaris sent this intelligence by courier to the Iberian capitals and, on occasions, even directly by wireless to the MI-6 wireless station—using, he thought, a trusted Abwehr wireless operator. For, as Curtis would continue: "Canaris had a code name and this appeared at the top of all intelligence emanating from him—it was a naval term." Could it have been Dreadnought? Curtis thought so. Equally, the code name Albatross rang a bell. But he was certain that Foord had told him that "to all intents and purposes Canaris was in the service of the Allies, not as an agent but in the same way that statesmen confide secrets to each other if it will bring them advantages at the bargaining table."

Foord's statement to Curtis would be supported by de Guingand, who knew more about Allied secret affairs as a whole than almost any other man. He would state:

> I distinctly remember being told that Canaris was the source of some of our most secret intelligence. Whether Canaris transmitted this material to us deliberately, or whether we obtained it through our ability to

read his command instructions, I did not know at that time. I had no reason to know. But after the war, I was told not once but several times at the highest level that, for ideological and political reasons, Canaris imparted high-level German command decisions to us.

And what was Canaris's motive? De Guingand thought: "Canaris was more afraid of the Russians than he was of us and, presumably, he wanted us to get ashore with the minimum of loss so that we would be able to bring the maximum power to bear upon the Russians and keep them out of Germany."

Further confirmation would come not from the Allied side but from one of Canaris's own compatriots, General Reinhard Gehlen, the man who had once been Roenne's chief and chief of intelligence at Fremde Heere Ost, and then became chief of the DNB, the postwar successor to the Abwehr. Gehlen stated that he was sure that Canaris had had "contact with the British secret service" and was not in the least surprised about the fact. He further remarked:

> I myself had contact with that organization. As chief of (Fremde Heere Ost) in 1944 I told a subordinate to communicate by wireless to the British secret service at Istanbul our appreciations of the Red Army's order of battle, and my appreciations of their strategic aims and intentions. The British were exceedingly grateful to me.

Gehlen would also write in his memoir, *The Service,* that MI-6 and the British military mission in Moscow passed his agents there material about the Russians. In particular, Gehlen would claim that he received through MI-6 "by devious means" an appreciation by Churchill of Russia's postwar intentions in Europe. These were surprising admissions, if Gehlen's story was true, for they showed that there were secret lines of communication between the British and German General Staff. It also gave rise to the speculation that if Fremde Heere Ost could transmit and receive from the British, Roenne and Michel at FHW might have been able to do likewise. As for Canaris, a man even more determined in his efforts to wreck Nazism, his years of service as chief of the Abwehr, his close association with the conspirators of the Schwarze Kapelle, and his myriad contacts in the world of secret intelligence, including his curious relationship with Menzies at MI-6, put him in an even better position to maintain, and use, secret channels of communication with the British.

In revealing the German order of battle before D-Day, Canaris would have attempted to do no more than he had done in the past: to thwart Hitler. But as winter gave way to spring, and the inevitable invasion neared, he would attempt an even bolder move. Abandoning the caution and indirection that had always characterized his clandestine activities, he would make a last, desperate, personal appeal to save Germany.

After his dismissal as chief of the Abwehr, Canaris had gone even deeper into the shadows of the Third Reich. There were reports that he was under house arrest at the Castle Lauenstein in Franconia; but they proved to be untrue. The castle was, in fact, the headquarters of the German economic warfare department and Canaris was its chief. His old enemies, Kaltenbrunner in particular, seemed to have lost interest in him as a quarry; the SD now saw him as an old Wilhelminian gentleman who had been put out to clover. None of the charges that had been made against him could be proven; the circumstances did not yet exist in which he might be placed in what the Nazis called "protective custody," and as far as Keitel and OKW were concerned, Canaris was the victim of a bureaucratic reshuffle, not the perpetrator of crimes against the state. Thus Canaris could now have been even more valuable to the Schwarze Kapelle than he had been as chief of the Abwehr. He was no longer under the continual observation of the SD, and as chief of economic warfare he could still travel widely and freely.

It can be presumed that Canaris remained in touch with Beck and Goerdeler in Berlin; and it may have been on their behalf that he emerged from the shadows and traveled to Paris on the most extraordinary mission in his long career of clandestinity. None of the Schwarze Kapelle's own accounts, none of the SD's accounts, and none of MI-6's or the Allies' official accounts would record that mission. But long after the war was over, there would be the testaments of eye witnesses.

By the late spring of 1944, Jade Amicol, the MI-6 *réseau* with its headquarters in the Lazarite convent in Paris, had become Britain's most important secret intelligence organization in northern France. Its operations were not confined to military espionage against the Wehrmacht; the organization had become a clearinghouse for political intelligence of all forms. With these new responsibilities, the *réseau* seems to have split into two parts with Colonel Arnould, the founder, looking after its military aspects and his partner, Major Philippe Keun, involved in its subtler political aspects. And in addition to its many other contacts in the anti-German underground, Jade Amicol was close to the Paris faction of the Schwarze Kapelle through an Austrian Catholic who was a member of the secretarial staff in the headquarters of Stuelpnagel. Keun would not survive the war; soon after D-Day he would be sold by a Frenchman in his own organization and murdered by the SD. But Arnould did survive, and he would state, in an interview in 1969, that through this secretary Canaris was able to make contact with Keun in Paris sometime in May 1944. Moreover, Arnould would state—and he was an officer in high standing with Menzies, who would arrange for him to receive the Distinguished Service Order, normally awarded to foreigners only if they had rendered Great Britain quite exceptionally valuable and distinguished service under fire or while on active service against the enemy in special circumstances—that the May contact was not an isolated one. Keun had apparently been in contact with Canaris in April.

Arnould went on to say that when he learned of this contact, he was alarmed,

> because I feared that the whole matter might be a trick by the Germans to find our headquarters. But Keun assured me it was not a trick and that Canaris was representing a group of high-ranking Germans who were anxious to get in touch with the Allied high command in London. He told me he must get this information to London without delay. He made the arrangements for an aircraft over our wireless set, which was hidden in the loft over the sacristy.

And, according to Arnould's recollections, ". . . Philippe flew to London on or about May 30, 1944."

That, then, was the nature of Canaris's extraordinary mission: to communicate once more directly with Menzies. But what did his message contain that warranted such grave personal risks, both on his part and on the part of Keun? Arnould said that he assumed it concerned an attempt by the military opposition to Hitler to open discussions for an armistice.

Without written records, any contact between Keun and Canaris, as well as the existence of a personal message from Canaris to Menzies, is open to question. But Keun did travel to England at this time and that fact was later confirmed by Commander Dunderdale, the liaison officer for MI-6 with the French secret services, a long-standing friend of the Keun family and Keun's sometime controller. Dunderdale said he went down to Manston, MI-6's forward airbase on the tip of the Kentish peninsula, to receive Keun personally. However, he was mystified by the story that Keun brought with him a personal communication from Canaris to Menzies. "Keun came over to receive instructions about the part Jade Amicol was to play in the invasion and had he brought a message with him I think he would have told me. Even if he had not told me I think I would have been told by Menzies. But Menzies said nothing." Nevertheless, Dunderdale agreed that he was not privy to everything that occurred between Menzies and Jade Amicol, and he confirmed that Canaris did have contacts with Menzies—as Menzies himself admitted. These, said Dunderdale, occurred at this time through Oswald Baron Hoyningen-Huene, the German ambassador at Lisbon, who was a fringe member of the Schwarze Kapelle. However, Dunderdale persisted in his objection to the story that Keun was the bearer of a message from Canaris to Menzies, observing: "It seems inconceivable that it happened this way, if it happened at all. In the first place, Canaris was far too wily an old bird to commit himself under circumstances where the messenger might very easily be captured. And Keun himself would have thought twice about carrying any message." However, Dunderdale became much less sure when he heard that, in addition to Arnould's testimony, Madame Henriette Frede, the Mother Superior of the convent in Paris, had stated that she had seen Keun walking with a man whom she later knew to be Canaris around the Lion of Belfort in the Place Denfert-Rochereau in the last week of May 1944. Finally, Dunderdale would say he was prepared to accept the story "tentatively" when he heard that Menzies had replied to the message, and that there had been a meeting between Canaris, Arnould and the Mother Superior at the convent just before the invasion. Thus it can be assumed that such a communication existed, that Keun was its courier, and that Dunderdale's objections were based on the fact that neither Keun nor Menzies told him about its existence. But as Dunderdale would admit: "There was no earthly reason why they should. Such matters were not my concern."

Nor, in spite of Menzies's position, were they his concern. How could he respond to such a communication? It would have been unthinkable for him to have acted without the authority of the Foreign Office. When he had received similar communications before, he had always referred them to Anthony Eden, the Foreign Secretary; and Eden had always instructed him to take no action. Dulles in Berne was in a like situation; he would state that when "I received a request from Canaris for a personal meeting on the German-Swiss frontier, Cordell Hull refused permission to accept." In both cases, the reasons were much the same. There was always the specter of another Venlo; no one could forget that two of MI-6's most important agents in western Europe had been kidnapped while, they thought, they were on business concerning the Schwarze Kapelle. Even without Venlo, there would have been the specter of the Russians, who suspected that Britain was so war-weary she was ready to talk peace. In January 1944, *Pravda,* the official Russian newspaper, had reproduced a story then circulating in the neutral press that British agents had met agents of Ribbentrop in a town in the Pyrenees. The British denied the story; but they remained cautious not to give the Russians any cause to suspect that the western powers were seeking a political termination to the war that would leave the Germans free to fight the Russians, nor to give Hitler any cause to suspect that there was a split in the Grand Alliance.

If Menzies at MI-6 was powerless to respond to Canaris's appeal, there was one bureau where the news of such a communication would have been extremely interesting, and that was the LCS. Wingate would not be able to remember whether either he or Bevan ever heard of the communication. But both were aware that such appeals had been made several times before. Wingate would recall:

> We received reports frequently about the German opposition [sic]. But the political authorities decided that no reliance could be placed on these. It had been decided long since that the war could only be ended by military means. Therefore, we did ask ourselves about the use that we could make of these contacts in order to assist our strategic deception operations. We decided that such overtures were examples of defeatism and of course where you have disaffected elements they are more liable to accept information which was to the disadvantage of Hitler. Perhaps this is what Bevan meant when he told me that we had people on the German Staff (who were being used by the LCS to sow its deceptions). The ability to put a word in the ear of the German Staff was worth divisions on occasions.

Thus the fate of Canaris's final overture was already sealed. He might better have saved himself the trouble. No accommodation could be offered. There could be only Unconditional Surrender. It was in this spirit that Menzies must have settled down to write his reply to Canaris—the last communication in the long years of their peculiar association. But here was another mystery. Why should Menzies have replied at all? Was it not too dangerous? Would the letter not have been Keun's and Canaris's death warrant had it been captured? Might it not have been a most valuable instrument for the German propagandists—if it had fallen into their hands—in stiffening the resolve of the *Feldgrau* and *Herrenvolk* and in splitting the Grand Alliance? Would it not have been more prudent for Menzies to meet the overture with disdainful silence? Perhaps; but his reply may simply have been the act of a gentleman, or Menzies, ever alert for an opportunity to "put a word in the ear of the German Staff," may not have wanted to end a channel of communication that had lasted for so long. At any rate, according to Arnould, Menzies did reply, and Keun returned to Paris with his letter.

Keun arrived back at the Convent of St. Agonie at about lunchtime "three or four days before the *débarquement*," and again, the events that followed were later described by eye witnesses—the Mother Superior and Arnould. The Mother Superior answered Keun's special knock at the chapel door and then led him through the chapel into the sacristy, where Arnould was waiting for him. The two men went into the Mother Superior's private room and there Keun told Arnould that he had brought a letter from London which must be given to Canaris without delay. Arnould immediately telephoned his contact at Stuelpnagel's headquarters, and they arranged to meet at a confessional at Notre Dame. Canaris was thought to be still in Paris, and at Notre Dame that afternoon. Arnould instructed his contact to get a message to Canaris, asking him to be at the windmill beside the racetrack at Longchamps at eleven o'clock on the morning of June 3.

Just before 11 A.M. next day, Arnould cycled past the windmill, which he considered a safe rendezvous because it was close to the copses of the Bois de Boulogne and because the windmill itself stood on high ground from which all roads leading into the area could be observed. Moreover, Arnould had a safehouse in the nearby suburb of Auteil to which he could escape. At about a quarter past eleven, Arnould saw Canaris—"a short man in a dark suit, easily identifiable because of his silver hair"—climb the steps to the windmill and then begin to walk around the pebble track, as if he was looking over the racecourse. Arnould approached Canaris from behind and, ensuring there were no witnesses either in the road below or on the windmill itself, spoke to him. He introduced himself as "Colonel Ollivier," a code name Canaris knew well, and said that he had received a letter for the admiral from London. He explained that it was too dangerous to bring by hand and could not be transmitted by post. Consequently, he invited the admiral to the convent that same evening at six o'clock. And Canaris—according to Arnould's own account of the encounter—agreed to be there.

It was an incredible rendezvous, for both men were risking everything. An even more incredible encounter was to follow that evening. At six o'clock Canaris arrived at the convent and rang the bell on the old door. It was answered by the Mother Superior, who asked him what he wanted. "Canaris seemed nonplussed," she would recall, "and replied that he had come to pray." He was, perhaps, unaware that the convent was MI-6 headquarters in France, and thought that he might be given the letter in the chapel. But Arnould had told the Mother Superior who was coming, and she had taken the precaution of confining her twelve sisters to their quarters so that none might observe the important visitor. She drew the bolts and asked the admiral to follow her. They crossed the nave, passed the little spiral stairs which led to the choir loft over the sacristy where Keun had his transceiver, walked down a narrow stone-flagged passageway toward the clinic and entered her own room.

There, Canaris was again confronted by Arnould. The table was set for what the Mother Superior later described as a "simple but wholesome dinner." The two men shook hands and while the Mother Superior was out of the room Arnould produced the letter. It was an ordinary white foolscap envelope unmarked by either name or address, and it appeared—from where Arnould stood—to contain two sheets of plain typewritten letter paper with a signature at the bottom. Canaris sat down in one of the Mother Superior's easy chairs to read the letter, and there was a deep silence in the room. But when he finished it, he seemed to go quite white and give a little gasp. "This is the finish for Germany," he said. "They will not give us any terms whatsoever. There must be unconditional surrender or nothing."

Canaris put the letter in one of his inside pockets, and the two men sat for a short while without saying a word until Canaris repeated, "Finis Germaniae!" Arnould then offered him some calvados, which the admiral refused with thanks, but he did accept an invitation to dine. The conversation over the meal was desultory. As Arnould recalled: "It was an agonizing meal. The admiral was clearly in great despair. He said nothing about the contents, but it was clear from the nature of our conversation that he had written to General Menzies about an armistice and he had been rejected."

Shortly after seven o'clock Canaris rose, thanked Arnould for his hospitality, wished him good luck, and asked to be shown out. Arnould escorted his visitor back down the corridor into the nave, where prayers were now being held, and so into the street. Canaris walked off up the rue de la Santé, a narrow cobbled road leading onto the

Boulevard Arago, and disappeared into the crowds of that sultry evening. He had failed, once again, to avert disaster for his homeland. Now no one could save Germany, for in Britain the clock had already been set ticking inexorably toward D-Day.

Vendetta

"VENDETTA," the last turn of the screw of special means during the pre-Neptune period, was issued to every Allied command at 0705 Greenwich Mean Time on May 1, 1944. It was a brief, pregnant message that read simply: "Word is Vendetta." While strictly speaking it was the code name for the threat against southern France from North Africa during Neptune, the promulgation of Vendetta would set in motion operations of an almost hemispherical nature during the month of May, all designed to produce uncertainty in the minds of the German high command and fear about their fate among the *Feldgrau*. The flames of Vendetta, fanned by the Supreme Command in London, ringed the German Empire. The Grand Alliance demanded that Turkey join "the cause"; and severe words were spoken to Rumania, Bulgaria, Hungary and Finland. In the Levant, the British 9th and 10th armies, which in fact had no more than a brigade of men apiece, appeared to be concentrating at Turkey's southern frontier, ready to march with the forty divisions of the Turkish army into Greece and Bulgaria. In the Balkans, special forces began raiding the Greek and Aegean islands with even greater frequency. In Yugoslavia, Tito's army of 800,000 partisans, now lightly equipped with artillery and tanks, intensified the volume of its aggressive defense; and the Germans retaliated with "Knight's Move," the code name of an operation to liquidate Tito and the partisan high command—an operation that almost succeeded. At the top of the Adriatic, Allied warships probed the defenses around Trieste as special agents continued to reconnoiter the entrance to the Ljubljana Gap. In January, America—Spain's only source—refused further supplies of petroleum products and Spain and Portugal were gradually being brought to heel by the increasing pressures of Allied diplomatic and economic warfare. And in Algeria, the

French army, reborn and rearmed with American equipment, appeared to be mounting an invasion of the Riviera coast of France, while the *maquis* in that region began sabotage operations that seemed to be a preparation for such an invasion. On the Biscay coast, the *maquisards* undertook similar operations that seemed to portend a large-scale uprising in concert with an Allied landing. It was the same story in northern France, Belgium, Denmark, Holland and Norway, where the resistance was at work like tens of thousands of deathwatch beetles burrowing into the prow of the Reich. In Scandinavia, rumors were still rife of Anglo-Russian landings to seize the nickel ore mines at Petsamo, rumors that were aggravated by the Russians, who were playing their part in Bodyguard by simulating the preparations for a seaborne assault. At Stockholm, an Anglo-American mission continued to seek, or so it seemed, bases from which to attack the Baltic coast of Germany.

Hundreds of incidents, indeed thousands, occurred right round the rim of the war. A general was kidnapped in Crete; an SD officer was murdered at Lyon; the Greek Sacred Heart Boat Squadron attacked a radar post on Rhodes; German aircraft crashed in flames at Athens and abrasive grease was found in their engines; three German soldiers vanished in a Commando raid on Sagvaag in Norway; F section agents blew up three compressors in the liquid oxygen factory at Boulogne-sur-Seine; saboteurs wrecked the Luftwaffe repair shops at Klovermarksvej in Denmark; a German leave train was derailed in the Ardennes; 300,000 liters of petroleum products were destroyed in a suspicious fire at Boussens in France; a sabotage team gave the manager of the ball-bearing factory at Aubervilliers a choice: either he put the plant out of action or the RAF would—he chose the former. Everywhere in Europe surreptitious, nerve-racking underground warfare sought to pin down the Wehrmacht as Gulliver was ensnared by the Lilliputians.

The Germans reacted very strongly to this incessant activity, particularly in France where, time and time again, they cut down the *maquis* —only to have them spring up in even greater numbers. The nervous, hysterical tenor of their reactions was just what the Allies hoped to achieve: a fear among the *Feldgrau* that they were surrounded by enemies who were omnipresent, clever and murderous. Adding to that fear was the ominous silence on the military fronts. The fighting in Italy was in a stalemate, but the Allied armies were preparing for "Diadem," the great offensive that would lead to the capture of Rome. On the Russian front, the guns were silent; the Red Army, honoring its commitment to Bodyguard, was waiting to launch its summer offensive at a time and place that would help Neptune. And in England, the build-up for the invasion continued as hundreds of thousands of men and millions of tons of equipment assembled for D-Day. The Germans knew that the storm would soon break. But would they discover where and when the Allies would invade?

To keep the enemy mystified about these key secrets of Neptune, the Allied deception agencies were busy putting the finishing touches to Fortitude and Quicksilver. During the month of May, as Montgomery's 21st Army Group, the invasion force, was secretly and silently assembling in the Gloucester-Falmouth-Brighton triangle, Patton's virtually nonexistent FUSAG was "assembling" in the Dover-Cambridge-King's Lynn triangle. Elaborate preparations had been made to give this "concentration" of troops the appearance of a massive force, and once those preparations were complete, German reconnaissance aircraft were allowed to intrude over the FUSAG zone. There, in the creeks, harbors and river mouths of eastern England, from Lowestoft and Yarmouth down to the Norfolk Broads, the Deben River, the Orwell, at Dover, Folkestone and the Thames Estuary, they spotted 400 "landing ships"—each in reality little more than tubular scaffolding, canvas and wood floating on oil drums. They had been manufactured at the film studios at Shepperton, near London, and then brought down by road. Smoke coiled from their funnels, they were surrounded by oil patches, laundry hung from the rigging, motorboats left wakes from ship to ship, and intruding aircraft could see their crews—over-age or unfit soldiers of units such as the 10th Worcestershires and the 4th Northamptonshires. Thousands of carefully shielded truck lights indicated the presence of large convoys, and lights over "hards" gave the impression of intense loading activity after dark. And behind this "invasion fleet," which was large enough to "land" the entire 1st Canadian Army, which did not as yet exist, the fields of East Anglia and Kent were crowded with tanks, guns, half-tracks, ammunition dumps, field kitchens, hospitals, troop encampments and fuel lines.

They, too, were fakes. Farmer Sydney George Cripps, of Chaul End, a tiny hamlet in the hills just off the Watling Street, the ancient Roman road, saw a line of trucks in one of his meadows late one May evening. It was a common enough sight and he took no further notice. But at dawn the next day he saw scores of tanks in the same meadow. Afraid that they would chew up his grass, Cripps was on his way to complain to the officer in charge when he noticed that the tanks had left no tracks. The only tracks in the thick, dewy grass were being made by some American soldiers who were dragging a device across the meadow behind a truck. Then Cripps saw something even odder. A bull was loose in the meadow and charged one of the tanks; but when its horns struck the side of the tank, it collapsed with a huge hiss like a balloon. The tanks—there were more than a brigade of them— were just that: balloons. And the American soldiers were making tracks for them in case a German reconnaissance plane came over with its cameras.

Sounds as well as sights were used to complete the deception. The ionosphere over FUSAG was filled by the sporadic wireless noises made by an army group, while it was silent over Montgomery's invasion force. German wireless intelligence men across the Channel heard radio chatter that had been compiled as a scenario in a book 8 inches thick, including the classic "1/5th Queen's Royal Regiment report a number of civilian women, presumably unauthorised, in the baggage train. What are we going to do with them—take them to Calais?" To confirm all the other indications that the main troop concentrations were in the Dover and Cambridge areas, signals engineers laid lines from Montgomery's real operations headquarters at Portsmouth to Dover Castle and released his wireless traffic from there. Then, to prevent the Germans from being able to inquire too closely into the truth of the information they were getting through intercepts, and to destroy their ability to find out where the Allied armies were really concentrating through the use of wireless direction finding, a series of air attacks were mounted against their wireless stations, including their signals intelligence headquarters near Cherbourg, which was leveled in a massive raid.

Leaks to the press added to the reality of FUSAG—chaplains were announced to have joined the army group which was "preparing for the invasion of Europe across the historic plains of Flanders." And there was yet another visual illusion designed to make the Germans believe that FUSAG was destined for the Pas de Calais. Preparations were being made for Pluto—the mnemonic for "pipeline under the ocean"—to be laid between southern England and Normandy to supply the invasion armies with petrol. To deceive the Germans about where such a pipeline would start—and therefore where it would terminate—Britain's finest architect of the period had been called in to create a vast but entirely fake oil dock at Dover.

Basil Spence, Professor of Architecture at the Royal Academy, member of the Fine Art Commission, one of the creators of the Vice-

roy of India's residence at Delhi, architect of the British Embassy in
Rome and the future Household Cavalry Barracks at Knightsbridge,
consultant for the extension to the Palais des Nations at Geneva,
architect for the new cathedral at Coventry—and a score of other such
projects—designed and built the phony oil dock with the aid of film
and theater stagehands. Made almost entirely of camouflaged scaffolding, fiber board and old sewage pipes, it occupied nearly 3 square
miles of the Dover foreshore, and it consisted of fake pipelines,
storage tanks, powerhouses, a fire brigade, anti-aircraft gun posts,
guardrooms, lorry parks, jetties—everything that a real oil dock would
have. Wind machines blew up clouds of dust to make it look as if rapid
progress was being made and to hide the fact that in reality there were
only a few score men at work there. The area was closely guarded by
military police. The King "inspected" the dock, and so did Montgomery. Eisenhower spoke to the "construction workers" at a dinner
party held at the White Cliffs Hotel in Dover; and the Mayor made
satisfied remarks about the "opening of a new installation, the precise
nature of which must remain secret until the war is over, but which
will bring the borough material benefits of consequence." The RAF
maintained constant fighter patrols overhead, as if to protect the installation; the Royal Engineers cloaked it each night with artificial fog
generated from smoke pots burning crude oil; and German reconnaissance aircraft were permitted to fly overhead—but only after they had
been "engaged" by the fighter patrols, and provided they were at
33,000 feet, where it was impossible for their cameras to pick out any
defects in the installation. Whenever German long-range artillery batteries on Cap Gris Nez attempted to shell it, as they did occasionally,
"hits" and subsequent "fires" were created from massive sodium
flares.

Fakery had become an immense industry in the interests of Fortitude and Quicksilver. East Anglia resembled an enormous film lot,
and no detail was spared. Livid vicars struck up angry correspondence
in the East Anglia newspapers about the "moral collapse" that had occurred since "the vast number of foreign troops"—and "particularly
American paratroopers and French and Polish tank units"—had "invaded the area." There was spirited discussion about the "immense
numbers of rubber contraceptives" found around "the American paratroop bases at Marham and Coggeshall." But, in essence, all this
fakery was designed primarily as physical confirmation for the reports
which the XX-Committee's double agents Garbo and Brutus had been
feeding, and continued to feed, the Germans about FUSAG. On May

19, 1944, as part of the process to build him up as a replacement for Tricycle, Brutus told his controllers by wireless that he had been posted to Patton's headquarters as a liaison officer between the Polish high command and FUSAG. This mundane job had been selected deliberately by the XX-Committee as a post where Brutus might have access to much without access to everything, for there was the constant threat that the Germans would ask him for more information than SHAEF was disposed to reveal. Having established himself in his new job, Brutus each night just before midnight began to send the entire FUSAG order of battle to his controller. This was stunning information for FHW to receive; but since it corresponded both with Roenne's own rigged estimates, with the reports of other agents and with the intelligence yield of aerial reconnaissance and wireless intercepts, Roenne had no recourse, after passing the intelligence through his analysis system, but to place the FUSAG order of battle before Hitler at Berchtesgaden.

As for Garbo, he, too, announced that he had been offered a new job—as translator by the chief of the Iberian subsection of the Ministry of Information. There, he explained, he would be privy to the secrets of a man who knew everything in Britain—Brendan Bracken, the minister and confidant of Churchill. But, as Garbo went on, he disliked very much the "idea of betraying the Führer by working for the British." Under the circumstances, since he could still obtain excellent intelligence by not working for the British, should he accept the post? His instructions came back immediately: Garbo must forget his scruples and accept the post. He did so, and a flow of even more deceptive information followed.

A feminine voice was also part of the XX-Committee chorus at this time. She was a beautiful young Argentinian whose father was at the Argentine Embassy in Vichy. In 1942, the young woman had visited her father, and while she was in France an Abwehr recruiting officer suggested that she might like to go to England (where her father had had important connections before the war) as an Abwehr agent. She accepted, but en route to London via Madrid, she went to the British and told them all. MI-6 helped her on her way and she landed in Bristol at the end of October 1942. In London, she was held by the security authorities for an extensive period; and then the XX-Committee assumed control of her at the beginning of 1943. She was codenamed "Bronx."

Bronx began as a secret ink letter writer, supplying the Germans with information supplied to her by the XX-Committee. Her work was considered so good by the Germans that they paid her a retainer of £25 ($120) a month, with expenses—a fair sum in those days—plus a number of bonuses. She corresponded with the Abwehr through the Bank of the Holy Ghost in Lisbon, which was also her own bank, and it was that connection which determined the next move in the game. Toward the end of 1943, the Germans, even then preoccupied with the invasion, provided Bronx with an interesting cipher to enable her to transmit more urgent and important information by commercial telegram. If she learned anything about the time and place of the invasion, she was to send a request to her bank along these lines: £100 indicated that the invasion would come in northern France; £125 would mean the Biscay coast; £150 would mean the French Mediterranean coast; £175 would mean the Adriatic; £200, Greece; £225, Denmark; £250, Norway; and so on. Further, if she put the purpose for which she needed the money into her telegram, it would indicate the month of the invasion.

Bronx, of course, passed the cipher on to the XX-Committee, which decided to put it to use for the purposes of "Ironside," the Fortitude operation designed to threaten the Bordeaux region and pin down the German 11th Panzer Division for as long as possible before, during and after D-Day. It was not expected in London that any stratagem would keep the division in place for very long; but then advantage was being measured in hours. Consequently, on May 15, 1944, Bronx sent this telegram to her bank through the Foreign Office (private telegrams could still be sent over commercial wires, provided the Foreign Office was allowed to handle them):

> *Envoyez vite cinquante livres. J'ui besoin*
> *pour mon dentiste.*

The cable meant: "I have definite news that a landing will be made in the Bay of Biscay in about one month"—around June 15, 1944, nine days after D-Day. This was just another of the "witty hors d'oeuvres" that preceded the "main course," the invasion; but as time would tell, it had a significant effect upon German reactions to Neptune.

The deception experts considered that it was not enough that the Germans learn of Allied military intentions in France only through wireless and aerial intelligence and the reports of agents whose veracity might be in question. How much better if there was someone of undoubted veracity who could report in person to the German General Staff on the enormous build-up in England for the invasion—and particularly on the existence of FUSAG. The LCS and the CSM had searched for such a man, and they found him in General Hans Cramer.

Cramer, the last commander of the Afrika Korps, had been captured in May 1943 at the Axis collapse in Tunisia. He was brought to England, and because his health had begun to deteriorate, it was decided to send him home in a repatriation program run by the Swedish Red Cross—but not before he had been of service to Fortitude. In May 1944 he was taken by road from his camp in south Wales to the "London Cage," the Combined Services Detailed Interrogation Centre in Kensington Palace Gardens. His route lay directly through the Neptune assembly area, and he was deliberately permitted to see immense build-ups of armor, shipping and aircraft. He dined with Patton, who was introduced as the "C-in-C of FUSAG," and he was received by various divisional commanders, all of whom laid emphasis on the fact that they were going to land at Calais. But what he was not allowed to know was where he had been; he was told that he had traveled through southern and eastern England when in fact he had been in central, south and southwestern England. He had no way of telling (except by the sun) where he had actually been, for ever since the Battle of Britain all signposts had been removed, and so had all place names on police stations, local government offices, shops, railway stations, and the like.

Cramer then embarked on the Swedish ship *Gripsholm* for passage to a German port and reached Berlin on May 23, 1944. He reported first to General Kurt Zeitzler, the Chief of Staff of the German army, and then to OKW at Berchtesgaden. Then, after a period of leave and a medical check, he was posted as a special adviser to the headquarters of General Leo Baron Geyr von Schweppenburg, the C-in-C of the German Panzerarmee in the West. Both at Berchtesgaden and Paris, Cramer evidently informed his superiors of what he had seen in Britain—and where he had seen it. For Goering would state after the war: "One of our generals . . . had been captured by the British and subsequently returned to us by exchange. Before his release [by the British] he was thoroughly indoctrinated by them and shown the vast stores of matériel and equipment along the southern coast of England. He came back to us with all those impressions (and) . . . a defeatist attitude." This was exactly what the LCS and the CSM had intended. The Cramer stratagem was, for all its simplicity, one of the most important instruments of corroboration for the existence of FUSAG. For who would distrust the report of a full *Gen-*

eral der Panzertruppen with the Knight's Cross of the Iron Cross with Oak Leaves?

Then came "Copperhead," a deception operation which was designed to reinforce the threat of an Allied invasion in the south of France. A romanticized version of the operation would become widely known after the war as the story of "Monty's Double." "The truth," according to Lieutenant Colonel J. V. B. Jervis-Reid, "was somewhat less romantic." It began on March 14, 1944, when, by chance, Jervis-Reid, the deputy chief of the CSM, happened to see a photograph of Lieutenant Meyrick Edward Clifton James, of the Royal Army Pay Corps stationed at Leicester, in the *News Chronicle*. James, in peacetime a minor actor on the English provincial stage, had appeared at an armed services theatrical show at the Comedy Theatre in London and the caption read: "You're wrong—His name is James!" For, as was quite evident in the photograph, James bore a very close resemblance to Montgomery.

Jervis-Reid conceived a scheme in which James would impersonate Montgomery. But at first the case did not look very promising; Montgomery was a strict teetotaler and James, investigation showed, suffered from serious bouts of alcoholism. Nevertheless, Jervis-Reid decided to pursue his scheme. He saw James at Leicester, gave him lunch, and explained that he wished to use him in a propaganda film to be made by the Army Kinematograph Service. James's reaction to the proposition betrayed much of the essence of his personality—a personality that was quite unlike that of Montgomery's arrogant self-assurance. As James would write afterwards: "I had an imaginary preview of a thrilling screen drama in which a glamorous enemy spy spreads alarm and confusion by vamping a pay clerk and persuades him to falsify the accounts." That, however, was not what Jervis-Reid had in mind. Despite his reservations, he "took rather a liking to the sad little fellow," and decided that, with close supervision and encouragement, James might work out. He arranged with his commanding officer to allow the paymaster to come to London on special duties; and James soon arrived for what was intended to be the biggest performance of his career.

The Copperhead plan proposed that James impersonate Montgomery and, under the direction of the CSM and A-Force, be paraded through Gibraltar and Algiers shortly before D-Day. The objectives were three: to lead the Germans to believe that, with Montgomery out of Britain, the invasion would not be launched across the Channel in the first week of June, as other reports and signs might indicate; to lead the Germans to believe that when the Neptune fleet sailed, it was just another exercise; and to pin down the four armored divisions (two of them SS) stationed south of the Loire by making the Germans believe that Montgomery was in command of Allied military operations from Africa and Italy against southern France.

James was separated both from his wife and from the bottle; and he was told he was impersonating Montgomery as part of training for a film production. He settled down well to the task of studying Montgomery from a distance, and then the two men were brought face-to-face aboard the C-in-C's personal train. James would recount: "The likeness struck me as uncanny. . . . On the stage it is something if you can resemble a man after using every artifice of make-up, but in this case there was no need for false eyebrows, padded cheeks, or anything of that kind." James had lost one of his fingers; but in all other physical respects, he and Montgomery seemed to be products of the same template. Their stances, build and walk were almost identical; and James found that he could imitate Montgomery's rapid, somewhat squeaky diction without trouble. As important, Jervis-Reid saw that James could develop Montgomery's air of authority. With that, he decided to go ahead with Copperhead—but still without telling James of the real purpose of the impersonation.

The paymaster was now introduced to the minutiae of his role, especially to such cocktail party and dinner table matters as Churchill's hours, Roosevelt's health, Eisenhower's ability, Smith's ulcer, Bradley's competence, Brooke's temper. Then James was outfitted by Myer and Mortimer, the military tailors, in a well-cut battledress with the scarlet gorgets of the Imperial General Staff, epaulets that included a general's crossed swords, four rows of decorations and honors, a black beret with two badges, the heavy Veldtschoen that Montgomery wore, a gold chain and fob, some handkerchiefs with the initials "BLM," a sheepskin flying jacket and a natty little cane. A trustworthy makeup artist was called in, trimmed James's mustache a shade, brushed up his eyebrows to make them bristle like Montgomery's and applied a touch of greasepaint to make his temples appear a little grayer. Now the likeness was indeed uncanny.

James was at last told what his mission was going to be—with the news that Montgomery had insisted that if James was going to impersonate him then he must be paid like him. But this did not smother James's alarm. He was, he would write, "overcome by the worst fit of stage fright I had yet had . . . I thought I looked as much like a successful general as a hypnotised rabbit." Nevertheless, he agreed to go through with the charade; and during the late afternoon of May 25, 1944, he was dressed, his false finger was put on, his beret set at the right angle, and then, traveling in a staff car, he was taken to the airfield at Northolt. With the minimum of flourish (but enough to permit gossip to circulate that it was Montgomery going on a tour), James boarded a Liberator and took off for Gibraltar. There was only one detail that had been overlooked; James, Jervis-Reid would recall, had hidden a hip flask of gin in his handkit.

The flight was due to land at Gibraltar shortly before breakfast time on May 26; and to make sure that James was fit and fresh for the morning, he was given a sleeping draught. Then everyone settled down for the night. But James got up again, perhaps because of the extreme cold, and went to the toilet in the rear of the aircraft. He was not missed at first, but when he was, his escort went after him—and found James nipping the gin. The pint flask was half empty. Worse, through the interaction of the gin and the sleeping draught, James was noticeably unsteady on his feet. Gibraltar was now only two hours away, and unless James could be sobered up quickly, it would be quite evident to everyone—not least the Liberator crew, which was not party to the stratagem—that the whole thing was a trick. Montgomery's loathing for alcohol and tobacco was as celebrated as the two badges on his beret. It was an emergency, and James was subjected to treatment that he was not likely to forget. His body was bared to the icy slipstream coming through the plughole in one of the cabin windows, he was made to vomit, he was kept walking up and down, he was thoroughly massaged and slapped, he was doused in cold water, and he was given a shave—in case he nicked himself. By the time the Liberator landed at Gibraltar, James was quite sober and, chastened, ready to begin his performance. Copperhead had been saved—for the moment.

When James disembarked, he gave the "Monty salute" to the small but impressive reception party, some men around the aircraft shouted "Up Monty!", the Spaniards working in the area were allowed to get a good look at the general, and then he was driven away to spend the night at Government House. The Governor, General Sir Ralph T. Eastwood, a man who had been at Sandhurst with Montgomery and knew all he had to know about Copperhead in order to cooperate convincingly, greeted him and there seemed little doubt that his arrival at both the airport and Government House was observed by German agents. Further, Eastwood gave a small party that evening at which "Montgomery" was introduced to two Spanish bankers, one of whom was thought to have connections with the SD, and they overheard James talking in a loud voice about "Plan 303." To the gratification of the A-Force representative on the spot, it was not long before the local counterintelligence office telephoned to state that all Gibraltar was abuzz with news that Montgomery was staying with the Governor, that he was talking about a "Plan 303," and that he was on his way the next morning to a conference at Algiers.

Driving back to the airfield the following morning—along a route which took the car through British engineers who were working on the roads—James was again put on public view. There were loud cries of "Good old Monty!" and "Up Monty!" as he flashed that famous salute. There were more such cries as the car swept through the main gates of the airfield, the guards gave a snappy present arms, and James got out close to his aircraft. Ceremonies were kept to a minimum, just as if a real general was traveling on active service. But to give time for a crowd to gather and observe the departure, the Liberator was allowed to develop a minor gremlin. Eastwood took James to the airport canteen for a cup of tea while the aircraft was being inspected, and there, James contrived to leave one of his "BLM" handkerchiefs for a Spanish servant to pick up, and within earshot of civilians, he again began to talk about "Plan 303." Finally, the aircraft was ready, and after a few last words with Eastwood, James boarded, the doors were closed and, within minutes, the Liberator was flying along the Queen of Spain's Chair on course for Algiers. So far, James's performance had been distinctly good, even brilliant. It seemed almost impossible for the Germans not to have known about "Montgomery's" visit; Algeciras, just across the bay from Gibraltar, was a main Abwehr outpost.

At Algiers, James was received with rather more ceremony at Maison Blanche airfield. Some French *spahis* formed a guard of honor; the huge figure of the Supreme Commander, General Sir Henry Maitland Wilson, could be seen towering like a pyramid out of the shimmering heat haze; and the British, American and French staff was formed up for James to meet. Then he was driven off to his quarters in the St. George Hotel overlooking the city. It was not long before all Algiers knew that Montgomery was in town; and from time to time his staff car, a pennant flying, outriders on both sides, was to be seen hurtling through the streets to one meeting or another. But then, the most incredible stories began to circulate at Eisenhower's headquarters in London that "Montgomery" had been seen staggering around the streets of Algiers with a cigar in his mouth. Whether or not the stories were true, "Montgomery," quite suddenly and for reasons that were never given out, vanished and Copperhead came to a rapid end.

Whatever had happened at Algiers, James was returned to a lieutenant's uniform, pay and privileges, and he was flown home not in his own personal aircraft but in the bucket seat of a DC-3 courier plane. At London, he was told that if he breathed a word of the operation he would be court-martialed; and he soon found himself back at his paymaster's desk. There, he encountered a new set of problems, for when he was unable to explain his absence, his colleagues began to gossip in the mess that he had been off on a bender, and his commanding officer wanted to court-martial him for being absent without leave. The War Office increased the confusion by telephoning James's commanding officer, who had been told nothing of the impersonation, to ask why a mere lieutenant had been drawing a general's pay and allowances. It was hinted that James had been fraudulent; and finally, a rumor spread that he had been in the Tower of London, arrested on suspicion of espionage.

It was not until the war was over that James could explain what he had done during those five weeks away from his desk. And then, in a ghostwritten memoir and a film called *I Was Monty's Double,* the most extravagant claims were made by him and on his behalf for the success of Copperhead. The facts were somewhat different. Nothing would appear in Abwehr documents captured after the war to show that the Germans had taken into their calculations the fact that "Montgomery" had visited the Mediterranean theater during this period. They were concerned about the threat of an Allied invasion in the south of France, but that concern was based on other, weightier, less melodramatic exploits—for example, the Vendetta comings and goings at Oran of the assault-trained U.S. 91st Infantry Division. But nothing was lost by Copperhead. The CSM had simply staged a performance—perhaps James's greatest performance—to an empty house.

Far more successful in aggravating German fear of an invasion of southern France was an operation called "Royal Flush." In a diplomatic maneuver conducted at the express instructions of Brooke, Marshall, Hull and Eden, the American and British ambassadors at Madrid called upon the Spanish Foreign Minister, General don Francisco Gómez Jordaña, to request the use of facilities at the port of Barcelona for the evacuation of Allied casualties in "impending operations." At the same time American and British diplomats appeared among the wharfingers of Barcelona, asking questions about the port's capacity to handle food and "other supplies," berthing arrangements and billeting facilities for surgical and nursing personnel. To all appearances, the Allies wished to turn the "Manchester of Spain" into a hospital for some great campaign shortly to be undertaken on the other side of the Golfe du Lion in southern France, a campaign that was indeed planned but for a later date. Would the Spanish government cooperate? The answer reached the Germans as quickly as it reached the Allies; yes Generalissimo Franco would be pleased to provide suitable space at Barcelona for 2000 hospitalized men and their attendants together with all dock, labor, warehouse and other facilities of the port. When this information was allied to intelligence about the activities of the American 91st Infantry Division, to the rapidly growing size of the French 1st Army in North Africa—an operation that was costing the United States $1.2 billion—and to the incessant prowling of reconnaissance ships and aircraft, OKW decided to keep its entire Army of the Riviera in place for the time being—including its panzer divisions.

Well before the Copperhead charade had run its course, Eisenhower had issued the last of a series of orders that marked the end of the Neptune preparatory period. After a long and careful study of the tides, the phases of the moon, the hours of daylight and the currents, Allied planners had agreed that only three days in early June— the 5th, the 6th and the 7th—filled all the basic requirements of Neptune. "Y-Day," that day when everything must be ready for the assault, was set for the 1st of June, and its code word was "Halcyon." June 5 was selected as the day of the assault, but the 6th and 7th would also be acceptable if bad weather interfered on the 5th. If the expedition could not sail on any one of these three days for any reason —particularly the weather—the next period during which all the natural factors would combine to favor Neptune would be between the 19th and the 22nd of June.

No one could predict what the weather might be during that first week in June. But with Halcyon set, Eisenhower ordered the great concentration of military force to begin in the counties of Cornwall, Devon, Somerset, Gloucestershire, Wiltshire, Dorset, Sussex and Surrey. On May 18, 1944, convoys—often 100 miles long—started to snake their way down quiet English roads to the embarkation points. Tanks with bridges over their turrets, and arms to lay them across ditches; tanks with trailers and strange nozzles to blast German positions with liquid fire; tanks with great bundles of wood overhead to lay in culverts and permit other tanks to move across; tanks with flails of chains to cut passages through minefields; armored cars, jeeps, ambulances, mobile headquarters, field kitchens, mobile hospitals, weapons carriers, half-tracks, Dodge and Bedford trucks by the thousands; mobile wireless and radar stations, anti-aircraft guns, self-propelled artillery, tank trucks—weapons and vehicles of every shape, every size, for every purpose, and in an abundance never before seen anywhere, advanced into the concentration areas to be loaded into the largest fleet in the history of maritime affairs. Yet such was the miasma of secrecy and deception that there were many who believed—as did Hitler—that the whole affair was mere shadowboxing. Eisenhower's diarist recorded on May 18: "Whitman [of the New York *Daily News*], a veteran war correspondent . . . told me that some correspondents believe there will not be an invasion, that talk of one is a giant hoax."

As the troops concentrated and tensions mounted, there were many portents and alarms. A Finnish professor announced that a comet would shortly appear over Europe, and Berlin radio urged the German people to ignore the old superstition that the phenomenon portended catastrophe. The women of Caddington in the Chilterns swore they saw the Angel of Mons in the night sky, just as it had been seen before the great battles in Flanders in the First World War. They refused to believe it when they were told that the vision was no more than a combination of flares and searchlights being tested to illuminate the ground at night. The world stood still for an hour on the evening of May 27 when a woman announcer on Berlin radio interrupted a program to declare: "Ladies and gentlemen, we have sensational news. Stand by for it later in this program. . . ." But the tension eased when Berlin radio later announced: "And now to the important news. In just a few moments you will hear a very talented Berlin artist play on a violin that was made in 1626."

The fears of ordinary people were magnified by the absence of news, but apprehension was no less great among those who knew all about Neptune. The Supreme Commander told his doctor that he was suffering from an almost intolerable ringing in the ear—a sign of extreme nervous tension. His diarist wrote: "Ike looks worn and tired. The strain is telling on him. He looks older now than at any time since I have been with him." And Eisenhower himself wrote in a letter to his friend General Brehon B. Somervell, in Washington:

   . . . tension grows and everybody gets more on edge. This time, because of the stakes involved, the atmosphere is probably more electric than ever before . . . we are not merely risking a tactical defeat; we are putting the whole works on one number. A sense of humor and a great faith, or else a complete lack of imagination, are essential to sanity.

Napoleon or Wellington might have expressed himself better, but the sense would have been the same.

Only Montgomery seemed quite impervious; like a monk, he worked and prayed in his caravan, venturing forth into the sunlight to speak to his men of the "holy crusade" on which they were about to embark. Other generals were apprehensive. On May 12, 1944, Smith had expressed the view that "our chances of holding the beachhead, particularly after the Germans get their buildup, are only fifty-fifty." Fifty-fifty—and it had taken the entire military, industrial, economic and intellectual resources of the Anglo-Saxon world four years just to mount the expedition.

Apprehension was manifested in different ways among the assault troops in the tented cities on the moors and in the valleys and forests of southwestern and southern England. They were well aware of the bitter fighting and bloodshed going on in Italy. Almost 150,000 men had been killed, wounded or declared missing since September 3, 1943, when the Allies first landed there. How much worse was Neptune going to be? For the Germans in France were ten times as numerous as they were in Italy; they had had four years since Dunkirk —four years almost to the day—in which to fortify the Channel coast. Some of the assault troops, it seemed, no longer cared what would happen to them. There were signs of severe morale problems among others, problems that would worsen if they were kept idle and waiting too long. Nor was Eisenhower always impressed by the officers he met during his visits to the assault divisions. His diarist would record: "I am concerned over the absence of toughness and alertness of the young American officers whom I saw on this trip. . . . They are as green as growing corn. How will they act in battle? . . . A good many of the full colonels also give me a pain. They are fat, gray and oldish. Most of them wear the Rainbow Ribbon of the last war and are still fighting it." Men of all ranks knew that many would be killed or wounded, burned or drowned. But if they were fearful, their mood, in the main, was one of compliance, as if the Far Shore and its dangers existed in dimensions other than time and place.

No expense or effort had been spared to ensure that Neptune would succeed. Eisenhower would command the finest expeditionary force ever to leave any shore, and he knew more about his enemy than any other commander in history. But no intelligence in war can ever be complete. There were gaps in SHAEF's knowledge, and one of them concerned the 352nd Infantry Division, a first-rate German fighting formation—despite the commanding general's claim that most of its newcomers were so undernourished that he had to build them up with special rations of Normandy buttermilk. This division had been located near St. Lô, at the base of the neck of the Cherbourg peninsula. But in May, it had inched forward and taken up a position overlooking what would become Omaha. Thus, instead of the two divisions of understrength and under-equipped infantry which the Americans believed were in the Atlantic Wall on the invasion coast of Calvados, there were three; and instead of the four battalions of infantry which the Americans expected to encounter at Omaha, there were two regiments, with a third close behind the coast in reserve. Furthermore, these men had created what an American naval historian would call "the best imitation of hell for an invading force that American troops (would encounter) anywhere." But not until the eve of D-Day would the Americans discover that the 352nd had moved up. And here was the mystery. On May 23, 1944, working with precisely the same intelligence that was available to the Americans, the British warned their forces that the 352nd might be encountered on D-Day. Then, on D–2, Brigadier E. T. Williams, Montgomery's intelligence officer, again warned in the *21 Army Group Weekly Neptune Intelligence Review,* which was circulated to the Americans as well as the British, that "It should not be surprising if we discovered that (the) 352nd Division has one regiment up and two to play." Granted the intelligence was only speculative, but it would later be suggested that it was withheld from the American commanders, with Eisenhower's knowledge and approval, in order not to increase the morale problems of the U.S. 1st and 29th divisions by informing them too far ahead that they would be facing a first-rate infantry division that had been tempered in the fires of the Russian front—as, indeed, had been the 352nd's lot before it arrived in Normandy.

Equally mysterious were the silence and inactivity of the enemy on the eve of D-Day. Where were the secret weapons? What were the Luftwaffe and the Kriegsmarine up to? The only German aerial activity just before the invasion was an occasional reconnaissance flight, the odd nuisance raid on London to keep everyone awake, and, on the night of May 30, a single attack in which a few bombs fell and caused casualties at an American ordnance base near Falmouth. Everyone assumed the Germans were saving their strength for the great contest on

D-Day; and when the Allied commanders obtained information that the enemy might use gas or some bacteriological weapon, they reiterated their standing orders concerning the detection and combatting of such attacks. Here lay another task for Bronx. She was induced to write a letter to her controller stating that the Allies had very large stocks of a germ warfare agent that created conditions like the bubonic plague. This story, intended to warn Hitler that if he used gas or germ warfare the Allies would retaliate, was supported by reports from other XX-Committee agents. But the troops need not have worried; Hitler, with his personal experience in the First World War of what it was like to be gassed, had no intention of using such weapons on D-Day.

It was now—on the eve of Halcyon time to assess the effects of Bodyguard and Fortitude. There was encouraging news from Italy. On May 23, an American patrol near Valmontone captured a German headquarters vehicle hidden in an olive grove, and papers found in armored cabinets were immediately sent to Allied headquarters at the royal palace in Caserta. When they were analyzed by G2 and A-Force, they revealed that Bodyguard was a triumph of strategic deception. For this was the German order of battle in May—and it would not change by D-Day:

Russian front: 122 infantry-type divisions, 25 panzer divisions plus one brigade; 17 miscellaneous divisions plus one brigade.

Italian and Balkans fronts: 37 infantry divisions plus two brigades; nine panzer and four miscellaneous divisions.

Western front including The Netherlands, Denmark and Norway: 64 infantry divisions plus one regiment; 12 panzer divisions plus two brigades; 12 miscellaneous divisions.

Reserves in Germany: three infantry divisions plus one brigade; one panzer division plus two brigades; four miscellaneous divisions plus two brigades.

In short, the Wehrmacht had dispersed its forces in response to Bodyguard's threats, a fact that was confirmed by Ultra; and it had no worthwhile reserves.

Ultra also revealed, in an intercept on the evening of May 30, that Fortitude, too, was a success—at least so far. A report of a conversation that Baron Oshima had held with Hitler at Berchtesgaden was decrypted, and it disclosed that Hitler still believed in the Fortitude and Quicksilver stories that there were eighty to ninety divisions in

Britain, with seven or eight airborne divisions; and he continued to hold the view that, while the invasion might well start elsewhere, for example in Normandy or Brittany, it would culminate in a main attack against the coast between the Seine and the Somme—the Pas de Calais. But what of the tactical situation in and around Normandy? How were Rundstedt and Rommel disposing of the forces under their command—particularly the panzers? Agents' reports concerning the 1st SS Panzer Korps Adolf Hitler, the most powerful German armored formation in the West, were encouraging. It was almost ludicrously simple to detect the movements of German divisions. As General Munro McCloskey, the commander of a USAAF special air squadron, would relate after the war, all that was necessary was to watch the laundry. The French intelligence service had gone into the laundry business and, through low prices and good work, had succeeded in capturing the custom of the German army. When the Germans moved, they collected all their laundry, and left behind forwarding addresses if it was not ready. The *Feldgrau* might be going to Valhalla, but they were not prepared to go without their linen. This form of surveillance revealed that, at Y-Day, neither of the corps's two SS panzer divisions, "Das Reich" at Toulouse and the "Adolf Hitler" between Brussels and Antwerp, had changed its position. This was regarded as significant intelligence at Supreme Headquarters, for if the Germans had seen through Fortitude, these powerful units would surely be moving toward the Calvados coast.

On the other hand, there was disquieting intelligence from Normandy. Rommel had suddenly made new dispositions in and around the Cherbourg peninsula that showed he might at least have obtained partial knowledge of Allied intentions. The 91st Airlanding Division, specialists in fighting paratroopers, and the 6th Parachute Regiment had moved inexplicably into exactly the area around St. Mère-Église where the American paratroop divisions were to land on D-Day. This movement was reported on May 29, and Leigh-Mallory, C-in-C of the air forces that would support Neptune on D-Day and the man who had prophesied disaster at Dieppe, delivered a solemn warning to Eisenhower. The arrival of the 91st, he said, meant that Allied paratrooper formations would be cut to pieces and that perhaps 50 per cent of the air transport force involved—some five hundred planes— would be lost. Eisenhower responded that, whatever the risks, the operation must proceed; without it, Neptune itself could not succeed.

Adding to the fear that, after all, the Germans had penetrated Neptune's strategies, was an appreciation of their estimate of Allied intentions in the West. Promulgated on May 25 by the British Joint Intelligence Committee, it was so secret that it was distributed on an "eyes only" basis to the actual force commanders and, in the Mediterranean, personally to Wilson, the Supreme Commander there. This appreciation, which seemed to spell a bloodbath in Normandy, stated:

1. *Area of main assault.* Main assault is expected against Northern coast of France from Boulogne to include Cherbourg inclusive. Although German High Command will until our assault takes place reckon with possibility that it will come across the Straits of Dover to Pas de Calais area, there is some evidence that Le Havre-Cherbourg areas [the actual Neptune area] . . . (are) regarded as likely and perhaps even the main point of assault.

That intelligence was bad enough, but if the JIC appreciation was accurate, then it seemed that the Germans also knew when to expect the invasion. "Enemy appreciates," the JIC signaled Wilson, "that Allied preparations are sufficiently advanced to permit operations any time now and that from the point of view of moonlight and tide first week in June is next likely period for assault." Neither was the JIC any more encouraging about the effectiveness of Vendetta's threats to the French Mediterranean coast, for as the report went on: "Enemy appreciates that while raids against French Mediterranean coast are possible at any time, Allied preparations for a major attack in this area are not yet completed." Similarly, the JIC doubted the effectiveness of Ironside's deceptions to threaten the Biscay coast. Only Fortitude North's operations against Norway, so it seemed to the JIC, were proving successful.

Under these circumstances, the code word for the next phase of the invasion—Halcyon—portended not tranquility and peace but the calm before a storm. It was issued to all formations at midnight May 31/June 1. Few knew that it had been issued; fewer still knew what it meant. But its consequences were felt throughout the land. As *The Times* (London) put it afterwards: "We have been as those speaking in whispers." All the multitudes of soldiers, sailors and airmen seemed to vanish. In the Queen's Head, the George and Dragon, the Star and Garter, the Good Queen Bess, the Sir Walter Raleigh, the Crown and Anchor, the George the Third, the Royal Steamer, the Wheatsheaf—in the pubs throughout England south of the line Humber-Mersey—for the first time in over a year only the locals came in to drink mild and bitter, to play dominoes and beer skittles. Silent Rapp, Skin Walbourne, Macadoo Machado, Lightning Ruberg—all the soldiers were gone. The troopers had stopped for a while, they had refreshed themselves, and now they had remounted and clattered on.

At Berchtesgaden, Hitler still retained absolute confidence in the outcome for Germany of the invasion. He believed that the invasions of North Africa had succeeded "only with the help of traitors." There would be, he said, no traitors in the West. Yet from time to time, at his noonday conference with his staff, he displayed sudden flashes of irritation and petulance at the Allies' stratagems. Following the diplomatic quarantine, for example, he declared that Allied invasion preparations were insolent posturing, a "completely bare-faced bluff." But petulant or not, Hitler was a better general than those around him, and a better military intellect than his enemies—Allied as well as German—gave him credit for. His critics had a tendency to sneer at what had become known as "Hitler's intuition." But between February and May of 1944, that intuition was at work to sniff out the secrets of Neptune—and it succeeded in a startling and dangerous fashion.

Hitler's conviction that the Allies' main assault would be directed against the Pas de Calais remained unchanged; but just as he had planned to invade England at more than one place in 1940, so it seemed probable that the Allies would have a similar strategy for their invasion in 1944. But where would these secondary and diversionary assaults come? Considerable thought was given to this question by *der Führer und Oberste Befehlshaber der Wehrmacht des Grossdeutschen Reichs*—as Hitler was thunderously styled in law; and at one time or another he saw threats—as the LCS and A-Force intended —everywhere from Petsamo to the Peloponnesus. But in February, Hitler grew sensitive to the dangers to Normandy and Brittany. On March 4, he regarded them as particularly threatened; and on May 6, following the noon conference, Jodl telephoned Blumentritt, a call that resulted in Blumentritt advising all headquarters that "The Führer attaches particular importance to Normandy and the defense of Normandy." Having commanded, he was obeyed—in the most thorough manner possible. Work on the fortifications along the Calvados coast was intensified, and the peninsula was reinforced with the troop movements that gave Leigh-Mallory such a fright. The mighty Panzer Lehr Armored Division was brought back from Hungary, whence it had gone to put down the rebellion, and the 21st Panzer Division was moved to Caen from Brittany. These were significant changes in the Normandy sector, changes that gave Eisenhower doubts about the sanctity of the secrets of Neptune. But at the same time Hitler did nothing to weaken the Pas de Calais front. It was from the Pas de Calais, in fact, that he intended to launch the secret weapon that the invasion armies had grown to fear. This was the V1, the ramjet 440-mph pilotless aircraft manufactured by Volkswagen at its Fallersleben plant, which cost only $600 to build and exploded with the force of a 4000-pound blockbuster bomb. The other V-weapons and the London gun had fallen short of expectations, and the production of the V1's was less than the 2000 rounds per month that had been visualized. Even so, Hitler was confident that they would turn the tide of battle, and on May 16, 1944, he issued orders concerning the bombardment of London. It was to be coordinated with heavy air attacks and an artillery bombardment of the British Channel towns by long-range conventional artillery in the Pas de Calais; and the exact time the offensive would begin was to be selected by Rundstedt, who would issue the code word "Junkroom." The 692 square miles of Greater London would be impossible to miss; the British capital would be turned into a flaming desert. Moreover, the flying bomb offensive would shatter the invasion before it had even sailed. But here again, Fortitude had infected the Fuehrer's thinking, for the V1 bombardment was tentatively scheduled to begin on or about June 16.

Hitler was less confident about the ability of another arm of the mighty Wehrmacht to repel an invasion, if and when it came. As he told Baron Oshima at Berchtesgaden on May 28, 1944, there was only one front about which he was really worried; and that was in the air. The Luftwaffe had fought the enormous air battles of the first months of 1944 with demonic energy and courage, but while the great numbers of aircraft that had been lost could be replaced, the loss of experienced aircrews left a gap in the ranks that could never be refilled. Operation Pointblank had achieved its objective. The Luftwaffe was beginning to buckle under the weight of Allied airpower. It was no longer able to defend Fortress Europe, and its aerial reconnaissance planes, which might have detected the fabrications of Fortitude and provided first warning of the approach of an invasion fleet, were rarely able to penetrate Allied defenses.

Hitler might also have been concerned about the Kriegsmarine. It, too, had been humbled by the Allied air forces—and Ultra. Yet it could at least alert German land commanders to the approach of Neptune. But Admiral Theodor Krancke, the German naval commander in the West, like other German commanders—and the Fuehrer himself —had based his counterinvasion strategy on preconceived notions of what the Allies intended to do. Krancke had made a long and thorough study of Allied amphibious warfare tactics and the natural conditions which must prevail before such a landing could take place. He believed that the Allies would attack during darkness, by moonlight, at full tide to permit the assault craft to sail in over obstacles, and in the immediate neighborhood of a large port but away from cliffs and shallow, rocky waters where currents were strong. He also believed that the Allies could and would not attack if the wind exceeded 24 knots, where visibility was less than 3 miles, and when the wave heights were higher than between 5 and 8 feet. Obedient to this philosophy, Krancke's main defensive measures—minefields and coastal artillery—were generally concentrated in areas other than those of the Bay of the Seine.

But Krancke was wrong, disastrously wrong; the Allies would attack at daybreak shortly after low tide, far from a large port, and at some points beneath sheer or high cliffs and in reefy waters where currents were strong. Moreover, the weather parameters, under certain circumstances, were wider than Krancke believed—due, doubtless, to some of the XX-Committee reports from England. As a result, the Kriegsmarine would be watchful for a different set of conditions from those which the Allies required.

Rundstedt was, by Y-Day, also uncertain about what the Allies intended, and his appreciations to OKW reflected his uncertainty. On April 24, 1944, he had written that he thought Normandy was in the danger zone; but his conception of the threatened area was very wide. It stretched about 175 miles (as the crow flies) from Caen to the mouth of the Scheldt. He had narrowed his focus by May 15 when he had stressed that the Allies "need to win large and capacious harbours"; and for that reason, he advised OKW, "Le Havre and Cherbourg are primarily to be considered for this purpose, Boulogne and Brest secondarily. The attempt to form a bridgehead rapidly on the [Cherbourg] peninsula in the first phase would therefore seem very natural." He came closer still to the truth on May 29 when, having examined the pattern of Allied air operations against the Seine bridges, he again concluded that the Allies might land in Normandy. In general, however, Rundstedt thought that the Allies might go for Cherbourg, but that their main thrust would come in the Pas de Calais.

Rundstedt's appreciations may well have been influenced by another clever stitch in the tapestry of Fortitude. Just as the Allies watched the 1st SS Panzer Korps of Sepp Dietrich because they were sure that these divisions would be committed to the Channel coast as soon as the Germans received any positive intelligence of Allied intentions, so Rundstedt had closely followed Garbo's reports concerning the location of the Guards Armoured Division, a crack British formation. His reasoning seems to have been that no general as blue-blooded as the commanding officer of the Guards Armoured, General Sir Allan Henry Shafto Adair (the 6th baronet, Harrow, Grenadier Guards, later governor of Harrow and Ensign of the King's Bodyguard of the Yeomen of the Guard), would ever allow himself to be very far from the main battle at H-Hour. But here, aware that snobbery often affected Rundstedt's judgment, the CSM played a merry ball. While proletarian armored divisions were moved into the concentration areas in great secrecy, the Guards Armoured was seen (and heard) moving from Brompton in Yorkshire to Hove on the Sussex coast as a component of FUSAG, not of Montgomery's army group. Between April 30 and May 28, 1944, in a series of reports which earned him the congratulations of Himmler, Garbo had related that there was considerable trouble in the divisional headquarters of the Guards Armoured. While on the road, the baggage had become mixed up and one unit of the division had received the mess silver of another. Moreover, to support this story, any German signaler listening in to the plain-language traffic on the division's wireless net would have heard sulphurous dialogue about the silver between generals, and triangularization would have revealed that the sharp words were coming from the FUSAG area.

Nevertheless, on Y-Day, Rundstedt's command, OB-West, considered that D-Day might be imminent, and its judgment was based on two main factors: the air battle and the state of the resistance. In the case of the former, Allied air activity had increased greatly, and the Germans detected that its main thrust was the destruction of supply lines. But the campaign was carried out in such a way that they could not deduce where the Allies would land. Resistance operations were plotted in the same way as air operations, and the parachuting of agents, weapons, ammunition and explosives at night—as well as the exchange of signals between aircraft and the ground—were extensively observed and charted. But here again, while the Germans detected an increase in these operations, they revealed nothing significant about the time or the place of the invasion. The German high command in the West was almost as ignorant about what the Allies would do as was the humblest *Feldgrau*.

Only Rommel and his intelligence officer, Staubwasser, had penetrated, but only partly, the smoke screens of Fortitude. On May 31, the two men met in Rommel's study at the Château de La Roche Guyon, and both felt sure that FHW had exaggerated its estimates of Allied strength within the British Isles. Further, Rommel was now certain that there would be only one landing, which would come either around the mouth of the Somme or of the Seine. There would not be, as OKW and OB-West estimated, "a number of major landings and diverting operations." It was also the OKW/OB-West consensus that the Allies would attack first with airborne troops, which could land only by day or at dusk, and that the aerial assault would be followed by major seaborne landings in darkness and at high tide. But because of the nature and extent of his "devil's garden," Rommel knew that it would be necessary to land assault engineers first to cut passages through the obstacles for the assault shipping. Such sapping could take place only in daylight and at low tide. Therefore, contrary to OKW and OB-West, Rommel and Staubwasser agreed that the airborne assault would come by moonlight, and the seaborne landings would take place at daybreak, just after low tide.

But when would the invasion come? The Allies certainly had the strength to make the assault wherever they wanted, said Rommel; but they could not choose *when* they would invade. That would be determined by natural conditions. Both men agreed that the Allies would require a guarantee of at least six days of settled weather—good June weather. Rommel then declared that there were only two periods in June when the moon, daybreak and tides would all combine to favor the operation. The first was between the 5th and 7th of the month, the second between the 12th and the 14th.

Rommel planned to go see the Fuehrer on the 5th to make another appeal for control of all the Wehrmacht's armored forces in the West, some of which Hitler had retained under his own command. If Rommel was to succeed in his plan to "Dunkirk" the Allies at H-Hour, he could not wait until the enemy had already established a foothold. He would need all the German panzer units at his immediate disposal to counter the landing; requesting their use through the normal channels would mean inevitable and possibly fatal delays.

Through Ultra the Allies had been able to read Rommel's angry protests about the disposition of the panzer forces. They had followed the debate as it went up to Hitler; they read the decision when it came down. Hitler retained control of four powerful panzer divisions in the West, which would constitute a reserve and would be held where they were. As Winterbotham would recall: "This, of course, was the plum we had been waiting for; had the final decision gone the other way it would have seriously jeopardized the chances of success of (Neptune) as it then stood."

Rommel intended to reopen the debate in person when he visited the Fuehrer at Berchtesgaden. But he realized he could not be absent from his command on the 5th—unless the weather was bad. Then he would go.

14

The Eve of D-Day

ON MAY 29, 1944, Eisenhower joined his battle headquarters at Southwick House, a mansion amid parkland on the lip of the hills above Portsmouth. Awaiting him was a telegram from Marshall in Washington. It announced that the American Chiefs of Staff would fly to London on June 7 "to be on hand in case major decisions by the Combined Chiefs of Staff were necessary" concerning Neptune, and to be present if "two possible eventualities" occurred which "might require action." The first was the "possible development of the situation where we have a very insecure hold on a beachhead and decision may be required as to whether to withdraw or to continue the operation." The second was that critical decisions might have to be taken "seven to eight days after D-Day, at which time a major German counterattack might be expected." For all its prosaic wording, the telegram reflected the grave anxieties of the Allied high command.

It was a Monday and the weather that weekend had been as gentle as a shepherd's call—as indeed it had been for much of the month. The skies were clear, the Channel smooth and blue, the winds calm, the moon in the right quarter. Having examined the charts for the next five days, and fairly satisfied that the weather would hold during the D-Day period, Eisenhower directed that the signal "Exercise Hornpipe plus six" be sent to all Commanders-in-Chief. It meant that D-Day was set for June 5, 1944. Eisenhower and his meteorological staff in the office next to the operations room hoped that it would stay that way. For the great machine called Neptune was beginning to turn. The troops and the vehicles of war were moving with precision down to the assault fleets, while follow-up formations were replacing them in the encampments under the woods and along the lanes of southern England. Every piece was being fitted into place for transfer across the

Channel to the Far Shore. But all the schemes of men notwithstanding, one factor alone would determine when, and if, the Allied armies would arrive at their destination in good order for immediate and perhaps decisive battle—the weather. Would the weather hold? Everything depended upon the facts contained in the six-figure code groups which flooded in from the weather-reporting ships, aircraft and stations arcing from Nova Scotia through Greenland, Iceland, the Faroes, Ulster, down to the Azores and the Canaries and across to Bermuda and the Caribbean.

It was lunchtime on May 29 when a group of signals came in from an aircraft plotting weather over Newfoundland which showed that the weather was beginning to change off the east coast of America. It was almost precisely at this same time that Eisenhower authorized a second important signal to be sent—"Halcyon plus 4." The code word, taken from the name of the bird of ancient fable that could calm the winds and the waves, meant to Marshall in Washington that D-Day was still scheduled for June 5. But even as it was being punched onto tape for radioteleprinting across the Atlantic, the weathermen began to plot the great whorls of what would come to be called "L5"—a disturbance that threatened Neptune itself.

There was disquiet among the members of Eisenhower's weather syndicate as L5 began to take shape. The syndicate included meteorological officers from the air forces, the Admiralty, the Air Ministry, the British weather central at Dunstable, and the U.S. Weather Services, all of whom communicated with the director, Group Captain John Stagg, an RAF meteorologist, and his deputy, D. N. Yates, an American air force colonel, over scrambled telephone conference lines to their headquarters which had been set up under the trees near Southwick House. All members of the syndicate received the same data and were expected to provide Eisenhower with a five-day forecast. But that in itself had proved to be an almost impossible task. For as G. K. N. Douglas, the leading British meteorologist and occasionally the spokesman for Dunstable, warned Stagg: "Unless Channel weather in 1944 turns out to be wholly exceptional, the production of regular forecasts which have any true scientific validity or worthwhile dependability is likely to be out of the question for more than two days ahead, or even, at times, more than twenty-four hours." Given this difficulty, in addition to the wide range of individual interpretations and opinions that prevailed among the group, the men of Stagg's syndicate rarely found themselves in complete agreement, and their squabbles often made them sound like fishwives rather than scientists. But now, in the crucial days that preceded Neptune, Eisenhower needed not arguments and opinions but an accurate assessment of what the weather over the Channel would be. It was up to Stagg to provide it.

The first signs of a crisis appeared on Thursday, June 1, as the ships of the heavy bombardment squadrons were preparing for their departure from Scapa and the sea lochs of Ulster and western Scotland the following day. There were enough indications of disturbances forming out in the Atlantic for Stagg to warn the Supreme Command that the weather prospects for the 4th, 5th and probably the 6th were not good. But the weather centers, he reported, were not sufficiently confident about the outlook to say more. Bull, SHAEF's operations officer, made the comment: "For heaven's sake, Stagg, get it sorted out by tomorrow morning before you come to the Supreme Commander's conference. General Eisenhower is a very worried man."

Stagg spent the rest of Thursday in constant telephone contact with the weather centers, but the data coming in from the special chain of warships and aircraft out in the Atlantic became more confused. Several deep depressions were forming rapidly between Newfoundland and Ireland, and the members of the syndicate could not agree on a forecast. Some believed that there would be no bad weather over the British Isles, some that there would be bad weather but that it would not involve the Channel or the Western Approaches, and the rest that a long period of disturbed weather in the Channel was inevitable. That night Stagg and Yates "wearied ourselves with discussion into a restless sleep. . . ."

The two men were up again before first light on Friday, June 2, examining the changes that had been reported while they slept. It was clear that the prospect had darkened, and as Stagg would recall of the charts lying on the table before him: "The whole north Atlantic ocean area appeared to be filled with a succession of depressions. . . . In all the charts for the 40 or 50 years I had examined I could not recall one which at this time of the year remotely resembled this chart in the number and intensity of depressions it portrayed at one time."

At the morning telephone conference, the weathermen again engaged in their usual wrangling and failed to arrive at a unanimous forecast. Stagg and Yates tended to support the view that the Channel would not escape very bad weather, with gale force winds and low cloud. Eisenhower was advised of this forecast later that morning, but Stagg decided against warning him of the dangerous disagreements between individual members of the syndicate. The Supreme Commander had problems already sufficiently arduous without burdening him with more. But another meeting was called for 9:30 that evening, and the moment was rapidly approaching when Eisenhower must decide whether or not to proceed with D-Day on the 5th.

By the evening telephone conference, the weather experts were still divided. Part of the syndicate was not only confident but certain that no bad weather would pass through the Channel, that cloud amounts would be small, and the wind speed would not exceed Force 4 throughout the period. This situation, the optimists declared, would hold from Sunday, June 3, through to Wednesday, June 7. But other members of the syndicate, including Stagg, thought the whole situation "untrustworthy." There was the potential for calamity in this disagreement, for if he accepted the optimists' opinion, passed it to the Supreme Commander, and he gave the order to proceed, the entire enterprise might be wrecked. Of the row that marked the conference, Stagg would note in his diary:

> Had it not been fraught with such potential tragedy, the whole business was ridiculous. In less than half-an-hour I was expected to present to General Eisenhower an "agreed" forecast for the next five days which covered the time of launching of the greatest military operation ever mounted (and) no two of the expert participants in the discussion could agree on the likely weather even for the next 24 hours . . . it was a desperate quandary from which I was saved only by the clock.

Stagg ran—literally—from the telephone conference to the Supreme Commander's conference.

Present in the bare, paneled room at Southwick House were Eisenhower, the three Commanders-in-Chief (Ramsay, Montgomery and Leigh-Mallory), their Chiefs of Staff, and the SHAEF chiefs of divisions. Breathless, Stagg opened the door and was greeted by Eisenhower with the words: "Well, Stagg, what have you for us this time?" Stagg, replying that the situation was now "potentially full of menace," gave his forecast: until at least Tuesday or Wednesday, the 6th and 7th of June, there would be much cloud and westerly winds of between Force 4 and 5. Eisenhower, who was still unaware of the disputes among the weathermen, pressed Stagg for his personal opinion, and Stagg—according to Tedder—replied: "If I answered that, Sir, I would be guessing, not behaving as your meteorological adviser."

Stagg and Yates then withdrew, half expecting news to reach them in the waiting room that the Supreme Commander had decided to postpone the launching of Neptune by twenty-four hours. As he waited, Stagg was possessed of terrible self-doubts. Had he been too pessimistic? If the Supreme Commander ordered a postponement, the first squadrons of the armada already at sea would have to scatter or turn back, and if they were spotted by enemy aircraft, surprise might be lost. But shortly, Bull came out of the meeting to tell Stagg that there would be no change of plans for the next twenty-four hours.

Stagg and Yates again spent a restless night, and at breakfast time on Saturday, June 3, Bull called at their quarters to ask whether anything new had developed. Stagg told him that there was no evidence of improvement. If anything, the weather was more complex. The outlook was "knife-edge marginal," and it could still "go either way by evening." Stagg later met Morgan by the lake in the park, and Morgan called out, "Good luck, Stagg; may all your depressions be nice little ones: but remember, we'll string you up from the nearest lamp post if you don't read the omens aright." Stagg would remember: "Though I could not foresee that happening whatever I did, the image haunted me, quite irrationally, that Saturday—and to this day it still does when under strain." For that Saturday was the day of the crucial decision. All the assault troops were now loading in the invasion craft, along with their tanks, guns and transport. Some convoys must begin to sail that evening if they were to be at the beaches on time at H-Hour, which was still set for Monday, June 5.

During the day, however, Stagg's despondency decreased, for he was proven correct in giving Eisenhower an adverse forecast for the 5th. That evening, he again barely reached the Supreme Commander's conference in time; and as he went into the meeting, Admiral Sir George Creasy, Ramsay's Chief of Staff, was heard to say, "There goes six foot two of Stagg and six foot one of gloom." It was meant well, but Stagg had nothing to say that would cheer the fifteen high commanders who were present. He outlined the weather picture, and then gave as the judgment of the syndicate the forecast that from June 4 until June 7 the weather in the Channel would be cloudy and stormy with winds of Force 5. The outlook after June 7 was uncertain, but Stagg thought there would be less persistent cloud once the cold front had cleared the Channel. After much question and answer, Eisenhower asked Stagg: "Now let me put this one to you. . . . Isn't there just a chance that you might be a bit more optimistic again tomorrow?" Stagg said there was no chance.

Stagg and Yates then withdrew to the anterooom; and an hour later,

Bull came out and stated that Eisenhower had made a provisional decision to postpone D-Day for twenty-four hours. But there would be a further meeting at 4:15 A.M. the next morning, Sunday, June 4, and Stagg and his syndicate must review the situation during the night and report again. Then, Eisenhower would make his final decision—to proceed or to postpone the operation.

When Stagg arrived at the 4:15 A.M. conference, he noted that the "tension in the room was palpable." The Supreme Commander was "serious and unsmiling," and at a nod from Eisenhower, Stagg informed the conference that there was no substantial change in his forecast. There was silence for a moment, and then after some discussion among the Commanders-in-Chief, the provisional decision of the night before was confirmed. Eisenhower told Smith to issue the code word to postpone D-Day by twenty-four hours—"Ripcord plus 24."

By this time, every ship (2010 in the American assault force, and 3323 in the British and Canadian) was in position, and every berth and every mooring in every port, river and creek was filled from Felixstowe on the North Sea to Milford Haven in Wales. Behind the assault forces were assembling those of the build-up, jamming the Bristol Channel, the Thames Estuary, the Humber, the Clyde and Belfast Lough—another thousand ships. Well over 2 million men—counting soldiers, sailors, airmen, and transportation and civil defense services —were in various stages of commitment to this first phase of D-Day. But now, through "Ripcord," the entire operation was placed in a state of suspended animation. It seemed inconceivable that the Germans would not detect the imminence of Neptune; it could almost be *sensed.*

Worse, major units were already at sea, including the heavy bombardment forces, the old merchantmen that would form the Mulberry breakwaters, and the seventeen convoys destined for Omaha and Utah beaches which were en route from their ports of embarkation in Cornwall and Devon. Ripcord caused little trouble to the heavy bombardment and Mulberry units; all they had to do was to mark time in the Irish Sea until they were given final orders. The danger lay with the small craft; one mine-sweeping force was only 35 miles from the Norman shore when it received the postponement order. It complied, and, astonishingly, the force was never detected by the Germans. Most of the convoys received the postponement order without difficulty and made about in the black, stormy night, although a number of the smaller, flat-bottomed landing craft were overturned and some lives were lost. But the message did not reach one convoy of 138 ships carrying troops of the U.S. 4th Infantry Division, and by 0900 on Sunday morning it was already 25 miles south of the Isle of Wight, steaming for the Far Shore. Unless the convoy was turned about, it would make its landfall off the Far Shore, there would be a disaster, and almost inevitably the security and surprise of Neptune would be lost.

Repeated efforts to contact the convoy by wireless had failed. Its speed was estimated at 8 knots, the sea was short and steep, and there were no naval craft in the vicinity capable of intercepting it. Aircraft were despatched, and flying at about 100 feet in fierce squalls, little Walrus pusher-engined biplanes hunted the convoy until it was spotted shortly before dark. One of the planes flew low over the commodore's ship to drop an official, signed and stamped message from naval headquarters, in cipher. But the canister missed and sank in the sea. The pilot of the Walrus scribbled a note instructing the commodore to return to anchor and refuel in Weymouth Bay, and then made a second pass. This time the canister landed on the ship. There was a danger that the commodore might ignore the message on the grounds of its informal wording, format and delivery, and for some forty-five minutes the ships steamed on. But finally the command ship ran up signals ordering the convoy to reverse. The disaster had been averted.

This was but the first of the events of that most extraordinary day in the history of the Supreme Command—Sunday, June 4, 1944. It was followed by news that Clark's army had captured Rome in what was a psychologically important but militarily hollow victory. Then Churchill's caravan of cars and motorcyclists arrived at Southwick House, filled their tanks, "diminished our supplies of Scotch like the devil," and disappeared into a storm that was, wrote Butcher, now raging in the Channel in "near-hurricane" proportions. Stagg awoke that morning after two or three hours' sleep in his tent, and as he walked over to the weather center, he noticed the clouds had thickened, the trees were swaying, and a wind of about Force 4 was running—just as he had predicted. The postponement of Neptune had been justified; but if there was no abatement in the weather, Neptune would have to be postponed again, not for one but for fourteen days. The moon and tides would then compel a fundamental change in the timing of the operation, and everyone recalled what had happened when the Dieppe raid was canceled and then remounted. Stagg knew that Eisenhower trusted him; and his forecast that day would almost certainly determine the fate of Neptune.

That morning as he examined the charts, Stagg saw that a cold front was moving toward the Channel that would pass through Portsmouth

later in the day or during the night. But this was not the only portent
he saw. While the general picture was extraordinarily confused, he
noted that one of the depressions in the Atlantic, at that time off Newfoundland, was intensifying and deepening, thus slowing its progres-
sion toward England. Stagg and Yates talked about the development
excitedly, for if their interpretation was correct, as Stagg would write:

> . . . then between the passage of the cold front and the approach of
> the depression there could be an interlude of improved weather, and
> this interlude if long enough and if it occurred at the right time might
> just allow the first two critical sets of assault landings to be launched,
> at dawn and at dusk, on the same day and that day could be Tuesday.

There was a danger that the Germans would also detect this devel
opment, but if they did not, they would surely believe that the weather
would remain too disturbed to permit an invasion, and Neptune would
catch them completely off guard. "Yes," Stagg wrote, "if it eventuated
and if the Supreme Commander could be persuaded to take advantage
of it, it might be a heaven-sent break."

If Stagg and Yates expected support from the syndicate, they were
mistaken. Stagg thought that the afternoon exchange of views would
be "short and happy." Instead, the conference was "the most heatedly
argumentative and most prolonged of the whole series: it lasted well
over two hours." The experts went back to their cubicles that evening,
put on their headsets, and the scrambler was switched on to dissolve
their words into what Stagg described as the sounds of a crowd of
"toothless parish councillors in some outlandish corner of Indo-
china." But this time the syndicate was in a sober and subdued mood.
For upon the outcome of this discussion would depend whether Neptune could be launched on Tuesday morning, or whether it must again
be postponed, risking all the dangers that such a delay would cause.
But if the experts were calmer, they still could not agree that a ridge of
fine weather would follow the storms now crossing the Channel. There
was a reasonably high degree of confidence that the weather would be
more favorable to Neptune from the afternoon of Monday the 5th into
Tuesday the 6th. But after that there was grave uncertainty.

At 9:30 P.M., Stagg was again in the conference room at Southwick
House; and it was now, measuring his words with the greatest care,
that he delivered the critical forecast. The atmosphere was, Stagg
would write, tense and grave as he said that—provided the forecast
was correct—cloud conditions would permit the heavy and accurate
aerial and naval bombardment with which Neptune would commence,

and that the wind after midnight on Monday would not be so strong, nor the cloud cover so thick, as to cause disorder among the airborne troops' fleets. Station-keeping at sea would be difficult but the waves, chop and wind should not seriously disorder the naval forces. In short, Stagg's forecast indicated weather that was tolerable, but far from ideal, for Neptune to proceed.

There was a brief debate. Ramsay reminded the commanders that there was only half an hour to make the final decision; if all the assault forces were to be at their assigned stations off the Far Shore for a D-Day on June 6, the signals had to go out now. Both Eisenhower and Smith stated that they felt the operation should proceed; and Smith added that to call off the invasion now meant they would have to wait until June 19 before Neptune could be tried again. Troops would have to be disembarked with great risk to security as well as to morale; there would be no moonlight for the airborne troops; and the longer the postponement the shorter the period of good campaigning weather on the continent, and the greater the possibility that Hitler would try to wreck the invasion with his V-weapons. Leigh-Mallory, on the other hand, doubted the ability of the air forces to operate effectively in the predicted cloud conditions; and Tedder agreed that air operations were going to be "chancy."

Eisenhower rejected these adverse views. He turned to Montgomery and asked: "Do you see any reason why we should not go on Tuesday?" Montgomery replied: "No. I would say—*Go!*" It was then, at 2145 hours, with the wind and rain beating on the windows, that the Supreme Commander announced his decision—perhaps the greatest decision of his life. "I am quite positive we must give the order . . . I don't like it, but there it is . . . I don't see how we can do anything else." With that declaration, Eisenhower gave the order to remount Neptune.

There remained the possibility, however, that the weather might become worse and the decision have to be reversed. There would be a final meeting at 4:15 A.M. the following morning. Stagg would note the paradox of the situation:

> (Neptune) had been postponed when the weather overhead was calm and clear; now in a gale of wind and rain the decision had been taken to proceed. Meteorologically I hoped it could be justified but at the moment it must have appeared a little mad to some of the Supreme Commander's military company.

On his way back to his caravan, the Supreme Commander encountered Merrill "Red" Mueller of NBC, one of the four correspondents attached to his headquarters. Eisenhower said to him: "Let's take a walk, Red." The two men disappeared into the oak wood and, as Mueller would recall, Eisenhower appeared to be "bowed down with worry." It was as if "each of the four stars on either shoulder weighed a ton." His mood was still somber when the high command gathered at Southwick House for the last time at 4:15 A.M. that Monday—the start of a new working week that would be one of the most memorable in history.

When Stagg reached the conference, he noted that "All were in battle-dress uniform except General Montgomery . . . he was dressed in a high-necked fawn-coloured pullover and light corduroy trousers. Facing them General Eisenhower seemed as spruce and immaculate as ever." The rest of the high command was settled into easy chairs and sofas; "faces were grave and the room was quiet." At a signal from Eisenhower, Stagg opened his report with the words: "Gentlemen, no substantial change has taken place since last time but as I see it the little that has changed is in the direction of optimism." It was his opinion that most of Tuesday would be just suitable for launching Neptune. The weather afterwards would be a "mixed bag" but it "might not be so bad as to jeopardize seriously the important buildup stages of the operation." When he had finished his report, Stagg would note:

> . . . the tension seemed to evaporate and the Supreme Commander and his colleagues became as new men. General Eisenhower had sat, turned sideways, facing me, taut and tense. Now a broad smile broke over his face as he said, "Well, Stagg, if this forecast comes off, I promise you we'll have a celebration when the time comes."

The meeting did not last long; and within the hour, Eisenhower sent an historic signal to all commands and the Combined Chiefs of Staff in Washington, a signal as historic as Nelson's "England expects . . ." "Halcyon plus 5 finally and definitely confirmed." D-Day would be Tuesday, the 6th of June. For better or worse, Neptune was irrevocably launched.

Another drama was being played out that extraordinary Sunday of June 4, 1944. The Prime Minister had sent for de Gaulle, who was flying in Churchill's private plane from Algiers to London, where it was quite possible that he might be arrested the moment he set foot on British soil. Criminal charges had been filed against him by a certain Dufour, and the case, the climax of the tedious and protracted troubles between de Gaulle and the British, had been simmering ever since.

Dufour, according to the Gaullistes, was an MI-6 agent who had attempted to infiltrate the French intelligence service in London. He was found to have misrepresented himself, and he was court-martialed by de Gaulle's commanders in England, and jailed at the French detention center at Camberley, just outside London. Dufour escaped, however, and filed a complaint with the British courts against de Gaulle and other French leaders claiming that he had been mistreated at Camberley. The British government had no power to quash the charges; once filed the case had to be heard unless it was withdrawn by the plaintiff. Nor, since de Gaulle had no official status at the time as a representative of any government, could the British grant him immunity or prevent him from being arrested if he returned to England and tried on charges that, had he been found guilty, would have resulted in his imprisonment.

Notified of the charges at his headquarters at Algiers, de Gaulle was outraged at this latest attempt "to spatter me with filth." He informed the Foreign Office that he considered the affair "an infamy," and there the matter rested until March of 1944 when he was again notified that the charges were about to be brought to trial. De Gaulle countered with charges of his own. Early in 1943, a Free Frenchman, Stephane Manier, who was employed by the Gaullistes to make broadcasts to Metropolitan France on the BBC transmitter at Accra, had returned to England, and as an alien, had been detained for interrogation by the British security authorities. Manier died—the British were unaware that he was suffering either from serious mental illness or malaria, or both—and his son, de Gaulle announced, intended to lodge a complaint against all MI-6 officers on French territory, Churchill and the entire British government. If the British could arrest de Gaulle, he could arrest Churchill.

De Gaulle would claim that he never heard of the "Affaire Dufour" again. He was quite wrong; Dufour had not withdrawn his charges, and on June 1, as the western world was about to embark on the most dangerous military operation in history, the War Cabinet had to decide whether to let de Gaulle come to England at all. No one could be sure that he was not what he claimed to be—the true leader of France. No one could be sure how the French *résistants,* or the French nation as a whole, would react if de Gaulle were indicted or jailed. But it was finally decided that he should be in London at the time of the invasion, if only to add his authority to SHAEF's orders to the *résistants* and to broadcast a message to the French people to keep calm. But what to do about the Dufour case which was about to come to trial? A special emergency Cabinet committee was formed to deal with the problem; and to settle or at least delay the case, Dufour was offered £1000 to withdraw his charges. Apparently Dufour agreed to settle, for de Gaulle was not arrested when he arrived in London early on June 4.

The French leader went immediately to Southwick House where he was met by Churchill who, in describing Neptune only in its broadest outlines and forbidding de Gaulle free rights of communication with his headquarters at Algiers, again treated him not with confidence but with suspicion. De Gaulle then met with Eisenhower, and as Butcher put it: ". . . Ike took them all on a Cook's tour of the war room, some of the really important stuff being tucked away out of sight." Eisenhower showed de Gaulle some maps and explained the Neptune plan, but he was careful to advise the French leader that the Allied landing in Normandy was diversionary in intent, and that the main landing would come in the Pas de Calais—a statement designed to give Fortitude an extra fillip.

However limited de Gaulle's role in Neptune would be, it was recognized that his was an important voice in France, and Eisenhower gave him a copy of the speech which he said he would like de Gaulle to make to the French people. Unfortunately, the speech lacked much in grandeur, and de Gaulle rejected it. He told Eisenhower he thought it stressed too strongly French obedience to the Allied command. He made similar objections to the speech that Eisenhower intended to broadcast, calling upon Frenchmen everywhere to obey the orders of SHAEF. This was too much; Eisenhower, who had other things to attend to, turned de Gaulle over to Smith; and de Gaulle, refusing an offer from Churchill to return to London by train, left Southwick House by motorcar with his own officers.

Back in London, de Gaulle was kept under a discreet but close watch by British security authorities to ensure that he kept the secrets of D-Day; and McClure, Eisenhower's chief of psychological warfare, Lockhart, the chief of PWE, and both Churchill and Eden again urged him to read the prepared speech. De Gaulle would not be budged. Eventually, he would broadcast to the French nation—but in his own words. De Gaulle's intransigence on this and other minor matters concerned with the liberation of his own country was one of the most extraordinary pieces of *folie de grandeur* in the history of the Second World War.

During the last few hours before D-Day itself, however, there was one area in which de Gaulle was acquiescent, and that was over the thorny and explosive question of the action that the French resistance would be ordered to undertake in support of Neptune. On May 30, Gubbins and Bruce had received an instruction from the Supreme Command directing them to set in motion the machinery for broadcasting all of the 325 *messages personnels* concerned with the assault phase of Neptune. Accordingly, on the evenings of June 1 and 2, the alert messages went out in their entirety; and the volume of these messages did not, it appeared from Ultra, alert the Germans to the imminence of the invasion, as had been feared. But then, on the eve of D-Day, came the difficult task of informing Koenig—and through him de Gaulle—that the action messages were also to be broadcast in their entirety.

That evening, the telephone rang at Gubbins's headquarters. It was Bull. Gubbins was to "request the approval" of Koenig to transmit all of the action messages. The request was a formality, for the messages were already being sent. Gubbins would recall his reaction: "Bull knew that this might provoke a national uprising among the French in France, to say nothing of what the French in London might do. But they had to go out. It was an operational necessity—one of those awful things that high commanders have to order in war."

With Bruce of the OSS, Gubbins made his way to Koenig's headquarters in Queen Anne Street, a quiet backwater of dainty houses round the corner from MI-6. Gravely, Gubbins explained their visit. Did Koenig object to the *messages personnels* going out en masse? Koenig, who knew that he was being presented with a fait accompli, thought for a short while. Then he said the French Committee of National Liberation could not and would not object. He would explain his reasons later: "This torrent of telegrams could have given some of the agents the impression that (the Allies had ordered) a national insurrection. But (I knew that) if the agents stuck to their orders (this would not occur)." He would go on to say that:

> . . . these orders . . . were so arranged (a) to let doubt exist as long
> as possible on the points where the landing would take place, and (b)
> to hinder to the maximum and at one blow the assembly . . . of the
> enemy's army, and (c) to demoralise the enemy, so that he would no
> longer feel secure at any point on our territory. . . .
> The resistance was to furnish its maximum effort during the first
> hours and days which followed H-Hour. That was one of its essential
> missions. It could not fail at the task.

In that moment of heroic acceptance, Koenig had gone a long stride toward the redemption of French honor. Gubbins and Bruce saluted and withdrew.

As the two men made their ways back to their headquarters, an announcer's curious, disembodied, almost sinister voice was reciting the list of action messages over the BBC, speaking slowly, then repeating them, and emphasizing every syllable: "The centipede is a mammal! . . . The crocodile is thirsty! . . . The doctor buries all his patients! . . . Flora has a red neck! . . . I hope to see you twice, darling, at the Pont d'Avignon. . . . Jacques needs Melpomene! . . . You may now shake the tree and gather the pears! . . . The tomatoes are ripe and ready for plucking at Perpignan! . . . The oleander is gorgeous in the Midi!" For nearly an hour, the voice droned on—and among the messages broadcast was the second line of the Verlaine couplet.

Apparently, the Germans had displayed no reaction to the alert messages; their broadcast was, after all, a fairly frequent occurrence. But how would they react to the action messages, particularly to the Verlaine? Would they put their armies on alert? Would they send up aircraft? Would they despatch the E-boats, submarines and destroyers they had assembled in French and Norwegian ports for just this moment? Would they man all their strong points? Would they begin moving their panzer reserves toward the coast? There was still time for them to prepare for the great battle now at hand. Never before had Ultra been watched so carefully.

At least one significant Ultra reached Eisenhower's headquarters in those last hours before D-Day. It was a weather Ultra, a decryption of the Luftwaffe's nightly weather report. In a long signal in a six-digit code that had been one of the toughest German codes for the Turing engine to break, the Luftwaffe predicted that disturbed weather conditions would persist in the English Channel throughout the current phase of the moon and tides. The Germans had not detected the brief interval of improved weather that Stagg's syndicate had predicted, and it was reasonable to hope that they believed the weather would preclude an attack that night.

If the weather Ultra gave the Allied high command some cause for confidence, another report from Foord's Operational Intelligence Centre created a spasm of alarm. Brissex agents watching the tank battalions of the Panzer Lehr near Orléans had seen rail activity that suggested they were preparing to move. A heavy tank train was loading at Châteaudun, and the ranks of tank flats in the yard at Orléans were "seen to be heavily loaded with AA, usually a sign of impending or actual movement," Foord noted in a hurried bulletin to Bull at Southwick House. "The evidence suggests that Panzerlehr (is) in the process of moving. . . . It is NOT clear where it (is) intended to go."

What was afoot? Had Rundstedt and Rommel got wind of something? Was the Panzer Lehr preparing to move toward Normandy? No one knew, and this time Ultra was silent. To the Supreme Command at Southwick House, and to Menzies, who spent much of the night at Broadway in the MI-6 signals center, Ultra's silence was both an encouraging and an ominous sign. If the Germans were moving to counter Neptune, the air would be crackling with signals—unless wireless silence had been imposed upon all commands.

At Storey's Gate, in the headquarters of the LCS beneath the pavements of Westminster, Bevan and Wingate talked late into the night. To relieve the acute tension, Wingate read from Churchill's *The World Crisis,* the book that had influenced British policy throughout the war to this climactic moment. His eyes fell upon Churchill's tribute to the men of the Imperial armies, "martyrs not less than soldiers," who fell by the thousands on the battlefields of the Somme in 1916. Would that holocaust be repeated on the beaches of Normandy? If Fortitude and Quicksilver were a success, there was a chance that it might not. What had they done in stitching together the cover and deception plans for Neptune that they should not have done; what had they left undone? These were the thoughts on the minds of both Bevan and Wingate; but for reasons he could not explain, Wingate would recall that he began to discuss the virtues of the gold standard.

At the Horse Guards, Brooke, the man who, perhaps more than any other, had shaped the strategy of the war, wrote in his diary that evening: "I am very uneasy. . . . At the best it will fall so very far short of the expectations of the bulk of the people, namely all those who know nothing about its difficulties. At the worst it may well be the most ghastly disaster of the whole war. I wish to God it were safely over."

Marshall's whereabouts that night would not be recorded, but Roosevelt spent the evening at the White House, where he was at last able to tell Mrs. Roosevelt that D-Day would be at dawn tomorrow. Such were the security precautions imposed upon the American press and radio that not more than ten people in a nation of 135 millions knew that the great invasion fleet had already left England from every port between Spurn Head and the Skerries.

Churchill spent the evening in his suite at Storey's Gate, drinking brandy with his secretary, Jock Colville. All who saw him that night would remember that he appeared to be brooding darkly, and was very silent.

In France, it had been the hottest Whitsun in memory. The countryside of the Île de France, with its great bend in the Seine, had been baked dry in the sunshine, and the nights had been sultry. But the weather broke in the early morning of June 4, and a storm moaned about the gables of the Château de La Roche Guyon. When Rommel rose just after daybreak, the grounds of the château were strewn with leaves and branches, and as he made his toilet the rain still beat heavily on the windows. Walter Stoebe, the Luftwaffe meteorologist, had forecast a disturbed period of weather for the next few days which, coming at a time when the moon and tides might otherwise have favored a landing, the Kriegsmarine had said would make it impossible for the Allies to undertake major combined operations for another two weeks. The storm around the château confirmed Stoebe's forecast, and Rommel decided he would go ahead with his trip to Germany the following day to see the Fuehrer about the disposition of the panzers, and to be with his wife on her birthday.

It was true that there were certain disconcerting signs from England. For one thing, a radio silence was in progress, and Rommel knew that in the desert this had often been the harbinger of an attack. But since March there had been several such silences, and all proved to have been used for training purposes or to keep the Wehrmacht alert, anxious and away from the urgent task of strengthening the fortifications of the Atlantic Wall. In the absence of favorable weather conditions, it was dismissed as another deception.

Throughout the German high command in the West, there was a sense that great events were close but not imminent. In a report dated June 4, Krancke observed that, while air reconnaissance in May had not been sufficient to give a clear picture of Allied preparations, he considered it "doubtful whether the enemy has yet assembled his invasion fleet in the required strength." In his weekly intelligence appreciation on that same day, Rommel urged that aerial reconnaissance of England's southern and southwestern ports be undertaken immediately; but the prolonged period of bad weather predicted for the Channel would make such flights impossible for the time being. That same weather was whipping up wave heights in excess of 5 to 8 feet on the Channel—much too high, in the German view, to permit a seaborne assault. Winds of Force 6 were predicted for the Pas de Calais, and of Force 7 at Cherbourg, with a cloud base of between 900 to 1800 feet—much too strong and low to permit an aerial attack or the use of paratroopers.

And so, at 6 A.M. on June 5, 1944, Rommel went on leave. With his aide, Lang, and his operations officer, Tempelhof, he was driven by his chauffeur, the faithful Daniel, down the carriageway of linden trees that led from the château, and out through the lanes onto the main highway. As he sped toward his home near Herrlingen, his headquarters informed OKW at Berchtesgaden that the armies might be stood down in this period of bad weather to give them some rest after a long period of watchfulness. OKW was also informed that Allied air operations continued to point to the "previously assumed focal point of the major landing"—the Pas de Calais.

That same day, Rundstedt reported: "The systematic continuation and noticeable intensification of enemy air attacks indicate a more advanced state of readiness for the descent." The report went on to estimate where the descent might occur:

> The main front between the Scheldt and Normandy is still the most probable place of attack. Its possible extension along the north coast of Brittany, including Brest, is not excluded. *Where* within this entire sector the enemy will attempt a landing is still obscure.

And Rundstedt ended his report with the words: "As yet there is no immediate prospect of the invasion."

It was quite clear that nobody at OKW suspected that the invasion was at hand—least of all Hitler. His diary revealed that on June 5 he attended a conference to discuss Portuguese tungsten imports, and the noon OKW conference was almost wholly taken up with the successful withdrawal of the 10th Army on the Italian front. Hitler then had a long session with Reichsminister Speer to discuss smoke-screening the Rhine bridges, he attended another conference to discuss building diesel trucks, and he was given a fecal examination by his physician—his meteorism was still giving him trouble.

The entire German high command was unanimous in its judgment on the eve of D-Day: whatever the Allies intended, the weather was too bad to permit an invasion during the first week of June. Neither Hitler, Rundstedt, Rommel, Krancke nor anyone else had the slightest idea that the assault fleet of over 6000 ships was already at sea. Rundstedt could not know that there would be a fair interlude between the storms over the Channel just long enough to make the invasion possible, even though the weather conditions during that period would be worse than those the Germans thought necessary for a large-scale amphibious assault. Allied victories in the little heralded weather war had systematically deprived the Germans of the means to forecast such subtle changes. It was for this moment alone that the weather war had been fought.

Because of the weather, the air and sea operations that would have detected the approaching armada were called off. No one reported that one flotilla of Allied minesweepers was already at work, cutting a passage through a German minefield lying across the path of the Utah and Omaha convoys, within sight of the shore of the Cherbourg peninsula near the Barfleur Light. Because of the weather, local leave was open to officers, and a war game to be held at Rennes, which a number of army and divisional commanders from the Normandy front were to attend, was not canceled. And because of the weather, Rommel would be absent from his post, for the third time, at a critical moment in his country's history. Although the Germans were, on the eve of D-Day, gravely unbalanced by the threats of Bodyguard and Fortitude, but for the weather, they might have been alert and waiting for Neptune. But no submarine, no aircraft, no radar set—not one officer or one man of the mighty Wehrmacht—detected the advance of the biggest force of warships in history. As General Warlimont, the deputy operations chief at German Supreme Headquarters, would record: "On 5 June 1944, . . . (OKW) had not the slightest idea that the decisive event of the war was upon them."

The Germans did, however, have one forewarning that Neptune was about to begin—the *messages personnels,* and, in particular, the Verlaine couplet. They had come to attach great importance to these messages, which were considered to be indicators of an invasion—but only one of a number. Wehrmacht intelligence staffs reported the broadcast of the alert messages on the nights of June 1 and 2; and on June 2, Colonel Oskar von Reile, the chief of the Abwehr's counterintelligence department in Paris, informed OKW and all higher headquarters in the West that several times between 1:30 P.M. and 2:30 P.M. on June 1 a British radio station had broadcast the first part of the Verlaine couplet, the alert message: "The long sobs of the violins of autumn." Reile's signal was with all commands—including Hitler's, Rundstedt's and Rommel's—by 7:55 P.M. on June 2. Had OKW, OB-West and Army Group B acted upon the intelligence available to them about the meaning of the *messages personnels*—intelligence that was close to the truth and which, oddly, had originally come from Canaris just before he was dismissed in February 1944—the armies in the West would have been put on alert to meet a probable invasion. But the German high command had heard the first line of the Verlaine and other alert messages in the past, notably on May 1, 1944. It had reacted then, only to find that nothing happened. As a result, Rundstedt had reserved for himself, with the permission of OKW, the sole right to alert his armies on the basis of the *messages personnels*. He took no action when informed of the broadcasts of June 1 and 2. In the absence of weather conditions favorable to an invasion, they were considered to be another false alarm.

The action messages, however, and in particular the second line of the Verlaine couplet—"soothes my heart with a monotonous languor" —had not been heard before. It was intercepted on the evening of June 5; in fact it was broadcast a total of fifteen times that day. The sheer volume and frequency of these broadcasts might alone have roused the Germans' suspicions, even if they had not known the approximate meaning of the Verlaine message. It was still not too late to alert the German armies, but only with reluctance did General Hans von Salmuth, the commanding general of the 15th Army between the Seine and the Somme—the Fortitude area—interrupt his bridge game to place his army in a state of alert on his own responsibility. But the 7th Army —in the Neptune area—was not alerted by its commanding general or OB-West, both of which were informed of the Verlaine intercept. Why it was not put on the alert would become one of the most impenetrable mysteries of the war, a mystery that centered around OB-West.

General Bodo Zimmermann, Rundstedt's operations officer at OB-West, would later claim that all commands in the West *were* put on alert. He would tell his postwar American interrogators that:

> At 2115 on 5 June 1944 (Meyer-Detring, his intelligence officer) reported the receipt of an urgent alarm message to the effect that the enemy radio had several times repeated a code word summoning the resistance movement to arise immediately throughout France. Practically, this signified the mobilisation of the resistance movement for the following night; the report was therefore taken very seriously. (Rundstedt) decided to transmit this fact, with a general warning, to all units and agencies concerned in its area.

In what amounted to legal testimony, for in certain respects his early release from Allied captivity depended upon the truth of his statements, Zimmermann then went on to say: "Army Group B, which was aware of the above report, was ordered by (Rundstedt) to comply with all the requirements of Alarmstufe II [maximum alert] throughout its entire coastal area [Wehrmacht District Netherlands, 15th Army *and* 7th Army]. . . ." Similar instructions were sent to

Army Group G in the south of France, by telephone and confirmatory teleprinter signals. This process was completed, said Zimmermann, by just after midnight—*before* any reports had arrived of landings in France. Thus—if Zimmermann's version was correct—the entire German group of armies, with the navy and the air force, should have been in a state of maximum alert by the time the first Allied soldiers started to land by parachute. But this was not the case.

Colonel Anton Staubwasser, Rommel's chief of intelligence, who was on duty at Château de La Roche Guyon that night, would tell his interrogators a quite different story. "At approximately 2200 hours," Staubwasser testified,

the 3rd General Staff Officer of the 15th Army informed me by telephone that one of these code words had again been intercepted, and that the 15th Army had therefore alerted its troops independently. I reported this matter immediately to (Speidel) . . . and, considering the circumstances that Headquarters Army Group B had *no records whatsoever* [Staubwasser's italics] by which to judge the import of the code word which had just been received, he ordered me to obtain a decision from (Rundstedt's headquarters, about whether to place the army group troops and 7th Army on alert).

At that moment, Speidel was giving a small dinner party for his brother-in-law, Dr. Horst, and for Rommel's friend, Ernst Juenger, in the château. It was virtually a meeting of the Schwarze Kapelle in the West, and those present talked much about the draft of a twenty-two-page document which Juenger, a philosopher and author, had prepared, so Speidel stated, at the request of Rommel, a document that was intended to be used by Rommel as the basis for an armistice with England and America. Following Speidel's orders, Staubwasser contacted Rundstedt's headquarters, and as he told his U.S. Army interrogators: "In the course of the ensuing conversations which I held personally, a special missions staff officer—after a short while—conveyed to me, by order of OB-West, the command to desist from alerting the troops." That was the reason, at least according to Staubwasser, that no alert was sent to the 7th Army on the invasion coast, and in turn no alert was sent by the 7th Army to 84 Corps, which bore responsibility for Utah, Omaha and most of the British sector. It would not be until 0215 that 7th Army ordered its divisions into the highest state of alert—by which time the airborne assault was under way.

What explanation was there for this fundamental difference in accounts between events at Rundstedt's and Rommel's headquarters? Who, in particular, was the "special missions staff officer" who ordered Staubwasser not to alert the troops? Hitler, later, would be convinced that there were either traitors or British agents at work at OB-West, claiming to have evidence that the British had impersonated Hans Baron von Boineburg-Langsfeld, the Commandant of Greater Paris and a member of the Schwarze Kapelle, who was, apparently, on leave at the time of the invasion. Hitler would order an investigation to be made into how it was that so many staff and field commanders were away from their posts on that particular night, why a war game had been scheduled the following day at Rennes, why the 15th Army was on alert but not the 7th Army. Speidel's conduct that evening would come under investigation by the Gestapo, and he would be arrested on suspicion that he had committed high treason. It would be asked why he entertained members of the Schwarze Kapelle that most important of all nights, and it would be suggested that he had not alerted 7th Army because he wanted the Allies to get ashore and capture France and Germany before western and central Europe were destroyed in battle, and before Russia reached Germany's eastern frontier. Later it would even be suggested that as reward for his schemes the Allies— and particularly the Americans—gave him a post in the NATO high command after the war. There would not be a shred of evidence to support any of these allegations and suspicions; indeed, there would be ample evidence that Speidel was absolutely loyal to his country, if not to the Nazi régime.

Nor would there be a shred of evidence to substantiate the suspicion that a British agent had infiltrated OB-West, although a story would go the rounds that an expert in the German language and military affairs, a certain "Sir John Hutchison," had undergone plastic surgery to perfect his resemblance to a German officer. It was Hutchison, so the story went, who told Staubwasser to desist from alerting 7th Army, was later responsible for giving the orders that sent certain key German combat forces off in the wrong direction, and even succeeded in planting a false copy of Neptune on Rundstedt, a plan revealing that the main Allied invasion would come in the Pas de Calais rather than Normandy. As unlikely as that story appeared to be, it was possible that Menzies did succeed in infiltrating the German high command in Paris at about this time. Major Alexander Scratchley, an SAS operations officer, would recall that just before the end of the war in Europe he received an order to plan the emergency exfiltration of a British agent who was in hiding in one of the Channel ports. He was in danger of being murdered by French patriots who thought he had been a German agent; he had been seen, Scratchley was told, "riding in Paris with Rundstedt and Goering and other German notables." The operation was mounted but just before take-off it was canceled. The agent had been murdered by the French.

Another explanation for the contradictory versions of the events at Rundstedt's and Rommel's headquarters might be found in communications difficulties and misunderstandings—or in the falsification of statements and documents by the officers concerned to avoid being held responsible for letting the German army sleep that night. Whatever the reason, the "sledgehammer of God"—as the Kaiser once called the German army—was without hands on the haft. The *Feldgrau* were at their ordinary posts on the Normandy front. At St. Lô, at the hour it should have been springing to arms, the staff of 84 Corps attended a birthday party for their commander, General Erich Marcks. A number of the divisional commanders in the corps were actually on the road to Rennes for the war games. At Le Mans, where the 7th Army had its headquarters, the commander, General Friedrich Dollmann, was also at Rennes, having ordered his Chief of Staff, General Max Pemsel, to *cancel* a practice alert which had been scheduled for that night because the troops, he said to Pemsel, need their sleep. Krancke was away from his headquarters in Paris, on his way to Bordeaux to inspect a submarine base. Rommel had arrived at his home in the Swabian Hills outside Herrlingen, had dined with his wife and his son Manfred, and had gone to his study for an hour to begin writing a memorandum to Hitler about the disposition of the panzers. Rundstedt had dined in his quarters and then gone to bed.

At Berchtesgaden the night was starry, the weather was calm, and, having spent part of the evening listening to some lieder with his mistress, Eva Braun, Hitler had taken a sleeping potion. He was fast asleep when Bull at Southwick House issued another historic signal—"Adoration from 0200." It was a signal in the Fortitude scenario. Wireless activity intended to make the Germans believe that major military movements were taking place in the FUSAG area opposite the Pas de Calais would commence at the same moment that the first waves of the airborne assault descended upon Normandy. The seaborne forces for the initial assault were beginning to enter the Bay of the Seine. Paratroop sky trains and bombers, antisubmarine and night fighters convulsed the silence of the skies as they made their way to the Far Shore. H-Hour for Neptune was at hand. There was nothing more the Supreme Command could do. Like Hitler, Montgomery and Eisenhower went to sleep.

PART

NORMANDY TO NEMESIS

JUNE 6 TO AUGUST 20, 1944

'Twas on a summer's day—the sixth of June:
I like to be particular in dates,
Not only of the age, and year, but moon;
They are a sort of post-house, where the Fates
Change horses, making history change its tune,
Then spur away o'er empires and o'er states,
Leaving at last not much besides chronology,
Excepting the post-orbits of theology.
'Twas on the sixth of June, about the hour
of half-past six—perhaps still nearer seven . . .

LORD BYRON, *Don Juan*

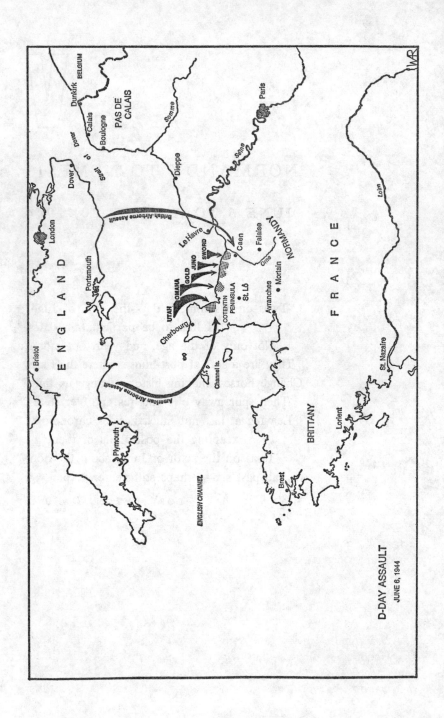

D-DAY ASSAULT
JUNE 6, 1944

D-Day

IN THE Bay of the Seine, in the shallows and meadows of the Norman shore, all was silent in the first few moments of June 6, 1944. D-Day began not with a cataclysmic air and naval bombardment, nor with the descent of airborne and seaborne armies. Conceived in secrecy, it commenced in stealth—with a series of deception and diversionary operations to confuse and distract the enemy.

It was eleven minutes after midnight when the first Titanic party leaped from a Stirling flying at 3000 feet above the Cherbourg peninsula. The first man away was Lieutenant Noel Poole, a Somerset bank clerk serving with the Special Air Service. Leading a party of three troopers, he jumped, struck the tail of the aircraft, fell into the scudding cloud with his parachute opening automatically, and landed —stunned—in a meadow about 5 miles due west of St. Lô on the road to Coutances. He lay in the wet grass, recovered, and then found a pigeon pannier that had been dropped with his stores. He wrote a message to London, put it in a cylinder on the bird's leg and released the pigeon. The signal read: "From Sabu 15 (Titanic 4) to HQ Airtps. NHP/1. Rang bell on leaving aircraft, received slight injuries on landing." Poole then gave a brief report on the situation. He was the first of the Allied soldiers to land on D-Day, and his was the first of the tens of millions of messages from France to England during Neptune. At 10 A.M. the following day, the pigeon was found by a village policeman fluttering on the tarmacadam of a country lane near Stokenchurch in Buckinghamshire.

A few minutes after Poole's party was dropped, a second Titanic party, commanded by Captain Harry "Chicken" Fowles, landed in the same general area, while overhead, to make it seem that these eight men were the advance party of an airborne brigade, more Stirlings flew in to drop two hundred of what the Germans would soon call "dolls"—the half-life-sized dummies of paratroopers. As the "dolls'" parachutes opened, hundreds of pintail bombs began to land and—on the principle of Roman candles—spurted parachute flares and Very lights into the sky. Thousands of rifle and machine-gun simulators dropped from the aircraft started to explode. At the same time, Poole and Fowles and their men set up boxes from which came the recorded, amplified sounds of more fire mixed with the thud of mortar bombs and soldiers' oaths and commands. Then, after about thirty minutes, silence returned to the meadows as Poole and Fowles and their men slipped away to hide up in some orchards.

Similar operations took place at Yvetot and Harfleur, near Le Havre; along the roads between Lisieux and Evreux; around the Forêt d'Écouves; near the Forêt de Cerisy; around Lessay, Villedieu-les-Poêles, and St. Hilaire-du-Harcourt. A rash of what seemed to be paratroop landings from company to brigade strength occurred in every area where sizable German mobile formations were stationed. Their purpose was to enmesh the local tactical anti-paratrooper formations in searches of the close Norman countryside as the real Allied airborne forces landed and established their airheads between Montebourg and Carentan, and astride the Orne Canal. Those "dolls" and noisemakers were to bedevil the German high command in Paris for the next few hours. In fact, Titanic would have an effect on Neptune out of all proportion to the handful of men, aircraft and technical devices used in the operation.

Even before midnight, throughout France, the men and women of the resistance gathered together, preparing to execute the acts of general guerrilla and sabotage that had been assigned to them. They had heard the call to action on the BBC; it was a moment of high emotion, a moment they had long been waiting for. In silent groups they crept from their meeting places in response to the clarion from London. Their main task, in the first few minutes of D-Day, was "Violet," SOE's plan to disrupt German telecommunications. Suddenly, all over the country, but particularly in the Neptune area between Le Havre and Avranches, the lines went dead as *résistants* dug up and spiked trunk cables and pulled down overhead wires. Operators left their switchboards, electrical power circuits fused and repeater stations exploded. From midnight on, Paris, Le Mans, Orléans, Lille, Dôle, Lyon, Tarbes, Bordeaux, St. Lô, Rouen, Avranches, Caen, Amiens—all vital German military centers—began to experience severe communications problems and sometimes total dislocation. Allied wireless and radar-jamming programs, which were carried on coincidentally with Violet, added to the chaos within the German command structure, particularly between divisions and regiments—the units that would have to fight the battle.

Other SOE plans would be put into effect in the hours and days ahead: "Vert" to sabotage rail communications and "Tortue" to disrupt German road travel, both intended to impede the rapid reinforcement of the Normandy front. All over France at shortly after midnight, aircraft approached their drop zones to spill loads of war stores and the special forces teams that would train and lead the resistance in guerrilla operations designed to harass the Germans from behind the lines. Among the most important of these teams were the French SAS troopers and the Anglo-American-French Jedburghs that were parachuted into Brittany to form a nucleus around which the sizable and brave Breton *maquis* could crystallize into fighting battalions. Lieutenant Nicholas Marienne and the men of the 4th SAS Regiment (Chasseurs Parachutistes) were one of the first special forces teams to land. At 0040 on D-Day they leaped from a Halifax into the bright moonlight over a drop zone on the moors near Vannes, hurtling past the twin rudders of the plane and arcing down through the clouds to the dark earth below, their parachutes breaking open behind them. The "Battalion of Heaven"—as the Bretons would come to call the SAS troopers—had begun to arrive.

As other Halifaxes dropped war stores, Marienne and his men landed amid the dolmens—megalithic remains similar to those at Stonehenge—and gorse of the moors. Almost immediately, they heard men nearby who were speaking an unfamiliar language. It was not French, and the men were not the *maquisards* in the Vannes area. They were probably Cossacks serving in the German army. There was a burst of machine-pistol fire and Corporal Bouetard, an SAS trooper who had been born in Brittany, was killed immediately. He was the first Allied soldier to lose his life on D-Day.

Just after midnight at Rundstedt's headquarters, a huge three-storey blockhouse in the side of a small hill on the rue Alexandre Dumas at St. Germain-en-Laye, the war room was almost silent. The duty officer sat in a little glass cubicle listening to his *deutscher Kleinempfänger*—a miniature wireless receiver. The late night Wehrmacht communiqué had been read, and it was now being followed—as it always was—with a record of Maria von Schmedes singing: "Another Beautiful Day

Draws to a Close." Rundstedt had retired at eleven o'clock, as had the operations officer, Bodo Zimmermann; Meyer-Detring, the intelligence officer, had gone on local leave. The Verlaine couplet apart, it looked like a relatively uneventful night—the usual bombing raids and resistance attacks, the usual *parachutage* and prowlings of Allied ships in the Channel. That was all.

There was not the slightest doubt in anybody's mind at the headquarters that the broadcast of the second half of the Verlaine couplet was a trick; certainly nobody really believed that the Allies would begin the *Grossinvasion* that night. The tides and moon conditions might be favorable, but the weather was not—visibility, wind, wave heights, surf conditions, all were unfavorable. Moreover, there were no reports of any significant increase in resistance activities. The Kriegsmarine duty officer, entering Krancke's opinion about the Verlaine couplet in the war diary for June 5, 1944, wrote:

> Although it is hardly to be assumed that the invasion will be announced in advance [over the BBC], it must be admitted that these (*messages personnels*) would certainly cause acts of sabotage in connection with the traffic and communications network, and also insurrections, all of which would pave the way for invasion proper.

Unlike his army and navy companions, however, the air duty officer was not satisfied that all was normal. That day, the Luftwaffe Y service had detected very unusual aerial activity over England and France. First there had been massive wireless tuning—far heavier than anything intercepted before—during the morning; and that always presaged aerial operations that night. Second, the long-range forecasting station at Bad Homburg, in the Taunus, using a statistical process based on a study of Channel weather over the past fifty years, had warned that the present bad weather might clear temporarily on June 6. Third, the Y service had intercepted many American Mercury broadcasts. Mercurys were weather intelligence flights; and what made the Luftwaffe suspicious was that the Americans usually made these flights in the daytime because they only bombed by daylight. Why were Mercury flights being made at night? There could be only one explanation: the Americans were about to undertake a night-time operation. The Luftwaffe duty officer decided that the circumstances were sufficiently suspicious to warrant despatching air patrols over land as a precaution. A few night fighters were therefore scrambled and were airborne by 0034. Their activity was instantly detected by the RAF Y service at Kingsdown in Kent. It was the first sign of German reaction on D-Day. But it was not considered a significant reaction, nor one that might be dangerous; the German night fighters were being vectored between Amiens in France and Deelen in Holland. Had they patrolled 100 miles or so to the west, they might have detected that the vast Neptune fleet had already entered the Bay of the Seine. But there, save for the tail end of Stagg's storm, the skies were empty.

Three miles offshore the British sector of Normandy, two midget submarines, the X-20 and the X-23, which had been lying in 11 fathoms of water for nearly two days, surfaced briefly at about 0020 to receive a signal from the Admiralty. The code word "Padfoot" came over very faintly from the control station near Portsmouth; it meant that the invasion fleet had entered the Bay of the Seine. The X-craft crews, sickened with stale air and the hyoscine and benzedrine tablets they had taken to forestall seasickness and fatigue, gulped some fresh air, and then the submarines bottomed to wait until it was time to surface again and act as beacons for the naval assault forces.

Admiral Sir Bertram Ramsay, at battle headquarters near Portsmouth, watched the plots uneasily. The great assault convoys had reached "The Spout"—the point at which all ships converged to enter the Bay of the Seine. A minesweeper, the USS *Osprey*, had hit a floating mine and sunk with the loss of six men—the first naval casualty of Neptune. But there was not the slightest indication that the Wehrmacht had awakened, and Ramsay reported to SHAEF operations at about 0030: "The assault forces in general are conforming to the plan."

At almost precisely that moment the first American Pathfinders—paratroopers dropped ahead of the main airborne assault forces to mark the airheads for the skytrains which were now approaching the Cherbourg peninsula—were landing on the wet Norman meadow grass. Their drop was chaotic. Confused by bad weather and encountering fierce fire from the ground, their Dakotas had been forced to weave, and so many had gone off course that only thirty-eight of the Pathfinders landed accurately. Some were killed, more were drowned when they fell with their heavy loads into low-lying pasture which the Germans had flooded with river water from the Merderet. Forty miles away, the British Pathfinders were more fortunate; they had not encountered flak when they made their landfall. But in both sectors, the paratroopers ran into stiff, immediate resistance from German patrols. One party of Pathfinders landed squarely on the lawn of the headquarters of Major General Josef Reichert's 711th Infantry Division at the easternmost end of the Neptune area. They were captured immediately by Reichert's intelligence officer.

At last the Germans were beginning to react, but their reaction was that of a drugged giant. The 7th Army stirred only sluggishly; the Titanic operations, together with the widely scattered Pathfinders' drop, made it impossible for anyone to know precisely what was happening; and as the resistance, obedient to Plan Violet, disrupted telecommunications, it became difficult and sometimes impossible for the German commanders to exchange information in a situation where minutes counted.

In the main room of the operations bunker of 84 Corps at St. Lô, the birthday party for the corps commander, General Erich Marcks, ended with the loyal toast and the singing of the German version of "Happy Birthday." The cathedral clock at St. Lô struck one as the general rose and thanked his officers. But while he was making his way stiffly up the stairs—he had lost a leg in action on the Russian front—a staff officer stopped him to say that unusual air activity was being reported in the Cherbourg peninsula. Marcks turned about and came down to the operations room to study the situation maps. When the telephone rang, he picked up the receiver, and, "as he listened, the General's body seemed to stiffen." Richter, the general commanding the 716th Division on the coast at Caen, reported that British paratroopers were landing east of the Orne. The news struck the officers round the table "like lightning." Was *this* the invasion?

Although the reports were spotty and confused, Marcks acted quickly. Three of his divisional commanders were already on the road to Rennes, and he ordered the divisional command posts to get them back. Then he called General Max Pemsel, the Chief of Staff at 7th Army headquarters at Le Mans, to announce that paratroopers were reported to have landed not only east of Caen but also in the triangle Coutances-Valognes-St. Lô in the Cotentin peninsula, the area in which the Titanic parties and the American Pathfinders had indeed landed. The time was 0211. Pemsel reacted immediately by placing the 7th Army in a state of full alert at 0215—approximately five hours after the Verlaine action message had been intercepted. Then he called General Friedrich Dollmann, the 7th Army commander, with the statement: "General, I believe this is the invasion. Will you please come over immediately?"

At Château de La Roche Guyon, Speidel had been awakened at 0215 by reports of paratroop landings and had telephoned Rundstedt at OB-West. Krancke and Field Marshal Hugo Sperrle (the Luftwaffe commander) were also on to Rundstedt at about this time; and as the Kriegsmarine war diary would show, none of them believed at that moment that this was a large-scale landing. Pemsel, however, did not share the Supreme Command's view. He called Speidel at 0235 to announce that the sound of ships' engines could be heard at sea off the east coast of the Cotentin, and that naval observers were reporting the presence of ships in the area around Cherbourg. Pemsel told Speidel that in his view this naval activity, when combined with that of the paratroopers, pointed to a major operation. But Speidel rejected his opinion on the grounds that some of the paratroopers had been found to be what he called "dolls," and some of the divisional commanders thought that the fuss was to do with bomber crews bailing out or with ordinary *parachutage* to the resistance. As Speidel himself would write later on: "It was not at all clear at first whether these were airborne landings in strength or just groups of parachutists dropped to provide a link between the French resistance forces and the invasion forces."

Pemsel placed Speidel's words in the 7th Army log: "the affair is still locally confined," and the "Chief of Staff of Army Group B believes that for the time being this is not to be considered as a large operation." Nevertheless, both the 7th Army and 84th Corps were now in the highest state of alert. Officers manned all switchboards and all operations rooms; the *Feldgrau* were rousted from their beds by sergeants and rushed to their positions; mobile patrols made for crossroads and village squares ready to be sent wherever paratroopers were reported. The giant was struggling to his feet and clearing his head, but Neptune's main airborne assault phase had already begun.

As skytrains disgorged thousands of Allied paratroops onto the Cotentin and astride the Orne, thirty Lancasters and Fortresses trailed their coats between Amiens and the German border, sowing the great foil blizzards of Window that would make it seem that a large bomber stream was heading for Germany. In these same aircraft, electronic warfare operators switched on their Airborne Cigar jamming transmitters to blot out surviving German reporting stations' broadcasts over northern France, while other jamming transmitters in Britain covered such frequencies as the Airborne Cigars could not tackle. At about 0230, the Kingsdown Y station intercepted a German controller ordering all fighters to scramble and those that were already airborne to vector on the ghost bomber stream. They did so and intercepted and shot down one of the Windowing Lancasters.

All but a few of the night fighters pursued the red herrings to the German border; those that were left to guard and search other areas were thoroughly confused by "Bagpipe" and "Chatter," transmitters in England which worked on the enemy's radio frequencies. Bagpipe produced sounds on the German air-ground systems that resembled those of some mad Scot playing the pipes; and Chatter passed false instructions to the German pilots, heckled the ground controllers and garbled their transmissions. Flight Lieutenant Alfred Price would recall one such operation:

> The German fighter controller recognised that fake orders were being fed into the system by the British, because of the faulty pronunciation (of the German). He warned the night fighters "Don't be led astray by the enemy" and "in the name of General Schmidt I order all aircraft to Amiens." Becoming increasingly angry, the German controller actually swore into the microphone, causing the ghost controller in England to remark: "The Englishman is now swearing!" The German controller shouted, "It is not the Englishman who is swearing, it is me!"

As the Luftwaffe prowled empty skies to the north, the great sky-trains were making their way safely to the British and American airheads in Normandy. Not one of the 1100 transports or their gliders would be lost through Luftwaffe activity. But Neptune's airborne army, particularly the American divisions, encountered other difficulties. The Americans' mission was to secure the causeways leading from Utah across the swamps and flooded areas onto the hard, dry ground of the interior—causeways that the Utah forces would have to use in order to get off the beaches. But heavy flak, bad weather and the early confusion of the Pathfinders created chaos for the Americans. The 101st Airborne Division dropped over an area of 25 by 15 miles. Sixty per cent of its equipment was lost or destroyed, and by 0300 some 1500 of its men were either killed, drowned, captured, or lying about in the meadows or in the swamps, wounded, stunned or out of action with broken limbs or sprains. Nevertheless, the 101st did manage to secure two important villages and their causeways to the beaches.

If the 101st's drop was a bad one, the 82nd's, which began at 0230, was worse. Its men were scattered all the way from Valognes in the north of the Cherbourg peninsula to Carentan in the south, and from St. Sauveur-le-Vicomte in the west to St. Martin-de-Varreville in the east, an area of 35 square miles. Only one stick out of three regiments was put down accurately on the three airheads; and the casualties—

particularly through drowning in the area's widespread inundations and swamps—were severe. The confusion was so great that it would be impossible to count the loss of life during the first hours of the 82nd's operations, and the division, at least temporarily, no longer existed as an integrated fighting unit. Yet the disaster was less severe in its consequences upon Neptune as a whole than it seemed. The scattered drops, when combined with surprise, the breakdown in German communications and the Titanic deception, thoroughly confused Rundstedt's, Rommel's and Dollmann's headquarters. Unable to determine, at least in the first hours of the assault, where the Americans were concentrating, they began to disperse their counterattack forces.

The mission of the British paratroopers was to establish a firm line on the Orne and secure the seaborne landings from an armored counterattack. Faring better than the Americans, they dropped well and managed to seize their objectives, even though the 21st Panzer Division was laagered but a few miles from the area. Had the panzers attacked, it might have been a different story. But they did not. General Edgar Feuchtinger, the commander of the 21st, was ready to strike, but his standing orders permitted no private enterprise. "I had been told," he would explain later, "that I was to make no move until I had heard from Rommel's headquarters." Partly due to the communications breakdown and partly due to the general confusion among the German high command, the 21st would not get into the battle until twelve hours after the airborne assault began.

At 0229, the USS *Bayfield,* an attack transport flying the two-star flag of Rear Admiral Don R. Moon and carrying the Utah beach commander, General J. Lawton Collins, arrived off Utah beach. She dropped anchor, the report, "Anchor holding, sir, in 17 fathoms," came back to the flag bridge, and the navigator announced that *Bayfield* was 11½ miles offshore. She was attended by troop transports, tank and infantry landing ships, control craft, and gunfire support ships; and the fleet had managed to get that close in without being spotted by German radar, the German navy or the Luftwaffe. At 0251 the American amphibious command ship *Ancon* anchored 11 miles off Omaha beach, again without being spotted by the German early warning defenses.

The long crossing—some ships had been at sea for two days—had been rough, but the fleet had managed to keep good station and only one of the 6100 vessels in the assault formations had been lost through enemy action. The leading ships had successfully picked up the lanes of dan buoys that marked the way through the German minefields, and as each attack transport arrived on station and anchored, it lowered the assault boats. From about 0315 onward, the troops began to file to the debarkation points as the assault boats heaved, pitched, ground and clanged against the sides of the transports. Still there was no German response. Where were the *Schnellboote,* the *Unterseeboote* and *Räumboote* that ordinarily infested the Channel, the boats that had inflicted the disaster upon Tiger? Where was the Luftwaffe? Why was there no naval gunfire? Had Neptune achieved surprise, or was this to be another Salerno, where the Germans had held their fire until the landing craft lowered their ramps into the surf? The enemy's inactivity caused much foreboding. Could the Germans be saving all their power, all their secret weapons, for one shattering counterstroke at that time when the assault troops were at their most vulnerable—in the grounded landing craft, seasick, wet, tired, laden down with ammunition, weapons and equipment, wading through the surf toward the shore?

Off the British and Canadian beaches of Gold, Juno and Sword, where three divisions were to assault the same area from which William the Conqueror had sailed for England in 1066, the story was the same. The lack of enemy activity was disconcerting, even sinister. It seemed incomprehensible that the Wehrmacht could be unaware that fifty-nine convoys of ships were spreading out along the 60 miles of the assault area. Thousands of paratroopers were landing in France; over a thousand bombers were plastering German strong points and coastal artillery batteries right round the Bay of the Seine. But apart from Luftwaffe intercepts, Ultra revealed very little German wireless activity. In fact, there was very little activity of any sort. The thought was inevitable; had the enemy something unforeseen up his sleeve? The fearful unreality of these last moments before H-Hour was intensified by the sight of the light at Barfleur, one of the world's tallest and most brilliant beacons. The Germans had left it burning that night. Was it because they thought it would give the appearance of normality to the Bay of the Seine?

The night was very dark, although there was a full moon. Occasionally the clouds split and a sliver of moonlight outlined a warship. Its crew, with steel helmets on and dressed in anti-flash clothing, looked like pikemen of the Middle Ages—as Ernest Hemingway, who would be in the fifth assault wave at Omaha, would write. Hemingway was not alone in invoking a vision of that other great invasion in the Bay of the Seine on August 20, 1415, when Henry V sailed from

England with 12,000 men to land at Harfleur and do battle with
Charles VI of France at Agincourt. What was about to happen here
would be more momentous than anything that had taken place before
in military history. Yet many quotations from Shakespeare's *Henry V*
seemed appropriate. Major C. K. "Banger" King of the British 3rd Infantry Division would remember the lines: "He that outlives this day,
and comes safe home/Will stand a tip-toe when this day is named."

At Bordeaux, Admiral Krancke took a telephone call at about 0200
from the C-in-C of Naval Group Normandy, who stated that paratroopers had landed near the heavy naval battery at Marcouf. Krancke
immediately telephoned his headquarters in Paris, to be informed that
the radar system was almost uniformly out of action in the area between Le Havre and Cherbourg—the Neptune area. But it was, he was
told, functioning spottily between Le Havre and Dunkirk—the Fortitude area. Krancke dressed and hastened across the dark courtyard to
the quarters of the admiral commanding Bordeaux; he was concerned
because he knew that the 15th Army had been in a state of maximum
alert since midnight; and he had heard from Rundstedt that the
Verlaine couplet had been broadcast.

For the moment, as he and the admiral commanding Bordeaux
talked in the drawing room of quarters built for one of Napoleon's admirals, Krancke was not disposed to believe that anything major was
afoot. How could the Allies invade on a night like this?—there was a
Force 6 wind running in the Channel and small ships like landing
craft could not navigate in such weather. But when at about 0230
Krancke's staff in Paris reported that "a fair number" of paratroop
landings were taking place along practically the whole of the Normandy coast between the Orne and the Vire, he became uneasy.
Together with the *Ozet* radar system, the Kriegsmarine was charged
with the task of patrolling the Channel to give the alarm if an invasion
fleet was approaching. The *Ozets* and patrols were supposed to be able
to detect the strength and thrust of any invasion fleet and provide
Rundstedt with the foreknowledge that would permit him to move his
panzers toward the threatened area. But on this night Krancke had
canceled all naval movements. There was not a Kriegsmarine ship at
sea. Not even the Allied minesweeping activity of the night before off
the Barfleur Light had alerted the Kriegsmarine. What was more,
because of Fortitude all the new-type German mines available to
Krancke had been laid off the ports between Le Havre and Dunkirk.
The Normandy minefields were laid with old-type mines, most of

which had been there for years and were so crusted with barnacles that nothing short of a direct hit with a bow at high speed would make them explode.

At 0309—according to the War Diary of German Naval Group West, if it is to be believed (there was some falsification of documents afterwards)—Krancke received a report which finally compelled him to act. The report stated: "North of Port-en-Bessin ten large craft located, lying some seven miles off the coast, thus indicating unloading activity." Now Krancke knew that a big attack was developing. At about 0400, he ordered the destroyers to sail from Royan for Brest, and sent some torpedo boats into the Bay of the Seine to see what was going on. He also began the procedure necessary for the submarine fleet to put to sea and engage the enemy. But then ECM deceptions began to cloud the picture; at 0400 the German radar chain reported enemy plots off Le Tréport in the Pas de Calais. Krancke ordered the minesweepers at Dieppe to investigate. They did so, reported seeing nothing, and returned to port. The War Diary noted: "Presumably plots were false."

The only major action between Krancke's forces and those of the Allies was fought at 0535, about an hour after the E-boats had finally managed to sail out of Le Havre. They encountered six heavy warships escorted by fifteen to twenty destroyers, but smoke screens laid by aircraft obscured the targets; the E-boats fired fifteen torpedoes, sank the Norwegian destroyer *Svenner,* and then turned for home. They were pursued by fighters which strafed them with cannon fire, and they were bombed as they entered Le Havre's inner harbor. The U-boat fleet fared no better. Just as the U-boats at Bordeaux were about to sail, their captains were told that their sortie had, for the moment, been canceled. It was possible that the Allies might land in the Bordeaux area. Ironside, the deception scheme to menace Bordeaux, had intervened.

The U-boats that did reach the Channel were quickly intercepted. For this German reaction had been anticipated by the Neptune planners and large air and sea forces had "corked" the Channel between Lands End and Ushant (the code name of the operation was in fact "Cork"). Endless chains of patrol aircraft were being flown; any aircraft making contact with a U-boat broke formation, attacked, reported the position of the craft, then rejoined the chain. "Rover" freelance aircraft collected the sighting reports, dropped beacons onto the target, and then guided in naval craft. In this manner—according to German sources—the first run of U-boats was attacked no less than

fifty times. Five boats were so seriously damaged that they were compelled to put into port, and two were sunk.

Thus it was that, during the first hours of D-Day, the once mighty
Kriegsmarine was not a factor. The vast Allied fleet had come through
the sea and electronic defenses of one of the world's mightiest powers;
and there had not been a single squeak on a radio or a blip on a
cathode-ray tube to warn the Germans. Krancke later sought to
explain this defeat in a report which stated: "The radar stations on the
Normandy coast did not record the approaching invasion fleet because
they were jammed by the enemy." But why did the jamming itself not
make the Germans suspicious and cause them to send aircraft and
ships to investigate? Because, said Krancke, when similar interference
in the past had been investigated, it was found to be enemy deception.
Once bitten, twice shy, he might have added. Finally, Krancke was
compelled to admit that Allied jamming, bombing and deception
measures had been so effective that it was possible to report a large
fleet in the Bay of the Seine only when "the ships could be recognized
by visual means."

Four minutes after the American amphibious command ship *Ancon*
had anchored 11 miles off Omaha beach at 0251, when he received
Pemsel's reports that engine noises could be heard out in the Bay of
the Seine, Rundstedt announced that he was no longer quite so sure
this was not a major operation. He told Zimmermann to get on to
Berchtesgaden and tell Führerhauptquartier what was happening, and
then he went to his quarters to dress. He was back in the war room,
drinking black coffee, by 0315 hours—the moment when the assault
boats were being lowered into the nasty chop of the Channel.

Now was the hour for Rundstedt to display that swift, formidable
logic for which he was renowned. But it was not until 0415—when,
still undetected, the first of the assault landing craft were leaving their
mother ships for the long run into Omaha—that he made up his mind.
Only then did he pronounce that the airborne landings were "definitely the opening phase of a (sea) landing to be expected at dawn."
He had received no forewarning from the German radar screen, the
Luftwaffe or the Kriegsmarine. But he still held one advantage: the
panzers. If he was to exercise that advantage, it was imperative to
order the panzer divisions to Normandy as fast as possible. If he left
them until after daybreak, naval and air bombardment might seriously
interfere with their movement. Furthermore, heavy ground mist
would develop around dawn; and that would help hide the panzers as

they closed up to the coast. But Rundstedt did not command all the panzers. Some of them were commanded by Rommel's headquarters; others were commanded by OKW and could not be deployed without Hitler's permission. After some hesitation, Rundstedt decided to act first and argue the case later. At 0430 he ordered the 12th SS Panzer Division, "Hitler Jugend" (between Paris and Caen) and the equally formidable Panzer Lehr (between Orléans and Caen) to begin to move up to the Calvados coast immediately. It was the right decision. But then Rundstedt made a mistake. He ordered General Kurt Meyer, the commander of the 12th SS, to send what was the equivalent of half the fighting force of his division to the coast north of Lisieux to deal with parachutists and a reported seaborne landing near Deauville. The parachutists were part of Titanic, and Rundstedt's orders constituted one of the early major diversions caused by the ghost airborne landings.

Rundstedt sent this signal to OKW advising of his action and requesting approval for his orders. It was a signal that reflected both his uncertainty and his concern about the situation.

> OB-West is fully aware that if this is actually a large-scale enemy operation it can only be met successfully if immediate action is taken. This involves the commitment on this day of the available strategic reserves . . . the 12th SS and the Panzer Lehr divisions. If they assemble quickly and get an early start they can enter the battle on the coast during the day.

It was *the* critical message of D-Day, for had OKW agreed to Rundstedt's action, it might have been possible for the Germans to launch an immediate, major counterattack that stood every chance of destroying the invasion at the water's edge.

When Rundstedt's message reached OKW, however, its critical nature was not at first realized. Somebody opened Jodl's door to see if he was awake, found he was asleep, and decided that the situation had not developed sufficiently for him to be disturbed. Equally, when OKW called Hitler's quarters at about 0500, nothing was said that caused instant action. The caller spoke to Hitler's naval *aide-de-camp*, Admiral Karl Jesko von Puttkamer, to say that some "extremely vague" messages had been received stating that there had been "some sort of landings in France." Puttkamer decided not to awaken the Fuehrer because "there wasn't much to tell him anyway and we . . . feared that if I woke him at this time he might start one of his endless nervous scenes which often led to the wildest decisions."

When Jodl did awake, and was told that landings were taking place and Rundstedt had ordered the panzer divisions to begin closing up to the Calvados coast, he was furious. At about 0630, the hour at which the seaborne landings were to begin, on Jodl's instructions General Treusch Baron von Buttlar-Brandenfels, the army operations chief at OKW, telephoned both Rundstedt and Speidel and objected violently to Rundstedt's "arbitrary employment" of the strategic panzer reserves. He ordered them to stop the movements and await Hitler's decision. As Zimmermann would remember: "When we warned that if we didn't get the panzers the Normandy landings would succeed and that unforeseeable consequences would follow, we were simply told that *we* were in no position to judge—that the main landing was going to come at an entirely different place anyway." Again, Fortitude was dominating the Germans' reactions.

Zimmermann tried to argue with Buttlar-Brandenfels; but the argument ended with Buttlar-Brandenfels exclaiming: "Nothing is to be done before the Fuehrer makes his decision. You are to do what you are told!" That was that; only one recourse was left to OB-West; Rundstedt must telephone Hitler. As a marshal of Germany he had the right to speak to Hitler personally at any hour if the need demanded, and by doing so at that moment he might have persuaded the Fuehrer to act immediately and decisively. But he did not, perhaps because he was somewhat hard of hearing and avoided using the telephone whenever possible, perhaps because he held the "Bohemian corporal" in such contempt that Hitler might call him, but he would never call Hitler.

At 0730, Jodl personally informed Rundstedt that the Hitler Jugend and the Panzer Lehr must not be committed without Hitler's instructions; the Hitler Jugend was to be halted at Lisieux and the Panzer Lehr was not to move at all. Thus, instead of the 500 tanks and 100 assault guns, and perhaps 40,000 panzer grenadiers as infantry that Rundstedt might have had for a three-division counterattack late on D-Day, all he would have were the 146 tanks and 51 assault guns of the 21st Panzer—and not even that division would be available for a single concerted thrust. The consequences of OKW's decision were immediately apparent to Zimmermann. He exclaimed later: "The first critical day was lost! The success of the invasion was already decided!" As for Rundstedt, he had breakfast and then spent much of the morning in his garden next door to the command post, pruning his roses.

At 0405, two hours before sunrise, the assault transports at Utah began to debark their troops into the landing craft. An 18-knot wind blew off the Cotentin peninsula to kick up the waves; the radar aboard the USS *Augusta,* General Bradley's command ship, washed in and out of the low clouds; and although the banging of the landing craft "made an ungodly racket," sailors on deck "spoke in whispers, as if the Germans could overhear." Still there was absolutely no sign that the enemy was awake. It was, all who were there would agree, quite eerie, and wholly unexpected.

At this same hour, other fleets approached other shores. Throughout the night, eighteen RAF and naval launches had been sailing at 8 knots toward the Calais coast. Each launch flew a 29-foot Filbert balloon, with a second anchored to a raft, and in each of the Filberts was a 9-foot radar reflector which gave back an echo that resembled a 10,000-ton attack transport. At a point about 15 miles off Beachy Head, the little fleet had split into two. Nine of the craft made for Cap d'Antifer, a headland north of Le Havre not far from Bruneval, where the "wizard war" of electronics had begun with the theft by paratroopers of a Würzburg radar back in February 1942. This fleet was called "Taxable." The rest of the fleet—"Glimmer"—proceeded up-Channel toward Boulogne.

At around 0100, operators in both fleets switched on their Moonshine apparatus, and at about 0200, a number of them observed signals on their green-glowing cathode-ray tubes. A German aircraft was interrogating them. They tuned into the search signals' wavelengths and started to Moonshine the German receiver, causing echoes that resembled an immense group of warships. The wizardry had begun.

As the two fleets came up toward the French coast's horizons, each was joined by a squadron of RAF bombers; 218 Squadron flew the Glimmer spoof and 617 Squadron joined Taxable. Using special radar devices which permitted the aircraft to navigate with great accuracy, both squadrons flew the very precise patterns which had been proved during Dr. Cockburn's trials at Tantallon Castle in Scotland in May. At predetermined intervals, the aircraft dropped bundles of Window, while above them other bombers used Mandrel radar jammers. Each formation was, in essence, a giant radar reflector covering an area of 256 square miles, and it appeared on the enemy radar screens as a great mass of shipping in the Channel. To ensure that no German patrol aircraft approached too closely and saw that this "invasion fleet" consisted of little more than rubber balloons and masses of thin aluminum strips, each formation was surrounded by several scores of Mosquito night fighters.

It was a nerve-racking night for the naval and air crews. The launches pitched, heaved and rolled so violently that few of those aboard were not very seasick. As for the air crews, they had to fly exact patterns for no less than four hours in high winds and turbulence that made every airframe shudder. One of the 617 Squadron crew members would recall:

> At the time I was rather concerned about what the Germans would do when they saw Taxable. We knew that we were bait and expected just about every night fighter in creation to roll up at any moment. Our Lancaster was packed full of Window, from nose to tail. If we were forced down in the sea there would be little chance of our getting out before the aircraft sank. We finished Windowing by 4 A.M., by which time it was just beginning to get light. The sky seemed to be full of transport aircraft and gliders: the Red Berets were going in. We hoped we had made things a little easier for them.

At the first hint of daybreak the next phase of the deception began. When the two ghost fleets reached points about 10 miles offshore, the launches switched on sound amplifiers as aircraft came in to blanket the area with smoke. Any German soldier on the shore would have heard bosuns' pipes, the rattle of chain cable through hawsepipes, warships' bugle calls, commands being shouted over loudhailers, the banging of landing craft against the sides of attack transports, the squeal of steam-powered derricks at work, the sounds of laboring engines. Just as Titanic had simulated the sounds of a major airborne landing, so Taxable and Glimmer simulated the sounds of a vast invasion fleet lying off the Channel coast between Cap d'Antifer and the long, wide beaches of Boulogne.

By this time, it was quite clear to the Germans that a major attack had begun between Cherbourg and Le Havre. Yet there were also indications of another, perhaps even larger attack between Le Havre and Calais. As naval operations reported to the OB-West command center in those incredibly confused first hours: "In the main, the landings are taking place off Houlgate and north of Caen," which was correct, "and also near Octeville and Montvilliers," which was incorrect. Moreover, suspicious resistance activities were reported to be taking place between Le Havre and Boulogne, particularly in the area of Le Tréport; and reports of paratroop landings had been received from around Yvetot, Octeville, Montvilliers and Le Tréport. Any sensible man looking at the situation maps, and knowing the British, would conclude that while Cherbourg looked like the target, Le Havre was the *real* one. Was it not written in Directive 51 that that was where the main attack would come?

As a result, the Germans responded to Taxable and Glimmer more positively than they did to the great Neptune fleet in the Bay of the Seine. Warships sailed, searchlights swept the areas off Cap d'Antifer and Boulogne, and the Taxable fleet was shelled by shore batteries. No German gun fired upon the Neptune fleet before H-Hour. But by the time German warships and patrol aircraft arrived to inspect Taxable and Glimmer, there was only some smoke and the wakes of small, fast craft, bucking the sea at high speed, heading for England. The ghost fleet had vanished.

At H-Hour, the Germans were still not certain where Neptune's airborne divisions were concentrating, nor where the major seaborne assault would occur. Such was the predicament of Major Friedrich-August Baron von der Heydte, the commander of the crack German 6th Parachute Regiment, 1750 highly mobile, young, well-armed paratroopers stationed at the eastern base of the Cherbourg peninsula. His regiment, which regarded itself as "fast and lean and deadly as a whippet," was specially trained to locate and destroy any Allied airborne force. Titanic parties had landed to the south of Heydte's command post at Periers, and the drop zones of the American 101st Airborne Division were to the north; but when he called corps headquarters to learn where the paratroopers were concentrating, he could not get through. The lines had been cut by the resistance. He did not reach corps headquarters until 6 A.M., and even then he was told only that the Americans were "north of Carentan." Heydte set his battalions on the march, but as day was breaking, he was compelled to climb the church steeple at the village of St. Côme-du-mont to get the intelligence he needed to deploy his regiment. He would never forget what he saw in the gray dawn light. It was, he would say, "overwhelming." The Neptune fleet lay before him from the shore to the horizon in a panorama that was so calm it reminded him of yachts on the Wannsee Lake at Berlin on a prewar Sunday afternoon.

Neptune went in behind a hail of 10,000 tons of explosive dropped from 2500 bombers, while 7500 fighters and fighter bombers combed the area and 600 warships shelled and rocketed the beaches. The first Allied seaborne forces landed at Utah, and here the American 4th Infantry Division was virtually unopposed. Even three and a half hours later there was still no accurate enemy fire, nor was there a counterattack. All the amphibious tanks and artillery managed to get ashore, and engineers and naval demolition parties quickly cleared lanes through Rommel's "devil's garden." Then they began the march inland to link up with the American paratroopers. It was a different story on the other beaches.

At Gold, the British 50th Division, veterans of the Western Desert and the Sicilian campaign, encountered tough resistance and would fail to capture either primary target: the little port of Bessin and the small town of Bayeux. At Juno, the 3rd Canadian Infantry Division came ashore on a rough sea. Many of the German strongpoints had survived the bombing and shelling, there was deadly sustained fire, and what should have been a swift assault became a battle of infiltration. The 21st Panzer Division, which dominated a 3½-mile gap between Gold and Juno, did not attack. But primarily because the Canadians' objectives—the capture of the Caen-Bayeux road and the big airfield at Carpiquet near Caen—were overambitious, they were not achieved. At Sword, where the British 50th Division landed to take Caen, the key to all Allied hopes, and to link up with the 6th Airborne, the troops encountered fiercer fire and more obstacles than had been expected. The division would not reach the paratroopers, who were in an almost desperate plight, until midnight on D-Day; and Caen would not be taken for twenty-seven days. But it was at Omaha—between Utah and Gold—that the situation was most serious; and when linked with the predicament of the two airborne divisions in the Cotentin, it seemed that Neptune's right wing might collapse entirely during D-Day.

The origin of the plight of the American 1st Division at Omaha was rooted in the Allied belief that the Germans had a battery of six 155-mm coastal guns on Pointe du Hoc, a blunt, triangular cape rising sheer for 120 feet from a narrow rocky shore. It was thought that these guns would dominate the landings at both Utah and Omaha, unless they could be knocked out; but since this could not be guaranteed, Bradley had decided that the shipping assembly areas must be located not closer than 11½ miles off the beaches. This meant that the Americans would have a rougher time getting in, and the job of the amphibious tanks would be particularly difficult. The American air forces had raided the guns three times between April 14 and D-Day; but more they had not dared do, for to display closer interest in Pointe du Hoc might have revealed to the Germans that the Americans intended to land there.

The second major factor that intruded at Omaha was the American intelligence failure to report in time that the area was defended by two complete regiments of the first-rate 352nd Infantry Division instead of one incomplete regiment of the inferior 716th Division. Intelligence reports had speculated on the whereabouts of the 352nd prior to D-Day, but there appeared to be no definite proof that it now defended Omaha. It was not until four hours before H-Hour that a message was flashed to Bradley, as his command ship *Augusta* entered the Bay of the Seine, warning that the 352nd had indeed moved up.

At H-Hour bad weather combined with bad intelligence to create chaos at Omaha. In the long run to the beach, twenty-seven of thirty-two amphibious tanks sank, all the artillery was lost, and the assault itself was inadequately supported by air and sea bombardment. Due to the bombardiers' anxiety not to hit the approaching landing craft, few of the 1285 tons of bombs hit their targets. Throughout the run-in period, the Germans held their fire. But when the assault craft reached the shore and landings began, they opened up with every weapon in their arsenal. Mist and smoke from the naval bombardment masked the landmarks, and the troops found themselves debarking in water that was often up to their necks, laden with heavy clothing and equipment, and wading through fire that intensified as they reached the high-water mark. Many were swept away and drowned, others were cut down by the withering fire. It was Dieppe and Salerno all over again.

As the assault progressed, the black, oily smoke of burning vehicles obscured the beach and flames tinged the mist a deep red. Dead and wounded by the hundreds were washed back and forth in the bloody froth of the surf. Ammunition boxes, rifles, jeeps, tanks, bulldozers littered the sand. The scene was one of such pandemonium and carnage that, for a time, Bradley considered switching the follow-up forces to either Utah or Sword and evacuating the remnants of the American assault forces from Omaha. But then the sun and wind cleared the mist, heavy and light naval units came in closer to roast the two German regiments in the bluffs, Allied fighter bomber squadrons flew over in full strength to keep the heads of the *Feldgrau* under their parapets, and by about nine o'clock the first men had Indian-crawled across the beaches and were beginning to get up into the dead ground of the lower bluffs. Many men died, but some got through; their example was followed by the hundreds of men digging in amid the dead kelp and old wood at the high-water mark. Sections became platoons, platoons became companies, and by noon the German commanders in their post on the Pointe et Raz de la Percée overlooking Omaha (who had earlier reported to the divisional commander that the invasion had been stopped on the beaches) began to see that the Americans had not been destroyed at all, and that they could not be stopped unless reinforcements came in.

Meantime, Rangers had succeeded in scaling Pointe du Hoc, hauling themselves to the top on rope ladders fired by rocket launchers. There, later in the day, they would discover that the battery of six guns which had dictated Bradley's tactics were not guns at all. They were telephone poles. The actual guns had been pulled out following the April and May bombing raids and hidden about a mile or two away where they were found and spiked by the Rangers. A German deception had almost destroyed the assault on Omaha. And now, as if to compensate, a British deception was to contribute to its eventual success.

The 352nd Infantry Division that defended the Omaha sector was understrength, short of equipment and even food supplies. Still, it was a much stronger formation than the Americans expected to encounter. It was commanded by General Helmuth Kraiss, who was dressed and on duty when, at 0200 on D-Day, he placed his division on maximum alert in response to reports of landings by enemy paratroopers. They were, although Kraiss did not know it, the Titanic parties that had been dropped south of where the actual airborne assault would land. Task force Meyer—as the 1750 men of the division's 915th Infantry Regiment were called—was ordered to the area to counter the landings; by 0400, traveling in wheezy French-driven Otrag trucks, or by cycle, the regiment was on its way through the winding narrow lanes of the *bocage*—close country of orchards and small meadows bordered by high hedges—in pursuit of nonexistent invaders. This task force was the sole main reserve for the German forces that took the brunt of the American assault at Omaha. The regiment, which was specifically charged with the task of making a counterattack if the Allies succeeded in penetrating the Atlantikwall in the 352nd's sector, would be enmeshed in the Norman countryside, "pursuing," as Foot put it, "TITANIC's spectral airborne army and a few American stragglers."

Meyer, the regimental commander, received specific instructions to keep in closest touch with Kraiss by radio in case it was necessary to order a countermarch. He drew a special radio from stores but it did not work. When the Americans touched down at Omaha and Kraiss realized that if he was to destroy the American landing he had to have the regiment back in the line as rapidly as possible, he could not get through to Meyer. It was just after 9 A.M. when Kraiss finally managed to reach Meyer with an instruction to return. At this point in the battle, it became necessary for Kraiss to order Meyer to split his force in two and send one half to Gold and one half to Omaha. Neither unit would reach its destination before late afternoon. At 11 A.M. the warmth of the sun burned off the ground mist, the sun broke through the clouds, and swarms of Allied fighters arrived to begin attacking the "very widely spaced march groups" of Meyer's task force which were now spread out over 20 square miles of countryside. The intensity of the bombardment was such that Meyer's counterattack was further delayed. Finally, at 3 P.M., Meyer reported that the enemy had anticipated his attack and was overrunning his spearheads with tanks. It was Meyer's last message; he was killed shortly afterwards.

By that time, the crisis for the Americans at Omaha was over. At nightfall they had a toehold, but it was not more than 1½ miles deep at any point. The fact that Task force Meyer was some 50 miles away from where it was needed at the critical time—at Omaha and Gold—had proved to be decisive. When it finally got back in position, it could do nothing to help repulse the assault. Titanic could be credited with the most effective tactical deception of all on D-Day.

It was not until ten o'clock on D-Day that Speidel decided the picture had cleared sufficiently to form an opinion of Allied intentions. He believed that the Normandy attack was an Allied diversion, but a situation was developing there that required Rommel's presence at La Roche Guyon. Fifteen minutes later Speidel was speaking to Rommel at the field marshal's home near Herrlingen. Speidel gave him his first complete briefing on the situation. Rommel listened, "shocked and shaken"; as one account would describe his reaction: "(Rommel) waited patiently until Speidel had finished the report and then he said quietly, with no tinge of emotion in his voice, 'How stupid of me. How stupid of me.'" He went into the breakfast room and Frau Rommel saw that "the call had changed him . . . there was a terrible tension." Rommel hurried through his breakfast and then telephoned his *aide-de-camp,* Captain Helmuth Lang, who was at his home near Strasbourg. Rommel was, Lang noted, "terribly depressed." They were due to go to Berchtesgaden that day to see Hitler and try to persuade him to allow Rommel greater control over the panzer divisions in the West. But not now. Rommel announced that he would return to La Roche

Guyon at one o'clock. Later, it would emerge that he was not told that the Verlaine couplet had been intercepted.

At that same hour, ten o'clock, having wakened from his drugged sleep, Hitler was informed of the landings. Admiral von Puttkamer and General Rudolf Schmundt, Hitler's army adjutant, took a prepared situation map into his suite at the Berghof. The Fuehrer, who was in his dressing gown, listened to the briefing and then sent for Keitel and Jodl. They declared that a full report from Rundstedt had not yet been received, but it was clear that a number of major landings had taken place between Cherbourg and Le Havre, and that more landings were either expected or were occurring. Jodl explained that he had countermanded Rundstedt's orders to the Hitler Jugend and Panzer Lehr divisions. Hitler approved and stated that, in his opinion, this might well be the opening of the invasion but that Allied intentions in Normandy were diversionary. He repeated this belief several times, and announced that any question of using the strategic reserves must await a clarification of the picture.

Hitler issued several commands that morning. He ordered Jodl to issue the code word "Junkroom," the command to begin the V1 bombardment of London, which meant little since the launch units were not ready to open fire. He gave instructions that Roenne was to make an estimate of the situation as rapidly as possible. Then he turned to the SS representative at Führerhauptquartier, Fegelein, and directed that a plan he had discussed with Himmler and Goering in April and May begin. Ever since the operations against Prosper, Hitler had taken a close interest in F section; and in his talks with Himmler and Goering, he had decided that when a major Allied landing took place in France, he would reveal to SOE that its most important circuits in Europe were under SD control. He believed it would "seriously unbalance the Allied high command to discover at this critical moment that the resistance movements they had relied on for support were penetrated by his minions." Then he went to his quarters to bathe and dress.

It was now about 11 A.M. and every panzer in the West—over 1600 of them—was fueled and armed with its crew ready to fold up the camouflage nets and begin to roll toward Normandy. The generals at all headquarters stood by their *Blitzfernschreiber* (high-speed teleprinters) awaiting Hitler's command to concentrate in preparation for an armored counterthrust to meet and destroy the invasion. All that was needed was for Rundstedt to receive from OKW the signal that had been worked out long before—"Initiate Case Three"—and all reserves would move into the battle. But the command did not come.

At the Strub Barracks, Roenne studied the maps, the incoming situation reports and the "Arabel" file, the German code word for Garbo's mission. The chief of FHW saw the situation as Fortitude had intended that he see it. "While the Anglo-Saxon enemy landing on the coast of Normandy," he wrote in his bulletin for the Fuehrer's noonday conference, "represents a large-scale operation, the forces employed comprise only a relatively small portion of the (Allied forces available). Of the sixty large formations [i.e., divisions] held in southern England only ten to twelve divisions including airborne troops appear to be participating so far." Then Roenne warned: "Not a single unit of the First United States Army Group, which comprises around twenty-five large formations north and south of the Thames, has so far been committed. The same is true of the ten to twelve combat formations stationed in central England and Scotland [i.e., the 4th Army]." His bulletin ended with the words: "This suggests that the enemy is planning a further large-scale operation in the Channel area, which one would expect to be aimed at a coastal sector in the Pas de Calais area."

That, on D-Day at least, was the decisive appraisal, an appraisal that corresponded with what the Fuehrer believed—and therefore became fact. It was nearing noon in France, the morning haze that might have concealed the panzers' movements from the Allied air force had burned off, and marauding Allied aircraft were thick overhead, rocketing and cannoning everything that moved. It was already too late to mount an effective counterattack that day.

At around noon, Roenne telephoned Staubwasser at La Roche Guyon in response to a signal from Staubwasser pleading for his help in freeing the panzers. "My dear Staubwasser," Roenne began, "the landing operation in Normandy (will) certainly not be the only attempted major landing by the Allies. A second such attack must be expected *definitely* in the (Pas de Calais) and therefore a withdrawal of troops from that sector (to assist in Normandy) cannot be allowed." As Staubwasser would recall, Roenne went on to state that FHW had "reliable information relating to a second major landing intended by the Allies." When Staubwasser began to protest, Roenne cut him short with the peremptory statement that Rommel's headquarters "had no data whatever to base any judgement." The two men replaced their telephones, then Staubwasser turned to an assistant and declared: "What can we do? Nothing!"

There was no noon conference at OKW that day. It was held at Klessheim Castle (distant from the command post of the entire Wehrmacht), the baroque palace under the Hohensalzburg Mountains which the Reich used as a guesthouse for visiting dignitaries. Hitler was entertaining the new Hungarian Premier, General Dome Sztójay, and he was in a sprightly mood when he met his staff and opened the conference with the words: "So, we're off." General Walter Warlimont, the deputy chief of operations, who was present, would record:

> . . . as we stood about in front of the maps and charts we awaited with some excitement Hitler's arrival and the decisions he would take. Any great expectations were destined to be bitterly disappointed. As often happened, Hitler decided to put on an act. As he came up to the maps he chuckled in a carefree manner and behaved as if this was the opportunity he had been awaiting so long to settle accounts with his enemy.

Still Hitler took no decisions about committing the strategic reserves to Normandy; he said he would think about the matter over lunch. He left the meeting and went off to brief General Sztójay in a paneled reception room. There, he exaggerated the strength of the German army in the West and the power of the secret weapons he was about to unleash against England, and he declared his absolute confidence in ultimate victory. Then Hitler led his entourage and the Hungarians in to lunch. He was still in good humor, apologized for the meatless meal, and is said to have quipped: "The elephant is the strongest animal—he also cannot stand meat!"

Just after two o'clock, Hitler suddenly emerged from the dining room and told Schmundt to inform Rundstedt that he could have control of the Hitler Jugend and the Panzer Lehr. But that was all—he must not touch any of the panzer or infantry units in the 15th Army. When the order reached the panzer divisions it was almost four o'clock. Only the lightest, fastest elements could reach Caen before darkness. The main elements would not be able to get into the battle before nightfall on the 7th, assuming that the Allied air forces permitted them to move at all.

The mighty Wehrmacht, the engine which had invented the *Blitzkrieg* and had once been powerful enough to subdue the entire continent, was sputtering along like an iron horse. This, apparently, did not worry Hitler. Later that afternoon he called at OKW on his way back to the Berghof where there was another message from

Rundstedt requesting the "Case Three" reserves. But again the Fuehrer took no action except to state that he could not permit Rundstedt to use these reserves until it became clear whether the Allies intended to make a second landing. Then he took a nap.

The Deceptions of D-Day

AT FIRST LIGHT on D-Day, Eisenhower strode across the duck-boards from his caravan to Southwick House. The sun was coming up in a series of pastel shades peculiar to England after a fierce rainstorm, the wind was still running high in the larches, the turf was soggy. But after the oppressive weather of the last few days, the day promised to be fresh, clear and cool. The Supreme Commander also looked fresh and cool, but he seemed to Curtis, whom he met on the duckboards, "a little rough around the edges, very much like a man who has tried to sleep all night and has failed."

News at that early hour was fragmentary. The invasion armada had crossed the Channel with virtually no interference from the enemy; all seaborne and airborne forces were ashore and consolidating. An aerial reconnaissance sweep of the panzer division assembly areas confirmed that tanks of the Panzer Lehr had been in the process of entraining on the eve of D-Day; but there was no further indication of movement. The single event that Eisenhower had once thought impossible had occurred; Neptune had achieved surprise. The stratagems of Fortitude and the well-kept secrets of the invasion itself had undoubtedly contributed to that surprise. But, in the final analysis, it was the weather that had caused the Germans to relax their vigilance. It was the weather, Stagg would record, that gave Eisenhower "the chance to get his first foothold on Europe." Eisenhower would later write to Stagg: "I thank the gods of war we went when we did."

Even with surprise, however, Neptune had gained no more than a foothold. The Germans were confused and uncertain in their reactions, but they were defending the beaches fiercely, and early reports from the American airborne divisions and from Omaha caused grave concern. Eisenhower had prepared a statement, which he carried in his breast pocket ready to issue in case the Allies lost the slight advantage they had gained. It read:

> Our landings in the Cherbourg-Havre area have failed to gain a satisfactory foothold and I have withdrawn the troops. My decision to attack at this time and place was based upon the best information available. The troops, the air and Navy did all that bravery and devotion to duty could do. If there is any blame or fault attached to the attempt, it is mine alone.

Although it was the British who had most dreaded the hazards of a cross-Channel attack, the attitude at Storey's Gate that morning was curiously optimistic. Brooke and the British Chiefs of Staff met in the map room shortly before 10:30 to hear the Joint Intelligence Committee's first appreciation of D-Day. Menzies had provided its chairman, Victor Cavendish-Bentinck, with the night's yield of Ultra and other intelligence, and Cavendish-Bentinck declared that not only did it appear that the enemy had been taken "largely by surprise," but that he also apparently continued to "expect several landings between the Pas de Calais and Cherbourg." Then he displayed a flash of confidence that would have astounded the Americans who were fighting so desperately at Omaha. He said: "We cannot estimate precisely when Germany's resistance will collapse . . . (but) we believe that faced with the situation outlined above Germany's defeat should occur before 1945." It was this appreciation that was sent to the White House Map Room, the Combined Chiefs of Staff at Washington, and the British military missions in Washington and Moscow. Meanwhile, Montgomery, the man who would fight the battle that had as yet scarcely begun, remained at Southwick Park. Like Rundstedt, he was pruning the roses in the garden outside his headquarters before he joined his command on the Far Shore.

At the Supreme Commander's order the invasion was announced at 0917. Lance Corporal Mary Parry, of the British army, fed a tape into a teleprinter autohead and SHAEF Communiqué 1 began to tick into the newsrooms of the world's press in London. The communiqué stated: ". . . Allied naval forces, supported by strong air forces, began landing Allied armies this morning on the northern coast of France." That was all. Eisenhower also ordered "Operation Topflite" to commence; and at 0917, in London, William S. Paley, the American radio adviser at SHAEF and later chairman of the board of the Columbia Broadcasting System, lifted the Sacred Line telephone—the special line from SHAEF to the BBC that was reserved for Neptune announcements—to give the prearranged code words: "Topflite at 0930." Two minutes later the BBC broadcast news of the landings, followed at 0948 by a series of canned addresses by the exiled leaders of the peoples of Europe—specially written broadcasts to confuse the Germans about the true nature of Allied intentions in northwest Europe, and to impress upon the members of the resistance the importance of obeying their orders. Neptune was ashore, but the security of the Allied beachheads would depend, in large measure, upon the continuing success of Fortitude.

Topflite was the political warfare phase of Fortitude on D-Day, and complete calm and authority were the keynotes of these epic broadcasts. The voice of Eisenhower himself led the way at ten o'clock. In his address, he referred to the Normandy landings as an "initial" assault. He asked for "discipline and restraint" among the resistance movements, and then, speaking to the French, he declared, "A premature uprising of all Frenchmen may prevent you from being of maximum help to your country in the critical hour."

Eisenhower was followed by King Haakon of Norway who, with an eye on the dictates of Fortitude North, declared that the "initial landing" was a "link in (a) great strategic plan." He asked the Norwegians not to "allow their enthusiasm to lead them into premature or unpremeditated acts." Professor Pieter Gerbrandy, Premier of The Netherlands, warned: "The enemy will not fail to employ any means of provoking or deceiving you," and declared: "As soon as more forceful action is required of you this will be made clear from here in unmistakable fashion."

Hubert Pierlot, the Prime Minister of Belgium, one of the key areas in Fortitude, then made a speech that hinted, as was intended, that the main attack would come shortly in Belgium.

> The hour so long awaited by you is near. Preliminary operations for the liberation of Europe have begun. This first assault is the certain signal for your deliverance. You are going to undergo difficult days, in a period of anxious waiting . . . be on the alert for false orders which might be issued by the enemy. . . . The only way to check the genuineness of any news is to make sure it is issued from an Allied radio station. Above all, distrust agents provocateurs. The moment of supreme combat has not yet come.

At his own insistence, de Gaulle would broadcast to the French nation in his own way, in his own time, and with his own script. That broadcast would not begin until 6 P.M. But at SOE headquarters in

Baker Street, where Gubbins had spent the night as the advance guards of the special forces teams—SAS, Jedburghs, Cooneys, F section organizers—were being parachuted into every corner of France, there were already signs that the resistance was not heeding calls for discipline and restraint. Scattered reports from the field seemed to indicate that France was catching fire from end to end. Gubbins was awaiting further reports when, at about eleven o'clock, there occurred one of those baroque moments that mark a memory forever. The controller of Station 53C, the wireless station near Bicester through which Baker Street kept contact with its staff and agents throughout Europe, called on the scrambler to advise that the SD command in Paris had come up with a signal for Gubbins from Butler, the wireless post under enemy control through which the Germans had discovered the meaning of the Verlaine poem. When the signal came through, it read: "Many thanks large deliveries arms and ammunition . . . have greatly appreciated good tips concerning your intentions and plans."

The signal was part of Hitler's plan to disconcert the Allies by revealing, at this critical moment, that the resistance movements were heavily penetrated. But the supreme irony of the signal was that the Germans had not acted upon the best tip of all. They had considered the broadcast of the Verlaine poem a deception when, in fact, it might have revealed the time the Allies would land. Gubbins read the message, and then directed that this reply be sent:

> Sorry to see your patience is exhausted and your nerves not so good as ours . . . give us ground near Berlin for reception organiser and W/T operator but be sure you do not clash with our Russian friends.

The exchange marked the end of German *Funkspiele,* but not the end of British wireless games. Garbo was still hard at work in the interests of Fortitude. Prior to D-Day, the XX-Committee and the Allied deception agencies had conceived an ingenious stratagem. It was the "Reid Plan," and it called for Garbo, through Kuhlenthal, his controller at Madrid, to inform the Germans that the opening phase of the invasion was under way as the airborne landings started, and four hours *before* the seaborne landings began. This, the XX-Committee reasoned, would be too late for the Germans to do anything to frustrate the attack, but would confirm that Garbo remained alert, active and well placed to obtain critically important intelligence.

According to the plan, Garbo was not only to reveal the fact that the invasion had begun, he was also to report the points of embarkation of the assault troops in England, the direction of the assault and the identities of the units involved. All this was potentially dangerous intelligence, but the Germans were bound to pick it up themselves within the first twenty-four hours of the landing. What, therefore, was the reason for passing it? It was the same as it had always been: to ensure the credibility of Garbo's future reports. After all—it was reasoned by the CSM when it discussed the Reid Plan with Smith and Bull at SHAEF—what would the Germans think of an agent who had *failed* to get wind of or to report upon an operation of the magnitude of Neptune?

The difficulty of the plan was that the German wireless station near Madrid which corresponded with Garbo closed down each night at midnight; the operators were in the habit of going out for a late dinner when the transmissions were finished for the day. Various tricks were employed to induce the Madrid station to stay open on the night of June 5/6 without alarming Kuhlenthal. All failed. The Royal Signalsman who transmitted Garbo's messages—for Garbo himself was never allowed to communicate personally with Kuhlenthal, nor to be close to a wireless set without an escort—could get no response from Madrid during the early morning hours of D-Day.

Garbo was back on the air shortly before noon of D-Day. It was too late to warn the Germans of Neptune, but not too late to encourage them to believe that the Normandy landings would be followed by other assaults. To substantiate that ruse, Garbo's operator transmitted the complete text of a PWE directive (which, of course, had been manufactured for the occasion) purporting to discourage speculation about other landings. The speeches already made by Eisenhower and the leaders of the governments-in-exile, which clearly implied future assaults, seemed to contradict this directive and Garbo commented on the inconsistency. Much would depend, he said, on what Churchill said to Parliament that day. But, he warned Kuhlenthal, a PWE directive calling for caution in discussing future assaults could only mean that future assaults were, in fact, planned.

The cat-and-mouse games of Fortitude continued on D-Day in the Chamber of the House of Commons. But not even the impending announcement by Churchill about what the *Daily Mail* would call "the greatest act of war in history" could make the Speaker change the ancient rituals of the House. First, the Chaplain read the Prayer, then the Speaker announced the death of an MP during the Whitsuntide recess, from which the House had just returned. Then he announced: "I have received a telegram from the Chilean Chamber of Deputies containing a copy of a resolution of friendship towards the British House of Commons." A low, approving cheer swept the House. "It will be your desire," the Speaker went on, "that I should send a suitable reply." There were more cheers. Then, as the Order of Business required, there came an hour of questions. Were soldiers securing their voting rights? Could not cheaper houses be built if interest did not have to be paid on the loans? Why was a disabled soldier refused a permit to open a shop in Wimbledon? What were the hours of employment in service canteens? Did political considerations enter into Allied Military Government appointments? Would the War Minister authorize the issue of berets to members of the women's army service? Sir James Grigg, the War Minister, replied that this was no time for new hats in the women's services. Sir Archibald Southby rose to chide the War Minister for his lack of gallantry; even if women were in the army they were entitled to a new hat in the spring.

It was so normal, so prosaic, that it must have seemed that nothing abnormal had occurred in world history that day. Then Lloyd George tottered in, a sign that perhaps something momentous had happened after all; he came only rarely those days. Montgomery's brother who was a Chaplain to the Forces also appeared. So did Mrs. Churchill. Then, at noon precisely, the Prime Minister entered the Chamber from behind the Woolsack. The cheers that greeted him gave way to some impatient muttering as Churchill announced: "The House should, I think, take formal cognisance of the liberation of Rome [which was captured by Mark Clark's army on June 5]." He spoke for nearly ten minutes describing this "memorable and glorious event," and then there was a pause. It lasted a few long moments before Churchill declared: "I have also to announce to the House that during the night and the early hours of this morning the first of a series of landings in force on the European Continent has taken place. . . . In this case, the liberating assault fell on the coast of France." The members assumed, as they were intended to assume, that other landings would fall on other countries, such as Belgium, Denmark and Norway. Fortitude's dissimulations had penetrated the House of Commons. Churchill went on to describe the assault and added, with Fortitude still in mind: "There are already hopes that actual tactical surprise has been attained. We hope to furnish the enemy with a succession of surprises during the course of the fighting."

The Prime Minister's canny address set the tone for the statements made by other Allied leaders that historic Tuesday. Roosevelt, speaking to the American nation of what he called "a mighty endeavor," remarked that "The Germans appear to expect landings elsewhere.

Let them speculate. We are content to wait on events." So far, the LCS had stage-managed the world leaders' pronouncements with cohesion and consistency; every address that day conformed to the requirements of Fortitude—with one exception. De Gaulle, in his broadcast to the French people at six o'clock that evening, made statements that at once were an insult to the Grand Alliance, an incitement to national insurrection in France, and a declaration that this was *the* invasion.

The LCS and the Supreme Commander's political advisers knew that the Germans would listen closely to de Gaulle's broadcast for clues about how Allied strategy would unfold. That was why SHAEF had prepared a speech for him. But de Gaulle rejected it, and in his own speech made no mention of further landings in France or else where. In fact, his address began with the words: "The supreme battle has begun! After so much struggle, fury, suffering, this is the decisive blow, the blow we have so much hoped for."

Worse was to follow. Despite SHAEF's anxiety not to precipitate a national uprising, de Gaulle's words to the French nation were highly inflammatory. "For the sons of France," he cried, "wherever or whoever they may be, there is a simple and sacred duty: to fight with all the means at their disposal." He instructed the resistance to obey the orders not of Eisenhower or SHAEF, but of the "French government" and of "French national and local leaders appointed by it," and it was clear that he considered himself to be the head of the French state, although he had no position in law. He made no reference whatever to Eisenhower or SHAEF. Nor was there a single mention of America or of any of the generals, admirals, air marshals, armies, air forces, navies, industries and economies that had made this day possible. He referred to England merely as "old England." To de Gaulle, the entire affair was "France's battle," although only a handful of Frenchmen and two or three French warships were involved in Neptune. De Gaulle, alone among the Allied leaders, had refused to cooperate in Fortitude. The consequences were inevitable. Staubwasser would recall that, in combination with Allied battle plans that accidentally fell into German hands on D+1, "de Gaulle's address . . . made us all [at Rommel's headquarters] absolutely certain that this was *the* battle and that any other suggestions were tricks." What chance did Fortitude have now?

That evening Garbo was on the air to Madrid again. How was he to explain the Prime Minister's suggestion in Parliament that there would be further landings in direct contravention of the PWE directive that sought to restrain such speculations? Garbo had the answer. He told Kuhlenthal that Brendan Bracken, the Minister of Information and a friend of the Prime Minister, had tried to dissuade Churchill from telling the House that the attack was "the first of a series of landings in force upon the European Continent," but Churchill had rejected the advice, stating that in his political position he was "obliged to avoid distorting the facts and that he was not going to allow his speeches to be discredited by coming events." With that piece of subtle, brilliant dissimulation, Garbo signed off until later that evening. And quite by chance, de Gaulle's address supported the fictitious PWE directive. Only he, so it might seem to the Germans, had obeyed the ban on speculations about future assaults.

At 11 P.M. Garbo came up with another message for Kuhlenthal. He was in a "flaming fury" because he had just learned that "my important signal of June 6, 0230 hours, was not transmitted until 0830 hours." Why was Madrid not listening as it had promised on that most critical of all nights? "Were it not for my faith in the Führer and the vital importance of his mission to save Europe from the twin tyrannies of Bolshevism and Anglo-American plutocracy," Garbo went on, "I would this very day give up my work, conscious as I am of my failure." Kuhlenthal, an avuncular man who thought his entire primary network in England was about to break up, sent a long signal of explanation to Garbo which ended: "I reiterate to you, as responsible chief of the service, and to all your fellow workers our appreciation of your splendid and valued work. I beg of you to continue with us in the supreme and decisive hours of the struggle for the future of Europe."

Garbo still ranked high in the esteem of his controller, but if Kuhlenthal had thought coolly and carefully enough, there was one aspect of that day's exchange of signals that might have made him suspicious. Garbo had been on the air so long that he had given the British radiogoniometrical stations ample time on three occasions to obtain a fix on his position and arrest him. Why was he able to stay on the air so long? Did he have a charmed life? Or was he being allowed to transmit by the British for the purpose of deception? These were questions that Kuhlenthal might well have asked himself. But instead of being suspicious, he sent a message to Berlin. In it he recommended Garbo for the Iron Cross.

The day's deception campaign ended as it had begun—with menacing rumbles from East Anglia where Army Group Patton was supposed to be waiting for the Germans to move the 15th Army out of the Pas de Calais before embarking for the main attack. Hitler, the primary target for that deception, had returned that evening to Klessheim Castle for a state banquet with his Hungarian visitors which lasted until 11 P.M. At a brief OKW situation report following the banquet, he repeated his belief that the Normandy landings were a diversion and then, business over, he took his visitors to a gramophone recital of Bruckner's 7th Symphony, a work which, Hitler said, reminded him of the Tyrolean dances of his youth. He went to bed as usual at about 2 A.M. It had been a grotesque day. The Fuehrer had spent its most important hours entertaining a minor central European leader when, had he not been perfectly certain that this was not the invasion, he might have been reacting to Neptune with all the ruthless speed and command for which he was renowned.

Meanwhile, Rommel had arrived back at Château de La Roche Guyon to discover that the panzers had managed to make only one strong counterattack that day in the Calvados. General Feuchtinger's 21st Panzer Division—the remnants of Rommel's favorite division in Libya—had penetrated the spot where the Canadian and British beachheads met and had driven down to the sea at the village of Luc-sur-Mer. But just before dusk a skytrain of five hundred aircraft and gliders brought in a brigade to help the British airborne division secure Neptune's left flank on the Orne. The Germans thought, however, that it was dropping in their rear to cut them off; and the panzer thrust died in confusion and bewilderment. Feuchtinger had tried to rally his men, but it was too late; it was almost dark. All that had really been achieved was a reminder of what the panzers might have done had Rundstedt and Rommel commanded three divisions of them. But the Hitler Jugend and the Panzer Lehr, the other two divisions that might have reached the beachheads that day, had not received their movement orders until late in the afternoon. The nightfall came in suddenly, and as Chester Wilmot, a BBC correspondent with the British paratroops, would write: "This was the time for counter-stroke. The assault forces were tired and strung out in a series of hastily-prepared positions. . . . The line was thin and there were gaps which cried out for exploitation. But the Germans were not in a position to take advantage of the opportunity that was offered that night and that night alone."

By the end of the day in London, the news from the Far Shore was thin, but it was clear that, despite the difficulties of the American airborne divisions and the near disaster at Omaha, there had not been a holocaust. The casualties were heavy (12,000 men would be reported killed, wounded and missing—against the 75,000 predicted if Neptune had not achieved surprise) and the material losses had been immense. But at Storey's Gate at midnight, where Bevan and Wingate were having a drink in the mess when Menzies came in, the general feeling was that Eisenhower and Montgomery had triumphed. "There was," Wingate would remember, "cause for satisfaction. But there had been little doubt that we would get ashore. Where the doubt arose was whether we should be able to stay ashore. Since this would be decided in the next three days, we went to our beds as early as possible that night."

It was quite true. The next three or four days would decide Neptune's fate. Hitler had only to order that Case Three be put in motion, and the full weight of the German panzers and the reserves of the 15th Army would descend upon the Normandy beaches, perhaps before the Allies were strong enough to resist such a counterattack. Furthermore, news of the activities of the French resistance at the end of D-Day boded ill for Neptune. To Gubbins's dismay, the Army of the Shadows had emerged into the bright sunshine, and there was now open fighting between the *Feldgrau* and the *maquisards* everywhere from the Ain to the Hautes Alpes, from the Franche-Comté to the Dauphine and the Savoy, from the Lande to the Côte d'Or and the Bas Rhin. Discipline was breaking down in an insurrection that was not wholly the work of firebrands or the politically ambitious; it was a genuine popular uprising, as passionate and as general as the French Revolution. And as rapidly as the resistance rose up, it was being cut down ruthlessly by the Germans. How much longer could it be counted on to harass and divert the enemy from behind the lines? How much longer could Fortitude sustain the fiction of an invasion of the Pas de Calais?

Sword and Stratagem

HAVING ISSUED his Order of the Day to the Allied armies fighting in Normandy—it began with the words: "The Lord Mighty in Battle!"—Montgomery joined his command on the Far Shore and established his headquarters in the parkland of the Château de Creully. There, he received General Sir Miles Dempsey, the C-in-C of the Anglo-Canadian 2nd Army, and General Omar N. Bradley, the Commanding General of the American 1st Army, just after daybreak on D+1. It was the first Allied command conference in Europe, and it took place at a time when the situation within the beachheads was giving rise to "considerable anxiety."

Nowhere had Allied operations succeeded as planned. The forces at Utah had failed to link up with the paratrooper divisions in the Cherbourg peninsula. Neither the British nor the Americans had joined their beachheads into a single consolidated front. The American penetration at Omaha remained slight and insecure; all the paratroop divisions were seriously disorganized and had suffered heavy casualties. In the British-Canadian sectors, the situation was somewhat easier. But none of the final D-Day objectives—and particularly Caen, which Montgomery regarded as the gate to Paris—had been achieved. Above all, the supply situation was not far short of catastrophic, and the weather—the element which Churchill said "hung like a vulture . . . over the thoughts of the most sanguine"—was expected to worsen before the navies could get additional supplies to the beachheads.

On the credit side, 83,115 British and Canadian troops were ashore, as were some 72,000 Americans. But these forces might be dislodged if the Germans attacked in strength while they were relatively disorganized and short of supplies. At the moment, the Germans were still scattered, due largely to the surprise achieved by Neptune, and as yet they were unaware of the Allies' true intentions. But they were gathering strength with the passage of every hour; and, unknown to the commanders at the conference, they had obtained intelligence of great importance. If that intelligence was used wisely and quickly, not only would Fortitude collapse but the Germans would also have a fair chance of defeating the invasion.

Late on D-Day, *Feldgrau* of the 352nd Infantry Division, picking over the debris of the battle for loot and intelligence, came across a small boat rocking in the surf near the mouth of the Vire. In the boat they found the corpse of an American officer who had been killed in the battle at Utah, and a briefcase was attached to the corpse by a chain. The briefcase was quickly in the hands of the operations officer of the 352nd, who saw instantly that—unless the documents had been fabricated and planted, which he thought entirely possible—here were the operational orders of the American 7th Corps at Utah. Then, during the late afternoon of D+1, troops of the 352nd who had been counterattacking the Americans at the seaside village of Vierville found the operational orders of the American 5th Corps at Omaha on the corpse of another American officer.

Thus, at the outset of the battle, the Germans had in their hands "the entire scheme of maneuver and order of battle for American units in the first phase of the invasion." While the documents contained nothing about Fortitude or about British plans, when they reached Pemsel's desk at 7th Army headquarters, it was possible for the Germans to deduce from them that Fortitude was a fiction. As Pemsel would put it: "The great expansion of the American bridgehead—according to the plan as far as the inner bay of St. Malo and eastward—led to the conclusion that this operation required such a large number of American forces that a second landing at another point [Pas de Calais] was not likely at all." Pemsel's opinion was important; more important still was that of Rundstedt, who received a digest of the plans early on the morning of June 8. Blumentritt would tell his American interrogators after the war that "(Rundstedt) already had the impression on June 7 that what was going on in Normandy was the actual invasion. The operations plan of the American 5th Corps . . . brought the certainty that this was the invasion."

It would always be a mystery that the officers concerned had been allowed to take the plans ashore; each was heavily stamped with the instruction: "Destroy Before Embarkation." But fate had provided Rundstedt and Rommel with what the Abwehr and the SD had failed to get: a detailed picture of American intentions in Normandy. The

Germans regarded these plans with some suspicion because of the ease with which they had been captured. Blumentritt would state that the documents might have been the product of "intentional loss and deliberate deception." However, they left neither Rundstedt nor Rommel in any doubt that Neptune was a strategic operation and not a diversion. With heavy reinforcements, they now knew exactly where to strike to disrupt the entire Neptune plan.

Rundstedt reacted accordingly; he telephoned the Fuehrer's headquarters at Berchtesgaden to request that Hitler—who had already been informed of the contents of the documents—and OKW release to him the seventeen divisions that had been earmarked in contingency planning for Case Three. As OKW deliberated, Rundstedt put into action a second plan in the event of an invasion. He replaced the Wehrmacht's field code (which he considered, with good reason, that the Allies might have penetrated) with a new system called "Rastor." Thus Montgomery was "effectively cut off from one of his most valuable sources of field intelligence," as one authority would later declare. Rastor was never really broken during the entire campaign.

Hitler approved Rundstedt's request; and so the critical moment in the history of the assault had arrived—at a time when the Allies were still ill-prepared to meet it. The situation in the British sector had improved, but the American position was still grave, although they had been given "invaluable respite" by another deception. During the late dark hours of D+1, both Rommel and Dollmann had received reports that three hundred air transports had dropped a brigade of paratroops in the Coutances-Lessay area west of St. Lô. Rommel had reacted by sending German reinforcements which were on the move to Normandy through the junction of the Breton and Cherbourg peninsulas to engage the paratroopers; and believing that the landing was the prelude to another seaborne assault, this time against the west coast of the lower Cherbourg peninsula, he had ordered "all available troops" to that area. The reports had proved to be false; it was a "Titanic" operation—another of Montgomery's master strokes based on Ultra intelligence—which had dropped more of the same dummy paratroopers that had bedeviled the Germans on D-Day. As bad, these forces, which were to be used against Omaha, as a result of a breakdown in communications had been out of contact with their higher command until daybreak on the 8th, and nearly a day was lost before they were back on the road toward the real American airheads.

German reinforcements from Brittany were also being harassed by the Breton *maquis,* and the SAS, Jedburghs and other special forces teams. Even so, the reports were ominous. Ultra showed that some six hundred German fighters and fighter bombers had been ordered from the defense of the Reich to advanced bases in Normandy, and by dawn on the 8th Rommel had three panzer divisions on the British front. Thus despite all the Allied advantages of tactical surprise, and technical ingenuity, the moment of supreme crisis was approaching with each hour. Unless Case Three could be frustrated or delayed, Neptune might yet be driven back into the sea.

Hitler's decision regarding Case Three was quickly known in London; Ultra, the Y service, aerial reconnaissance, special forces teams— all reported German moves that indicated a grand assembly of the German army in the west at Normandy. At Montgomery's, Bradley's and Eisenhower's headquarters, and at Storey's Gate, the situation was viewed with mounting concern. Marshall and the U.S. Chiefs of Staff were due to arrive in London to be present with the British Chiefs of Staff to "handle any eventuality that might arise"—a euphemism for withdrawal. The fact that this reaction had been anticipated did not lessen the tension for the Allied high command. Every weapon in the Allied arsenal—aerial warfare, guerrilla and deception— would have to be employed to prevent a rapid German assembly in Normandy. No one doubted the overwhelming might of the Allied air forces nor the determination and bravery of the French *maquis*. But the moment had now come to establish whether the German high command really believed men like Garbo and Brutus—and whether strategic deception could still be an effective weapon of war.

It was against just such a situation as had now arisen—the implementation of Case Three—that Dericourt had been used to plant the false *messages personnels* on the Germans in 1943. On June 7, the BBC had broadcast a mixture of dummy and real alert messages to the resistance groups of northern France and Belgium. Then, on the 8th, Eisenhower, working through his former G2, General J. F. M. Whiteley, who was now a deputy chief in SHAEF operations, ordered SOE to broadcast the action messages. They went out that same day (at 2:30 P.M., 7:30 P.M. and 9:30 P.M.), as an odd, disembodied French voice in a broadcasting basement in London began apparently incoherent references to flowers and scents: carnations, violets, iris, heliotrope, jasmine. It was SHAEF's intention to order "general harassing action and guerrilla," combined with the "sabotage of specific railway, road and telecommunications targets," in northern France and Belgium, and the many well-organized *réseaux* in the Ardennes and Belgium sprang immediately to their assigned tasks. But due to the heavy concentrations of German forces in the Pas de Calais, there were actually very few *réseaux* in that area; the dummy messages were broadcast to make the Germans believe that there were a great many more pockets of active resistance than there really were. That was the purpose of the Dericourt stratagem. Both real and dummy alert messages had been broadcast in the past to deceive and alarm the Germans, for it was known that they regarded the messages as harbingers of an Allied attack. But now, to reinforce Fortitude, the action messages, both real and false, were also broadcast; and to a listening German intelligence officer, the great number of messages, combined with the activities of the *réseaux* which actually existed in northern France and Belgium, could only portend a major Allied operation in the Pas de Calais.

In a pattern of activity which was designed to be seen by the Germans as identical to that which preceded Neptune, Allied special forces and intelligence teams were parachuted into the Pas de Calais and submarines and motor torpedo boats began to appear off the French Channel beaches north of the Seine. On the English side of the Channel, the activities surrounding the fictitious FUSAG were intensified, activities that also portended a major military move. Large numbers of dummy craft, with a goodly sprinkling of real ships, particularly ships that could be used for bombardment, appeared to be gathered in great strength at ports and anchorages along the coast opposite Boulogne. The ports and "hards" were discreetly illuminated by "Paradise" lights to make it seem to German reconnaissance aircraft that the Allies were loading the ships by night. The German Y service was allowed to hear a noticeable increase in wireless traffic between SHAEF and Combined Operations Headquarters at Dover and Chatham. The wireless points of the eleven divisions of FUSAG, which, according to the scenario of Adoration, had been discreetly chattering with each other for the benefit of German ears, went silent— a sign that they were beginning offensive operations. The navies sortied to lay great smoke screens between The Wash and Dover. Minesweepers set forth to clear passages through the minefields around Calais. The ionosphere was crowded with the radiotelephone conversations of ground and air crews preparing for some mammoth operation. Allied air and naval forces began a violent bombardment of the "landing beaches" between Le Havre and Antwerp. In short, every sign pointed to an imminent invasion of the Pas de Calais.

At the same time, the Allied high command could not risk depending solely upon deception to delay a concentration of German forces upon Normandy. Powerful units were already moving toward the beachheads, and to disrupt and delay that movement Eisenhower unleashed the air forces on the French market towns and transportation centers in the Neptune lodgment area. The plan had originated with the man who now commanded the assault forces, Montgomery, its objective to create what 21 Army Group called "choke points," blocking the towns and villages through which the Germans must move with rubble and cratering. The U.S. 8th Air Force had objected to the plan; the targets were considered "unsatisfactory for air attack," and as an after-action report would state: "The stand of the 8th Air Force was based on the risks to civilian life and property." Montgomery's headquarters was adamant; the choke points must be created. But the 8th Air Force was equally adamant; it would not do the job. The case was taken to Supreme Headquarters, and the after-action report noted: ". . . SHAEF, motivated by military expediency, directed that the attack be made."

Leaflets were dropped to warn civilians to evacuate the threatened towns, but when the attacks were over, the devastation was complete. Among the towns very heavily hit was Caen, the capital of Calvados, with a population of about 52,000 and the world's main center for Norman art. Villers Bocage, the gateway to the Bocage Normand with a population of about 1500, was obliterated. The charming and serene little city of St. Lô (population about 10,000) became "the capital of ruins." Pontaubault on the Sélune, a small place with a quaint old bridge over which the Germans had to pass in order to get from Brittany to Normandy, was very badly damaged. In Coutances (6000), only the Cathédrale Notre Dame, one of the most beautiful examples of Norman Gothic art, was still standing when the dust and fire that consumed the rest of the city had settled. Thury Harcourt (1200), the gateway to the Suisse-Normande, became a lifeless ruin. The cathedral "Lisieux of St. Teresa" at Lisieux (2000) survived, but almost everything else in the quaint old city founded in Gallo-Roman days was destroyed. So was Falaise (5500), the seat of the earliest Norman dukes and noted for the horse fair held there ever since William the Conqueror. Vire (6000), the picturesque cloth-working town, was so heavily damaged as to be unrecognizable when its inhabitants returned; as was Argentan (6100), from which the four knights set out to murder Thomas Becket at Canterbury in 1107.

It was one of the most brutal uses of aerial power in history, but the campaign, when allied to the destruction of the Seine, Loire and

Meuse bridges and of the French railroad system, produced a situation in which, in general, the German soldiers in troop trains moving toward Normandy would be compelled to detrain about 50 miles from the front. They would then be forced to move—usually on foot, except at night when the German truck trains could make their runs—up to the front, often under fighter bomber attack. The choke points would also prevent the rapid movement of food, fuel, arms and ammunition; and the chaos that would develop when armored and troop columns tried to move through the choke points could only be straightened out by the use of voice radio or low-grade cipher wireless traffic—time did not permit more secure enciphering. This, in turn, would enable the Allies to learn with great rapidity where most of the German formations were, and with their overwhelming aerial power to attack them again and again.

As the aerial campaign produced chaos and fear, so the deception campaign hoped to produce indecision whose effects might be as important to victory as the more tangible effects of the bombing, Allied ground operations and the activities of the resistance. To substantiate the flurry of bogus activity surrounding FUSAG, the Allied high command brought Brutus into play. In a message dated June 8, 1944, he told his controller in Paris that he had seen "with my own eyes the Army Group Patton preparing to embark at east coast and south-eastern English ports." He reported Patton as stating that "now that the diversion in Normandy is going so well, the time had come to commence operations around Calais." The King, Churchill, Eisenhower and Brooke had all visited the FUSAG command post at Dover Castle, and "General Marshall of the American army comes here from Washington on the 9th or 10th of June to see Patton and the troops off." The troops available for the assault included, according to Brutus, "at least five airborne divisions," a "sea force of at least ten divisions," and "FUSAG will have 50 divisions, some of them being here already."

This message was—Bevan would later claim—"on Hitler's desk within one half-hour of its transmission from London." Then, to support Brutus, the faithful Garbo sent a signal for Kuhlenthal on June 9 that took no less than 120 minutes to transmit. In a general review of the situation as seen by the entire Garbo mission in England, he told of the concentration of landing craft in the Orwell and Deben and of the dispositions of the Allied armies after D-Day. Like Brutus, he stressed that Neptune was a diversion and that there were still many more divisions left in England for a second strike. He concluded: "I transmit this report with the conviction that the present assault is a trap set with the purpose of making us move all our reserves in a rushed strategic redisposition which we would later regret."

Roenne, significantly, was among the first to react to the accelerating tempo of Fortitude. The mass of intelligence indicating an imminent invasion of the Pas de Calais was too credible to ignore, and after consultation with Keitel and Jodl, Roenne issued this signal from FHW to all commands in the West: "In all probability major landing by enemy on the Belgian coast is to be expected on June 10." And as the first warning to Rundstedt and Rommel that Hitler might reconsider the movement of Case Three forces to Normandy, Roenne added: "Withdrawal of our forces from 15th Army sector untenable."

Would Hitler stop the movement of the Case Three reserves? Some 500 tanks and perhaps 50,000 of Germany's élite fighting men were already on the march toward Normandy, but of those forces only the paratroop divisions in Brittany and the armored and infantry divisions in the Pas de Calais, less than a day's march away under normal circumstances, were close enough to the Normandy beachheads to pose an immediate threat to Neptune. Surely, now was the time for Hitler to display that "active and bold imagination," that "astute grasp of military matters" with which an American official study of the battle would credit him. Now was the moment for the employment of traditional German military thought and training: defeating an enemy by a decisive act rather than by a strategy of gradual and cumulative attrition. Everything would depend upon whether the Fuehrer continued to believe the fictions of Fortitude. If he did not, the Allies would be in for the fight of their lives in Normandy.

Hitler began the day of June 9 decisively enough; he ordered the 9th and 10th SS Panzer Divisions—360 tanks, including Panthers and Tigers, and 35,000 men—to France from central Poland, where they were resting after having put down the Hungarian rebellion and then destroying the mighty Russian offensive at Tarnopol. But these forces could not affect the decision in Normandy; while they had taken only a week to get from France to Hungary before the invasion, it would take them three weeks to get back. What Rommel and Rundstedt needed were the armored and troop divisions in reserve in the Pas de Calais. These divisions were now committed to the battle. But just before the OKW noon conference, Roenne telephoned Colonel Friedrich-Adolf Krummacher, Hitler's personal intelligence officer and the link between the intelligence and evaluation agencies and OKW. Speaking in his rapid, high-pitched voice, Roenne launched into an attack on

OKW's decision to permit the movement of the 15th Army's panzer and infantry reserve to Normandy. He said he had definite intelligence that the enemy was about to launch a large-scale operation from the east of England; the German Y service had intercepted and decrypted a message to the Belgian resistance on the night of the 8th. This, he said, indicated large-scale guerrilla action beginning on the 9th. It would therefore be madness, he said, to permit the reserves to continue to march. Krummacher replied that he was just off to the noon conference with the Fuehrer and assured Roenne that he would "present your points with all the emphasis at my command."

At the conference, Hitler heard Jodl report Roenne's views. He was concerned, for it confirmed what had been his belief all along—that despite the information in the captured American documents, Normandy was only a diversion. But Hitler would not make up his mind about whether to issue fresh orders to the 15th Army panzers and infantry. He said he would make his final decision at the midnight conference. But before that conference, Jodl gave Hitler a message with the observation that perhaps the Fuehrer should read it in conjunction with the orders to the resistance movements and the news that Marshall was arriving shortly to inspect Army Group Patton headquarters at Dover Castle. The message was from Kuhlenthal, and it was his appreciation of Garbo's report:

> After a personal exchange of views in London with my agents . . . and after considering the massive concentration of troops in eastern and southeastern England which are taking no part in the present operations, I have come to the conclusion that the (Normandy) operations are a maneuver. Its purpose is to entice our reserves into the bridgehead in order that the decisive assault can be launched at another point. . . .

At midnight on June 9/10, Hitler pronounced: the movement of the panzer and infantry divisions from the Pas de Calais to Normandy must not only be stopped, the 15th Army must also be strengthened. The orders were with Rundstedt and Rommel during the night; and they brought both field marshals to the brink of resignation. For they recognized that with these divisions they might win the Battle of Normandy; without them they stood no chance of victory. The war, wrote Zimmermann, was lost at that point. From now onwards—at least until mid-July—Hitler, Jodl and Roenne would remain convinced that Army Group Patton was about to land at the Pas de Calais and would refuse permission to Rommel and Rundstedt to call upon the forces there to help in Normandy. The second stage of Neptune, the consolidation of the beachheads in Normandy, had ended in an Allied victory. The German Supreme Command and the General Staff had been outwitted and outgeneraled. The dimensions of that victory were soon apparent in the Martians' order of battle estimates. On D+4 it had been estimated that the Germans would have twenty-one and a half divisions in the line against an estimated sixteen of the Allies. As a result of the bombing, the destruction of the Germans' communications, resistance activity and Fortitude, they had only ten and a half divisions facing the Allies in Normandy.

Back in London, Marshall and the other American Chiefs of Staff had arrived on June 10. They gathered at Storey's Gate that day and the next with their British colleagues; and there, in an atmosphere that was "heavy with tension and pipe and cigarette smoke combined with a faint aroma of good whiskey," they watched the outcome of this critical playing of the cards. Wingate would remember:

> It was a frightful moment—there were those big red blobs on the war maps moving towards Normandy all the time. Were all the bridges out over the Seine? Had the Germans built underwater bridges? Would the tanks have to come round through Paris, where we had left the bridges intact? Ought we not to bomb the bridges over the Seine in Paris? Had Garbo overplayed his hand? That was the sort of thing that was being discussed. Then Joan Bright [a secretary who kept the most secret intelligence file] knocked on the door, came in, and said there was a message which might interest us; she had just put it in the "Black Book" [the book in which all Ultras were filed]. Brooke and Marshall went to have a look. They were all smiles. We looked at the Ultra—and there it was: Hitler had cancelled Case Three. We'd won, and what an astonishing moment that was! We knew then that we'd won—there might be very heavy battles, but we'd won. There was nobody more astonished than Bevan, for I don't think he thought that we'd really pull it off. Brooke's attitude was the oddest. He said if Hitler was such a bloody fool why had it taken us so long to beat him? Then he stalked off. The P.M. came in with Stewart Menzies and the P.M. said this was the crowning achievement of the long and glorious history of the British Secret Service—or something like that.

4

The French Revolt

BY D+4, the Allies had completed the second stage of Neptune successfully: the consolidation of the beachheads into a single front. Now began the third stage: the battle of the build-up in which the Allies sought to bring ashore sufficient strength to break out of the beachhead while the Germans struggled to contain them and, simultaneously, to assemble the forces needed for the counterblow that, they hoped, would drive Neptune back into the sea. Here, both sides were seriously handicapped. For the Allies, the worst summer weather since 1900 was wrecking all the carefully laid troop and supply schedules. Shortly, a severe storm would destroy one of the Mulberry harbors and sink or badly damage some eight hundred ships, landing craft, tugs and ferries—four times as many ships and stores as had been lost on D-Day. Moreover, the very shallowness of the beachhead— nowhere was it much more than 6 miles deep—made it always difficult and often impossible to bring in more troops and stores.

But if Montgomery's position was bad, Rommel's was worse. Almost immediately, he began to suffer from the effects of Allied aerial superiority, naval gunfire, and the cumulative results of the long strategical and tactical pre-invasion bombing campaign. Even without the Case Three reserves, he had the men, tanks, guns and stores to launch a great counterstrike; his problem was to assemble them in the right force at the right place and at the right time. But the railways were out and truck convoys could, generally, move only by night. Petrol, oil and ammunition shortages began to occur because, through Fortitude, the Germans had concentrated their main supply dumps in the Pas de Calais. Due to calculated attacks before the invasion against the German ball-bearing and automotive industries, all vehicles—tanks included—developed high rates of unserviceability. The infantry was compelled to move up on foot, cycles, horse-drawn vehicles, and motor transport that was in varying degrees of decrepitude; and such movement as was possible was liable to sudden, murderous air attack and disruption by the *maquisards*. The Luftwaffe might have helped protect Rommel's transport and supply routes, but for all practical purposes, like the Kriegsmarine, it had been eliminated as an effective fighting force.

The defense of the Reich was left to the army; but in addition to his other problems, Rommel's command was rapidly breaking up. Marcks, the commanding general of 84 Corps in the invasion area, was caught on the open road and killed by fighter bombers; Dollmann, the 7th Army commander, was soon to die—suicide was rumored—in the Banque Mutuelle at St. Lô. In the first stages of the invasion, six of Rommel's divisional commanders and some twenty of his other senior commanders would be killed or rendered hors de combat. All this, combined with Hitler's refusal to release the Case Three reserves, left Rommel at a distinct disadvantage. Even so, the Germans were still enormously powerful in the West. With remarkable ingenuity, Rommel was managing to get some divisions up to the line, although rarely as organic units. But if he could find the means to move them, and if he could divine precisely what the Allies intended, he had 1 million men and 1600 tanks which he could employ against the wafer-thin sliver of Europe that was all the Allies had gained in their immense attack.

Montgomery's original battle plan rested on the ability of the British and Canadian troops to break out of the beachhead, capture Caen and sweep across the flat plains of the Seine. But informed by Ultra of the Germans' gathering strength which, when combined with the lag in the Allied build-up, would probably make that objective impossible, Montgomery altered his strategy. He decided that the British and Canadians should still make every effort to take Caen, but the primary objective of their campaign would be to draw German panzer forces to the Caen sector so that Bradley's American army might have a better chance to break out in the St. Lô sector with a right hook against lesser opposition. It was a complete reversal of roles that was dictated by intelligence derived from Ultra; and this new strategy would become the basic principle of the battle in Normandy. Thus the deception agencies would be charged with an additional task. While they continued to maintain the threat to the Pas de Calais, they also had to make Hitler, Rundstedt and Rommel believe that Caen was the main Allied objective in Normandy, not St. Lô. In fact, the reverse was true.

But powder—not principles—wins battles, and Montgomery knew that he was inviting disaster by luring the panzers into the Caen sector unless their power could be severely blunted. On Rommel's orders, General der Panzertruppen Leo Baron Geyr von Schweppenburg, the former German military attaché in London and son of the Master of Horse to the King of Württemberg, had taken command of the Panzer Army in Normandy; and Ultra revealed that the German armor was beginning to concentrate. The 17th SS Panzer Grenadier armor had moved into the woods of the Forêt de Cerisy; the 9th and 10th SS Panzer divisions—the units that Hitler had sent east to meet the threats of defection of Hungary and Rumania—had been ordered back to Normandy; the 2nd SS Panzer Division, "Das Reich," was en route north from Toulouse, and large numbers of Panther tanks at the panzer training ground at Mailly-le-Camp near Paris were being readied for the battle. The 1st SS Panzer Division was lurking east of the Seine, the 21st Panzer as well as the Panzer Lehr were already in action; and all units would come under Schweppenburg's control when they reached the front. Ultra also disclosed that he was planning a great counteroffensive in the direction of Caen that was intended to split the beachhead in two. It was imperative, Montgomery decided, to eliminate Schweppenburg. But where was he? Where was his headquarters?

The Allied wireless intelligence services had located heavy wireless signals traffic coming from La Caine, a hamlet 12 miles south of Caen. The volume of the traffic bespoke an army headquarters; reconnaissance aircraft were sent over as unobtrusively as possible, and their photo coverage showed a cluster of wireless vans, office caravans and tents inexpertly camouflaged under the trees of an apple orchard. Ultra surveillance soon revealed that it was indeed Schweppenburg's headquarters and with him as an adviser was none other than General Cramer, the officer who had been repatriated just before the invasion and who ever since his return had been busy telling everybody about Army Group Patton.

In order to confirm that this was Schweppenburg's headquarters, the RAF sent over a single fighter bomber. Flying at low altitude, and slowly, the pilot saw Schweppenburg himself with his officers, claret stripes down their trousers, watching other fighter bomber operations nearby through their fieldglasses. An hour later, on the evening of June 9, the RAF attacked and wiped out the headquarters, burying Schweppenburg and Cramer in their foxholes. All the staff officers were either killed or wounded; and the wireless vans, so essential to the command of moving panzers in close country, were destroyed. At about the same time, Lancasters plastered the tank concentrations at Mailly-le-Camp, while Mitchells and Bostons saturated the Forêt de Cerisy to knock out the 17th SS's supporting counterattack. Yet another of Rommel's hopes for a speedy panzer thrust disappeared; and Staubwasser, Rommel's chief of intelligence, would comment ruefully after the war, when he learned of Ultra: "We would have been much better off without wireless."

Meanwhile, the deception agencies spun new webs to tie down German forces in areas remote from the main battle—with varying degrees of success. Fortitude North sustained the menace to Scandinavia, but there were indications that threats to the Balkans were beginning to wear thin. Turkey still refused to join the Grand Alliance, and the stratagems of Zeppelin, Russian maneuvers and the activities of the Balkans partisans had failed to prevent Hitler from ordering the 9th and 10th Panzer SS Divisions to Normandy. The German 1st Army, and particularly the 11th Panzer Division, continued to guard the Biscayan coast in response to the threats of Ironside; but in spite of similar threats to the Riviera coast, the powerful Das Reich panzers were moving north, while German forces that garrisoned Brittany had also been ordered to the beachhead.

Where deception failed, the Allies looked to the French *résistants,* and the special forces teams that led them, to delay and disrupt the concentration of German forces during the build-up period. But the *maquis,* disregarding orders for discipline and obedience, had, in many areas, boiled over into open rebellion. While this action would result, as an SAS appreciation for 21 Army Group noted on June 20, in delays to the Germans' movements that "have far exceeded general expectations," there was a grave danger ahead. The Germans were retaliating with such savagery that, as the appreciation went on to state:

> . . . after the initial wave of enthusiasm raised by the Allied landing, and in view of the counter-measures taken by the enemy, Resistance will tend to fall off considerably as a result of casualties unless it is wholeheartedly supported with arms and equipment and, where possible, by the presence of Allied troops. . . .

In the first few days after the invasion, the *maquis* had risen up in virtually every corner of France—uprisings that, in most cases, did little to help the Allied armies in Normandy. Just as SHAEF had feared, the rebels were ferocious, not only in their attacks against the Germans but also against resistance groups of a different political stripe, and suspected collaborators and traitors. The German reaction was equally ferocious, and the rebels were cut down wherever they could be found. The bloodshed was appalling; the casualties would never be computed with accuracy. It all added up to a single word: anarchy. Alarmed by the situation, both Eisenhower and Koenig broadcast to the French nation on June 12, stating that all that was required of the resistance outside the main areas of the battle was to *obey their orders exactly*. These orders called for limited operations, not a general insurrection. But it was too late; an unquenchable forest fire had begun.

The political repercussions were inevitable. The Gaullistes accused the high command of ordering the rebellion despite its agreements not to do so. A formal protest was lodged by the "Commandement Supérieur des Forces Françaises en Grande Brétagne et Délégation Militaire du Gouvernement Provisional de la République Française" (as de Gaulle now styled his organization) that SHAEF had issued instructions over the BBC during and after D-Day that called for a national insurrection. It was a serious charge, for unless it was answered satisfactorily, the French insurgents might turn against the Allies as well as the Germans. SHAEF ordered an investigation. General A. S. Nevins, of the G-3 operations section at SHAEF, instructed McClure, the chief of the political warfare section, to find out what had happened, and in particular to look into the activities of a certain Mme Aubrac who, de Gaulle's headquarters had claimed, had issued the instructions.

McClure quickly established that no call for a national insurrection had been made by SHAEF, by any of the American or British broadcasting authorities, or by Mme Aubrac, who was a well-known radio personality on the BBC. Moreover, his investigation showed, no such order had been issued by either the British or the American broadcasting stations in Algiers. But a check with the special report of the American Foreign Broadcasting Intelligence Service, which monitored all major radio stations' outputs, revealed that de Gaulle's own stations at Algiers and Brazzaville had made some highly inflammatory broadcasts during the D-Day period. Baron Emmanuel d'Astier de la Vigerie, a passionate Gaulliste who would become chief of de Gaulle's Service d'Action Politique en France, had gone on the air to declare that Frenchmen everywhere had "one sacred duty—the liberation of France." He had also made such statements as: "The French people will rise in their entirety to take part in the annihilation of the enemy."

The investigation cleared SHAEF of any direct responsibility for the insurrection, although the volume of *messages personnels* broadcast during the D-Day period helped spark the highly explosive atmosphere of the moment. The demands of deception also played a part in fanning the flames of rebellion; and this time, as recently declassified documents would reveal, there could be no doubt that the French resistance had been deliberately manipulated. The Fortitude after-action report would plainly state that the deception agencies sought to mislead the Germans about Allied intentions by "methods of manipulation" that included: "(1) . . . giving resistance groups intentionally misleading information. (2) . . . maneuvering resistance groups so that their observed activities will be consistent with our deception scenario. (3) . . . controlling radio traffic with groups."

But the causes of the tragedy that swept through France could not be attributed solely to SHAEF, the Gaullistes or deception. In the final assessment, they could be traced to the belief that the *messages personnels* represented a general call to arms when in fact they called for only limited action, and to the failure of the *maquisards* themselves to obey their orders precisely. Lack of security, inexperience in clandestine warfare and political rivalry among the *résistants* added fuel to the fire; and the Germans, too, were responsible in some cases for inciting open rebellion so that the *résistants* could be destroyed. Thus, de Gaulle's charges were unfounded, but his bitterness over the deaths of so many of his countrymen would remain to color the relations between his postwar government and the governments of both Britain and America.

As the flames of rebellion leaped from province to province, the Allied high command watched events in Brittany with special concern, for here the *maquis* had a role that was of high importance to both Neptune and Fortitude. In support of Neptune, the Bretons were charged with cutting Brittany off from the rest of France and, in particular, with delaying the movement toward Normandy of the fighting units of the 145,000 German troops that garrisoned the peninsula. At the same time, in support of Fortitude, their activities were partly intended to make the Germans fear another major Allied invasion. While there were a number of plans for actual landings in Brittany, and at one stage Montgomery considered using one or all of them to break Rommel's stranglehold on Normandy, the Allies would not invade the peninsula from the sea. However, the Bretons would be called upon to take part in a major military action when Patton's 3rd Army moved to capture the peninsula and its valuable ports. Thus, the scope and intensity of clandestine activity were greater in Brittany than anywhere else in France.

To arm, train and lead the Breton *maquis,* scores of special forces teams had parachuted into the peninsula from D-Day onwards. Three-man Jedburgh teams went in to form a nucleus around which the *maquis* could rally. Cooneys were dropped to cut road and rail links with the French interior. F section agents came in from air and sea to try to get both left and right wings of the resistance to obey SHAEF. And the men of the SAS 4th Regiment (Chasseurs Parachutistes) — the Battalion of Heaven—landed to establish two heavily armed re-doubts behind enemy lines. This flood of agents did not go unnoticed by the Germans. In a broadcast over Radio Paris, they warned the French people to beware of these "provocateurs . . . who, though outwardly polite and expressing love for our country, may be members of the Intelligence Service." "We all remember Colonel Lawrence," the broadcast continued on a somewhat hysterical note. "Who knows but that this man Lawrence, who was reputed to have been killed in a motor-cycle accident, is still wandering about the world? In any case, a large number of lesser Lawrences have descended . . . like a plague of locusts." The warning was wasted on the Breton *résistants;* they wel-comed these "lesser Lawrences," particularly the men of the Battalion of Heaven, with open arms.

The moon was very brilliant in clear skies when the first men of the Battalion of Heaven arrived over the moors and copses of Brittany. It was 0045 on D-Day when Lieutenant Jules Deschamps jumped out of a Halifax, followed by his radio operator, seven SAS troopers and Jed team Frederick, their mission to establish "Samwest," one of the two Breton redoubts, near the old walled city of Guingamp in the center of heavy German paratroop concentrations. The drop was entirely successful and within hours the base had been set up in the Forêt de Duault from which special forces teams and the *maquis* were to sally forth to harass the Germans and, when they heard the action message, "Le chapeau de Napoléon est-il toujours à Perros-Guirec?", to rise up in a full-scale rebellion more or less coincidentally with the entry of the Allied armies into the peninsula. Almost immediately thousands of *maquisards* began to gather at the base, but none of the good for-tune of mermaids—the heraldic symbol of the region—would attend Samwest.

The *maquisards* of the area rose exuberantly to their task, but their rivalries, lack of discipline and indifference to security caused trouble from the start. They assembled in great groups to greet new arrivals and collect drops of arms and stores; their staccato Breton chatter could be heard for miles across the moors. Jed team Frederick would report that one reception committee was "assisted by an enormous crowd of onlookers of both sexes, most of whom were smoking, which we did not consider very wise as the boches were in a town only five miles away."

Capitaine Jules Leblond, the SAS commander of Samwest, encountered similar indiscretions. As he climbed out of his harness amid the dense gorse and undergrowth of the Forêt de Duault on D+4, he was shocked by the indiscipline he found among both the troopers who had preceded him and the *maquisards* who had gathered around them. "There was," his after-action report would state, "a continual procession of visitors—sightseers and well-wishers—round the base." Leblond gave "strict orders to forbid sightseers access to the base, but these orders were indifferently carried out as the paratroops tended to fraternise with all the world, without distinction or mistrust." The result was inevitable; alerted by the crowds proceeding to Samwest, the Germans began to infiltrate the camp. Three suspected agents—two men and a woman—were arrested, and after interrogation, as team Frederick would tell Gubbins, "One woman and one man were shot and daggered respectively."

The *maquisards* at Samwest were equally brutal in their treatment of the Germans. Frederick's report would state:

> Without our knowledge some of the young patriots were armed with weapons which had been dropped the previous night to the SAS and they congregated that evening in a farm about 200 yards from the base —none of them being trained to handle a weapon like a Sten gun. As chance would have it a car containing two boche officers stopped at the farm to ask the way to Carhaix. One officer entered the room where these young patriots were having supper and quite politely asked for directions. The answer he received was about five slugs in his belly. Holding his stomach in place with one hand he regained the car and a grenade was thrown at the patriots while the men in the car escaped.

To attack a German paratroop officer was to invite retribution without mercy. It came on June 12 when the Germans burned down a farm from which Samwest obtained all of its water and some of its food. Despite his strict orders not to come out into the open until he heard the signal "Napoleon's hat" from London, Leblond sent a party of thirty SAS troopers to the rescue of the farmers. As he put it in his report to London: "I did not want the enemy to know of our presence in the forest, but on the other hand I thought it would have a disastrous effect on morale if we let a farm be burned within a kilometre of the base without raising a hand." There was a battle between the Germans and the troopers—ten Germans were killed, two troopers were badly wounded, and the Germans withdrew. Two truckloads of Germans kept watch on the base while the third went off to find reinforcements. They returned in a convoy of thirteen truckloads, put the torch to five farms on the way (burning the two wounded SAS corporals alive in one farmhouse), and Leblond decided—as were his orders—to avoid a pitched battle and disperse the base. As the SAS troopers, the Jedburghs and the *maquisards* crept out by darkness, a sapper blew up Samwest's ordnance dump—all of which had been brought in at great cost and danger to supply what London hoped would become a redoubt of 35,000 men. The *maquis* scattered, the SAS troopers and the Jeds melted away among the menhirs, and Leblond and a small party of men, hiding on the moors by day and marching by night, made for "Dingson," the second Breton redoubt, which had been established amid the strange dolmens of the Landes de Lanvaux, a plateau outside Vannes, the first capital of Brittany. But Dingson, too, was marked for disaster.

Dingson was established at La Nouette farm near the village of St. Marcel; and when the first party of SAS troopers arrived on the evening of June 9, they discovered that the *maquisards* were already extremely well organized. Their leader had assembled sufficient cattle to feed five hundred guerrillas, together with a butchery, kitchen, bakery, electric dynamos to feed the wireless sets, a repair shop for motor vehicles, a tailor, cobblers, a small hospital, and a chit system for the purchase of wine and groceries in the village. Moreover, the *résistants'* intelligence showed that the Germans did not have the slightest idea that Dingson existed. That soon changed, again because of the Bretons' exuberance and lack of security.

On the night of June 10/11, "Le Manchot"—the one-armed man, the code name for Commandant Henri Bourgoin, the commanding officer of the Battalion of Heaven—arrived by parachute to take charge of the Dingson redoubt. He was shocked by the indiscretion of the Bretons. The base covered 1200 acres, inside 3500 men had already gathered, and Bourgoin was

> surprised by the village-fair atmosphere that reigned at la Nouette: lights on all sides, patriots coming and going feverishly in the most as-

tonishing costumes. All the neighboring civilians were at the landing. People were everywhere—in the lofts, in the farm, in the stables, in the fields, in the woods. An extraordinary exaltation had taken hold of the *maquisards* at the sight of these men coming from the sky to arm and guide them.

There were also about a thousand Russian soldiers who had deserted the Wehrmacht, hanging about the fringes of the base begging for food. *Maquisards* en route to the base had stopped at every café for miles around for some wine, chitterlings and directions, and before long only the blind, deaf and dumb could fail to know the location of the base.

The Germans attacked Dingson in brigade strength at dawn on June 18, the same day that Leblond and his party, fleeing the destruction of Samwest, reached the redoubt. The *Feldgrau* sprayed the tinder-dry woods with tracers and started forest fires. Jed team George, which was stationed at the redoubt, radioed London on the emergency frequency, asking for air support and stating: "Dingson under attack by considerable enemy force. . . . The situation will become desperate unless a low flying attack can be made on the enemy." The attack was ordered by Montgomery's headquarters and a group of Thunderbirds streaked over from Normandy to rake the ground around Dingson with fire and bombs. They came too late. Bourgoin, realizing that he was up against a very large force of German paratroopers, gave the order to disperse. His men waited until dark, prepared the arms dump for destruction—the RAF had poured in no less than 890 containers of arms, ammunition and stores to Dingson, enough for 5000 men with part stores for another 5000—and broke camp in small parties. As they moved out across the moors, the night was lit with a terrific flash followed by the roar of an explosion. Dingson's arms dump had gone up. The destruction of the Allied redoubts in Brittany was now complete.

Bourgoin, many SAS troopers and Jed team George got away safely; but fifty troopers and two hundred *maquisards* were killed or missing. The Germans were known to have taken thirty-five prisoners, who were given collective absolution by a German priest, shot, and buried as "unknown Germans." Scores of farms were burned down and the *Feldgrau,* believing their adversaries were terrorists, spared nobody who they thought had helped the Battalion of Heaven. But like the survivors of Samwest, the remnants of Dingson re-formed in smaller groups, and under their command the Breton *maquis* again began to multiply. Soon there would be—according to British agents who were sent in to investigate the two disasters—8000 armed and 22,000 unarmed *maquisards* at work in the peninsula. The RAF, now supported by the USAAF, supplied them with hundreds of containers of fresh arms and stores. The Germans could not extinguish the fires of the Breton insurrection.

For all their early misfortunes, however, the Jedburghs, the *maquisards,* the Battalion of Heaven, and the other special forces teams had important success in delaying the movement of the Germans out of Brittany into Normandy. Rommel's strategy was to ring the bridgehead with infantry while he regrouped his panzers for a counterthrust. But he could never quite get enough infantry when he needed it. Due to a combination of guerrilla activity and bombing in Brittany, the 77th Infantry Division took thirteen days to make a two-day journey; the 165th Infantry Division began to leave Lorient on D-Day, but was still not complete at the front by June 16; the 275th Infantry Division, which began to leave the Vannes area on June 7/8, was still arriving on the 14th, and one battalion took eight days to make a single day's journey. Parachute battalions encountered similar troubles, and these were major—if not decisive—delays. The Germans had to fight their way out of Brittany, and to greater or lesser degrees, every German division ordered to the front had much the same experience. Among them was the 2nd SS Panzer Division, Das Reich, one of the best and most formidable fighting formations in the world. Its long journey from the Périgord to Normandy would become one of the epics of guerrilla warfare.

SS Brigadeführer und Generalmajor der Waffen-SS Heinz Lammerding was the commanding general of Das Reich, one of the four SS panzer divisions in France on D-Day. Das Reich usually consisted of some 20,000 of the most battle-hardened fighting men of the SS (almost double that of an average U.S. armored division), and its order of battle included seventy-five self-propelled assault guns, seven light tanks, fifty-seven medium tanks and ninety-nine heavy tanks. Part of the 1st SS Panzer Korps "Adolf Hitler," the division's battle honors were very long. It had helped conquer The Netherlands, had plowed through France from the German frontier to the Spanish border, and was to have been one of the spearheads of the Wehrmacht in the invasion of Britain. It had captured Belgrade, it had defeated a Russian army near Smolensk in the great battle of Yelnya in August 1941, and it was the spearhead of the German offensive south of Borodino that took the army to within a few miles of the outskirts of

Moscow. It had helped prevent the Russians from recapturing the Donetz industrial basin, had led Hitler's great armored strategic counteroffensive at Kursk and had fought a hundred smaller battles. Now it was well rested and fed in the Périgord just outside Montauban, the ancient city of pink-stone arcades on the Tarn River, hated and feared by the *maquis* and very closely watched by MI-6 and BCRA agents.

It was expected at SHAEF that the Germans would rush this élite division to Normandy to meet Neptune on D+3, and the routes it would have to take to get to the beachhead with such speed were the direct rail and road routes through Brive, Limoges, Poitiers, Tours, Le Mans and Caen. It therefore became the objective of all arms—particularly F Section of SOE and the RAF—to delay the movement of Das Reich. In exactly the same way that Spanish irregulars under British control confounded Napoleon's "hurricanes" of heavy cavalry during their march on Madrid in the Peninsula War, so the descendants of the descendants of the *Grande Armée* were to confound the modern "hurricanes"—the panzers of Das Reich—on the long, hot and lonely roads through the Périgord, the Limousin, and the Dordogne.

The Allied air forces led the attack, destroying the road and rail bridges over the Loire between the Atlantic and Orléans in raids intended to prevent the German panzers in southern France from crossing the river. Then, on the evening of June 7, the RAF's 617 Squadron —the "Dambusters," who were renowned for their precision bombing and were equipped to carry the 12,000-pound "earthquake" bomb, the heaviest of the Second World War—was ordered to destroy the Saumur-Parthenay railroad tunnel under the Loire, the last main route open between the south and Normandy. The squadron was airborne at dusk, and when it reached its destination, the commander, Group Captain Leonard Cheshire, flying his Mosquito, dive-bombed his red markers from 3000 feet squarely into the tunnel mouth. Within a few minutes the earthquake bombs were streaking down in what was their first operational use. There were a series of direct hits or near misses, and one bomb bored it way through 70 feet of earth and chalk to explode inside the tunnel itself. The tunnel collapsed.

On the ground, in the first hours of D-Day, "Wheelwright" struck, and although its members came from every part and were of every faith—some with very long police records—Wheelwright was one of F section's best *réseaux*. It was controlled by George Starr, the famous "Hilaire," who was among the longest-surviving F section agents in the field; he had landed from a felucca in November 1942. He posed as a retired Belgian mining engineer who had become rich in the

Congo, to explain away his odd French accent and the fact that he had very large sums of money and no visible means of support. As a man he was secure, prudent, attractive, brave and popular; and although Gascons historically had little love for foreigners, and none at all for the representatives of distant capitals, including Paris, he had become the virtual controller of all Gascony. His specialty was in cutting communications, and he and his men had caused much trouble for the *Feldgrau* in the south during 1943, frequently putting telephone lines and power stations out of order for many days. Wheelwright was based on Agen, a crossroads town in the Périgord where Starr could keep an eye on both Das Reich and the 11th Panzer Division stationed near Bordeaux; and at almost precisely the same moment that Lammerding received his orders from Rundstedt to begin moving to Normandy, Wheelwright parties blew up a large part of Das Reich's petrol dumps.

Short of fuel, Lammerding turned to the railways. But here, "Pimento" was at work. Pimento was Anthony Brooks, the youngest and also the longest-surviving F section organizer. An Englishman raised in the French cantons of Switzerland, he began clandestine life as a part-time helper on an escape line across the Pyrenees, exfiltrated himself to London, volunteered for and was taken on by F section. He was just twenty when on the night of July 1/2, 1941, he was parachuted into the Limousin to begin work with a small but skillful band of *cheminots* to interrupt rail traffic in southern France. His D-Day mission was to cut the south of France off from the rest of the country and from Italy; and at H-Hour, Pimento struck. He stopped all traffic on the line between Toulouse and Montauban, effectively halting Das Reich's supply, munitions and bridging trains—bridging trains that were now needed to cross the Loire. His men also saw to it that every single train leaving Marseilles for Lyon was derailed at least once during its journey; and this in turn made it difficult if not impossible for Das Reich to go east in order to get northwest into Normandy.

With the rail lines cut, Das Reich was forced to move out under its own power, but not before Lammerding had found enough petrol to do so. However, the line of march took the division through one of Wheelwright's sub-sectors between Bergerac and Périgueux. And there in the lovely valleys of the Dordogne, the Vézère, the Auvézère, the Isle and the Dronne, the *maquis* had set some vicious traps. Baron Philippe de Gunzbourg's *maquisards* were everywhere in the red-tiled, brown-stone villages and the granite outcrops that hung over the roads, beside old bridges and older Gallic and Roman ruins, in the caves and grottos of that part of France where Richard the Lionheart was said to have been mortally wounded. They executed some audacious ambushes, planted cyclonite landmines that looked like cow droppings, sniped at tank commanders standing in their turrets, and held up the line of march by placing upturned soup plates, which looked like the humps of buried landmines through a tank's periscope, across the roads.

When Das Reich had extricated itself from Wheelwright, it ran into "Quinine," a Jedburgh team that had been dropped into the low mountains of the Corrèze, near the village of that name close to the main road from Tulle to Clermont-Ferrand. Commanded by Major T. MacPherson, an officer of the Queen's Own Cameron Highlanders who was now working for SOE, Quinine equipped a *maquis* of "some dozen ragged ill-armed men," blew a small bridge on the main road, and then waited—for Lammerding was known to be diverting heavy units of Das Reich around the *maquis* on the normal road to Normandy. When a company of Panther tanks came into view, the twenty-seven men now in the group held the Germans at the bridge at Bicteroux for six hours. Twenty of the *maquisards* were killed. Then Das Reich ran into "Digger," an F section *réseau* in the Corrèze whose leader, Harry Peluevé, had just been caught and was in prison removing a bullet from his thigh with a spoon. Digger's men had suffered much; too much to forgive. They struck again and again in those winding hill roads; many a stormtrooper was shot, many a tank's tracks came off.

It was now D+7 and before Das Reich had even sighted the Loire it still had to deal with "Fireman," "Shipwright," "Wrestler," "Ventriloquist"—and "Bulbasket," an SAS party of fifty men and armored jeeps which had landed northwest of Limoges, the great ceramics center, at 0137 hours on D-Day. Bulbasket had been put in for just this purpose: to harass (and to help the *maquis* harass) German armor moving to Normandy from the south. Their intelligence was as good as gold; Captain J. E. Tonkin, Bulbasket's commander, learned that OB-West had sent petrol trains to provide fuel for Das Reich. When the fuel had been nicely cached at Châtellerault (between Poitiers and Tours), he radioed the target information to London and a squadron of Mosquitos came over and "secured the best petrol fire they had known." Four hundred SS men—probably of Das Reich—were detached to clean out Bulbasket; but the SAS melted into the woods, providing London with another target while on the run: an SS camp west of Limoges. The RAF came over again and, Bulbasket claimed, killed a further 150 of the stormtroopers. But Bulbasket's luck would finally run out; it was later trapped in a wood by an SS infantry battalion, some thirty of the SAS troopers were killed or captured and executed on the spot, and the rest of the team was evacuated to London by Dakotas.

By this time, the temper of the SS was dangerously frayed. As Captain C. S. S. Burt, of the Scots Guards, the leader of a team called "Dickens" which was operating in the same area, put it: "The enemy were extremely nervous." The roads were often littered with German corpses, the railway embankments dotted with locomotives and trains that had been derailed, the roads with disabled or charred German vehicles. The harassment took every form; Jedburgh team "Hamish" hijacked a truckload of butter, and twenty-eight *maquisards* held up the leading elements of "Der Führer" regiment, a unit of Das Reich, on the narrow road at the outskirts of the town of Souillac, for forty hours, while the rest of the division was bunched up on the roads around and subjected to constant air attacks and sniping.

A major explosion across the route of Das Reich occurred at Tulle, a small crossroads town on the Corrèze beneath the Plateau de Millevaches between Limoges and Clermont-Ferrand. On hearing of the actions being fought against the main force of Das Reich just to the south, the *maquisards* in and around Tulle rose and killed the German garrison in the Manufacture des Armes, the École Normale, and the Hôtel La Tremolière. Colonel Bouty, the Mayor, proclaimed the liberation of the town and set about fortifying it. But Lammerding declared that Tulle would pay with "blood and ashes" for the massacre of the German garrison. Armored vehicles fought their way into the town and SS panzer grenadiers rounded up some five hundred men and a few women. Of these, the SS commander, Sturmführer Walter, selected ninety-nine men, women and boys and hanged them from the balcony railings of the houses along the Pont Neuf. Lammerding, two or three of his officers, and a German woman secretary who had worked in the Manufacture des Armes watched the executions from the terrace of the Café Tivoli, "drinking, smoking cigarettes and listening to gramophone records."

The German reaction to another incident was even more vicious. One of Das Reich's battalion commanders, a popular man, was either sniped at and killed in his command vehicle or ambushed, taken prisoner and then shot by the *maquisards* at the village of Oradour-sur-Vayres, about 25 miles west of Limoges. The next morning, a detachment of SS troopers from Das Reich ringed the village of Oradour-sur-Glane—the wrong village but one lying in approximately the same area—and assembled the entire population in the village square. The regimental commander informed the community, mainly farm workers, that arms and explosives were hidden in the village, and that the villagers had been harboring terrorists. He announced that an identity check would be made, and ordered the men to remain where they were and the women and children to go to the church. This, under SS escort, they did. The men were machine-gunned to death where they stood. The church door was locked and the troopers set fire to the church. Of the 652 inhabitants, 642—245 women, 207 children, 190 men—were killed. The massacre at Oradour-sur-Glane would be called "the most horrible and shameful page of the history of German war crimes," and Lammerding was branded a war criminal. He vanished after the war and was never arrested, but he was sentenced to death in absentia. Two of his unit commanders were executed by the French, and the eighteen men in the SS detachment were sentenced to prison terms of between five and twelve years. The leader of the detachment, Major Otto Dickmann, was never brought to trial; he was killed in action in Normandy a week or two later.

Das Reich continued to trudge north and finally crossed the Loire, but it still had more F section *réseaux* to fight before it got to Normandy; Ventriloquist, Headmaster and Scientist all harried it before it reached the frontline "so thoroughly mauled that when they did eventually crawl into their lagers . . . heaving a sigh of relief that at last they would have real soldiers to deal with and not these damned terrorists, their fighting quality was much below what it had been when they started." It would be correct for SOE to claim that: "The division might be compared to a cobra which had struck with its fangs at the head of a stick held out to tempt it; the amount of poison left in its bite was far less than it had been." As important was the time it had taken the division to make the march. It did not arrive until D+17; SOE would maintain:

> The extra fortnight's delay imposed on what should have been a three-day journey may well have been of decisive importance for the successful securing of the Normandy bridgehead. Affairs in the bridgehead went so badly for the allies in the first few days that the arrival of one more first-class fully-equipped overstrength armoured division might easily have rolled some part of the still tenuous allied front right back on to the beaches, and sent the whole of NEPTUNE awry.

In all, the French would claim, 4000 men of Das Reich were killed, wounded or missing in the march to Normandy from the Périgord. Moreover, several score of the pride of Krupp—the sullen *Sturmgeschütz* and broad-tracked Panthers—lay tipped on their sides, broken and burned, gutted testaments to the power of what Byron once called "the shirtless patriots" of guerrilla warfare.

Even before Das Reich was on the line, however, it was clear that the Allies were winning the battle of the build-up. Both their tactical and supply positions had improved, while the Germans were still fighting a holding battle, and the reinforcements and supplies necessary to launch a major counterthrust had not yet arrived. The Allies had twenty-nine and a half first-rate, full-strength divisions (some were almost the size of corps) in the beachhead. The Germans had managed to bring in only sixteen and a half, and many of these were exhausted and badly chewed up when they did reach the line. Of the panzer divisions made available to Rommel, only four—the 2nd, the Panzer Lehr, the 21st and the 12th SS—were at the front more or less complete. The élite 1st SS Panzer was still being held down by Fortitude in the Pas de Calais. The 116th Panzer was in the same sector but for a different reason: Rommel's decision to keep at least one dependable army division in reserve to put down any SS opposition to his plans for "an independent termination of the war in the west." Forward elements of 9th and 10th SS Panzer divisions had reached the French frontier, but their regiments were being forced by Allied air activity to detrain at Fontainebleau and make the long march up to the front by night. Of the panzer divisions in southern and southwestern France, only Das Reich was on the move toward Normandy. The 9th Panzer was being pinned down by Vendetta on the Mediterranean coast, Ironside still preoccupied the 11th Panzer on the Biscay coast; and both divisions, along with other elements of Blaskowitz's Army Group G, would suffer the brutal and persistent harassment of *maquisards*. Key infantry units which were so badly needed if Rommel was to be able to withdraw and concentrate the panzers for a counterattack were still straggling in from Brittany. Without the forces necessary to oppose them, it would be, it seemed, only a matter of days before the Allies cracked and began to seep through the German dyke around Normandy. Deception and the war of special means had proved to be an invaluable adjunct to the methods of more conventional warfare. Yet the battle was far from being won, and Hitler had one weapon left in his arsenal that might delay and disrupt the inexorable Allied build-up. In the weeks ahead this weapon, the V1, would pose a grave threat to Neptune and Allied strategy.

5

Rommel

By MID-JUNE, Normandy had become an immense killing ground. The Allies and the Germans were locked together among the hedgerows and orchards in what Rommel would tell his son was "one terrible bloodletting. Sometimes we had as many casualties on one day as during the whole of the summer fighting in Africa in 1942. My nerves are pretty good, but sometimes I was near collapse. It was casualty reports, wherever you went. I have never fought with such losses. If I hadn't gone to the front nearly every day, I couldn't have stood it, having to write off literally one regiment every day."

Rommel's supply position was even worse. He needed 2500 tons of food, ammunition, war stores and petrol and oil supplies daily if his armies were to be kept fighting. But through air and guerrilla operations he never received more than 400 tons of all sorts. It was, as he said to Staubwasser one evening, a preposterous situation. The army in the Pas de Calais was sitting by the seaside doing nothing, but was still receiving most of the reinforcements and stores, while his army in Normandy was rapidly being destroyed. Yet Rommel himself could not be sure that the Allies did not intend to land in the Pas de Calais. At times he said he believed that Normandy *was* the invasion, but as he had written to his wife on June 10 (even though he had only just read the captured American 5th and 7th Corps orders): "It's quite likely to start at other places soon." On June 13 he wrote again. "It's time," he said, "for politics to come into play. We are expecting the next, perhaps even heavier blow to fall elsewhere in a few days."

At the root of Rommel's predicament was Hitler's determination to command the battle in Normandy himself. "My functions in Normandy," Rommel would tell his son, "were so restricted by Hitler that any sergeant-major could have carried them out. He interfered in

everything and turned down every proposal we made." Even
worse for Rommel, Hitler and OKW continued to believe the
fictions of Fortitude, and their command decisions reflected that
belief. Apparently convinced of the veracity of reports from agents in
England, mesmerized by the specter of Patton (who was reported
here, there and everywhere), arrogant in the conviction that their military judgment was right and all others' wrong, Hitler and the German
Supreme Command ignored the advice and pleas of their western commanders. The battle in Normandy was being fought from Berchtesgaden.

Roenne, too, remained convinced of the existence of Army Group
Patton. Staubwasser would later testify that Roenne called him personally "every two or three days . . . right up to the end of July" to
"emphasize" that FHW had "reliable information relating to a second
major landing intended by the Allies on the west coast of France or
the coast of Belgium." To support these telephone calls, Roenne sent
"almost daily" teleprinter reports that the number of divisions in the
British Isles ready for action exceeded the number of divisions then in
Normandy, that these formations had powerful air and naval forces at
their disposal, and that until they appeared in action nobody could be
certain that the main blow would not fall upon the Pas de Calais.
When Staubwasser, who knew something of the method by which
Roenne had arrived at his estimate of Allied strength in England,
challenged his figures, "Baron von Roenne insisted that the opinion
held by his department was correct, emphasizing that (Rommel's
headquarters) had no data whatsoever to base any judgment on in this
matter, and that therefore the strengths of the Allied forces assumed
by his department *must* serve as a basis for all planning carried out by
Army Group B." It was very curious behavior for the man who was
originally responsible for exaggerating the estimates of Allied strength.
Had he come to believe his own exaggerations, or was he acting on
some other motive?

As the casualties continued to mount in Normandy and the needed
replacements and reinforcements did not arrive, Rommel took another
step down the road to treason. Without the 15th Army, he had little
hope of inflicting such heavy losses on Neptune that the Allies would
be forced to seek terms, and he realized that unless he acted now he
would have nothing left either to save or to bargain with in any negotiations with the Grand Alliance. Accordingly, he invited Hitler to the
Château de La Roche Guyon for a conference, determined, if the
Fuehrer rejected his proposals, particularly concerning the use of the

15th Army, to have him arrested by troops who were loyal only to Rommel. Hitler accepted his invitation but elected to meet at W2, an underground command post near Soissons; he was far too wily to meet Rommel at the château.

Hitler arrived at W2 on June 17, escorted by his entourage. There, under the wooded hills of the Aisne, at a post which had been built for the Fuehrer to direct the invasion of England four years before, Hitler, Rundstedt and Rommel confronted each other. The Fuehrer, pale and weary from lack of sleep, toyed nervously with his colored pencils and his spectacles as Rommel described the state of the battle. The field marshal was himself close to nervous exhaustion, for the fighting had reached a degree of ferocity that had few parallels, even in Russia. That very day American troops were penetrating the last German line of defense before Cherbourg.

For thirty minutes Rommel told how the *Feldgrau* were fighting with "unbelievable courage and tenacity," but that infantry divisions were being reduced to battalions. He spoke of the overwhelming weight of Allied firepower; of the strength of the Allied divisions in the bridgehead; of the failures of the Luftwaffe, the Kriegsmarine and the intelligence services to provide any assistance that might help the men at the front. In particular, arguing with what Staubwasser would call "a combination of strategical and intuitive reasoning," he sought to persuade Hitler that the captured 5th and 7th Corps plans provided incontrovertible evidence that Normandy was *the* invasion.

The conference was interrupted for lunch. There, moodily, Hitler played with a dish of rice and vegetables which one of his escorts had tasted first, and began a monologue that was, Speidel would write, a "strange mixture of cynicism and wrong intuition." Hitler had ordered the V1 campaign against England to begin on June 12; even as he spoke, London was being subjected to what one observer would describe as an intermittent drizzle of malignant robots that seemed harder to bear than the storm and thunder of the blitz. Hitler talked "endlessly about the V-weapons which were going to decide the war," and stated that the existence of these weapons alone would *compel* the Allies to invade at the Pas de Calais. When Rommel protested that the Norman campaign was being directed from an armchair behind the front and declared, "You are asking us to have confidence in you, but you don't yourself trust us," Hitler grew even paler. After lunch, Rommel turned upon Hitler "with complete ruthlessness" and explained what he thought about the military and political situation. He prophesied the collapse of the German front in Normandy, stated that

not even the V-weapons could prevent that collapse, and ended with a
bold and memorable question: Did Hitler continue to believe that this
war could be won? Hitler brushed the question aside with an order:
"Look after your invasion front, and don't bother about the continuation of the war."

With that remark, Hitler propelled Rommel beyond any consideration of loyalty to the régime. He was now determined to make an
end to the war. Speidel would write:

> Rommel was under no illusion regarding the harshness of the peace
> conditions which had to be expected. But he placed his hope in a mod-
> est measure of statesmanlike insight, psychological intelligence, and
> political planning in Allied considerations. He no longer counted on
> Allied sympathy or similar sentiments. But he trusted the sober brains
> of the Great Powers.

From now on, as Walter Bargatzky, a lawyer on Stuelpnagel's staff
who was charged with the legal planning involved in the *coup d'état,*
would declare, Rommel could "hardly be restrained and wanted to get
things moving without delay." He received the emissary of the
Schwarze Kapelle in Berlin, Lieutenant Colonel Caesar von Hofacker,
a cousin of Stauffenberg's, whose assignment was to integrate the
conspirators' operations with those of Rommel. Hofacker informed
Rommel of the current plans to assassinate the Fuehrer, and as Bargatzky, who was a confidant of both, would state: "The (German)
Army in the west was supposed to surrender at the same time." Bargatzky, who later became president of the German Red Cross and a
leading official in the postwar West German Interior and Health
ministries, would also reveal that Speidel had "made it his business to
take all the larger SS units in France and have them engaged in battle
on the Normandy front on the day of the uprising so as to protect Paris
against their possible intervention." It was a statement that would bear
out Speidel's contention that Rommel had planned to keep army
panzer units out of the battle for as long as possible so that they might
be fresh, intact and available for any counterrevolution that the SS in
France might launch. Indeed, all combat arms of the SS would be
deeply committed to the battle.

Rommel made plans to send six German military emissaries, including Stuelpnagel and Speidel, across the lines to negotiate an armistice,
offering the complete evacuation of the occupied territories in the
West and the withdrawal of the German army to the old Siegfried
Line. They would ask for the immediate cessation of the bombing of

the German heartland, and in return, Rommel would stop the V-weapon bombardment of London. The armistice—not Unconditional Surrender—was to be followed by peace negotiations. On the eastern front, the struggle was to be continued by a holding action along a shortened line. Rommel had no doubt, Bargatzky would state, that he could master the SS. Nor did he expect a rebuff from the Allies. He was convinced that his "friend" Montgomery would give him an armistice and a separate peace, believing completely that such matters were in Montgomery's hands.

But first Rommel decided he would give Hitler "one more chance" to make "the correct deductions of the situation." He resolved to go to Berchtesgaden to confront the Fuehrer. On June 29 he and Rundstedt arrived at the Berghof. But Hitler was in no mood to talk with his marshals. He kept them waiting for six hours; and when he received them, much was discussed yet little decided—particularly in regard to Rommel's insistence that the 15th Army must be allowed to go to the help of the 7th.

Rundstedt demanded greater freedom of action, pointing out that the high commander on the spot could take more immediate, surer action than a commander 600 miles from the front. At this, Hitler looked sharply at the old field marshal, and Rundstedt knew that his days were numbered. Rundstedt also demanded at least some of the infantry divisions of the 15th Army to form a line behind which the panzers could be concentrated for a counteroffensive. Hitler replied only that he would consider the matter and issue a new directive. In the meantime, said the Fuehrer, repeating what he had said ever since D-Day, victory was to be gained by "holding fast tenaciously to every square yard of soil." Rommel protested that such a strategy was impossible. He alluded to the fact that the Russians had opened their summer offensive, and after feinting in various directions to tie up the forty-seven panzer divisions the Wehrmacht had in the East, the Red Army had destroyed thirty divisions, torn a gap in the German lines and was about to enter East Prussia. Bulgaria, Rumania, Hungary, Finland—all were contemplating surrender. The Wehrmacht was confronted with revolution in every one of the occupied countries. The Allied breakout in Normandy was both inevitable and imminent. The skies were growing dark for Germany.

Hitler listened frostily and then replied that Rommel had not considered the fact that this was England's war and that England was being forced out of it. When that happened, through the V1 campaign and his strategy of keeping the Allies penned up in Normandy, the entire Grand Alliance would collapse and Germany would be able to consume the pieces at her will. In the meantime, Hitler ordered, Rundstedt and Rommel must hold the line. That was an imperative. Detailed orders would follow.

Rommel and Rundstedt withdrew from the meeting, the former quite clear in his own mind that Hitler's policy was insane and that, if the German army was not to suffer the fate intended for the British, Hitler must be removed and an armistice obtained. The two marshals emerged gratefully into the fresh, clean air of the alpine evening, both convinced that they would be dismissed from their commands. They made their way to OKW quarters at the Strub Barracks to bathe, dine, wine, and to talk about the gravity of the situation in the East and the West. During the conversation Rommel spoke of a remarkable similarity between the Fuehrer and King Lear. Finally, Rundstedt, the "last of the German knights," broke up the discussion with a formal bow and wandered off to bed. He had drunk a lot of champagne and was a little tipsy.

When the two field marshals returned to their headquarters late in the evening of June 30, Hitler's directive awaited them. It dealt almost wholly with detail, and said little or nothing about the use on the 7th Army front of the 15th Army's infantry divisions. This meant that the panzer divisions under Rommel's command, designed for attack, would have to be used for defense; and even if the time came when it would be possible to mount a counteroffensive, they would probably be too weak through attrition to be effective. Neither could they be replaced once they had been chewed up. Situation reports awaiting Rommel revealed that the panzers were even now in danger. The army commanders demanded an immediate evacuation of the "killing ground" of Caen, where most of the panzer divisions were concentrated, and retirement to a new line beyond the range of the naval guns which were causing appalling casualties and disruption in the assembly areas. Rommel sent the appreciations to Rundstedt that same night, Rundstedt read them, and then penned a personal signal to the Fuehrer in which he endorsed the army commanders' and Rommel's opinions. Hitler sent this reply:

> The present positions are to be held. Any further breakthrough by the enemy will be prevented by tenacious defence or by local counterattacks. Assembly (of the armor) will continue and further mobile formations will be released (from defensive operations) by infantry divisions as they arrive.

Rundstedt's premonitions of dismissal proved to be correct. On July 2, Colonel Borgmann, one of Hitler's adjutants, arrived at Runstedt's headquarters, gave the field marshal a letter from the Fuehrer stating that he was relieved of command on the grounds of ill-health, and handed him the Oak Leaves to his Iron Cross. Geyr von Schweppenburg had also been sacked for his defeatist attitude, and when Rommel heard of Rundstedt's dismissal, he said to Speidel, "I shall be next."

On July 3, Field Marshal von Kluge arrived to succeed Rundstedt; and at their first conference, held at the Château de La Roche Guyon, relations between Kluge and Rommel were distinctly cool. Kluge, after several weeks in the Fuehrer's presence, had taken up the appointment of C-in-C West convinced once more of Hitler's greatness. He was also convinced of his ability to eject the Allied armies and was in no mood to discuss—at least sympathetically—Rommel's ideas for an "independent termination of the war in the west." Neither was he prepared to honor any of the assurances he had previously given the Schwarze Kapelle. Shown into Rommel's study by Speidel, Kluge carried his baton and wore all his medal ribbons, which Rommel usually did not.

It was not long before the two marshals were displaying their dislike for each other. After disagreeing fundamentally about the state of the battle in Normandy, Kluge delivered a severe censure upon Rommel. He stated that the dismissal of Rundstedt was the outward sign of Hitler's dissatisfaction with the high command in the West and—according to Speidel—declared that "Rommel himself did not enjoy the absolute confidence of the Führer." Rommel, said Kluge, was "not carrying out the Führer's orders wholeheartedly." Then he became threatening: "Field Marshal Rommel, even you must obey unconditionally from now on. This is good advice that I am giving you."

At this point Rommel flushed, and the conversation became so heated that he ordered Speidel and Tempelhof, his operations officer, both of whom were present, to leave the room. As they departed Rommel could be heard demanding that Kluge draw his "own conclusions from the general situation" and that he "withdraw his accusations at once." Rommel was heard to insist that he would set a time limit by which this must be done and he advised Kluge "not to form any opinions until he had conferred with his army commanders and with the troops and had made a tour of inspection at the front."

Kluge accepted the advice—and changed his mind about the situation in the West. He made a two-day tour of inspection and, according to Speidel, said that he had "not been able to escape the overwhelming evidence of the facts, the unanimous views of all the military commanders, and the logic of the situation; he had temporarily been bemused by Hitler's phrases. He took back all his accusations." From then on, Kluge veered closer to the conspirators' plans, tried not to interfere with control of the battle, and sought harmony with the ruffled Rommel.

Meanwhile, an eerie and remarkable incident had occurred at the front which suggested to Rommel that it might not be so difficult to get in touch with Montgomery. On July 2, as Bargatzky was actually drafting a letter for Rommel which he recommended be taken through the lines to the Allied high command by a "trustworthy German doctor," a section of German panzer grenadiers in the sector of the American 1st Infantry Division near Caumont heard with astonishment an American voice speaking German break in on their radio circuit. According to the German report of the incident, the voice called: "*Achtung! Achtung!* We call the German commander in this sector! We have important news for him!" The German commander came to the set to see what the Americans wanted, and the voice explained that they wished to repatriate a number of women, most of them nurses who had been captured at Cherbourg when that city fell to the Americans on June 26. Would the Germans take them back? After consulting with his superiors, who in turn notified Speidel, the Germans agreed to accept the nurses and suggested that a local truce be arranged to allow them to pass through the lines.

At three o'clock that afternoon, the guns went silent. Incredulous grenadiers and GI's alike, men with pink hedge roses stuck in their helmets for camouflage, rose out of their hides in meadows that were rich with clover and tall grass and saw three American officers coming down the road from the direction of the hamlet of Sept Vents. The American party was led by Captain Quentin Roosevelt, a G2 with the 1st Infantry, and Captain Fred Gercke, a prisoner of war interrogator. With them were eight German women. From out of a hedge stepped a Major Heeren, the commanding officer of the 2nd Panzer Reconnaissance Battalion of the 2nd Panzer Division of General von Luettwitz— one of the two panzer divisions which Rommel had intended to keep out of the line to deal with "internal enemies" when the rebellion came. There was a brief conversation and the nurses were transferred at 3:10 P.M. But the guns did not begin to fire again for four hours. Why did the truce last so long? Was it the outcome of a German initiative, camouflage to conceal the passage of a letter such as Bargatzky had drafted for Rommel? The official British answer was that no communication was received from Rommel at that or at any other time.

Then, on July 9, there was a second such truce in the same area, near the hamlet of Sept Vents. Captain Roosevelt, accompanied by Lieutenant Erhardt Dabringhaus and Lieutenant Kenneth J. Calligan, having failed to raise the Germans on the wireless, proceeded from the lines of the American 26th Infantry Regiment under cover of the white flag. The guns on both sides immediately went silent as the three men walked down the road shouting "Hello"—a brave thing to do. The time was 3 P.M. A German sergeant appeared out of some bushes with two soldiers, all of whom—according to Roosevelt's report—"looked completely flabbergasted." The Americans told the Germans that they wished to hand over nine more women who had been captured in Cherbourg, two nurses and seven secretaries. The sergeant, explaining that it was his duty to do so, insisted upon blindfolding the Americans. Then a Hauptmann Branns appeared, ordered that the blindfolds be removed, and announced that he would accept the women. There was a conversation about the state of the war. The Hauptmann declared, "What a pity it is we are fighting Americans," and at that point ambulances appeared with the women inside. Two of the women gave the salute "Heil Hitler!" to the Hauptmann, who did not reply, except to make the ungallant statement, having looked the women over, that "there is not much of interest here"; the prisoners were all between forty and fifty.

The exchange completed, the envoys returned to their respective lines and the fighting resumed. But again, the truce lasted about three hours, although it had taken less than fifteen minutes to hand the women over. They had much to report about the opulence of the Americans and the excellence of their treatment; for a last lunch they had been given orange juice, pea soup, fricasseed chicken with peas and carrots, fruit cocktails, and cigarettes. This was clearly the purpose of the exchange—an attempt by the Americans to prove the truth of their propaganda claims about the handsome treatment German deserters would receive. In fact, three Germans at Sept Vents did desert. But, again, why did the truce last so long? Was there some sort of reply made to a letter sent across on July 2? Once more the official British position—for Montgomery had high command in France at that time—was that no letters of any sort passed between the lines. All that was ever said about these incidents was a statement by Sir John Wheeler-Bennett, writing from his special place in the British secret intelligence apparatus: "With the knowledge that (a local truce) was now possible, Rommel (inspected) his frontline positions and (discussed) the position with his subordinate commanders. The outcome of his observations was embodied in a report to the *Führer* . . . couched in the terms of an ultimatum."

In the report, which was dated July 15, Rommel for the first time abandoned the careful phraseology and diplomatic niceties which had hitherto marked his correspondence with the Fuehrer. He pointed out flatly that Hitler's policies were failing. "The situation on the Normandy front is growing worse every day and is now approaching a grave crisis," he wrote. He spoke of the enemy's "enormous" concentrations of artillery and tanks, and of his own "huge" material losses. He declared that of the 97,000 men he had lost, including 2360 officers, only 6000 replacements had arrived at the front, with another 4000 promised. Against the enemy's power, Rommel wrote, "even the bravest army will be smashed piece by piece"; and drawing the Fuehrer's attention to the existence of idle divisions on the Pas de Calais front, he warned that "In these circumstances we must expect that in the foreseeable future the enemy will succeed in breaking through our thin front . . . and thrusting deep into France." He ended:

> The troops are everywhere fighting heroically, but the unequal struggle is approaching its end. It is urgently necessary for the proper conclusions to be drawn from this situation. As C-in-C of the Army Group I feel myself in duty bound to speak plainly on this point.

As protocol demanded, Rommel sent the letter to Kluge for forwarding to Hitler. But Kluge, aware that the letter might bring Rommel's relief and court-martial, held on to it for a day or two. Kluge needed Rommel in the West. For despite their intense dislike for each other, the two field marshals had agreed upon a pact. The revolution should begin not in Germany, as the Schwarze Kapelle intended, but in France. Kluge and Rommel had decided that if the opportunity arose they would open the front and permit the Anglo-American armies to march to the western borders of Germany with the assistance—not the opposition—of the Wehrmacht. The strategic objective: to allow the western powers to occupy Germany before the Russians did. Kluge had once again committed himself to conspiracy.

On the evening of the 15th—the same day that Rommel wrote to the Fuehrer—he walked with Staubwasser through the grounds of the Château de La Roche Guyon toward the two mighty cedars where there was a bench overlooking the Seine. After some long minutes of silence, Rommel said: "Staubwasser, I have given him his last chance. If he does not take it, we will act." The field marshal was silent as they walked on. But when they sat down on the bench, it was evident that Rommel was facing a personal crisis of the greatest magnitude. Suddenly he placed his head in his hands and murmured: "Oh Staubwasser! This war must be brought to an end!"

In spite of his despair, and for all the disadvantages with which he was fighting the battle, Rommel had succeeded in imposing a near stalemate upon the Allies. He had sealed off the beachhead, forcing the Allies to fight the sort of battle they feared the most—a dull killing match in country where they could not employ their armor or their airpower with decisive effect. It had become a battle that, for the British, was all too reminiscent of Flanders and the Somme.

Bradley had finally succeeded in capturing Cherbourg, fourteen days later than the Neptune plan anticipated, but twice Montgomery had tried to take the other key town in Normandy—Caen—and twice the *Panzertruppen* stopped him. Neptune was being strangled. Except in the Cotentin, the lodgment was little more than 10 miles deep. Bad weather still interrupted supply schedules and there were serious ammunition shortages. Moreover, the fierce fighting generated a crisis in the troops' morale. Eisenhower, particularly, was deeply shocked when he visited the lodgment and discovered that in one hospital alone there were over a thousand cases of SIW (self-inflicted wounds), men who had shot themselves through the foot or some other non-vital part of their bodies to get out of the firing line.

The causes of the near stalemate were many. The Allies were virtually trapped in the difficult "hedgerow country," a terrain where the normal horizon was 75 to 150 yards, where one man well dug into a hedge could hold back five, where it was impossible to use tanks, where artillery was rarely completely effective, and where the best weapons were carbines, pistols, bayonets, knives and mortars. The persistent rains prevented the Allies from using their airpower and turned the countryside into bogs. The German tanks, and particularly their 88-mm anti-aircraft artillery piece, were superior to Allied weapons. German strategy and tactics in containing the beachhead were excellent, and Rommel's armies, outnumbered and outgunned, were fighting with a stubbornness and heroism that came in part from loyalty to their commander and in part from the realization that they could not surrender.

The methods of conventional warfare alone seemed insufficient to break the German stranglehold, so the British looked anew into their armory of special means to produce, in the first place, "Hellhound." Aware (probably through Ultra) that Hitler and the German high command were directing the battle in Normandy from Berchtesgaden, the Allies prepared to launch a massive air strike against the headquarters by the U.S. 15th Air Force in Italy. Hellhound, the code name of the operation, was first mentioned in a "Redline" signal—Eisenhower's personal communication—to the Mediterranean Allied Air Force Headquarters on June 15. American photographic reconnaissance aircraft made a series of runs over Berchtesgaden during the next four days, and by June 24, intelligence mosaics had been produced and were ready for distribution for the briefing of the bomber groups. But then, mysteriously, MAAF was ordered to hold its hand. No explanation was ever given, and the operation was not mounted. Why? Only one reason appears probable; a raid against Berchtesgaden might destroy *the* key Ultra source—OKW itself—without killing Hitler.

But the British did have another plan: "Gaff," an operation that had been conceived by the special operations planning syndicates as early as March 1944, its objective to kill or kidnap the man who continued to symbolize Germany's military skill, tenacity and heroism—Rommel. The mission had not been mounted before or during the invasion, largely because of the failure to locate his headquarters accurately. But in the second week of June, Rommel's headquarters had been discovered and, with the mounting crisis over the near stalemate in Normandy, Montgomery gave his approval for the operation which, he hoped, would help break the deadlock.

Just after D-Day, Lieutenant Colonel William Fraser, of the 1st SAS Regiment, had dropped into the Morvan Mountains between Dijon and Nevers, his mission to establish "Houndsworth," another large SAS redoubt in enemy territory. Eighteen officers and 136 troopers with armored jeeps and artillery would be parachuted to the base to harass the Germans as they came up from the Côte d'Azur to Normandy. It was a bold operation, for the nearest Allied forces would be in Normandy, 300 miles away.

When Fraser and his wireless operator landed, they buried their parachutes in the thick humus, and then made their way to a thicket close to a small stone bridge over the Cure, a stream coming out of the mountains near Château Chinon, a town about 180 miles southeast of Paris. Fraser's orders were to make contact at the bridge with an F section agent, Louis, who would lead him to the headquarters of a *maquisard* called Camille. Camille was then to take him on to the Houndsworth advance party, which had gone in just after H-Hour. Intelligence-gathering formed no part of Fraser's operational orders.

At dawn, as arranged, Fraser saw a middle-aged man in a cloth cap and a baggy double-breasted suit coming down the narrow lane toward the bridge, driving some cattle. Fraser called out the passwords: *"Je cherche la maison de Charles."* The man replied: *"Vous voulez dire de Monsieur Dupont?"* It was Louis, but he demanded further evidence of Fraser's identity, and Fraser replied that he would signal London to broadcast the words *"Le médecin a les cheveux gris"* over the BBC at 1:30 P.M. the following day. Not until Louis heard those words would he take Fraser to Camille. But they began a march that lasted thirty-six hours. Finally, the men stopped by a brook and Fraser's operator tuned in to London. Fraser and Louis had spoken little until that moment; but when he heard the music of the French song *Sur le pont d'Avignon*—the idioform for the SAS in France—and the words, *"Le médecin a les cheveux gris,"* Louis broke into smiles and laughter. Three hours later they were with Camille, who, as they arrived, was trying three suspected agents of the Gestapo. One of them, a Belgian, was taken behind a clump of rhododendrons and shot.

At the base, Fraser met an aristocratic-looking Frenchman who had been staying at the nearby Château de Vermot and who introduced himself as "M. Defors, chief game warden of all the French colonies before the war," and now "the owner of an estate near the Château La Roche Guyon." What Defors had to say electrified Fraser. The château was Rommel's headquarters. Would it be possible for Fraser to go there and kill the field marshal, Defors asked, because his presence was making the local inhabitants afraid they might be bombed? Fraser determined to make the sortie, and began to gather all the data necessary from Defors. It would be, he discovered, a simple matter to approach the château, although the area was very heavily guarded by German troops. From a wood on the bank of the Seine opposite the château, a sniper could shoot at the field marshal at a range of about 400 yards, as he walked in the Italian gardens. There were *maquisards* at Vernon upon whom Fraser could rely for a safehouse, an air drop, and a landing field.

At 1645 on June 14, 1944, Fraser sent this message to London:

From HOUNDSWORTH 102. Very reliable source states Rommel's headquarters at Chateau delaroche Guyon 50 miles W of Paris 10 miles WNW of Mantes on the right bank of Seine. Rommel there on 25 May and Staff permanently there. Rommel arrives left bank of Seine, crosses by motor launch. Walks and shoots in Foret de Moisson. Send maps from this area to area of Mantes also three snipers rifles. Would prefer you not to send another party for this job as consider it is my pigeon.

The next day at 1330 Fraser followed up this message with another:

From HOUNDSWORTH 102. Request permission to start for Rommel's headquarters in one week's time. Have excellent contacts on route and in that area.

At Moor Park, the country mansion just outside London built by Henry VIII for Anne Boloyn which was now an SAS headquarters, Fraser's messages were examined by Brigadier R. W. McLeod, the SAS commander, and Major Alexander Scratchley, the Duke of Norfolk's trainer and, for the moment, an SAS intelligence officer. The difficulties of the mission were obvious immediately. Fraser was more than 200 miles from the château, he would have to move through areas that were stiff with German troops and the *Geheime Feldpolizei,* and Rommel might not be there even if he succeeded in getting through. Moreover, Fraser's present assignment was too important, for Houndsworth was to cut the route the Germans were expected to use to bring the 9th Panzer Division from the south to Normandy. They wirelessed back:

For FRASER. Regret must forbid your personal attack on Rommel. Appreciate you consider him your pigeon but your task to remain in command present area. This pigeon will be attacked by special party.

Fraser made two attempts to get McLeod to change his mind; but McLeod was adamant. He wirelessed Houndsworth: "Regret decision must stand."

There had been other indications—probably intelligence derived from the Y service—that Rommel was headquartered at the château, and RAF photo-reconnaissance planes had been prowling around the area. Additional confirmations came from F section which had a *réseau* in the vicinity; indeed, the Comtesse Y. de la Rochefoucauld, a relative of the duc, was a sub-agent. With that information, McLeod decided to go ahead with Gaff, and the plan was issued as SAS Brigade Operation Instruction 32. The orders were terse and to the point. The objective of the plan was to "kill, or kidnap and remove to England, Field Marshal Rommel, or any senior members of his staff," and while the instruction observed that "it is preferable to ensure the former rather

TOP SECRET

Copy No. .5...

HQ SAS Tps/TSB/5/G

SAS BRIGADE OPERATION INSTRUCTION No. 32

Operation GAFF - OC 2 SAS Regt

INTENTION

1. To kill, or kidnap and remove to England, Field Marshal ROMMEL, or any senior members of his staff.

INFORMATION

2. Recent information regarding the location and movement of ROMMEL is contained in:-

i) SHAEF letter, 18 Jul 44, copy attached as Appendix A.

ii) Two signals from HOUNDSWORTH dated 14 and 16 Jul stating that reliable information obtained from the owner of the estates around ROMMEL's HQ indicated that this HQ is at Chateau DE LA ROCHE, near LA ROCHE GUYON N.5572; that ROMMEL was there on 25 Jun; that his staff is there permanently; that he crosses the R. SEINE by motor launch and walks and shoots in the FORET DE MOISSON on the left bank.

iii) A signal from HAFT dated 18 Jul saying that ROMMEL's Tac HQ is at BAGNOLES Y.9798 (HAFT has been asked for further details).

METHOD

3. This must be left to you and you will submit your detailed proposals as soon as possible to this HQ.

4. The following points should be borne in mind:-

If it should prove possible to kidnap ROMMEL and bring him to this country the propaganda value would be immense and the inevitable retaliation against the local inhabitants might be mitigated or avoided. Such a plan would involve finding and being prepared to hold for a short time if necessary, a suitable landing ground.

5. To kill ROMMEL would obviously be easier than to kidnap him and it is preferable to ensure the former rather than to attempt and fail in the latter. Kidnapping would require successful two-way W/T communication and therefore a larger party, while killing could be reported by pigeon.

6. The possibilities of dropping to reception arranged by SFHQ should be investigated.

ACKNOWLEDGE.

c/o HQ Airborne Tps (Main),
APO, England.
WBKS/MAJ
20.7.44

/Distribution

Brigadier,
Commander,
SAS Troops

SAS Brigade Operation Instruction No. 32—Operation "Gaff"—the special order authorizing a plan "to kill, or kidnap" Field Marshal Rommel, an operation that was mounted even as Rommel sought to arrange an armistice and the surrender of his armies in France.

than to attempt and fail in the latter," it also noted that "If it should prove possible to kidnap Rommel *and* bring him to this country the propaganda value would be immense and the inevitable retaliation against the local inhabitants might be mitigated or avoided."

Gaff was assigned to a specially trained party of SAS troopers—it consisted of one officer and six men—which already existed under the command of a man whose *nom de guerre* was "Raymond Lee." He was a captain in the International Squadron of the SAS, a unit made up of men of such nationalities as Algerian *pieds-noirs*, Corsicans, Sicilian *mafiosi*, anti-Communist Bulgarians and the like, which had been formed with the express purpose of committing special acts of warfare such as the assassination of enemy commanders. Evidently Lee was expert, trusted and brave; for an unspecified task while on operations in the Mediterranean he had received the Distinguished Service Order. Lee and his men were prepared for action when this letter was received by Brigadier McLeod from Montgomery's headquarters:

> It is understood that General Montgomery has agreed to this operation and confirmation is expected shortly from 21 Army Group. Plans should therefore be proceeded with as quickly as possible.

By this time, the intelligence dossier on Rommel and his headquarters was very detailed. It described the routes that Rommel used to travel to and from the château, and noted in particular that he usually left his headquarters when going on inspection trips at between five and six o'clock in the morning, returned usually at about six o'clock, dined at about seven-thirty, and after dinner often went for a stroll in the grounds—grounds that were open to a shot from the woods on the other bank of the Seine.

On July 10, Lee and the rest of the Gaff party had been fully briefed, and were sealed in an apartment near Broadcasting House in London to await any final orders and transport to the special duties airfield at Harrington in Northamptonshire. That same day SAS headquarters reported to Montgomery's headquarters:

> SAS 116. secret. SAS ready to send party to end Rommel existence and/or any ersatz staff officer at his headquarters. Will try to arrange for his transmission to this country if you will suggest date most suitable to you for his interrogation in this country.

During the evening of July 15—the same evening that Rommel said to Staubwasser that the war must be brought to an end—the Gaff party was taken in a closed van to Harrington, for a takeoff that night. But at the last moment it was decided to postpone the mission; the weather over the drop zone near Dreux was reported bad. Lee and his men were told that they would go in when the weather cleared. Thus at the very moment that Rommel was preparing to surrender, the British were planning to kill him. Gaff was remounted late in the afternoon of July 18 and the party was parachuted into the woods between Orléans and Vernon on or about the night of the 18th or 19th. But by then it was too late. Fate had caught up with Field Marshal Rommel.

The V1

Tиe V1 flying bomb campaign against "Target 42"—the German cipher for London—began six days after D-Day. It did not come as a surprise to the Allied air defense authorities. There had been much physical, wireless and technical evidence that the attack was impending. Moreover, the Germans had advised their key agents in London such as Garbo to move out of the capital, and from this it was deduced that the long-awaited onslaught was about to begin.

The opening salvo in what was intended to be a mass attack of a thousand missiles was, however, as the RAF would have said, something of a fizzle. So effective had been the Allied air forces' pounding of the launch sites, supply trains and storage depots that the Germans had only ten rounds ready for launch when they received the order for the attack to begin. Of these, four crashed upon launch, two failed to hit England at all, and only four got anywhere near the aiming point— Tower Bridge in central London. The first crashed at the Thames Estuary near Gravesend, 20 miles from the bridge. The second fell even further away, at Cuckfield just north of Brighton, startling only the crows. The third fell near Sevenoaks in Kent, startling everybody. The fourth came down at Bethnal Green, one of the most densely populated quarters of London. It struck a railway bridge, killed six people and seriously injured thirteen others. They were the only casualties of the night.

The attack was hardly the holocaust that the Fuehrer demanded and desired; and it seemed to Churchill, at his Cabinet meeting the following morning, that Hitler's secret weapon was just another bluff after all. Cadogan reflected the jubilation of those present when he wrote in his diary: "Not v. impressive. Hope some will return and fall in Germany! They didn't fly higher than 8,000 ft. and only 250 mph.

at most. A sitting target (for the British air defences)!" The Chiefs of Staff regarded the attack as a baffling anticlimax, for they had been expecting at least four hundred missiles—each carrying 1 ton of high explosive—to rain down upon London. But there were less optimistic counsels, among them Dr. R. V. Jones of MI-6. He thought the opening salvo was a misfire—as it was. He called Lord Cherwell, the Prime Minister's personal scientific adviser, to urge the Cabinet to be cautious. But Cherwell "exuberantly chuckled" that "The mountain hath groaned and given forth a mouse!" Jones replied: "For God's sake don't laugh this one off!" Cherwell would not listen; and neither would the Chief of the Air Staff, Portal. He decided that the 3000 Flying Fortress sorties which he had ordered against the 60-odd known launching sites should be reduced to 1000 and the balance be given to SHAEF to support the armies in France.

The jubilation had vanished when the Chiefs of Staff and the Cabinet met on the morning of June 16. The previous day seventy-three V1's had fallen on London and a new ordeal for the city had begun—at the same moment that Neptune was struggling to stay ashore in Normandy. The destruction of the missiles in flight and the bombardment of the launching sites became top priorities. Anti-aircraft equipment which was being used to protect Neptune from harassment by the Luftwaffe was withdrawn, and Eisenhower was asked to take "all possible measures to neutralise the supply and launching sites subject to no interference with the essential requirements of the Battle of France." Accordingly, on June 18, Eisenhower ordered that "*Crossbow* [the code name for the V1] targets would now rank higher than anything for the Allied bomber force 'except the urgent requirements of the battle.'"

That same day, a V1 hit the Guards Chapel at Wellington Barracks, only a few yards from the heart of the main nerve center of the British war machine—10 Downing Street, the Foreign Office, Parliament, MI-6 headquarters, the War Bunker at Storey's Gate and Buckingham Palace. It was a Sunday, the chapel was packed with worshipers. Elisabeth Sheppard-Jones would recall what happened just before both her legs were blown off:

> The congregation rose to its feet. . . . In the distance hummed faintly the engine of a flying bomb. "We praise thee, O God: we acknowledge Thee to be the Lord," we, the congregation, sang. The dull burr became a roar, through which our voices could now only faintly be heard. "All the earth doth worship Thee: the Father everlasting." The roar stopped abruptly as the engine cut out. . . . The *Te Deum* soared

again into the silence. "To Thee all Angels cry aloud: the Heavens, and all the Powers therein." Then there was a noise so loud it was as if all the waters and the winds in the world had come together in mighty conflict, and the Guards' Chapel collapsed upon us in a bellow of bricks and mortar. . . . One moment I was singing the *Te Deum,* and the next I lay in dust and blackness, aware of one thing only—that I had to go on breathing.

In that moment of explosion, some 80 Guards officers, men and their relatives were killed and about another 120 were badly injured. Mrs. Churchill was close by, visiting her daughter Mary who was on duty with the Hyde Park flak battery; they saw the bomb descend toward Downing Street and people falling flat on their faces. Among them was Menzies, who was on his way from MI-6 headquarters to the chapel to attend the service. That day other V1's fell in Wandsworth, Croydon, Lewisham, Camberwell, Woolwich, Greenwich, Beckenham, Lambeth, Orpington, Coulsdon, Purley, West Ham, Chislehurst and Mitcham. No longer a mere threat, Hitler's secret weapon was generating a crisis of magnitude.

Churchill, who was at Chequers that Sunday, returned to the capital immediately and ordered that the House of Commons, which had been bombed out in the London blitz of 1940 but had since returned, should evacuate to Church House, "whose modern steel structure offered somewhat more protection than the Palace of Westminster." A sense akin to terror began to spread through the capital; there was little panic, but the "grating roar that resembled a badly-tuned motorcycle engine" soon dominated all life in London and southern England. As one social historian would put it:

> Of all the bombs that descended upon the British Isles between 1939 and 1945 none is remembered with more bitter loathing. The first unmanned aircraft, with its harsh-sounding engine, scuttling remorselessly across the sky like some science-fiction monster, seemed even more sinister than the bombers which preceded it . . . to have one's house wrecked or one's family killed just when this seemingly interminable war was drawing to a close seemed not merely tragic but pointless.

Churchill ordered Bomber Command to make a maximum effort against Berlin as retaliation; and on the night of June 21/22, 1944, some 2500 RAF bombers attacked the German capital in the heaviest raid so far in the Second World War. They were followed, during the daylight hours, by 1000 American heavy bombers and 1200 long-range fighters. The death and destruction in Berlin were enormous, but Hitler's V1 campaign continued.

By June 25, the Germans had launched more than 2000 bombs, hundreds of which penetrated British defenses and fell upon London and the surrounding areas. Destruction and dislocation were severe, and the government began an evacuation of women, children, the elderly and hospital patients that would total nearly 1 million people. The evacuation placed an enormous strain on roads and railways that were already carrying capacity loads to the ports for the battle in Normandy; and this, in turn, caused serious delays in the shipment of supplies that were desperately needed on the Far Shore. But more important than all else was the strain that the V1's put on the civilian population. Would it hold up under the attack? If it did not, Britain would have to sue for peace just as Hitler had predicted.

On June 27, Herbert Morrison, the Home Secretary, delivered to the Cabinet a warning that was at once more serious and somber than any he had delivered in the entire course of the war. The V1 bombardment had already destroyed or damaged over 200,000 houses, and literally millions of panes of glass had been blown out of Londoners' homes. Unless the glassmaking industry was capable of producing enough glass to replace them before winter set in, there would be disastrous losses in manpower through illnesses. Furthermore, shattered sewage systems posed the threat of epidemics, and the Ministry of Works, Morrison reported, was "finding it difficult to keep up with the damage caused." Hundreds of people were homeless and rations might have to be reduced because rail services, already overtaxed by the demands of Neptune and the evacuation, were also suffering damage. No less grave was the anxiety caused by the continual bombardment. "After five years of war," Morrison declared, "the civil population (is) not capable of standing the strain of air attack. . . ."

What was to be done? As a first step the War Cabinet ordered the mass movement of anti-aircraft artillery to the south coast—over 2000 guns and anti-aircraft rocket launchers were positioned there overnight. The second step was an intensification of Allied aerial bombardment of the launch sites and storage depots. To help the air forces, Menzies and Gubbins directed their agents in France to increase their efforts to locate the targets; and one agent in particular—"Wizard"—came through with intelligence of great importance.

Wizard was W. J. Savy, a lawyer turned F section organizer and close friend of Antelme, who had saved him from the live embers of the Prosper disaster by whisking him out of France to London aboard a Dericourt Lysander. Savy returned to France early in 1944 to act as Antelme's treasurer and quartermaster, but when Antelme was captured, he went to ground in Paris and joined another *réseau*. Savy kept his eyes and ears open and on a trip to Creil, near Paris, in March, he heard a whisper from a man who grew mushrooms in the great caves at St. Leu d'Esserent nearby. The Germans, said the mushroom man, had taken over the caves and were building a spur railway line up to them. Their roofs were being lined with concrete and shorn up with steel and wood; narrow-gauge rail tracks were being laid inside them, and anti-aircraft and machine-gun posts were also being constructed. Savy suspected, correctly, that they were to be some kind of arms dump. He flew to London just before the invasion to report and then returned after D-Day to continue his surveillance. Late in June, he discovered what the Germans were storing in the caves—2000 V1's. The intelligence was wirelessed to London in Savy's special one-time pad cipher.

Delayed by bad weather, the RAF did not find the correct conditions for a precision attack for several days. But on the night of July 4/5, 227 Lancasters carrying 4000-pound "cookies" hit the caves and the road and rail links leading into them. German night fighters rose to their defense and claimed thirteen bombers, but seventeen more Lancasters of 617 Squadron, each carrying a 6-ton earthquake bomb, slipped through. Eleven of the earthquake bombs hit the specially marked caves accurately and stove them in, while the "cookies" wrecked the gun and rail systems.

The next day, Savy's mushroom man reported that all the entrances and approaches to the caves had been blocked and that inside many of the V1's were buried in chalk, limestone and earth. Could the Germans dig them out and open up the entrances? Yes, said the mushroom man, they could—and were doing so already. Savy passed the news to London, SOE told Bomber Command, and on the night of July 7/8, 228 Lancasters came in low and buried the V1 dumps in a welter of high explosive. It was probably SOE's most important intelligence contribution of the Neptune period, for it denied to the Germans about a quarter of the missiles available to them in France.

The aerial campaign against the V1 would prove to be a costly diversion from the demands of the land battle in France. The Allies were forced to deflect a fifth of their strength in the air toward tackling the problem. It was also a costly campaign in terms of lives and aircraft; some 3000 airmen lost their lives in these operations, along with some 500 aircraft. The British were responsible for the air defense of England, and the main burden was borne by the RAF, but the dead were not only British. There were many Americans, among them Lieutenant Joseph Kennedy, of the United States Navy, the eldest son of the American ambassador in London in 1940, and the brother of future President John F. Kennedy. Lieutenant Kennedy took off from an airfield in East Anglia in a B-24 Liberator bomber crammed with 22,000 pounds of high explosives and set course for the great earthworks at Mimoyecques, a suspected rocket storage depot. Soon after Kennedy took off, a second Liberator became airborne. The plan was for Kennedy to fly to a point close to the target; then he and his co-pilot would bail out, leaving their aircraft under the radio control of the second Liberator which would direct it to Mimoyecques, where it would crash into the target. But there was an accident—the precise nature of which would never be established—and the Liberator blew up over Suffolk, killing both Kennedy and his co-pilot. Their bodies were never found.

While attack and defense measures against the V1 were being employed by the military, the British secret agencies set in motion a third measure—deception. The scheme was proposed by Dr. R. V. Jones at a meeting with MI-5 and MI-6 on July 1. The secret agencies were faced with a dilemma. Agents working for the XX-Committee were being asked by their German controllers to report the fall of the V1's, a request they could not ignore. But, said Jones, if they spotted the shots accurately, they would be giving aid and comfort to the enemy, who would continue to aim the missiles on Tower Bridge with grievous consequences to London. And if they lied, aerial reconnaissance would reveal that they had done so, and the Germans would suspect that they were under control. Furthermore, the Germans kept records of the firing time of each missile, and although they could not be certain of the location of impact, they knew the time of impact within a minute or two. Jones's scheme solved the dilemma. He proposed that XX-Committee agents report on the missiles that had fallen north of London using the impact times of missiles that had actually fallen south of the capital. Thus, Jones thought the Germans would conclude that the V1's were falling long and shorten the range by decreasing their flight times. That, in turn, would cause the missiles to fall in open country south of London.

Before the plan could be employed, approval had to be obtained. The XX-Committee took it up with Sir Findlater Stewart, the chairman of the Home Defence Executive, who was a member of the Committee and of the LCS; and he took it to Duncan Sandys, Churchill's son-in-law, the former commander of Britain's first rocket-firing regiment, and now chairman of the War Cabinet's Crossbow Committee, the organization established by Churchill to coordinate all intelligence and counteraction. Sandys took the plan to the War Cabinet, it was approved, and XX-Committee agents began to transmit the rigged fall of shot.

By a fortunate coincidence, an old friend of the XX-Committee was sent to England by the Germans at about this same time to report the fall of the V1's. His name was Edward Chapman, and his XX-Committee code name, "Zigzag," was an apt description of his career. A former Coldstream Guardsman and safe-blower, he had deserted in 1939 and had been captured by the Germans in 1940 while hiding on the Channel Islands. He volunteered for work with the Abwehr as a sabotage agent in England and, because of his knowledge of explosives, he was accepted. After extensive training at the Abwehr's espionage school in a château near Nantes, he was given a contract worth £15,000 to sabotage the de Havilland aircraft works at Hatfield in Hertfordshire. An aircraft was laid on to drop him near Ely in December 1942 but the British were waiting for him. Through Ultra, the security authorities were able to follow the movements of enemy agents, including Zigzag, well before they arrived in England. Masterman would write: ". . . we knew a great deal about ZIGZAG before his arrival, and elaborate preparations had been made with regional and police authorities to secure him quickly and without advertisement as soon as he arrived."

Zigzag was collected as he stepped out of his parachute shrouds; but upon interrogation, he proved to be on the side of Britain rather than Germany, and he agreed (in return for a pardon) to work for the XX-Committee. A violent explosion was rigged at de Havilland (together with suitable damage, arranged by some special effects and scenery experts from the Old Vic); Zigzag reported his coup (as did the British press, which was allowed to breathe fire at the ineptitude of the security services) by wireless; and then arrangements were made for him to "escape." This he did in January 1943, posing as a steward aboard the steamer *City of Lancaster,* bound for Lisbon.

Nothing more was heard of Zigzag until the middle of 1944 when, as Masterman put it, "News . . . trickled through to us of a mysterious figure at Oslo—a man speaking bad German in a rather loud high-pitched voice clad in a pepper-and-salt suit, displaying two gold teeth and enjoying the amenities of a private yacht. This we thought must be ZIGZAG, and so it was."

Zigzag returned to England out of the night sky near Cambridge at the end of June, with two wireless sets, cameras, £6000, and a contract with the Germans for £100,000 to report the fall of shot of the V1's. The XX-Committee promptly put him to work passing doctored information. But then he was overheard by MI-5 officers telling his story in a public house. His case was "terminated" and he was quietly locked up, although the XX-Committee continued to use his wireless, cipher and security checks to relay the doctored information. Zigzag did not reappear until after the war, when he was to be seen frequenting the edges of Belgravian society, and later came into the possession of a Rolls-Royce and a health farm.

The XX-Committee campaign to deflect the fall of the V1's was not entirely successful. The Germans did indeed shorten their range, but the missiles began to fall not on open country, but on the working-class quarters south of the Thames, sparing the wealthier areas north of the river. Herbert Morrison protested. He demanded that the secret agencies seek only to confuse the German's aim, rather than deflect it; and he advocated precisely what Hitler believed that the Allies must do: invade the Pas de Calais to destroy the missile launching sites. Morrison insisted that the deception campaign be stopped immediately. As an historian of the incident would write: "M.I.5 was not authorised to interfere with Providence." Morrison's protests were quietly ignored, and the deception campaign continued to the end. But Hitler's use of the V1 as a weapon of indiscriminate destruction and terror seemed, at the time, immoral in itself, and it would lead the British to consider an even deadlier form of retaliation—poison gas.

It was a trying moment in the history of the Anglo-American alliance. The battle in Normandy was going slowly and badly as the weather continued to interrupt supply schedules. The weather also provided cover for the V1's, making the job of interception and destruction by fighters extremely difficult. Churchill, under the fearful strain of events in Normandy and the accelerating V1 campaign, wanted to abandon Anvil, Marshall's plan for an invasion of southern France to open up Marseilles as a port of entry for fresh U.S. divisions and supplies. He proposed instead to strengthen the Italian campaign, which was going well, cross the Alps, and march upon Austria and Germany from the south. This suggestion brought the sharpest and rudest rejection by Roosevelt in the history of the alliance so far, a rejection that was caused in part by what the Americans regarded as Montgomery's failure to break the German front in Normandy. The

American attitude was uncompromising and blunt. Anvil would proceed.

It was in this context that the British Chiefs of Staff began to consider the use of poison gas. On July 4, a note from the Chiefs of Staff Secretary to the Joint Planning Staff at Storey's Gate stated:

> At their meeting today, the COS instructed the JPS to examine the desirability and practicability of using gas as a retaliation for Crossbow attacks. The report should consider the use of gas (a) against the Crossbow area alone, (b) as a general retaliation against Germany.

While the JPS was studying the implications of using gas, Menzies brought new and serious information to Cadogan. On July 10, he reported that a German long-range rocket had fallen in Sweden accidentally, and the Germans there were attempting to recover its remains; one party had entered the area, which was sealed off, behind a funeral cart, posing as mourners. Menzies wanted permission to "buy" the rocket's remains from the Swedes in exchange for two squadrons of tanks. Cadogan agreed, so did the Swedes, and two Mosquitos were sent to Stockholm to pick up the remains. After they were examined in London, they proved beyond doubt what had hitherto been a source of argument and speculation: that Hitler had a missile even more powerful than the V1. It was the V2, a liquid-fuel rocket capable of carrying 1 ton of aluminized explosive to London; and a V2 attack would not be long delayed.

On July 13, in light of this worrying news and after studying the JPS report, Churchill sent a minute to the Vice Chiefs of Staff directing that:

> A comprehensive examination should be undertaken of the military implications of our deciding on an all-out use of gas, principally mustard gas, or any other method of warfare which we have hitherto refrained from using against the Germans, in the following circumstances:
>
> (a) as a counter-offensive in the event of the use by the enemy of flying bombs and/or giant rockets developing into a serious threat to our ability to prosecute the war; or, alternatively
>
> (b) as a means of shortening the war or of bringing to an end a situation in which there was a danger of stalemate.

The memorandum reflected the gravity with which Churchill saw the situation.

Consideration of the use of poison gas was undertaken at the highest levels and a new report from the JPS was ready on July 16. It was handed in for study as Churchill was busily promoting another deadly idea: that the RAF should select one hundred small, undefended German towns and wipe them out one by one until Hitler stopped using his missiles. The report was a chilling assessment of the advantages and disadvantages of poison gas; it stated, however, that "British use of gas in Europe would achieve an initial tactical surprise, but would thereafter restrict Allied movements." It therefore ruled out gas warfare. But it did not entirely rule out bacteriological weapons.

The JPS had studied the use of a bacteriological agent codenamed "N"—probably anthrax; and as the report stated:

> There is no known prophylactic against "N." If it can be used in practise, the effect on morale will be profound. It is improbable that the Germans will initiate biological warfare. There is no evidence to show whether they are in a position to retaliate in kind, were we to initiate it. . . . There seems to be little doubt that the use of bacteriological warfare would cause heavy casualties, panic and confusion in the areas affected. It might lead to a breakdown in administration with a consequent decisive influence on the outcome of the war. . . . If the claims of N are substantiated, its use could probably make a substantial change in the war situation.

But the report concluded that "There is no likelihood of a sustained attack being possible before the middle of 1945." That was that; Churchill dropped the matter. But, for a moment at least, the almost unbearable tensions caused by the V1 bombardment and the stalemate in Normandy had weakened the war's ultimate moral restraint; as one historian of the period would point out: ". . . the possibility exists that the JPS report of 16 July might have reached a different conclusion if Britain's development of the mysterious 'N' had been a year further advanced."

Britain was forced to endure Hitler's aerial bombardment; and casualties and damage—most of them in London—were severe. In all, the Germans would launch 10,500 V1's against England, 2400 of which got through the defenses. Some 1.5 million houses were destroyed or damaged, 6200 people were killed and 18,000 were seriously injured. But the weapon, though terrible, was not conclusive. It did not compel Eisenhower to change his plans and land in the Pas de Calais, as Hitler was convinced that it must. Moreover, Hitler had made a fundamental mistake in directing fire at London. The 630 square miles of that great city could absorb the punishment. Had the bombs been launched against the south coast ports—Dover, Folkestone, Margate, Portsmouth, Southampton—the damage and casualties would have so dislocated Neptune's supply schedules that the Germans might have regained the initiative in France. But Hitler's desire for vengeance against the Allies for the bombardment of German cities prevailed over wiser counsels. He used the V1's not to obtain a strategic advantage, but for revenge—yet another mistake that would cost him the war.

Goodwood

For all the flaming magnitude of the battle in Normandy, the secret war which went on behind it—the war in which the Germans sought to establish the Allied plan of campaign and strength while the Allies sought to delude the Germans on those very points—was, in manpower terms, a comparatively small affair. Yet seemingly minute incidents could—and did—provide intelligence that dictated the plans and actions of high commanders and the movements of armies and air forces. On occasions they could dictate the fate of multitudes—even the outcome of the battle for France itself. Such an incident occurred at Cherbourg.

When the SHAEF Counter-Intelligence War Room was formed behind the cover address "Post Office Box 100, Parliament Street, London, S.W.1," its chief, Colonel Dick Goldsmith White, a schoolmaster turned spymaster, issued what was known as the Detailed Counter-Intelligence Instruction No. 1, a document that became the canon for the immense counterintelligence operations that accompanied Neptune. The instruction outlined the aims of Allied counterintelligence activities, chief among them to "prevent the operation of enemy intelligence or subversive elements within the theatre." And in this area of operations, the instruction warned of a particular problem.

> The Continent of Europe has been under enemy occupation for four years and the enemy have had unrivalled opportunities for organising espionage and sabotage. There is reason to believe that the Abwehr, the (Gestapo) and the (SD) organisations will have established a co-ordinated system consisting both of individual agents and of underground German and pro-German organisations, which is designed to go into operation in the event of an Allied invasion of Western

Europe. Even though the Abwehr and (Gestapo) and (SD) administrative officials will have been withdrawn and are unlikely to be
captured in the advance, the system of espionage and sabotage agents
will remain in the areas liberated by the Allied Forces.

Goldsmith White's organization thought it likely that these "stay-
behind agents" (as they were called) would be especially located at
ports, at villages or towns near airfields, and at the centers of road
nets, their task to report by wireless the movements of Allied forces.
And because they might have "submerged" themselves in their com-
munities over a period of four years and have civilian occupations,
they would be difficult to uncover. In the event, Goldsmith White's
warning proved to be accurate; over 200 German stay-behind agents—
often of Alsatian stock but sometimes pro-Nazi Frenchmen or women
—would be detected in France, and over 1800 clandestine arms dumps
would be unearthed.

The first of these stay-behind agents was detected transmitting from
Cherbourg by American radiogoniometrical units shortly after the city
was captured on June 26. Once a small Channel port, Cherbourg had
been transformed by a succession of French monarchs of the last two
centuries into a great naval base and trans-Atlantic port-of-call. Hitler
had further transformed it into one of the most formidable fortresses
of the Atlantikwall; and as the Allies moved to take the city, he wired
its commandant: "Even if the worst comes to the worst, it is your duty
to defend the last bunker and leave to the enemy not a harbor but a
field of ruins. . . ." Cherbourg fell, but not before the Germans did
as they had been ordered. As Colonel Alvin G. Viney, a U.S. Army
port engineer, reported after he surveyed the scene, "The demolition
of the port of Cherbourg is a masterful job, beyond a doubt the most
complete, intensive, and best-planned demolition in history." It would
be months before the port was restored to full capacity, but it was only
three weeks before the first cargo was unloaded across the beaches;
the Fuehrer had reckoned without British maritime skill and American prodigies of reconstruction. The facilities of Cherbourg were soon
able to compensate for the loss of one of the Mulberries, but it was important to conceal this fact from Hitler. If he believed that the Allies
were having severe supply problems, it was reasoned at Montgomery's
headquarters, he might continue to try to smash the beachheads by
incessant counterattacks—a battle that only the Allies could win, for
their manpower and supply difficulties were much less great than the
Germans'.

Few German agents were so devoted to the Fuehrer that they were prepared to give their lives for him. "George," as the stay-behind agent who was discovered transmitting from Cherbourg was code-named, was no exception. He had been captured with his set, operating codes, instructions and transmission schedules intact, and X2, the OSS counterpart of the XX-Committee, had all the necessary ingredients for a wireless game. Moreover, George's particular mission at Cherbourg had been to report to his controller in Paris on the state of the harbor and whether the Allies were able to use it as a supply base. Why should he not continue his reports? On July 25 George reopened communications with Paris, and in response to the urgent requests of his controller, began to relay messages on Allied progress in reconstructing the harbor—all carefully fabricated to make it seem that Cherbourg was not fit for a fighting and supply base, and would not be so for some time to come. Other stay-behind agents were used to play the same game. The Germans were fed deceptive information about Allied intentions, and unknowingly revealed their own intentions by the questions they put to the captured agents. With that information, combined with Ultra and the yield of the Y service, Montgomery was able to piece together an intelligence picture of remarkable accuracy. It came, it would appear, none too soon.

By the beginning of July, the Germans had succeeded in sealing off the Allied lodgment area so effectively that when Bradley began his great offensive to take the key town of St. Lô, the Battle of the Hedgerows became what the Allies feared most—a slaughter yard. Bradley finally captured the town, but his army of twelve divisions advanced only 7 miles in seventeen days and lost 40,000 men, seriously impairing the fighting capability of two-thirds of his army. So brutal was the battle that, as one American officer reported:

> Over a stretch of . . . days, you became so dulled by fatigue that the names of the killed and wounded they checked off each night, the names of men who had been your best friends, might have come out of a telephone book for all you knew. All the old values were gone, and if there was a world beyond this tangle of hedgerows . . . where one barrage could lay out half a company like a giant's club, you never expected to live to see it.

Bradley's ammunition supply became short, his supply of reinforcements worse. He was compelled to call for 25,000 infantry replacements by the fastest transportation possible. He was told they did not exist in England and therefore would have to be brought from the United States. For both the Americans and the Germans alike—as

General Dietrich von Choltitz, the German corps commander around St. Lô, would state—it was "the most monstrous bloodbath, the likes of which I have not seen in eleven years of war."

Montgomery, too, was in serious trouble on the British front, and the tenuous brotherhood of arms forged for D-Day between American and British generals and fighting men began to crack. Criticism of Montgomery's command became more vocal. His own countrymen, Air Marshal Sir Arthur Tedder, the deputy Supreme Commander, and General Sir Frederick Morgan, the former COSSAC and now an assistant Chief of Staff to Eisenhower, were two of his bitterest critics. They joined the important group of Americans who openly advocated that Montgomery be replaced or, at least, that Eisenhower should take command of the battle. Montgomery be relegated to the command of the British and Canadian armies, and Bradley be given command of an American army group. To counter this criticism, Montgomery launched another attack against the Caen fortress—for the SS had turned the "Norman Athens" into a citadel—on the morning of July 8, behind a force of 467 Lancasters and Halifaxes which dropped 2560 tons of bombs. The bombardment shattered part of the German line, and on the 10th, the British and Canadians at long last captured the city. But they got no further; the bombardment had tossed about the blocks of stone with which much of Caen was built like cubes of sugar. The roads were choked with rubble, pocked with hundreds of craters, and Montgomery's attack stalled before he could get across the Orne and onto the road to Paris. The SS closed ranks and once again Montgomery was checkmated.

There was more bad news for the Allies. On June 30, Hitler had held a major conference at the Strub Barracks at Berchtesgaden to plan the long-delayed armored counteroffensive in Normandy, at last penetrating, so it seemed, the fogbanks of Fortitude. Analyzing the situation with remarkable clarity and perception, Hitler said he recognized that the Allies still retained the means to land in great strength anywhere between the North Sea and the Mediterranean coasts of Europe, and that he was "reasonably sure" that they would land on the Riviera coast—as indeed a Franco-American army would on August 15. He still believed that the Pas de Calais must be the Allies' primary objective in order to destroy the V-missile bombardment of London. But, he said, it must be remembered that the Allies had already disembarked their best troops in Normandy.

With that remark, it was clear that Fortitude was beginning to wear thin. Moreover, OKW situation reports of the next few days revealed that, while the intentions of Army Group Patton remained "the big question mark," Hitler thought "the troops in Britain were definitely second-string." Worse still for Montgomery in his present predicament, Hitler went on to state in a letter of instruction on July 8: "If they conduct a landing operation in the Pas de Calais, it (can) only be a diversionary operation." Except for Hitler's conviction that the V1 launching sites in the Pas de Calais "constituted a challenge which the Allied armies (cannot) ignore," it seemed that Fortitude was in danger of collapsing completely. The threat to Montgomery was readily apparent. If he could not break the thin German line that was holding him now, how could he hope to break it if Hitler finally agreed to let Rommel have the services of the first-rate divisions defending the Pas de Calais?

But Colonel Wild and the CSM did not intend to permit Fortitude to evaporate yet awhile. Throughout this period, Fortitude follow-through operations had been launched in quick succession to keep the deception alive. There was a British naval feint off Boulogne on June 24, intensive Allied aerial reconnaissance on either side of Dieppe that same day, and heavy smoke-screening by naval units off the southern coast of England. Resistance movements were once again alerted by a combination of real and dummy *messages personnels,* and an American staff study would note that, on the basis of those messages, and information obtained from the Belgian underground, Hitler had declared on June 30 that, since the tide and moon conditions between the 6th and 8th of July "would be like those prevailing on the night of the invasion in June," the 15th Army should receive "appropriate alert orders." The American study went on to describe the measures that had been used to reinforce this latest threat to the Pas de Calais: "As if to keep the Germans on edge during the night of 6/7 July the wire net in Belgium was disrupted; then during the night 7/8 July Third Air Fleet, which was monitoring radio channels, reported that the same picture prevailed (in Britain) as on the night of the invasion." Heavy air attacks about daybreak carried out by 2000 bombers accompanied by hundreds of fighter escorts added to and emphasized the scale of the threat.

Plainly, the LCS and CSM had come a long way since the "one-man band" operations of Garbo. When before in history had 2000 bombers with perhaps another 1000 fighters—more aircraft than existed in the entire German air force—been used solely for the purposes of stratagem? It was the most impressive display of force in support of cover and deception so far in the Second World War. But evidently it was not quite enough. For on July 8, Hitler gave orders for "Lüttich," a surprise night offensive in great strength to be launched by four SS and three army panzer divisions—perhaps 100,000 men and 500 tanks—against the British at Caen. They were to jump off without artillery preparation. Air support would be provided on the grandest scale possible, and Goering would be ordered to deploy yet another new and formidable secret weapon, the ME262 jet fighter. Hitler had been informed that the first of these jet fighters would be ready for service around July 15; many more were on the production lines, and he was convinced that with them the Luftwaffe would regain aerial superiority.

Rommel was given tactical command of Lüttich, and, expanding the scale of the attack, he envisaged using two more panzer divisions and an infantry division. This, exactly, was the magnitude of the force which the Allies had expected to meet on D+4. Moreover, to enable Rommel to pull the panzers out of the line for concentration, Hitler at long last agreed that Normandy should have the 15th Army's reserves of one panzer division (the 116th) and six infantry divisions. The first of these divisions began to move on July 13, a date that marked the beginning of the end of Fortitude's influence on the campaign.

Montgomery was soon informed of Hitler's and Rommel's intentions. Intelligence gleaned from Ultra, the Y service and the stay-behind agents under Allied control—all pointed to the looming threat. In due time, the code name and even the details of Lüttich would become known to the Allies; and with that information, it was not difficult for Montgomery to launch a series of shrewdly timed and placed attacks to throw Rommel off balance and compel him to keep his panzers on the line rather than concentrating them for a counteroffensive. But if these tactics disconcerted the timetables for Lüttich, they did not permit Montgomery to break out of the bridgehead. That he had to do at any cost before the new German infantry and armor arrived.

Throughout the brutal fighting in Normandy, and in spite of the criticisms that were being leveled against him, Montgomery, as an American official history would declare, "directed the tactical operations on the Continent with what might have seemed like exasperating calm." The reason for his calm, de Guingand, his Chief of Staff, would remember, was his belief that the Germans would soon break. The Americans were suffering heavy casualties, but they were doing what he wanted them to do: kill Germans. American casualties could be replaced; the much heavier German losses could not. Meanwhile, he was systematically destroying German armor and infantry; and once the armor had been written off, the German front would collapse with a thunderclap.

The Allied high command, however, did not share Montgomery's calm. Eisenhower, infected with the unease of a situation in stalemate, wrote Montgomery to call for a full-blooded offensive to break the deadlock. Montgomery said he had such plans in mind, and on July 10 he conferred with Bradley to lay the groundwork for "Goodwood," a mighty offensive in which the British army would attempt to crack the German lines at Caen. A few days later, the American army would attempt a similar breakout at St. Lô in an operation called "Cobra." The objective of the two-pronged attack was the encirclement and destruction of the 7th Army and the Panzer Army West. It was an ambitious plan without any guarantees of success, for Montgomery had barely managed to capture Caen, and Bradley was still battling for every mile in the difficult hedgerow country before St. Lô. But everyone recognized the imperative of an immediate offensive to shatter the German lines.

To provide full-scale cover and deception for Goodwood and Cobra, new life had to be breathed into Fortitude; and it was now that Fortitude South II, which was also known as "Rosebud," began to flower. Its object was to maintain the fiction that the million men of FUSAG still waited to invade the Pas de Calais if the Germans were unwise enough to reinforce the embattled 7th Army with idle divisions from the 15th. Rosebud was controlled not by British deception agencies this time, but by American. The man in charge was Colonel Harris of the Special Plans Branch, and it was his task to maintain the illusion that land, naval and air forces existed in England that were even larger than those of the Normandy assault. With the help of the Royal Navy and the American fleet, he was to convey to the enemy that three immense assault armadas—"Fox," "Mike," and "Nan"—were still gathering at ports and creeks between The Wash and the Thames, armadas that consisted, in reality, of immense numbers of "Big-bobs," the rubber or timber and canvas "landing ships" that had been used in the earlier phases of Fortitude South. Furthermore, he was to convince the Germans that an entirely new tactical air force—the 8th—had arrived in Britain from America for the operation, a force which, in reality, was composed of nothing more than hundreds of rubber bags that when inflated resembled, to German reconnaissance aircraft, the presence of entire squadrons of fighters. The land forces of Rosebud were but a variation of the original Quicksilver order of battle, consisting of a collection of British and American formations that existed only as skeleton units—or did not exist at all.

Rosebud got underway immediately, using the same variety of special means that had characterized earlier Fortitude deceptions—wireless chatter interspersed with ominous silences, warning reports from XX-Committee double agents, intensification of reconnaissance flights over the Pas de Calais, increased numbers of messages sent by SOE to resistance groups in the 15th Army sector, and a corresponding increase in sabotage and guerrilla activities in northern France and Belgium. At the same time, plans were laid for naval, air and military movements that would suggest large-scale assault exercises of the type that had preceded Neptune. These exercises, with code names like "Haircut," "Moustache," "Vanity I" and "II," "Jitterbug," "Filmstar," "Honeysuckle," "Viola I," "II" and "III," were scheduled to begin in the last days of July; and finally, the "invasion" itself would be launched against the Pas de Calais on August 14—almost the same time span that had occurred between the Neptune exercises and the Normandy assault.

Plainly, Rosebud was intended to create the maximum amount of anxiety within German headquarters during the period that would begin with an attempt to break the stalemate in Normandy and end with the Anvil assault across the Mediterranean beaches of France. But the deception agencies had a problem. Patton, the man who had been so conspicuously built up as the commander of the Pas de Calais assault, had arrived in France to assume command of the 3rd Army, and it would be difficult, if not impossible, to conceal his presence for long.

During the last several weeks, Patton had been extravagantly advertising himself in England. Beautifully tailored in a tight-fitting, brass-buttoned battle jacket, pink whipcord jodhpurs, gleaming riding boots with spurs, carrying a crop and accompanied by his white bulldog Willie, he had been busy delivering the same bellicose and profane speech to troop concentrations throughout Britain and Ulster. In his shrill, boyish voice he spoke of the glories of battle, of the greatness of the American fighting man, of death, honor, duty, manhood. It was an extraordinary performance, and one young soldier who heard him would write: ". . . you felt as if you had been given a supercharge from some divine source. Here was the man for whom you would go to hell and back."

Patton had moved his headquarters from Peover Hall south to the embarkation area on the last day of June; and on the morning of July 6, carrying with him the six volumes of Edward Freeman's *History of the Norman Conquest* from which he hoped to learn what the roads were like in Normandy and Brittany, he boarded his Dakota for France. He landed at a forward airstrip just behind Omaha beach and stepped out of the plane to be greeted by hundreds of troops. He made a speech, of course. Standing in his jeep, he began by warning all who heard him that he was "the Allies' secret weapon," and that they were forbidden to mention that they had seen him in France. Then he declared:

> I'm proud to be here to fight beside you. Now let's cut the guts out of those krauts and get the hell on to Berlin. And when we get to Berlin, I am going to personally shoot that paper-hanging goddammed son-of-a-bitch [Hitler] just like I would a snake.

With that, he drove off in a cloud of dust to Bradley's headquarters in a wooded field south of Isigny.

Patton had had his private D-Day. That was the trouble. The Germans could not fail to hear that he was in France and soon they must hear that he was in command not of an army group about to invade the Pas de Calais, but of an army in Bradley's sector. How was the Fortitude threat to be maintained? The answer was simple; Patton had to be "demoted." In a letter to Smith on July 10 Eisenhower directed that it should be leaked out that "Patton has lost his high command because of displeasure at some of his indiscretions, and that he is reduced to army command." That, of course, would be a serious statement to make about a general in an army where promotions or demotions were often decided by press comment. But, in fact, there would be some justification for spreading the story. Patton was indeed guilty of a serious indiscretion.

Ever since his arrival in France, Patton had sat fuming and restless at his command post in an old apple orchard near the Cotentin village of Néhou, near the Douve River. He became "obsessed with the fear that the war would be over before he got into it"; and he worried that "all the glory would go to others, while he was forced to sit idle watching the cider apples growing." He began to expound a theory to newsmen that two armored divisions, preceded by a heavy concentration of artillery fire, could crack the German line at St. Lô, end the bloodletting, enable the Allies to get the Breton ports and, at the same time, sweep into the center of France to surround the German army. If only "that fart," as Patton was thought to have called Montgomery on at least one occasion, was not in command.

On July 12, Bradley briefed Patton on Cobra which, curiously, called for the very operation that Patton had expounded to the newsmen: a bold, two-division attack on a narrow front preceded by a massive artillery barrage in the vicinity of St. Lô. Patton immediately did what he had promised not to do—tell his staff—and Colonel Charles C. Blakeney, his press officer, went to the correspondents' camp to announce that Patton's plan had been accepted. In consequence, the 3rd Army correspondents began to brag about their foreknowledge to their 1st Army colleagues, and they, in turn, complained to Bradley's press officer. The fat was in the fire with a vengeance; it was the grossest leakage of Bradley's operational plans, and Bradley, for a time, considered replacing Patton. But the demands of the battle made that impossible, and it was decided instead to use this indiscretion as the main reason for Patton's "demotion."

There was a second reason—and one that was less justified than the first. Shortly after the Cobra breach, word began to spread that Patton was allowing his troops to take women with them to France. The story, which caused a storm among the more puritanical of the American women's organizations, had its origins in an incident for which Patton bore no responsibility. At Omaha, on July 14, two Negro soldiers, "Pfc. Watson" and "Pvt. Dayton," were found to have smuggled a young woman from Firamsarn, Wales, to France in a DUKW amphibious truck. The two men were tried on charges of transporting the woman "for immoral purposes"; Watson was sentenced to ten years' hard labor, Dayton was found not guilty.

Patton may or may not have cooperated in his "demotion," but it soon became common knowledge among the American press corps that he had been "replaced" by General Lesley J. McNair, the sixty-one-year-old Chief of Army Ground Forces, a military establishment figure of power and influence who had built the American army from a tiny group of professionals into an immense machine of 10 million men in just over two years. McNair had graduated from West Point in 1904, eleventh in a class of 124; he had served with the Funston Expedition to Veracruz and on Pershing's expedition to the Mexican border. At thirty-five, he had been the youngest general to serve in Pershing's army in France in the First World War; he had been professor of Military Science at Purdue, had commanded an artillery brigade between the wars, had been Commandant of the Command and General Staff College at Fort Leavenworth, and was reputed to be a military intellectual. Thus the Germans, in looking at his credentials, would certainly believe that he was the sort of man who could be expected to hold high operational command.

McNair was not told what his command would be when he saw Marshall at the Pentagon shortly before his departure from Washington on or about July 12. But it was clear that he did not expect to find that he had been given command of nothing more than a paper tiger. McNair and Eisenhower met at Southwick House on July 15, and when McNair came out of the meeting, Curtis noted that "he was white with fury. I had never seen a man looking quite so angry or disappointed." Word of a "row" began to spread, but McNair acceded to his appointment, and the American press was manipulated to make it seem that he was in Europe to command an army group.

There were no stories about Patton's "demotion," but rumors abounded which inevitably reached the Germans through XX-Committee agents such as Garbo and Brutus. The Germans had indeed discovered that Patton was in France—largely through the Cobra indiscretion—and the news spread rapidly, threatening to destroy Fortitude completely, unless Brutus or Garbo could give a convincing explanation. This they tried to do between July 12 and 18. In a series of telegrams, Garbo "revealed" that FUSAG "had undergone important changes" because of the "necessity to send immediate reinforcements to Normandy." But these forces were being replaced by units fresh from the United States, and FUSAG now consisted of the American 9th Army (which existed in fact), the American 14th Army (which was bogus), and the British 4th Army (which consisted of a few second-string brigades). Brutus reported that the "milking" of FUSAG had caused a severe row between Eisenhower and Patton and that Patton had, in consequence, "been displaced as Commander-in-Chief of FUSAG by another senior General, General McNair." In a signal of elaboration he announced that "(The changes and demotion) have caused quite a stir at our headquarters."

Patton's indiscretion had clearly threatened the continuing success of Fortitude, but Roenne was not yet quite disposed to write off the story that the Allies would invade the Pas de Calais, although in weakened strength. It seemed that Hitler, too, wavered in his opinion, if only temporarily, that FUSAG would not now make a major strike across the English Channel. Thus, it was possible that Patton's "demotion" was interpreted by Hitler as a piece of what the Germans called "blossoming," their word for military deception operations. It may have appeared eminently plausible that the publicity surrounding

Patton was a delicate attempt to distract the Germans' attention from FUSAG and the Pas de Calais. All in all, it was as beautiful a piece of dissimulation as there had ever been.

It was at about this same time that a new element—perhaps the most dramatic of all—entered the Allied games of deception and maneuver. Ever since April 1944 there had been rumbles of brewing revolution among the German General Staff. Now, as the Americans and British were stalled in Normandy, it seemed that an attack on Hitler might be imminent, an attack that would, even if it was unsuccessful, cause a profound dislocation among the German high command and provide Montgomery with a strategical advantage that might help break the deadlock. If it was successful and the Nazi régime was toppled, western Europe might be liberated, and Germany occupied, without further loss of blood. Surely now was the time to enter into serious negotiations with the Schwarze Kapelle; surely now was the time to soften the terms of Unconditional Surrender to encourage the conspirators to act.

The Allies were well informed about the conspiracy with intelligence derived from many sources. Dulles had filed repeated warnings to the White House and the OSS in the early weeks of July. Theodore Steltzer, a high German officer at Oslo and a member of the Schwarze Kapelle who was in close contact with Milorg, the Norwegian intelligence organization, had passed information about the plot to Milorg in mid-July and Milorg passed it to London immediately, receiving a cipher signal acknowledging receipt. Both the OSS and MI-6 had received similar reports from the Schwarze Kapelle's representative in Sweden, Robert von Mendelsohn, a German banker and an intimate of Canaris. On July 11, the British captured Joachim Count von Helldorf, an SS soldier and the son of the police president of Berlin, Wolf-Heinrich Count von Helldorf, one of the leading figures in the plot. Helldorf said under interrogation that he was to have taken part in the plot, revealed the names of the senior conspirators, and said that the execution of the *coup d'état* could not be long delayed.

There is also evidence that officers of the German General Staff were in touch with the Allies at this time. Gehlen, the chief of the Fremde Heere, would later testify that Colonel Hansen, Canaris's successor, met " 'an emissary of Churchill' on a lonely road somewhere in southern France," to discuss the "all-important question of whether the British government would be prepared to negotiate an armistice with a new German government if Hitler were overthrown." Hansen also sent Otto John to Madrid to inform his contacts that an attack against Hitler was imminent.

Then there was the curious situation of Roenne. Gehlen, Roenne's superior at Fremde Heere, would claim that: ". . . it is the duty of every sophisticated intelligence service to keep open a channel of communication with the enemy's intelligence service" and state that: "I was able to keep such channels active during the Third Reich." Is it conceivable that Roenne himself—or his assistant Michel—had these same channels available to them? Were they using them for Schwarze Kapelle business; and were the British, in turn, using them to sow the deceptions of Fortitude to FHW? It would perhaps explain Roenne's adamant conviction of the existence of Army Group Patton. There would be many indications that this was precisely what was happening during the Fortitude period, but no direct proof.

There was some proof, however, that Fellgiebel—the man who ran Gehlen's and Roenne's communications and who was now providing the conspirators with super-secret telephone and teleprinter lines to be used during the revolt—had wireless contact with the British in the period immediately before Goodwood. Fellgiebel's *aide-de-camp,* Colonel Joachim Arntz, would state at a Combined Services Detailed Interrogation Centre session in London on April 11, 1945, that Fellgiebel had told him on May 22, 1944, at Führerhauptquartier that Hitler and his staff were to be assassinated, that the German forces in France would then be withdrawn to the German frontier, the Allies were to be asked for an armistice, and that to discuss terms he had "made contact with His Majesty's Government."

Finally, at a meeting with Hansen at the end of June or the beginning of July, General Ulrich Liss, a former chief of FHW, who was at Berlin to recover from wounds he had received while commanding an infantry division on the Russian front, received instructions to be ready to fly to Stockholm immediately Hitler was dead. His job, he would state, was to get in touch with General Kenneth W. D. Strong, a British officer whom Liss had known when he was a deputy military attaché in Berlin, and who was now Eisenhower's chief of intelligence, to "arrange a channel along which most confidential communications could pass."

In short, the Allies had many reports of the imminence of a revolution in Germany. They could continue to demand Unconditional Surrender; they could agree to an armistice, if the revolution succeeded, and undertake a bloodless liberation of Europe and conquest of Germany; or they could encourage the conspirators and then attack to take advantage of the chaos that a revolution would inevitably cause in the German command structure. It seemed that the British, at least, chose the last course. For on July 6, as the Allied failure to break out from the Neptune bridgehead was reaching crisis proportions, the British government changed its tune dramatically. For the first time, it acknowledged the existence of the Schwarze Kapelle, and encouraged it to revolt. In a speech to the House of Commons that day, Clement Attlee, the deputy Prime Minister, made a declaration that was at once a fundamental change of attitude, an olive branch, and an incitement to rebellion. Attlee stated:

> So far as His Majesty's Government are concerned, it has repeatedly been made clear in public statements that we shall fight on until Germany has been forced to capitulate and until nazism is extirpated. It is for the German people to draw the logical conclusion. If any section of them wants to see a return to a regime based on respect for international law and for the rights of the individual, they must understand that no one will believe them until they have themselves taken active steps to rid themselves of their present regime. The longer they continue to support and to tolerate their present rulers, the heavier grows their own direct responsibility for the destruction that is being wrought throughout the world, and not least in their own country.

Nothing could be clearer: kill Hitler *now* and we may be able to talk peace.

A week after Attlee's statement, the Prime Minister dropped a similar bombshell. Reminded by an MP of his advice to the Germans to overthrow "their Nazi taskmasters," and "asked what statement he could make to encourage them to do so," Churchill declared on July 12: "I am very glad to be reminded of that statement, to which I strongly adhere. I think it has been repeated in other forms by the Foreign Secretary and other Ministers. At any rate, it would certainly be a very well-advised step on the part of the Germans."

Would the Americans offer similar encouragement to the conspirators? There had been no reaction to Dulles's previous warnings when, on July 18, he sent another L-Document to the White House and the OSS, informing them that the plot had now definitely crystallized around the Home Army and Amt Mil, and reporting that the conspirators believed "that the next few weeks represent the final opportunity to initiate steps to overthrow Hitler and his organization and to set up a 'respectable government.'" Dulles's informant was Gisevius, who was even then in Berlin at great personal peril ready to open communications with Dulles if the plot succeeded. But still the Americans kept silent. Dulles would later write:

> In reviewing my notes of those days (July 1944) I find that the "Breakers" group was encouraged to proceed by a . . . statement in the House of Commons by Mr. Attlee. . . . They were also heartened by a statement made about the same time by Prime Minister Churchill, recommending that the German people should overthrow the Nazi government. I urged that some similar statement be made from America as I was convinced that whatever the result of (the revolt) might be, the fact that an attempt was made to overthrow Hitler, whether or not successfully, would help to shorten the war. Nothing of this nature was done.

In Berlin, meanwhile, Stauffenberg and Beck were indeed completing their plans for rebellion. Stauffenberg, who on July 1 had been appointed Chief of Staff of the Home Army and in this post would have direct personal access to the Fuehrer, had decided to undertake the attack on Hitler himself. Professor Sauerbruch, the German surgeon who was a friend and doctor to both Stauffenberg and Beck, advised against it; the dual role of assassin and leader of the revolt would be too much for any man, let alone one suffering from Stauffenberg's physical disabilities. Stauffenberg replied that earlier he might have agreed, but it was now too late; there would be no going back—the situation was too grave. Indeed it was, for while the German line in Normandy was groaning, the Russians had torn a huge hole in the front line in the East; the twenty-seven divisions of Army Group Center had simply disintegrated and, as bad, Army Group North was about to be cut off in East Prussia. Tresckow, the Chief of Staff to the C-in-C of the shattered army group, reported to Beck on July 8 that Russian tanks would be outside Berlin in ten days, and that a third offensive was expected against the southern part of the front. However, the conspirators in Berlin were encouraged by Hofacker's report that Kluge was now party to Rommel's schemes, although he believed that his plans to negotiate with Montgomery to end the war in the West were probably impracticable. Kluge's view was that if the war was to be ended, "action" in Berlin and at OKW was imperative. Rommel, reported Hofacker, was also tending toward this point of view, and wished to assure Stauffenberg that once action had been started in Berlin and at OKW he would give it his full support in France.

But bad luck continued to dog the conspirators. On July 11, Stauffenberg flew to a conference at Berchtesgaden, intending to kill Hitler on that day. Hitler was present, but Himmler and Goering were not; and at that stage Stauffenberg considered that the assassination of all three was necessary if the coup was to succeed. On July 13, Führerhauptquartier moved to Rastenburg; and it was there that Stauffenberg flew on July 15, again intending to assassinate Hitler. The plotters, confident of success this time, issued all preliminary signals for Valkyrie, but again, some evil providence stood at Hitler's side. Neither Himmler nor Goering was at the conference—perhaps because they, like so many others, had heard rumors of a plot—and Stauffenberg abandoned the attempt for a second time.

The day dealt the conspirators two more grave blows before it was done. Keitel heard of the Valkyrie signals and was so suspicious that it would be impossible again to camouflage Valkyrie as a "training exercise." Then it was learned that General von Falkenhausen, the Military Governor of Belgium and a key member of the Schwarze Kapelle in the West, had been suddenly relieved of command and ordered to return to OKW. Coming on top of the arrests of several important members of the Schwarze Kapelle in Berlin, and the knowledge that Himmler had issued a warrant for the arrest of Goerdeler, it was clear to Stauffenberg that there was a traitor in their midst and that unless they acted immediately there might be none of the hierarchy left.

The next day—the 16th—Stauffenberg met Beck at his home in the Goethestrasse and it was decided that he would kill the Fuehrer at the first possible moment, whether Himmler and Goering were present or not. That evening, another meeting took place, this time at Stauffenberg's home at Wannsee, and the conspirators agreed that they could not now hope to secure a modification of Unconditional Surrender. But no matter what the future might bring, Hitler must be killed "to prove to the world and to future generations that the men of the German resistance movement dared to take the decisive step and to hazard their lives upon it."

A similar urgency infected Rommel. On July 17, he toured the front, talking first to General Heinz Eberbach, the commander of the Panzerarmee on the British front, and then to General Sepp Dietrich, the commander of the 1st SS Panzer Korps, Adolf Hitler. Both assured him of their loyalty in the event of a *coup d'état*. The SS General Paul Hausser, the new commander of the 7th Army, and the SS General Wilhelm Bittrich, the commander of the 2nd SS Panzer Korps in Normandy, had also agreed to support him—an almost certain guarantee of a successful rebellion, for the prospect of civil war between the midnight black of the SS and the field gray of the army was now removed. But at this most crucial moment in the long history of the conspiracy, fate again intervened.

At four o'clock that afternoon, Rommel left Dietrich's headquarters for the Château de La Roche Guyon. With him in the car—a six-wheeled Mercedes staff car with a folding top and glass winding windows—were his aide, Lang, Corporal Holke, whose duty was to look out for marauding aircraft, and a Major Neuhans. They were on the Livarot road approaching a hamlet with the ironic name Sainte Foy-de-Montgommery when, at about 4:20 P.M., Holke warned that two low-flying RAF Typhoons were banking toward them behind a clump of poplars. Staff Sergeant Daniel, Rommel's driver since before El Alamein, put on speed to get to another clump of poplars, there to hide until the Typhoons had passed. But just before he reached a road leading into the first houses of Sainte Foy-de-Montgommery, the Typhoons came roaring in above the tree tops, their 20-millimeter cannons spewing shells. The Mercedes was struck in the left side from the rear by the explosive shells, any one of which could wreck an armored car, and as Rommel turned round to look at the planes he was hit by flying glass and stone. He was struck in the left temple and the left cheek and was instantly unconscious. Sergeant Daniel, who was mortally wounded, lost control of the car. It hit a tree stump, careened across the road and stopped in a stormwater ditch. Rommel was thrown from the car into the road, where he was lying when another plane came in to strafe the tarmacadam. Lang and Holke ran into the road and brought Rommel, who was bleeding heavily from the wounds in his face, under cover.

When the fighters disappeared, Lang stopped a passing German car and drove Rommel, who was still unconscious, to Livarot; and there, in front of the war memorial, he met Marcel Lescene, the Mayor and chemist, who was taking his evening calvados in a café on the square. Lescene would later recall:

> I saw a tank officer who was very distraught. He asked me if the village had a doctor and I said it had but I did not know where he was at this hour. I decided myself to go to the hospital and there I saw an officer whom I knew was at least a general because he wore red tabs and broad red stripes on his breeches, and because of his high boots.
>
> I noticed he had a large open wound above his left eye and was bleeding from the ears. He was unconscious. I took his pulse, which was weak, and gave him two injections of etherated camphor. Then the commander of the German garrison hastened up and removed the seat from the back of his car, put Rommel onto the floor and drove him off

to the military hospital at Bernay. I myself did not give Rommel the ghost of a chance of surviving those wounds.

His wounds were serious indeed. At the Luftwaffe hospital on the airfield at Bernay, three German doctors found that Rommel had a fracture of the base of the skull, two fractures of the left temple, and his left cheekbone had been broken in. His left eye was badly damaged, the scalp was badly torn, and he was seriously concussed.

When the news reached Rommel's headquarters and was relayed to all his subordinates, an immediate air of catastrophe and tragedy descended upon the officers and the men whom he had led. It was thought that he might die that night and Speidel would write:

> Rommel was in fact eliminated in the very hour that his Army and his people could spare him the least. All those who were groping with his help to find a way to a new and better world felt themselves painfully deprived of their pillar of strength.

Ernst Juenger, the historian and philosopher who was active in the conspiracy and was a close friend of Rommel's, felt compelled to write:

> The blow that felled Rommel on the Livarot road on 17 July 1944 deprived our plan of the only man strong enough to bear the terrible weight of war and civil war simultaneously, the only man who was straightforward enough to counter the frightful folly of the leaders of Germany. This was an omen which had only one interpretation.

A few hours after Rommel was struck down, the RAF delivered the mighty opening stroke of Goodwood, and Montgomery launched 1500 tanks and 250,000 men against the German lines around Caen. They jumped off into the cornfields by ghostly artificial moonlight, hundreds of powerful searchlights playing upon the undersides of the clouds. Scores of flame-throwing tanks howled and screeched as they burned the SS out of their foxholes. Preceded and attended by an aerial bombardment of unheard-of strength—1700 heavy and 500 medium bombers dropped 7000 tons of bombs on an area of little more than 20 square miles—three tank divisions and three armored brigades moved forward behind a rolling barrage laid down by almost the entire artillery of the British 2nd Army; 45,000 shells fell upon the 2nd SS Panzer Korps alone in a few hours. Eight hundred fighter bombers took wing to give the army close support, and one RAF group alone flew 1800 rocket missions against German tanks and emplacements. It was the most concentrated and furious attack of the Second World War in western Europe.

Kluge was taken completely by surprise; misled by deceptive information supplied by stay-behind agents, he expected the attack from another direction three or four days later, and had gone to Poitiers for a conference. Even so, Goodwood was destined to fail. Montgomery's armies penetrated six of the seven deep lines of defense around Caen, and for a time it seemed that the fate of the German army in the West was in the balance. But then the British ran up against the seventh and last line of defense—the anti-tank screen guarding the entrance to the plains and Paris. The *Feldgrau* held the line until finally, on the 20th, Montgomery called the operation off. The British had lost 500 tanks and 5000 men, and all that had been captured was the industrial suburb of Caen and some 40 square miles of new territory.

The failure of Goodwood caused the most serious outcry at SHAEF so far. Tedder, believing that all the airpower used in Goodwood had been expended for nothing, declared bitterly that "we [the air forces] have been had for suckers." Morgan thought the situation "had the makings of a dangerous crisis." Cadogan snorted in his diary: "Monty . . . does a lot of publicity stuff in his sweater and beret. I don't believe he's a general at all, but just a Film Star." Eisenhower fidgeted and Churchill announced that he would go to Normandy to see what the situation was for himself.

But the commanders who were loudest in their criticism knew the least. Montgomery's tactics had forced the best of the Germans' armor and infantry to concentrate in the Caen sector, and Goodwood had torn them to pieces. Kluge realized that his armies could not withstand another such attack—an attack that he knew must come. But where— from the cornfields and hamlets around Caen, or amid the wild roses and hedgerows near St. Lô? Standing over his chinagraph maps in the Forêt d'Écouves, Kluge decided that Paris and the flying bomb launch sites must be the primary Allied objectives, and he, as well as the other German generals, considered the British and Canadian forces under Montgomery far superior to the American forces under Bradley in fighting capability. The attack would come from the Caen sector as soon as Montgomery had regrouped. But Kluge was quite wrong. The Breton ports were the main Allied objective; and the attack would come where Kluge least expected it, and where his defenses were now the weakest—from the American sector at St. Lô.

Under cover of the Rosebud phase of Fortitude, Bradley's Cobra offensive was scheduled to open on July 20, the same day that the

Schwarze Kapelle would attempt to assassinate Hitler. Was there a connection between these climactic events? The Allied high command had ample warning of the Schwarze Kapelle's intentions, and by a remarkable coincidence—if it was a coincidence—the decision to launch Cobra on the 20th was confirmed between Montgomery and Bradley on the 18th, shortly after the conspirators had decided to assassinate Hitler at the first possible moment. Had the Allied high commanders been informed of that decision; had they in any way encouraged it? If so, all of the labyrinthian strategies, stratagems and special means of the secret war against Hitler might be said to have led up to this single moment. History seldom allows for such oversimplifications; but on the evening of the 19th, as the sun went down over the Norman countryside, Montgomery did something he had never done before and would not do again. He directed his provost marshal to seal off his headquarters until further orders. No one was to be allowed in or out unless he had a special pass that showed him to be on the most urgent business. And that same evening, in Berlin, Stauffenberg took absolution from his priest and prepared for the morrow.

July 20, 1944

8

JULY 20, 1944, broke over Berlin in an airless, sweltering dawn. Once again Stauffenberg wrapped the British-made bomb (SOE stores captured in France) in some shirts in preparation for another attempt to assassinate the Fuehrer. He placed the package in his briefcase and then set out by car for Rangsdorf Airfield, en route to Führerhauptquartier in the East Prussian woods at Rastenburg.

For Stauffenberg, it was an ideal opportunity. All the Nazi hierarchs would be at their headquarters near the Wolfsschanze (the Wolves' Lair), on hand for a meeting between Hitler and Mussolini; only Goebbels would be in Berlin. The success of the *coup d'état* would hang upon the conspirators' ability—after Hitler was dead—to immure the Nazi high command in those thick woods far from Berlin during the first critical hours of the seizure of power; and, if everything went according to plan, it would be a relatively simple matter to prevent a counterrevolution simply by pulling the plugs on telephone, telegraph and wireless communications from the Wolfsschanze. Moreover, Hitler had moved to Rastenburg only six days before, all the communications posts there were not yet fully manned, and because the Red Army was only 100 miles away, some of the essential parts of the communications equipment had actually been dismantled ready for quick evacuation.

At about nine o'clock, Stauffenberg, who was accompanied by Lieutenant Colonel Werner von Haeften, his *aide-de-camp,* fellow conspirator and friend, boarded the special Ju-52 trimotor transport aircraft which had been provided by Eduard Wagner, the Quartermaster General of the army, to enable him to be independent of routine transportation and to get back to Berlin quickly after the assassination. Three hours later, the aircraft landed and Haeften ordered the pilot to be fueled and ready to return to Berlin at any time from noon onwards.

Stauffenberg and Haeften then left the airfield for the 10-mile drive to the Wolfsschanze. They noticed that the security precautions, always careful, were today extremely thorough, although nobody actually searched either of the two men, both of whom were carrying bombs. The care with which papers and the car were searched led afterwards to the belief that the SS may have got wind of the fact that an assassination attempt was imminent. Indeed, Schellenberg would later state that he had received "indirect hints" of the plan. But if Rattenhuber, the chief of the SS bodyguard, had any suspicions, he did not show them when Stauffenberg arrived at the gate for entrance into the Fuehrer's personal compound. He asked Stauffenberg only to hand over his pistol, probably influenced by the thought that a one-eyed, one-armed man with three fingers would never be able to work a pistol or a bomb with the speed and accuracy necessary to kill the Fuehrer in a crowded room.

Stauffenberg interrupted his journey to the conference briefly at "Anna," the code name for the army's headquarters at the Wolfsschanze, to talk with Fellgiebel, the man who had the essential task of cutting the Führerhauptquartier's communications after the bomb had exploded. What they said is not known, but Fellgiebel knew precisely what he had to do; indeed, he had planned the isolation action. With the help of his *aide-de-camp,* Colonel Arntz, he was to cut the five communications centers at Rastenburg, including those of the Fuehrer, the SS and Leopold (the party communications center). The other two would be cut by the SS itself as the result of instructions Fellgiebel would give after the attack.

Stauffenberg then called on Keitel to present a résumé of what he intended to report to the Fuehrer. Keitel ordered Stauffenberg to be brief as Mussolini was expected at the Wolfsschanze later that afternoon. Then, just before 12:30 P.M. Keitel and Stauffenberg, accompanied by two other officers, left for the map room where the conference was to be held. On the way, Stauffenberg asked Keitel to excuse him for a moment, remarking that he had forgotten to pick up his cap and belt. Keitel assented and Stauffenberg went into the anteroom of Keitel's suite, opened his briefcase and, with an instrument rather like a pair of sugar tongs, squeezed and broke the glass capsule in the fuse. At that moment the bomb was primed as a chemical began to eat away noiselessly at the wire which restrained the detonator. Keitel, irritated that Stauffenberg was taking so long, called to him to hurry up.

Stauffenberg emerged almost immediately and first Keitel and then his adjutant suggested they might carry Stauffenberg's briefcase. Stauffenberg declined with a murmur of thanks.

They entered the map room, another of those anonymous buildings at the Wolfsschanze which caused Jodl to describe life there as a "cross between a cloister and a concentration camp." Located in the gloomy twilight of the forest, the map room adjoined Hitler's private quarters. Normally, the conference would have been held in one of the concrete-lined bunkers. But today, because of the chaos caused by preparations for an evacuation, it was to be held above ground in a large wooden hut built upon concrete and stone pillars and roofed with tarred felt. The hut had three windows, and was furnished with two small tables at either end of a large, heavily built map table covered with situation maps.

Keitel and Stauffenberg entered the room at approximately 12:40 P.M. About a score of people were present, but Himmler, Goering and Ribbentrop were not there. General Adolf Heusinger, deputy Chief of the General Staff, was reporting on the situation in the East, while Hitler, his back to the door, followed the briefing on the situation maps. He was wearing his usual gray tunic and black trousers. Keitel interrupted the briefing to present Stauffenberg. Hitler looked up somewhat sharply, cast his gaze over Stauffenberg's black eye patch and his mutilations, and said he would take his report next. Keitel moved to Hitler's side while Stauffenberg went to the corner of the table at Hitler's right. He placed the briefcase which contained the bomb on the floor close to Colonel Heinz Brandt, the man to whom Schlabrendorff had addressed the "Cointreau-bottle bomb" at Smolensk on March 13, 1943. Then he said: "I will leave this here for the moment. I have to make a telephone call." Brandt found the briefcase in his way and moved it so that it rested against the heavy, thick upright support of the table on the side farthest away from Hitler.

Stauffenberg left the hut, went to some turf at Bunker 88 about 100 yards away and lit a cigarette. Inside the hut, Heusinger was just finishing his gloomy report. Keitel looked up and said to General Walter Buhle: "Where's Stauffenberg?" Buhle went to look in the anteroom and then returned. "I can't find him," he said. "He went to make a telephone call." Keitel became irritated, for Heusinger was on the last part of his report:

> *Der Russe dreht mit starken Kräften westlich der Düna nach Norden ein. Seine Spitzen stehen bereits südwestlich Dünaburg. Wenn jetzt nicht endlich die Heeresgruppe vom Peipussee zurückgenommen wird, dann werden wir eine Katastrophe . . .*

At that moment—at the utterance of the word *"Katastrophe"*—the bomb exploded. Jodl said afterwards, "It was as if a great chandelier were coming down on your head." A thunderous bang shattered the central table, the roof fell in, the windows were blown out, and the room was filled with heavy smoke shot with orange flame. The explosion killed the official stenographer immediately, mortally wounded two generals and a colonel, seriously injured one general and one colonel, and inflicted lesser injuries on four more generals.

Stauffenberg, certain that he had killed the Fuehrer and anxious to get out of the Wolfsschanze before Rattenhuber sealed the place off, left immediately. He and Haeften were stopped at the last checkpoint by the SS guard, but Stauffenberg went to the telephone in the guardpost and got Rittmeister von Moellendorf, an officer of FHW and a fellow conspirator, on the line. Moellendorf ordered the guard to let Stauffenberg pass. He opened the heavy electrified gate and Stauffenberg swept through. Within twenty minutes he was airborne over the Masurian Lakes.

But Hitler had not been killed. The heavy upright support had deflected the blast away from him. His hair was set on fire, his right arm was paralyzed—temporarily—and both his eardrums were affected by the pressure waves. One of his trouser legs was blown off, and a weighty object had fallen across his back and buttocks. He was bruised, as he complained later, "like the backside of a baboon." Nevertheless, he behaved very calmly as he was led away from the ruin by Keitel, his right arm hanging slack at his side, his hair singed, and a livid cut across the sallow skin of his face.

Even with Hitler still alive, all was not lost. If Fellgiebel cut the communications as planned, the *coup d'état* could continue with every promise of success. This Fellgiebel proceeded to do. Almost immediately after the explosion, he ordered Arntz to see to it that all communications between Rastenburg and the outside world were cut while he found out what had happened. Arntz complied; both Anna and Leopold were shut down and the switchboards were manned, as the emergency contingency plan required, by officers of the Führerhauptquartier signals regiment. They were under orders not to complete any circuits without Fellgiebel's permission. But then, having cut two of the five communications centers, Fellgiebel's nerve failed him when he looked out of the window and saw the procession of blackened men—Hitler included—walking away from the blasted hut. He did not proceed with his plans to isolate the remaining centers, presumably because by doing so he would have implicated himself. Neither did he report to Beck or Olbricht in Berlin the outcome of the explosion, as he had agreed to do. Keitel came over to Fellgiebel's hut and told the signalmaster to resume communications; and this he did. With that action the plot began to collapse. Knowing that his part in the conspiracy would come to light, Fellgiebel declared to Arntz: "I am not going to shoot myself. One should not make these creatures think that one is afraid of them. I am going to play this game to the end, knowing that Hitler will not enjoy his triumph for long." Then, according to Arntz, they sat down together and talked at length of the immortality of the soul. Fellgiebel was arrested that same night on Keitel's orders and was subsequently hanged.

As for Hitler, he recovered with extraordinary rapidity and went to the Wolfsschanze railroad station to meet Mussolini. Surrounded by bodyguards and wearing a heavy black cloak to conceal his right arm, which was in a sling, he was in a strange, almost hysterical mood when he greeted the Italian dictator. They shook hands and embraced, and then Hitler told Il Duce what had happened. "Duce, an infernal machine has just been let off at me," he said. The chauffeur drove them through the tall pines to the Wolfsschanze and they went straight to the wreckage of the hut. There, Hitler, amid the rubble, said to a horrified Mussolini:

> I was standing here by this table; the bomb went off just in front of my feet. . . . Look at my uniform! Look at my burns! When I reflect on all this. . . . it is obvious that nothing is going to happen to me; un-doubtedly it is my fate to continue on my way and bring my task to completion. . . . What happened here today is the climax! And having now escaped death in such an extraordinary manner, I am more than ever convinced that the great cause I serve will be brought through its present perils and that everything can be brought to a good end.

Hitler, hitherto so calm, now began to speak like a prophet. He assured Mussolini of the New Roman Empire and that, the disasters of the hour notwithstanding, the Reich would live for a thousand years. Il Duce responded fervently:

> . . . you are right, Fuehrer. . . . heaven has held its protective hand over you. . . . After the miracle that has occurred here in this room today it is inconceivable that our cause should suffer from misfortune.

The two dictators then left the scene; and Hitler, who thought at first that the bomb had been dropped from an airplane or thrown at him through a window, learned that Stauffenberg had been responsi-ble. When he also learned that the Valkyrie order had been issued by the Home Army and that war district commanders inside and outside the Reich had begun to secure the administrative and communications centers under their control, the Fuehrer realized that the attempt on his life was not an isolated incident but part of a carefully prepared *coup d'état*. Furious, he spoke again and again of the treachery of his generals and the perfidy of the British secret service. Convinced that the British were involved in the plot, Hitler ordered as retaliation a maximum V1 strike against London to begin that very night. He demanded "continuous fire at maximum tempo with an 'unrestricted expenditure of ammunition,'" and his orders were obeyed. One hundred and ninety-three rounds were catapulted during the night of July 20/21—almost twice the usual rate of fire; and a further two hundred rounds were launched the following night in the heaviest attack so far in the V1 campaign. (One missile exploded near Brooke's London home as the field marshal lay asleep; he was not harmed but the building was rocked to its foundations.) In spite of his desire for revenge, Hitler was mistaken. The British were not directly involved in the *coup d'état;* at most, they had merely encouraged the conspirators to act, possibly in coincidence with the culmination of Fortitude and the Cobra offensive. Nevertheless, Hitler would claim that he had evidence that Count Helldorf, the police chief of Berlin, had been in league with MI-6; and he would be even more certain of British involvement when he learned that the bomb was of British manufacture.

While every one of the men in the hut had been injured by the explosion, the Nazi high command reacted with speed and efficiency to restore order and calm. Goering, Ribbentrop, Doenitz and Himmler, who were in their headquarters or personal trains nearby when the bomb went off, had rushed to their Fuehrer's side, and Hitler ordered Himmler to Berlin immediately to suppress the revolt and restore Nazi authority in the capital. Then a doctor came to examine his injuries and found that Hitler's back, buttocks and legs were peppered with wood splinters, he had slight flashburns about the face and hands, his hair and eyebrows had been singed, and his eardrums had been slightly damaged. The doctor would later report that the Fuehrer was unable to hear higher harmonics such as those in the prelude to *Lohengrin*. But oddly, the shock of the explosion had cured, although only temporarily, the palsy which afflicted his right hand and arm. Hitler said ruefully to the doctor that, while he was delighted to be rid of the affliction, "the treatment was not one that he could recommend"—a remark that showed he was a good deal less affected by the incident than his enemies would have wished. But Hitler's composure did not last long; it soon became evident that he had been badly

shaken by the blast, both physically and psychologically. Eugen Dollmann, Hitler's personal representative at Mussolini's court—and the
SS general who would later betray him and start the negotiations with
Dulles for the surrender of the German army in Italy—would describe
the Fuehrer's behavior that afternoon:

> At five o'clock there was a big tea party; it was amazingly interesting,
> all of them were there, in the Führer's GHQ, and over tea they all
> began arguing and shouting at one another, each one putting the blame
> on the other because the war had not yet been won! Ribbentrop raved
> against the generals, because they had betrayed us to England, and the
> generals raved in their turn against Ribbentrop and Doenitz. The Füh-
> rer kept pretty quiet the whole time, and Mussolini was very reserved
> too . . . all of a sudden someone happened to mention the 30th of
> June 1934 [the "Night of the Long Knives"]. The Führer leapt up in a
> fit of frenzy, with foam on his lips, and yelled out that he would be re-
> venged on all traitors, that Providence had just shown him once more
> that he had been chosen to make world history, and shouted about
> terrible punishments for (the) women and children [of the conspira-
> tors]. . . . He shouted about an eye for an eye and a tooth for a
> tooth for everyone who dared to set himself against divine Providence.
> It was awful, and it went on for half an hour! I thought to myself, the
> man must be mad. I don't know why I didn't go over to the Allies there
> and then. . . . Meanwhile more tea was served by the footmen in
> white (when) a telephone call came through from Berlin to say that
> order had not yet been restored there. The Führer answered the call,
> and started yelling again, gave full powers for shooting anyone they
> liked. . . . Then came the lovely bit: "I'm beginning to doubt if the
> German people is worthy of my great ideas." At that of course there
> was a tremendous to-do. They all wanted to convince the Führer of
> their loyalty. Doenitz and Göring came out with all they had done,
> Doenitz told him about the blue-eyed boys in blue—damned rubbish—
> and Göring started having a row with Ribbentrop, and Ribbentrop
> shouted at him: "I am still the Foreign Minister, and my name is *von*
> Ribbentrop!" Göring made a pass at him with his [Reichsmarschall's]
> baton. I'll never forget that scene. The Führer was in a very peculiar
> state at that time. It was the time when his right arm began to develop
> a tremor. He sat there . . . eating his coloured pastilles . . . and then
> suddenly he'd break out like a wild animal, and wanted to get at every-
> one, women and children too, into the concentration camp with the
> lot of them, he was the one Providence had chosen, and so on.

In Berlin, at about noon, the leaders of the Schwarze Kapelle
gathered at the headquarters of the Home Army on the Bendlerstrasse, prepared to issue the Valkyrie orders as soon as General

Olbricht, the deputy C-in-C of the Home Army, received a telephone message from Fellgiebel telling him that the Fuehrer was dead. At the same time General von Haase, the Commandant of Greater Berlin, gave his garrison troops, which included some of the best infantry and armored units in the army, guarded preparatory orders to ensure that they were kept in their barracks ready for deployment at a moment's notice. Beck arrived and John, who was also present, would note that he was "still suffering from the consequences of a dangerous stomach operation, was then 64 years old, and looked in his brownish lounge suit more like a kind old gentleman making a social call than the man to replace Hitler as Head of the German Reich." Witzleben, who would be designated C-in-C of the Wehrmacht, entered the conspirators' room, erect, impressive, hawklike, in the full uniform and medals of a Field Marshal. Hoepner, the panzer general, was there, too, in full uniform—which he had been forbidden by Hitler to wear again—to give the orders to the Panzerarmee.

The atmosphere was extremely tense as the conspirators awaited the call, and, John would record: "The tension grew as the hands of their watches advanced from hour to hour. But the expected telephone call from General Fellgiebel did not come." One P.M., 2 P.M., 3 P.M.—the hours passed without word from Rastenburg. Then, between 3:30 and 3:45 P.M., Haeften called from Rangsdorf Airfield where he had just landed with Stauffenberg. With annoyance he demanded to know why no car had been sent to meet them. Colonel Mertz von Quirnheim, Olbricht's Chief of Staff, the plotter who took the call, asked what had happened at Rastenburg. Was Hitler alive or dead? Haeften replied that the attack had taken place and that Hitler was dead. With that information—at about four o'clock—Olbricht issued the Valkyrie orders to all commands. In Berlin, Haase's troops prepared to march upon the government quarter, and the commanding generals of every war district in Germany and the empire were ordered to secure their headquarters and cities against "an SS revolt." The revolution had begun.

Olbricht's next move was to try to bring Fromm, his superior as the C-in-C of the Home Army, into line. Fromm had dallied with the conspiracy, and with his outright support, the plotters might obtain the services of over 3 million men in Germany who were in uniform—men on leave, garrison troops, anti-aircraft gunners, naval and air personnel, and the like. Olbricht went to Fromm's office, informed him that the Fuehrer had been murdered at Rastenburg by the SS, and suggested that he put Valkyrie into effect "in order to safeguard law and order which in view of Hitler's sudden death might be disturbed by an uprising of radical elements, particularly from among foreign workers." But Fromm was not to be rushed. He stated that as C-in-C of the Home Army he could "initiate such weighty measures only when he had assured himself personally that Hitler was, in fact, dead."

Olbricht, believing that the line to Rastenburg had been cut, suggested that Fromm ring Keitel. This Fromm did, and to Olbricht's surprise got Keitel on the line. Fromm asked him what was happening at Rastenburg as the wildest rumors were circulating in Berlin that Hitler had been killed. Keitel replied: "That is all rubbish. An attempt was made upon the Führer, but it failed. He has merely been slightly injured. He is now with the *Duce*." And, Keitel asked ominously, where was Fromm's Chief of Staff, Stauffenberg? After a few minutes of discussion, Fromm replaced the telephone and gave a direct order that Valkyrie was not to be put into effect. Incredulous at the news that Hitler was still alive, Olbricht went into his own office and found that Valkyrie orders had already gone out by teleprinter.

Just before five o'clock, Stauffenberg arrived with Haeften from Rangsdorf and was greeted by Beck. Was Hitler alive or dead? Stauffenberg, sweating heavily in the heat inside the headquarters, replied: "I saw it myself. I was standing with Fellgiebel at Bunker 88 when the explosion occurred. It was as though a fifteen centimetre shell had hit the *Barracke!* It is impossible that anyone could have survived." Olbricht then told Stauffenberg of Fromm's conversation with Keitel, and Stauffenberg went to Fromm's office. Hitler was undoubtedly dead, he announced, but Fromm countered with Keitel's report. Thereupon Stauffenberg declared coldly: "Field Marshal Keitel is lying as usual. Hitler is dead." At that moment Olbricht broke in to say that "Under these circumstances we have given the order for the proclamation of a State of Emergency to the (war district) commanders." Fromm, almost speechless with rage, leaped to his feet and roared: "What does it mean: WE? This is insubordination. Who has given such an order?" Olbricht replied that Quirnheim, his Chief of Staff, had issued the order. Fromm summoned Quirnheim to his office and declared that he was under arrest.

At that point Stauffenberg told the astounded Fromm: "Herr Generaloberst, the Führer is dead. I myself ignited the bomb. No one escaped alive." Fromm gained his composure and replied: ". . . the attempt has failed. You must shoot yourself." Stauffenberg said: "I shall do nothing of the kind." Olbricht now spoke. "Herr Generaloberst, this is the last chance to take action to save our country from total ruin. If we don't strike now, all will be lost." Fromm, who had heard enough of treason for one day, glowered at Olbricht. "Are you involved in this affair?" he demanded to know. Olbricht said that he was. Fromm then declared: "You must all consider yourselves under arrest." At this, Olbricht dropped all pretenses and announced: "That is where you are mistaken, Herr Generaloberst. We, in fact, arrest you." Fromm went for his pistol and, as John recorded, "a regular rough and tumble ensued." Fromm was overpowered and, exhausted, surrendered himself and his pistol, which he had tried to use. Olbricht then declared him to be their prisoner and told him to remain quietly in the room next door. An armed officer was placed on the door, but inexplicably nobody thought to lock it.

It was about 5:30 P.M. when Stauffenberg, Olbricht and Quirnheim left Fromm to continue with the Valkyrie operations. Witzleben appointed Hoepner to replace Fromm; and for a time it seemed that the coup might succeed, especially when the Munich war district commander reported that he had the city under Valkyrie control. But in Berlin, in the hours ahead, the revolution would degenerate into an artless, inefficient mess that could have only one outcome—the firing squad and the hangman. One fact remained, however; at this critical moment in European history, the Schwarze Kapelle's two principal contacts with the Allied Supreme Command—Gisevius and John—were present as witnesses to what became the final spasms of morality and conscience of the Third Reich. John had arrived from Madrid the day before, by air, alerted to the imminence of the assassination by a code word in a letter from his brother. If the attack was successful, he had made arrangements in Madrid which would enable Hansen, the chief of Amt Mil, to get through to Eisenhower.

Gisevius had returned to Berlin on July 13, even though he knew that Himmler had placed his name on the "wanted" list. But Gisevius had powerful police friends in the Nazi hierarchy. Count Helldorf, the police chief of Berlin, and Artur Nebe, the chief of the Reich detective service, were both friends and fellow conspirators. It was still possible to hide in Berlin, even though agents and informers were everywhere; and Gisevius did so, in the basement of the home at 31 Nuernbergerstrasse of Theodor Struenck, a captain in the Abwehr and a close associate of Oster, who was under house arrest at Dresden throughout this period.

Gisevius spent the first part of July 20 in Helldorf's office overlooking the bomb wreckage of the Alexanderplatz; Helldorf was awaiting a telephone call from Olbricht to begin operations to arrest Kaltenbrunner, Schellenberg and the chief of the Gestapo, Mueller, and to seize control of civilian life in the capital. The afternoon was sweltering, and the heat when combined with the tension made ordinary human actions all but impossible. The hours ticked past in a rising tide of anxiety and nervousness, for everyone at police headquarters knew that if the coup succeeded they would be the new rulers of Germany; if it failed they would probably be corpses by midnight.

The telephone call from Olbricht to Helldorf came at about four o'clock; and shortly afterwards Helldorf rushed excitedly into the room where Gisevius and the other conspirators were waiting and cried: " 'It's starting!' Olbricht had just telephoned him to hold himself in readiness; there would be an important message within half an hour." Just before 4:30 P.M. Helldorf reappeared. He almost shouted: "Gentlemen, we're off! Olbricht has just given me an official order to report at the Bendlerstrasse: he says the Fuehrer is dead, a state of siege has been proclaimed, and he has urgent orders to deliver to me in the name of Colonel-General Fromm."

Helldorf and Gisevius then drove to the headquarters of the Home Army; but when they passed through the guard, Gisevius became alarmed. Why was the Bendlerblock not surrounded by tanks and loyal troops of the Grossdeutschland Guard—the unit responsible for keeping order in Berlin—as had been arranged? And if they were admitted so readily, how would the SS be received if it came? Uneasily, Helldorf and Gisevius mounted the great marble staircase where they were met by Olbricht and Stauffenberg, who had just come from the airport. Of that elegant, maimed figure, Gisevius would record:

> Stauffenberg's appearance was impressive. Tall and slender, he stood breathless and bathed in perspiration. Somehow the massiveness of the man had been reduced; he seemed more spiritualized, lighter. There was a smile of victory on his face; he radiated the triumph of a test successfully completed.

Then Beck, looking very ill and drawn, joined the group. As Gisevius went on: "We greeted one another with a silent, deeply felt clasp of the hands. What could be said at such a moment?" Olbricht announced that the Fuehrer had been the victim of assassination that afternoon, the Wehrmacht had taken over the direction of the government, and a state of siege was being proclaimed. The Berlin police were hereby subordinated to the army, which was now under the command of Witzleben, and Helldorf was to carry out all army orders.

Helldorf made a short, sharp bow and started to leave the room. But as he was doing so, according to Gisevius, Beck said: "One moment, Olbricht. In all loyalty we must inform the chief of police that according to certain reports from headquarters Hitler may not be dead . . ." Olbricht did not let him finish and cried: "Keitel is lying! Keitel is lying!" Stauffenberg "laughed triumphantly . . . and Helldorf, (Count) Bismarck [the deputy chief of police, who was also present] and I looked at one another in utter consternation. All at once the fiction was being torn to shreds. Suddenly we were confronted with the brutal reality of the *Putsch*." It was Beck who now spoke. The revolution must go forward, he declared, adding: "It doesn't matter whether Keitel is lying. What is important is that Helldorf must know what the other side has asserted about the failure of the assassination. . . ." He asked that all present maintain their solidarity.

John was sitting on the stairs during this meeting, eating a plate of sausage salad, and he would report that Count Schwerin (a relative of the man whom Canaris had sent to London to see Menzies in 1939 in a last attempt to avoid war) came up and said, "We shall need every man we can get tonight." John asked when he should be able to speak to Beck or Olbricht about the memorandum to be laid before Eisenhower, and Schwerin replied: "Out of the question—useless now —wait a bit!" John insisted that Hansen and he should leave for Madrid the moment the position was clear.

The position was not clear, and at that point the revolt received another body blow. The task of General Fritz Thiele, the chief of signals at the Bendlerblock, was to ensure that only the Schwarze Kapelle's signals traffic was sent and received. But when he got no call from Fellgiebel, he telephoned Rastenburg and spoke to Arntz. Arntz reported that there had been an explosion and casualties, but Hitler was alive. Thereupon, sure that he would be among the first to be arrested and executed, Thiele tried to reinsure himself. He called his watchmasters together and, according to one who was there, gave "a spirited speech in which he pointed out how reprehensible the attempt had been, demanded loyalty to the Führer and criticised the plotters most severely." His staff interpreted his statement literally—and hurried away to cut the Schwarze Kapelle's communications. The Valkyrie orders had already gone out and Witzleben's proclamation to the Wehrmacht had been transmitted. But from about 6 P.M. on, while the plotters were given the impression that their traffic was being sent out under the highest priority to all parts of the German Empire, it was, in fact, piling up in out trays and baskets "for enciphering." The Schwarze Kapelle was, without its knowledge, effectively quarantined.

Yet the revolt might still succeed—or at least prosper—if the troops obeyed their Valkyrie orders. Goebbels, the Reichsminister for Propaganda and the only Nazi leader in Berlin that day, was at his office near the Brandenburg Gate when he saw from his window—at about six o'clock—that troops fully equipped for combat had surrounded the building and were establishing machine-gun posts and roadblocks. Goebbels knew what was afoot; he had been told of the events at Rastenburg in a telephone call from Hitler. After taking a packet of cyanide pills from his desk drawer—"just in case"—he ordered one of his assistants to go into the street and establish what the soldiers proposed. The assistant returned to report that the troops had been told that the SS had assassinated Hitler, that the army was forming a provisional government, and that their orders were to seize Radio Berlin and the Propaganda Ministry and place Goebbels in protective custody.

Albert Speer, who was with Goebbels, would record the subsequent actions of the cunning Reichsminister. Goebbels learned that the troops were under the command of Major Adolf Remer, an officer known to be ardently *führertreu* who was merely carrying out his orders in obedience to Valkyrie—no more. Goebbels sent his assistant back into the street with an invitation. Would Remer kindly come to his office to clarify the situation? The Reichsminister was confused and anxious to avoid any bloodshed. Speer described the scene when Remer came into the office, his pistol holster unfastened:

> Goebbels seemed controlled, but nervous. He seemed to sense that everything hung on this, the fate of the uprising, and thus his own fate as well. . . . First, Goebbels reminded the major of his oath to the Fuehrer. Remer replied by vowing his loyalty to Hitler and the party. But, he added, he must obey the orders of his commander. . . . Goebbels retorted with the ringing words: "The Fuehrer is alive!" Seeing that Remer was at first taken aback and then became obviously unsure of himself, Goebbels added at once: "He's alive. I spoke to him a few minutes ago. An ambitious little clique of generals has begun this military putsch. A filthy trick. The filthiest trick in history."
>
> The news that Hitler was still living was evidently an enormous relief to this perplexed young man, recipient of an incomprehensible order to cordon off the government quarter. Happy, but still incredulous, Remer stared at all of us.

Goebbels had won the first hand, and, using his mesmeric gifts, he proceeded, according to Speer, to win Remer over completely.

> Goebbels now pointed out to Remer that this was an historic hour, that a tremendous responsibility before history rested on his shoulders. Rarely had destiny afforded a single man such a chance. . . . Now the Propaganda Minister played his highest card: "I am going to talk to the Fuehrer now, and you can speak to him too. The Fuehrer can give you orders that rescind your general's orders, can't he?" . . . Within seconds Hitler was on the phone.

Goebbels spoke to Hitler and then handed the receiver to Remer. At the precise moment that the army was occupying the government quarter of Berlin, Remer, snapping to rigid attention, took the instrument. The only hope left for the conspirators in Berlin was that Remer might conclude that the voice on the other end of the line was an impostor, and decide to carry out his orders. But as chance would have it, while thousands of majors had never exchanged a word with Hitler, Remer had met the Fuehrer; only a few weeks before he had received from Hitler personally the oak leaf cluster to his Knight's Cross of the Iron Cross. The voice cried down the line from Rastenburg: "Do you recognize me, Major Remer? Do you recognize my voice?" Remer, still standing very rigidly to attention, replied: *"Jawohl, mein Fuehrer!"* Those three words sealed the fate of the conspiracy; Remer saluted Goebbels and Speer—the latter had taken no part in dissuading him from carrying out his orders—and left the office. Obedient to the Fuehrer's command, Remer instructed his company commanders to keep the troops in their places, but to secure the government quarter *against* the conspirators. Such were the consequences of the *Fahneneid,* the strength of the Nazi faith, the belief of the ordinary German officer that an order must be obeyed without question, the magic of Hitler.

By 7 P.M., the headquarters of the Home Army was practically surrounded by Remer's men. But believing that his signals were still being transmitted to all parts of the German Empire—and that he was being obeyed—Stauffenberg continued to issue orders; and John would recall that ". . . from the telephone conversations which I overheard it seemed that everything was going forward somehow." In reality, except for a few telephone lines, the conspirators were cut off from the outside world; and when Berlin radio announced that the attempt on Hitler's life had failed, it was clear that the Nazis had managed to frustrate the Valkyrie orders and still controlled the means of public communication. The revolt in Berlin was beginning to collapse, but there was still a chance that it might succeed in the West. General Stuelpnagel had called from Paris with the most encouraging news of the day; he had, he reported, ordered the arrest of all SS officers in the West and, subject to Beck's authority, they would be executed the following morning.

Everything now depended upon Marshal von Kluge. Would he or would he not support the coup? Beck called La Roche Guyon, and when Kluge, who had been appointed C-in-C of Army Group B as well as Supreme Commander in the West after Rommel's wounding, came to the phone, he explained to him in a quiet, firm voice what the situation was. Then he said: "Kluge, I now ask you clearly: Do you approve of this action of ours and do you place yourself under my orders?" Gisevius was listening on a handset attached to Beck's telephone, and he recorded: "Kluge stammered a few phrases that were apparently the outburst of a tormented soul. It was impossible to make anything of them; yes was no and no was yes." Then Beck demanded: "Kluge, in order to remove the slightest doubt, I want to remind you of our last conversations and agreements. I ask again: Do you place yourself unconditionally under my orders?" Gisevius recounted: "Kluge remembered all the conversations, but . . . he would have to confer with his staff. He would call back in half an hour." "Kluge!" Beck exclaimed as he replaced the receiver. "There you have him!"

Nightfall had come and Berlin was in total darkness, except for some searchlights sweeping the skies. Goebbels had obtained Hitler's approval to order Remer's troops to invade the Bendlerblock and arrest the conspirators. But the situation was still confused; no one was sure who was in control of the government quarter. Against this background of doubt, a battalion of army panzers arrived at SS headquarters on the Fehrbellinerstrasse and swung its 75-mm guns almost into the windows and doors of the great, gray building. Obedient to their Valkyrie orders, the men were ready to fire upon anyone who tried to stop them from occupying the building. But then someone intervened to countermand those orders. An officer of high rank rushed up and declared:

> You're crazy. The Führer is alive. The attempt has failed. Everything has been betrayed. There's no sense in carrying on! I can give you only one piece of advice. Go back home! You can't save anything now! You can only lose your head here!

A doctor with the panzers would later testify that the officer was General Heinz Guderian, the Inspector General of Armored Forces.

Guderian himself would declare that he was nowhere near SS headquarters at that hour; he was returning to his home near Deipenhof, having been out walking his dogs. Whatever the truth, the next day Guderian was appointed Chief of the General Staff in place of Zeitzler, whom Hitler had dismissed on the spot for suspected complicity in the coup. And whoever gave the panzers the order to withdraw, it was obeyed. Had they attacked SS headquarters, it would have drawn the army, including Remer's unit, into strife with the SS, and the conspirators might have had a chance to regroup and reorganize. But they did not. The last hope of the conspiracy had been extinguished.

Speer, having heard of the impending attack on the Bendlerblock, and fearing bloodshed, drove there to see if he might act as an intermediary. "In totally blacked-out Berlin," he would write, "the Bendlerstrasse headquarters was illuminated by searchlights—an unreal and ghostly scene." It "seemed as theatrical as a movie backdrop brightly lit inside a dark studio." Troops had now sealed the area off completely; their arms were drawn and loaded and they expected a gunfight. Kaltenbrunner (Heydrich's successor) and Otto Skorzeny (the Nazi commando leader) had charge of the attack operations. Speer found them standing under the trees across the road from the Bendlerblock. They "looked like phantoms and behaved as such," Speer would write. "Everything seemed muted; even the conversation was conducted in lowered voices, as at a funeral."

Inside the great building, the last drama was being enacted. Between 10 and 11 P.M., a group of officers on Fromm's staff who had remained loyal to Hitler moved against Stauffenberg. They entered his office with pistols drawn, overpowered Olbricht and wounded Stauffenberg in the back as he tried to get away through the door into an adjoining office. Fromm succeeded in overpowering the officer guarding his door and took command. All the conspirators were arrested, and at precisely the same time, troops entered the building from the street. There was no resistance; many of the conspirators who remained at large in the building had forgotten even to bring their pistols with them.

Beck was tending the wounded Stauffenberg when Fromm entered the room. According to Hoepner's testimony to the Gestapo, this conversation ensued:

Beck: I have a pistol here, but I should like to keep it for my private use.

Fromm: Very well, do so. But at once.

> *Beck:*   At this moment I am thinking of earlier days.
> *Fromm:* We do not wish to go into that now. Will you kindly go
> ahead!

Beck said a few more words, put the gun to his head, and fired. The bullet grazed the top of his head, and Beck, reeling, cried: "Did it fire properly?"

"Help the old fellow!" Fromm said to two officers who were standing near Beck. "Take away his gun!"

> *Beck:*   No! No! I want to keep it!
> *Fromm:* Take the gun away from him; he hasn't the strength.

While the two officers busied themselves with Beck, Fromm turned to Olbricht, Stauffenberg, Quirnheim and Haeften, and declared: "And you, gentlemen, if there is anything you want to put in writing, you still have a few moments." He left the room, returned five minutes later and said:

> Are you finished gentlemen? Please hurry, so that it will not be too hard for the others. Now, then, in the name of the Führer a court-martial, called by myself, has taken place. The court-martial has condemned four men to death: Colonel of the General Staff Mörtz von Quirnheim, General of Infantry Olbricht, this colonel whose name I will no longer mention [Stauffenberg] and this lieutenant [Haeften].

Fromm spoke to a lieutenant at his side: "Take a few men and execute this sentence downstairs in the yard at once!" The four men were led away. Then Fromm turned to Beck and demanded: "Well, what about it?"

Beck, dazed, managed to answer: "Give me another pistol." One of the men gave him a gun and Fromm stated: "You have time for a second shot!"

Beck put the pistol to his head, fired, and again failed to kill himself. It was said that Fromm then declared to a sergeant in the room, "Give the old man a hand," and that the sergeant executed Beck with a shot through the temple. Whatever the case, there was a shot and Beck was dead. Stauffenberg, Olbricht and their comrades were taken to the cobbled yard below; and there, illuminated by the headlamps of an army truck, they faced a firing squad. In the instant before the volley, Stauffenberg was heard to cry: "Long live the eternal Germany!" Shots rang out and the four men fell dead. Later that night, their corpses, along with that of Beck, were thrown on the back of a truck. They would have no known grave. It was an inglorious end to a brave conception.

Fromm, ordered by Kaltenbrunner not to shoot any more of the conspirators, descended to the street. Speer saw "a massive shadow (appear) against the brightly illuminated background of the Bendler-strasse. In full uniform, all alone, Fromm approached us with leaden steps. . . . 'The putsch is finished,' he began, controlling himself with stern effort. 'I have just issued the necessary commands [to cancel Valkyrie]. . . . General Olbricht and my chief of staff, Colonel Stauffenberg, are no longer living." Twenty minutes later, after a muffled conversation with Kaltenbrunner, Fromm was himself placed under "protective custody." In summarily executing the leaders of the Schwarze Kapelle, he had attempted to eliminate the witnesses to his dalliance with treason. But Witzleben and Hoepner lived to indict Fromm for complicity in the plot. He was arrested, court-martialed and executed.

The revolution in Berlin had failed; Himmler and the SS were again in firm control. In the weeks that followed, a manhunt of unprece-dented thoroughness and ruthlessness embraced all of Germany as everyone involved in the plot was arrested, tried and executed. Remarkably, both John and Gisevius escaped. Although he was being hunted by the SD, John left the country routinely by air for Iberia, survived various plots by Schellenberg to capture or kill him, and was eventually exfiltrated by MI-6 to England where Menzies got him a job in the Political Warfare Executive. Gisevius, who managed to get away from the Bendlerblock before it was surrounded, went on the run and hid in various friends' homes. Dulles would hear nothing from him for many weeks until a message arrived by the hand of a courier who was able to get to Switzerland despite the Gestapo *ratis-sage*. The message read:

> . . . von Kluge holds the key to the situation. . . . (He) would be ready to cooperate with the western Allies in order to facilitate a more rapid occupation [by the Anglo-American armies] if a suitable officer . . . were sent him as an intermediary. . . . The Army is deeply out-raged and shocked by the events which have occurred since 20th July . . . it is only necessary now for the Allies to strike hard and the entire German structure will collapse.

This was extraordinary intelligence, but it had traveled too slowly to be of use. It was, apparently, written by Gisevius on July 25, but it did not reach Dulles until August 17. It was given special dissemination at the White House as an L-Document the following day, but by that time a tumult had struck the front in France. Gisevius remained in hiding until he was finally able to escape to Switzerland, using Gestapo documents manufactured by the OSS and smuggled to him by one of Dulles's couriers. The OSS looked after its own.

Canaris also escaped the *ratissage*—at least for the moment. In fact, he seems to have been remote from the center of the 20th of July plot. He was at home in Berlin that day, and when he was told of the attack upon Hitler, he said, "Good heavens! Who did it? The Russians?" Later he drove out to Eiche, where his economic study group met, to approve a staff telegram of congratulations to the Fuehrer on his most felicitous escape.

Hitler's escape had, indeed, been felicitous, and in the collapse of the coup the Schwarze Kapelle had suffered its greatest, and final, misfortune. It was Goebbels who delivered the epitaph to the entire conspiracy: "If they hadn't been so clumsy! . . . What dolts! What childishness! When I think how I would have handled such a thing. . . . To hold so many trumps and botch it—what beginners!"

Goebbels was quite correct. These ranking members of the German General Staff, the military clique that had conquered almost all of Europe with ruthlessness and efficiency, had failed in the simple task of seizing control of a few square miles of their own capital. Yet the revolt in Berlin had come within an ace of success. It was a different story in France. There, the conspiracy failed not because of inefficiency, but because of the ambivalence of Field Marshal von Kluge.

Kluge spent the day of July 20 conferring with his army commanders, Eberbach and Hausser, and with the corps commanders involved in repulsing Goodwood. The meeting took place in the cool woods near the Panzer Army headquarters; Kluge wanted no repetition of the Ultra incident of June 10 when Schweppenburg's headquarters had been wiped out. According to Wilhelm Ritter von Schramm, the German military historian: "None of those present knew anything about the events (at Rastenburg) and Berlin, or of the careful preparation (for the assassination of Hitler). . . . None had any direct connection with the conspirators. None the less, even under the comforting shelter of the trees, all had the feeling of oppression and foreboding. All felt the approach of defeat. . . ."

The German commanders could not conceal their pessimism. Eberbach spoke of having lost 40,000 men and receiving only 2300 replacements. Dietrich described his orders as "mad" and "impossible," and complained of the policies from Führerhauptquartier that were causing a "mad waste of men." All present agreed that it was unlikely that the Allies would make a second landing in northeastern France; why then were three armies kept idle in other parts of France while the army group in Normandy was being "ripped in pieces like a rotten cloth"?

The conference droned on over the hood of Kluge's staff car, as did the drumfire, the sound of nemesis, from the direction of Caen. The generals agreed that the German armies must withdraw from France before they were finally destroyed. But Kluge said there could be no further retreat; the "line in the vicinity of Caen must be held at all costs." Then Kluge declared: "We will hold, and if nothing can be found to better our situation basically, then we'll die like men on the battlefield." With that, the conference ended. The generals returned to their troops and Kluge drove off to La Roche Guyon.

The severe thunderstorm of the afternoon was dying away when the field marshal arrived at the château at about six o'clock. He strode through the Hall of Arms to his study (Rommel's former office) to look at the day's message file before bathing and dining; and what he saw on his desk—a message stamped *"Blitz Geheim"*—was the most astounding signal of his thirty-four years as a soldier. Hitler had been assassinated and Beck declared acting Chancellor of Germany. Witzleben had issued a proclamation that he, Witzleben, had been entrusted with full powers as Commander-in-Chief of the Wehrmacht, and Kluge was ordered to eliminate the SS leadership in France.

Kluge had still not absorbed the full import of the message when Blumentritt, his Chief of Staff at St. Germain-en-Laye, was shown into the study. At that moment his telephone rang and Kluge was informed that General Fromm was on the line from the Bendlerstrasse. It was not Fromm; it was the call from Beck, who explained the situation in Berlin and asked Kluge to support the revolt and put himself under his command.

The revolt of July 20 was quite possibly the first revolution in history to be orchestrated by telephone, an instrument which all German general officers had been taught to distrust. Kluge wavered for a moment; he did not want to commit himself in a call that was perhaps being monitored by the Gestapo. Then he took the receiver, listened and in response to Beck's plea for support he replied, according to the historian Ritter von Schramm's version of the call, "I must first consult with my people here. I shall ring you back in half an hour." Kluge would not ring back.

Then the telephone rang again. It was General von Falkenhausen. He, too, had just spoken to Beck and was calling Kluge to establish what he proposed to do. Again, Kluge refused to commit himself, and Falkenhausen rang off, promising to keep in contact during the evening.

It was then that Kluge received the *Blitzfernschreiben,* a copy of Witzleben's proclamation as the new C-in-C of the Wehrmacht. It was the first official news he had received and its tone and authority had the effect of persuading him that Hitler was indeed dead and that he must join the conspiracy. Schramm recorded:

> Between 7:30 and eight o'clock Kluge was all for siding with the Berlin Resistance; he had as much as said so to Blumentritt. The obvious thing to do in the West was to try and get an armistice as Rommel had planned. But how? There was no long discussion.

Blumentritt would remember: "Kluge turned to me and said 'Blumentritt, an historic hour has come. First we must get on to Wachtel and get him to stop the V1 fire.'"

Kluge's decision to halt the V-weapons fire on London and southern England, which was reaching its most intensive stage, was the first political step of consequence he took that evening. He considered, evidently, that the cessation of the bombardment would be the olive branch to which the Allies would respond. Schramm wrote:

> . . . it was natural that Kluge should think of stopping the V-attack as the first thing to be done after Hitler's death. That would make it easier to negotiate with the Allies for a cessation of the air war, a cessation which would be the price asked for a voluntary evacuation of the occupied areas. Evacuation was the next stage; on that there was agreement.

Kluge's telephone rang yet again. It was Zimmermann from OB-West, and the message he read to Kluge shattered that moment of extraordinary relief and elation. Keitel at OKW had announced that Hitler was alive and almost uninjured after an assassination attempt and he directed all commanders to ignore any orders received from anyone but himself and Himmler. Kluge, Blumentritt remembered, looked thunderstruck as he replaced the receiver. He declared that if Keitel's message was true, there could be no thought of independent action aimed at an armistice.

Kluge turned to Blumentritt and Speidel and ordered: "Find out what is true and what is false. We must get at the facts first and until then let things stay as they are." Kluge left the room to bathe and change for dinner, and when he returned, Blumentritt was able to inform him that the Fuehrer was alive. Kluge announced that it had been a "bungled business" and poured himself a glass of sherry. He then declared to Blumentritt: "You know, or you strongly suspect, that I was in contact with 'these people.' I needn't tell you my reasons. But when I was, there was still hope. Today I am without hope, for hope is now without meaning."

Then Kluge walked toward the windows overlooking the Italian gardens and began to speak of his dalliance with treason:

> In the summer of '43 messengers from Beck and Witzleben came twice to me when I was in command of Army Group Centre at Smolensk. They tried to win me over to certain political plans. At first I spoke with them at length; the second time, I had my doubts. I broke off the conversation and asked them to leave me out of this highly dubious business. They went on to Guderian who had just been sacked. But he too turned a deaf ear. We should, of course, have reported it.

Two staff cars swept up the drive. In them were General Stuelpnagel; Colonel Eberhard Finkh, the quartermaster of the German army in the West; and Colonel Caesar von Hofacker, the principal link between the Berlin and Paris arms of the conspiracy. The three men had come from Paris, where Stuelpnagel, as Military Governor of France, had crossed his personal rubicon without hesitation. That afternoon, upon hearing of Hitler's death, he had ordered the immediate arrest of the senior officers of the SS and the SD. Having set the machinery in motion for the seizure of power in France—the first step toward an armistice with the Allies and the evacuation of German-occupied Europe—Stuelpnagel had come to the château to ensure Kluge's support.

Kluge received the three men immediately and informed them that he had heard news that the Fuehrer was not dead. The elegant Stuelpnagel seemed unfazed, and there and then Hofacker began to speak:

> Field Marshal, what has happened in Berlin is not decisive. Much more so are the decisions which will be taken in Paris. I appeal to you, for the sake of the future of Germany, to do what Field Marshal Rommel would have done, what he said he would do in the secret conference I had with him in this very room on July 9. Cut free from Hitler and yourself take over the task of liberation in the West. In Berlin power is in the hands of Colonel-General Beck, the future Head of the State; create the same *fait accompli* here in the West. The army and the nation will thank you. Put an end in the West to bloody murder; prevent a still more terrible end and avert the most terrible catastrophe in German history.

Kluge sat with an unmoved face throughout Hofacker's address. Then the field marshal rose suddenly and declared: "This is the very first I've heard about any such assassination attempt." Blumentritt's account of the events that evening follows:

> (Kluge) behaves as if he were very indignant about the whole thing. Silence. Stuelpnagel pales slightly and says: *"Herr Feldmarschall,* I thought you knew all about it." Kluge says "Good heavens, man, I had not the *slightest inkling,* otherwise I shouldn't have been out at the front. . . ."

Stuelpnagel was obviously stunned. Schramm recorded:

> (He) felt himself suffocating. He could not bear to be longer in this gloomy room. . . . He walked into the terrace garden. There were blooming the summer roses with their almost unearthly sweetness, perfuming the coming-on of night. Stuelpnagel walked past without noticing them. He was filled with one shattering thought: all was over . . . at this very moment the troops in Paris were arresting the SS and the Gestapo on . . . (his) orders.

Blumentritt's account continues:

> Then Stuelpnagel comes in from the balcony and you can see that he must have gone through a terrific mental upheaval. Then Kluge, the very figure of a country squire, says "Well Stuelpnagel, you'll stay and have a meal." We sit down to dinner—it must have been late, 9 o'clock at least. . . . During the meal Kluge talks like a book about some battle in the front line, drinks, raises his glass—"your health"—and behaves as though nothing were up. Stuelpnagel eats hardly anything and takes only a sip or two. All at once Stuelpnagel says: "But I've already taken steps. I've given the order to arrest the SD in Paris." Kluge jumps up from the table: "Heavens alive, man, you couldn't do that without my consent! Well, my dear Stuelpnagel, you'll have to save your own skin, then!" To me he said: "Ring up and see whether action has already been taken!"

Blumentritt returned from the telephone to report that the entire SS and SD hierarchy—including the Nazi ambassador Otto Abetz, and such dangerous individuals as Knochen, Boemelburg, Kieffer and Goetz—had all been arrested by picked troops of the army and were to be executed in the morning. Kluge wanted no share of the responsibility and declared: "My dear Stuelpnagel, I must ask you to give orders immediately that the SD are to be released. The best thing would be for you to get into civvies and disappear somewhere or other."

It was now nearly 11 P.M. Kluge walked with Stuelpnagel to the door of the château. "You must get back as quickly as you can to Paris and release the arrested men," he told Stuelpnagel. "The responsibility is wholly yours." Then Stuelpnagel rallied. He said: "We cannot withdraw now, Field-Marshal. Events have spoken for us." Hofacker said, "It is your honour that is at stake and the honour of the army and the fate of the nation is in your hands." Kluge replied: "It would be so if the swine were dead." But no, he could and would do nothing. He could not betray the *Fahneneid*. As the two men took formal leave of each other, Kluge advised Stuelpnagel to "Regard yourself as suspended from duty." Blumentritt, appalled that this instruction would mean Stuelpnagel's death warrant, whispered to Kluge: "We've got to help him." As Kluge and Stuelpnagel went down the stone steps into the courtyard where the cars were, Kluge again advised the Military Governor of France to "Get into civilian clothes and disappear somewhere." Stuelpnagel saluted the Commander-in-Chief and was driven off into the night. They had not shaken hands.

Kluge walked back up the steps into the château, went to his study and wrote this signal:

> To the Führer and the Supreme Commander of the Armed Forces. Thanks to a merciful act of Providence, the infamous and murderous attempt against your life, My Führer, has miscarried. On behalf of the three branches of the Armed Forces entrusted to my command, I send you my congratulations and assure you, My Führer, of our unalterable loyalty, no matter what may befall us.

Then he penned an Order of the Day to the armies:

> The Führer lives! The war effort at home and the fighting at the front goes on. For us there will be no repetition of 1918, nor of the example of Italy! Long live the Führer!

He gave the order to an aide for immediate transmission, and, as a final gesture before retiring, picked up the telephone and ordered the operator to get him a *Blitz* call to Rastenburg. There he spoke to Jodl and reported Stuelpnagel's actions.

At about 0130, the field marshal slipped gratefully between the cool sheets of his bed. If he cared to, he could hear the rising fury of the guns in the distance.

The news that an attempt had been made on the life of Hitler reached Eisenhower in France where he was visiting the front. At daybreak on the 21st, Curtis was shaving in his tent after a long night's work on the order of battle estimates. He would recall:

> One of Eisenhower's aides rushed up the duckboarding as I was shaving and told me the old man wanted to see me right away. I knew from his attitude that something was up and I rushed off with the shaving soap still on my face, not even bothering to put a shirt on. Eisenhower was in the operations tent and he said to me: "Holy smoke, Curtis! There seems to be a revolt going on among the Krauts. What does it mean?" He seemed to have been taken by surprise, and I always wondered why. Dulles knew all about it, and we got his warnings. I replied: "Sir, there have been rumors about this on and off for at least three weeks." Then I told him what I knew—stuff obtained mainly from Dulles—and he said: "Well, it looks good for Cobra!" He added a remark that I always remembered and thought important. "I wonder whether the Prime Minister knows about this."

Churchill had spent the evening of July 20 in the wardroom of the British cruiser *Enterprise,* lying off the beaches at Arromanches. The officers were singing songs and ended with "Rule Britannia." Although it is not clear whether he knew what had happened in Berlin at that hour, Churchill rose and recited one of the verses: "The nations not so blest as thee/Must in their turn to tyrants fall:/While thou shalt flourish great and free,/The dread and envy of them all."

Churchill certainly knew of the attentat on the morning of July 21, but Eisenhower made no formal pronouncements about the abortive revolt, nor did Roosevelt. And it was not until the 23rd, when Churchill was visiting a forward RAF base in Normandy, that he said anything publicly. Then, according to the *New York Times,* he remarked with "an acid grin" to a group of five hundred airmen gathered around him:

> There are grave signs of weakness in Germany. They are in a great turmoil inside. Opposite you is an enemy whose central power is crumbling. They missed the old [here Churchill used either the word "bugger" or "bastard," but the *Times* reported the word "bounder"] —but there's time yet. There is a very great disturbance in the German machine. Think how you would feel if there was a revolution at home and they were shooting at Cabinet Ministers. . . . Britain stands today as high as she ever stood in a thousand years.

Later, Churchill would admit that he had been wrong about the Schwarze Kapelle—the only resistance movement in German-occupied Europe that had not received the active support and encouragement of the Allies. The attempted assassination and *coup d'état,* even though they had failed, were "exhilarating" to the Allied high command; for they signaled the beginning of the end of the Nazi stranglehold on Germany, and could only serve to benefit the Allies in the psychological, political and military arenas of the war. But there were those, Dulles among them, who saw in the failure of the plot a greater and more far-reaching failure. Wilhelm Hoegner, one of Dulles's agents in Bavaria, who spoke with Dulles and his assistant Gaevernitz on July 21, would remember: "I never saw them so completely downtrodden. They had always hoped that through a sudden downfall of Hitler, the war would be ended before the Soviet Russians entered Berlin. A quick peace agreement with a democratic German regime would have prevented that. But now all was lost; the continuation of the war would provide the Russians with a pathway to the Elbe in the heart of Europe. American policy had suffered a terrible defeat."

9

The Breakout

SIMPLE SOUNDS foretold the next Allied move in Normandy: the all-night rumble of tanks here, a fragment of intercepted radiotelephony there; an artillery barrage here, a mortar-stonking there. Jays and crows cawed and hopped from bough to bough, disturbed by troops creeping up to jump-off positions in copses. The clang of a cooking pot against a spade; the sizzle of a Very light flare, fired off as patrols made their way back to their lines before dawn; a cough, a grunt, a shout in the dawn twilight—all these and a thousand other signs were the harbingers of the great battle now to be fought.

Kluge, sensing that the decisive battle was in the wind, wrote to the Fuehrer on July 21:

> I can report that the front has held . . . as a result of the magnificent valor of the troops and the resolution of the commanders. . . . However, the moment is approaching when the front will break. . . . And when the enemy has erupted into open terrain . . . orderly and effective conduct of the battle will hardly be possible.

He signed and sealed the letter and—because it was so secret and sensitive—it was taken to Rastenburg by armed guard.

The document could not have arrived at a worse moment for Kluge. As Himmler hunted down the members of the Schwarze Kapelle—Canaris, Oster, Witzleben, Tresckow, Goerdeler, Fellgiebel, Roenne, Hansen, Helldorf, Gehre, Schlabrendorff, Hofacker, Stuelpnagel, Falkenhausen were all in jail or about to be arrested—Hitler learned that Kluge *and* Rommel had been involved in plots to kill him. The atmosphere at Führerhauptquartier became pregnant with the need for cleansing and revenge. Everywhere Hitler saw traitors, particularly in his signals, intelligence and supply services; everywhere he saw connections between "blueblooded German swine" and the "international aristocracy." Yet considering that he had almost been assassinated, Hitler was remarkably calm when he read Kluge's letter. For the moment, military realities dominated his thinking; on July 23 he ordered that plans be drawn up for the withdrawal of the German army from France, and that all Todt construction workers in the Pas de Calais begin to restore the Siegfried Line, the fortifications on Germany's western frontier. This latter order was quickly decrypted by Ultra and provided Montgomery and Bradley with their first clear intelligence about Hitler's predicament after July 20.

Calamity confronted the Fuehrer from all sides. Turkey broke off relations with Germany—at long last. Army Group South was surrounded in the Ukraine. There was—again at long last—a revolution in Rumania and Hitler lost the Rumanian oilfields. Bulgaria revolted a few hours later. Bodyguard's chickens had finally come home to roost. Yet still the Fuehrer was not ready to admit defeat. He directed that the entire resources of Greater Germany be fully, ruthlessly and immediately mobilized for the defense of the Reich, and took special measures to ensure the loyalty of the armed forces. He sent an order to all fronts announcing that everyone who gave up ground would be shot. Of propositions that he should negotiate with one side or the other, Hitler declared: "Anyone who speaks to me of peace without victory will lose his head, no matter who he is or what his position."

The Fuehrer gave Germany a choice: victory or, in the event of defeat, national suttee, with himself applying the torch. He believed, with even greater intensity, that only he could save the Reich, and his behavior grew increasingly disturbed. Guderian, the new Chief of the General Staff, would write:

> . . . the deep distrust (Hitler) already felt for mankind in general, and for General Staff Corps officers and generals in particular, now became profound hatred. A by-product of the sickness from which he suffered is that it imperceptibly destroys the powers of moral judgment; in his case what had been hardness became cruelty, while a tendency to bluff became plain dishonesty. He often lied without hesitation and assumed that others lied to him. He believed no one any more. It had already been difficult enough dealing with him; it now became a torture that grew steadily worse from month to month. He frequently lost all self-control and his language grew increasingly violent.

At this conclusive moment in the war, Hitler seemed close to madness. Thus, the failure of the assassination had served the Allied cause after all; and the Allies made no attempt to kill Hitler by aerial bombardment, as might have been quite easy. There was always the possibility that among the Nazis there would be a more formidable successor. As Churchill said, while Hitler remained in power, the Allies could not lose the war.

Guderian was only one of a wholesale replacement of "unreliable" officers by those who were *führertreu*. The events of July 20 and the following days shook the German command structure severely and its morale began to crack. Cadogan would record that on July 23 he authorized the dispatch of a British agent, Colonel X, to Holland where the German C-in-C, General der Infanterie Hans Reinhard, had told another British officer of his wish to consider surrender. It was the first positive overture from a German high commander since Arnim had surrendered in Tunisia in May 1943.

But what of the commanders and the troops who still held the line in Normandy? Would they collapse, as the Allies hoped they might? In fact, they would go on fighting with all their old tenacity. Zimmermann told his American interrogators after the war:

> And now came the psychologically baffling aspect. . . . The front kept right on fighting as though nothing had happened. . . . Why did not thousands and tens of thousands lay down their arms and end the war? The answer was simple. It was because in the high emotional tension of battle, in this physical and moral over-exertion, this murderous struggle, the individual was so completely and intensely pitched to the moment of combat, to the "you or me" of fighting, that any convulsions outside the focus of this tension, no matter how strong they might be, only touched him on the fringe of his consciousness. Figuratively speaking, the combat soldier was in another world. . . . They did not have the time nor were they in a mental state to concern themselves with matters beyond the perimeter of their struggle. They saw also with their own eyes that any further attempt at a change [of government in Germany] would let loose another St. Bartholomew's massacre. So the army silently went on doing its duty, though with the bitter subconscious knowledge that an unavoidable catastrophe was impending.

Zimmermann added as an afterthought: "But for the existence of unconditional surrender, we might well have folded up right there and then." That policy had not been modified, however, and so the Germans went on fighting hopelessly—and savagely.

Kluge's attention remained firmly fixed on the Caen front. He was convinced that Montgomery would strike there; and the Allies, aware of that belief through Ultra, did everything they could to encourage it. Staubwasser would report the presence of very strong naval forces between Le Havre and Cap d'Antifer, aerial reconnaissance activity between Le Tréport and Ostend, and a "marked increase in partisan activity—attacks and acts of sabotage in Belgium and border areas of northern France." Rosebud was at work. But if it now seemed unlikely that the Allies would attempt another land assault, Staubwasser warned that the German high command had to "reckon with Allied large-scale air landings." Where? All the evidence pointed to the Caen front.

Meanwhile, Bradley prepared to unleash Cobra on the St. Lô front. The offensive, which was originally to have begun on July 20, had been postponed because bad weather prevented the massive aerial bombardment necessary to cut a path through the German lines. Cobra was rescheduled to open at midday on July 24, but bad weather forced another cancellation. That morning, Air Chief Marshal Sir Trafford Leigh-Mallory, who was at Bradley's command post, saw that the weather would still prevent the precise bombing necessary if Americans troops were not to be hit. He ordered a postponement, but through a signals delay his order did not reach the bomber groups until it was too late to turn back the first wave of the aerial assault. Three hundred bombers dropped 550 tons of high explosive and 135 tons of fragmentation bombs, some of which fell upon the American 30th Infantry Division, killing 25 men and wounding 131.

Cobra was off to a bad start. The morale of the Americans was badly shaken; and worse, it seemed to Bradley that the accident would alert the Germans and that he would lose the surprise he had hoped for. The Germans did respond with a large volume of artillery fire on the three American assault divisions in the area; and Kluge said to Hausser, the commander of the 7th Army on the American front, "Without any doubt, there's something new in all this air activity. We have got to expect a heavy enemy offensive somewhere." But remarkably, he still looked for the attack on the British front, and made arrangements to be there on the 25th.

The dawn broke fair that day. General Fritz Bayerlein, the commander of the Panzer Lehr Division on the American front, noticed that the heavily wadded cloud of the day before was breaking up. But except for occasional small-arms fire, the front was quiet. It remained that way until about eleven o'clock, when his scouts began to report sounds like "an orchestra of bass viols tuning up." The Cobra air armada was approaching, and within ten minutes an infernal agitation had begun.

The area to be drenched was very small: about 7000 by 2500 yards of Norman earth, bounded by the little villages of Amigny–La Chapelle–Le Mesnil Eury. But into that area in the next hour or two the Americans poured 140,000 shells, while 1800 bombers dropped 3300 tons of bombs. They were followed by 380 medium bombers which dropped over 650 tons of high explosive and fragmentation bombs; and they, in turn, were followed by 550 fighter bombers which dropped more than 200 tons of bombs and hundreds of napalm canisters. The world seemed to shake. One account of the assault noted:

> The bombardment transformed the main line of (German) resistance from a familiar pastoral *paysage* into a frightening landscape of the moon. Several hours after the bombing, the village priest of la Chapelle . . . walked through the fields and thought he was in a strange world.

A thousand *Feldgrau*—one-third of Bayerlein's fighting men—were killed; the blasts destroyed or overturned so many of his tanks that only a dozen or so were left operable. Three of the Panzer Lehr's battalion command posts were destroyed. A parachute regiment attached to the division virtually vanished. Bayerlein recorded that men went mad and "rushed dementedly round in the open until they were cut down by splinters." He was among the few divisional commanders to survive. "Housed in an old Norman château, with ten-foot walls," he reported, "we were rather better protected than the others." But even so "the ground shuddered," and "quick glimpses outside showed the area shrouded by a pall of dust, with fountains of earth spewing high in the air."

The attack was devastating, but the bombardment and the power punch on land that followed merely dented the German lines; and that same evening at his command post, Bradley declared sadly that even that dent had not been obtained without grievous cost. During the aerial assault the lead bombardier of one heavy formation had trouble with his bombsight, and misjudging the intended point of impact, he dropped his bombs and a great cloud of dirt and dust obscured the red markers laid by the artillery. The rest of the formation dropped their bombs on the lead aircraft's salvo, and the ordnance of thirty-five heavy and forty-two medium bombers fell upon the 30th Infantry Division. In the second disaster in two days, the bombs killed 111 and wounded 490 men of Old Hickory.

Among the casualties of the accidental bombing was General Lesley J. McNair, who had gone forward that day to the 30th Infantry's advanced positions to watch the bombardment and the assault. Whether McNair should have been in France at all would long be debated, for during the critical breakout operations it was imperative to maintain the Fortitude threat. Eisenhower, seeking to keep Fortitude alive, cabled Marshall for a replacement, and General John L. de Witt was selected. Mrs. McNair was told nothing beyond the fact of her husband's death, and the general was buried secretly in an apple orchard near Bradley's headquarters. All news was suppressed, correspondents were not told that the most senior American general ever to be killed in action had just died, and censors were given instructions to prevent any leakages. The LCS needed time to cover its tracks, and this was done by Brutus on July 26 with a telegram to his controller that read:

> I have learned that General McNair (the commanding general of First United States Army Group) has been killed in Normandy. He had gone there to consult with General Montgomery and to inspect the German coastal defences. Here at FUSAG this loss is considered very serious. It is thought that a successor will be appointed immediately to command the FUSAG operations.

Cobra struck again in the dawn mist of July 26, while Montgomery intensified his efforts to distract Kluge's panzers, praying that they might be held just a little longer around Caen—a prayer that was answered. American armor, supported by one of the greatest artillery barrages in history, was committed to the Cobra attack, and for the next two days the entire front was engulfed in "the elemental mingling of earth, air, fire and water" of an enormous battle. The troops inched forward with no time to bivouac, no time to light fires; they ate cold beans and dozed where they collapsed when the sun went down.

The *Feldgrau* fought like demons, but the dent in their lines became a bulge and, finally, on the morning of the 28th, they had had enough. In single-file, dirty, weary, they began to fall back; and the *Panzerkampfwagen,* covered with the branches of cider apple trees, rumbled south through the seafront villages of the western Cherbourg peninsula. The German commanders had decided to make a new line along the ridges of the Suisse-Normande at the base of the peninsula. The Americans arose that morning expecting another day of bloody fighting. Units of the 30th Infantry Division, the men who had been so badly punished by their own air force's bombs, moved out; an hour passed, two, three, and there was no sign of resistance. It seemed impossible, but the *Feldgrau* had gone; the hedgerows were empty. The German line had broken.

That day, the next and the next, Americans poured into the breach; a rivulet became a stream, the stream an olive-green tide in pursuit of the retreating Germans. Kluge could not stem the flood. He reported that the front was *"eine Riesensauerei"*—one hell of a mess. In reality, there was no front, no flank but the sea. Bradley's armor rocketed south with all the velocity of a hollow-charge shell, and the Allied air forces flew a larger number of missions than had ever been flown before. Kluge commanded the tatterdemalion ruins of an army that had once been the cocks of Europe. Gone were the precise formations, the battle flags, the polished boots and pressed field gray. The 7th Army was a rabble, and Hausser and his staff only narrowly escaped capture. But despite the speed and ferocity of the American advance, the German armor, paratroopers and panzer grenadiers got away.

It was the eve of Judgment Day for the Germans in the West; and Hitler, who was at last convinced that there would be no further Allied landings along the Channel coast, gave Kluge permission to begin removing some of the infantry divisions that garrisoned the Pas de Calais—but not all. The V1 launch sites must be protected just in case the Allies did attempt another landing. Nevertheless, this decision effectively marked the end of Fortitude, which would pass into history as perhaps the greatest deception of any war. Hitler also decided that OKW should establish a command post in Alsace-Lorraine whence he would go to direct the battle in the West personally. He would tell Kluge, he announced, "only enough of future plans for the Commander-in-Chief West to carry on immediate operations." The reason, he said, was because "the broad strategic plans of the Reich . . . would be known to the Allied powers almost as soon as the details reached Paris." Hitler still suspected that traitors in his signals and supply systems were responsible. He remained in complete ignorance of Ultra. The man who had proclaimed himself to be the greatest military strategist of all time had been outwitted by the modern refinements of two of the oldest tricks in the lexicon of war—deception and cryptanalysis.

Meanwhile, in Normandy, the British and Canadians continued to slug it out around Caen like refreshed pugilists who had been too long on the ropes; and the Americans were moving so fast that at times Bradley himself knew where the spearheads were only from air reconnaissance reports of villages bursting into the red, white and blue of the tricolor—a sign that the enemy had departed. But as yet the breakout had not become a breakthrough. That could not be claimed until Bradley's army had taken Avranches, the town of Jean No-Feet and the Salt Tax Revolution of the seventeenth century.

By dawn on July 31, all attention—German as well as Allied—was focused on Avranches, a hill resort of 7000 people overlooking Mont-St.-Michel, where there was a single stone bridge over the broad estuary of the See River. If the American armor was to get into Brittany without delay, and if the Germans were not to re-form and hold a new line along the river, that bridge had to be taken undamaged and immediately. It was. Tanks of the 4th Armored Division captured and secured Avranches and hurtled on along the coast road with its constant views of the strange conical ghost of Mont-St.-Michel hanging in the mist. They approached the second town of critical importance—Pontaubault and its old, thirteen-arch stone bridge over the second river barrier, the Selune. Surely the Germans would have blown this bridge? They had not. Pontaubault and its bridge were taken by American tanks and infantry during the late afternoon of July 31. The Americans stood at the gateway to Brittany and to central France.

The stalemate in Normandy was ended, and the success of the epic charge across Normandy generated an even greater wave of relief and optimism in the Allied high command than the success of the landings. At last, Allied armor could begin to move. Eisenhower reported to Marshall: "Paris and the Seine have come within reach." Montgomery, in a directive to Bradley, announced that the destruction of the 7th and Panzer Army west of the Seine would "hasten the end of the war." Colonel Dickson, Bradley's G2, opined of the German army that "Only discipline and habit of obedience to orders keeps the front line units fighting," and that "It is doubtful that the German forces in Normandy can continue for more than four to eight weeks as a military machine." "In the next four to eight weeks," Dickson added, "the current situation may change with dramatic suddenness into a race to reach a chaotic Germany."

For Hitler, it must have seemed that it was ten minutes to midnight on the clock of destiny. His armies were in disarray everywhere. The Russians had broken the main Finnish-German defense lines, and Finland seemed about to desert her alliance with Germany. Twenty-five of the thirty-three divisions of Army Group Center were trapped in central Russia. On the southern front, the Wehrmacht had been compelled to abandon the Crimea. In Italy, the German army was in general—although orderly—retreat to the last lines of defense in the north. And now in France, the front had burst wide open.

Yet Hitler still refused to accept OKW's advice to withdraw his armies to the German frontiers and make the nation into a fortress on easily defensible lines. He remained obdurate in his contention that the Grand Alliance was a flimsy structure which would collapse with a single massive defeat. Britain, he said, was war-weary and would seek a political settlement if he could keep France as a base for his missiles, his new jet *Blitzbombers,* and his revolutionary hydrogen-peroxide-fueled submarines. Withdrawal would mean the beginning of the end for Germany. Accordingly, he sent Kluge new orders. The front, through which at that moment a hundred American fighting battalions and a thousand armored fighting vehicles were streaming, must be restored with infantry while German armor gathered to deliver the Allies a blow they would not forget. It was Operation Lüttich again, and this time it was imperative that the tactic succeed. All he needed, said Hitler, was bad weather and good fortune.

On August 1, Bradley's new command, the 12th Army Group, was established, and Patton's army—the 3rd—was activated as the fangs of Cobra. With remarkable resource, Patton, often directing traffic personally, managed to get seven divisions across the two-lane bridge at Pontaubault in six days. The weather, which had been generally wet and cloudy ever since D-Day, suddenly turned hot and dry—tankmen's weather. One of the two combat commands of General John S. Wood's 4th Armored Division made 40 miles in an afternoon—faster than Rommel in 1940—to reach Brittany's capital city, Rennes, by early evening of August 1. Although Rennes was once described by Augustus Hare as "the dullest, as it is almost the ugliest" city in France, the cupolas of the Hôtel de Ville seen through the blood-red haze of a setting sun and the dust of a preparatory bombardment by massed Thunderbolts and Bostons were, after the maddening Battle of the Hedgerows, one of the world's greatest skylines. But the euphoria was only momentary; German panzer grenadiers stopped the advance and Wood was compelled to withdraw. He left the city to the infantry and, with orders to do so, made another dart, this time to the ancient city of Vannes, on the Golfe de Morbihan about 70 miles from Rennes. His tanks rocketed across the undulating moors of the Landes de Lanvaux and entered the town at 9 P.M. on August 5. With that stroke, Patton's army had severed the Breton peninsula—along with some 70,000 *Feldgrau*—from the rest of France. Nearly 100,000 Germans were now cut off, if the garrison in the Channel Islands was counted.

The great prize of the Breton campaign was the port of Brest, which would be used to supply the Allied forces spilling out of Normandy. While Patton turned the greater part of his army east toward Le Mans, he ordered General Robert W. Grow, the commander of the American 6th Armored Division, to take Brest. Grow was delighted; he had "received a cavalry mission from a cavalryman." But to some such an order was madness. Brest was 200 miles away and the peninsula bristled with *Feldgrau*. What kind of opposition would Grow meet on the narrow roads; was it wise to leave his flanks and rear exposed? It would depend upon the Breton *maquis*.

Since the collapse of Samwest and Dingson in June, Gubbins and Bruce had made enormous efforts to restore the clandestine situation in Brittany. They had poured Jeds into the peninsula: "Horace," "Hilary," "Felix," "Giles," "Gilbert," "Francis," "Gerald," "Guy," "Gavin." Dingson was reestablished, along with two smaller bases, "Grog" and "Wash." Nearly 200 tons of arms and explosives had been delivered by August 1. Some 30,000 Bretons were armed, another 50,000 carried grenades and acted as couriers and guides. The French parachutists of the SAS—the Battalion of Heaven—were now at work in small do-or-die bands along the two main highways that ran through the peninsula. For the moment, the entire Breton operation was commanded in the field by Bourgoin—Le Manchot, the "One-armed Man" who was so elusive that the Germans had placed a million francs on his head. Casualties had been heavy—40 per cent of his men were killed, and, in the nature of the fighting, nobody took any prisoners—but they were now an effective force that had managed, as Eisenhower would state in a special Order of the Day to mark Breton underground operations, to surround the Germans with "a terrible atmosphere of danger and hatred which ate into the confidence of the leaders and the courage of the soldiers."

At about the same time that Grow received his orders to take Brest, SFHQ wirelessed its orders to the Jeds and the other leaders of the Breton *maquis*. Now, instead of destroying, they were to preserve. They were ordered to keep all bridges open and intact, capture all German road demolition points and remove the charges, mask or mark all German artillery and anti-tank gun positions. They were to keep the roads to Brest open; and above all, the great stone viaduct at Morlaix was to be seized, held and German-laid demolition charges defused. On August 2, a hundred French SAS troopers were dropped near Morlaix, and after a brief but fierce battle, they took and held the bridge. The Germans responded, sending a battalion of the 2nd

Parachute Division to retake and destroy the bridge. If they succeeded, Grow's tanks advancing on Brest would be stopped on the
wrong side of the gorge.

Jed team Giles had been operating clandestinely on the Rennes-
Brest highway in the Montagnes Noires ever since landing in Brittany
on July 6. Now, with the receipt of the idioform *Le xérès est un vin
d'Espagne,* Giles was ordered to come out in the open in support of
the SAS troopers holding the bridge at Morlaix. Commanded by Bernard Knox, Giles positioned 2000 *maquisards* in the bush and hillside
copses along the Rennes-Brest road between Châteauneuf and
Châteaulin to intercept units of the 2nd Parachute Division moving
toward Morlaix. Before dawn, they scattered hundreds of tirebursters,
which resembled the little black turds of the Finistère hill sheep or the
big ocher feces of the milch cows, and exploded the moment a vehicle
ran over them. Giles laid on bazooka, light machine-gun and grenade
parties, and then they waited.

At about ten o'clock on August 3, a battalion—perhaps a thousand
German paratroopers—was discovered moving out of Châteaulin toward Pleyben, a pretty town on the Brest-Nantes canal. Giles resited
some of his attack parties further to the west. And then, as the
Feldgrau came trudging up the road behind their slow-moving motor
transport and guns, Giles opened fire. Several score of the paratroopers fell in the first minutes, while trucks and trailers caught fire as
the tirebursters exploded and the bazooka shells and machine-gun fire
struck home. The paratroopers quickly dispersed into the countryside,
where *maquisard* killing parties set out after them on what they called
"*boches* hunts." In that brief moment of violence, some thirty paratroopers were killed, about twenty wounded, and some thirty captured. The wounded were killed on the spot by the *maquisards,* and
the captured men were brought before Knox for interrogation. As the
rest of the German battalion withdrew into Châteaulin and the villages
in the area, the captured men were also shot. Knox would explain in
his report to SFHQ:

> They were all from the 2nd Paratroop Division, and all of them were
> Hitlerites to a man. They admitted to the atrocities they had commit-
> ted, refused to believe that the Americans had taken Rennes, refused to
> discuss the Hitler regime, and refused to explain why they had French
> jewelry, money and identity cards on them. They were all very young
> (one of the worst was only 17) and they were all subsequently shot
> by the FFI. Even if we had tried to prevent this shooting, we would
> have been powerless—these men had burned farms and farmers with
> their wives and children all the way along the road.

The German attempt to retake Morlaix failed, and that same day—August 3—Giles and the other special forces teams in Brittany heard that quaint but heroic call to arms: *Le chapeau de Napoléon, est-il toujours à Perros-Guirec?* General Koenig came to the microphone in London and declared:

> French people of Brittany, the hour of your liberation has come! The provisional government of the French Republic calls for the national uprising! French people of Brittany, workers, peasants, officials, employees! The time has come for you to take part, with or without weapons, in the last battle. . . . French people of Brittany! The whole of France salutes you! The whole of France will follow you in the national insurrection!

They were immortal words, not heard in France since the Revolution. They were followed by the *Marseillaise* and—as a signal that they were also meant for the SAS—the lilting idioform music of *Lilliburlero.*

Like their ancestors in guerrilla, the Chouans and the Companions of Jehu, the Bretons rose almost to a man that day. The towns and villages of the peninsula became bright with tricolors as the Jeds and the Battalion of Heaven issued the ancient command: *Formez-vous vos bataillons!* The Germans retreated and by the evening of August 6, Grow's armored columns were at Brest. The port would not fall for another month, but the war of movement had ended and a flashfire of killing swept Brittany as the *maquisards,* out of control, sought out individual or small parties of Germans and their collaborators and killed them in what would come to be called "the joys of liberation."

A few days later, General de Gaulle would give the order over the BBC for the commencement of an insurrection throughout France with the words that it was the "simple and sacred duty" of every Frenchman to "take part in the supreme war effort of the country." "Frenchmen!" de Gaulle declared, "The Hour of Liberation sounds! Join the French Forces of the Interior! Follow the directives of their leaders! The National Uprising will be the prelude of liberation! *Français! L'heure de la libération sonne!*" The broadcast ended with massed choirs singing—and massed bands playing—the *Marseillaise.*

With that order, the French boil burst, a rebellion began in Paris, and the five German armies in France would find themselves in various states of siege. It was an uprising comparable to the Commune of 1871. All were involved—schoolteacher, postal worker, trade unionist, priest, scholar, writer, shopkeeper, mayor, policeman, architect, cable layer, aristocrat, hedge-dweller, vineyard worker, egg-packer, Communist, petrol pump attendant, Catholic, retired officer, rationing clerk, printer—all engaged in random but often clever actions of combined mulishness and systematic sabotage and guerrilla. Ammunition trains destined for Lyon—a classic case—found themselves at Hamburg. Locks failed to work, canal levels dropped, roadmenders pulled up paving stones in the path of panzers, trains were delayed, signals locked, points jammed, sugar got into the petrol, goods trains were improperly put together so that wagons destined for Metz were routed to Marseilles, telephone boxes became a jumble of incorrect connections, German mail addressed to Paris ended up at Turin, pylons collapsed through "frost," cows wandered in front of ambulances.

To organize roving packs of guerrillas into flank guards for Patton's spearheads, Gubbins and Bruce began to build a necklace of Jedburghs along the Loire from Nantes to Montargis, and the flames of insurrection leaped from Loire Inférieure to Anjou, the Touraine, the Sologne, the provinces of Orléans. Team "George," led by Cyr of the OSS, traveling from Brittany hidden under hundreds of lice-ridden hens in the back of a wheezy old wood-burning Renault, arrived to anchor the necklace in the woods around Ancenis. Hundreds of shirtless ones, carrying .22 rifles, shotguns and spears fashioned out of hay-knives, rallied to his command post and were sent out to watch the fords over the Loire for Germans seeking to take Patton in the side. Team "Dickens" landed near the south bank of the Loire in the province of that name; "Harold" came down in the Deux-Sèvres; "Ian" into the Vienne; "Andy" into the Haute Creuse; "Hugh" and "Hamish" in the Indre between the Creuse and the Cher; "Isaac," "Harry" and "Verveine," "Haft 105" and "Gain" landed north of the Loire; "Canelle" and "Gingembre" came down near the point where it rose.

William Colby of team "Bruce" would find himself and his two French comrades dropping into the streets of Montargis, the town due south of Paris which Hitler had ordered transformed into a fortress. He would join the SOE Donkeyman réseau led by the baleful figure of Roger Bardet, the most notorious double agent in France—a sinister matter that would cause the future chief of the CIA to debate thirty years later whether he had been some sort of pawn in a wireless game. A squadron of DC-3's would bring Captain Roy Farran and twenty armored jeeps bristling with machine guns to an airfield near Rennes, whence they would set forth in a great arc across France as far as the Vosges, slashing at the capillaries of the Germans' retreat routes. Ian Fenwick, the Punch cartoonist, landed in the gap between the Loire and the Seine to shoot up the tails of German convoys—an operation in which Fenwick would be killed and ten of his troopers caught and executed by the outraged Kieffer, an act that led, in turn, to Kieffer's execution. The culmination of the insurrection would be the liberation of Paris itself by the resistance, while throughout France many Germans would find themselves in much the same plight as did General Botho H. Elster, the officer in command of one of three columns of the German 1st Army retreating from the Biscay region. The column stretched for nearly 30 miles between Poitiers and Châteauroux: 750 officers, 18,850 men, 10 women, 400 cars, 500 lorries, 1000 horse-drawn vehicles. Harried by the *maquisards* of Jed team Hugh, Elster approached the American command and in the interests of humanity begged to be permitted to surrender to regular troops rather than to the *maquisards*. The Americans accepted his surrender. A report to the Supreme Commander of resistance operations in August would state: "The work of the resistance during the period under review has led largely to the liberation of a great portion of France." The report noted more somberly: "The achievements of the FFI have not been made without severe losses, but in almost every case these have been far lower than those of the enemy. As was anticipated . . . the value of resistance, as a strategic factor, has had a definite effect on the course of the military operations undertaken in France." As a tribute, Eisenhower agreed that *maquisards* should be allowed to paint the Allied white star on their vehicles.

In Brittany, the main battle had obscured the fact that behind the massed movements of armies, the vast comings and goings of air and sea armadas, the greatest clandestine operation in history had succeeded in diverting, harassing and cutting German forces off from the rest of France, forces that might have changed the course of the battle in Normandy. Eisenhower, in a special proclamation to the Bretons and the special forces teams, would acknowledge their contribution. The Battalion of Heaven, the Jeds and their "Groupes Mobiles d'Attaque"—as the shirtless, shoeless patriots of Brittany came to be called—had tied up countless *Feldgrau* in a bloody, interminable battle of the shadows. Then, when the breakout occurred and Grow's and Wood's tanks entered the peninsula too fast for the infantry to keep apace, the *maquisards* kept the roads open and the bridges intact, protected the Americans' flanks, acted as guides, and took care of prisoners—tasks that would have tied down tens of thousands of Patton's men and slowed down his spearheads. Finally, the *maquisards* formed themselves into infantry battalions and helped first to encircle and then to destroy the Germans holed up in the ports.

With the peninsula safe, Gaulliste bureaucrats arrived to form the first État Major on the soil of France. It was the "Mission Aloes"—a bitter plant—come to take command of Brittany from Le Manchot. The first party dropped to a Jed team Frederick reception (one of its number, an officer who would later come to be called "one of the fathers of modern Europe," refusing at the last moment to jump) on August 4, just behind Grow's tanks. Then, a few days later, ten Halifaxes towing Waco gliders appeared over the Landes de Lanvaux north of Vannes. The gliders cast off, whistling down to another Frederick reception (clandestinity was still necessary for, while the American armor had passed through, isolated pockets of Germans still fought in the rear) with their cargoes of armored jeeps, wirelesses, typewriters, mimeograph machines, heavier weapons, folding desks—equipment for the État Major du Commandement Supérieur des Forces en Grande Brétagne et Délégation Militaire du Gouvernement Provisional de la République Française. The men of the Steward of France had come to claim the keys. A new régime was established and the covert campaign in Brittany in support of Neptune was virtually over.

The État Major would give little credit to the indomitable Le Manchot and his men. The Gaullistes would give no public credit at all to the Jeds and the other special forces teams. Le Manchot would lead his Battalion of Heaven down the Champs Élysées on victory day and then go into obscurity in Brittany, honored only by the Bretons. But the Bretons would not forget the Jeds. As Knox and the men of team Giles loaded their jeep with bedding, petrol cans, wireless, guns and stores, and prepared to move off quietly from outside their safehouse at Plessis, Legal, Knox's FFI assistant, and the Communists' Groupes Mobiles d'Attaque marched up. They formed ranks around the jeep and, in the ragged manner of partisans the world over, presented arms. Then Legal stepped forward and, quite forgetting that Knox was an American, delivered a little speech.

> We regret that it was not possible to do more and do better. The lack of matériel, a certain amount of incohesion and some petty political rivalries were our handicap. Nevertheless it was with great joy that we acclaimed (you as) the first parachutists and we tried to give of our very best in assisting (you) to hunt the common enemy, "the Boches." We can never thank you sufficiently for what you have done for us and the liberation of our country. Furthermore, we regret deeply

that certain untoward incidents cause a shadow on those happy days. No doubt they will be smoothed out in the near future. That is our most fervent desire, the desire of our Frenchmen of the "Resistance" who are your comrades of days gone by as well as of the future.

To His Britannic Majesty, to you Sir, and to your proud warriors who were our liberators and our comrades, I and my fellow Frenchmen of the Resistance send our sincere thanks and best wishes for the good fortune and prosperity of your country—which we consider, a little, our own.

Götterdämmerung

10

On August 2, 1944, the Turing engine (there were more than ever now at work) in Hut 3 at Bletchley unbuttoned a signal that would prove to be the most decisive cryptanalytical revelation of the campaign in France. It was the Fuehrer's order to Kluge to mount Lüttich at Mortain, a charming town on the Cance in the hills of lower Normandy. As the five-figure groups were first decrypted into German and then translated into English, exalted sentences began to take shape. "The decision in the Battle of France depends on the success of (Lüttich). . . . The C-in-C West has a unique opportunity, which will never return, to drive into an extremely exposed enemy area and thereby to change the situation completely." Supported by all the aircraft the Luftwaffe could scrape together—three hundred planes— the main elements of eight armored divisions were to strike through Mortain and recapture Avranches, thereby cutting Patton's army off from the rest of the American forces. An infantry division was to be put in to support the armored thrust, and the auguries were promising; only elements of one tank and one infantry division stood in the way of Lüttich. H-Hour was set for midnight, August 6.

The Ultra reached MI-6 headquarters at just about the same time that Kluge received the Fuehrer's orders at his forward command post near Alençon. It covered two whole sheets of quarto-size Ultra paper, and Winterbotham recognized its importance immediately. He placed the Ultra in a red leather Despatch Box for Churchill at 10 Downing Street, and sent a copy by teleprinter to Eisenhower's headquarters at Southwick Park. Tedder was on the scrambler line within the hour; were there any indications that Hitler might be bluffing? Winterbotham would recall that he telephoned Hut 3 "to make quite sure that the original German version was in Hitler's own distinctive style and language. They told me we had no reason to doubt it on any score, and the signal had without doubt come from Fuehrer headquarters." Winterbotham called Tedder back and told him it was "absolutely copper-bottom, gilt-edged and gold-plated."

With that, the Supreme Commander decided to fly immediately to Bradley's command post, to be on hand when the attack began.

Kluge, who was at least an excellent general, saw the dangers of Lüttich immediately and signaled Führerhauptquartier: ". . . an attack, if not immediately successful, will lay open the whole attacking force to be cut off in the west." He pointed out that in order to concentrate the necessary panzer power to attack at Mortain he would have to withdraw the armored divisions from the Caen front, thus his forces would be vulnerable to a breakthrough by the British. His signal to Hitler was decrypted by Ultra on August 3, and the debate that followed was watched with intense interest at various Allied headquarters. Winterbotham recalled: "Now the vital question was who was going to win the argument, Hitler or Kluge? My money was on Hitler. This was once again his chance to show his doubting armies that he still remained a genius and to rekindle the Hitler myth. . . . Hitler didn't keep us waiting long."

The Fuehrer replied that all risks must be taken, announcing that he would give Kluge 140 fresh tanks and some 60 armored cars, to make a rough total of armored fighting vehicles at Kluge's disposal of about 400 units—a powerful force for two American divisions to have to fight. Still Kluge protested. In a final signal to Führerhauptquartier, as Winterbotham would write:

> Kluge staked his whole career on trying to stop this attack. In his last signal he pulled no punches and boldly stated that it could only end in disaster . . . one could get a glimmer of his utter hopelessness from his signals. He must have known it was the end for him anyway.

The Fuehrer did not comment on Kluge's signal. He merely ordered him to proceed with Lüttich, an order which was known to the Allies within the hour. Then a second intelligence factor entered into the game of frustrating Lüttich and destroying the German army in the West. George, the stay-behind agent at Cherbourg, and "Mr. Desire," his sub-agent at Avranches, were ordered to report on the state of various bridges that the Lüttich force would have to cross to get to Avranches. Thus through Ultra, Montgomery and Bradley knew every detail of Lüttich, and through the questions put to the stay-behind agents, they could even deduce the time schedules for the attack.

General Leland S. Hobbs, the commander of the 30th Infantry Division, assumed command of Mortain at 8 P.M. on August 6, four hours before Lüttich H-Hour. The fifty-four-year-old infantry officer knew very little about the dispositions of friendly troops—and, for that matter, of the whereabouts of the enemy. His division was extremely tired after a long march, and it took over positions that were virtually unprepared for a major defensive battle. Fortifications and communications were inadequate, but above all the 30th had no intelligence that a major offensive was building up in the sector in front of them. The Allied high command may have known about the details of Lüttich right down to the last nut and bolt but none of this intelligence had filtered down to Hobbs's headquarters.

Hobbs's first move was to secure Hill 317, a 1030-foot peak which dominated Mortain and the countryside around it. On a clear day it was possible to see Avranches, which was just 20 miles away on the coast. As the seven hundred officers and men of three companies dug into their positions on the hill, a number of portents suggested unusual German activity in the area: odd, brief messages on German radiotelephone links; a good deal of aerial activity, the disturbed flight of crows, jackdaws and partridges in the woods to the east of Mortain; the rumble of tanks in the distance. The men on Hill 317 thought they could see the torches of military police guiding armored columns on the move. They could, but they were not American columns; they were German.

Suddenly, without preparatory artillery fire which would have alerted the defenses, the Germans attacked. Tanks carrying SS storm-troopers emerged from the woods, swept around Hill 317, entered Mortain and captured the U.S. command post in the Hôtel de la Croix-Blanche. Then the panzers fanned out through the 30th Division's defenses, one arm of the attack taking the village of Le Mesnil Adelée on the See River, while the other arm advanced on St. Hilaire on the Selune. At dawn the Germans were within 10 miles of the Avranches-Pontaubault road. At one point the panzers were only a mile from Hobbs's command post at the hamlet of La Bazoge; and at another point the 30th Division was in danger of complete disintegration. As Hobbs would report: "With a heavy onion breath that day the Germans would have achieved their objective."

But at dawn three elements intervened to blunt the attack. The first was the German failure to take Hill 317; and from their commanding view of the German assembly areas, the men on the hill could direct great volumes of artillery fire to break up the German columns. The second element was the ground mist. The Germans expected that heavy mist between sunup and eleven o'clock would give cover for their tanks from Allied fighter bombers. But the mist lifted quickly and exposed the panzers to massed Typhoon aerial rocket attacks; no fewer than ten squadrons were airborne just after 8 A.M., bombarding the panzers as they tried to shove through the *bocage*—the very country in which the Germans had stopped the Americans' armor so often before in the Cherbourg peninsula.

The third element that contributed to the failure of the initial assault at Mortain was the curious behavior of General Gerhardt Count von Schwerin, the commander of the 116th Panzer Division, and the same officer who had tried to negotiate an understanding with Menzies, Cadogan and Godfrey on behalf of Canaris and Beck in London in 1939. Scheduled to participate in the assault, Schwerin's division had simply not appeared; and General der Panzertruppen Hans Baron von Funck, who commanded Lüttich, set out to discover what had happened to it. Where the hell had Schwerin been? Where were his panzers? Schwerin was quite indifferent to Funck's anger. He explained that he had no confidence in Lüttich; therefore he felt he could not take part in the attack. But there was more to it than that—as Funck and Kluge knew. Schwerin had lost hope of victory. Involved in the 20th of July conspiracy, he despised the régime, and Kluge in particular. Even if his neck was at stake, he was not going to have his division chewed to pieces in a lost cause far from Germany. He was going to keep it intact to defend the Fatherland.

Schwerin was guilty of flagrant disobedience and he was relieved of command at 4 P.M. on August 7. His men, who were devoted to him, began to mutter ominously; in fact, later at Aachen, they would indeed revolt against the SS. But now they did as they were told; they joined the assault. But the lead tanks were stopped when they ran into a hail of American cannon fire and RAF rocketry. The Luftwaffe got nowhere near the battle, and neither did the reinforcements that Kluge had hoped to get from the 15th Army at the Pas de Calais. Then, just before midnight on the 7th, the 1st Canadian Army struck Kluge's northern flank from the Caen sector. Spearheaded by massed formations of tanks and armored troop carriers, the great Canadian thrust penetrated the first line of the German defenses. To blast a path through the second, 1000 RAF night bombers, their targets marked for them by green flares and starshells, came over just after one o'clock. The Canadians pressed the attack, and at dawn, when Kluge spoke to Eberbach, the general commanding the panzers, his voice was heavy with anxiety. "We didn't expect this to come so soon," he said, "but I can imagine it was no surprise to you." Eberbach replied: "No, I have always waited (expected) it and looked toward the morrow with a heavy heart."

Kluge called Lüttich off, only to be blamed by Hitler for the failure of the offensive. The Fuehrer regarded Lüttich as the master stroke that would restore the German position in France. He declared that Kluge had displayed poor judgment in selecting the direction and time of the attack. He decided he could no longer rely on Kluge, and assuming command of the battle himself, he ordered a resumption of Lüttich with the words: "Greatest daring, determination, imagination must give wings to all echelons of command. Each and every man must believe in victory." Kluge foresaw only disaster, but as he told Eberbach, ". . . the order is so unequivocal that it must be obeyed."

Eisenhower, Montgomery and Bradley were informed through Ultra of the Hitler-Kluge exchange, and, like Kluge, they immediately recognized the vulnerability of the German situation. The initial thrust of the Lüttich offensive had created a dent in the Allied lines, and the Allied commanders realized that if the Germans continued to hold their present position, Bradley's forces might have time to slip around their southern flank, while Patton's armored spearheads, which were advancing toward Le Mans, might swing up from the southeast and Canadian forces descend from the north to encircle and destroy the German armies in Normandy. But the Allied commanders needed forty-eight hours to move their armies into position. How, then, could they lure the Germans into biting so deeply into the Allied front that they would not be able to escape?

Bradley, a former schoolmaster whose modesty and mildness obscured his genius as a military commander, conceived a plan to gain the necessary time. It was called "Tactical Operation B." As a rule, the Americans disliked the British practice of giving grand or symbolic code names to their special operations, but in spite of its colorless name, Tactical Operation B was the last of the great deceptions of the French campaign, a masterpiece of imaginative military thinking that represented the final flowering of one of Wavell's principal dictums of deception: feigned retreat while planning to attack. Its objective was to *encourage* the Germans to resume Lüttich or at least to delay their withdrawal from Mortain; and to achieve that, the plan proposed a "display of weakness by our forces in this area."

Montgomery approved Tactical Operation B, and Harris and Ingersoll of the Special Plans Branch, with the cooperation of Strange-

ways's R-Force and the XX-Committee, were given the responsibility
for its execution. By August 9, Harris and Strangeways had arrived at
their scenario. The "story for enemy consumption" was that:

> . . . delay on the Brest Peninsula is seriously inconveniencing us. Our
> growing army is straining supply on the beaches. We know that we
> cannot drive East beyond the Seine until we have developed the Brest
> Peninsula ports, and we are very chastened by the length of time it
> took to put Cherbourg in condition. Moreover, the commanders of
> both the 4th and 6th Armored Divisions at Lorient and Brest have for
> days been complaining that they have neither the infantry nor artillery
> to reduce the ports, that their supply lines are in danger, that they are
> short gasoline and ammunition and that their equipment is in bad
> shape. Both commanders *urgently* request infantry, corps artillery and
> supplies.

Armed with that script, a chorus of double agents, including
George, Garbo and Brutus, immediately began to report to their controllers the details of the American predicament. Then they announced that:

> Faced with this situation . . . General Bradley has made a decision.
> It is to order the daring General Patton to clean up his situation by
> sending adequate forces of infantry and artillery into the peninsula
> *quickly* to reduce the fortresses of St. Malo, Brest and St. Nazaire.
> These forces shall be in the strength of two or three infantry plus one
> armored division. . . .

In short, the Germans were told that Bradley was stripping the Mortain front; and if they believed that three or four divisions were being
diverted to the Brest peninsula, they would also believe they had
nothing to fear at Mortain.

Allied troops did begin to move into Brittany, but they were only
the 1200 men of the U.S. 23rd Headquarters Special Troops—men
trained in deception and equipped to simulate the movement of much
larger forces. Company "C" impersonated an entire armored division;
Company "A" made noises like an infantry division. Tactical Operation "Nan" simulated the westward movement of a second infantry
division; Tactical Operation "Oboe" sounded like yet a third infantry
division proceeding toward St. Nazaire. False unit insignia were
painted on the vehicles and the men wore false shoulder patches for
the benefit of unlocated stay-behind agents known to be transmitting
from the Avranches, Brest and Lorient areas. It was a movement
wholly of "special effects," conducted much as Hollywood might use a

few hundred extras to create the impression that thousands of men were on the move. Meanwhile the real divisions under Bradley's command silently took up their positions on Kluge's southern flank, the Canadians were poised to the north and Patton rocketed toward Le Mans.

The effect of Tactical Operation B on the enemy can only be estimated by subsequent events. Kluge, fearful of encirclement and annihilation, remained reluctant to remount Lüttich, but obedient to Hitler's orders, he moved units of the 9th, 10th and 12th SS Panzer divisions away from the British sector at Caen toward the Mortain front. Other German forces, including units of the 9th Panzer, which had finally left Bordeaux when the Ironside threat evaporated, were moved into the area immediately behind Mortain. Hitler appointed Eberbach to command the great new thrust and decreed that all forces must be ready to resume the attack on August 11. Eberbach declared that this was impossible, but Hitler demanded no further delay and, to satisfy Eberbach's persistent requests for more forces, ordered parts of the 11th Panzer Division, which was being held in the south to meet the Vendetta threats and the actual menace of Anvil, to proceed immediately to the Mortain sector. But finally, on the night of the 11th, even Hitler recognized the vulnerability of the German position. He suspended all other orders and gave permission for the 7th Army to begin withdrawing from the Mortain area. But Bradley had gained his forty-eight hours, and the circle around the German forces was virtually complete.

The withdrawal of the forward elements of the 7th Army brought relief to the 30th Infantry Division at Mortain and to the defenders of Hill 317. Of the seven hundred men who had been on the hill, only three hundred walked off. For six days and nights, they had paralyzed all German movements in the area, and over one hundred enemy tanks and self-propelled guns lay beneath them as testimony to their extraordinary tenacity and heroism. Theirs was one of the finest small unit actions of the war. In all, over three thousand Americans were killed or wounded at Mortain, but they had broken the German lance; and Hitler, contemptuous of American fighting ability, was—as with so much else—proved quite wrong.

By August 13, it was apparent that Tactical Operation B had succeeded, for on that day Kluge's nightmare of encirclement was becoming a reality. The 5th Panzer Army and the 7th Army were practically surrounded in what would come to be called the Falaise Gap—a name to rank with Stalingrad as the cenotaph of German military might. For it was here, amid the hills and valleys around the small town where William the Conqueror was born, that Army Group B met its end. In an area that stretched from Falaise to Mortain, eight German divisions with all their equipment were more or less encircled by the Americans to the south and west, and the British and the Canadians to the north and northwest—trapped like rats in a demijohn. Fighter bombers by the thousand bombarded and machine-gunned the German troops as Allied infantry and armor pressed in from all sides. Medium bombers and the shells of massed artillery increased the German agony. It was a seething, bloody cauldron which the Germans would come to call *"der Kessel von Falaise."* A British soldier, R. M. Wingfield, would write:

> Hundreds of men were coming towards me. They were German. They were from the Falaise Gap. I never want to see men like them again. They came on, shambling in dusty files. . . . They were past caring. The figures were bowed with fatigue, although they had nothing to carry but their ragged uniforms and their weary, hopeless, battle-drugged bodies.

It would be estimated that some 10,000 Germans were killed and another 50,000 captured at Falaise. Total German losses to this date would be close to 300,000 men, with a further 100,000 trapped in the Channel fortresses. Such was the price of the Normandy campaign.

On August 14, Kluge went to the front to see if he could break the Allied ring around his armies. He spent the night at Dietrich's headquarters at the castle of Fontaine l'Abbé near Bernay. Then, at dawn on the 15th—a day that would leave history with one of its most momentous mysteries—he set out to attend a meeting with two of his commanders at the village of Necy. He was to meet them in the village church between ten and eleven o'clock. With him were his son, a wireless truck, a small escort and some aides. The fact that he had taken his wireless truck—and his son—would lead to speculation that the purpose of the trip was something other than to confer with his army commanders.

The weather was hot and perfect for aerial attackers; Kluge and his party were soon under fire and two of their vehicles were destroyed. They tried to avoid attackers by going across country, through fields and woods, but they were again caught by *Jabos* near Ammeville. The wireless car was hit and burned, and the chief operator was killed while his assistants were all wounded. Cut off by the swarming planes, Kluge, exhausted, could go no further and collapsed into a ditch while his aide, a Lieutenant Tangermann, found a bicycle and rode to the rendezvous. When he got to the church at Necy, there was nobody there; the commanders had come and gone. Tangermann returned to Kluge but by now OKW, OB-West and Army Group B were all extremely alarmed. Kluge was declared missing and Hitler looked around for a new C-in-C West. He selected Field Marshal Walter Model, and while Model was being brought to Rastenburg for a briefing, Hitler placed Hausser in temporary command of Army Group B.

Kluge would not turn up at Eberbach's headquarters until 10 P.M. that evening. He had been missing for seventeen hours, and Hitler became convinced that he had attempted to surrender the German armies in the West to Montgomery that day. Both he and Keitel would maintain that Kluge was in radio contact with the British. Keitel would state that Kluge's wireless messages were intercepted by a special Horchkompanie set up after Hitler's suspicions were aroused by the ceasefires that accompanied the exchange of nurses early in July. At an OKW conference on August 31, Hitler would declare that "August 15th was the worst day of my life." His forces in France were crumbling; French and American armies began landing on the Riviera coast; and as Guderian would state: "Hitler was desperate . . . when Kluge had failed to return. . . . He imagined that the field marshal had established contact with the enemy." And that prospect produced one of the most violent storms witnessed since the afternoon of July 20.

Had Kluge attempted to surrender? Hitler thought so. At the staff conference on August 31 he stated:

> Field Marshal von Kluge planned to lead the whole of the Western Army into capitulation and to go over himself to the enemy. . . . It seems that the plan miscarried owing to an enemy fighter-bomber attack. He had sent away his staff officer, British-American patrols advanced, but apparently no contact was made. . . . Nevertheless the British have reported being in contact with a German general.

Time Magazine, in a report published on June 25, 1945, and obtained, presumably, from Patton, would give the following account of Kluge's missing hours:

> *The Road to Avranches*—One day last August (Kluge) suddenly left his headquarters on the Western Front. . . . With some of his staff, Kluge drove to a spot on a lonely road near Avranches in northwestern France. There he waited, hour after hour, for a party of U.S. Third

Army officers with whom he had secretly arranged to discuss surrender. They did not appear. Fearing betrayal, Kluge hurried back to his headquarters.

The correspondent explained that "On the day of the rendezvous, Allied air attacks blocked the Third Army party's route to Avranches. By the time the U.S. negotiators arrived, Kluge had gone." This story —and other identical stories in the American (but not the British) press—received some confirmation from Dulles, who would later write that Kluge made "a futile attempt to surrender to General Patton's army somewhere in the Falaise Gap. . . ."

Neither Sibert, the G2 of the 12th Army Group, Strong, Eisenhower's G2, nor de Guingand, Montgomery's Chief of Staff, would provide the slightest substantiation for the story. There was, however, important evidence that surrender was on the mind of the German high command in the first and second weeks of August, despite the collapse of the Schwarze Kapelle plot. A document discovered in the OSS files at the National Archives in Washington in 1974 revealed that the German General Staff did, in fact, make at least one serious attempt at surrender during this period. The document, which was prepared by the OSS Committee on Dissemination of Intelligence and given special limited circulation on August 11, 1944, to the President, the Secretary of State and the Joint (but *not* the Combined) Chiefs of Staff, reported approaches to the OSS at Lisbon by Heinz Carl Weber, who, the report stated, was "in charge of all German mineral purchasing operations in Lisbon as representative of the *Reichswirtschaftsministerium.*" According to the report, Weber's overture had been made through a "thoroughly reliable source"—either Baron Hoyningen-Huene, the German ambassador, or one of his deputies, for there were contacts of a special nature between the English, American and German embassies in Lisbon. Weber, the report stated, had "received a message from German General Headquarters to find out how the United States would react to the following proposal: Germany would surrender unconditionally to the Western Allies and meet any industrial or territorial demands, provided the latter act at once to occupy the Reich and keep out the Soviet." The OSS document declared that "the report may merit attention in view of the channels employed and the apparent sincerity of the source."

There, then, was a chance to end the Second World War. The German army had been defeated in France and, it appeared, was willing to turn against the Nazis in the same way that the army of Italy had done. If the overture was accepted, might it not remove the need for the western powers to fight their way to Berlin, Vienna and Prague, leaving the Germans to take care of the Nazis? But if the emissary was given any reply at all—and there would be no evidence of a reply—it could only have been those fateful words that Canaris heard so many years before aboard the quarter deck of HMS *Glasgow:* "I am empowered neither to proffer nor to accept any terms other than unconditional surrender." The war was to go on for another nine months, during which time the continent would suffer more devastation than during the whole of the preceding five years.

Kluge had been able to do nothing to break the iron ring around his armies in the Falaise Gap; and on August 17, he was back at the Château de La Roche Guyon. The noise of battle was now very close as American tank columns crossed the Seine near Mantes. But Kluge appeared to care nothing for his own safety or for that of his headquarters. He was preoccupied with the signal he had received from OKW. It read: "The Commander-in-Chief West and the Commander-in-Chief Army Group B, Field Marshal von Kluge, is placed on the reserve list. At the same time Field Marshal Model is appointed Commander-in-Chief West and Commander-in-Chief Army Group B." The coldness of the signal, its very brevity, was an insult. Worse was to come. Model, a tall, monocled Nazi who had distinguished himself during the various retreats on the Russian front, arrived at the château that evening, and after exchanging formal salutes, he handed Kluge a letter. It instructed Kluge to report forthwith to Führerhauptquartier. That could mean only one thing.

Blumentritt arrived from St. Germain-en-Laye to meet the new C-in-C, and he went into Kluge's study to say goodbye. There, in the gloom, he found the field marshal bending over a map on a table. Kluge looked up, greeted his former Chief of Staff, tapped the map with his pencil, and then said: "Here at Avranches all my military reputation went. Do you remember the book which the old Moltke wrote which saved the honour of his opponent Benedek? There is no Moltke for me." It was a reference to Moltke's chivalry in protecting the reputation of the defeated Austrian general, Benedek, at the Battle of Sadowa on July 3, 1866, during the Seven Weeks' War. Blumentritt sought to console the fallen field marshal, but Kluge declared: "It's all up with me." And so it was. Hitler knew that Kluge had been involved in Operation Flash in March 1943. He had also been implicated in the July 20 plot, had lost Normandy, and now he was suspected of attempting to arrange an armistice with the Allies in the West. There was more than enough against him to warrant Kluge's arraignment on suspicion of high treason—and almost certain execution.

Blumentritt assured Kluge that responsibility for the Lüttich disaster could not and would not be laid at his door. But Kluge repeated despairingly: "No, no! It's all up with me." He prepared to return to Germany, as Model received orders that same night to begin the withdrawal of the German army from France. It was, as Sir John Wheeler-Bennett would observe, the nemesis of the power of the German General Staff, that instrument of German might which had twice in half a century brought the Reich to the verge of world hegemony. Now Germany stood on the brink of disaster. It was a process that had begun that day at the Siegessäule when the General Staff swore the *Fahneneid* to the new Fuehrer; one that ended in a botch assassination attempt at the *Wolfsschanze*.

That evening, Kluge sat down in his study to write a letter to the Fuehrer. For a man about to die, a man whose armies were destroyed and whose enemies were close to the very room where he was writing, it was an astonishing letter. Even when it no longer mattered, Kluge excused himself, his officers and his men for the German defeat. He blamed it on the insufficient numbers of tanks, anti-tank weapons, supplies and personnel available in the West—a direct tribute to the efficacy of Bodyguard. He wrote that it had been impossible to withdraw the panzer divisions in time because of the lack of infantry— a direct tribute to the efficacy of Fortitude. And then, revealing his moral ambivalence even to the end, Kluge concluded the letter with these words:

> Should the new weapons in which you place so much hope, especially those of the air force, not bring success—then, my Führer, make up your mind to end the war. The German people have suffered so unspeakably that it is time to bring the horror to a close.
>
> I have steadfastly stood in awe of your greatness, your bearing in this gigantic struggle, and your iron will. If Fate is stronger than your will and your genius, that is Destiny. You have made an honourable and tremendous fight. History will testify this for you. Show now that greatness that will be necessary if it comes to the point of ending a struggle which has become hopeless. I depart from you, my Führer, having stood closer to you in spirit than you perhaps dreamed, in the consciousness of having done my duty to the utmost.

Just before dawn on August 18, the day upon which the Germans began their retreat from France, Kluge, his *aide-de-camp* and a small escort drove down the lane of linden trees from the Château de La

Roche Guyon and headed for Germany. The little column stopped briefly at the Forêt de Compiègne, where Kluge got down from his six-wheel command car to stretch his legs. Then the convoy started again and headed into the battlefields of the First World War. Near Verdun, Kluge told his chauffeur to stop for a meal. They were between Clermont-en-Argonne and Dombasle. Kluge spread a rug under a tree, asked his *aide-de-camp* Tangermann for some paper, and wrote a letter to his brother. He gave it to Tangermann with instructions to post it, and then said: "Get everything ready in about a quarter of an hour and then we'll go on."

Kluge had no intention of going on. At about 3:20 P.M. on the afternoon of August 18, 1944, Field Marshal von Kluge, the man who had almost captured Moscow and was now disgraced by a small group of Americans on a hill called 317, the man who for a few fleeting seconds might have ended the Second World War in the West, took his life. He bit into a phial of potassium cyanide and was dead in an instant.

Epilogue

THE SUICIDE of Field Marshal von Kluge marked, at least symbolically, the end of Neptune and Fortitude and, it seemed to the Allied Supreme Command, the war itself. As a SHAEF intelligence bulletin announced on August 23, 1944: "Two-and-a-half months of bitter fighting, culminating for the Germans in a bloodbath big enough even for their extravagant tastes, have brought the end of the war in Europe within sight, almost within reach. The strength of the German armies in the West has been shattered, Paris belongs to France again, and the Allied armies are streaming towards the frontiers of the Reich."

In fact, victory was still nine months away; and Neptune, one of the great acts of human courage and intellect, would deteriorate into dull carnage. Hitler had time to rally and rebuild his armies, and the road to Berlin would be a long and costly one. Conventional warfare superseded the war of special means, Eisenhower took command of the battle from Montgomery, football replaced cricket. The large-scale use of deception, in particular, ended with the success of Neptune. The Soviet General Staff formally canceled its participation in Bodyguard on September 29, 1944, a significant date in the evolution of the Cold War. The common goals and global cooperation that had made Bodyguard possible evaporated as each of the three big powers began to fight the final battles with separate political objectives.

The decline in the use of Churchill's "sinister touches" and "elements of legerdemain" was attended by a severe increase in casualties. During Neptune—when stratagem dominated—the Americans suffered 133,326 casualties (34,133 dead); the British and Canadians lost a further 83,825 men (16,138 dead). During the march to Germany—a campaign not noted for its brilliance of military thought or conduct—

the casualties would number 418,791 Americans (86,000 dead) and 107,000 Britons and Canadians (25,000 dead); moreover these figures did not include air force, French or civilian casualties, all of which were immense.

So bitter and apparently interminable would the fighting become, as the Allied armies began to penetrate Germany, that Eisenhower would send a signal to the Combined Chiefs of Staff on November 22, 1944, declaring that it was of "vital importance that we should redouble our efforts to find a solution to the problem of reducing the German will to resist." The matter went to Roosevelt, who agreed and wired Churchill that a message should be broadcast to the German people defining Unconditional Surrender in kindlier terms that he had hitherto permitted, and urging them to join "in this great effort for decency and peace among human beings." It would be, by implication, an invitation to revolt. But this time it was Churchill who, after discussing the President's proposal with the War Cabinet, advised against such a broadcast. Anything which looked like appeasement, he wired Roosevelt, would "worsen our chances, confess our errors, and stiffen the enemy resistance."

Nevertheless, both Sibert and Dulles would try, through their secret contacts, to make the German General Staff revolt again. But it was too late; the Schwarze Kapelle no longer existed. With the failure of the July 20 plot, all serious resistance to Hitler and the Nazi régime ended. Everyone who was suspected of taking part in the conspiracy was rounded up and, group by group, appeared before various bloody assizes, stripped of rank, decorations, privileges, honor. Their families often disappeared in what Hitler called the *"Nacht und Nebel"*—the decree of the Night and the Fog. Wives were taken into custody, apparently to await death by execution or by malnutrition; children were given out to SS families so that the names of the conspirators would not be perpetuated. Clutching at their trousers, in crumpled and dirty civilian clothes, deprived of their belts, braces, ties, even their false teeth, lest they tried by suicide to thwart the executioner, the conspirators stood before their Nazi judges. In almost all cases, death by hanging—the ultimate insult in the German *Offizierskorps*—was the sentence.

The first hangings took place in Plötzensee Jail in Berlin on August 8, 1944, when Field Marshal von Witzleben, General Stieff, General Fellgiebel and Colonel Hansen were among those who appeared on its gallows. Erich Stoll, a film cameraman employed to record their deaths, described the scene. Each defendant came into the execution chamber and a hemp loop was placed around his neck. He was lifted up by the executioners, the upper loop of the rope was hung on what resembled a butcher's meathook, and then the condemned man was allowed to drop.

Very few of the conspirators survived. Schlabrendorff and Mueller did, even though they were arrested; a bookkeeping error is thought to have saved them. Speidel, too, survived. Both Gisevius and John escaped from Germany. Colonel Michel was never arrested, but his chief, Roenne, was. He was executed on the evening of October 11, 1944. His last act was to write a letter to his mother in which he said he would die in the spirit of the "thief on the cross at Jesus's side." The total number of people executed, or who killed themselves, in the wake of the July 20 plot will never be known; many simply disappeared or were killed out of hand by the Gestapo. The lowest estimate would be 400, the highest 7000.

After the war, an attempt was made by the West German government to honor the Schwarze Kapelle dead. Streets and squares were named after the leaders, and the 20th of July was proclaimed a national day of remembrance. But neither the dead nor the day would be really remembered. Schlabrendorff recalled that Tresckow said to him, just before he blew his head off with a grenade on the Russian front:

> Now everyone will turn upon us and cover us with abuse. But my conviction remains unshaken—we have done the right thing. Hitler is not only the arch-enemy of Germany, he is the arch-enemy of the whole world. In a few hours' time I shall stand before God, answering for my actions and for my omissions. I think I shall be able to uphold with a clear conscience all that I have done in the fight against Hitler. . . . The worth of a man is certain only if he is prepared to sacrifice his life for his convictions.

In the West, and particularly in Washington, the fate of the Schwarze Kapelle was received with indifference. Only for Rommel would there be expressions of admiration and regret. Hurriedly evacuated from France—his guards heard that both Gaff and the SS were after him—he was taken home to recover. This he did, with surprising speed. He spent his last days, his left eye covered with a black bandage, writing his version of the campaigns in Africa and Normandy. He blamed his defeat in Africa on the failure of Hitler and Mussolini to supply him adequately. He remained unaware to the end that it was Ultra that had ensured his defeat. Of the battle in France, he contended that "My functions . . . were so restricted by Hitler that any sergeant-major could have carried them out." He never admitted that he had been outwitted and outgeneraled, commenting only upon ". . . the well-thought-out, guileful method with which the Englishman wages war." And of the entire war, his last observation was that "it was all without sense or purpose."

Rommel, implicated in the Schwarze Kapelle conspiracy by Hofacker, received orders on October 13, 1944, to report to Führerhauptquartier. He refused to go, and the next day two OKW generals arrived at his house. They asked to speak to Rommel alone, and when they had done so, they went to wait outside. Manfred Rommel found his father looking pale; Rommel said: "I have just had to tell your mother that I shall be dead in a quarter of an hour . . . the house is surrounded and Hitler is charging me with high treason." He then went on: " 'In view of my services in Africa,' I am to have the chance of dying by poison. The two generals have brought it with them. It's fatal in three seconds. If I accept, none of the usual steps will be taken against my family, that is against you. They will also leave my staff alone."

The field marshal summoned his *aide-de-camp* Hermann Aldinger, and said: "I'm to be given a state funeral. I have asked that it should take place in Ulm. In a quarter of an hour, you, Aldinger, will receive a telephone call from the Wagnerschule reserve hospital in Ulm to say that I've had a brain seizure on the way to a conference."

Rommel got into the generals' car. Twenty minutes later, the telephone rang at his villa. He was dead. Frau Rommel received this telegram from Hitler: "Accept my sincerest sympathy for the heavy loss you have suffered with the death of your husband. The name of Field Marshal Rommel will be for ever linked with the heroic battles in North Africa." Somewhat later, she received a letter from the War Graves Commission:

> The Führer has given me an order to erect a monument to the late Field Marshal, and I have asked a number of sculptors to submit designs. I enclose some of them. . . . I think that the Field Marshal should be represented by a lion. One artist has depicted a dying lion, another a lion weeping, the third a lion about to spring. . . . I prefer the last myself but if you prefer a dying lion, that, too, could be arranged.
>
> The slab can be made immediately, as I have special permission from Reichsminister Speer. Generally monuments cannot now be made in stone, but in this special case it can be made and quickly shipped. . . .

Such was the manner of the death of the modern Sisera.

Had Kluge not taken his own life, he might have suffered a similar fate, or worse—arrest, a trial and death without honor. But his suicide forestalled any final assessment of his part in the Schwarze Kapelle conspiracy. How much did Kluge know of the 20th of July plot? Did he attempt to surrender the German armies in the West to the Allies? These questions would remain unanswered until the spring of 1975 when the last remaining portion of the files of the U.S. War Department Historical Commission's Intelligence Branch were opened at the National Archives to reveal the existence of a sworn statement by Dr. Udo Esch, of the German Army Medical Corps, to Special Agent Montford H. Schaffner. The statement was made on October 23, 1945 and concerned "von Kluge's participation in the July 20 Putsch and his subsequent suicide."

Esch was Kluge's son-in-law and the director of a military hospital in Paris. He had been very close to Kluge, both on the Russian and French fronts, and he stated: "From my father-in-law's assertions and actions I have always taken him for an opponent of nazism." Esch also stated that he had taken part in the conference between Kluge, Goerdeler and Tresckow in Berlin in 1943, offering corroborative evidence that the meeting had occurred, and that Kluge participated in the plot. More important was Esch's testimony about Kluge's involvement in the conspiracy after he replaced Rundstedt as C-in-C West. He stated that he saw his father-in-law "almost daily" and "learned that the plot was maturing." Esch further remarked: "My father-in-law asked me to provide poison for him and the others in case the plot miscarried." He complied with the request, making up seven ampules of waterless acid cyanide in the laboratory of the University of Leipzig while on leave. When he returned to Paris, the ampules were given to the leaders of the conspiracy.

Esch's testimony revealed that both Kluge and Rommel had known that the attack on Hitler was imminent, and that Kluge had said on July 19 that it would occur the very next day. It was possibly conclusive evidence that Kluge had been kept intimately acquainted with the plans of the Schwarze Kapelle, in spite of the fact that he denied knowledge of the plot when the conspirators came to La Roche Guyon the evening of the 20th to beg for his assistance and support. But Esch stated that Kluge did, in fact, attempt to surrender to the Allies. He testified:

> After this failure (of the assassination), my father-in-law considered surrendering the Western Front to the Allies on his own authority, hoping to overthrow the nazi regime with their assistance. This plan he

only discussed with me, at first, and I doubt that even General Speidel, his Chief of Staff, was informed about it. He very much doubted (that the Waffen-SS and the Luftwaffe would cooperate), but he hoped to succeed by surprise.

The means by which Kluge proposed to surrender were not revealed; Esch testified only that "He went to the front lines but was unable to get in touch with the Allied commanders." This, presumably, occurred on August 15. And what happened when he failed? Esch continued: "On his return he found Field Marshal Model as his successor and an order to report to *Führerhauptquartier.*" Esch did not see his father-in-law again. Kluge, fearing arrest if he returned to Germany, took the cyanide capsule that he had been given by his son-in-law. Esch himself was subsequently arrested as an accessory to the plot and taken to the SD jail on the Prinzalbrechtstrasse. He was placed in the cell formerly occupied by Field Marshal von Witzleben, who had just been executed, and told that he could expect death by hanging. Then, mysteriously—only he and Speidel left that terrible place alive—he was released, probably through Rundstedt's intervention. He was ordered to reenlist in the German army "owing to the lack of surgeons," and on March 30, 1945, he surrendered voluntarily to the U.S. 17th Airborne Division near Munster.

When the war finally ended, the fate of the German General Staff, once so mighty, resembled the collective fate of the Emperors of Byzantium. During his twelve years as Fuehrer, Hitler created twenty-six Field Marshals and Grand Admirals. Few escaped his own fury; and those who did survive did not escape the retribution of the Grand Alliance. All either were shot, committed suicide, were compelled to commit suicide, or were jailed by the Allies. The Chiefs of the General Staff fared no better. All suffered similar ends. Of the estimated 2500 generals of the Wehrmacht, 786 are known to have died in the war. Of these, 253 were killed in action, 44 died of wounds, 81 committed suicide, 23 were executed by Hitler, 41 were executed by the Allies for war crimes, and 326 died of other or unknown causes. Those captured by the Americans or the British were imprisoned; of those captured by the Russians, many died in jail.

The toll among the SS generals was even greater. Thirty-two were killed in action; four died of their wounds; two were executed by Hitler for treason; fourteen were executed by the Allies for war crimes; five died from unrecorded causes; nine died from natural causes while on duty; eight died in jail; four were executed by the West German government; and sixteen committed suicide. Thus ninety-four of the generals of the inner cabal of Nazidom died, from all causes, but most significant was the number of suicides—the ultimate signal of fear and despair—both in the army and the SS. Ninety-seven German generals died by their own hands. In the Kaiser's war, Germany lost 63 generals in combat and 103 through other causes; only 3 committed suicide.

The German General Staff, founded by Scharnhorst and Gneisenau as the guardians of the Reich, was extinguished, just as Stalin and Roosevelt intended. With it went Prussian militarism although, ironically, no sooner was the war over than it was revived in another form by the Americans. German generals—mostly those who had been connected with the Schwarze Kapelle—were given high and honored places in NATO councils and commands, and once again yesterday's enemies became today's friends. Stalin lived to see the destruction of one traditional enemy—Germany—and the exhaustion and bankruptcy of another—Britain. But the architect of Soviet victory and Russia's emergence as a major world power would be confronted by another power that had discovered its strength on the battlefield—America.

Stalin's hostility toward the Anglo-American bloc derived, in part, from his conviction that the western powers had deliberately contrived to let Russia and Germany fight each other into exhaustion and thereby establish world hegemony for capitalism; the war had been won, so it was said, with "British brains, American brawn and Russian blood." Hence, the Soviet Premier's belief that Britain in particular had attempted to delay, and even betray to the Germans, Allied plans for a cross-Channel invasion. Stalin was also convinced that the Allies had attempted to reach an agreement with the Schwarze Kapelle to overthrow Hitler and, with Germany, to pursue the war against Russia. In an effort to prove that suspicion, the Russians, in 1954, kidnapped one of the Schwarze Kapelle's emissaries to the West, Otto John, who had become chief of the Bundesamt für Verfassungsschutz, West Germany's equivalent of the FBI or the Special Branch. John was taken to East Berlin and then to Moscow, where he was interrogated at great length, as he explained when he subsequently escaped, about his wartime contacts with the western powers. They concentrated, John later wrote, "in particular on my knowledge of alleged secret agreements between the British government and the German Resistance in the event of a successful *coup d'état* against Hitler." But John apparently failed to convince his interrogators that he had not arranged a deal, for the Russians repeated their allegations often and publicly.

The hostility between East and West that would color the postwar decades did not diminish with Stalin's death in 1953, even though he was instantly dishonored by his successors. Of the triumvirs that had commanded the war against Germany, only Churchill now remained. Roosevelt died of a sudden, massive brain hemorrhage in April 1945, before the war was over, and the difficult business of directing America's course through the postwar world had fallen to his Vice President, Truman, and then to the obscure general Roosevelt had picked to command the battle in Europe, Eisenhower.

Of other American generals who had engineered the Allied victory, Marshall, as Secretary of State, would secure an honored place in history with the Marshall Plan, which helped restore the war-shattered economy of Europe. Bradley, retiring as chairman of the Joint Chiefs of Staff, would become the president of a watch company. Patton was relieved of command of the 3rd Army by Eisenhower just after the end of the war for stating publicly that America had been fighting the wrong enemy—Germany instead of Russia—a sentiment that many in both America and Britain would come to share. It was Patton's last indiscretion; he died shortly after of a broken neck received in a road accident.

Among the British generals, Morgan, the first planner of Overlord and Neptune, became chief of the British atomic energy authority and "father" of the British hydrogen bomb. But he would die in straitened circumstances, living in a semi-detached house in a London suburb like any low-rung civil servant. Montgomery, the master of Neptune strategy and tactics, was criticized even in retirement for his conduct of the battle, but while Ultra and deception remained highly classified secrets, he could not bring their existence to his own defense. Even so, both Montgomery and Brooke would be honored by their countrymen as the greatest generals since Wellington and Kitchener. But with peacetime and the publication of memoirs and reminiscences, the alliance of generals created for Neptune fared no better than the Grand Alliance. Eisenhower, according to Brooke, had "a very, very limited brain from a strategic point of view," while Montgomery said that "as a field commander he was very bad, very bad." Eisenhower, in turn, declared that Montgomery was a "psychopath," and "I eventually just stopped communicating with him. . . . I was just not interested in keeping up communications with a man who just can't tell the truth." Bradley remarked that "Montgomery was detestable and I never spoke to him after the war." Neither did Montgomery speak to Bradley; and with the publication of Brooke's memoirs, which were remarkably candid, Churchill refused either to see or speak to Brooke again.

The post-war squabbles of the Allied high commanders revived interest in the strategical controversies that had so often divided them during the war. Whose advocacy would history finally declare to be correct: the British or the American? D-Day was indeed "a close-run thing," and it seemed to many historians of the period that Brooke's strategy of peripheral warfare to weaken German resistance to the invasion was fully justified. Marshall was thought to have been extremely unwise in advocating such an attack in 1942 and 1943. But then, once again, documents recently made public from America's secret archives indicated that Brooke's strategy may have needlessly prolonged the war. Martian Intelligence reports, declassified on April 1, 1975, revealed that on ten occasions between July 1942 and October 1943, the commanders of the German army in France, with their transportation advisers, had met with French railway authorities to discuss measures to evacuate German forces. It was known that during the summer of 1943, at the time of the Starkey feint, Hitler withdrew forces from the western front in response to the pressures on the Russian and Mediterranean fronts. The Martian reports revealed that even earlier, in July of 1943—the very time that Marshall advocated as the most suitable for a cross-Channel attack—German transportation authorities seemed to have planned for an evacuation of some 750,000 German soldiers by rail alone.

All armies have contingency plans for such operations, and the evidence is not conclusive that Hitler considered a retreat into Fortress Germany at this time. But it would seem possible that Marshall was correct in assuming that the Germans were so weakened and over-extended during the summer of 1943 that they might not have been able to resist an assault against France. The outcome of such an assault must remain a matter for conjecture, however. At best the Allies might have succeeded in capturing the Breton peninsula as a base for future operations on the continent—a strategy that Marshall had advocated as early as 1942. At worst, Hitler might have been able to push the invaders back into the sea; and Brooke was surely correct in insisting that whenever the Allies attempted to get ashore in France, they should be certain that they would be able to stay ashore.

Churchill, the champion of the British strategy, was voted out of office soon after the end of the war; but he would return to power to preside over the disintegration of the Empire and the decline of Britain's primary place in the world, both of which he had declared he would not permit. In a very real sense, he had won the battle but had lost the war. His employment of stratagem and special means was a decisive factor in the Allied victory, although in his own account of the war, and in the accounts of other writers, history would be left with the impression that the Germans had been tricked mightily, especially during Neptune; but few knew exactly how.

The mysteries that began almost immediately to surround the strategies and stratagems of Neptune originated largely with the British. While the Americans were disposed to keep few secrets about their contributions to victory, the British had their eyes on the political realities of the future. As Wingate would explain: "We wanted no articles in the *Reader's Digest* about how the Allies had outwitted the German General Staff. It was felt that we might have to take the Russian General Staff on." Yet for all the secrecy, no one doubted the importance of Jael, Bodyguard and Fortitude in the Allied strategy and tactics that led to victory in Normandy and the liberation of France. Eisenhower left several testaments to the skill, craft and malevolence of the covert war that attended D-Day. In his Report to Congress in 1945, he said that the Allied armies on D-Day "achieved a degree of tactical surprise for which we had hardly dared to hope." In a secret signal to Marshall on July 6, 1944, he declared that Fortitude and Bodyguard had been "remarkably effective," and that the deception campaign had "paid enormous dividends." Bradley, in an after-action report on Fortitude to the Supreme Commander, was moved to write more fully:

> Operation Fortitude . . . was responsible for containing a minimum of 20 enemy divisions in the Pas de Calais during the first crucial months of the invasion. The enemy was led to believe—and reacted to—a long inventory of opportune untruths, the largest, most effective and decisive of which was that (Neptune) itself was only the prelude to a major invasion in the Pas de Calais area. . . . Best testimony to the effectiveness with which this misinformation influenced the enemy's command decisions is the historic record of the enemy's committing his forces piecemeal—paralysed into indecision in Normandy by the conviction that he had more to fear from Calais.

Harris and Ingersoll of the Special Plans Branch, both of whom had been intimately involved in the strategical and tactical deceptions of Neptune, would add to the chorus of praise. In a postwar report to Joint Security Control entitled "Appreciation of Deception in the European Theater," they admitted that they had "entered deception operations in the United Kingdom with grave misgivings as to their value." They had, in fact, succeeded in destroying the first cover plan proposed for Neptune. But now they reported of Fortitude that: "There is no doubt whatever that enormous losses were avoided by the successful achievement of surprise, which was the deception's first objective." They added, however, that:

> The overwhelming success of the Fortitude operations was followed by a period of partial and/or indifferent success during the remainder of the campaign on the Continent. No over-all strategic deception was attempted. Tactical deception, despite a record of successful minor manipulations of enemy intelligence, was characterized by a succession of wasted opportunities.

With victory, the secret agencies that had engineered Fortitude—the LCS, the CSM, and the XX-Committee—were disbanded, at least officially. Bevan, however, kept the LCS alive by holding a dinner party for its members each year at his club. He also made the work of historians extraordinarily difficult by getting each member of the LCS and its satellite organizations to swear never to discuss publicly what it was they had done. Not until 1970 did this agreement begin to break down, and then only partially. Bevan returned to his job in the City and became a Privy Councillor. Wingate became chairman of the Gold Commission, a businessman and an author. But something soured him and, living peacefully in a handsome country house under the church steeple at the Wiltshire hamlet of Barford St. Martin, he remarked on occasion that "the service of the Crown is but dust and ashes." Masterman resumed his academic career and became Vice President of Oxford University, Provost of Worcester College, Governor of Wellington College, a Fellow of Eton, chairman of the Committee on the Political Activities of Civil Servants and a member of the BBC General Advisory Council. He received the Royal Order of the Crown of Yugoslavia (an odd echo of the Tricycle network), and in the early 1970's , in a complicated intrigue against the British government, his after-action report of the XX-Committee's activities was published by the Yale University Press and became a best-seller.

Of the other members of the LCS, Fleetwood Hesketh became an MP and Lord of the Manor of North Meols; Baumer retired from the army as a major general and became a successful business entrepreneur in Washington, D.C.; Wild spent his declining years at his club, the Cavalry, evading historians; Wheatley returned to writing novels about spies and black magic; Fleming died elegantly on the grouse moors; Clarke remained as mysterious and impenetrable as ever, and was rarely heard or seen outside his own small circle. Andrade, seen from time to time at one of his clubs, lectured a little dottily—so his pupils thought—about physics, mathematics and philosophy. But he would become, in fact, a director of two of the world's leading research institutes, the Davy Faraday and the Royal Institution, and a member of the Council of the Royal Society. Thus the men who had caused so much confusion and mayhem would resume their peaceful lives and, in all probability, die tranquilly in their beds. All deplored the new society they had done so much to create.

The spirit, and the methodology, of the LCS would live on, however, and return to haunt the western Allies. The British had been extremely careful to reveal to the Russians only as much of their deception machinery as was necessary to ensure their cooperation in Bodyguard. But the Russians were quick to adopt and apply this unique weapon of modern warfare. Just how quick was revealed in a reply to a letter sent by Bevan to the British Military Mission at Moscow in July of 1944 requesting the views of the mission "as to what policy (he) should pursue vis-à-vis the Russians in any large-scale cover plans which he may be called upon to prepare." Evidently the success of Bodyguard led Bevan to consider further cooperation with the Russians in this sphere of activity.

The response to Bevan's question was discouraging. The correspondent, identified only as "Bolton," Bevan's "representative at the (British) embassy," said that General Brocas Burrows, the Chief of the British Military Mission, felt that the Russians "distrusted and hated the whole thing." They had played their part in Bodyguard, but they had consistently refused to reveal anything about the special means they had used. "We know, in general," Bolton wrote, "their intelligence system is nothing like so highly developed as ours, and the impression that we derive from their treatment of *Bodyguard* is that they have no special organisation comparable with yours." He believed that Russian successes against the Germans "may have been due to careful concealment, rather than to deception." He added, moreover, that the Russians had displayed a lack of understanding of the intricacies of geopolitics and military matters, and, as important, that their machinery for the execution of global deceptions was slow and cumbersome. Bodyguard's successes, Bolton went on—ominously for the postwar world—had made "a big impression here," but he doubted that the Russians were likely "to divert brain-power to this specialised form of warfare."

In the light of later events, it would appear that Bolton was quite wrong in his assessment. If there were deficiencies in the Russian intelligence services, they were eliminated, and the Russians soon established a massive deception organization of their own. Russian intelligence and deception would work together with great effectiveness in the jousts of the postwar world, as Britain and America discovered at their own cost. It would be interesting to speculate whether Bodyguard had not been the catalyst in Russia's increased proficiency in these fields, and whether, to obtain Russia's cooperation in surprising Hitler on D-Day, the western powers had not revealed too much about their secret methodology.

Having indeed "set Europe ablaze," SOE shut up shop surrounded by a rather rascally reputation. As someone wrote in the last days, it would be "happy and handy / If Bodington baffled the coastguards / By smuggling in claret and brandy, / And super-de-luxe dirty postcards." It was a reputation that was not wholly deserved, and Churchill is said to have remarked: "we may feel sure that nothing of which we have any knowledge or record has ever been done by mortal men which surpasses the splendour and daring of their feats of arms." Eisenhower, too, commended SOE. On May 31, 1945, he wrote to Gubbins to "express my great admiration for the brave and often spectacular exploits of the agents and special groups under control of Special Force Headquarters." On the other hand, Marshal of the Royal Air Force Sir Arthur Harris, the C-in-C of Bomber Command, damned the Ministry of Economic Warfare, which controlled SOE, as "amateurish, ignorant, irresponsible and mendacious." The suspicions about sacrifice and betrayal of SOE agents persisted and there was considerable speculation about the true causes, and the reasons for, a fire which consumed many of SOE's archives just before it shut down. So persistent were the allegations against SOE, in fact, that the Foreign Office took the unusual—in Britain—step of replying publicly. They were, said the Foreign Office spokesman, monstrous and repugnant.

Rightly, no blame ever attached to Gubbins for the peculiar circumstances that often surrounded the deaths of SOE agents, or for the several thousands of their helpers who also lost their lives. After the war he disappeared from public view, only to reappear briefly as one of the men behind an Anglo-American plot to overthrow the Communist government in Albania. Then he became the chairman of a carpet factory and finally went back to where he had come from, and where he wished to die—among the crofters of the Isle of Harris in the Outer Hebrides. Buckmaster also dropped from public view, appearing occasionally at Gubbins's side at church ceremonies to honor the dead. But the mysteries about SOE and F section would linger on.

The double agents who were controlled by the XX-Committee fared better than many SOE agents. The main double agents involved in the Neptune cover plans all survived the war, and Tate, who had helped tie down some 400,000 German fighting men in Norway until the end of the war, was actually transmitting to his controller in Germany on the day the Third Reich surrendered. Garbo disappeared, with his Medal of the British Empire *and* his Iron Cross, surely the only man in history to wear the cross patonce alongside the cross-pate on the same dinner jacket. Treasure found she was not suffering from leukemia and settled contentedly in Canada. Brutus stayed in London, wrote a book and became a printer. Tricycle emerged from the shadows to publish his memoirs in 1974. But most of the double agents were like old soldiers; they simply faded away. So did their controllers and wireless men. Kuhlenthal, who did his country more damage than most men, died in his bed in 1965.

MI-6 casualties were, like those of SOE, very heavy; it lost possibly half its agents in Europe. Philippe Keun, co-chief of Jade Amicol in Paris, was sold to the Germans by a Frenchman in July 1944, and executed in a concentration camp in September of that year. Best and Stevens came back, unhonored. Stevens spent his last years on a miserable pension, trying to make ends meet by translating German books into English for London publishers. Gibson, the man whose intelligence started the main attack on Enigma, fetched up in Rome, became a local notable in commerce, and then, probably for financial reasons, killed himself. Dunderdale, a rich man, retired in the late 1960's, content, as he put it, after "40 years of legal thuggery" to spend his last years in his workshop, hand-crafting electronic devices and equipment—and going out twice each week to serve hot meals to incapacitated old-age pensioners.

The war over, MI-6 was, so it was said, all past and no future. In fact, it began rebuilding a service that would become, in other, new dimensions, the equal of the old. Its wartime staff was gradually replaced, and because of the secrecy that cloaked MI-6's work in intelligence and counterintelligence in general, and Ultra and deception in particular, the world was left with the feeling that it had accomplished little. It had accomplished a great deal; quite apart from its other triumphs, MI-6 had Ultra to its credit.

Ultra, so decisive in Neptune, continued to play an important role in the Allied pursuit of the German armies in France. The enemy generals, remaining unaware, as once was said, that "all wireless is treason," still trusted Enigma; and shortly after the breakout in Normandy, the Turing engines at Bletchley received assistance from an unexpected quarter. Toward the end of August or the beginning of September 1944, General Troy Middleton's U.S. 8th Corps was besieging the great port of Brest; and Hitler, to persuade the troops defending the city that they had not been forgotten, ordered the Luftwaffe to fly in a special consignment of Iron Crosses. The German signals corps learned of the flight and it was decided to include something else in the parcel—the Wehrmacht's Enigma keys for the coming quarter.

A Heinkel III transport flew the mission and dropped its cargo. But the parcel fell wide of the target and landed close to a U.S. battalion headquarters. An American soldier saw it coming down on its parachute in the moonlight, collected it when it landed, heard the rattle of metal—Iron Crosses—and opened it. If this particular type of consignment had been American or British, it would have burst into flames or exploded at that moment. But, despite German thoroughness and ingenuity, there was no self-destruct apparatus built into the parcel. The soldier gave the Iron Crosses to his friends as trophies of battle, and put the rest of the package—a quarter-inch file of pink and biscuit-colored documents, none of which, again, had been specially treated to self-destruct—to one side.

When the sun came up the next morning, the documents were examined more closely and were taken to a Lieutenant Finkelstein, one of the G2's on Middleton's staff. He saw instantly what they were: the *M-Schlüssel,* the German book of Enigma keys, an intelligence prize of the greatest importance. Finkelstein handed the documents over to Ensign Angus McLean Thuermer of the Forward Intelligence Unit of the U.S. 12th Fleet (and in 1974 a personal assistant to the director of the CIA), and Thuermer, in turn, took them to the unit commander. They were then rushed to London where the data was fed into the Turing engines, and Bletchley was able to decrypt the Wehrmacht's current wireless messages much faster than might otherwise have been the case.

It was an intelligence coup that enabled the Allies to score another military victory—the entrapment of a remnant of the German armies in France at the Battle of the Mons Pocket. Through Ultra, the Allies learned that the survivors of the Falaise Gap, streaming westward toward the Siegfried Line, had been formed into a provisional army near Mons. The Americans threw up powerful roadblocks across their line of retreat and the ensuing action was "like shooting sitting pigeons." Some 25,000 men, the remnants of 20 divisions, were captured, while the air forces claimed the destruction of 850 motor vehicles, 50 armored fighting vehicles, 650 horse-drawn vehicles and another 500 men. Thus, as the U.S. army's official history would state, "These potential defenders of the (Siegfried Line) were swept off the field of battle." But for the capture of the *M-Schlüssel* at Brest, the Americans might not have known of the existence of this force before it got back to Germany.

It was, effectively, Ultra's last triumph in the war in Europe. The light that it had cast for so long upon the secrets of the enemy began to dim in the fall of 1944 when the Germans finally realized that Enigma might have been penetrated—a realization that came about not through the careless use of Ultra, but through treason on the part of a member of the staff of Prince Bernhard of The Netherlands. Allied security authorities had long been concerned about Bernhard's "apparent inability to choose trustworthy and loyal advisers and assistants," as an OSS appreciation would state. The future Prince Consort and leader of the Dutch government-in-exile in London was thought to have made "questionable" and "unfortunate" selections of men for his entourage. But it was not until after the invasion that Bernhard, who as C-in-C of Dutch Forces was accredited to SHAEF, made his "worst selection," according to the report: "that of a certain Mr. Lindemans, who was accepted by the Prince as his confidential agent." The report did not exaggerate, for Lindemans was a German agent, and a very clever and dangerous one at that.

Christiaan Antonius Lindemans, then aged about twenty-seven, had been recruited as an Abwehr agent in 1943 by Lieutenant Colonel Herman Giskes, the Abwehr officer in Holland who succeeded in decimating SOE's Dutch section. He had, it appeared, offered his services in return for the release of his mistress and his younger brother, both of whom were loyal members of the Dutch resistance movement. Codenamed "King Kong" by Giskes (Lindemans was 6 feet 3 inches tall and weighed 260 pounds), he was put to work against the Dutch underground with appalling results. According to SHAEF Counter-Intelligence Report No. 4 for the week ending November 10, 1944, Lindemans was "an important agent" whose information "led to the arrest of over 250 resistance members."

The same report revealed that in late June or early July 1944, Lindemans (apparently on Giskes's orders) infiltrated the British sector of the Normandy beachhead. He was, it seemed, an ardent and knowledgeable member of the Dutch underground, and he so impressed his British interrogators that he was taken onto the staff of a British intelligence unit commanded by a Canadian captain. In due course, Lindemans succeeded in ingratiating himself with Bernhard, who now commanded the Dutch Forces of the Interior and spent much of his time with the British and Canadian forces that were nearing Holland.

On or about September 15, while with the Canadians and Bernhard's staff in Brussels, Lindemans was sent by the Canadian intelligence officer back into Holland apparently to warn Dutch underground resistance leaders not to send downed Allied pilots over the escape line from Holland into Belgium; it had been, presumably, penetrated by the Germans. Lindemans either was captured by, or surrendered to, a German patrol in no-man's-land on the Belgian-Dutch frontier near Valkenswaard. He demanded to see Giskes, and Giskes directed that he be taken without delay to Driebergen. There, Lindemans revealed all that he had learned during his brief stay on the other side of the line. He had learned a great deal. First he told of the build-up for Montgomery's great airborne and land attack to take Arnhem and cross the Rhine into northern Germany (information which, apparently, the Germans did not believe). Then Lindemans revealed the secret that the Allies, against seemingly impossible odds, had been able to keep for more than four years—Ultra.

By September 1944, the German signals security chiefs were beginning to suspect that Enigma might be a principal source of the Reich's agony. Whether traitors had revealed all his plans to the Allies, as Hitler continued to believe, or whether the Allies had in some way managed to penetrate German ciphers, the security of Enigma was in question; and possibly as a result of Lindemans's information, the Wehrmacht began late in 1944 to replace it. The task of manufacturing and distributing new machines, and of retraining the thousands of operators involved, proved to be impossible in the short time left to the Third Reich, and the Wehrmacht continued to use Enigma. However, German suspicions about its security almost certainly played a part in the extraordinary precautions which OKW adopted to protect the secrets of its Ardennes counteroffensive at Christmas 1944. When Hitler was planning the offensive, he directed that none of his orders, nor any orders relating to the attack, be sent by wireless. He was obeyed to the letter, and Ultra suddenly dried up. The Allies had obtained order of battle intelligence, as well as aerial reconnaissance and prisoner of war intelligence, all of which suggested that the Germans were preparing for an imminent offensive. But because the American intelligence staffs—and particularly Sibert's at 12th Army Group—had become over-dependent upon Ultra not only as their primary source of intelligence but also as confirmation of other less reliable and trusted sources, no action was taken. The result was, for Eisenhower and Bradley, near catastrophe. The Germans obtained complete surprise and but for the fortunes of war they might have split the American and British armies and inflicted a defeat from which the western powers would not have quickly recovered.

After Ardennes, the Germans resumed the use of Enigma on wireless, and the Turing engines were still clicking the day the Russians entered Berlin and Hitler committed suicide. The war against Germany was over, but Ultra continued to exercise a powerful, and ironic, influence in the secret war. In June 1945, before the surrender of Japan, Franco, partially in response to American economic and political pressure, decided to expel the Japanese diplomatic mission at Madrid. But the Pentagon, through Ultra, was gleaning important information from the Enigma-enciphered reports of the Japanese missions at all the neutral capitals, and its intelligence chiefs requested that the State Department do nothing to force the neutrals to terminate relations with Japan. The request was considered favorably by the "Committee of Three"—the Secretaries of State, War and the Navy, virtually the highest decision-making body under President Truman—and thereafter American policy toward the neutrals, which had been very rough, became much more benevolent.

In military operations against Japan in the Pacific, Ultra also continued to function until the war's end; and a document released by the United States government on February 4, 1974—one of the only two documents so far discovered in the National Archives with the word "Ultra" stamped upon it—would provide an answer to one of the most controversial mysteries of the entire war: why President Truman decided to use the atomic bomb against Hiroshima (on August 6, 1945) and Nagasaki (on August 9, 1945) when, as many believed, the Japanese had already notified the Allies of their intention to surrender.

So enormous were the casualties and destruction, so far-reaching the consequences in the postwar world, that Truman was often reviled for that decision. It was said that the Anglo-American powers wanted a quick end to the war against Japan to prevent Russian intervention in the Far East. Most recently, Charles Mee, an American historian and the author of *Meeting at Potsdam,* would contend that Truman and Churchill "wished to make the Russians more manageable in Europe," and that the use of the bomb under those circumstances was "wanton murder." Truman, however, would insist during his lifetime that he was motivated primarily by the desire to force Japan into rapid Unconditional Surrender, and thus save countless Allied lives. The Ultra document, a signal from Tokyo to the Japanese ambassador in Moscow, decrypted by the American Ultra service on July 12, 1945 —twenty-five days before the first A-bomb was dropped—substantiated Truman's claim, and provided compelling justification for his decision to use the bomb.

The contents of the Ultra signal revealed that the Japanese Emperor had indeed decided to surrender; but a memorandum analyzing the signal from General John Weckerling, the deputy G2 at the Pentagon, to General Thomas T. Handy, the deputy Chief of Staff of the United States Army, warned that ". . . the Japanese governing clique was making a well coordinated, united effort to stave off defeat. . . ." According to Weckerling, the signal indicated that the Japanese were prepared to offer "attractive terms of peace, including withdrawal of Japanese troops from all occupied territories to appeal to U.S. and British war weariness," and thus prevent an invasion and occupation of Japan. The Japanese were further prepared to block Russia's entry into the war in the Far East by "offering renunciation of Japanese rights under the Portsmouth Treaty . . . and concessions in Manchuria."

In short, the terms contemplated by the Japanese smacked more of a bargain than of surrender. Still, it might be argued, was not a surrender with strings attached morally preferable to the use of the atomic bomb? Perhaps—if the Allies had positive assurance that the Emperor's will would prevail. Weckerling stated in his memorandum that while the Emperor wished to surrender and had "personally intervened and brought his will to bear in favor of peace," there were still powerful militarist elements in the Japanese armed services who wished to continue the war with "prolonged desperate resistance." There was a danger, then, as General Clayton Bissell, the G2 of the U.S. army, wrote in reply to Weckerling's analysis, that the militarists might repudiate the Emperor's terms even if the Allies accepted something less than Unconditional Surrender. In that case, an occupation force might be ambushed, or the Japanese army might continue the battle in the remotest parts of the Pacific in order to exhaust the will to fight of the western powers.

The situation was further complicated by the inability of American cryptographers to penetrate all the Japanese secret ciphers and thus determine a full picture of their intentions. Debating this aspect of the situation, Bissell stated:

> Although some of the major Japanese Army (crypto) systems are in a stage of solution where most of the messages are solved within four to eight days after date of transmission and some are read within a few hours, there are other Army systems that are not solved and messages cannot be read for many weeks if at all . . . in view of the many unsolved Army systems, Japanese orders for general or isolated repudiation of the surrender could easily escape detection.

Given the uncertainties of the Japanese military and political situation, and the far-flung nature of their empire where a war might continue almost indefinitely, there was only one way to ensure that Japan surrendered unconditionally—the use of a weapon that would forcibly demonstrate the futility of further resistance. Truman's decision to use that weapon was the direct outcome of intelligence gleaned from Ultra; he was, as he would claim, motivated primarily by the desire to end the war, although the effect of his decision upon the Russians and, indeed, upon the politics of the postwar world as a whole, were undoubtedly secondary considerations.

Thus, Ultra made a final, grim contribution to victory in the Second World War. The teleprinters from Bletchley in Winterbotham's office went silent, and he would record that he "handed back to Stewart Menzies the key to those red boxes which had done so many journeys between my offices and No. 10, Downing Street." Winterbotham resigned from MI-6 immediately; he was honored with the rank of Commander of St. Michael and St. George, although he would not receive a knighthood. He became chief of public relations at BOAC; and then he retired to a farm in Devon where, in 1974, he completed work on a memoir about Ultra that the British security authorities allowed to be published.

Winterbotham's statements ended nearly thirty years of silence about this extraordinary intelligence victory, a silence that obscured the part Turing had played in its history. Tragically, the astonishing mental effort which resulted in the machine that broke Enigma would also break Turing. In 1954, while working on Britain's first computer, MADAM, he began an experiment in his home at Adlington Road, Wilmslow, Cheshire, based on the supposition that he was a scientist stranded on a remote and uninhabited island with only the equipment he could build himself and the chemicals he could manufacture from what he could find. He began to make certain chemicals, among them potassium cyanide.

Why he should have chosen to make such a deadly poison would never be established; but he did, building a rudimentary electrolysis machine and scraping some gold from his watch fob to produce it. Then, again for reasons that were inexplicable, he got into bed, coated an apple with some of the cyanide, bit the apple, and died. When his housekeeper arrived for work on the following morning, she detected a strong smell of almonds—cyanide's smell—and found Turing dead in his bed, the apple beside him. The verdict was suicide. Knowing nothing of his contribution to Allied victory in the Second World War (for it was still a secret), the coroner pronounced pompously: "I am forced to the conclusion that this was a deliberate action, for with a man of this type one can never be sure what his mental processes are going to do next. Here was a brilliant mathematician with unusual mental achievements. He might easily become unbalanced and unstable." Such was the last official pronouncement upon the man who, with his colleague Knox, had enabled the Allied high command to know what the German high command was planning almost, at times, from hour to hour.

Menzies, the man behind Ultra and the chief of MI-6 who commanded much of the Allies' intelligence and counterintelligence battle with the Germans, retired after the war to his home at Luckington. But when the Cold War began to dominate the politics of the western world, he was recalled to his post by Churchill, who was back at 10 Downing Street, and remained in office until the Philby scandal broke. The discovery that there was a Russian spy in the center of Britain's secret intelligence apparatus ruined Menzies's reputation publicly. As the man who had appointed Philby in the first place, he was compelled to offer his resignation; and it was accepted. All Menzies's triumphs were largely forgotten, particularly by his enemies. Quite unfairly—for Menzies knew nothing of the affair—his reputation suffered a second major blow when one of his wartime assistants and friends was arrested on charges of major fraud.

Surrounded by criticisms that he was a "witless, upperclass snob"—criticisms that he might have countered had he been able to discuss such secret matters as Ultra and Bodyguard publicly—Menzies returned to the life of a country gentleman. He brooded upon Philby's betrayal, and as his moods became blacker and his despair greater, he eventually decided, or so it was said afterwards, to commit suicide.

The story went that he shot his two gray hunters, closed the house, and went to London where he killed himself. In fact this story was quite untrue, for his death certificate read:

> Stewart Graham Menzies, Male, 78 years, of Bridges Court, Lucking-ton, Wiltshire, Knight Commander of the Bath, Knight Commander of St. Michael and St. George, Distinguished Service Order, Military Cross, Major General: Death—1 (a) Bronchopneumonia (b) Cere-bral vascular accident (c) Ischaemic heart malaise. Certified by T. G. Hudson, M.B., Date of Death 29 May 1968.

Only later would it become clear that Ultra had been Menzies's trump card. Throughout the war, it had been unnecessary for him to deploy his service conventionally in an attempt to penetrate the enemy security screens and obtain Germany's secrets. The Allies learned those secrets in large measure through Ultra and through the revela-tions of the conspirators of the Schwarze Kapelle. Thus Menzies was left free to deploy his men in great strength on deception operations in support of Jael/Bodyguard, and also overseas, on operations to de-stroy or control the enemy secret services to protect the secrets of the Allies. It is small wonder, then, that Churchill is said to have regarded Menzies as one of the men who were indispensable to victory in the Second World War. Eisenhower's career, in particular, owed much to MI-6 and the GC&CS at Bletchley Park. In a letter written to Menzies at the end of the war, he did not mention Ultra, for even the code name would remain classified until 1974, but his tribute was unmis-takable.

> Dear General Menzies,
>   I had hoped to be able to pay a visit to Bletchley Park in order to thank you, Sir Edward Travis, and the members of the staff personally for the magnificent services which have been rendered to the Allied cause. I am very well aware of the immense amount of work and effort which has been involved in the production of the material with which you have supplied us. I fully realize also the numerous setbacks and difficulties with which you have had to contend and how you have always, by your supreme efforts, overcome them. The intelligence which has emanated from you before and during this campaign has been of priceless value to me. It has simplified my task as a com-mander enormously. It has saved thousands of British and American lives and, in no small way, contributed to the speed with which the enemy was routed and eventually forced to surrender. I should be very grateful, therefore, if you would express to each and every one of those

engaged in this work from me personally my heartfelt admiration and sincere thanks for their very decisive contribution to the Allied war effort.

Sincerely,
Dwight D. Eisenhower

Few of Menzies's principal adversaries of the Abwehr and the SD escaped Allied retribution at the end of the war. Kaltenbrunner, Heydrich's successor as chief of the SD, was hanged. Kieffer, Knochen and Goetz were all executed by the British or French for war crimes. Schellenberg served a period in prison, was released, and died in the 1950's of a liver complaint. That left only Canaris, and riddles. What was Menzies's relationship with that mysterious man? Was he, or was he not, a British agent?

Menzies pondered these questions for a long time, in the lowering gloom of a winter's day at Luckington in 1964. Then he replied:

Canaris was never a British agent in the accepted sense of that term. The fact that I had contact with him is liable to misinterpretation, but the fact is that all sophisticated intelligence services maintain contact with their enemies. Canaris never betrayed his country's secrets to me or to anyone else on the British side, although his men did. On the other hand, he did give me assistance. For example, I wanted to get the wife of a colleague of mine out of occupied Europe; I made the fact known to Canaris through channels, and in due course she came out.

The silence in the parlor at Luckington was very intense, and Menzies, perhaps struggling with his innate belief that he should keep silent while, at the same time, wanting to say something about his old enemy, eventually went on:

Canaris was a German patriot, a religious man, a monarchist, a conservatist, and a traditionalist. He was a man in a powerful position who wanted to do something about the situation—to save Germany and Europe from ruins. He thought I might be able to help, and he did contact me and ask me to meet him on neutral territory with a view to putting an end to the war. I spoke to Anthony Eden about it, and Eden forbade me even to reply—Venlo was still very much on everybody's mind. Furthermore, if I had gone to see Canaris the fact would soon have been known to the Russians and they would have thought that the British were dickering with a peace with the Germans aimed against the Russians. The result was that I never saw Canaris. But I did like and admire him. He was damned brave and damned unlucky.

If Canaris was not actually working for the British, it is clear that he was working against Hitler. And ironically, just as Ultra proved to be

Menzies's trump card, so it was Canaris's undoing. Political considerations aside, it was unnecessary for the Allies to treat with Canaris
and the other conspirators of the Schwarze Kapelle, offering certain
concessions in return for useful intelligence. In almost every case, the
Schwarze Kapelle could not provide any information that was not already known through Ultra. Furthermore, the existence of Ultra
stained Canaris's personal reputation. As Professor H. R. Trevor-
Roper, the Regius Professor of Modern History at Oxford and a wartime MI-6 officer, would explain, Ultra was *the* decisive source of
intelligence of the Second World War; and in order to protect its security, it was insinuated that the material supplied by Ultra was coming
"from Canaris." What better explanation for the remarkable intelligence reaching Churchill and Roosevelt and their higher commands? Thus it was that ambassadors and high administrators were
led to believe that it was none other than Canaris, that "notorious
right-wing intriguer," who was behind the priceless secrets on their
conference tables. The *ruse de guerre* succeeded, but it also tarnished
the bright and honored place that Canaris might otherwise have held
in history.

For a time after the war, no one knew what had become of Canaris.
Then it emerged that he had been betrayed by Hansen, who told his
Gestapo inquisitors that Canaris had been conspiring against Hitler
for years. Hansen also revealed that Canaris had kept diaries, volumes
that covered Hitler's activities and those of the Nazis from the "Night
of the Long Knives" on June 30, 1934, when Canaris, shocked by the
murders of Schleicher and Bredow, first realized that Hitler was a dangerous and incorrigible revolutionary whose every activity must be
watched and recorded. Anxious to find these diaries, Kaltenbrunner
sent Schellenberg to arrest Canaris; and shortly after lunch on July 23,
1944, he did so. The bell rang at Canaris's home in the Dianastrasse of
Schlachtensee, a lakeside colony of comfortable houses where he lived
alone with his Polish cook and Algerian manservant, having sent his
family into the provinces to escape the bombing. When the frail white-
haired man saw who had come, he said: "Somehow I felt that it would
be you. Please tell me first of all, have they found anything in writing
from that fool Colonel Hansen?" Schellenberg answered quite truth-
fully: "Yes; a notebook in which there was among other things a list
of those who were to be killed." Then Schellenberg went on: "But
there was nothing about you or participation on your part." Canaris
replied, still standing on the doorstep: "Those dolts on the General
Staff cannot live without their scribblings." Then he invited Schellen-

berg and his companion, SS Hauptsturmführer Baron von Voelkersam, into his home.

Schellenberg was under orders from SS Obergruppenführer Mueller, the chief of the Special Commission ordered by Himmler to investigate the Schwarze Kapelle and the 20th of July plot, to place Canaris under honorable protective custody at the Sicherheitspolizei school at Fürstenberg in Mecklenburg. When Schellenberg had explained his mission, Canaris said with resignation:

It's too bad that we have to say good-bye in this way. But we'll get over this. You must promise me faithfully that within the next three days you will get me an opportunity to talk to Himmler personally. All the others Kaltenbrunner and Mueller—are nothing but filthy butchers, out for my blood.

Canaris, evidently, hoped that his hold over Himmler was still strong enough to save him from investigation, trial and execution for treason. Schellenberg agreed to the request, but then, in a completely official voice, he gave Canaris the "German Chance"—the opportunity to commit suicide if he chose. Canaris refused with the words: "No, dear Schellenberg, flight is out of the question for me. And I won't kill myself either. I am sure of my case, and I have faith in the promise you have given me."

Canaris was held at Fürstenberg until Mueller sent for him. Then he was brought to Gestapo headquarters in the Prinzalbrechtstrasse in Berlin, where he was held in cells that were crammed with members of the Schwarze Kapelle. Because of his eminence, Mueller elected to interrogate Canaris personally—within the limits permitted him by Himmler. But Canaris, as eel-like as ever, was more than a match for the blunt, bullet-headed Mueller. He denied all knowledge of the 20th of July plot, but said that he had known of earlier plots because it was his duty as chief of the Abwehr to know what was happening in the Reich. He had not told Himmler of these conspiracies because he wanted to establish their extent—and had been prevented from doing so often enough by the clumsiness of the Gestapo itself.

Very cleverly, Canaris wound Mueller in a skein of half-truth. But then the interrogation was handed over to Walter Huppenkothen, the subtle lawyer from the Rhineland. Under his questioning, Canaris made the one single terrible mistake of his career. Confident that his friend and fellow conspirator, Major Werner Schrader, the Abwehr's representative at army headquarters at Zossen, had destroyed them, he admitted that he had kept diaries. They contained only personal matters and he had given them to Schrader for safekeeping at Zossen because he feared they might be destroyed in the aerial bombardment of Berlin. But Schrader had not destroyed Canaris's diaries; he had committed suicide without destroying any of the Schwarze Kapelle's archives.

Huppenkothen sent a team to Zossen, and inside a big Pohl-schroeder safe, they found a mass of documentation, including a number of red, gray and black files on one of the shelves—Canaris's diaries. There, despite the orders of various high officials, including Halder, to destroy the documents, was the entire history of the conspiracy, from its inception in 1934 over the murders of Schleicher and Bredow, through the Vatican negotiations to Flash in 1943. There was much detail about Oster's betrayal of Case Yellow, and a total of fifty-two of the files contained what would be called "important military information sent in by German agents abroad, decoded and dealt with by Dohnanyi. Many of their reports had been deliberately doctored by additions and omissions before being passed on to the Wehrmacht."

It was all the evidence Himmler needed to hang Canaris and Oster; but oddly he did not do so. He used it to convict other members of the conspiracy, and then ordered the documents destroyed. As for Canaris and Oster, Himmler kept them alive. Why? It can only be assumed that Himmler feared that if Canaris was put to death, his friends would release a dossier to the world press—a dossier which, it was said, had been kept by Canaris on Himmler ever since the Nazis had seized power.

Canaris and Oster were held in various concentration camps for many months, along with such important prisoners as Halder, Best and Stevens; and as the Americans closed in on south Germany in the spring of 1945, both men found themselves at Flossenburg. Canaris spent his last days alone in a cell, reading Kantorowicz's *Friedrich II, von Hohenstauffen*. Then on the evening of April 8—twenty-nine days before the end of the war in Europe and with one of Patton's tank columns less than 100 miles away—he was taken before a "court" and was charged with high treason and conspiracy to murder Hitler. Canaris again denied all the charges laid against him, and in a final statement asked to be allowed to go to the Russian front as a common soldier. This was refused, and he was taken away for immediate execution. Oster was brought in on identical charges, and he, too, was found guilty and sentenced to death. Oster was executed in the early hours of April 9, 1945.

At some stage during the return to his cell Canaris was beaten up and his nose was broken. Alone in his cell just before his execution, using prison Morse tapped out on a pipe with a spoon, Canaris transmitted this message to Lieutenant Colonel H. M. Lunding, the former chief of the Danish secret service, who was in the next cell:

I . . . die . . . for . . . my . . . country . . . and . . . with . . . a . . . clear . . . conscience . . . you . . . as . . . officer . . . will . . . realize . . . that . . . I . . . was . . . only . . . doing . . . my . . . duty . . . to . . . my . . . country . . . when . . . I . . . endeavored . . . to . . . oppose . . . Hitler . . . do . . . what . . . you . . . can . . . for . . . my . . . wife . . . daughters . . . theyve . . . broken . . . my . . . nose . . . I . . . die . . . this . . . morning . . . farewell.

It was, in effect, Canaris's last will and testament. Just before daybreak on April 9, 1945, Lunding, who was looking through a hole in his cell door, saw Canaris being dragged naked down the corridor of the cell block. Dr. Joseph Mueller, Canaris's secret envoy to the Vatican, who was also in the same block, later testified that an SS officer told him that Canaris was hung from the ceiling in the execution chamber by an iron collar. His executioners thought he was dead and took him down; but when they found that he was still alive, they started the execution over again. Canaris, in all, took thirty minutes to die. His corpse was then incinerated and his ashes tossed into the winds. He was given no grave and no monument. But one of his former enemies would rise in Parliament in 1947 to make a testament to Canaris and his fellow conspirators. He said of the German opposition to Hitler that it "belonged to the noblest and greatest (of resistance movements) that have ever arisen in the history of all peoples." The man who made the testament was Churchill.

Whether the conspirators of the Schwarze Kapelle were considered heroes or traitors to the German state, the fact remained that they constituted the only anti-Nazi resistance movement that did not receive the active support of the western powers. There are no documents presently available to historians to substantiate the belief, so strongly held by Stalin and by Hitler himself, that the Schwarze Kapelle and the Allied secret agencies reached some form of understanding that culminated in the climactic events of the last weeks of July 1944. But then, until quite recently, no references to Ultra could be found in the declassified documents of the Second World War, and Ultra surely existed. If evidence of a pact between the Allies and the Schwarze Kapelle does exist, it might be contained in the secret files of MI-6 and OSS(SI), which may never be declassified. If it does not—if, in fact, the Allies offered little more than verbal encouragement to the conspirators, history is left with a haunting question: Was D-Day necessary?

Charles V. P. von Luttichau, an eminent German-American military historian, would express an opinion shared by many Germans who were opposed to the Nazi régime:

> D-Day was one of the greatest political blunders of all time. If Great Britain and the United States had uttered a single word publicly of encouragement to the conspirators then Montgomery and Eisenhower would have walked ashore, and Rommel would have been there to salute them. As it was, Great Britain and the United States were determined to destroy Germany as they destroyed the Austro-Hungarian Empire in World War I; and in their blind hatred of Germany they failed to see the greater enemy beyond the horizon—Russia. Only fools could have failed to perceive that the real enemy was Russia and that one day the western powers would need a strong and democratic Germany to act as a counterweight to Bolshevism. By their actions towards the anti-Hitler conspiracy they sealed the fate of Europe and the world in a pact of blood on D-Day. It is all too hideous to look back upon, and we are paying for that blunder to this day.

Von Luttichau was both right and wrong. Certainly the course of history would have been altered if the Allies had been able to walk ashore on D-Day. But to hold the Allies solely responsible for the phenomenon of Hitler, and his continuation in power even to the moment of his suicide in a ravaged Berlin, is to absolve the conspirators of the Schwarze Kapelle, and the German people themselves, of their share of the responsibility. And if the western powers were slow to perceive a new enemy, their aid and support to the old enemy, virtually without parallel in history and motivated by both humanitarian and political aims, did result in a strong and democratic Germany.

Churchill, among the first of the western leaders to recognize the Russian menace and to regret that the Anglo-American alliance had dealt so ruthlessly with those who represented the social, political and even military conscience of Germany, died in 1965, in his ninety-first year, his reputation already beginning to suffer with hints of amoral stratagems in his conduct of the war. His part in Coventry, Dieppe, the manipulation of resistance forces, Bodyguard, Fortitude, the use of Ultra and deception and so many of the other major strategies and stratagems of the Second World War, including D-Day itself, will undoubtedly be subjects for endless debate. But in 1974, on the occasion of the centenary of his birth, the *New York Times* acknowledged his permanent place in history:

> But what a man! The familiar sound of that voice . . . reminds us again that at rare moments in history one man of courage and vision—and eloquence—can make all the difference, not merely for Britain but for the world. . . . Where and when will Britain or *any of us* again find such inspiration?

The year 1974 also marked the thirtieth anniversary of D-Day, and men in great numbers who had taken part in Neptune once again visited the Far Shore. There on the beaches of Normandy, so it is said, one can hear the sounds of old battles in the wind. It is the same phenomenon that one hears on the gentle rises at Waterloo. For those who require monuments, there are strange, rust-red shapes sticking out of the sea, looking so remote from present history that they might have been there since the days of Richard the Lionheart. They are the remnants of the merchantmen sunk as breakwaters for the Mulberry harbors. The seas wash over these relics, rising and falling with the fierce tides. But they are not destroyed. They remain as a testament to that time and place where the fates changed horses and history changed its tune.

Author's Note

Bodyguard of Lies has taken much longer to research and write than I could have expected. It was first registered at the Office of the Chief of Military History in Washington, D.C., at the time of the Cuban Missile Crisis in 1963, when I was at the Pentagon for the *Daily Mail,* London, waiting to record what we thought might be the Armageddon. I was surprised to find in that most distinguished institution of American military learning that, apart from a few references of a minor nature in its card index, there were no documents on cover and deception operations pertaining to Overlord and Neptune. One of the cards did state that there were thirty-eight cover and deception plans concerning the invasion in existence, but they were in the custody of the British Cabinet Offices in London. That seemed most strange to me for, of course, the United States armed forces had played an important part in the campaign. Moreover, I was informed in a semi-official manner at the OCMH that I would have very great difficulty in getting the materials I wanted. In its own official histories of the campaign, the OCMH itself had not been permitted to use even the term "cover and deception." General John R. Deane, I learned, had been threatened with court-martial for mentioning, in his account of his wartime assignment as chief of the U.S. Military Mission to Moscow, the names of some of those involved in cover and deception operations—proceedings that were dropped only through the direct intercession of General Eisenhower, who was then Chief of Staff of the United States Army. I also learned that two official historians, both writing on the authority of Eisenhower, had tried and failed to include chapters on cover and deception in their works. There were files concerning Bodyguard and Fortitude in the records of SHAEF and in the archives of the Joint Chiefs of Staff, I discovered, but because they were still classified even twenty years after the war, I could not see them.

In England, the situation was no more encouraging. When I approached the Ministry of Defence for documentation in 1964, I received a letter reminding me of the Official Secrets Act. The Foreign Office agreed to give me a verbal briefing, provided I submitted a list of questions beforehand; and when I rejected the suggestion, I was advised that "The Foreign Office will slit your gizzard if you go too far." With that it was apparent that I would have to look elsewhere for information and I tried a fresh tack—approaching those who had taken part in Bodyguard and Fortitude for interviews. Again I met with a wall of silence; indeed, one man warned me that if I persisted he would have me "horsewhipped." But General Sir Stewart Menzies was more cordial. In two long interviews, we discussed a number of matters, notably Canaris and Cicero, but since he had not commanded the British deception apparatus, Menzies could not, or would not, discuss Bodyguard and Fortitude. Nor did he mention Ultra.

There, in 1964–65, the trail seemed to end. I still knew little about cover and deception, and I did not know that Ultra had even existed. It was not until 1968, during a long stay at the Hoover Institution for War, Revolution and Peace at Stanford, California, that I was able to learn more about Bodyguard and Fortitude. Then I met General William H. Baumer, who told me of Plan Jael. A document entitled *A Short History of COSSAC, 1943–1944,* which, unaccountably, had been declassified, added to my knowledge of Overlord and Neptune, and a number of histories and memoirs began to appear that threw some new light upon the whole affair. Finally, in 1969, as I was walking along a beach in the northeastern United States with a distinguished military man, I heard about Ultra. "You know," he said, "that your people and ours were reading the German and Japanese command ciphers for the better part of the war." It was an incredible revelation. Others almost as incredible were to follow, and gradually the story began to fall into place.

I had learned a truth about historical research. The more you know, the more people are inclined to talk to you. I renewed my efforts to interview men who had been personally involved in Overlord and Neptune, on both the Allied and the German sides. I met General Reinhard Gehlen in Washington and again, under circumstances of authentic Teutonic mystery, at Starnberg-am-See in Bavaria. In France, I met Colonel Claude Arnould, the former co-chief of MI-6's *réseau* in Paris, Jade Amicol. In England, Ronald E. L.

Wingate, H. R. Trevor-Roper, R. Fleetwood Hesketh and John H. Bevan all talked to me about deception and related matters. My knowledge of Ultra expanded considerably through meetings in Hampshire and London with Wilfred F. Dunderdale and in Devon with Frederick W. Winterbotham. In the United States, General Omar N. Bradley, Allen W. Dulles, General Edwin L. Sibert and General Baumer, among many others, contributed to my understanding of Overlord and Neptune. I am extremely grateful to these men and the many other people who granted me the privilege of personal interviews during the course of my research. Those whose names may be used are listed below with the ranks or positions they held during the span of years covered by the book.

Although many officials involved in the invasion agreed to talk with me, I still was unable to find the necessary documentation. That, for all practical purposes, was not forthcoming until 1971–72. During that period, the American authorities at last began to liberalize their attitude toward the secret matters of the Second World War. Even so, the material available to me was but a trickle at first; and the rules were as exasperating to the many archivists, historians and librarians who attempted to help as they were to me. All of the men and women who aided my research are listed below with my thanks. Among them, Charles B. MacDonald, Charles V. P. von Luttichau and Detmar Finke at the OCMH and Robert Wolfe, George Wagner, Thomas E. Hohman, William Cunliffe, John E. Taylor and Tim Nenninger at the National Archives must be singled out for special thanks.

Almost all of the barriers finally came down in Washington early in 1975 when, ironically, work on the manuscript was virtually complete. But in the special contexts of Bodyguard, Fortitude and Ultra, it may be regarded as significant that none of the documents cited in *Bodyguard of Lies* was obtained from official British sources. Why all this secrecy both in London and Washington? I discovered the answer in the flood of documents that were finally declassified in Washington in the spring of 1975. There, in the records of the U.S. Joint Chiefs of Staff, was clear evidence of an agreement to prevent any access whatsoever to secret documents concerning cover and deception, and cryptanalytical matters, in the Second World War.

It was a complicated intercession that apparently originated with Colonel John Bevan of the LCS, who objected to the publication and distribution of a report of American authorship on Allied cover and deception operations in the European theater, submitted to the War

Department late in 1944. General Clayton Bissell, the G2 of the War Department, acceded to many of Bevan's requests; all references to Ultra would be eliminated from the report. But the British sought to widen the restrictions; in a memorandum to the U.S. Joint Chiefs of Staff, dated August 5, 1945, they requested that all those concerned with compiling the official histories of the war not "be given access to any original special intelligence material." They further proposed that the British Chiefs of Staff "write up important battles, using personnel already indoctrinated," and it was this information that would be given to official historians for incorporation in their volumes. The U.S. Joint Chiefs debated the proposal; and while they doubted that such Draconian restrictions would be effective, they agreed, in a memorandum to the British Chiefs of Staff, dated September 7, 1945, that "it is desirable and necessary to take appropriate action to insure the protection of sources of signal intelligence in connection with the preparation of official histories."

At about the same time, President Truman added the weight of his authority to the restrictions surrounding Ultra. In a memorandum dated August 28, 1945, to the Secretaries of State, War and the Navy, the Attorney General, the Joint Chiefs of Staff, and the Directors of the Budget and the Office of War Information, he wrote:

> Appropriate departments of the Government and the Joint Chiefs of Staff are hereby directed to take such steps as are necessary to prevent release to the public, except with the specific approval of the President in each case, of:
>
>> Information regarding the past or present status, technique or procedures, degree of success attained, or any specific results of any cryptanalytic unit acting under the authority of the U.S. Government or any Department thereof.

That directive muzzled all public discussion of Ultra in the United States for the next thirty years.

Meanwhile, steps had also been taken to guard the secrets of cover and deception. In a memorandum to the U.S. Joint Chiefs dated May 25, 1945, from Joint Security Control, which was working closely with the LCS, it was recommended that "The existence of a cover and deception organization, or parts thereof, must be guarded now and in peacetime at a TOP SECRET level." It was further requested that "Despatches and correspondence with respect to cover and deception plans and reports" be classified Top Secret; and equipment used in deception might only be downgraded in classification "in a manner similar to that for secret weapons." These proposals were also adopted by the Joint Chiefs, and again history was denied knowledge of the unique operations that had contributed so significantly to victory.

So rigid were the restrictions surrounding cover and deception that history would even be denied knowledge of Patton's role in these operations. Soon after his death, the Joint Chiefs of Staff seem to have tried to make posthumous amends for the way Patton's name and reputation had been used in Fortitude. Because of the agreement between the American and British governments to keep such matters Top Secret, they applied to the British for permission and the request was referred to Colonel Bevan. Speaking on behalf of Bevan, Brigadier A. T. Cornwall-Jones replied to the Joint Chiefs that although Bevan had "tried his best to produce something that would be of value," he had however "reluctantly been driven to the conclusions that it would be impossible to prepare any story which would not give away facts that the British Chiefs of Staff are particularly anxious to conceal and which the Combined Chiefs of Staff have agreed should not be revealed." Evidently Eisenhower had also been consulted on the matter, for Cornwall-Jones wrote that he "immediately understood and, I believe, satisfied the Secretary of War that publication of General Patton's activities during this period would be undesirable." But to avoid the suspicion that the British military authorities might be "trying to hide something from you," Cornwall-Jones appended what he called a "very secret account of General Patton's activities." The account, of some eight paragraphs—little more than desk diary notes—concerned Patton's role in the deception scheme to hide the Anzio landings. There was no mention of his part in Fortitude.

At the time, there seemed to be a number of sound and sensible reasons for putting such restrictions in force, notably the fear that the western powers might soon find themselves at war with the Soviet Union, and Ultra and the LCS might function as they had in the past. There may have been some hope that the Russians would adopt a cipher machine system similar to Enigma—a hope that was surely dashed when Philby revealed the existence of Ultra to the Russians —but Enigma was employed by secondary powers in the 1950's and 1960's, and the Turing engine still had its uses. Ultra, from its uncertain beginnings at Bletchley, had become a secret of the utmost importance in the conduct of international affairs.

The methodology of deception would find similar application in the postwar world, but in guarding that secret the western powers may have had their eyes on the past as well as on the future. The discovery of the uses to which resistance movements in both German-occupied countries and Germany itself were put for the purposes of deception—to mention only one of the most carefully guarded secrets of Allied methodology—was bound to generate new controversies about the conduct of the war. And, indeed, it has. Further, governments, and particularly the British government, are always reluctant to reveal their secrets, whatever those secrets may be, and the long tradition of secrecy for the sake of secrecy is difficult to break. But whatever the motives of those who attempt to conceal them, the facts of history will out; and while my research might have been made infinitely easier if the documents I sought had been available to me from the very first, I would have been denied the pleasure of searching for, and finally, finding them.

It was, however, a time-consuming task, and it might not have been completed at all were it not for the understanding, patience and support of my publishers, Harper & Row, and two of its editors, Cass Canfield, Sr., and M. S. Wyeth, Jr. There are others at Harper & Row and elsewhere to whom I am also indebted: Kitty Benedict, an editor whose early memoranda on my subject proved the spur to proceed; Florence Goldstein, Victoria Schochet, Lynne McNabb, Harriet Stanton, Sallie Gouverneur, Anne Adelman, Stephen Hardiman, and Edmée Busch Reit. I am especially grateful for the craftsmanship of my editor, Burton Beals, who helped me across many a minefield and through many a maze. To everyone concerned with the publication of *Bodyguard of Lies* I would like to make a most sincere expression of thanks. I must also say that while no effort has been spared to ensure that the facts in these pages are accurate, the responsibility for error is mine alone.

ANTHONY CAVE BROWN

Washington, D.C., 1975

Interviews

Colonel Claude Arnould, Co-Chief, Jade Amicol, MI-6 *réseau*, Paris

Robert Aron, French resistance historian

Dr. Walter Bargatzky, lawyer on the staff of the German Governor-General of Paris and Northern France

Lieutenant Colonel William H. Baumer, representative of the U.S. War Department, General Staff, on the London Controlling Section

Major D. Baxter, The Northamptonshire Regiment (unit involved in the Fortitude North and Quicksilver stratagems)

His Grace the Duke of Beaufort

Brigadier R. F. K. Belchem, Chief of Operations, 21st Army Group

Colonel Alexander Berding, Chief, OSS X2, 12th U.S. Army Group

Brigadier General Thomas J. Betts, Deputy Chief, G2, SHAEF

Colonel John H. Bevan, Controller of Deception, London Controlling Section, Joint Planning Staff, War Cabinet, London

Lieutenant General Omar N. Bradley, Commanding General, 1st U.S. Army; 12th U.S. Army Group

Detective Inspector George Brown, Special Branch, Scotland Yard

Colonel the Honourable David K. E. Bruce, Chief, OSS, London

Lieutenant Colonel Robert E. Button, Signals Intelligence, 12th U.S. Army Group

Dr. Robert Cockburn, Telecommunications Research Establishment, Great Britain

Major William E. Colby, team leader, Jedburgh team Bruce, Yonne, France

Lieutenant Colonel Ian Collins, operations officer, Special Air Service

W. Greville Collins, resident of Luckington Manor and neighbor of Stewart Menzies

Ian Colvin, an intermediary of Canaris with the British government

R. H. S. Crossman, Section Chief, Political Warfare Executive, London

Lieutenant Colonel Thomas J. Crystal, G2, U.S. 19th Corps

Lieutenant Colonel James O. Curtis, Jr., member, G2, SHAEF

Major General John R. Deane, Chief, U.S. Military Mission, Moscow

Major General Francis W. de Guingand, Chief of Staff to General Sir Bernard Montgomery, North Africa, Sicily, Italy, northwest Europe

D. Sefton Delmer, Chief, Research Unit, Political Warfare Executive, London

Lieutenant Commander Norman Denning, The Admiralty, London

Lieutenant Colonel Harold C. Deutsch, OSS, Chief, Research and Analysis Division, Political Intelligence Section, European Theater

Colonel Benjamin A. Dickson, G2, 1st U.S. Army

Allen W. Dulles, Chief, OSS, Switzerland

Commander Wilfred F. Dunderdale, officer of MI-6

Lieutenant Commander Ian Fleming, assistant to the Director of Naval Intelligence; Chief, Deception Sub-section, The Admiralty, London

Captain M. R. D. Foot, Special Air Service

Sister Henriette Frede (courier for Jade Amicol), Mother Superior, Convent of St. Agonie, Paris

General Reinhard Gehlen, German General Staff, Chief, Fremde Heere Organization

Father Robert A. Graham, Jesuit priest at the Vatican and editor of the *Cattolica Civiltica*

General Sir Colin McVean Gubbins, Chief of Special Operations Executive

Captain S. A. Hector, Chief Constable, Coventry, 1940

Lieutenant Colonel Roger Fleetwood Hesketh, Committee of Special Means, SHAEF

C. Holland-Martin, member of the design committee of the Turing engine

Air Commodore R. Ivelaw-Chapman, O/C RAF Station, Elsham Wolds, Lincolnshire, and member of the Planning Staff, Air Ministry, London

C. D. Jackson, Section Chief, Office of War Information, London

Lieutenant Colonel J. V. B. Jervis-Reid, Executive Officer, Committee of Special Means, SHAEF

Captain J. F. Johnston, staff member, 4th Army

H. M. Keen, designer of the Turing engine

Georges B. E. Keun, father of Major Philippe Keun

D. F. Kingston, member of the household of Captain Robert Treeck

Major B. M. W. Knox, team leader, Jedburgh team Giles, Brittany

Oliver Knox, son of Alfred Dilwyn Knox

General Ulrich Liss, German General Staff, Chief, Fremde Heere West

Colonel Samuel Lohan, Ministry of Defence, London

J. G. Lomax, agent of Ministry of Economic Warfare, Istanbul, Ankara, Lisbon, Berne

Lieutenant Commander Donald McLachlan, liaison officer between The Admiralty and the London Controlling Section

Colonel R. M. MacLeod, team leader in Quicksilver

Mrs. Lesley J. McNair, wife of General Lesley J. McNair, Commanding General, U.S. Army Ground Forces, Washington, D.C.

General Sir James Marshall-Cornwall, Vice-Chief, Imperial General Staff

Major J. C. Masterman, XX-Committee

General Sir Stewart Graham Menzies, Chief, MI-6

Colonel Lothar Metz, Fremde Heere West

Colonel Wilhelm Meyer-Detring, German General Staff, G2, OB-West, Paris

Lieutenant Colonel C. J. Moore, Royal Corps of Signals

General Sir Frederick W. Morgan, COSSAC and Deputy Chief of Staff, SHAEF

Dr. Josef Mueller, an emissary of Canaris to the Vatican

Major Airey Neave, officer of MI-9 and G.S.O. (i), 21st Army Group

Major Albert W. Norman, Historian, 12th U.S. Army Group

Dr. Forrest C. Pogue, Historian, ETOUSA

Lieutenant Noel Poole, team leader, Titanic, June 6, 1944

Flight Lieutenant Alfred Price, electronics officer, RAF Bomber Command

Colonel J. H. Randewig, Chief, Wireless Intelligence Service (West)

Colonel J. D. Ricketts, The Worcestershire Regiment (unit involved in the Quicksilver stratagem)

Major Dwight Salmon, Historian, AFHQ

Lieutenant Colonel Walter Scott, Royal Corps of Signals, Middle East and SHAEF

Major Alexander Scratchley, Special Air Service

Major General Edwin L. Sibert, G2, ETOUSA; G2, 12th U.S. Army Group

Brigadeführer SS Otto Skorzeny, team leader, SS special forces

Air Marshal Sir John C. Slessor, C-in-C Coastal Command; C-in-C RAF Mediterranean and Middle East; Deputy to Air C-in-C, Mediterranean Allied Air Forces

Colonel Anton Staubwasser, German Staff, Fremde Heere West; G2 to Field Marshal Erwin Rommel

Major General Kenneth W. D. Strong, Chief, G2, SHAEF

Dr. F. E. Terman, Director, Radio Research Laboratory, Harvard University

General Sir Andrew Thorne, C-in-C, Scottish Command

Lieutenant (jg.) Angus McLean Thuermer, Forward Intelligence Unit, 12th Fleet, U.S. Navy

Major H. R. Trevor-Roper, officer of MI-6

Major Ronald E. L. Wingate, Executive Officer, London Controlling Section

Squadron Leader Frederick W. Winterbotham, Deputy Chief of MI-6 in charge of Ultra security and dissemination

Captain Inzer Wyatt, member of a Special Liaison Unit for Ultra

Archivists, Historians and Librarians

D. C. Allard, Chief, Operational Archives Branch, U.S. Navy, Washington, D.C.

W. Arenz, Head of Documents Center, Militargeschichtliches Forschungsamt, Freiburg

T. B. Bates, Archives Branch, Imperial War Museum, London

A. D. Bauer, Berlin Documents Center, U.S. Forces, Berlin

Magda E. Bauer, Historian, U.S. Army, Washington, D.C.

Don Chetwynd, Coventry News Service, Coventry

C. J. Child, Acting Librarian and Keeper of the Papers, Foreign Office Library, London

David L. Christensen, Research Associate, University of Alabama, Tuscaloosa, Alabama

E. S. Costrell, Chief, Historical Studies Division, Historical Office, State Department, Washington, D.C.

William Cunliffe, Acting Chief, Modern Military Records, National Archives, Washington, D.C.

B. J. Day, Naval Library, Home Division, Ministry of Defence, London

P. B. Devlin, Office of the Keeper of College Library and Collections, Eton College, Eton

Major A. J. Dickson, Curator, Household Cavalry Museum, Cavalry Barracks, Windsor

William R. Emerson, Director, Franklin D. Roosevelt Library, Hyde Park, New York

Detmar Finke, Chief Archivist, U.S. Army, Washington, D.C.

L. Fisher, Institute of Contemporary History and Wiener Library, London

E. R. Flatequal, Chief, Archives Branch, National Archives, Washington, D.C.

Oberstleutnant T. E. Forwick, Militarchiv, Freiburg

Corporal Major C. W. Frearson, Keeper, Household Cavalry Museum, Cavalry Barracks, Windsor

Lieutenant Commander J. W. Frere-Cooke, Curator, Royal Navy Submarine Service Museum, Portsmouth

Michael Garrod, Press Office, Home Office, London

Kenneth Glazier, Chief, Western Section, Hoover Institution on War, Revolution and Peace, Stanford, California

C. Haase, Niedersachsisches Staatsarchiv, Hanover

F. Hallworth, Librarian, Devizes, Wiltshire

R. Helliwell, City Librarian, Winchester

F. J. Heppner, Assistant Chief, Modern Military Records, National Archives, Washington, D.C.

Anton Hoch, Institut für Zeitgeschichte, Munich

T. E. Hohmann, Chief, Modern Military Records; Deputy Chief, Declassification and Review Board, National Archives, Washington, D.C.

F. von Hueck, Deutsches Adelsarchiv, Marburg

L. A. Jacketts, Chief, Archives Section, RAF, Ministry of Defence, London

H. John, Washington National Records Center, Suitland, Maryland

Captain Terry Johnson, Declassification Officer, AFHQ records, Washington National Records Center, Suitland, Maryland

Leo Kahn, Foreign Documents Centre, Imperial War Museum, London

Lieutenant Commander P. J. Kemp, Chief, Naval Historical Branch, Ministry of Defence, London

A. G. Kogan, Research Guidance and Review Division, Historical Office, State Department, Washington, D.C.

W. Krolinski, Zentralbibliothek der Bundeswehr, Düsseldorf

Carrie Lee, Modern Military Records, National Archives, Washington, D.C.

William Lewis, General Archives Division, Washington National Records Center, Suitland, Maryland

Lieutenant Commander R. W. Mackay, Chief, Declassification Section, U.S. Navy Archives, Washington, D.C.

Bryan Melland, Historian and Archivist, Cabinet Office, London

Françoise Mosser, Archives Departmentales du Morbihan, Vannes

K. M. Murphy, Library, University College of Swansea, Wales

Abraham Nemrow, Clerk of Court, U.S. Army Judiciary, Washington, D.C.

Tim Nenninger, Modern Military Records, National Archives, Washington, D.C.

Peter Pagan, Director, Bath Municipal Libraries and Victorian Art Gallery, Bath

Edward Reese, Modern Military Records, National Archives, Washington, D.C.

W. S. Revell, Historical Section, Air Ministry, London

G. D. Ryan, Declassification Branch, Modern Military Records, National Archives, Washington, D.C.

John Saltmarsh, Historian, King's College, Cambridge

P. J. Sanhofer, Militarchiv, Freiburg

Patrick Strong, Keeper of College Library and Collections, Eton College, Eton

J. E. Taylor, Archivist in Charge of OSS Records, National Archives, Washington, D.C.

H. L. Theobald, Cabinet Office, London

D. J. Urquhart, Director, The National Lending Library for Science and Technology, Boston Spa

R. Wagner, Enemy Documents Section, National Archives, Washington, D.C.

Phillip Warner, Historian and Tutor, Royal Military Academy, Sandhurst

P. F. Whitby, Imperial War Museum, London

J. W. Willis, Imperial War Museum, London

R. Wilson, U.S. Army Records, Washington National Records Center, Suitland, Maryland

Robert Wolfe, Chief, Enemy Documents Section; Chief, Modern Military Records, National Archives, Washington, D.C.

Carol Zangara, Modern Military Records, National Archives, Washington, D.C.

Hannah Zedlick, Archivist, Office of the Chief of Military History, Washington, D.C.

Glossary

Abwehr: The secret intelligence and counter-espionage service of the German General Staff

Admiralstab: German naval staff

Adoration: Code name for Fortitude South wireless deception and silence operations

A-Force: The deception organization in the Mediterranean and Middle East

Amt Mil: The intelligence acquisition section of the German General Staff, successor to the Abwehr

Ankara Committee: The Anglo-American organization responsible for intelligence in the Middle East, the Balkans and the eastern Mediterranean

Anvil: Code name for the Anglo-American invasion of southern France in August 1944 (later, Dragoon)

Avis: See *messages personnels*

Barbarossa: Code name for the German invasion of Russia in 1941

Battalion of Heaven: 4th SAS Regiment (Chasseurs Parachutistes), a force of Frenchmen trained in guerrilla warfare dropped behind German lines from D-Day onward

BCRA: Bureau Centrale de Renseignements et d'Action, the secret intelligence service founded by de Gaulle

Berne Report: German diplomatic documents leaked in 1943–44 to Allen W. Dulles, OSS chief at Berne

Bertram: Code name for British cover and deception operations to conceal Montgomery's Lightfoot offensive in North Africa in 1942

Bigot: The SHAEF code word indicating that a document contained information about Neptune and required special security handling; also used to denote an individual with knowledge of Neptune

Bodyguard: Code name for the strategic cover and deception operations to conceal Allied intentions in northwest Europe in 1944; formerly Plan Jael

"The Bomb": Engineers' slang for the machine used to decode Enigma-enciphered messages

Brissex: British secret intelligence teams dropped in France prior to D-Day

Case Green: Code name for German operations to occupy Czechoslovakia

Case White: Code name for German operations to invade Poland

Case Yellow: Code name for German operations to invade The Netherlands, Belgium and France

Cobra: Code name for Bradley's offensive to break the German lines at St. Lô in July 1944

Cockade: Code name for the LCS's major strategical deception scheme in 1943, designed to draw off German strength from the Russian and Italian fronts by threatening an Allied invasion of western Europe

Combined Chiefs of Staff (CCS): The Anglo-American supreme command in Washington, D.C.

Combined Intelligence Committee (CIC): The Combined Chiefs of Staff intelligence evaluation organization in Washington, D.C.

Commando Supremo: The Italian supreme command

Cooneys: Special forces teams trained to disrupt German communications in Brittany during Neptune

COSSAC: Chief of Staff, Supreme Allied Commander, the headquarters of the Combined Chiefs of Staff at London established in 1943 to execute Cockade and plan for Overlord and Neptune

Crossbow: Code name for the Allied aerial campaign against V1 launch sites

CSM: Committee of Special Means, the SHAEF department responsible for the execution of cover and deception plans; also called Ops B

Diadem: Code name for Allied military operations in Italy in concert with Neptune and Overlord

Enigma: The name of the enciphering machine used extensively throughout the Wehrmacht, by the Abwehr and by the Axis nations

Etappe: Etappendienst, the secret supply and intelligence organization of the German navy

Fahneneid: The oath of allegiance sworn by the German armed services to Hitler

Feldgrau: The German soldier, a term derived from the field-gray color of his uniform

FH: Fremde Heere, the intelligence evaluation section of the German General Staff

FHO: Fremde Heere Ost, the section of Fremde Heere responsible for evaluating intelligence about Russia and other nations east of Germany

FHW: Fremde Heere West, the section of Fremde Heere responsible for evaluating intelligence about the western Allies

Flash: The code name of the unsuccessful operation to assassinate Hitler in 1943 by placing a bomb aboard his aircraft

Forschungsamt: The communications intelligence service of the Luftwaffe and, later, a dependency of the Nazi Party intelligence services

Fortitude: Code name for the tactical cover and deception operations to conceal the secrets of Neptune

Fortitude North: Code name for the Fortitude cover and deception operations directed at the Scandinavian countries

Fortitude South: Code name for the Fortitude cover and deception operations directed at the Channel coast of France and Belgium

Fortitude South II: Code name for the Fortitude South cover and deception operations carried on after D-Day; also called Rosebud

F section: The section of SOE concerned with special operations against the Germans in France and French territories

Führerhauptquartier: Hitler's headquarters

FUSAG: First United States Army Group, the almost wholly fictitious Allied force supposedly assembled in southeastern England to invade the Pas de Calais in 1944

Gaff: Code name for the special operation to kill or kidnap Rommel in France in 1944

GC&CS: Government Code and Cipher School, the cover-name for the main British cryptanalytical organization, a dependency of the Foreign Office located at Bletchley

German General Staff: The small, élite military hierarchy responsible for army planning which functioned under the direction of OKW

Glimmer: Code name for the deception operation that simulated the presence of an invasion fleet off Boulogne on D-Day

Goodwood: Code name for Montgomery's offensive to break the German lines at Caen in July 1944

Halcyon: Code name for Y-Day, when all preparations for the invasion of Normandy were complete

Huff-duff: High Frequency Direction Finding, a method of locating enemy ships and land stations by taking bearing on their radio traffic

Husky: Code name for the invasion of Sicily in 1943

Interallié: Early MI-6 *réseau* in Paris in 1940–41

Ironside: Code name for the cover and deception operations directed at Bordeaux and the Biscay coast; a component of Fortitude South

Jade Amicol: The main MI-6 *réseau* in Paris and northern France in 1943–44

Jael: Code name for the cover and deception operations to conceal Allied intentions in Europe in 1943; later called Plan Bodyguard

Jedburghs: Special forces teams consisting of one American, one Briton and one Frenchman trained to organize and lead the French *maquis*

Joint Chiefs of Staff (JCS): The American high command in Washington, D.C.

Joint Intelligence Committee (JIC): The name given to the highest intelligence evaluation services in both London and Washington

Joint Planning Staff (JPS): The British military planning organization, of which the LCS was a part

Joint Security Control (JSC): The American organization under the Joint Chiefs of Staff responsible for the security of military and cryptanalytical operations, and the coordination of deception operations; the American counterpart of the LCS

Jubilee: Code name for the Allied raid on Dieppe in August 1942

Jupiter: Code name for Churchill's proposal to invade northern Norway

Kondor Mission: German intelligence network in Cairo

Kriegsmarine: The German navy

LCS: London Controlling Section, the organization within the Joint Planning Staff at Churchill's headquarters responsible for devising and coordinating strategic cover and deception schemes in all theaters of war

Lightfoot: Code name for Montgomery's offensive at El Alamein in October 1942

Lisbon Report: Documents describing German rocket and missile development passed to the British in Portugal in 1943

London Group: The section of SOE responsible for special operations in western Europe

Luftwaffe: The German air force

Lüttich: Code name for the German counteroffensive in Normandy in August 1944

Magic: American code name for intelligence derived from decrypting Japanese Enigma-enciphered wireless traffic

Martians: Code name for the COSSAC/SHAEF intelligence evaluation organization in London

Menace: Code name for the unsuccessful Anglo-French operation to occupy Dakar in 1940

Messages personnels: The British system of communicating with *réseaux* in western Europe, usually by voice code broadcast by the BBC; also called Avis

MI-5: The British counterintelligence and security service

MI-6: The British Secret Intelligence Service

MI-9: A section of the War Office responsible for creating escape routes in Europe

Mincemeat: Code name for the deception operation in 1943 using a corpse carrying false documents to persuade the Germans that the Allies intended to invade Greece and southern France, not Sicily; also codenamed Trojan Horse

Moonshine: An electronic device used to amplify and return the pulses of German radar and thus simulate large numbers of approaching ships or aircraft

Mulberry: Code name for the two amphibious harbors anchored off Normandy to supply the Allied invasion forces

Neptune: Code name for the invasion of Normandy, the assault phase of Operation Overlord

OKW: Oberkommando der Wehrmacht, the German supreme command

Organization Todt: German paramilitary construction engineers and workers

Oslo Report: Documents describing German weapons development programs delivered anonymously to the British Embassy, Oslo, in 1939

OSS: Office of Strategic Services, the U.S. secret intelligence and special operations service

OSS (SI): The secret intelligence branch of the OSS

OSS (SO): The special operations branch of the OSS, the American counterpart of SOE

Ossex: American secret intelligence teams dropped in France prior to D-Day

Overlord: Code name for Allied strategic plans and operations in northwest Europe in 1944–45

Overthrow: Code name for deception operations to suggest that the Allies would invade western Europe in 1942

OWI: Office of War Information, the American political warfare agency

Pointblank: Code name for the Allied Combined Bomber Offensive against German cities and industries prior to D-Day

Princes: The underground secret intelligence service in Denmark

PWE: Political Warfare Executive, the British political warfare agency

Quicksilver: Code name for those cover and deception operations concerning FUSAG and threats to invade the Pas de Calais; a component of Fortitude South

Rankin: Code name for Allied contingency plans in the event of the collapse of Germany

Ratissage: Literally, a rat-hunt, secret service jargon for a counter-espionage manhunt

Reichskanzelei: Literally, Reich Chancellory, Hitler's headquarters in Berlin

Réseau: Literally, a nest, a term applied to clandestine intelligence or espionage organization in German-occupied territories

R-Force: The deception organization at Montgomery's headquarters

Roundup: Code name for proposed American strategical and tactical operations in France in 1942–43; *see also* Sledgehammer

Rutter: Code name for the proposed Allied raid on Dieppe in July 1942; postponed and later mounted as Operation Jubilee

SAS: Special Air Service, a British military organization trained to carry out special missions behind enemy lines

Schwarze Kapelle: Literally, Black Orchestra, the name used by the Nazi Party to describe members of the German military services and the Abwehr conspiring to overthrow Hitler

SD: Sicherheitsdienst, the intelligence and counter-espionage arm of the SS

Sealion: Code name for the German plan to invade Britain in 1940–41

SHAEF: Supreme Headquarters, Allied Expeditionary Force, acronym for the Anglo-American command established to plan and execute Overlord and Neptune under the Combined Chiefs of Staff in Washington, D.C.

SIM: Servizio Informazione Segreto, the Italian secret service

Skye: Code name for those cover and deception operations concerning the creation of a fictitious Anglo-American force in Scotland preparing to invade Norway; a component of Fortitude North

Sledgehammer: Code name for the American proposal to invade France in 1942

SLU's: Special Liaison Units, MI-6 personnel attached to all higher Allied headquarters to disseminate intelligence derived from Ultra and protect its security

SOE: Special Operations Executive, the secret British organization created in 1940 to raise, arm, fund and train patriot armies in German- and Japanese-occupied territories and nations allied to the Axis

Special Plans Branch: The deception organization at Bradley's headquarters

SS: Schutzstaffel, the political-military order of the Nazi Party through which Hitler ruled Germany and German-occupied territories

Starkey: Code name for the deception operations to lure the Luftwaffe to battle and threaten an invasion of the Pas de Calais in the summer of 1943; a component of Cockade

Strategy and Policy Group: The section of the Joint Chiefs of Staff with responsibility for examining and developing American military and political policies

Sussex: Code name for the operation to drop American and British intelligence teams in France prior to D-Day; *see* Brissex, Ossex

Taxable: Code name for the deception operation that simulated the presence of an invasion fleet off Cap d'Antifer on D-Day

Telecommunications Research Establishment (TRE): The British radar and wireless research and development organization

Tindall: Code name for the deception operations to suggest an Anglo-American invasion of Norway in 1943; a component of Cockade

Titanic: Code name for airborne deception operations on D-Day which simulated large paratroop landings in the Neptune area of France

Torch: Code name for the Anglo-American invasion of North Africa in 1942

Ultra: Code name for intelligence derived from decrypting German Enigma-enciphered wireless traffic

Valkyrie: Code name for the German plan to suppress internal disorders which became the instrument through which the Schwarze Kapelle hoped to seize power from Hitler and the Nazi Party

Vendetta: Code name for the cover and deception operations directed at southern France; associated with Fortitude South

Wadham: Code name for the deception operation to threaten an Anglo-American invasion of Brittany in 1943; a component of Cockade

Wehrmacht: Literally, war machine, a term used to denote German military forces

Window: British code name for the foil strips dropped from aircraft to obstruct German radar reception

X2: The counterintelligence and agent-manipulation branch of the OSS

XX-Committee: The MI-5 organization for the control and manipulation of double agents

X-Gerät: A radio-navigation device used by German bombers for blind bombing in 1940

Y service: Technical communications intelligence services of both the German and the British armed forces

Zeppelin: Code name for the cover and deception operations directed at the countries of southern and southeastern Europe in 1943–44

Sources and Notes

The names of authors cited in the Sources and Notes refer to their published works which are listed in the Bibliography.

The abbreviations listed below are used in the Sources and Notes for the names and locations of certain libraries, collections and archives; the names and locations of certain documents; and the designations of certain military units.

AFHQ	Air Force Headquarters
BAOR	British Army of the Rhine
CCS	Combined Chiefs of Staff
CIAP	Copy in Author's Possession
COS	Chiefs of Staff
COSSAC	Chief-of-Staff Supreme Allied Command
CSDIC	Combined Services Detailed Interrogation Center
DRB	Diplomatic Records Branch
ED	Eisenhower Diary, Eisenhower Library, Abilene, Kansas
EDS	Enemy Documents Section
EPF	Eisenhower Personal File, Eisenhower Library, Abilene, Kansas
ETOUSA	European Theater of Operations, United States Army
FBIS	Foreign Broadcasting Intelligence Service
FC	Fraenkel Collection, Thaxted, England
FCC	Federal Communications Commission
HI	Hoover Institution on War, Revolution and Peace, Stanford, California
IWM	Imperial War Museum, London
JCS	Joint Chiefs of Staff
JSC	Joint Security Control
KC	Karlsruhe Collection, United States Air Force Historical Branch, Maxwell Air Force Base, Montgomery, Alabama
MAAFHQ	Mediterranean Allied Air Forces Headquarters
MAFB	Maxwell Air Force Base, Montgomery, Alabama
MID	Military Intelligence Division
MMR	Modern Military Records
NA	National Archives, Washington, D.C.

OAB	Operational Archives Branch, U.S. Navy, Washington, D.C.
OCMH	Office of the Chief of Military History, U.S. Army, Washington, D.C.
OMR	Old Military Records
ONI	Office of Naval Intelligence
OPD	Operations and Plans Division
OSS	Office of Strategic Services
OUP	Of Unknown Provenance
PRO	Public Records Office, London
R&A	Research and Analysis
RUSI	Royal United Services Institute
SAS	Special Air Service
SC	Shuster Collection, Modern Military Records, National Archives, Washington, D.C.
SDA	State Department Archives
SDDLRS	State Department Division of Libraries and Reference Services, Washington, D.C.
SGS	Secretary, General Staff
SHAEF	Supreme Headquarters Allied Expeditionary Force
USDA	United States Department of the Army
USFET	United States Forces European Theater
USJCS	United States Joint Chiefs of Staff
WDGS	War Department General Staff
WDGSS	War Department General and Special Staffs
WNRC	Washington National Records Center, Suitland, Maryland

PROLOGUE

Sources

Historical Sub-Section, Office of the Secretary, General Staff, SHAEF, *A Short History of COSSAC 1943–1944,* May 1944, Center for Military Studies, U.S. Army, Washington, D.C.; SHAEF SGS 381, *Bodyguard,* MMR, NA.

Notes

page
1 "pale skin . . ." Philby, p. 78.
2 "true to the . . ." Foot, p. 12.
3 "As the big . . ." Eisenhower in a letter to Gen. Brehon Burke Somervell, April 4, 1944, ED, p. 1627.
4 "It still seemed . . ." Churchill, *The Second World War,* Vol. 5, p. 514.
5 "Battles are won . . ." Churchill, *The Great War,* Vol. 1, p. 498.
7 "The dermal . . ." Norman Holmes Pearson, in a foreword to Masterman, p. xvi.
7 "Proustian complexity," Foot, p. 12.

page

8 "to approach . . ." SHAEF Psychological Warfare Division, Memorandum to SHAEF Ops, "Policy and Methods of Black Warfare Propaganda Against Germany," November 10, 1944, MMR, NA.

8 "to drive a wedge . . ." William J. Donovan, Director, OSS, Memorandum to the USJCS, "Over-all Strategic Plan for U.S. Psychological Warfare," February 22, 1943, Record Group 218, Records of the USJCS, JSC 385, MMR, NA.

8 "Nothing quite like . . ." Foot, p. 12.

9 "It was Churchill . . ." Wingate, p. 185.

9 "Looking back . . ." Baumer interview.

10 "nine hundred chariots of iron," *et seq.,* Old Testament, Judges 4.

11 "In war-time, truth . . ." Churchill, *The Second World War,* Vol. 5, p. 338.

11 "It was going . . ." Morgan interview.

PART I: THE ORIGINS OF SPECIAL MEANS

1. ULTRA

Sources

Information concerning Menzies was obtained from the libraries of the *Sunday Times, Sunday Telegraph,* and *Daily Mail,* London; Ellerman's Wilson Line, Ltd., Hull (M. W. Webster, Archivist); Westonbirt School (Margaret Newton, Headmistress); *Eton College Chronicles* and Eton Archives (Patrick Strong, Keeper of College Library and Collections); Household Cavalry Museum, Cavalry Barracks, Windsor (Maj. A. J. Dickson, Curator, and Cpl. Maj. C. W. Frearson, Keeper); *War Diary, 1914, 2nd Life Guards,* and an unpublished account of the charge of Zwartelen by Cpl. Maj. T. L. King, Household Cavalry Museum, Cavalry Barracks, Windsor.

Notes

epigraph

"In the high ranges . . ." *et seq.,* Churchill, an epigraph to Hyde, *Room 3603,* p. ix.

page

15 "It is difficult . . ." Churchill, *The Second World War,* Vol. 1, p. 261.

17 "The natural inquisitiveness . . ." *Die Schreibende Enigma-Chiffriemaschinen,* undated pamphlet, cited by Kahn, p. 421.

18 "a chance that . . ." *et seq.,* Review and analysis of Bertrand in *The Rearguard,* Munich, No. 29 and 30, July 15, 1974, *et seq.*

20 "tall, with a rather . . ." Winterbotham, *The Ultra Secret,* p. 14.

21 "A sonnet written . . ." Sara Turing, citing Alan Turing, p. 134.

22 "a permanent place . . ." *The Times,* London, June 16, 1954.

22 "In answer to . . ." Sara Turing, p. 67.

22 "wild as to hair . . ." *et seq.,* Sara Turing, quoting Sir Geoffrey Jefferson, p. 58.

page
22   "raven plucking . . ." Dunderdale interview.
25   "There was no . . ." Keen interview.
27   ". . . it was just . . ." Winterbotham, *The Ultra Secret,* pp. 15–16.
29   "guard the very . . ." Standing Orders of the Household Cavalry, p. 51.
30   "most select families . . ." *et seq.,* Henry Legge-Bourke, *The King's Guard,* London: Macdonald, 1952.
30   "fair to see . . ." *et seq.,* Churchill, *The Great War,* Vol. 1, p. 62.
31   "gather all . . ." Rowan and Deindorfer, p. 70.
34   "played his hand . . ." Dilks, p. 234.
34   "intellectual twilight . . ." Page, *et al.,* p. 110.
35   "the unique experience . . ." Winterbotham, *The Ultra Secret,* pp. 2–3.

2. COVENTRY

Sources

Information concerning Ultra during the Battle of Britain and in the Coventry raid, as well as its use throughout the war, was derived in part from interviews with Frederick W. Winterbotham, and from "Results of Ultra Based on a Study of the OCMH Chronology for 1939–1944," a memorandum from Winterbotham to the author, dated June 1971, prior to the publication of his own book, *The Ultra Secret.*

Notes

page
37   "You have sat . . ." Churchill, citing the speech made by the Rt. Hon. L. S. Amery, *The Second World War,* Vol. 1, p. 594.
37   "would certainly . . ." *ibid.,* p. 599.
37   "troops of the hunter . . ." Churchill, *The Second World War,* Vol. 2, p. 217.
38   "A proper system . . ." *ibid.,* p. 218.
40   "Conduct of Air and Sea Warfare . . ." KC.
40–41 "All depends . . ." Royal Institute of International Affairs, entry for June 20, 1940.
41   "We must regard . . ." Churchill, BBC broadcast, September 11, 1940.
42   "I was struck . . ." *et seq.,* Winterbotham, *The Ultra Secret,* p. 59.
43   "It was Goering's . . ." Winterbotham interview.
44   "exclusively against . . ." *New York Times,* November 10, 1940.
46   "sadly and badly . . ." Lee, p. 104.
46   "It is a striking . . ." *Royal Air Force, 1939–1945,* Vol. 1, p. 210.
47   "all the Civil . . ." *et seq.,* S. A. Hector, in a letter to the author, March 3, 1974.
47   "I switched on . . ." *Life,* December 23, 1940.

page
48 "A report was . . ." Unsigned, unpublished monograph, IWM.
49 "the greatest attack . . ." *New York Times,* November 16, 1940.
49 "Coventry is now . . ." *ibid.,* November 17, 1940.
49 "martyred City." *The Times,* London, November 16, 1940.

3. SPECIAL MEANS OPERATIONAL

Sources

Führer Conferences on Naval Affairs, 1946, Naval Intelligence Division, The Admiralty, London; ONI, *Etappes, The Secret German Naval Intelligence and Supply Organization,* 1946, OAB; OSS, R&AB, *Chronology of Principal Events Relating to the USSR,* Part II: "USSR in the War, 22 June 1941–2 September 1945," September 25, 1945, SDDLRS, DRB, NA; Relevant papers of ONI and U.S. Naval Attaché at London, OMR, NA.

Notes

page
50 "sizeable escape . . ." Foot, p. 5.
51 "All his life . . ." *et seq.,* Wingate, pp. 189–90.
51–52 "Practically all . . ." *et seq.,* "Aids to Surprise with Particular Reference to Deceiving, Mystifying and Confusing the Enemy on the Battlefield," British memorandum, presumed to be War Office in origin, with an appendix entitled "Ruses and Stratagems of War," a note by Field Marshal Sir Archibald Wavell, HI.
53 "separate war," JSC, OPD, WDGS, "Cover and Deception," Memorandum to the USJCS, May 14, 1945, Record Group 218, Records of the USJCS, JCS 498/10, MMR, NA.
57 "This timely . . ." Churchill, *The Second World War,* Vol. 3, p. 194.
58 "We are entering . . ." Churchill, *The Second World War,* Vol. 2, p. 493.
59 "We have got . . ." Churchill, *The Second World War,* Vol. 3, p. 106.
59 "an Admiralty muddle," Winterbotham interview.
63 "It is not necessary . . ." McLachlan, p. 161.
63 "They had . . ." *ibid.,* p. 400.
63 "foul baboonery," Churchill, *The Great War,* Vol. 3, p. 1392.
64 "so far as . . ." Churchill, *The Second World War,* Vol. 3, p. 316.
64 "If Hitler invaded . . ." *ibid.,* p. 331.
64 "The prospects for . . ." *et seq.,* Dilks, p. 420 ff.
66–67 ". . . if the Germans . . ." *et seq.,* Masterman, p. 8.
67 "most favorable impression," *ibid.,* p. 56.
67 "I can catch . . ." *et seq.,* Popov, pp. 169–70.
68 "'gigantic boiler . . .'" Churchill, *The Second World War,* Vol. 3, p. 540.
68 ". . . we had won . . ." *ibid.,* p. 539.

4. THE SEARCH FOR A STRATEGY

Sources

Combined Operations Headquarters Reports C.B. 04244, "The Dieppe Raid (Combined Report), 1942," and C.B. 04244(I), "The Raid on Dieppe, Lessons Learnt," October and September 1942, OCMH; OUP, "Digest of Operation Roundup," with "Notes on Operation Sledgehammer," June 1944, OAB; Adm. E. Weichold, "The German Naval Defense Against the Allied Invasion of Normandy," Interrogation report by ONI, undated but probably 1945, OAB; Adm. F. Ruge, "Coast Defense and Invasion," ONI Report to Chief of Naval Operations, OAB; SHAEF, "German Report on Dieppe," SHAEF/116G/4/Int, MMR, NA; Gerd von Rundstedt, *et al., OB-West—A Study in Command,* Ms. No. B633, OCMH; SHAEF, "German Appreciation Cotentin Peninsula Landing of 14 Aug 42," TDS/SHAEF/86/24 February 1944, MMR, NA; SHAEF, "Cotentin Landing 14 Aug 42," Reports by the 320th Infantry Division, TDS/SHAEF/86/24 February 1944, MMR, NA; German Admiralty, Intelligence Division, "Radio Intelligence Report on Dieppe Landing," August 19, 1942, EDS, NA; Abwehrstelle Paris to Military Governor France and C-in-C West, "Report Concerning Foreknowledge of Dieppe Raid," EDS, NA.

Additional information concerning German foreknowledge of the Dieppe raid is derived from a series of letters and articles: David Irving, *Daily Telegraph,* London, September 9, 1963; *Evening Standard,* London, October 1, 2, and 14, 1963; Capt. S. W. Roskill, *Daily Telegraph,* London, November 4, 1963; *Der Spiegel,* Hamburg, November 6, 1963.

Notes

page
70   "a blend of . . ." R. Harris Smith, p. 2.
70–71 "Witnessed a demonstration . . ." *et seq.,* U.S. Army Intelligence Division, Correspondence 1917–41, "A Cipher Machine," Record Group 165, Records of the WDGSS, OMR, NA.
75   "virulent anti-Semite," Farago, *The Game of the Foes* (New York: Bantam, 1973), p. 430.
75   "to the attention . . ." *ibid.,* p. 434.
77   "to prevent . . ." Joint U.S. Staff Planners, "Establishment of a Security Committee for Military Operations," Note by the Secretaries, May 2, 1942, Records of the USJCS, Joint Planning Staff files, MMR, NA.
79   "has my heart . . ." Churchill, *The Second World War,* Vol. 4, p. 281.
80   "This country is . . ." Alanbrooke, Vol. 1, pp. 292–93.
80   "totally unprepared," OSS, R&A Report No. 9, "Morale in the British Armed Forces," March 21, 1942, in OSS R&A files, DRB, NA.
80–81 "Whether we are . . ." Alanbrooke, Vol. 1, p. 358.
81   "hanging on . . ." *ibid.,* p. 357.
81   "In the light of . . ." *ibid.,* p. 354.
81   "a good general . . ." *ibid.,* p. 358.
81–82 "at long last . . ." Matloff and Snell, *1943–1944,* p. 13.

page
82 "In the early days . . ." Eisenhower, *Crusade in Europe*, p. 320.

84 ". . . a premature Western . . ." Alanbrooke, Vol. 1, p. 371.

84 "We discussed . . ." *ibid.*, p. 370.

84 "We are making . . ." *et seq.*, Sherwood, p. 577.

85 "full understanding . . ." *et seq.*, Churchill, *The Second World War*, Vol. 4, p. 305.

85 "Roosevelt (is) getting . . ." Alanbrooke, Vol. 1, p. 397.

85 "wheedle," *et seq.*, Stimson and Bundy, p. 214.

85–86 "We hold strongly . . ." Churchill, *The Second World War*, Vol. 4, p. 342.

86 "river of blood," *et seq.*, Sherwood, pp. 590–91.

87 "Operations in France . . ." Churchill, *The Second World War*, Vol. 4, pp. 344–45.

87 "supreme political crisis," Sherwood, p. 592.

87 "No responsible British . . ." Churchill, *The Second World War*, Vol. 4, p. 391.

88 "I am most . . ." *ibid.*, p. 395.

88 "Unless you can . . ." *ibid.*, pp. 396–97.

89 "The fall of . . ." *ibid.*, p. 398.

89 "However, I thought it . . ." *ibid.*, p. 457.

90 "It is sad . . ." Masterman, p. 108.

90 "A man whose . . ." F. W. Winterbotham, in a note to the author, 1974.

91 "I feel damn . . ." Sherwood, p. 609.

91 "All was therefore . . ." Churchill, *The Second World War*, Vol. 4, p. 404.

92 "Judged by this . . ." Liddell Hart in Taylor, *Churchill Revised*, p. 225.

92 "I cannot help . . ." Alanbrooke, Vol. 1, p. 430.

92 "All depends upon . . ." Churchill, *The Second World War*, Vol. 4, p. 405.

93 "The coastal regions . . ." *New York Times*, June 9, 1942.

93 "full understanding . . ." Churchill, *The Second World War*, Vol. 4, p. 305.

93 "The troops will . . ." Robertson, p. 144.

94 "As a result of . . ." *Führer Order*, OKW/WFSt, 551213/42, EDS, NA.

95 "From available intelligence . . ." Churchill, *The Second World War*, Vol. 4, p. 457.

97 "Even before we . . ." Flower and Reeves, citing Munro, p. 443.

97 "One question worried . . ." *ibid.*, p. 447.

97–98 "and in a stage . . ." *et seq.*, *ibid.*, p. 443.

98 "We bumped on . . ." *ibid.*, p. 444.

98 "the whole sky . . ." *ibid.*, p. 446.

98 "No armed Englishman . . ." Report of the German C-in-C (Rundstedt), "Dieppe Raid," September 3, 1942, issued by the Canadian General Staff Historical Section (GS), November 1946, Army Headquarters, Ottawa.

99 "They will not . . ." *ibid.*

page
99 "In London they . . ." Germany to North America, August 29, 1942,
       FBIS, FCC, NA.
99 "My general impression . . ." Churchill, *The Second World War*, Vol.
       4, p. 467.
99 "Looking back . . ." *ibid.*, p. 459.
100 "It is a lesson . . ." Moran, p. 73.
100 "This bloody affair . . ." Alanbrooke, Vol. 1, p. 488.
100 "Several of the . . ." *ibid.*, p. 541.

5. ALAM HALFA

Sources

Reports of the U.S. Military Attaché at Moscow, in Records of the USJCS,
JSC 381, MMR, NA; Reports of the Military Attaché at Cairo, OMR, NA; R. P.
Serle, ed., *The 2/24th Australian Infantry Battalion*, Melbourne: Jacaranda Press;
Maj. Gen. R. F. H. Nalder, *The History of the British Army Signals in the
Second World War*, London: Royal Signals Institution, 1953.

Notes

page
102 "We have a . . ." Churchill, *The Second World War*, Vol. 4, p. 69.
103 "a jubilant shout . . ." Desmond Young, citing Rommel, p. 15.
103 "From the moment . . ." *ibid.*, p. 16.
103 "Where Rommel is . . ." Desmond Young, citing "Hauptmann Hart-
       mann," p. 23.
103 "trying to minimise . . ." *et seq.*, *ibid.*, pp. 23–24.
107 "There exists . . ." Desmond Young, p. 7.
108 "We had foreseen . . ." Churchill, *The Second World War*, Vol. 4,
       p. 320.
109 "beloved of the . . ." Germany to North America, July 21, 1942,
       FBIS, FCC, NA.
110 "I should say . . ." Alanbrooke, Vol. 1, p. 471.
110 "so afraid . . ." Churchill, *The Second World War*, Vol. 4, p. 431.
110 "for a very great . . ." *ibid.*, p. 430.
110 "at least the ice . . ." *ibid.*, p. 435.
111 "cast off . . ." *et seq.*, Dilks, p. 471.
111 ". . . all the talk . . ." Churchill, *The Second World War*, Vol. 4, p.
       442.
112 "Rommel, Rommel, Rommel . . ." Alanbrooke, Vol. 1, p. 450.
113 ". . . what messages they were!" Kahn, p. 473.
115 "The consequences of . . ." Scott interview.
119 "We examined . . ." Mosley, citing Sadat, p. 82.
119 "Now is the . . ." *ibid.*
119 "with a Saarland . . ." *et seq.*, *ibid.*, p. 86.
123 "It happened that . . ." *ibid.*, citing Sadat, p. 161.

page
124 "I was taken . . ." Churchill, *The Second World War*, Vol. 4, p. 464.
124 "The ensuing battle . . ." *ibid.*, p. 467.
124 "At any moment . . ." *ibid.*, p. 468.
125 "Condor calling." *et seq.*, Mosley, p. 167.
126 "this false information . . ." Churchill, *The Second World War*, Vol. 4, p. 490.
126 *"Zip* now equal . . ." *ibid.*, p. 489.
126 "The assault force . . ." Rommel, p. 277.
127 ". . . the British command . . ." *ibid.*, p. 284.
127 "proceed methodically . . ." de Guingand interview.

6. EL ALAMEIN

Sources

U.S. Naval Institute Proceedings, *The Italian Navy in World War II*, Annapolis: U.S. Naval Institute, 1957; C-in-C U.S. Naval Forces, Northwest African Waters, to C-in-C U.S. Fleet, "Recommendation for Special Organization for Deceptive Warfare," with staff memorandum re "Special Operations" and "Organization and Function of 'A-Force,'" in Records of the USJCS, CCS 434/2, MMR, NA; Documents relating to the security of Torch, Record Group 218, Records of the USJCS, CCS 334, JSC, NA; Sundry documents in The Goodfellow Papers, an OSS collection, HI.

Notes

page
128 "He was . . ." Slessor interview.
130 "Well there it is." De Guingand interview.
131 "the enemy would become . . ." Barkas, p. 202.
137 "a heavy heart," *et seq.*, Rommel, p. 293.
138 "Don't worry . . ." *et seq.*, Desmond Young, pp. 147–48.
138 "But really . . ." Warlimont, p. 298.
143 "To Field Marshal Rommel . . ." *et seq.*, Rommel, pp. 320–21.
144 "Whether I survive . . ." *ibid.*, p. 363.
144 "There was . . ." *et seq.*, *ibid.*, p. 365.
145 "Generals who had . . ." Bullock, p. 689.
145 *Herr Generalfeldmarschall . . ."* L Document 44499, August 17, 1944, OSS German Section, MMR, NA.
145 "You must excuse me . . ." Desmond Young, p. 155.
145 "Flying back . . ." Rommel, p. 369.
146–47 "I should have . . ." *et seq.*, Desmond Young, pp. 161–62.

PART II: THE ROOTS OF CONSPIRACY

1. CANARIS

Sources

Items from the OSS file on Canaris, CIA Headquarters, Langley, Virginia; *Log of the Coaler* Baden (companion to *Dresden*), OUP, in English, perhaps a translation by The Admiralty, IWM; "Extracts from the Log of the *Dresden*," with "Comments," *Naval Review*, undated, IWM; Oberstleutnant-zur-See Canaris, "Aktenvermark," October 5, 1915, a personal report of the *Dresden* engagement and escape from South America, Box 431 PG75155, Kriegsmarine Archives, Freiburg; Account of the ambush of U-35 by Commandant Pradeau, in *Les marines, sociaux et politiques d'un ancien Officier de Marine*, OUP, undated, FC; Adm. Arnauld de la Perière, "Account of the Ambush of U-35," FC; Lt. Cdr. Arnauld, "Transfer of Lt. Commander Canaris off Cartagena," OUP, 1916, Kriegsmarine Archives, Freiburg; "Bericht Kapitänleutnant Canaris über Abholung durch 'U-35,' von Trefflinie bei Cap Tinoso," a signed report of his escape from Cartagena by Canaris to the Admiralstab, undated, Box 161 PG61579, Kriegsmarine Archives, Freiburg; H. B. Gisevius, "Admiral Canaris, die Sphinx der deutschen Spionage," *Weltwoche*, March 1, 1946; Helmut Krausnick, "Aus den Personalakten von Canaris," Vol. 10, No. 3, July 1962, Institut für Zeitgeschichte, Munich; *Outbreak of Hostilities Between Britain and Germany*, British Blue Book, London: HMSO, 1940; ONI, "Reports on Lieutenant Commander Wilhelm Canaris," a file of attaché reports dated April–July 1928, Record Group 38, Records of the Office of the Chief of Naval Operations, OMR, NA.

Notes

epigraph
"Gehlen: Don't you think . . ." A conversation between General Reinhard Gehlen and General Edwin L. Sibert, Room 303, Army and Navy Club, Washington, D.C., November 1968.

page
151   "If England wants . . ." Bullock, p. 548.
151   "Naturally . . ." Colvin, *Canaris*, Maidstone, U.K.: George Mann, 1973, p. 95.
152   "I am speaking . . ." *The Times*, London, September 4, 1939.
153   "I must warn you . . ." Colvin, *Master Spy*, p. 55.
155   "inefficient, intriguing . . ." Lohan interview.
155   "grey fox . . ." Wheeler-Bennett, *Nemesis of Power*, p. 598.
155   "trapeze artist . . ." Louis Rivet, "L'énigme du service renseignements allemands sous le régime hitlérien," *Revue de Défense Nationale*, July 1947, Paris.
155   "extraordinarily intelligent . . ." Marras interrogation, OSS Bern, February 7, 1945, in OSS file on Canaris, *op. cit.*

page
155 "I have ascertained . . ." Colvin, *Master Spy*, p. 256.
155 "Canaris betrayed . . ." Skorzeny interview.
155 "served the enemy . . ." Colvin, *Master Spy*, p. 256.
155 "one of the bravest . . ." Dulles interview.
155 "shrouded even now . . ." Gehlen, p. 27.
156 "He is one . . ." Zeller, p. 24.
156 "damned brave . . ." Menzies interview.
157 "spies and assassins . . ." Rowan and Deindorfer, p. 62.
158 "kill or capture," Menzies interview.
161 "What I want," Fleming, p. 194.
162 "reasonable and sees . . ." Colvin, *Canaris, op. cit.*, p. 39.
162 "The 'Canaris group' . . ." Interrogation of Franz Maria Liedig, an extract from *Interim* (British army intelligence review), "The German Intelligence Branch and 20th July," No. 14, December 17, 1945, in the private collection of a former MI-6 officer.
162 "It is difficult . . ." J. R. R. Tolkien, *The Lord of the Rings*, London: Allen & Unwin, 1966, p. 171.

2. THE SCHWARZE KAPELLE

Sources

In addition to the sources cited in the Bibliography, information concerning the Schwarze Kapelle in this chapter and throughout the book has been derived from: Interrogations by U.S. Army Historical Section, Germany, of Leading German Generals, SC; SHAEF Counterintelligence Sub-Division, G2, Evaluation and Dissemination Section Report No. 12, "Anti-Nazi Groups in Germany and Austria," February 6, 1945, MMR, NA; Albert Speer, Interrogation Report 19, "Politicians and Politics in Nazi Germany," U.S. Group Control, Office of the Director of Intelligence, Field Information Agency (Technical), January 1946, MMR, NA; Otto A. W. John, "Some Facts and Aspects of the Plot Against Hitler," undated memorandum, OUP, HI; Berlin District Interrogation Center, Consolidated Interrogation Report, "The Political and Social Background of the 20th July Incident," September 10, 1945, *World War II, Underground Movements, Germany,* OCMH; Gen. Georg von Sodenstern, *Events Leading Up to 20th July 1944,* Ms. No. B499, undated, OCMH; Günther Blumentritt, *20 July 1944,* Ms. No. B272, circa 1946, OCMH; Rudolph von Gersdorff, *History of the Attempt on Hitler's Life,* Ms. No. A855, circa 1946, OCMH; Erich Zimmermann and Hans-Adolf Jacobsen, eds., *Germans Against Hitler, 20 July 1944,* Bonn: Press and Information Office of the Federal Government of Germany, 1960; Franz von Papen, "The Schwarze Kapelle and 20th July as Seen from the German Diplomatic Service," OUP, no date but circa 1945–46, located in an MI-6 collection, CIAP; Walter Huppenkothen, "Chief SS Interrogator's Report on the Aims, Connections and Personalities of Members of the Plot Against Hitler," OUP, no date, possibly an MI-6 interrogation, CIAP; F. L. Belin, "Hitler's Generals," OSS promulgation, November 10, 1942, MMR, NA; Johannes Blaskowitz, "Strife Between German Military and Political Powers," State Department

Interrogation Report, OSS German Section, MMR, NA; Horace Schacht, "How Hitler Came to Power," "Schacht's Attempt at Putsch," "Failure of the German General Staff to Keep Its Oath and Curb Hitler," State Department, Special Interrogation Report, September 25, 1945, OSS German Section, MMR, NA; OSS Switzerland, Report No. 34495, "Background of Attack upon Hitler," OSS German Section, MMR, NA; *Documents on German Foreign Policy, 1918–1945*, Series D, Vols. 4 and 8, 1951 and 1954, Washington, D.C.; "Judgment in the Trials of Walter Huppenkothen," Bavarian Landesgericht, February 1951 and November 1952, HI; OSS R&A Report No. 2458, "The Process of the Collapse of the German Armies," August 29, 1944, SDDLRS, NA.

Sources pertaining to this chapter in particular include: Hans Speidel, *Beck Against Hitler,* an undated monograph, OCMH; Fabian von Schlabrendorff, "Gestapo Report of the Investigation into the Indictment of Fritsch," Appendix, Schlabrendorff, *The Secret War Against Hitler;* Office of the U.S. Chief of Counsel for War Crimes, Sundry testimonies, interrogation summaries and interrogation reports of W. Schellenberg, November 1945–January 1947, MMR, NA.

Notes

page
163   "sole bearer of . . ." Wheeler-Bennett, *Nemesis of Power*, p. 334.
164   "Orders of a superior . . ." Shulman, pp. 9, 11.
164   "General Beck . . ." Liedig interrogation, *op. cit.*
165   "I wonder why . . ." *et seq.*, attributed to Bredow in O'Neill.
166   "The events of . . ." *et seq.*, Liedig interrogation, *op. cit.*
166   "It may be . . ." Goerlitz, p. 289.
168   "I swear by God . . ." Wheeler-Bennett, *Nemesis of Power*, p. 339.
168   "This is a fateful . . ." Gisevius, p. 279.

3. FRIEND OR FOE

Sources

Walter Tachuppik, "Canaris und Heydrich," *Die Zeitung,* November 7, 1941.

Notes

page
170   "does not love . . ." *et seq.*, Deacon, pp. 272–73.
172   "such matters as . . ." Menzies interview.
174   "Party Member Reinhard . . ." Höhne, p. 192.
174   "incredibly acute . . ." Schellenberg, p. 30.

4. THE PLOT BEGINS

Notes

page
180   "Hitler's criminal procedure . . ." Liedig interrogation, *op. cit.*
181   "my daily bread . . ." *et seq.,* Bullock, pp. 32, 34.
181   "Why didn't you . . ." *et seq.,* Goerlitz, p. 326.
183   "A war begun . . ." *ibid.,* p. 339.
183   "The elimination of . . ." Report of Gen. George C. Marshall, Chief of Staff, United States Army, to the President of the United States, November 6, 1945, Library of Congress, Washington, D.C.
183   "The only one . . ." Deutsch, p. 90.
185   "through yielding to . . ." *et seq.,* Colvin, *Master Spy,* p. 67.
185   "Everything is decided . . ." *et seq., ibid.,* p. 70.
186   "utmost frankness and . . ." Wheeler-Bennett, *Nemesis of Power,* p. 411.
186   "I am as certain . . ." *ibid.,* p. 412.
186   "I have found . . ." Colvin, *Master Spy,* p. 72.
187   "What he . . ." *et seq., ibid.,* p. 75.
187   "rivalries, prejudices . . ." Liedig interrogation, *op. cit.*

5. THE OUTBREAK OF WAR

Sources

Reports of the U.S. Military Attaché at Berlin, 1929–41 OMR, NA; Reports of the Director of Military Intelligence to the Chief of Staff of the U.S. Army, 1919–1939, OMR, NA; Statement by G. J. Sas to Deinstag, Report 2128/58, March 16, 1948, Institut für Zeitgeschichte, Munich.

Notes

page
189   ". . . Hitler's mental condition" *et seq.,* Dilks, pp. 141, 143.
189   "Hitler's death . . ." *et seq., The Times,* citing *Der Spiegel,* London, August 5, 1971.
190   "We were being . . ." Dilks, pp. 166–67.
190   "Shortly before I . . ." McLachlan, p. 245.
191   "officers of the military . . ." The diary of General Sir James Marshall-Cornwall, excerpts provided the author by Marshall-Cornwall.
192   "Hitler had decided . . ." *et seq.,* Aster, pp. 235–36.
192   "a good deal . . ." *et seq.,* Marshall-Cornwall diary, *op. cit.*
193   "There will probably . . ." Shirer, *The Rise and Fall of the Third Reich,* p. 41.

page
193   "I have struck . . ." Wheeler-Bennett, *Nemesis of Power*, p. 446.
194   "Our enemies . . ." *et seq.*, Bullock, p. 526.
194   "bloodthirsty thanks . . ." International Military Tribunal, Document No. L-3 PS 798, NA.
194   "Have no pity . . ." *et seq.*, Bullock, p. 527.
195   "greatest strategist . . ." H. R. Trevor-Roper, "The Mind of Adolf Hitler," in Hitler, p. xxv.
195   "Peace has been . . ." Wheeler-Bennett, *Nemesis of Power*, p. 451.

6. CONSPIRACY AT THE VATICAN

Sources

Reports of the U.S. Military Attaché at Rome, 1939–41, OMR, NA; George O. Kent, "Pius XII and Germany: Some Aspects of German-Vatican Relations 1933–43," *American Historical Review*, 70 (1964); Dr. Josef Mueller, Sundry statements re Canaris and Heydrich, OUP, undated, Vols. 14B, 15, 16A, 17, 18D, Dr. Mueller, FC.

Notes

page
197   "One day . . ." International Military Tribunal, Document No. 3047–PS 769, NA.
197   "these things," Liedig interrogation, *op. cit.*
199   "An eagle hunts . . ." *et seq.*, Boveri, p. 248.
200   "It is Hitler . . ." Deutsch, p. 117.
201   "The German Opposition . . ." *ibid.*, p. 121.
201   "The Pope is . . ." *ibid.*, p. 120.
204   *"Schmarren,"* *et seq.*, *ibid.*, p. 134.
205   "Cannot someone put . . ." *ibid.*, p. 196.
205   "human being and . . ." *ibid.*, p. 197.
205   "We have no . . ." *ibid.*, p. 224.

7. THE VENLO INCIDENT

Sources

MID Papers, WDGS, German Section, 1939–41, OMR, NA.

Notes

page
207   "The political overthrow . . ." Schellenberg, p. 89.
207   "encouraged," *et seq.*, Menzies interview.
207   "marvellous oysters," Schellenberg, p. 90.

page
208   "on the highest . . ." Menzies interview.
209   "Several old Party . . ." *et seq.*, Schellenberg, p. 94.
211   "bloodier than the Somme." Gubbins interview.

8. "ADROIT INTRIGUE"

Sources

Command and Commanders in Modern War: Harold C. Deutsch, "The Rise of the Military Opposition in the Nazi Reich," with commentary by Charles V. P. von Luttichau and Peter Parct; and Walter Warlimont, *et al.*, "The Military View," Proceedings of the Second Military History Symposium, USAF Academy, May 2–3, 1968. Also Karl Brandt, "The German Resistance in American Perspective," an address at the memorial convocation for the dead of July 20, 1944, July 20, 1954; S. J. Sas, "Het hegon in Mei 1940," *Der Spiegel*, Hamburg, October 7 and 15, 1953; General Adolf Heusinger, "Military Participation in the Conspiracy of 20 July 44," Final Interrogation Report No. 30, January 10, 1946, HQ USFET Military Intelligence Service Center, SC.

Notes

page
212–13   "violent, bitter . . ." *et seq.*, Donald Watt and Ian Colvin, "1940s Anti-Nazis Who Never Were," *Daily Telegraph*, London, January 1 and 2, 1971.
213   "the long-awaited . . ." Deutsch, p. 289.
213   *"Conditio sine qua . . ." et seq., ibid.*, pp. 294–95.
213   "contained a broad . . ." *et seq., ibid.*, pp. 296–98. Mueller's recollections of his negotiations at the Vatican were related to the author in an interview before the publication of the Deutsch account.
214   "unusually serious . . ." *ibid.*, citing Halder interview, p. 312.
214   "You should not . . ." *et seq., ibid.*
215   "carefully formulated," *et seq., ibid.*, pp. 336–37.
216   "wangle a botched-up . . ." Watt and Colvin, citing Cabinet Minutes, *op. cit.*
216   "No German . . ." Deutsch, citing Leiber interview, p. 340.
216   "deep in the ink," *et seq., ibid.*, pp. 343–44.
217   "his own *gendarme*," *ibid.*, citing Neuhausler interview, p. 344.
218   "he could not . . ." *et seq., ibid.*, pp. 345–46.
219   "well-wishing German . . ." R. V. Jones, "Scientific Intelligence," *Journal of the Royal United Services Institute*, February 19, 1947.
220   "Tremendous strides . . ." General Board, U.S. Forces, Europe, "V2 Rocket Attacks and Defenses," a report on the characteristics and effectiveness of the German A-4 (V2) long-range rocket, Anti-aircraft Artillery Section, 1945, OCMH.
220   "It seemed quite . . ." Cockburn interview.
223   "There is no . . ." Deutsch, pp. 99–100.

page
224   "to cause . . ." Liedig interrogation, *op. cit.*
224   "funeral banquet," *et seq.,* Deutsch, pp. 328–29.
225   "complete tactical surprise . . ." Churchill, *The Second World War,* Vol. 2, p. 30.

9. CANARIS AT WORK

Sources

OSS Dublin Reports Nos. A2630-1-2-3-4-5, March 11, 1943, MMR, NA; OSS Report No. N5400, "German Espionage in Ireland," March 16, 1944, MMR, NA; Military Intelligence Division, War Department General Staff, "Ireland," a report by the Military Attaché, Dublin, July 26, 1944, MMR, NA; OSS file on Canaris, *op. cit.;* Gen. Walter Warlimont, "The Führer's Headquarters," Interrogation Report No. 9, October 24, 1945, HQ USFET Military Intelligence Service Center, SC.

Notes

page
226   "I appeal . . ." *et seq.,* Bullock, p. 592.
228   "(If we could) . . ." Delmer, *Black Boomerang,* p. 137.
229   "I am sorry . . ." *ibid.*
230   "You know . . ." Liss interview.
230   *"fons et origo,"* Masterman, p. 36.
232–33 "the German forces . . ." *et seq.,* Fleming, p. 179.
233   "with the certainty . . ." *et seq.,* Farago, *The Game of the Foxes,* p. 223.
233   "had some connection . . ." *et seq.,* Fleming, p. 182.
234   "rotten to its . . ." Farago, citing Goetz's "testament," *The Game of the Foxes,* p. 224.
234   "German agents have . . ." OSS R&A Report No. 2087, "An Introduction to the Irish Problem," May 23, 1944, MMR, NA.
236   "strange old buzzard," *et seq.,* Farago, *The Game of the Foxes,* p. 513.
237   "The admiral asks . . ." *et seq.,* Colvin, *Master Spy,* p. 149.
237–38 "sought to overbear . . ." *et seq., ibid.,* p. 151.
238   ". . . in Spain (Canaris) . . ." *ibid.,* p. 155.
239   "destroy Yugoslavia . . ." *et seq.,* Bullock, p. 635.

10. THE ASSASSINATION OF HEYDRICH

Sources

Files of the Personal Staff of the Reichsführer SS, Group T-175, NA; General Files, SS, Koblenz and Freiburg; Berlin Documents Center, Microfilm Groups 580–611, NA; Ernst Kaltenbrunner, "The Kaltenbrunner Report," edited by the

Archiv Peter für Historische und Zeitgeschichtliche Dokumentation, Stuttgart; Sundry interrogations of W. Schellenberg, *op. cit.*

Notes

page
242 "secret documents prepared . . ." Amort and Jedlicka, Introduction.
244 "the section dealing . . ." *ibid.*, p. 122.
245 "political unreliability," *et seq.*, Walter Schellenberg, *War Room: 14.8.45 Brigadeführer SS Schellenberg, Autobiography, Compiled During His Stay in Stockholm June 1945,* OUP, in the collection of a former MI-6 officer.
245 "Heydrich's Decalogue," Amort and Jedlicka, p. 147.
251 "was one . . ." Manvell and Fraenkel, *Himmler,* pp. 139–40.
251 "your murdered chief," *et seq.*, Schellenberg, p. 336.
251 "deceptive features . . ." Hohne, citing Dr. Bernard Wehner, p. 560.
251 "choked with emotion," *et seq.*, Schellenberg, p. 338.
251 "almost feminine . . ." Alan Bullock, citing "Herr Harprecht, a young German journalist," in the Introduction to Schellenberg, p. 15.
252 "A live spy . . ." Masterman, p. 54.

11. OPERATION FLASH

Sources

CSDIC, Report SRGG 1347, "A Conversation Between General Eberbach and General Blumentritt," August 19, 1945, in a private collection, CIAP; *Field Marshal Günther von Kluge,* Form 201, OCMH; European Command, United States Army, Ethint 5, "An Interview with General W. Warlimont, Circumstances of the 20th July Incident: Was Von Kluge a Traitor?" August 3, 1945, MMR, NA; "Statement by M. Wallenberg," *Svenska Dagbladet,* Stockholm, September 4, 1947; Hans-Adolf Jacobsen, ed., *July 20, 1944, The German Opposition to Hitler as Viewed by Foreign Historians,* Bonn: Press and Information Office of the Federal Government of Germany, 1969; Charles de Cosse-Brissac, "Collapse of the Wehrmacht," *Revue de Défense Nationale,* Paris, March 1946; Martin Blumenson and J. Hodgson, "Hitler Versus His Generals in the West," *United States Naval Institute Proceedings,* 82: 1036–1287; Gen. Rudolph Baron von Gersdorff, "Events Leading Up to Planned Attempt on Hitler's Life on 15 March 1943," Intermediate Interrogation Report No. 34, HQ USFET Military Intelligence Service Center, SC.

Notes

page
253–54 "the strongest terms," *et seq.*, Schellenberg, p. 198.
254 "could see . . ." Alan Clark, *Barbarossa,* p. 206.
255 "vain, cowardly," Goebbels, p. 92.

page

255 "Gone were the days . . ." Wheeler-Bennett, *Nemesis of Power*, p. 526.

256 "Half my nervous . . ." Halder, p. 57.

257 "On the basis . . ." Speer, pp. 325–26.

257 "We didn't even . . ." *ibid.*

258 "To land first . . . " McLachlan, p. 82.

258 "The real triumph . . ." Masterman, p. 110.

259 "Once again . . ." Speer, pp. 325–26.

259 "Had the enemy . . ." *et seq.*, Roskill, Vol. 2, p. 213.

260 "Gibraltar received . . ." Colvin, *Master Spy*, p. 187.

260 "Stalingrad is no longer . . ." Alan Clark, *Barbarossa*, p. 269.

263 "Gentlemen . . ." Rundstedt, *et al.*, Ms. No. B633, *op. cit.*, Annex II, Part 2.

264 "But, my dear Führer . . ." *ibid.*

264 "I am a soldier . . ." *et seq.*, Moll, p. 73.

267 "As always, . . ." Fabian von Schlabrendorff, "Our Two Tries to Kill Hitler," *Saturday Evening Post*, July 20, 1946.

PART III: HIGH STRATEGY AND LOW TACTICS

1. CASABLANCA

Sources

Anfa Reports and Minutes in CCS/JCS files, MMR, NA; Reports and Minutes of the 55th–60th meetings of the Combined Chiefs of Staff, MMR, NA; USJCS, draft history, *The War against Germany*, Part 3, "Casablanca through Trident," Record Group 218, Records of the USJCS, MMR, NA; Report by Joint Strategic Survey Committee, "German Strategy in 1943," February 10, 1943, Record Group 218, Records of the USJCS, JSC 214, MMR, NA; "Germany (12-10-42)," Sec. I, Record Group 218, Records of the USJCS, CCS 381, MMR, NA.

Notes

epigraph

" 'Cover' was carried . . ." attributed to Churchill.

page

274 "They swarmed down . . ." Matloff and Snell, *1943–1944*, p. 107.

274 "In matters touching . . ." Ingersoll, p. 71.

275 "kind of dark . . ." Alanbrooke, Vol. 1, p. 540.

275 "opposed as much . . ." *et seq.*, Matloff and Snell, *1943–1944*, p. 25.

276 "I heard the words . . ." *et seq.*, Sherwood, p. 696.

276 "If you were given . . ." R. E. Dupuy, *Men of West Point*, New York: Sloane, 1952, p. 324.

276 "its effect was . . ." John Slessor, "Grand Strategy and the Second World War," *The Listener*, London, November 22, 1956.

page

276 "the despairing ferocity . . ." Menzies interview.
277 "There is much . . ." *et seq.*, Popov, p. 245.
277 "can be . . ." *et seq., ibid.*, p. 246.
277 "You know, my dear . . ." Colvin, *Master Spy*, p. 193.
277 "Now no honorable . . ." Armstrong, p. 133.
278 "extraordinary dangers," *ibid.*, p. 162.
278 "To compel . . ." *ibid.*, p. 167.

2. THE BATTLE OF THE ATLANTIC

Sources

"Report of the Proceedings of Convoy SC122," OAB; "Report of the Proceedings of Convoy HX229," OAB; "Reports of Commander Task Force 24," U.S. Atlantic Fleet, April 13, 1942, OAB; "Report of the Flag Officer, *Newfoundland*," to the Secretary, Naval Board, Ottawa, OAB; A collection of signals from C-in-C Western Atlantic to escorts, 1943, OAB; Excerpts from the *History of the U.S. 21st Weather Reporting Squadron*, USAF Historical Branch, MAFB; Intelligence Division, Chief of Naval Operations, "Ifni Radio Station Intelligence Reports," June 28, 1943, MMR, NA; OSS Collected Reports on German Radio and Weather-Reporting Stations, October 1, 1942, to February 5, 1944, MMR, NA; *The U.S. Coast Guard in World War II*, Washington, D.C.: Government Printing Office, 1944–53; C-in-C Allied Naval Expeditionary Force, "Operation Neptune Weather Criteria," OAB; Gen. R. E. Lee, U.S. Military Attaché, London, "Interception of Axis Weather Reports," Report to the MID, Washington, D.C., May 31, 1941, Record Group 165, Records of the WDGSS, OMR, NA; Canadian Intelligence Service, "Meteorological Security," with "Report on Arctic Operations," Record Group 218, Records of the USJCS, CCS 385, MMR, NA; Office of Naval History, *A History of Etappes*, OAB.

Notes

page

279 "groping and drowning . . ." attributed to Churchill.
280 "dreadfully emaciated," *et seq.*, Oliver Knox interview.
281 "national calamity," Wingate interview.
281 "The service he . . ." "Report on the Death of A. D. Knox to the Fellows of King's," King's College, Cambridge (John Saltmarsh, Historian).
282 "German heroism . . ." Germany to North America, November 20, 1942, FBIS, FCC, NA.
282 "Our submarines . . ." Flower and Reeves, p. 418.
282 "The new-moon night . . ." Wolfgang Frank, p. 116.
283 "American impetuosity . . ." Slessor interview.
286 "a serious disaster . . ." Roskill, Vol. 2, p. 366.
286 "the Germans never . . ." *et seq., ibid.*, pp. 367–68.

page
288   "After examining all . . ." *ibid.,* p. 364.
288   "the combination . . ." *ibid.,* Vol. 3, p. 16.
289   "descendant of . . ." *ibid.,* p. 64.
290   "the whole great . . ." *ibid.,* p. 68.
290   "one of the most . . ." *ibid.,* p. 69.
291   "I noticed . . ." *ibid.,* p. 86.
291   "No more mortifying . . ." *The Times,* London, February 17, 1942.
291   "We shall fight . . ." Roskill, Vol. 3, p. 87.
292   "accurate intelligence . . ." *ibid.,* p. 88.
292   "If really bad . . ." Eisenhower, *Crusade in Europe,* p. 240.

3. THE LCS AND PLAN JAEL

Sources

R. E. L. Wingate, A memorandum to the author on the history, structure, authority, responsibilities and working methods of the London Controlling Section; SHAEF SGS 381, Pre-Invasion File, MMR, NA; SHAEF, *A short History of COSSAC 1943–1944, op. cit.;* Plan Cockade, SHAEF G2 202BX/2/Int, in SHAEF Pre-Invasion File; Plan Zeppelin, SHAEF 18209/Ops (b), in SHAEF Pre-Invasion File; Helmuth Greiner, The Greiner Series: "OKW World War II," Ms. No. C-065b, SHAEF Historical Division, OCMH; JCS Memorandum, "Deception Policy 1943 Covering Germany and Italy," March 22, 1943, Record Group 218, Records of the USJCS, CCS 184/1, MMR, NA; "Deception Policy 1943 (Germany and Italy)," (Final), April 3, 1943, Record Group 218, Records of the USJCS, CCS 184/3, MMR, NA; William J. Donovan, Director, OSS, Memorandum to the USJCS, "Overall Strategic Plan for U.S. Psychological Warfare," *op. cit.;* OSS, Psychological Warfare Analysis, January–September 1943, OUP, Record Group 218, Records of the USJCS, MMR, NA; Col. H. D. Kehm, memorandum for the Assistant Chief of Staff, OPD, WDGS, "Conference on Deception," May 29, 1943, Record Group 218, Records of the USJCS, MMR, NA; OUP, possibly OPD, Memorandum to the USJCS, "Final Report for the Washington Anglo-American Cover and Deception Conference, June 2, 1943," Record Group 218, Records of the USJCS, CCS 385, MMR, NA; Gen. A. C. Wedemeyer, for JSC, "Deception Planning and Execution," Record Group 218, Records of the USJCS, MMR, NA.

Notes

page
300   "Colonel Bevan played . . ." Deane interview.
300–01 "I do not think . . ." Bevan interview.
301   "Bevan and Churchill . . ." Baumer interview.
301   "most famous political . . ." Charles Graves, *Leather Armchairs,* New York: Coward-McCann (1964), p. 13.
301   "think nine ways . . ." Baumer interview.
302   "preoccupied not so much . . ." *et seq.,* Sampson, pp. 202, 203.

page

303 "collecting old scientific . . ." *Who's Who,* London: A. & C. Black, 1970.

304 "waves of confusing . . ." Greiner, *op. cit.*

305 "perfect oil-can," Moran, p. 121.

305 "to induce the . . ." SHAEF, *A Short History of COSSAC, op. cit.*

305 "contain the maximum . . ." Plan Cockade, *op. cit.*

4. MINCEMEAT

Notes

page

309 "One has to be . . ." *et seq.,* Warlimont, pp. 326–27.

309 "Here is where . . ." *et seq., ibid.,* p. 341.

309–10 ". . . the shadow of . . ." Deakin, p. 176.

310 "Anybody but a damned . . ." Wingate interview.

312 "Colonel R. Meinertzhagen . . ." Wingate interview.

313 "once and for . . ." Richard Meinertzhagen, *Army Diary 1899–1926,* London: Oliver & Boyd, 1960, p. 224.

313 "Why shouldn't we . . ." Montagu, p. 25.

315 "the body was . . ." *ibid.,* p. 30.

316 "He is quiet . . ." *et seq., ibid.,* p. 65.

318–19 "I regard the situation . . ." Deakin, p. 194.

320 "a wholly reliable . . ." *ibid.,* p. 347.

320 "Following the impending . . ." *ibid.,* p. 348.

5. QUEBEC

Sources

CCS Trident Meeting, *Official Trident Conference Book,* MMR, NA; CCS Quadrant Meeting, *Official Quadrant Conference Book,* MMR, NA; Gen. Thomas T. Handy, "Conduct of the War in Europe," Memorandum to the USJCS, Record Group 218, Records of the USJCS, MMR, NA.

Notes

page

323 "to delay Germany's . . ." CCS 135/1, 135/2, CCS 134, January 4, 1943, Record Group 218, Records of the USJCS, MMR, NA.

324 "disturbed," *et seq.,* Pogue, *George C. Marshall,* Vol. 3, p. 187.

324 "about who . . ." Arthur H. Vandenberg, Jr. (ed.), *The Private Papers of Arthur H. Vandenberg,* Boston: Houghton Mifflin, 1952, pp. 48–49.

324 "In preparing for . . ." Matloff and Snell, *1943–1944,* p. 217.

page
325 "able to justify . . ." *ibid.*, p. 216.
325 "We cannot now . . ." *et seq.*, Stimson and Bundy, pp. 436–38.
326 "very undiplomatic language . . ." Leahy, p. 175.
326 "took the offensive," *et seq.*, Quadrant Conference Book.
327 "belt buckle . . ." Morgan interview.
327 "entire US-UK strategic . . ." *et seq.*, Matloff and Snell, *1943–1944*, p. 221.
327 "opportunistic," Quadrant Conference Book.
327 "gloomy and unpleasant . . ." *et seq.*, Alanbrooke, Vol. 1, pp. 705–7.
328 "Our talk was . . ." *ibid.*, p. 708.
328 "To my great . . ." *ibid.*, p. 710.
329 "feeling the inevitable . . ." *ibid.*, p. 718.
329 "I knew that . . ." Churchill, *The Second World War*, Vol. 5, p. 514.
330 "I never again . . ." MacDonald, p. 178.
331 "Evidently a most critical . . ." Churchill, *The Second World War*, Vol. 5, p. 126.

6. THE SCHWARZE KAPELLE (1943)

Sources

Sundry interrogations of W. Schellenberg, *op. cit.*; A collection dealing with various aspects of the plot against Hitler, including CSDIC reports, reports by various agencies including OSS and MI-6, almost wholly immediately postwar in origin, OUP, possibly MI-6, CIAP; State Department Special Interrogation Report, "Conversations of Fritz Kolbe with Harold C. Vedeler: Activity as an Allied Agent During the War, Personalities and Agencies in the Foreign Office, Activities of Sofindus," September 23–24, 1945, Wiesbaden, SDA, NA; OSS Report No. A27627 Concerning Baron Hoyningen-Huene, April 11, 1944, MMR, NA; "Peace Overtures," a collection of documents relating to anti-Nazi peace gestures, Record Group 218, Records of the USJCS, MMR, NA.

Notes

page
334 "Since the generals . . ." *et seq.*, Kramarz, p. 122.
336–37 "could not bring . . ." Bethge, p. 704.
337 "counter-espionage," *ibid.*, p. 713.
337 "Drones Club." Bartz, p. 125.
338 "The only thing . . ." Bethge, p. 815.
339 "During the years . . ." Schellenberg, pp. 407–8.
339 "a matter of serious . . ." *et seq.*, *ibid.*, p. 406.
339 "were reassuring," *et seq.*, *ibid.*, p. 407.
340 "Be pleased to . . ." Alanbrooke, Vol. 1, p. 726.
341 "I was able . . ." *et seq.*, Schellenberg, p. 407.
341 "You would be as . . ." Wheeler-Bennett, *Nemesis of Power*, pp. 570 ff.
342 "not interested." *ibid.*, p. 574.

page
342 "must be removed . . ." attributed to Kluge in Zeller.
343 "to persuade . . ." Dulles, citing a memorandum from Jacob Wallenberg, *Germany's Underground*, p. 142.
344 "I should be glad . . ." *et seq., ibid.*
344 ". . . the group's leaders . . ." Liedig interrogation, *op. cit.*
346 "Philby's job . . ." Page, *et al.*, p. 159.
347 "And what a yield . . ." Dulles interview.
347 "Sincerely regret . . ." Dulles, *Secret Surrender*, p. 23.
348 ". . . the *Wehrmacht* . . ." *et seq.*, John, p. 128.
348–49 "she told me . . ." *ibid.*, p. 134.
350 "There is no doubt . . ." Sherwood, p. 791.

7. STARKEY

Sources

SHAEF G2, SHAEF/201DX/3/Int, *Enemy Reactions to Tindall*, MMR, NA; COSSAC/44DX/Int, *Enemy Reactions to Wadham*, MMR, NA; COSSAC/41DX /Int, *Enemy Reactions to Starkey*, MMR, NA; HQ 12th Army Group, *Operation Wadham*, in SHAEF SGS 381, Pre-Invasion File, *op. cit.*; SHAEF G6, *BBC Warnings to Resistance Groups*, File No. 000.77-I, MMR, NA; Intelligence Branch, COSSAC 182X, in SHAEF SGS 381, Pre-Invasion File, *op. cit.*; Gen. J. E. Upton, Deputy Chief, Theater Group, OPD, WDGS, Memorandum to Gen. Handy and Gen. Hull, "Tactical Report on Air Operations from Great Britain, September 1943," October 10, 1943, OPD (Great Britain) file, MMR, NA; Memorandum from London, CM-In-7887, to OPD, WDGS, "8th Air Force Operations during 9th September 1943, Dispatched in Support of Special Operation Starkey," September 10, 1943, OPD (Great Britain) file, MMR, NA; OPD (France), Record Group 165, Records of the WDGSS, MMR, NA; Selected AFHQ Records, WNRC.

Notes

page
352 "There was a certain . . ." Wingate interview.
353 "an elaborate camouflage . . ." *et seq.*, SHAEF, *A Short History of COSSAC, op. cit.*
354–55 "the deception by . . ." *et seq., Operation Cockade*, PWE Plan, COS (43) 384 (o) July 18, 1943, in COSSAC/41DX/Int, *op. cit.*
357 ". . . the PWE plan . . ." Jacob L. Devers, in a letter to George V. Strong, August 24, 1943, in COSSAC/41DX/Int, *op. cit.*
358 "Will someone . . ." Frederick Morgan, a note in HQ 12th Army Group, *Operation Wadham, op. cit.*
358 "An unofficial source . . ." Director of Press and Publicity, War Office Report, August 19–25, 1943, in Intelligence Branch, COSSAC/ 182X, *op. cit.*
358 ". . . the liberation of . . ." *New York Times*, August 19, 1943.

page
358   "may come any day . . ." *et seq.*, Press Digest, in COSSAC/41DX/
       Int, *op. cit.*
358   "before the leaves . . ." Director of Press and Publicity, War Office
       Report, *op. cit.*
359   "ARMIES READY . . ." *New York Times*, August 19, 1943.
359–60 "discontinue," *et seq.*, in COSSAC/41DX/Int, *op. cit.*
360   "suggested," *et seq.*, Brig. H. Redman, British Joint Staff Mission,
       Offices of the CCS, Washington, D.C., to Gen. John R. Deane, "Cock-
       ade Directive," Record Group 218, Records of the USJCS, CCS 385,
       MMR, NA.
361–62 "disappointing manner," *et seq.*, in COSSAC/41DX/Int, *op. cit.*
362   "What is all . . ." Delmer, *The Counterfeit Spy*, p. 87.
362   ". . . it would appear . . ." in COSSAC/41DX/Int, *op. cit.*
362   "The movements . . ." Liddell Hart, *The German Generals Talk*,
       p. 231.
363   "practically denuded," in COSSAC/41DX/Int, *op. cit.*
364   "balls-up," Morgan interview.

8. PROSPER

Sources

Maj. Gen. Sir Colin Gubbins, "Resistance Movements in the War," Lecture to
the RUSI, January 28, 1948; William J. Donovan to Brig. Gen. John R. Deane,
"A Proposal to Make Use of Certain Facilities and the Services of Certain
Persons in France and America with a View to Aiding the War Effort," February 20, 1943, Record Group 218, Records of the USJCS, MMR, NA.

Notes

page
366   "of formed bodies . . ." *et seq.*, Foot, p. 4.
367   "And now set . . ." *ibid.*, p. 11.
367   "stabbing attacks," *et seq.*, *ibid.*, p. 12.
368   "a skein so . . ." Deacon, p. 344.
369   "brave, ambitious . . ." Foot, p. 198.
370   "the persevering efforts . . ." *ibid.*
371   "at least one . . ." *ibid.*, p. 290.
374   "95 per cent . . ." *ibid.*, p. 121.
375   "There was nothing . . ." An unsigned, undated note in the SAS Oper-
       ations and Intelligence Section files, CIAP.
376–77 "In the middle . . ." *et seq.*, Foot, p. 308.
377   "Suttill . . ." *ibid.*, p. 309.
380   "exceptional character," *ibid.*, p. 199.
380   "Evidently . . ." *ibid.*, p. 178.
382   "authentic confusion." *ibid.*, p. 449.
382   "An assertion," *ibid.*, p. 307.

page
382 ". . . to send a few . . ." *ibid.,* p. 308.
382 "The staff concerned . . ." *ibid.,* p. 278.
383 "We never used . . ." Wingate interview.
383 "In the *Starkey* . . ." in COSSAC/44DX/Int, *op. cit.*
384 "The truth is . . ." *et seq.,* Foot, p. 290.
385 "The fact that . . ." *ibid.*
386 "We know he is in . . ." *et seq., ibid.,* p. 303.
386 ". . . when—if ever— . . ." *et seq., ibid.,* p. 301.
387 "great ability and . . ." *et seq.,* Foot, p. 299.
388 "the British secret service . . ." Fuller, *Double Webs,* p. 215.
388 "(he was) dressed . . ." *France-Soir,* Paris, June 8, 1948.
389 "to work for them . . ." *et seq.,* Fuller, *Double Webs,* p. 67.
389 "very mysterious," *et seq., France-Soir,* Paris, June 9, 1948.
390–91 "strategic sacrifice," *et seq.,* Fuller, *Double Webs,* p. 208.
391 "he could reveal . . ." *ibid.,* p. 210.
391 ". . . I can sleep . . ." *ibid.,* p. 246.

9. THE INTELLIGENCE ATTACK

Sources

Foreign Office citation of Sister Henriette Frede, CIAP; A Report of Operations, The Enemy Terrain and Defense Section, G2, HQ 12th Army Group, June 2, 1945, provided the author by Gen. E. L. Sibert; US Strategic Bombing Survey, "V-Weapons (Crossbow) Campaign" and "V-Weapons on London," USAF Historical Branch, MAFB; MI-6 Interrogation Report of Otto John, CIAP; Jeremy Bennett, *British Broadcasting and the Danish Resistance Movement 1940–45: A Study of the Wartime Broadcasts of the BBC Danish Service,* Cambridge: Cambridge Univ. Press, 1966; Erik Lund, *A Girdle of Truth,* Denmark: Institute of Communication Research and Contemporary History, Arhus University, 1970; Cecil von Renthe-Fink, German Minister to Denmark, Final Interrogation Report, OI FIR 36, Military Intelligence Service, USFET, MMR, NA.

Notes

page
395–96 "All signs point . . ." *et seq.,* Harrison, Appendix D.
404 "expressed surprise . . ." Irving, *The Mare's Nest,* p. 35.
404 "The Chiefs of Staff . . ." *ibid.,* p. 38.
405 "The petrol instructions . . ." Jones, "Scientific Intelligence," *op. cit.*
405 "Hitler and members . . ." Irving, *The Mare's Nest,* p. 89.
407 "promised greatly . . ." *et seq., ibid.,* p. 91.
407 "This evening nobody . . ." *ibid.,* p. 104.
408 "It seemed particularly . . ." *ibid.,* p. 114.
419 ". . . it was the elimination . . ." *ibid.,* p. 211.

10. TEHERAN

Sources

CCS, JCS and COS Minutes and Documents Concerning the Cairo-Teheran-Cairo Conferences, MMR, NA, and HI; State Department Minutes and Documents Concerning the Cairo-Teheran-Cairo Conferences, SDA, NA, and HI; Valentin Berezhkov, "The Teheran Meeting," *New Times,* Moscow, June, July, and August 1948; Reports of the U.S. Military Mission to Moscow, November 1943–June 1944, MMR, NA; JCS 533, 127th Meeting, "Reaffirmation of Over-All Strategic Concept and Basic Undertakings," undated, MMR, NA; JCS 606, "Collaboration with the USSR," Note by the Secretaries, November 22, 1943, MMR, NA; CCS 586, "Information on Overlord for Soviet General Staff," June 2, 1944, MMR, NA; Gen. Sir Hastings Ismay to Joint Staff Mission, Washington, D.C., "Cover and Deception Plans 1944, Teheran Agreement with Soviet Union," January 21, 1944, Record Group 218, Records of the USJCS, MMR, NA; Charles E. Bohlen, *The Bohlen Minutes,* SDA, NA; Dr. Forrest C. Pogue, chapter notes for *The Supreme Command* (Pogue study), OCMH.

Notes

page
421   "I do not think . . ." ED, p. 988.
421   "child's play." Matloff and Snell, *1943–1944,* p. 335.
422   "I wish our . . ." Alanbrooke, Vol. 2, p. 74.
422   "a most underhand," Pogue study, *op. cit.*
422   "probable British proposals . . ." *et seq.,* JCS 533, 124th Mtg., Item 3, "Recommended Line of Action at Next US-British Staff Conference (European-Mediterranean Strategy)," undated, MMR, NA.
423   "very cautious stand," JSC 533, 123rd Mtg., November 15, 1943, MMR, NA.
423   "Amen." JSC 533, Mtg. with President, November 15, 1943, MMR, NA.
424   "General Marshall . . ." Matloff and Snell, *1943–1944,* p. 330.
424   "On the way here . . ." Moran, p. 141.
425   "a formidable-looking . . ." *ibid.,* p. 139.
425   "Brooke got good and nasty . . ." Pogue, *George C. Marshall,* Vol. 3, p. 305.
425   ". . . I have noticed . . ." Moran, p. 141.
425   "Sure, we are . . ." *et seq., ibid.,* p. 142.
427   "This conference . . ." *ibid.,* p. 143.
427   "The difference between . . ." *et seq.,* Sherwood, pp. 783–84.
428–29   "I have been commanded . . ." *et seq.,* Roosevelt, pp. 181–82.
429   "very direct question," *et seq.,* Churchill, *The Second World War,* Vol. 5, p. 329.
429–30   "Nothing more can . . ." *et seq.,* Moran, pp. 148–49.
430   "without the slightest . . ." Dilks, p. 581.

page
430 "rounded up . . ." *et seq.,* Churchill, *The Second World War,* Vol. 5, p. 330.
430 "You are pro-German . . ." Moran, p. 152.
430–31 ". . . I was not . . ." *et seq.,* Churchill, *The Second World War,* Vol. 5, p. 330.
432 "In war-time . . ." Churchill, *The Second World War,* Vol. 5, p. 338.
433 "Agreed that . . ." Bohlen, *op. cit.,* November 30, 1943.
433 "against the almost . . ." Sherwood, p. 802.
433 "invaluable, and indispensable," *et seq.,* Churchill, *The Second World War,* Vol. 5, pp. 369–70.
433 "front man," *et seq.,* Ingersoll, pp. 76–78.

11. CICERO

Sources

Christopher Buckley, *Five Ventures—Iraq–Syria–Persia–Madagascar–Dodecanese,* London: HMSO, 1954; Sir John Lomax, "The Legend of Cicero," a letter in the *Daily Telegraph,* London, no date; Miscellaneous Collection of German Foreign Ministry Documents by Franz von Papen and Ludwig Moyzisch Concerning Cicero, EDS, NA; State Department Special Interrogation Report, "Conversations of Fritz Kolbe," *op. cit.*

Notes

page
435 ". . . the enemy . . ." SHAEF SGS 381, *Bodyguard, op. cit.*
436 "This is the time . . ." D. N. Brunicardi, "Aegean Enterprise," *An Cosantioir,* Dublin, no date, HI.
439 "dark eyes kept . . ." *et seq.,* Moyzisch, p. 31.
440 "At first glance . . ." Schellenberg, p. 388.
440 "To Ambassador . . ." Moyzisch, p. 43.
441 "My astonishment grew," *et seq., ibid.,* p. 54.
442 ". . . we sought to . . ." Schellenberg, p. 391.
442 "there might just . . ." Moyzisch, p. 135.
443 "the bank-notes . . ." Bazna, p. 196.
444 "Assistant Military Attaché." "Obituary of Montague R. Chidson," *The Times,* London, October 4, 1957.
445 "We always thought . . ." Dunderdale interview.
445 "whitewash the stupidity . . ." Lomax interview.
446 "I knew about . . ." Bazna, p. 109.
447 "Of direct practical value . . ." Dulles, *Secret Surrender,* p. 24.
447 "Since a leak . . ." *et seq.,* Dulles interview.
448 "security reasons," Harrison, p. 485.
449 "The greater . . ." Masterman, p. 9.
449 "Of course Cicero . . ." Menzies interview.
450 "Enemy intentions . . ." Warlimont, p. 401.

PART IV: COVER AND DECEPTION

1. EISENHOWER, SUPREME COMMANDER

Sources

Neptune Monitor Daily Intelligence Reports January 1, 1944–June 5, 1944, MMR, NA; Counter Intelligence Corps (US) School, *History and Mission of the CIC in World War 2*, OCMH; SHAEF 2DX/12/Int, *Overlord, Disruption of Enemy Lines of Communication*, MMR, NA; SHAEF 2DX/16/Int, *Overlord, Enemy Reactions*, MMR, NA; "Planning for Deception Plans for Cross-Channel Operation," Vols. 1 and 2, Record Group 218, Records of USJCS, CCS 385, MMR, NA; "Outline Plan for Political Warfare—Overlord," Record Group 218, Records of the USJCS, CCS 385, MMR, NA; CCS, "Memo on Friction Between Members of the U.S. and British Armed Forces," OPD, WDGS, Records of the WDGSS, MMR, NA; Special Plans Branch, 12th U.S. Army Group, "Report on Operation Fortitude and Cover and Deception in the European Theater of Operations" (the "Harris Report"), a collection of reports prepared by Col. William A. Harris and his staff, Record Group 319, Records of the (US) Army General Staff, MMR, NA.

Notes

epigraph

"My Christmas message . . ." T. J. T. and E. P. T., *There Is a Spirit in Europe, A Memoir of Frank Thompson,* London: Gollancz, 1947, fly-leaf.

page

454　"They're over-paid . . ." OWI Bureau of Special Services, "A Pilot Study of American Sentiment Toward the British," March 29, 1943, NA.

455　"With a broad smile . . ." Stagg, p. 17.

455　"It must be . . ." *et seq.,* Alanbrooke, Vol. 1, pp. 527–28.

456　". . . it wearies me . . ." ED, p. 1063.

456　"The planning stages . . ." Gen. W. B. Smith, "Document for Inclusion in Historical Records Concerning General Eisenhower's Critical Decisions," a memorandum to Historical Section, SHAEF, February 22, 1945, OCMH.

457　"much more marked . . ." CCS Study, "British Reaction to U.S. Troops in the United Kingdom," August 24, 1942, MMR, NA.

457　"My colleagues . . ." Churchill, *The Second World War,* Vol. 6, p. 8.

458　". . . whatever further assaults . . ." *et seq.,* 21 AG/00/Int/1101/15, "Reaction to Overlord of Enemy Land Forces in the West based on Intelligence up to March 8, 1944," in SHAEF 2DX/16/Int, *op. cit.*

460　"It is to my . . ." Churchill, *The Second World War,* Vol. 5, p. 602.

460–61　"Germany will be capable . . ." *et seq.,* Strategy and Policy Group,

page

WDGS, "United Nations Course of Action in Europe in the Event Overlord is Canceled," in American-British Conversations (ABC Papers), USJCS file, MMR, NA.

461 "attractive at first . . ." Joint Strategic Survey Committee, WDGS, "Probable Russian Reaction to Anglo-American Operations in the Aegean," in ABC Papers, USJCS file, MMR, NA.

462 "As I saw the problem . . ." Churchill, *The Second World War*, Vol. 5, p. 377.

463 "advance on," *et seq.*, Jackson, p. 170.

463 "eyes and ears . . ." Blumenson, citing Lucas, *Anzio*, p. 89.

463 "I am far too . . ." *ibid.*, p. 91.

464 "I felt like . . ." *ibid.*, p. 93.

465 "(Canaris) was pressed . . ." *et seq.*, Westphal, p. 240.

465 "Anzio was my . . ." Moran, p. 202.

465 "first attempt . . ." Warlimont, p. 410.

466 "If we succeed . . ." *ibid.*, p. 411.

466 "We should . . ." Churchill, *The Second World War*, Vol. 5, p. 431.

466 "The ease with . . ." *et seq.*, *ibid.*, p. 432.

466 ". . . It is absolutely . . ." *et seq.*, ED, February 18, 1944.

467 "The Boche has . . ." *ibid.*, February 22, 1944.

468 "send into the south . . ." Churchill, *The Second World War*, Vol. 5, p. 434.

2. THE GERMAN SUPREME COMMAND

Sources

Gen. Hans Speidel, OCMH Ms. No. B720, *Reflections and Views of General-feldmarschall Rommel, C-in-C Heeresgruppe B*, March 31, 1945, MMR, NA; Speidel, Ms. No. B721, *Background for July 20, 1944, Ideas and Preparations of GFM Rommel for an Independent Termination of the War in the West and for Putting an End to Nazi Despotism*, OCMH; Field Marshal Karl Rudolph Gerd von Rundstedt, Special Interrogation Report, February 1, 1946, Historical Section, Canadian Army, SC.

Notes

page

469 "in spite of . . ." FBIS, FCC, Daily Reports, January 1, 1944–September 1, 1944, NA.

470 "rapidly progressive . . ." "Hitler as Seen by His Doctors," OUP, undated, presumed to have originated with U.S. Group Control Council (Germany), Office of the Director of Intelligence, located in an MI-6 file in private hands.

470 "spiritual derangement," *et seq.*, "Special Interviews of A. Speer by O. Hoeffding," U.S. Group Control Council (Germany), Office of the Director of Intelligence, located in an MI-6 file in private hands.

page
471–72 "It is evident . . ." *et seq.*, Rommel, p. 465.
   473 "gifted with a . . ." *et seq.*, Hitler, p. 52.
   473 "At no place . . ." Rommel, p. 465.
474–75 "The Fatherland . . ." *et seq.*, Rundstedt, *et al.*, Ms. No. B633, *op. cit.*
   476 "devil's garden." *ibid.*
   476 "He will do . . ." Pogue study, *op. cit.*
   476 "an independent . . ." Speidel, Ms. No. B721, *op. cit.*
   477 "some figure . . ." Wheeler-Bennett, *Nemesis of Power,* p. 606.
   477 "that he was . . ." Desmond Young, pp. 196–97.
   477 "When the government . . ." Hans Speidel, *Invasion, 1944,* New York: Henry Regnery, 1950, p. 71.
   477 "I believe it . . ." Desmond Young, p. 197.
477–78 "in perhaps . . ." *et seq., ibid.,* pp. 200–201.

3. BODYGUARD

Sources

SHAEF SGS 381, *Bodyguard,* and SHAEF SGS 381, *Fortitude,* MMR, NA; Plan Zeppelin, Plan Vendetta, Plan Ironside, SHAEF G3, SHAEF/18209/Ops (b), June 3, 1944, MMR, NA; Plan Zeppelin, Intelligence Section, Office of the Director of Operations and Intelligence, MAAFHQ, WNRC; Deception Plans, S (B) 641/Int, Intelligence Section, Office of the Director of Operations and Intelligence, MAAFHQ, WNRC; Vendetta Conference Minutes, April–June 1944, MAAFHQ, WNRC; Relevant documents in the "Harris Report," *op. cit.;* Relevant documents in Record Group 218, Records of the USJCS, MMR, NA; OSS, *The PW Weekly, Psychological Warfare Analysis,* Printed for the Planning Group, OSS, R&A files, DRB, NA; Relevant documents in the files of the U.S. Military Mission to Moscow, Record Group 334, MMR, NA; Relevant documents in Record Group 226, Records of the OSS, MMR, NA; War Cabinet, London Controlling Section, "Report by Colonel John H. Bevan (Britain) and Lieutenant Colonel W. H. Baumer (America) Regarding Their Visit to Moscow," LCS (44) 10, April 2, 1944, and "Brief of Report by Colonel J. H. Bevan and Lt.-Col. W. H. Baumer Regarding Their Visit to Moscow in Connection with Plan Bodyguard," April 26, 1944, in Strategy and Policy Group files, OPD, WDGS, MMR, NA.

Notes

page
   482 "To complete . . ." *et seq.,* "PWE/OWI Outline Plan for Political Warfare, including Joint PWE/OWI and SOE/OSS (SO) Political Warfare Plan," August 12, 1943, Record Group 218, Records of the USJCS, CCS 385, MMR, NA.
   484 "musicians and choristers," Wingate interview.
   484 "I like all this," Note by Eisenhower on a Bodyguard memorandum, in SHAEF SGS 381, *Bodyguard, op. cit.*

page

485 "necessary organization . . ." "Final Report of the Washington Anglo-American Cover and Deception Conference," with annexes, Record Group 218, Records of the USJCS, CCS 385, MMR, NA.

485 "we find ourselves . . ." *et seq.,* "Plan Bodyguard, Report by the Joint Staff Planners"; and "Plan Bodyguard, Memorandum from the United States Chiefs of Staff," Record Group 218, Records of the USJCS, CCS 385, MMR, NA.

486 "active pursuit and . . ." 21 AG, Counter-intelligence Instruction No. 1, April 1944, CIAP.

486 ". . . there was always . . ." Morgan, p. 239.

487–90 "He seemed to . . ." *et seq.,* The personal diary of Maj. Gen. William H. Baumer, copy provided the author by Gen. Baumer.

490 "I thought Kuznetzov . . ." Deane, p. 147.

491 "very enthusiastic . . ." *ibid.,* p. 148.

491 "suddenly the lines . . ." Deane interview.

492 "I had never . . ." Deane, p. 14.

493 "We felt no . . ." Bevan and Baumer interviews.

493 "they put us . . ." Baumer diary.

494 "loaded with crossings out . . ." Baumer interview.

4. THE BALKANS

Sources

"German Anti-Guerrilla Operations in the Balkans, 1941–1944," USDA Pamphlet, 1954, OCMH; S. G. Walker, "Imperial Strategy and the Middle East," lecture, RUSI, March 1949; OSS R&A Report No. 2458, "The Process of Collapse of the German Armies," August 29, 1944, SDDLRS, NA; Military Intelligence Service, Washington, D.C., Italian Air Attaché Reports, Turkey, OSS files, SDDLRS, NA; Intelligence Division, Office of Chief of Naval Operations, Report on German Activities in Turkey and the Balkans, May 27, 1944, OSS R&A file, MMR, NA; OSS R&A Report No. 1742, "The Anti-German Opposition in Bulgaria," February 29, 1944, U.S. Board of Economic Warfare, NA; U.S. Joint Intelligence Committee Middle East, OSS Reports on Bulgaria, Nos. 6283-4-5-90-91, August 14–September 9, 1943, OSS files, MMR, NA; OSS dissemination No. A-18720, "Reactions of Bulgarian Officers," January 17, 1944, MMR, NA; The Foreign Service of the United States, U.S. Consulate General, Istanbul, "An Analysis of the Situation Following the Death of King Boris 3," to Secretary of State, Washington, D.C., September 6, 1943, OSS files, MMR, NA; Helmut Heiber, *The Death of Czar Boris,* Institut für Zeitgeschichte, Munich, 1964; *Germany and Her Allies in World War II,* Vols. 1 and 2, Ms. No. P108, OCMH, MMR, NA; Maj. E. W. Sheppard, "The Eastern Mediterranean in British World Strategy," *The Fighting Forces,* London, February 1948; OSS R&A Report No. 1502, "The Role of the Local Dynasties in the Balkans," April 1944, SDDLRS, NA; Gen. Edgar Feuchtinger, *History of the 21st Panzer Division,* OCMH Ms. No. B441, circa February 1947, MMR, NA; Gen. Sylvester Stadler, *Combat Reports of the 9th SS Panzer Division,* OCMH Ms. No. B470,

March 30, 1947, MMR, NA; Ambassador Frohwein to Reichsminister Ribbentrop, Report on the Vermehren Affair, February 20, 1944, in *Auswärtiges Amt, Büro des Staatssekretärs, Akton, Turkei,* November 1, 1943–April 30, 1944, CIAP; OSS Switzerland, Background Story on German Occupation of Hungary, April 4, 1944, in OSS R&A file, MMR, NA; SHAEF Theater Intelligence Section Martian Report No. 88, "The Move of the 9th SS Panzer Division Hohenstaufen from the Amiens Area (18–24 February 1944)," March 15, 1944, OPD files, MMR, NA.

Notes

page
496   "cause the peoples . . ." "Outline Plan for Political Warfare," *op. cit.*
497   "was to carry . . ." Kallay, p. 78.
497   "political adventurer," *et seq., ibid.,* p. 179.
497   "the Allied bombers . . ." *ibid.,* p. 199.
498   "We propose that . . ." *et seq., ibid.,* pp. 370–71.
499   "publication shall in . . ." *et seq., ibid.,* p. 374.
499   "By concluding . . ." *ibid.,* pp. 376–77.
500   "a small, secret . . ." *et seq., ibid.,* pp. 379–80.
500   "With deep consternation . . ." *ibid.,* p. 496.
501   "Fate has willed . . ." *ibid.,* p. 438.
503   "everything was in . . ." Cretzianu, p. 96.
503   ". . . my stay . . ." *ibid.,* p. 110.
504   "elected to strip . . ." "Operations in Support of Neptune, Results," Folder 12, the "Harris Report," *op. cit.*
504   "if I had . . ." Warlimont, p. 415.

5. FORTITUDE NORTH

Sources

Earl F. Ziemke, "The Northern Theater of Operations, 1940–1945," USDA Pamphlet, December 1959, OCMH; Plan Fortitude (final), February 23, 1944, in SHAEF SGS 381, *Fortitude, op. cit.;* C-in-C Home Fleet to The Admiralty and SHAEF, "Naval Plans for Operations in Support of Fortitude North," April 2, 1944, in SGS 381, *Fortitude, op. cit.;* COSSAC to All Commands, "Notes on Wireless Deception and Silences," December 9, 1943, in SGS 381, *Fortitude, op. cit.;* COSSAC, "Early Plans for Mespot (later Fortitude)," July 22, 1943, in SGS 381, *Fortitude, op. cit.;* Sir R. E. L. Wingate, a note to the author on Plan Fortitude, July 1971; Col. R. M. MacLeod, a note and letters to the author on the activities of the British 4th Army, 1963–64; Jeremy Bennett, *British Broadcasting and the Danish Resistance Movement 1940–45, op. cit.;* A collection of German Foreign Office telegrams, September 1943–June 1944, *Auswärtiges Amt file Büro England,* EDS, NA; Testimony of Walter Schellenberg taken at Horsbruck, Germany, by Lt. Col. Smith W. Brookhart, Jr., IGD, May 8, 1946, OUP but presumed to be depositions for International Military

Tribunal (Nuremberg), MMR, NA; Relevant documents in the "Harris Report," *op. cit.;* Relevant documents in Record Group 218, Records of the USJCS, MMR, NA.

Notes

page
510   "A broad plan . . ." SHAEF/18209/Ops (b), June 3, 1944, in SGS 381, *Fortitude, op. cit.*
514   "Rory, old boy . . ." *et seq.,* Delmer, *The Counterfeit Spy,* pp. 117–18.
515   "were just . . ." MacLeod interview.
515   "Captain R. V. H. Smith . . ." *et seq.,* Johnston interview.
519   "they were eventually , , ," Bevan interview.
519   "A diplomatic threat . . ." SHAEF/18209/Ops (b), June 3, 1944, in SGS 381, *Fortitude, op. cit.*
519   "secret negotiations . . ." Gordon and Dangerfield, p. 1.
519   "By law . . ." *ibid.,* p. 14.
521   "a judicious mixture . . ." *ibid.,* p. 90.
521   "my only friend . . ." Höhne, p. 13.
522   "Beware . . ." *et seq.,* Dulles interview; Kolbe conversations, *op. cit.*
522   "a novel method . . ." Farago, *The Game of the Foxes,* p. 543.
524   "was told bluntly . . ." *et seq., ibid.,* p. 553.

6. FORTITUDE SOUTH

Sources

J. L. Hodgson, R Study, "Fear of Allied Intentions," OCMH; Plan Quicksilver, Plan Skye, SHAEF/18209/Ops (b), in SGS 381, *Fortitude, op. cit.;* Relevant documents in the "Harris Report," *op. cit.;* Documents relating to Gen. George S. Patton, Record Group 218, Records of the USJCS, MMR, NA; BAOR, Intelligence Review, File on Colonel "M," March 1946, Bundesarchiv, Koblenz.

Notes

page
532   "blistering epistle . . ." Farago, *Patton,* p. 343.
532   "reprehensible conduct." *ibid.,* p. 356.
532   "inspecting amphibious forces," *et seq.,* Metz interview.
533   "You persistently . . ." Farago, *Patton,* p. 376.
533   "master of flattery," *et seq.,* ED, p. 1017.
533   "Whoever picked . . ." *et seq.,* Farago, *Patton,* pp. 386–87.
534   "It has now . . ." *ibid.,* p. 407.
534   "Patton appreciated . . ." *ibid.,* p. 400.
535   ". . . since it is . . ." *ibid.,* p. 417.

page

536 "I am thoroughly . . ." Eisenhower letter to Patton, April 28, 1944, EPF.

536 "You probably are . . ." *et seq.,* Farago, *Patton,* pp. 421–22.

536 ". . . this last . . ." *ibid.,* p. 423.

536 "51, a swarthy . . ." J. Edgar Hoover, "The Spy Who Double-Crossed Hitler," *American Magazine,* May 1946.

539 "2/lt. N, of . . ." *et seq.,* Johnston interview.

539 "Speculations, guesses, . . ." Masterman, p. 146.

540 "An agent who, . . ." *ibid.,* p. 147.

540–41 "Connoisseurs of double . . ." *et seq., ibid.,* p. 114.

541 "Only later did . . ." *ibid.,* p. 116.

542 "The one-man . . ." *ibid.,* p. 142.

543 "I received . . ." Bleicher, pp. 58–59.

545 "rough-hewn Slavic . . ." Farago, *The Game of the Foxes,* p. 619.

546 "broken off . . ." Johnston interview.

547 "He was interrogated . . ." Masterman, p. 56.

548 "Yugoslav of good family, . . ." *ibid.,* p. 138.

549 "A V-mann dispatch . . ." Delmer, *The Counterfeit Spy,* p. 156.

550 "It was not . . ." Masterman, p. 151.

551 "small consolation," *et seq., ibid.,* p. 154.

552 "The Führer attaches . . ." Blumentritt to all commands, letter, May 8, 1944, with note of conversation with Jodl on May 6, 1944, CIAP.

552 "He was an . . ." Liss interview.

555–56 "The multiplicity . . ." *et seq.,* FHW *Lagerberichte,* October 1943– February 1944, EDS, NA.

557 ". . . it is known . . ." Staubwasser, Ms. No. B782, *op. cit.*

558 "had a reputation . . ." Gehlen, p. 44.

558 "tall, sporty . . ." *et seq.,* Col. Anton Staubwasser, in a letter to Gen. E. L. Sibert concerning Col. Michel, March 1972, CIAP.

7. NUREMBERG

Sources

1st Air Corps (Luftwaffe) *War Diary,* and scattered associated documents, KC; "RAF Bomber Command Intelligence Narrative of Operations No. 774," PRO, London; RAF Bomber Command, "Report on Night Photographs No. P1," Air 24/268, PRO, London; RAF Bomber Command, "Casualty Report, Nuremberg, Night, 30/31 March 1944," Air 14/2674, PRO, London.

Notes

page

561 "a necessary preliminary," Masterman, p. 9.

562 "We never gave . . ." Masterman interview.

page
562 "On at least . . ." de Guingand interview and letter to the author, April 26, 1970.
562 ". . . to bait the . . ." Carroll, p. 217.
562 "cruel expedient," *ibid.*, p. 221.
563 "One of the . . ." ED, p. 1600.
563 "no other propaganda . . ." *et seq.*, Carroll, p. 221.
563 "General Spaatz . . ." ED, p. 1219.
563 "more than ordinary . . ." Craven and Cate, p. 31.
563 "had to bother . . ." *et seq.*, Becker, p. 353.
564 "ambush," Royal Institute of International Affairs, p. 243.
565 "Since the war . . ." Price, pp. 198 ff.
565 "This was," Webster, Vol. 3, p. 207.
565 "The German form . . ." Shirer, *The Rise and Fall of the Third Reich,* p. 287.
566 "mounting apprehension," Campbell, p. 8.
567 "The blood is . . ." *ibid.*, p. 158.
568 "the Germans were known . . ." *et seq.*, Middlebrook, p. 106.
569 "we were assured . . ." Campbell, p. 21.
569 "it should be . . ." *ibid.*, p. 62.
571 "The fighters were . . ." *ibid.*, p. 65.
572 "The enemy . . ." RAF Bomber Command, Minutes from Chief Signals Officer, "Report of Operations Night 30/31 March 1944," PRO, London.
572 "You could see . . ." Flight Lieutenant Alfred Price, "The Greatest Air Disaster Ever—Black Friday," a memorandum to the author.
572 "I knew things . . ." *ibid.*
573 ". . . one could navigate . . ." Middlebrook, p. 158.
573 "It was the story . . ." Campbell, p. 103.
574 "The air over . . ." *ibid.*, p. 126.
574 "Bloody hell!" *ibid.*, p. 132.
574 "It certainly appeared . . ." *et seq.*, *ibid.*, p. 130.
575 "Fighter activity . . ." Middlebrook, p. 250.
575 ". . . I always had . . ." Campbell, p. 152.
576 "In sending the . . ." Campbell, p. 178.
577 "THEY KNEW . . ." RAF Bomber Command, "Raid Plot, Nuremberg, Night, 30/31 March 1944," Air 14/3221, PRO, London.
577 "It was caused . . ." Campbell, p. 157.
577 "strange," *ibid.*, p. 147.
579 "the larger the prize . . ." Masterman, p. 9.
579 "The enemy has . . ." Goering Order of the Day, KC.

8. AERIAL STRATAGEMS

Sources

SHAEF SGS 373, *Military Objectives for Aerial Bombardment,* MMR, NA; W. Gaul, "The German Air Force and the Invasion of Normandy, 1944," ONI, OAB; "Effect of Enemy Air Raids Before and During the Invasion," a Luftwaffe intelligence report, OUP, USAF Historical Branch, MAFB; Col. T. G. Lanphier, deputy for Air G2, "Axis Air Forces, Strength and Disposition," and documents concerning French civilian casualties, in OPD files, MMR, NA; Minutes of the 6th Meeting of the Scientific Advisory Committee on Radio Aids, Countermeasures Against Enemy RCMs and Jamming, London, April 20, 1944, CIAP; Joint Board on Scientific Information Policy, Electronics Warfare, a Report on RCMs, November 19, 1945, Washington, D.C.; Radio Research Laboratory, Harvard University, "The Operational Use of RCM in the ETO," 1945, in the private collection of Dr. F. E. Terman; Office of Scientific Research and Development, "History of the Radio Research Laboratory, March 21, 1942– January 1, 1945," in the private collection of Dr. Terman; Lt. Col. Combaux, "Communications–a Weapon of War," *Revue de la Défense Nationale,* Paris, October 1946; Sir Robert Cockburn, a letter to the author, January 4, 1970; Omar N. Bradley, "Effect of Air Power on Military Operations, Western European," Report of Air Effects Committee, 12th Army Group, U.S. Army, Wiesbaden, July 15, 1945.

Notes

page
581   "grave and on . . ." ED, April 3, 1944.
581   "we should build . . ." EPF.
581   "I am not prepared . . ." memorandum for the prime minister, Record Group 218, Records of the USJCS, CCS 385, Section I, MMR, NA.
582   "put his hand . . ." Dunderdale interview.
582   "The French railway . . ." *New York Times,* May 24, 1944.
585   "The station is . . ." Herington, p. 36.
585   "absolutely vital . . ." "Cover and Deception in Air Force Operations, European Theater of Operations," Informal Supplementary Report to Joint Security Control, the "Harris Report," *op. cit.*
587   "varied so widely," Harrison, p. 179.
587   "No single factor . . ." Report of the Supreme Commander to the CCS on Operations in Europe of the AEF, June 6, 1944, to May 8, 1945, EL.

9. SECURITY

Sources

SHAEF SGS 380.01/4, *Security for Operations,* MMR, NA; "Bigot Procedure," in OPD files, MMR, NA; T. Hughes, Cabinteely, County Dublin, Eire, letter to U.S. ambassador, Dublin, March 1961, concerning the crash of Gen. Smith's aircraft, in Composite Accessions, 1970, Box 1, EL; OSS R&A Report No. 30131, "The Attitude of the Eire Government on Various Points Connected with the War," March 11, 1943, Record Group 226, MMR, NA; OSS R&A Report, "An Introduction to the Irish Problem," May 23, 1944, Record Group 226, MMR, NA; Lt. J. F. Murdock to Secretary of the Navy, Report of the Loss of LST 531, May 2, 1944, OAB; Lt. H. A. Mettler to C-in-C U.S. Navy,

Action Report Concerning LST 289, May 2, 1944, OAB; Ens. D. G. Harlander to Secretary of the Navy, Report of the Loss of LST 531, May 2, 1944, OAB; Lt. J. F. Murdock, *Film Record Report of the Loss of LST 507 in Normandy Invasion Exercises,* Film Record No. 263, OAB.

Notes

page

592 "Urging others . . ." Norman Longmate, *How We Lived Then,* London: Hutchinson, 1971, p. 95.

592 "It will go hard . . ." Eisenhower letter to British Chiefs of Staff, March 6, 1944, in SGS 380.01/4, *op. cit.*

593 "The rules of . . ." Eisenhower letter to Montgomery, Bradley, Ramsay, Leigh-Mallory, February 23, 1944, in SGS 380.01/4, *op. cit.*

594 "There lurked . . ." Betts interview.

594 "The clumsy . . ." ED, p. 1160.

595 "I had no choice." Bradley interview.

595 "There were officers . . ." Bradley, p. 224.

595 "I simply . . ." Miller letter to Eisenhower, April 25, 1944, EPF.

595 "I know of . . ." Eisenhower letter to Miller, April 27, 1944, EPF.

597 "details of impending . . ." *et seq.,* Eisenhower-Stark correspondence, May 21 and 23, 1944, OAB.

597 "shakes," Eisenhower letter to Marshall, May 21, 1944, EPF.

598 "Was it really . . ." Eisenhower Foundation, *D-Day: The Normandy Invasion in Retrospect,* University Press of Kansas, 1971, p. 170.

599 "additional aircrew." Ivelaw-Chapman interview.

602 "disclosed a crescendo . . ." Schellenberg, p. 366.

606 "We know exactly . . ." *et seq.,* Ellsberg, p. 155.

607 "did not quite . . ." Farago, *The Game of the Foxes,* p. 549.

609 "a great deal of . . ." OSS Report A22884A, "Ireland as a Source of Information to the Germans," March 16, 1944, Record Group 226, MMR, NA.

609–10 "continues to operate . . ." *et seq.,* The U.S. Government to the Irish Prime Minister, February–March 1944, Documents on American Foreign Relations, NA, pp. 625–26.

610 "designed to isolate . . ." *New York Times,* March 15, 1944.

611 "many false alarms . . ." *New York Times,* March 27, 1944.

612 "The exercise concerned . . ." Ingersoll, p. 103.

614 "There was a whole . . ." *ibid.,* p. 104.

10. THE WIRELESS GAME

Sources

"Use of Intelligence in Cover and Deception," "Enemy Source of Information," and "Methods of Manipulation," the "Harris Report," *op. cit.*

Notes

page
620 "nice assessment . . ." Masterman, p. 10.
622 "A splendid, vague, . . ." Foot, p. 337.
622 "strong and flexible . . ." *ibid.*, p. 336.
622 "too emotional . . ." Fuller, *Double Webs*, p. 25.
622 "really stuck . . ." *et seq.*, Foot, p. 337.
624 "London had twigged." *ibid.*, p. 341.
626 "imperial fury," *ibid.*, p. 342.
629 "The first part . . ." Staubwasser, Ms. No. B782, *op. cit.*
630 "in order to . . ." *et seq.*, Foot, p. 328.
631 "The ways of headquarters . . ." Fuller, *Double Webs*, p. 208.
632 "I know that . . ." Baumer interview.
632 "into a sandy . . ." Foot, p. 429.

11. THE FRENCH LABYRINTH

Sources

Coordinator of Information, "French Attitudes Toward the British (Spring 1942)," July 20, 1942, Record Group 226, MMR, NA; HQ Airborne Troops, selected files in a private collection; HQ 21st Army Group, Minutes of a Conference on Destruction of Enemy Telecommunications, May 16, 1944, CIAP; Capt. D. A. Bayly Pike, A Report on Destruction of Overhead Telephone Lines, May 19, 1944, CIAP; "Telecommunications Targets for Destruction at H-Hour," OUP, no date, CIAP; 21st Army Group, Memorandum on SAS Tasks for Inclusion in 21st Army Group Plan for Delaying of Enemy Reserves, May 10, 1944, CIAP; SAS Brigade Operations Instructions, CIAP; "Organization and Command of SAS Troops for Special Operations," December 1943, CIAP; Appreciation on Control of Resistance in France, no date, HQ Airtps/TS/25006/0/Liaison, CIAP; Appreciation of Employment of SAS Troops in Overlord, no date, HQ Airtps/MS/2500/40/G, CIAP; Notes of a Meeting Held at 21st Army Group to Consider the Various Roles of SAS, SOE and PWE in Overlord, March 1, 1944, CIAP; A Memorandum on Factors Affecting SAS Operations, May 1944, CIAP; Brig. R. W. MacLeod, "Appreciation of the Tasks Which Should Be Undertaken by SAS Troops in Overlord," March 14, 1944, CIAP; Col. I. Collins, "Delaying Enemy Reserves in Invasion Battle," June 27, 1943, and "Uniformed Airborne Guerrilla Force," August 1943, CIAP; B. M. W. Knox, "After-action Report of Jedburgh team Giles," CIAP; OSS, "Performance and Potential of French Resistance," Memorandum from Donovan to Marshall, July 9, 1944, Record Group 165, Records of the WDGSS, MMR, NA; U.S. Joint War Plans Committee, "French Collaboration in the Invasion of Europe," JWPC 229, in CCS 350.05, MMR, NA; Sundry documents concerning the rearmament of French military and resistance forces and security in Algiers, OPD 336, Security Section 1, Cases 1 through 17, Record Group 165, Records of the WDGSS, MMR, NA.

Notes

page
636 "the sun . . ." Gubbins interview.
638 "These *Avis* . . ." *et seq.*, in *BBC Warnings to Resistance Groups, op.*
cit.
639 "We call him . . ." R. Harris Smith, p. 68.
639 "Gestapo-like methods," OSS R&A Report No. 2553, "The Organization of the French Intelligence Services," January 11, 1945, MMR, NA.
641 "It is clear . . ." *et seq.*, Foot, pp. 231–32.
641 "bad faith . . ." Foot, p. 232.
642 "If this were . . ." Deacon, p. 347.
644 "discretion incarnate," Foot, p. 364.
648 "*Patriot Forces* . . ." *et seq.*, Plan Torrent, in SHAEF SGS 381,
Fortitude, op. cit.
649 "While we were . . ." Knox interview.
649 "You will go . . ." HQ Airborne Troops, Jedburgh file, in a private
collection.
650–51 "In order that . . ." *et seq.*, EPF.

12. CANARIS'S LAST THROW

Sources

General Leo Baron Geyr von Schweppenberg, "Reflections on the Invasion,"
Military Review, 1961; Peter de Mendelsohn, "Speidel's Story," *New Statesman
and Nation*, London, October 29, 1949.

Notes

page
655 "comprehensive conference . . ." *et seq.*, Speidel, Ms. No. B721, *op.*
cit.
659–60 "pertinent questions," *et seq.*, USJCS and the Joint Intelligence Committee (US), "Effect of Unconditional Surrender Policy on German
Morale," memorandum and associated documents, February 10, 1944,
JIC 159/JCS 718 Series, MMR, NA.
660 "they were up . . ." Dilks, p. 620.
661 "white alley," ED, April 16, 1944.
661 "In conversation . . ." *et seq.*, JIC 159/JCS 718 Series, *op. cit.*
661 "In the German . . ." SHAEF intelligence digest, located in U.S.
1st Army After-Action Report, HI.
662 "Justice . . ." *Hansard*, London, May 25, 1944.
663 "begging before . . ." *et seq.*, Churchill letter to Eisenhower, in
SHAEF SGS 380.01/4, *Security for Operations, op. cit.*
665 "I first heard . . ." *et seq.*, Gen. James O. Curtis, Jr., memorandum

page
for the record of conversations with the author, witnessed by Luther Nicols, Berkeley, California, May 16, 1968, original in author's possession.
665   "I distinctly remember . . ." *et seq.*, de Guingand interview.
666   "contact with . . ." *et seq.*, Gehlen interview.
666   "by devious means," Gehlen, p. 103.
668   "because I feared . . ." Arnould interview.
668–69 "Keun came over . . ." *et seq.*, Dunderdale interview.
669   "I received . . ." Dulles interview.
670   "We received . . ." Wingate interview.
671   "three or four . . ." *et seq.*, Arnould interview.
672   "Canaris seemed . . ." *et seq.*, Frede interview.
672   "This is the . . ." *et seq.*, Arnould interview.

13. VENDETTA

Sources

Allied Forces Headquarters, Information and News Censorship Branch, *Plan Vendetta*, WNRC; Air Vice Marshal Sir T. Elmhurst, "The German Air Force and Its Failure," *Journal of the Royal United Services Institution,* November 1946; Col. R. M. Adams, Historical Office, Royal Signals Institution, London, letter to Brig. W. Scott re Lt. Col. F. K. Austin, November 11, 1970, CIAP; letters and documents concerning Quicksilver, Big Bob and Flake from Robert Shearer, Lt. Col. G. A. C. Danby, A. C. Walsh, P. M. Kemp, and excerpts from *The History of the Northamptonshire Regiment* (p. 321 ff.) and "Firm," Activities of the 10th Worcestershire Regiment, 1944, CIAP; JSC, *Plan Royal Flush,* with State Department, SHAEF and Joint Chiefs signals and annexes, May 26, 1944, OPD 381, MMR, NA.

Notes

page
677–78 "1/5th Queen's Royal . . ." *et seq.*, Johnston interview.
679   "idea of betraying . . ." Delmer, *The Counterfeit Spy*, p. 178.
680   *"Envoyez vite . . ."* Masterman, p. 161.
681   "One of our . . ." Special Staff, U.S. Army, An interview with Reichsmarschall Hermann Goering, Eucom:HD:OHGB:Ethint 30, July 1, 1945, MMR, NA.
682   "The truth . . ." Jervis-Reid interview.
682   "I had an imaginary . . ." James, pp. 5–6.
682   "took rather a . . ." Jervis-Reid interview.
683   "The likeness struck . . ." *et seq.*, James, p. 88.
688   "Whitman . . ." ED, p. 1265.
688   "Ladies and gentlemen . . ." *New York Times*, May 29, 1944.
688   "Ike looks . . ." ED, May 12, 1944.

page
688   ". . . tension grows . . ." Eisenhower letter to Somervell, April 4, 1944, EPF.
689   "our chances . . ." ED, May 24, 1944.
689   "I am concerned . . ." *ibid.*, April 28, 1944.
690   "the best imitation . . ." Morison, p. 115.
690   "It should not . . ." *21 Army Group Weekly Neptune Intelligence Review*, June 4, 1944, OPD 315, MMR, NA.
693   "*1. Area of main* . . ." *et seq.*, MAAF, Intelligence Section, Office of the Director of Operations and Intelligence, "Enemy Appreciations of Planned Intentions," May 25, 1944, Record Group 331, AFHQ microfilm, WNRC.
693   "We have been . . ." *The Times*, London, June 7, 1944.
694   "only with the . . ." Wilmot, p. 143.
694   "completely bare-faced bluff." Warlimont, p. 408.
694   "The Führer attaches . . ." Blumentritt to all commands, *op. cit.*
696   "need to win . . ." Rundstedt, *et al.*, Ms. No. B633, *op. cit.*
698   "a number of major . . ." *ibid.*
698   "This, of course . . ." Winterbotham, *The Ultra Secret*, pp. 127–28.

14. THE EVE OF D-DAY

Sources

Phillip M. Flammer, "Weather and the Normandy Invasion," *Military Review*, June 1961; ZY Detachment, 21 Weather Squadron, 9th USAF, The Albert F. Simpson Historical Research Center, MAFB; J. M. Stagg, "Meteorology in War," Meteorological Office Library, Bracknell, Berkshire, England; Memorandum on weather forecasts, May 26, 1944, in SHAEF SGS 000.91, *Meteorological Matters*, MMR, NA; Air Marshal Sir Trafford Leigh-Mallory, *Despatch*, Supplement to the *London Gazette*, December 31, 1946; SHAEF G2 (Int), Daily Intelligence Digests, June 7, 1944–May 1945, MMR, NA; Gen. Walter Bedell Smith, "Eisenhower's Six Great Decisions," *Saturday Evening Post*, June 8, 1946; RAF Kingsdown, Y Service Report, June 5/6, 1944, OUP, OCMH; SHAEF, Office of the Chief of Staff, memorandum on the events of June 5/6, 1944, Document for Inclusion in Historical Records, February 22, 1945, OCMH; Col. Anton Staubwasser, "The Alert Problem during the Night of the Invasion (June 5–6, 1944)," a memorandum to Gen. Speidel with a copy to Gen. E. L. Sibert, CIAP; Staubwasser, "The Enemy as Seen by Oberkommando of Heeresgruppe B Before the Invasion (Time: End of May–Beginning of June 1944)," Ms. No. B675, OCMH.

Notes

page
700   "to be on hand . . ." *et seq.*, Memorandum for the Record, Office of the Chief of Staff, May 31, 1944, MMR, NA.
700   "Exercise Hornpipe . . ." in SHAEF SGS 380.01/4, *Security for Operations, op. cit.*

page

701 "Halcyon plus 4." in SHAEF SGS 380.01/4, *Security for Operations, op. cit.*

701 "Unless Channel weather . . ." Stagg, p. 38.

702 "For heaven's sake . . ." *ibid.*, p. 69.

702 "wearied ourselves . . ." *et seq., ibid.*, p. 80.

703 "untrustworthy." *et seq., ibid.*, p. 86.

703 "Well, Stagg . . ." *et seq., ibid.*, pp. 87 and 88.

704 "knife-edge marginal," *et seq., ibid.*, pp. 90–91.

704 "There goes six . . ." *et seq., ibid.*, pp. 96 and 98.

705 "tension in the . . ." *et seq., ibid.*, p. 102.

706 "diminished our supplies . . ." ED, June 4, 1944.

707 ". . . then between . . ." *et seq.*, Stagg, pp. 107 and 108.

707 "toothless parish . . ." *ibid.*, p. 40.

708 "chancy." *et seq., ibid.*, p. 114.

708 "I am quite positive . . ." Ryan, p. 58.

708 "(Neptune) had been . . ." Stagg, p. 115.

709 "Let's take a . . ." *et seq.*, Ryan, p. 55.

709 "All were in . . ." *et seq.*, Stagg, p. 116.

709 ". . . the tension . . ." *ibid.*, p. 118.

709 "Halcyon plus 5 . . ." in SHAEF SGS 380.01/4, *Security for Operations, op. cit.*

710 "to spatter . . ." de Gaulle, *War Memoirs,* Vol. 2, p. 244.

710 "an infamy," *ibid.*, p. 246.

711 ". . . Ike took them . . ." ED, June 4, 1944.

712 "request the approval," *et seq.*, Gubbins interview.

712 "This torrent of . . ." *et seq.*, Gen. Pierre Koenig, Memorandum on Matters Concerning *Messages Personnels* on the Evening of June 5, 1944, copy provided the author by Robert Aron.

713 "seen to be . . ." *et seq.*, SHAEF G2 Daily Intelligence Digest, June 7, 1944.

714 "martyrs not less . . ." Churchill, *The World Crisis, 1916–18,* Pt. I, New York: Scribners, 1927, p. 197.

714 "I am very . . ." Alanbrooke, Vol. 2, p. 206.

715 "doubtful whether . . ." *et seq.*, Ellis, p. 129.

717 "On 5 June . . ." Warlimont, p. 422.

718 "At 2115 on . . ." *et seq.*, Rundstedt, *et al.*, Ms. No. B633, *op. cit.*

719–20 "At approximately . . ." *et seq.*, Staubwasser, Ms. No. B675, *op. cit.*

721 "riding in Paris . . ." Scratchley interview.

PART V: NORMANDY TO NEMESIS

1. D-DAY

Sources

HQ German 7th Army, *War Diary,* IWM; Assessment of the Luftwaffe on the night of D-Day, a Luftwaffe report, OUP, no date, USAF Historical Branch, MAFB; Robert Cockburn, The Moonshine Operations of June 6–7,

1944, a memorandum dated June 13, 1944, in Cockburn's private collection; RAF Kingsdown Y Service Report, in 8th USAAF After-Action Report on Chronology of Developments in Normandy, Intelligence Section, USAF, OCMH; Lt. Col. Charles A. Taylor, "Omaha Beachhead," 1946, OCMH; R. G. Ruppenthal, "Utah Beach to Cherbourg," 1947, OCMH; J. W. Arnold, USNR, "NOIC Utah," *U.S. Naval Institute Proceedings*, Annapolis, 73 (June 1947): 671–81; Lt. Cdr. L. Ware, Special Historical Observer for the Commander, U.S. Naval Forces, Europe, Vol. 1: *Planning the Invasion*, Vol. 2: *War Diary, Naval Force "U,"* OAB; Commander, U.S. Naval Forces, Europe, "Plan Neptune," Sections 1–32, OAB.

Notes

epigraph

" 'Twas on a summer's . . ." Byron, *Don Juan*, Canto IV.

page

725 "From Sabu 15 . . ." HQ Airborne Troops, Titanic file, CIAP.

728 "Although it is . . ." *War Diary*, (German) Naval Group West, June 1–30, 1944, OAB.

729 "The assault forces . . ." Adm. Sir Bertram Ramsay, *Despatch*, Supplement to the *London Gazette*, October 7, 1947.

730 "as he listened . . ." *et seq.*, Ryan, p. 129 (Greenwich, Ct: Fawcett, 1960).

730 "General, I believe . . ." *ibid.*, p. 127.

731 "It was not at all . . ." Speidel, *Invasion 1944, op. cit.*, p. 77.

731 "the affair is . . ." Ryan, p. 129.

732 "The German fighter . . ." Price, p. 184.

733 "I had been told . . ." E. Feuchtinger, *History of the 21st Panzer Division from the Time of Its Formation until the Beginning of the Invasion*, February 18, 1947, OCMH Ms. No. B441, EDS, NA.

733 "Anchor holding . . ." Morison, p. 93.

735–37 "a fair number," *et seq., War Diary*, (German) Naval Group West, *op. cit.*

737–38 "definitely the opening . . ." *et seq.*, Rundstedt, *et al.*, Ms. No. B633, *op. cit.*

738–39 "extremely vague," *et seq.*, Ryan, p. 147.

740 "made an ungodly . . ." Morison, p. 94.

741 "At the time . . ." Price, p. 108.

741 "In the main . . ." *War Diary*, (German) Naval Group West, *op. cit.*

742 "fast and lean . . ." American military attaché report on German paratroopers, Cairo, November 14, 1942, in OSS R&A file on Crete, MMR, NA.

742 "north of Carentan," *et seq.*, Maj. Friedrich-August Baron von der Heydte, *Operations of the 6th Parachute Regiment*, Ms. No. B839, EDS, NA.

745 "pursuing," Foot, p. 387.

746 "very widely spaced . . ." Lt. Col. Zeigelman, *History of the 352nd Infantry Division*, OCMH Ms. No. B432, EDS, NA.

page
746   "shocked and shaken," *et seq.,* Ryan, p. 222.
747   "seriously unbalance . . ." Foot, p. 347.
748   "While the Anglo-Saxon . . ." *et seq.,* Rundstedt, *et al.,* Ms. No.
         B633, *op. cit.*
748   "My dear Staubwasser," *et seq.,* Staubwasser, Ms. No. B782, *op cit.;*
         and Staubwasser interview.
749   "So, we're off." *et seq.,* Warlimont, p. 427.

2. THE DECEPTIONS OF D-DAY

Sources

   Maj. Kenneth W. Hechler, "The Invasion," an interview with Genfldm
Wilhelm Keitel and Genobst Alfred Jodl, Ethint 49, SC; Hechler, "From the
Invasion to the Ruhr," "Eastern vs. Western Fronts," "High Level Strategy,"
a series of interviews with Reichsmarschall Hermann Goering, July 21, 1945,
Ethint 30, OCMH; Hechler, "Invasion and Normandy Campaign," an inter-
view with General Jodl, July 31–August 2, 1945, SC; Hechler, "The Invasion,"
"The Battle of Normandy," "Cherbourg," "Replacement of von Rundstedt,"
"Normandy Breakthrough and Mortain Counterattack," "Eberbach," "Retreat
toward the German Frontier," a series of interviews with General Warlimont,
July 19–20, 1945, SC; Relevant documents in the "Harris Report," *op. cit.*

Notes

page
751   "a little rough . . ." Curtis interview.
751   "the chance . . ." *et seq.,* Stagg, p. 125.
752   "Our landings . . ." EPF.
752   "largely by surprise," *et seq.,* JIC appreciation in Chiefs of Staff
         (British) Brief, War Cabinet Papers, Piece 79, PRO.
752   ". . . Allied naval forces . . ." SHAEF Psychological Warfare Di-
         vision, Plans in Support of Overlord, April 30, 1944, Record Group
         331, MMR, NA.
753   "Topflite at 9030." *et seq.,* SHAEF, G3, D-Day Proclamations, in *BBC
         Warnings to Resistance Groups, op. cit.*
754   "Many thanks . . ." *et seq.,* Gubbins interview.
755   "the greatest . . ." *Daily Mail,* London, June 7, 1944.
755–56 "I have received . . ." *et seq.,* An essay by William Barkley, Gallery
         Correspondent, *Daily Express,* London, June 7, 1944.
756   "a mighty endeavor," *et seq., New York Times,* June 7, 1944.
757   "The supreme battle . . ." *et seq., The Times,* London, June 7, 1944.
757   "de Gaulle's address . . ." Staubwasser interview.
758   "obliged to . . ." *et seq.,* Delmer, *The Counterfeit Spy,* pp. 183–84.
758   "flaming fury," *et seq., ibid.,* pp. 184–85.
759   "This was the time . . ." Wilmot, p. 287.
760   "There was," *et seq.,* Wingate interview.

3. SWORD AND STRATAGEM

Sources

Letter, Maj. Gen. Harry J. Maloney to Gen. Omar N. Bradley, Subject: Loss of two U.S. Corps operational orders, January 25, 1949, in Geog. M. France 314.4 (Normandy), OCMH; German Summary of U.S. 7th Corps order captured in Normandy, EDS, OCMH; U.S. 5th and 7th Corps operational orders with annexes, OCMH; Oberstleutnant Ziegelman, *Additional Information About the Operational Plan of 5 (US) Corps Captured on June 7, 1944, in the Sector of the 352nd Infantry Division*, September 3, 1947, OCMH Ms. No. B636, EDS, NA; An Account of the Operations of (British) 2nd Army in Europe, copy of Gen. Sir Miles Dempsey, IWM; 12th Army Group, G2, Report of the Air Effects Committee, Frankfurt, 1945.

Notes

page
761   "considerable anxiety," Ellis, p. 217.
761   "hung like a vulture . . ." Wilmot, citing Churchill, p. 293.
762   "the entire scheme . . ." *et seq.*, Blumentritt, *et al.*, *The Capture of U.S. 5th Corps Operational Orders*, OCMH Ms. No. B637, EDS, NA.
763   "effectively cut off . . ." Scott interview.
763   "invaluable respite," *et seq.*, Wilmot, pp. 298–99.
764   "handle any eventuality . . ." Marshall, Note for Conference with General Brooke, EPF.
764   "general harassing . . ." SHAEF 17240/17/Ops (a), June 7, 1944, in *BBC Warnings to Resistance Groups*, *op. cit.*
765   "Paradise," Plan Paradise, in SHAEF SGS 381, *Fortitude, op. cit.*
766   "unsatisfactory . . ." *et seq.*, "Sunday Punch in Normandy," After-Action Report of the U.S. 8th Air Force, OUP, MMR, NA; and G2 (Air) 12th Army Group, "Effect of Air Power on Military Operations," in the private collection of General E. L. Sibert.
767   "with my own eyes . . ." *et seq.*, Wingate interview.
767   "on Hitler's desk . . ." Bevan interview.
767–68   "I transmit . . ." Wingate interview.
768   "In all probability . . ." *et seq.*, Staubwasser, Ms. No. B782, *op. cit.*
768   "active and bold . . ." Hodgson, R Study, *op. cit.*
769   "present your points . . ." Delmer, *The Counterfeit Spy*, p. 16.
769   "After a personal . . ." *ibid.*, p. 18.
770   "heavy with tension . . ." *et seq.*, Wingate interview.

4. THE FRENCH REVOLT

Sources

SOE Monthly Progress Reports to SHAEF for May, June, July, August 1944, CIAP; Capt. J. Kerneval, "Report of Jed Team Felix on Operations 7 July–23

August 1944," CIAP; Lt. S. R. Trumps, OSS, "Report of Jed Team Ronald on Operations," CIAP; Capt. R. Marchant, R. Pariselle, "Reports of Jed Team Hillary on Operations," CIAP; *War Diary*, (German) Inspectorate of the Armistice Commission, CIAP; Brig. Gen. A. S. Nevins, Chief Operations Section, SHAEF, "D-Day Propaganda to French," June 17, 1944, in *BBC Warnings to Resistance Groups, op. cit.* Michel de Galzain, *"Le Bal du Ciel,"* a monograph provided by the Mairie, Vannes, Brittany, CIAP; SFHQ, London, "9th (May 1944), 10th (June 1944), 11th (July 1944) Reports of Operations to SHAEF," CIAP; Sgt. O. A. Brown, Royal Armoured Corps (on detachment to Team Quinine), "Quinine Radio Report," CIAP; Capt. J. E. Tonkin, "Bulbasket Report," CIAP; HQ SAS Troops, "Operations in Brittany," Report to the B.G.S. 21st Army Group, August 21, 1944, CIAP; C. B. MacDonald, "France 1940–1944," Working Paper for the Special Operations Research Office, Washington, D.C., 1968; 3rd French Paratroop Battalion, "Report of Cooney Operations," circa August 1944, CIAP.

Notes

page

774   "We would have . . ." Staubwasser interview.

774   "have far . . ." *et seq.,* Lt. Gen. F. A. M. Browning, Commander, Airborne Troops, 21st Army Group to Headquarters 21st Army Group, "Progress Report SAS Operations 5–20 June 1944" June 22, 1944, CIAP.

775   "one sacred duty . . ." *et seq.,* FBIS Survey for period June 6–July 6, 1944, FCC, NA.

776   "methods of manipulation," *et seq.,* "Cover and Deception, Definition and Procedure," the "Harris Report," *op. cit.*

777   "provocateurs . . ." *et seq.,* Broadcast transcript in SAS Brittany file, CIAP.

778   "assisted by . . ." Capt. Paul Aguirec, "Report on Jed Team Frederick on Operations 9 June–27 August 1944," CIAP.

778   "There was . . ." *et seq.,* Capitaine Jules Leblond, "Report on Operations of 4th French Parachute Battalion and on the Present Situation in Brittany, 6 June–13 July 1944," CIAP.

778   "Without our knowledge . . ." Aguirec report, *op. cit.*

779   "I did not want . . ." Leblond report, *op. cit.*

779   "surprised . . ." Roger Le Hyaric, *"Les patriotes de Brétagne,"* a monograph provided by the Mairie, Vannes, Brittany, CIAP.

780   "Dingson under attack . . ." Capt. P. Cyr (US), "Report on Operations of Jed Team George," CIAP.

780   "unknown Germans." Maj. O. A. J. Cary Elwes, "Report of Operations of 'Operation Lost' in Brittany," CIAP.

784   "some dozen . . ." Maj. T. MacPherson, "Report of Operations of Team Quinine," CIAP.

784   "secured the best . . ." Foot, p. 404 ff.

785   "The enemy were . . ." Capt. C. S. S. Burt, "Report of Operations of Team Dickens," CIAP.

page
785 "blood and ashes," *et seq.*, Cookridge, p. 340.
786 "the most horrible . . ." *ibid.*, p. 341.
786 "so thoroughly mauled . . ." *et seq.*, Foot, p. 398.
786 "The extra . . ." *ibid.*, p. 397.

5. ROMMEL

Sources

HQ USFET, Public Relations Division, "20th July and Rommel," USFET Release 282, September 4, 1945, CIAP; Drew Middleton, "The War as Rommel Fought It," *New York Times Book Review*, May 17, 1953; 2nd Panzer Division, *Bericht über Rückkehr der 2 DRK–Schwesterngruppe aus amerik, Gefangenschaft an die 2 Pz Div. nachrichtl.*, MIRS/W 1044, EDS, NA; PWD, Report of Transfer of Red Cross Nurses, September 21, 1944, HI; Intelligence Section, Office of the Director of Operations and Intelligence, MAAFHQ, *Operation Hellhound*, Record Group 331, AFHQ microfilm, WNRC.

Notes

page
788 "one terrible . . ." *et seq.*, Rommel, p. 496.
788 "My functions . . ." *ibid.*, p. 495.
789 "every two or three . . ." *et seq.*, Staubwasser, Ms. No. B782, *op. cit.*; and Staubwasser interview.
790 "unbelievable courage . . ." *et seq.*, Speidel, Ms. No. B720, *op. cit.*
791 "Rommel was under . . ." Speidel, Ms. No. B721, *op. cit.*
791 "hardly be restrained . . ." *et seq.*, Dr. Walter Bargatzky, "Personal Recollections of the 20th of July 1944 Insurrectionary Movement in France," Baden-Baden, October 20, 1945, HI.
792 "one more chance," *et seq.*, Speidel, Ms. No. B721, *op. cit.*
793 "The present positions . . ." Hodgson, R Study, *op. cit.*
794 "I shall be next." Staubwasser interview.
794–95 "Rommel himself . . ." *et seq.*, Speidel, *Invasion 1944, op. cit.*, p. 105.
795 "trustworthy . . ." Bargatzky, *op. cit.*
795 *"Achtung"* German 47th Corps HQ, *Gespräch zwischen deutscher Kommandostelle und einer amerikanischen Dienststelle am 2/7/44, Beginn 14:00 Uhr,* Mirs/W 1043, EDS, NA.
796 "Hello," *et seq.*, U.S. 1st Infantry Division AA Report, "Transfer of Red Cross Nurses," with G2 Annexes, OCMH.
796 "With the knowledge . . ." Wheeler-Bennett, *Nemesis of Power*, pp. 631–32.
797 "The situation . . ." *et seq.*, Rommel, pp. 486–87.
798 "Staubwasser . . ." *et seq.*, Staubwasser interview.
800 *"Je cherche . . ." et seq.*, Operation Houndsworth, Operational and (Fraser) Personal File, CIAP.

page
800–01   "From HOUNDSWORTH . . ." *et seq.*, Operation Houndsworth, Signals File, made available to the author by private sources.
801, 802   "kill or kidnap . . ." *et seq.*, SAS Brigade Operation Instruction No. 32, Operation Gaff–OC 2 SAS Regiment, HQ SAS Tps/TSB/5/G, with annexes, CIAP.

6. THE V1

Sources

U.S. General Board Reports on V1 and V2, 1945–47, MMR, NA; War Cabinet and Chiefs of Staff files 1944, PRO; U.S. Navy, Report of the Disappearance of Lt. (jg.) J. Kennedy, USN, OAB.

Notes

page
805   "Not v. . . ." Dilks, p. 639.
806   "exuberantly . . ." *et seq.*, Irving, *The Mare's Nest*, p. 234.
806   "all possible measures . . ." *et seq.*, *ibid.*, p. 236.
806   "The congregation . . ." Flower and Reeves, pp. 584–85.
807   "whose modern steel . . ." Churchill, *The Second World War*, Vol. 6, p. 37.
807   "grating roar . . ." *et seq.*, Longmate, *How We Lived Then*, *op. cit.*, p. 490.
808   "finding it . . ." *et seq.*, Parkinson, pp. 326–27.
811   ". . . we knew . . ." Masterman, p. 122.
811   "News . . ." *ibid.*, p. 171.
812   "M.I.5 was not . . ." Irving, *The Mare's Nest*, p. 257.
813–14   "At their meeting . . ." *et seq.*, War Cabinet Paper, Secretary's Standard [i.e., Sensitive] File, COS 1944, PRO.
814   ". . . the possibility . . ." Parkinson, p. 342.

7. GOODWOOD

Sources

SHAEF G2 (CI), Counter-Intelligence Digests, September–October 1944, in 6th Army Group G2 Records, MMR, NA; G2 Section, FUSAG, Policy Book for CI Branch, date uncertain, CIAP; G2 12th Army Group, CI Organization and Operations, date uncertain, CIAP; U.S. 1st Army, *Report of Operations*, Vols. 1–12, OCMH; General E. L. Sibert, G2 12th Army Group and G2 FUSAG, notes for National War College lectures, dates uncertain, CIAP; Exhibit 4: "Use of Intelligence in Cover and Deception," and Exhibit 6: "Fortitude South II (Rosebud)," in the "Harris Report," *op. cit.*; WDGS, "Biography of Lesley James McNair," OCMH; CSDIC, Interview with Count Helldorf,

PW Paper 12, August 4, 1944, CIAP; Lt. Col. H. P. Persons, Instructor, Command and General Staff College, "St.-Lô Breakthrough," *Military Review,* March 1951; Interrogation of Robert v. Mendelssohn, OUP, handwritten on H.M. Government note paper, undated, CIAP.

Notes

page

816 "prevent the operation . . ." *et seq.,* GSI (b), HQ 21st Army Group, Detailed Counter-Intelligence Instruction No. 1, May 5, 1944, CIAP.

817 "Even if the . . ." Harrison, p. 426.

817 "The demolition . . ." *ibid.,* p. 441.

818 "Over a stretch . . ." Blumenson, *Breakout and Pursuit,* p. 176.

819–20 "the most monstrous . . ." *et seq.,* Hodgson, R Study, *op. cit.*

821 "directed the tactical . . ." Blumenson, *Breakout and Pursuit,* p. 9.

823 ". . . you felt . . ." *ibid.,* p. 428.

824 "the Allies' secret weapon," *et seq., ibid.,* p. 478.

824 "Patton has lost . . ." SHAEF SGS 381, *Fortitude, op. cit.*

824 "obsessed with the . . ." Delmer, *The Counterfeit Spy,* p. 226.

825 "for immoral purposes," HQ Advance Section, Communications Zone, ETO, U.S. Army, Office of the Staff of the Judge Advocate General, Record of Trial by General Court Martial of Pfc. —— . . . Pvt. ——, August 6, 1944, Clerk of the Court, JAG, U.S. Army, Washington, D.C.

826 "he was white . . ." Curtis interview.

826 "revealed," *et seq.,* Delmer, *The Counterfeit Spy,* p. 227.

827 "an emissary . . ." *et seq.,* Gehlen, p. 99.

828 ". . . it is the duty . . ." *ibid.,* p. 103.

828 "made contact . . ." CSDIC (UK) Report, Interrogation of Oberstleutnant Arntz, SIR 1610, April 11, 1945, CIAP.

828 "arrange a channel . . ." Liss interview.

829 "So far as His . . ." *Hansard,* July 6, 1944.

829 "their Nazi taskmasters," *et seq.,* Charles Eade (comp.), *The Dawn of Liberation, War Speeches by the Rt. Hon. Winston S. Churchill,* London: Cassell, 1945.

829 "that the next . . ." "Germany: Nazi Opposition Reports Progress," Document L89970, July 18, 1944, OSS German Section, MMR, NA.

830 "In reviewing . . ." Dulles, *Germany's Underground,* pp. 140–41.

831 "to prove . . ." Wheeler-Bennett, citing Tresckow, *Nemesis of Power,* p. 627.

832 "I saw a tank officer . . ." Detmar H. Finke, U.S. Army Archivist, Attack on Field Marshal Rommel, Medical Report, a letter to Dr. R. A. Davis, Department of Surgery, Northwestern University, Chicago, May 8, 1958.

833 "Rommel was in fact . . ." *et seq.,* Speidel, Ms. No. B721, *op. cit.*

834 "we [the air forces] . . ." ED, July 20, 1944.

834 "had the makings . . ." Ellis, p. 353.

834 "Monty . . ." Dilks, p. 649.

8. JULY 20, 1944

Sources

Gen. Günther Blumentritt, *Three Marshals, National Character, and the July 20th Complex*, February 15, 1947, Ms. No. B344, OCMH; Standartenführer Kopkow (member of Gestapo investigation team), Account of the Plot of July 20th, an interrogation report, OUP but presumed MI-6 or BAOR G2 service in origin, undated, but circa 1946, CIAP; CSDIC (WEA), Report on Heinz Lorenz, BOAR/Int/B3/PF582, November 20, 1945, CIAP; Fabian von Schlabrendorff, Answers to Questionnaire re 20th July, MI-6 in origin, undated, unsigned typescript, CIAP; CSDIC (UK), Report of Conversation between General der Flieger Bodenschatz and an RAF Officer, SRGG 1219 (C), undated but immediately postwar, CIAP; MI-6 Report 1583, "Eyewitness Account of 20th July: PW from F. U. Grenadier Regiment on Guard Outside the Hut at Rastenburg," unsigned, undated, CIAP; Nicholas Count von Below, Interrogation Report, "Events at Führerhauptquartier," marked 032/Case No. 0279, OUP but presumed MI-6, undated, unsigned, CIAP; Sgt. A. Croy, Civilian Interrogation Camp, BAOR, Secret Documents left by Canaris in the care of Frau von Haase, to the CO, Documents Section, GSI (b), BAOR, November 27, 1949, CIAP; B. H. Liddell Hart, 3rd Interrogation of General Blumentritt, OUP, presumed GSI (b), BAOR, CIAP; CSDIC (UK), Report of Conversation between General Blumentritt and a British Army Officer, June 7, 1945, SRGG 129 (C), CIAP; Dr. Georg Kiesell, *Das Attentat des 20 Juli 1944 und seine Hintergruende*, Description of Gestapo activity following assassination attempt by a leading member of the RSHA Amt IV, OUP, CIAP; Totentafel, a list of names, ranks, dates of execution, addresses of next-of-kin, situation of surviving dependents, of 130 people shot or otherwise executed in connection with July 20, 1944, OUP, CIAP; Baronin Funck (*née* Frau M. von Haase), "The Growing of the Opposition Until July 20, 1944," November 26, 1945, OUP, but presumed British G2, CIAP; Gen. Georg Thomas, *Gedanken und Ereignisse, Aufzeichnung vom July 20, 1944*, FC; MI-14, War Office, London, Report of Executions at the Plötzensee, OUP, CIAP; Notes of an Interview between B. H. Liddell Hart and Gen. Rohricht (GOC 59th Corps) concerning the association of Rundstedt and Kluge with conspiracies and bomb plot, undated, OUP but presumed British G2 in origin, CIAP; Interrogation of Field Marshal Gerd von Rundstedt by Liddell Hart on events of July 20, 1944, OUP, CIAP; Walter Huppenkothen, Interrogation Report, USFET/CIC, July 20, 1944, including British questionnaire, dated May 17, 1946, CIAP; Martin Bormann, Report of July 20, 1944, Rundschreiben Nr. 155/44, undated, HI; Walter Schellenberg, MI-6 Interrogation concerning July 20, "Hansen und Canaris," undated, handwritten document, CIAP; Extracts from the diary of Dr. Erwin Giessing, ENT specialist who treated Hitler just after attentat, OUP, undated, CIAP.

Notes

page
837   "indirect hints," Schellenberg, MI-6 interrogation, *op. cit.*
838   "cross between . . ." Payne, p. 433.

page
838–39   "I will leave . . ." *et seq.*, Wheeler-Bennett, *Nemesis of Power*, pp. 640–41.

840   "I am not . . ." CSDIC (UK) Report, Interrogation of Oberstleutnant Arntz, *op. cit.*

840   "Duce, an infernal . . ." *et seq.*, Deakin, p. 708.

840   "I was standing . . ." *et seq.*, Payne, p. 511.

841   "continuous fire . . ." Irving, *The Mare's Nest*, p. 260.

841   "the treatment . . ." A remark made to Gen. Jodl, reported in *Besprechung der Führer* for July 31, 1944, OCMH.

842   "At five o'clock . . ." A conversation between SS Gen. Eugen Dollmann and SS Gen. Georg Elling, CSDIC Report CMF/X 194, July 22, 1945, CIAP.

843–45   "still suffering . . ." *et seq.*, John memorandum, *op. cit.*

846–47   "It's starting! . . ." *et seq.*, Gisevius, pp. 533–35.

847   "We shall need . . ." *et seq.*, John memorandum, *op. cit.*

847   "a spirited speech . . ." GSI (b) 21 Army Group, Interrogation Report of Otto Werth, late Wachtmeister im Nachrichtendienst, August 23, 1945, BA/907/Int, CIAP.

848   "just in case," Speer, p. 490.

848   "Goebbels seemed . . ." *et seq.*, *ibid.*, p. 492.

849   "Do you recognize . . ." *et seq.*, Gisevius, p. 556.

849   ". . . from the telephone . . ." John memorandum, *op. cit.*

850   "Kluge, I now . . ." *et seq.*, Gisevius, p. 551.

850   "You're crazy . . ." MI-6 interrogation record of an unnamed German doctor with the battalion, CIAP.

851   "In totally . . ." *et seq.*, Speer, p. 493.

851–52   "Beck: I have . . ." *et seq.*, Gisevius, pp. 563–64.

853   "a massive shadow . . ." Speer, p. 495.

853   ". . . von Kluge . . ." Document L42251, August 17, 1944, OSS German Section, MMR, NA.

854   "Good heavens!" Colvin, *Master Spy*, p. 236.

854   "If they . . ." Speer, p. 496.

854   "None of those . . ." Schramm, p. 31.

854   "mad," *et seq.*, *ibid.*, p. 32.

855   "line in the . . ." *et seq.*, Hodgson, R Study, *op. cit.*

855   "I must first . . ." Schramm, p. 46.

856   "Between 7:30 . . ." *ibid.*, p. 50.

856   "Kluge turned . . ." CSDIC Report SRGG 1347, "A Conversation Between General Eberbach and General Blumentritt," *op. cit.*

856   ". . . it was natural . . ." Schramm, p. 51.

856   "Find out what . . ." *et seq.*, *ibid.*, p. 52.

857   "bungled business," *ibid.*, p. 54.

857   "You know . . ." *et seq.*, *ibid.*, p. 55.

857   "Field Marshal . . ." Schramm, p. 59.

858   "This is the . . ." CSDIC Report SRGG 1347, *op. cit.*

858   "(He) felt . . ." Schramm, p. 60.

858   "Then Stuelpnagel . . ." *et seq.*, CSDIC Report SRGG 1347, *op. cit.*

859   "You must get . . ." *et seq.*, Schramm, p. 64.

859   "To the Führer . . ." *et seq.*, Hodgson, R Study, *op. cit.*

page
860   "One of Eisenhower's . . ." Curtis interview.
860   "an acid grin," *et seq., New York Times,* July 24, 1944.
861   "exhilarating," G2 estimate, July 24, 1944, in First United States Army Report of Operations, OCMH.
861   "I never saw . . ." R. Harris Smith, p. 221.

9. THE BREAKOUT

Sources

OB-West War Diary *Anlagen* July–August 1944, EDS, NA; U.S. 30th Infantry Division, *Workhorse of the Western Front,* Unit History Collection, OCMH; Col. T. J. Crystal, U.S. 19th Corps G2, "Reports," in the Crystal Collection, HI; History of the (U.S.) 120th Infantry Regiment, Unit History Collection, OCMH; U.S. 8th Air Force, "Report of Operation 494," Albert F. Simpson Library, MAFB; U.S. 1st Army, *Report of Operations,* Vol. 1, OCMH; U.S. 3rd Army, *Report of Operations,* Army and Navy Club Library, Washington, D.C.; Brig. R. W. MacLeod, "Report of Operations in Brittany as at 16 July 1944," CIAP; Captain S. J. Knerly, "Report of Operations of Jed Team Gerald, 7 July–23 August 1944," CIAP; Scipion (code name), "Report of Operations of Jed Team Hugh," undated, CIAP; Maj. J. V. Summers, "Report of Operations of Jed Team Horace on Operations in Brittany 17 July–15 September 1944," CIAP; Maj. B. J. Cliffe, "Report on Visit to 1 SAS Regiment in France," October 2, 1944, CIAP; Capt. J. H. Cox, "Report of Operations of Jed Team Ivor," CIAP; Senior Intelligence Officer, Combined Operations Headquarters, "Brittany and Lucky Strike," May 14, 1944, CIAP; Capt. Bennett, "Report of Operations of Jed Team Daniel," August 14, 1944; Brig. R. W. MacLeod, "Report on Visit to Southern Morbihan," August 19, 1944, CIAP; Director of Tactical Investigation, War Office, *SAS/SOE Operations in Brittany,* CIAP; Director of Tactical Investigation, War Office, *Organisation and Development of Resistance in Brittany,* October 12, 1944, CIAP; Gen. Koenig, EMMFFI missions, *Aloes, Muguet, Lilal, Oeille, Héliotrope, Violette,* with intelligence and communications annexes, CIAP; *le Général de Corps d'Armée Koenig, Commandant des Forces Françaises de l'Intérieur, ordre à Commandant Bourgoin, Commandant le 4e Bataillon SAS, 90, Londres, le 1er Août 1944,* CIAP; Gen. Fritz Bayerlein, 21st Panzer Division, Ms. No. A902, OCMH.

Notes

page
862   "I can report . . ." *et seq.,* Hodgson, R Study, *op. cit.*
863   "Anyone who . . ." Payne, p. 519.
863   ". . . the deep distrust . . ." Guderian, p. 272.
864   "And now came . . ." Rundstedt, *et al.,* Ms. No. B633, *op. cit.*
865   "marked increase . . ." *et seq.,* Staubwasser, Ms. No. B782, *op. cit.*
865   "Without any doubt . . ." Hodgson, R Study, *op. cit.*
865   "an orchestra . . ." Blumenson, *Breakout and Pursuit,* p. 238.

page

866 "the bombardment . . ." *ibid.*, p. 240.

866 "rushed dementedly . . ." *et seq.*, Bayerlein, Ms. No. A902, *op. cit.*

867 "I have learned . . ." Delmer, *The Counterfeit Spy*, p. 235.

868 "*eine Riesensauerei*," *et seq.*, Hodgson, R Study, *op. cit.*

869 "Paris and the Seine . . ." EPF.

869 "hasten the end . . ." Pogue study, *op. cit.*

869 "Only discipline . . ." *et seq.*, G2 Report, July 31, 1944, in U.S. 1st Army, *Report of Operations, op. cit.*

871 "received a cavalry mission . . ." Blumenson, *Breakout and Pursuit*, p. 370.

871 "a terrible . . ." Foot, citing Eisenhower, p. 408.

872 "They were all . . ." "Report of Operations of Jed Team Giles," *op. cit.*

873 "French people , , ," *et seq.*, Radio France, Call to Breton Insurrection, 0700, August 6, 1944, in *BBC Warnings to Resistance Groups, op. cit.*

875 "in the interests . . ." *et seq.*, SFHQ September Report to Supreme Commander, CIAP.

876 "We regret . . ." "Report of Operations of Jed Team Giles," *op. cit.*

10. GÖTTERDÄMMERUNG

Sources

U.S. V Corps in the ETO, OCMH; Capt. Martin Blumenson, "The Mortain Counterattack," *Army*, 8 (July 1958): 30–38; Count G. von Schwerin, "The 116th Panzer Division," unnumbered U.S. Army interrogation report, OCMH; Gen. Walter Warlimont, *Circumstances of the 20th July 1944 Attempt, op. cit.*; *Günther von Kluge, deutscher Generalfeldmarschall*, ME-KI (v. Kluge+) 2.11.1963 137*** Aus: Internat.: Biograph Munzingerarchiv, Lieferung 44/63, CIAP; Blumentritt, *von Kluge on 15 August 1944*, Ms. No. B034, OCMH; German Army, Form 202, "von Kluge, Günther," OCMH; Martin Bormann, "File on Kluge," OCMH; Heinz Eberbach, Ms. No. A922, OCMH; MIRS London, Kluge to Hitler, Letter, August 18, 1944, CIAP.

Notes

page

878 "The decision . . ." Hodgson, R Study, *op. cit.*

878 "to make quite . . ." Winterbotham, *The Ultra Secret*, p. 149.

879 "absolutely copper-bottom . . ." Winterbotham interview.

879 ". . . an attack . . ." Hodgson, R Study, *op. cit.*

879 "Now the vital . . ." Winterbotham, *The Ultra Secret*, pp. 149–50.

879 "Kluge staked . . ." *ibid.*, p. 151.

880 "With a heavy . . ." U.S. 30th Infantry Division, *Workhorse of the Western Front, op. cit.*

882 "We didn't expect . . ." *et seq.*, Hodgson, R Study, *op. cit.*

page
882–83 "display of weakness . . ." *et seq.,* "Tactical Operation B," Folder 15, the "Harris Report," *op. cit.*
885 "Hundreds of men . . ." R. M. Wingfield, *The Only Way Out,* London: Hutchinson, 1945, p. 27.
886 "August 15th . . ." HQ USFET, Information Control Division, Intelligence Section, "Transcript of Fragments of Hitler's Conference of August 31, 1944, at the Wolfsschanze, Westphal and Krebs Present," CIAP.
886 "Hitler was desperate . . ." Guderian, p. 296.
886 "Field Marshal von Kluge . . ." HQ USFET, "Transcript of Hitler's conference of August 31, 1944," *op. cit.*
886 *"The Road to Avranches . . ." et seq., Time,* June 25, 1945.
887 "a futile attempt . . ." Dulles, *Germany's Underground,* p. 188 ff.
887 "in charge of . . ." *et seq.,* OSS Interoffice Memo, "German Economic Agent Seeks Allied Contacts in Lisbon," L Document 42255, August 11, 1944, based upon OSS Official Despatches, Lisbon, August 7 and 8, 1944, MMR, NA.
888 "The Commander-in-Chief . . ." Hodgson, R Study, *op. cit.*
888–89 "Here at Avranches . . ." *et seq.,* Rundstedt *et al.,* Ms. B633, *op. cit.*
889 "Should the new . . ." Hodgson, R Study, *op. cit.*
890 "Get everything . . ." Schramm, p. 205.

EPILOGUE

Sources

CIC/CCS Intelligence Reports for June–December 1944, MMR, NA; Theater Intelligence Section Martian Report 87, Annex V1, "Plans for the Evacuation of German Troops by Rail from France," of uncertain date but promulgated no later than March 31, 1944, OPD, WDGS files, Overlord Section, MMR, NA; Dr. Louis de Jong, Director of the Netherlands State Institute for War Documentation, Amsterdam, "Report prepared for the Second International Conference on the History of the European Resistance, 1939–1945, Milan 26/29 March 1961," HI; Angus McLean Thuermer, letter to the publisher concerning the capture of the Enigma keys at Brest; Minutes, Committee of Three, June 5, 1945, "Top Secret Ultra," in Assistant Secretary of War Safe File 334.8, Record Group 107, MMR, NA.

Notes

page
891 "Two-and-a-half . . ." SHAEF G2 report, August 23, 1944, in SHAEF Record Group 331, MMR, NA.
892 "vital importance . . ." *et seq.,* Loewenheim, *et al.,* pp. 603–6.
893 "thief on the cross . . ." Zimmermann and Jacobsen, *Germans against Hitler, 20 July 1944, op. cit.*
893 "Now everyone . . ." Schlabrendorff, p. 157.

page
893 "My functions . . ." *et seq.,* Manfred Rommel, monograph, in Rommel, p. 495.
894 "I have just . . ." *et seq., ibid.,* p. 503.
894 "Accept my . . ." *ibid.,* p. 505.
894 "The Führer . . ." Desmond Young, p. 222.
895–96 "von Kluge's participation . . ." *et seq.,* War Department Historical Commission Report, "Field Marshal von Kluge and the Plot of 20th July 1944," prepared by Lt. Col. O. J. Hale, SC.
897 "in particular . . ." John, p. 312.
898 "a very, very . . ." *et seq.,* Ryan, *A Bridge Too Far,* New York: Simon & Schuster, 1974, p. 65.
898 "psychopath," *et seq., ibid.,* p. 76.
898 "Montgomery was . . ." Bradley interview.
900 "We wanted no . . ." Wingate interview.
900 "achieved a degree . . ." Eisenhower Report, *op. cit.*
900 "remarkably effective," *et seq.,* Eisenhower to Marshall, July 6, 1944, in SHAEF 370.2, *Fortitude,* MMR, NA.
900 "Operation Fortitude . . ." HQ 12th Army Group, Bradley to Eisenhower, Cover and Deception, European Theater of Operations, 18 November 1944, in SHAEF 370.2, *Fortitude, op. cit.*
900 "entered deception operations . . ." *et seq.,* "Appreciation of Deception in the European Theater," in the "Harris Report," *op. cit.*
901 "the service . . ." Wingate interview.
902 "as to what . . ." *et seq.,* Overlord file of the U.S. Military Mission to Moscow, a copy of a letter from "Bolton" to Col. J. H. Bevan, July 19, 1944, MMR, NA.
903 "happy and handy . . ." Foot, p. 419.
903 "express my great . . ." *ibid.,* p. 442.
903 "amateurish . . ." Webster, Vol. 3, p. 88.
904 "40 years . . ." Dunderdale interview.
906 "like shooting . . ." Blumenson, *Breakout and Pursuit,* p. 683.
906 "These potential . . ." *ibid.,* p. 684.
906 "apparent inability . . ." *et seq.,* OSS, R&A Report No. 2947, "Prince Bernhard, The Future Prince Consort of the Netherlands, an examination of the personal history, character and constitutional position," March 30, 1945, MMR, NA.
906 "an important agent," *et seq.,* SHAEF Counter-Intelligence Report No. 4, November 10, 1944, in 6th Army Group CI file, MMR, NA.
909 "wished to make . . ." *et seq.,* Charles Mee, *Meeting at Potsdam,* New York: M. Evans, 1975, p. 83.
909–10 ". . . the Japanese . . ." *et seq.,* Operations Division, WDGS, "Ultra: The 'Starts' File," Executive 17, Item B, Record Group 165, Records of the WDGSS, MMR, NA.
910 "handed back . . ." Winterbotham, *The Ultra Secret,* p. 186.
911 "I am forced . . ." Report of the death of A. M. Turing, *Wilmslow County Express,* Cheshire, U.K., June 10, 1954, obtained by Mrs. G. M. Barry.
911 "witless, upperclass . . ." Winterbotham interview.

page
912   "Stewart Graham . . ." Menzies's death certificate, Somerset House, London, CIAP.
912   "Dear General Menzies," Eisenhower to Menzies, in Eisenhower-Menzies file, EL.
913   "Canaris was never . . ." *et seq.*, Menzies interview.
914   "from Canaris." Trevor-Roper interview.
914–15 "Somehow I felt . . ." *et seq.*, Schellenberg, p. 410.
916   "important military . . ." Bartz, p. 163.
917   "I . . . die . . ." Colvin, *Master Spy*, p. 248.
917   "belonged to the . . ." Zimmermann and Jacobsen, *Germans against Hitler, 20 July 1944, op. cit.*, p. 64.
918   "D-Day was one . . ." Charles V. P. von Luttichau, a note to the author, May 1975.
919   "But what . . ." *New York Times*, November 30, 1974.

AUTHOR'S NOTE

Notes

page
924   "be given access . . ." *et seq.*, CCS 334, Record Group 218, Records of the USJCS, and JCS 385, MMR, NA.
924   "Appropriate departments . . ." OPD 311.5, MMR, NA.
924   "The existence of . . ." *et seq.*, CCS 334, Record Group 218, Records of the USJCS, and JCS 385, MMR, NA.
925   "tried his . . ." *et seq.*, Cornwall-Jones to JSC, April 17, 1946, including "Information Concerning General Patton," undated, CCS 201, "Patton, General," Record Group 218, Records of the USJCS, MMR, NA.

Bibliography

Alanbrooke, Viscount. *Diaries*. Edited by Sir Arthur Bryant. 2 vols. London: Collins, 1957–59.

Alexander of Tunis, Earl. *Memoirs, 1940–45*. Edited by J. North. London: Cassell, 1962.

Alsop, Stewart, and Braden, Thomas. *Sub Rosa: The OSS and American Espionage*. New York: Harcourt, Brace & World, 1964.

Ambrose, Stephen E. *The Supreme Commander: The War Years of General Dwight D. Eisenhower*. New York: Doubleday, 1970.

Amort, C., and Jedlicka, M. *The Canaris File*. Translated by M. Parker and R. Gheysens. London: Wingate, 1970.

Armstrong, Anne. *Unconditional Surrender*. New Brunswick, N.J.: Rutgers Univ. Press, 1961.

Aron, Robert. *De Gaulle Before Paris: The Liberation of France, June–August 1944*. Translated by Humphrey Hare. New York: Putnam, 1962.

————. *France Reborn: The History of the Liberation, June 1944–May 1945*. Translated by Humphrey Hare. New York: Scribners, 1964.

Aster, Sidney. *1939: The Making of the Second World War*. New York: Simon & Schuster, 1974.

Astley, Joan Bright. *The Inner Circle*. London: Hutchinson, 1971.

Attlee, Clement R. *As It Happened*. London: Heinemann, 1954.

Avon, The Earl of. *The Eden Memoirs*. London: Cassell, 1960–1965. Vol. 3, *The Reckoning*, 1965.

Barkas, G. *The Camouflage Story*. London: Cassell, 1952.

Bartz, K. *The Downfall of the German Secret Service*. Translated by E. Fitzgerald. London: Kimber, 1956.

Bazna, Elyesa. *I Was Cicero*. Translated by Eric Mosbacher. New York: Harper & Row, 1962.

Bekker, Cajus. *The Luftwaffe War Diaries*. New York: Doubleday, 1968.

Belgium, The Official Account of What Happened, 1939–40. Published for the Belgium Ministry of Foreign Affairs, New York, 1941.

Bernstein, Jeremy. *The Analytical Engine: Computers—Past, Present and Future*. New York: Random House, 1963.

Bertrand, G. *Enigma ou le Plus Grande Enigme de la Guerre 1939–1945*. Paris: Librairie Plon, 1973.

Best, S. P. *The Venlo Incident*. London: Hutchinson, 1950.

Bethge, Eberhard. *Dietrich Bonhoeffer*. London: Collins, 1970.

Birse, Arthur H. *Memoirs of an Interpreter*. New York: Coward, McCann, 1967.

Bleicher, Hugo. *Colonel Henri's Story*. Translated by Ian Colvin. London: Kimber, 1954.

Blumenson, Martin. *Breakout and Pursuit*. Washington, D.C.: Department of the Army, 1961.

——. *Anzio: The Gamble That Failed*. Philadelphia: Lippincott, 1963.

——. *The Patton Papers 1940–1945*. Boston: Houghton Mifflin, 1974.

Bonhoeffer, Dietrich. *Letters and Papers from Prison*. Rev. ed. Edited by Eberhard Bethge. New York: Macmillan, 1967.

Boveri, Margaret. *Treason in the 20th Century*. Translated by Jonathan Steinberg. New York: Putnam, 1963.

Bradley, Omar N. *A Soldier's Story*. New York: Henry Holt, 1951.

Brickhill, P. *The Dam Busters*. War Classics series. London: Evans, 1966.

Buckley, Christopher. *Norway; The Commandos; Dieppe*. Popular Military History series. London: HMSO, 1951.

Buckmaster, Maurice J. *Specially Employed*. London: Batchworth, 1952.

Bulloch, John. *M.I.5*. London: Barker, 1963.

Bullock, Alan. *Hitler—A Study in Tyranny*. Rev. ed. New York: Harper & Row, 1963.

Butcher, Harry. *My Three Years with Eisenhower*. New York: Simon & Schuster, 1946.

Campbell, James. *The Bombing of Nuremberg*. New York: Doubleday, 1974.

Carré, M.-L. *I Was The "Cat."* Translated by M. Savill. London: Four Square Books, 1961.

Carroll, Wallace. *Persuade or Perish*. New York: Houghton Mifflin, 1948.

Catton, Bruce. *The War Lords of Washington*. New York: Harcourt Brace, 1948.

Churchill, Right Hon. Winston S. *The Great War*. 3 vols. London: George Newnes, 1933.

——. *The Second World War*. 6 vols. London: Cassell, 1948–54.

Ciano, Galeazzo. *The Ciano Diaries, 1939–1943*. New York: H. Fertig, 1973.

Clark, Alan. *Barbarossa: The Russian-German Conflict, 1941–1945*. New York: Morrow, 1965.

Clark, Mark W. *Calculated Risk*. New York: Harper & Bros., 1950.

Cline, Ray S. *Washington Command Post: The Operations Division*. Washington, D.C.: Department of the Army, 1951.

Collier, Basil. *The Defence of the United Kingdom*. London: HMSO, 1957.

Collier, Richard. *Ten Thousand Eyes*. New York: Dutton, 1958.

Collins, Larry, and Lapierre, Dominique. *Is Paris Burning?* London: Gollancz, 1965.

Colvin, Ian. *Master Spy*. New York: McGraw-Hill, 1951.

——. *Vansittart in Office: The Origins of World War II*. London: Gollancz, 1965.

Combined Operations Command. *Combined Operations. Great Britain*. New York: Macmillan, 1943.

Connell, J. *Auchinleck: A Critical Biography*. London: Cassell, 1959.

——. *Wavell*. Edited by M. Roberts. 2 vols. London: Collins, 1969.

Cookridge, E. H. *Inside S.O.E.* London: Barker, 1966.

Cookson, John, and Nottingham, Judith. *A Survey of Chemical and Biochemical Warfare.* London: Sheed & Ward, 1969.

Craig, Gordon A., and Gilbert, Felix, eds. *The Diplomats 1919–1939.* 2 vols. Princeton, N.J.: Princeton Univ. Press, 1953.

Craven, Wesley F., and Cate, James L., eds. *The Army Air Forces in World War II.* 6 vols. Chicago: Univ. of Chicago Press, 1949–58. Vol. 3, *Europe: Argument to VE Day, January 1944 to May 1945,* 1951.

Cretzianu, A. *The Lost Opportunity.* London: Cape, 1957.

Cunningham, Andrew B. *A Sailor's Odyssey.* New York: Dutton, 1951.

Dalton, Hugh. *Memoirs.* London: Muller, 1953–62. Vol. 2, *The Fateful Years,* 1957.

Dansette, A. *Histoire de la Liberation de Paris.* Paris: Fayard, 1959.

Deacon, R. *A History of the British Secret Service.* London: Muller, 1969.

Deakin, F. W. *The Brutal Friendship: Mussolini's Last Years.* London: Weidenfeld & Nicolson, 1962.

Deane, John R. *The Strange Alliance: The Story of Our Efforts at Wartime Cooperation with Russia.* New York: Viking, 1947.

De Gaulle, Charles. *Appels et Discours, 1940–1944.* Published clandestinely, 1944.

———. *War Memoirs.* 3 vols. New York: Simon & Schuster, 1958–1960.

De Guingand, Sir Francis W. *Operation Victory.* New York: Scribners, 1947.

———. *Generals at War.* London: Hodder & Stoughton, 1964.

De Launay, J., ed. *European Resistance Movements, 1939–1945: In English, French and German.* 2 vols. London: Pergamon, 1960–64.

Delmer, Sefton. *Black Boomerang.* New York: Viking, 1962.

———. *The Counterfeit Spy.* New York: Harper & Row, 1971.

Dennett, Raymond, and Johnson, J. E., eds. *Negotiating with the Russians.* Boston: World Peace Foundation, 1951.

Deutsch, Harold C. *The Conspiracy Against Hitler in the Twilight War.* Bloomington, Minn.: Univ. of Minnesota Press, 1968.

Dewavrin, André. *Souvenirs.* Paris: Librairie Plon, 1951.

Dilks, David, ed. *The Diaries of Sir Alexander Cadogan 1938–1945.* New York: Putnam, 1972.

Doenitz, Karl. *Memoirs.* London: Weidenfeld & Nicolson, 1959.

Dourlein, Peter. *Inside North Pole.* London: Kimber, 1953.

Dulles, Allen W. *The Craft of Intelligence.* New York: Harper & Row, 1963.

———. *Germany's Underground.* London: Macmillan, 1947.

———. *The Secret Surrender.* New York: Harper & Row, 1966.

Dupuy, Richard E., and Dupuy, Trevor N. *The Encyclopedia of Military History.* London: Macdonald, 1970.

———. *The Military Heritage of America.* New York: McGraw-Hill, 1956.

Ehrlich, B. *The French Resistance.* London: Chapman and Hall, 1966.

Ehrman, J. *Grand Strategy, August 1943–September 1944.* London: HSMO, 1956.

Eisenhower, Dwight D. *Crusade in Europe.* New York: Avon, 1968.

———. *General Eisenhower on the Military Churchill: A Conversation with Alastair Cooke.* New York: Norton, 1970.

———. *The Papers of Dwight David Eisenhower: The War Years.* Edited by Alfred D. Chandler, Jr. 5 vols. Baltimore: Johns Hopkins Press, 1970.

Ellis, L. F., and Warhurst, A. E. *Victory in the West.* Vol. 1. United Kingdom Military History series. London: HMSO, 1962.

Ellsberg, Edward. *The Far Shore.* New York: Dodd, Mead, 1960.

Essame, Hubert, and Belfield, E. M. G. *Normandy Bridgehead.* New York: Ballantine, 1970.

Farago, Ladislas. *The Broken Seal: "Operation Magic" and the Secret Road to Pearl Harbor.* New York: Random House, 1967.

———. *The Game of the Foxes: The Untold Story of German Espionage in the United States and Great Britain during World War II.* New York: McKay, 1971.

———. *Patton—Ordeal and Triumph.* New York: Obolensky, 1964.

Farran, R. *Winged Dagger: Adventures on Special Service.* London: Collins, 1948.

Feis, H. *Churchill, Roosevelt, Stalin: The War They Waged and the Peace They Sought.* Princeton, N.J.: Princeton Univ. Press, 1957.

Fergusson, Bernard. *The Watery Maze: The Story of Combined Operations.* New York: Holt, Rinehart and Winston, 1961.

First Infantry Division, U.S. Army. *Danger Forward, A History with Introduction by Hanson W. Baldwin.* U.S.: Albert Love Enterprises, 1947.

Fitzgibbon, Constantine. *The Shirt of Nessus.* New York: Norton, 1957.

Fleming, Peter. *Operation Sea Lion.* New York: Simon & Schuster, 1957.

Flicke, W. F. *Rote Kapelle.* Düsseldorf: Hilden, 1949.

———. *War Secrets in the Ether.* 2 vols. Washington, D.C.: National Security Agency, 1954.

Flower, Desmond, and Reeves, James, eds. *The Taste of Courage: The War 1939–45.* New York: Harper & Bros., 1960.

Foot, M. R. D. *S.O.E. In France.* London: HMSO, 1966.

Foote, Alexander [pseud.]. *Handbook for Spies.* New York: Doubleday, 1949.

Ford, Corey. *Donovan of OSS.* Boston: Little, Brown, 1970.

Ford, Corey, and McBain, Alastair. *Cloak and Dagger: The Secret Story of OSS.* New York: Random House, 1946.

Forrestal, James. *Diaries.* Edited by Walter Millis. New York: Viking, 1951.

Frank, Owen. *The Eddie Chapman Story.* London: Wingate, 1953.

Frank, Wolfgang. *The Sea Wolves.* Translated by R. O. B. Long. New York: Rinehart, 1955.

Freidin, Seymour, and Richardson, William, eds. *The Fatal Decisions.* Translated by Constantine Fitzgibbon. New York: Sloane, 1956.

Fuller, J. F. C. *The Second World War, 1939–1945: A Strategical and Tactical History.* New York: Duell, Sloane & Pearce, 1949.

Fuller, Jean Overton. *Born for Sacrifice.* London: Pan, 1957.

———. *Double Webs.* New York: Putnam, 1958.

———. *Madeleine.* London: Gollancz, 1952.

———. *The Starr Affair.* London: Gollancz, 1954.

Funk, Arthur L. *Charles de Gaulle: The Crucial Years, 1943–44.* Norman, Okla.: Univ. of Oklahoma Press, 1959.

Galland, Adolf. *The First and the Last: The German Fighter Force in World War II.* Translated by M. Savill. London: Methuen, 1955.

Garby-Czerniawski, Roman. *The Big Network*. London: Ronald, 1961.

Garlinski, J. *Poland, S.O.E. and the Allies*. Translated by P. Stevenson. London: Allen & Unwin, 1969.

Gehlen, Reinhard. *The Service: The Memoirs of General Reinhard Gehlen*. Translated by David Irving. New York: World, 1972.

Gilbert, Felix. *Hitler Directs His War*. New York: Oxford Univ. Press, 1950.

Gisevius, H. B. *To the Bitter End*. Translated by R. and C. Winston. London: Cape, 1948.

Giskes, H. J. *London Calling North Pole*. London: Kimber, 1953.

Goebbels, Joseph. *Diaries, 1942–1943*. Edited and translated by Louis P. Lochner. New York: Doubleday, 1948.

Goerlitz, Walter. *History of the German General Staff, 1657–1945*. Translated by Brian Battershaw. New York: Praeger, 1953.

Gordon, David L., and Dangerfield, R. J. *The Hidden Weapon: The Story of Economic Warfare*. New York: Harper & Bros., 1947.

Grunberger, Richard. *The Twelve Year Reich. A Social History of Nazi Germany, 1933–1945*. New York: Holt, Rinehart and Winston, 1971.

Guderian, Heinz. *Panzer Leader*. New York: Ballantine, 1972.

Guillaume, P. *La Sologne au Temps de l'Heroisme et de la Traison*. Orleans: Imprimerie Nouvelle, 1950.

Hagen, Louis. *The Secret War for Europe*. New York: Stein & Day, 1969.

Halder, H. *Hitler as Warlord*. Translated by P. Findlay. London: Putnam & Co., 1950.

Harris, L. H. *Signal Venture*. Aldershot, U. K.: Gale and Polden, 1951.

Harrison, Gordon A. *Cross-Channel Attack*. Washington, D.C.: Department of the Army, 1951.

Hassell, Ulrich von. *The Von Hassell Diaries, 1938–1944*. 1947. Reprint. Westport, Conn.: Greenwood Press, 1971.

Hassett, William D. *Off the Record with F.D.R., 1942–1945*. New Brunswick, N.J.: Rutgers University Press, 1958.

Haukelid, Knut. *Skis Against the Atom*. Translated by Lyon. London: Kimber, 1954.

Hayn, F. *Die Invasion*. Heidelberg: Vowinckel, 1954.

Henderson, Sir N. *Failure of a Mission*. London: Hodder & Stoughton, 1940.

Herington, John. *Air Power Over Europe, 1944–1945*. Canberra: Australian War Memorial, 1963.

Hislop, J. *Anything But A Soldier*. London: Michael Joseph, 1965.

Hitler, Adolph. *Hitler's Secret Conversations, 1941–1944*. New York: Farrar, Straus and Young, 1953.

Hoegner, W. *Der Schwierige Aussenseiter*. Munich: Isar Verlag, 1959.

Hoettl, Wilhelm. *The Secret Front: The Story of Nazi Political Espionage*. Translated by R. H. Stevens. New York: Praeger, 1954.

Höhne, H. *The Order of the Death's Head: The Story of Hitler's SS*. Translated by R. Barry. London: Secker & Warburg, 1969.

Höhne, Heinz, and Zolling, Hermann. *The General Was A Spy: The Truth about General Gehlen and His Spy Ring*. New York: Coward, McCann & Geoghegan, 1972.

Howarth, P., ed. *Special Operations*. London: Routledge, 1955.

Hull, Cordell. *Memoirs*. New York: Macmillan, 1948.

Hunt, Sir David. *A Don at War*. London: Kimber, 1966.

Hyde, H. M. *Cynthia*. London: Hamish Hamilton, 1966.

——. *Room 3603: The Story of the British Intelligence Center in New York During World War II*. New York: Farrar, Straus, 1952.

Ingersoll, R. *Top Secret*. New York: Harcourt Brace, 1946.

International Military Tribunal. *The Trial of the Major War Criminals before the International Military Tribunal, Nuremberg, 14 November 1945–1 October 1946*. London: HMSO, 1947–49.

Irving, David. *The German Atomic Bomb*. New York: Simon & Schuster, 1968.

——. *The Mare's Nest*. Boston: Little, Brown, 1965.

Jackson, W. G. F. *The Battle for Italy*. British Battles series. London: Batsford, 1967.

James, Clifton. *I Was Monty's Double*. London: Rider, 1954.

John, Otto. *Twice Through the Lines*. Translated by R. H. Barry. Harper & Row, 1973.

Joslen, H. F., ed. *Orders of Battle: 1939–1945*. Vol. 1. United Kingdom Military History series. London: HMSO, 1960.

Kahn, David. *The Codebreakers*. New York: Macmillan, 1967.

Kallay, Miklos. *Hungarian Premier: A Personal Account of a Nation's Struggle in the Second World War*. New York: Columbia Univ. Press, 1954.

Kennedy, Sir John. *The Business of War*. London: Hutchinson, 1957.

Kimche, J. *Spying for Peace*. London: Weidenfeld & Nicolson, 1961.

King, Ernest Joseph, and Whitehill, W. M. *Fleet Admiral King*. New York: Norton, 1952.

Kirkpatrick, Lyman B. *The Real CIA*. New York: Macmillan, 1968.

Knatchbull-Hugessen, Sir H. *Diplomat in Peace and War*. London: John Murray, 1949.

Kramarz, J. *Stauffenberg—The Life and Death of an Officer*. Translated by R. H. Barry. London: Deutsch, 1967.

Langelaan, G. *Knights of the Floating Silk*. London: Hutchinson, 1959.

Leahy, W. *I Was There*. New York: Whittlesey, 1950.

Leasor, J. *War at the Top*. London: Michael Joseph, 1959.

Lee, Asher. *Blitz on Britain*. London: Four Square, 1960.

Lerner, Daniel. *Psychological Warfare Against Nazi Germany: The Skywar Campaign D-Day to VE-Day*. Cambridge, Mass.: MIT Press, 1971.

Leverkuehn, P. *German Military Intelligence*. Translated by R. H. Stevens and Constantine Fitzgibbon. London: Weidenfeld & Nicolson, 1954.

Lewin, Ronald. *Rommel as Military Commander*. Military Commanders series. London: Batsford, 1969.

Liddell Hart, B. H. "The Military Strategist," in A. J. P. Taylor, *Churchill Revised*. New York: Dial Press, 1969.

——. *The German Generals Talk*. New York: Morrow, 1948.

——. *History of the Second World War*. 2 vols. New York: Putnam, 1972.

Livry-Level, P. *Missions dans la RAF*. Caen: Ozanne, 1951.

Loewenheim, Francis W., *et al. Roosevelt and Churchill: Their Secret Wartime Correspondence*. New York: Saturday Review Press, 1975.

Lomax, Sir John. *The Diplomatic Smuggler*. London: Barker, 1965.

Longmate, Norman. *If Britain Had Failed*. New York: Stein & Day, 1974.

MacCloskey, Monro. *Secret Air Missions*. New York: Richards Rosen, 1966.

MacDonald, Charles B. *The Mighty Endeavor: American Armed Forces in the European Theater in World War 2*. New York: Oxford Univ. Press, 1969.

McKee, Alexander. *Last Round Against Rommel: Battle of the Normandy Beachhead*. New York: New American Library, 1964.

McLachlan, Donald. *Room 39: A Study in Naval Intelligence*. New York: Atheneum, 1968.

Macmillan, Harold. *The Blast of War, 1939–1945*. New York: Harper & Row, 1967.

Maiskii, Ivan. *Memoirs of a Soviet Ambassador; The War: 1939–1943*. Translated by Andrew Rothstein. New York: Scribners, 1968.

Majdalany, Frederick. *The Battle of El Alamein: Fortress in the Sand*. New York: Lippincott, 1965.

———. *The Fall of Fortress Europe*. Crossroads of World History series. New York: Doubleday, 1968.

Manvell, Roger. *Conspirators*. New York: Ballantine, 1971.

Manvell, Roger, and Fraenkel, Heinrich. *The Canaris Conspiracy*. London: Heinemann, 1969.

———. *Himmler*. New York: Paperback Library, 1972.

Marshall, George C. *Reports to the Secretary of War*. Washington, D.C.: Government Printing Office, 1943, 1945.

Marshall, Samuel L. A. *Night Drop: The American Airborne Invasion of Normandy*. Boston: Little, Brown, 1962.

Martienssen, A. *Hitler and His Admirals*. London: Secker & Warburg, 1948.

Maser, Werner. *Hitler's Letters and Notes*. Translated by Arnold Pomerance. New York: Harper & Row, 1974.

Mason, David. *U-Boat: The Secret Menace*. New York: Ballantine, 1968.

Masterman, J. C. *The Double-Cross System in the War of 1939–1945*. New Haven: Yale Univ. Press, 1972.

Matloff, Maurice, and Snell, Edwin M. *Strategic Planning for Coalition Warfare, 1941–1942*. Washington, D.C.: Department of the Army, 1953.

———. *Strategic Planning for Coalition Warfare, 1943–1944*. Washington, D.C.: Department of the Army, 1959.

Medlicott, William Norton. *The Economic Blockade*. 2 vols. History of the Second World War: United Kingdom Civil series. London: HMSO, 1952.

Michel, Henri. *Jean Moulin l'Unificateur*. Paris: Hachette, 1964.

———. *The Shadow War: European Resistance, 1939–1945*. New York: Harper & Row, 1973.

Middlebrook, Martin. *The Nuremberg Raid*. New York: Morrow, 1974.

Millar, George. *Horned Pigeon*. London: Heinemann, 1946.

Moll, Otto E. *Die deutschen Generalfeldmarschälle, 1939–1945*. Rostatt/Baden: Pabel Verlag, 1961.

Montagu, Ewen. *The Man Who Never Was*. War Classics series. London: Evans, 1966.

Montgomery, Viscount. *Normandy to the Baltic*. London: Hutchinson, 1947.

———. *The Memoirs of Field Marshal Lord Montgomery*. Cleveland: World, 1958.

Moran, Lord. *Churchill: Taken from the Diaries of Lord Moran*. New York: Houghton Mifflin, 1966.

Morgan, Sir F. *Overture to Overlord*. London: Hodder & Stoughton, 1950.

Morison, Samuel E. *The History of United States Naval Operations in World War II*. 14 vols. Boston: Little, Brown, 1947–1962. Vol. 11, *The Invasion of France and Germany, 1944–1945*, 1957.

Mosley, Leonard. *The Cat and the Mice*. New York: Harper & Bros., 1959.

Moyzisch, L. C. *Operation Cicero*. Translated by H. Fraenkel and Constantine Fitzgibbon. London: Wingate, 1950.

Munro, Ross. *Gauntlet to Overlord: The Story of the Canadian Army*. Toronto: Macmillan, 1946.

Neave, Airey. *Saturday at M.I.9: A History of Underground Escape Lines in Northwest Europe in 1940–1945*. London: Hodder & Stoughton, 1969.

Nelson, O. L. "National Security and the General Staff." Washington, D.C. *Infantry Journal*, 1946.

Nicholas, E. *Death Be Not Proud*. London: Cresset, 1958.

Norman, Albert. *Operation Overlord, The Design and Reality: The Allied Invasion of Western Europe*. Harrisburg, Pennsylvania: The Military Service Publishing Co., 1952.

O'Connor, Raymond G. *Diplomacy for Victory: FDR and Unconditional Surrender*. Norton Essays in American History series. New York: Norton, 1971.

Olden, Rudolf. *Hitler*. Translated by Walter Ettinghausen. New York: Covici-Friede, 1936.

O'Neill, Robert J. *The German Army and the Nazi Party, 1933–1939*. London: Cassell, 1966.

Page, Bruce, *et al. The Philby Conspiracy*. New York: Doubleday, 1968.

Papen, Franz von. *Memoirs*. Translated by Brian Connell. New York: Dutton, 1952.

Parker, T. W., and Thompson, W. J. "Conquer. The Story of the Ninth Army, 1944–1945," Washington, D.C. *Infantry Journal*, 1947.

Parkinson, Roger. *A Day's March Nearer Home*. New York: McKay, 1974.

Pash, Boris. *The Alsos Mission*. New York: Award, 1969.

Patton, George S., Jr. *War As I Knew It*. Boston: Houghton Mifflin, 1947.

Payne, Robert. *The Life and Death of Adolf Hitler*. New York: Praeger, 1973.

Pendar, Kenneth. *Adventure in Diplomacy: Our French Dilemma*. New York: Dodd, Mead, 1945.

Philby, Kim. *My Silent War*. New York: Grove, 1968.

Phillips, William. *Ventures in Diplomacy*. Boston: Beacon, 1953.

Pinto, Oreste. *Friend or Foe?* New York: Putnam, 1954.

Piquet-Wicks, E. *Four in the Shadows*. London: Jarrolds, 1957.

Playfair, I. S. O. *et al. The Mediterranean and the Middle East*. 3 vols. London: HMSO, 1954–1960.

Pogue, Forrest C. *George C. Marshall*. 3 vols. [to date]. New York: Viking, 1963–.

———. *The Supreme Command*. Washington, D.C.: Department of the Army, 1954.

Popov, Dusko. *Spy-Counterspy*. New York: Grosset & Dunlap, 1974.

Price, Alfred. *Instruments of Darkness*. London: Kimber, 1967.

Robertson, Terence. *Dieppe: The Shame and the Glory*. London: Hutchinson, 1963.

Roosevelt, Elliott. *As He Saw It*. New York: Duell, Sloane & Pearce, 1946.

Rommel, Erwin. *The Rommel Papers*. Edited by B. H. Liddell Hart. Translated by Paul Findlay. New York: Harcourt, 1953.

Root, Waverly. *Secret History of the War*. 3 vols. New York: Scribners, 1945–46.

Roskill, S. W. *The War at Sea, 1939–1945*. 3 vols. London: HMSO, 1954–56.

Rothfels, Hans. *The German Opposition to Hitler*. Translated by L. Wilson. London: Wolff, 1961.

Rowan, Richard W., and Deindorfer, Robert G. *The Secret Service: Thirty-three Centuries of Espionage*. New York: Hawthorn, 1967.

Royal Air Force, 1939–1945. 3 vols. London: HMSO, 1953–54.

Royal Institute of International Affairs. *Chronology of the Second World War*. London: Royal Institute of International Affairs, 1947.

Rozek, Edward J. *Allied Wartime Diplomacy: A Pattern in Poland*. New York: Wiley, 1958.

Ruge, F. *Sea Warfare, 1939–1945: A German Viewpoint*. Translated by M. D. Saunders. London: Cassell, 1957.

Ryan, Cornelius. *The Longest Day*. London: Gollancz, 1960.

Sampson, Anthony. *Anatomy of Britain*. New York: Harper & Row, 1962.

Saunders, H. St. George. *The Red Beret*. London: Michael Joseph, 1950.

Schellenberg, Walter. *The Schellenberg Memoirs*. London: Deutsch, 1956.

Schlabrendorff, Fabian von. *The Secret War Against Hitler*. Translated by H. Simon. London: Hodder & Stoughton, 1966.

Schramm, Percy. *Hitler: The Man and the Military Leader*. Translated by Donald S. Detwiler. Chicago: Watts, 1971.

Schramm, Ritter von. *Conspiracy Among Generals*. Translated by R. T. Clark. London: Allen & Unwin, 1956.

Schulze-Gaevernitz, Gero von, ed. *They Almost Killed Hitler; Based on the Personal Account of Fabian von Schlabrendorff*. New York: Macmillan, 1947.

Sherwood, Robert E. *Roosevelt and Hopkins: An Intimate History*. New York: Harper & Bros., 1948.

Shirer, William L. *Collapse of the Third Republic: An Inquiry into the Fall of France in 1940*. New York: Pocket Books, 1971.

———. *The Rise and Fall of the Third Reich: A History of Nazi Germany*. London: Secker & Warburg, 1960.

Shulman, Milton. *Defeat in the West*. London: Secker & Warburg, 1947.

Smith, Gaddis. *American Diplomacy During the Second World War, 1941–1945*. New York: Wiley, 1965.

Smith, R. Harris. *OSS: The Secret History of America's First Central Intelligence Agency*. Berkeley: Univ. of California Press, 1972.

Smyth, Howard M., and Garland, Albert N. *Sicily and the Surrender of Italy*. Washington, D.C.: Department of the Army, 1965.

Snell, John L. *Illusion and Necessity: The Diplomacy of Global War, 1939–1945*. Boston: Houghton Mifflin, 1963.

Soustelle, Jacques. *Envers et Contre Tout*. 2 vols. Paris: Laffont, 1947–50.

Soviet Commission on Foreign Diplomatic Documents, Correspondence Between the Chairman of the Council of Ministers of the USSR and the Presidents of the USA and the Prime Minister of Great Britain During the Great Patriotic War of 1941–1945. Moscow: Foreign Languages Publishing House, 1957.

Spears, Edward. *Assignment to Catastrophe.* 2 vols. London: Heinemann, 1954.

Speer, Albert. *Inside the Third Reich: Memoirs of Albert Speer.* New York: Avon, 1970.

Stacey, C. P. *Canada's Battle in Normandy: The Canadian Army's Share in the Operations 6 June–1 September 1944.* Ottawa: The King's Printer, 1946.

———. *Official History of the Canadian Army in World War II.* Ottawa: The Queen's Printer. Vol. 3, *The Victory Campaign Operations in North-West Europe, 1944–45,* 1960.

Stagg, J. M. *Forecast for Overlord.* New York: Norton, 1972.

Stanford, Alfred Boller. *Force Mulberry.* New York: Morrow, 1951.

Stettinius, Edward R. *Roosevelt and the Russians: The Yalta Conference.* Edited by Walter Johnson. New York: Doubleday, 1949.

Stimson, Henry L., and Bundy, McGeorge. *On Active Service in Peace and War.* New York: Harper & Bros., 1948.

Strawson, John. *Hitler as Military Commander.* Military Commander series. London: Batsford, 1971.

Strong, Sir Kenneth W. D. *Intelligence at the Top: Recollections of an Intelligence Officer.* New York: Doubleday, 1969.

Strutton, B., and Pearson, M. *The Secret Invaders.* London: Hodder & Stoughton, 1958.

Sweet-Escott, B. *Baker Street Irregular.* London: Methuen, 1965.

Sykes, Christopher. *Troubled Loyalty.* London: Collins, 1968.

Taylor, Telford. *Sword and Swastika: Generals and Nazis in the Third Reich.* New York: Simon & Schuster, 1952.

Templewood, Viscount. *Ambassador on Special Mission.* London: Collins, 1946.

Thompson, G. R., and Harris, D. R. *The Signal Corps: The Outcome.* Washington, D.C.: Department of the Army, 1966.

Thompson, R. W. *D-Day: Spearhead of Invasion.* London: Purnell's, 1968.

Tickell, J. *Moon Squadron.* London: Wingate, 1956.

Tompkins, Peter. *Italy Betrayed.* New York: Simon & Schuster, 1966.

Toynbee, Arnold, ed. *Hitler's Europe: Survey of International Affairs, 1939–1946.* Oxford: Oxford Univ. Press, 1954.

Toynbee, A. J., and Toynbee, V. M., eds. *The War and the Neutrals.* Oxford: Oxford Univ. Press, 1956.

Trevor-Roper, Hugh R., ed. *Hitler's War Directives, 1939–1945.* New York: Holt, Rinehart and Winston, 1965.

Truman, Harry S. *Memoirs.* 2 vols. New York: Doubleday, 1958.

Turing, S. *Alan M. Turing.* Cambridge: Heffer, 1959.

U.S., Chief of Counsel for Prosecution of Axis Criminality. *Nazi Conspiracy and Aggression.* 8 vols. Washington, D.C.: Government Printing Office, 1946–47. Supplements A and B. 2 vols. 1947–48.

U.S., Department of the Army, Army Forces, Far East. *Operational History of Naval Communications: December 1941–August 1945.* Washington, D.C.: Office of the Chief of Military History, no date.

U.S., Department of the Army, Seventh Army. *The Seventh Army in France and Germany, 1944–1945.* 3 vols. Heidelberg: Seventh Army, 1946.

U.S., Department of State. *Foreign Relations of the United States, 1943, Europe.* Washington, D.C.: Government Printing Office, 1964.

Verrier, Anthony. *The Bomber Offensive.* New Yolk: Macmillan, 1968.

Vomecourt, Phillipe de. *Who Lived to See the Day.* London: Hutchinson, 1961.

Walker, David E. *Lunch With A Stranger.* London: Wingate, 1957.

Ward, Irene. *F.A.N.Y. Invicta.* London: Hutchinson, 1955.

Warlimont, Walter. *Inside Hitler's Headquarters, 1939–45.* Translated by R. H. Barry. New York: Praeger, 1966.

Watson-Watt, Sir Robert. *The Pulse of Radar.* New York: Dial, 1959.

Webb, A. M., ed. *The Natzweiter Trial.* War Crimes Trials series. London: Hodge, 1949.

Webster, Sir Charles. *The Strategic Air Offensive Against Germany, 1939–1945.* 4 vols. London: HMSO, 1961.

Weizsäcker, E. *Memoirs.* London: Gollancz, 1951.

Werth, A. *Russia at War, 1941–45.* London: Barrie and Rockcliff, 1964.

Westphal, S. *The German Army in the West.* London: Cassell, 1952.

Wheeler-Bennett, John W. *Munich, Prologue to Tragedy.* New York: Duell, Sloane & Pearce, 1948.

——. *The Nemesis of Power: The German Army in Politics, 1918–1945.* London: Macmillan, 1953.

——, ed. *Action This Day.* London: Macmillan, 1968.

Whitehead, Donald. *The FBI Story: A Report to the People.* New York: Random House, 1956.

Whiting, Charles. *Patton.* New York: Ballantine, 1971.

Wiener, Jan G. *The Assassination of Heydrich.* New York: Pyramid, 1969.

Wighton, C. *Pinstripe Saboteur.* London: Collins, 1952.

Williams, Mary H. *Chronology, 1941–1945.* Washington, D.C.: Department of the Army, 1960.

Wilmot, Chester. *The Struggle for Europe.* London: Collins, 1952.

Wilson, Field Marshal Lord. *Reports by the Supreme Allied Commander, Mediterranean, to the Combined Chiefs of Staff, Washington, D.C.* London: HMSO, 1946–48.

Wingate, Sir Ronald. *Not In The Limelight.* London: Hutchinson, 1959.

Winterbotham, Frederick W. *Secret and Personal.* London: Kimber, 1969.

——. *The Ultra Secret.* New York: Harper & Row, 1974.

Wiskemann, Elizabeth. *The Rome-Berlin Axis.* London: Collins, 1969.

Woollcombe, R. *The Campaigns of Wavell, 1939–1943.* London: Cassell, 1959.

Woodward, E. L. *British Foreign Policy in the Second World War.* United Kingdom Military History series. London: HMSO, 1962.

Wright, Robert. *Dowding and the Battle of Britain.* London: Macdonald, 1969.

Wrinch, P. N. *The Military Strategy of Winston Churchill.* Brookline, Mass.: Boston University Press, 1961.

Young, Desmond. *Rommel, the Desert Fox.* New York: Harper & Bros., 1950.

Young, Gordon. *Cat With Two Faces.* New York: Putnam, 1957.

Young, Kenneth. *Churchill and Beaverbrook: A Study in Friendship and Politics.* London: Eyre & Spottiswoode, 1966.

Zeller, Eberhard. *The Flame of Freedom: The German Struggle Against Hitler.* Translated by R. P. Heller and D. R. Masters. London: Wolff, 1967.

Ziemke, Earl F. *Stalingrad to Berlin: The German Defeat in the East.* Washington, D.C.: Department of the Army, 1968.

Index

EUROPEAN THEATER OF OPERATIONS, WORLD WAR II

Allies of the Axis

Neutral Nations

Countries Occupied by Germany

Furthest German Advance into Russia
and North Africa

The Major Cover and Deception
Operations of Plan Bodyguard

Faroe Is.

Shetland Is.

Orkney Is.
(Scapa Flow)

SCOTLAND

NORTH SEA

Edinburgh

N. IRELAND

EIRE

Dublin

FORTITUDE NORTH

FORTITUDE SOUTH

DE

Coventry

ENGLAND

London

NETHER-
LANDS

Ha

BELGIUM

Col

IRONSIDE

English Channel

Le Havre

Cherbourg

Dieppe

Paris

Nur

Brest

ATLANTIC OCEAN

Bay of Biscay

FRANCE

Vichy

SWITZERLAND

Bordeaux

Marseilles

PORTUGAL

Lisbon

Madrid

SPAIN

Barcelona

ROYAL FLUSH

VENDETTA

SA

Tangier

Gibraltar
(Br.)

SPANISH
MOROCCO

Oran

Algiers

Casablanca

Kasserine

MOROCCO
(FRENCH)

ALGERIA
(FRENCH)

TUNISIA
(FRENCH